The Book of Job, a Revised Text and Version;

THE BOOK OF JOB

OXFORD UNIVERSITY PRESS
London   Edinburgh   Glasgow   Copenhagen
New York   Toronto   Melbourne   Cape Town
Bombay   Calcutta   Madras   Shanghai
HUMPHREY MILFORD
Publisher to the University

THE BOOK OF
JOB

A REVISED TEXT AND VERSION

BY

C. J. BALL

WITH PREFACE

BY

C. F. BURNEY

OXFORD
AT THE CLARENDON PRESS

PREFACE

IN responding to Dr. Ball's request that I should write a preface to his commentary on the Book of Job I feel very strongly that I run the risk of appearing lightly to commit an act of intolerable assumption. Dr. Ball was well known as an accomplished Hebrew scholar when I was a child in the nursery. He guided my first steps in the study of Hebrew; and throughout my life I have been and still am his pupil, gaining from him a store of knowledge and inspiration for which it is impossible adequately to express my obligation. All Hebrew scholars who matter are well aware of his preeminent gifts, and will joyfully welcome his detailed and critical discussion of the most difficult book in the Old Testament. If, then, I undertake the task which gratitude and affection forbid me to decline, I must be understood to be addressing myself to younger scholars to whom Dr. Ball's reputation may not be so familiar as it is to an older generation.

Perhaps the most striking characteristic of the present commentary is its originality and freshness. The writer does not profess laboriously to have studied and digested the works of all former scholars upon the Book of Job; I suspect indeed that there are many such which he has not troubled to consult. This, in my opinion, is all to the good. Biblical exegesis labours under the burden of volumes which are, mainly if not wholly, commentaries upon other commentaries. Such a Rabbinic method of exegesis, if intelligently performed, has a certain value; yet it can hardly be doubted that it has a serious tendency to stifle originality of thought, and not seldom (we may suspect) it is the mark of the kind of scholarship which is incapable of reaching original conclusions. Dr. Ball is a scholar who has a mastery, and a knowledge of cognate languages which in breadth and depth is unique; and with this he combines a feeling for literary style and a shrewd common sense such as few scholars can claim. If he be thought to deal somewhat drastically with the text of Job, it must be remembered that this text presents problems which call for drastic treatment by the scholar who possesses the equipment for the task; and it cannot be doubted that Dr. Ball is such a scholar. In this respect his work speaks for itself. Those of us who have worked for many years at the text of the Old Testament may have been responsible for the suggestion of a large number of emendations in corrupt and difficult passages; yet few indeed are the passages in which we can flatter ourselves that we have actually recovered the original, and settled the textual difficulty once and for all. I have read through Dr. Ball's proof-sheets with great care, and have also listened with delight to his verbal discussion of many of the difficulties in the text of Job, and I am convinced that in not a few textual problems he has actually reached finality, whilst in others his criticisms and suggestions rarely fail to illuminate the point at issue. One marked characteristic of his method which has always impressed me is that he carries his hearer or reader with him in such a way that the conclusion can often be divined before it is stated; and this is the best kind of proof of sound reasoning and critical acumen.

Dr. Ball's volume is not merely a commentary on the text of Job. It is a storehouse of material for the enrichment of the Hebrew Lexicon. This results, in the main, from his profound knowledge of the Babylonian language—a knowledge which is essential to progress in Hebrew studies, but in which the great majority of our professed Old Testament students are unfortunately lacking. In the present work the supreme value of such knowledge is illustrated by the writer's masterly translation and discussion of the text of 'the Babylonian Job' on pp. 12 ff.

For myself one of the most interesting and valuable features of the book is the elucidation of the original biliteral forms of Semitic roots by reference to Sumerian. In this Dr. Ball holds the position of a pioneer; and students who have not read his 'Ser... ... Sumerian' (Hilprecht *tribute Volume*, 1909) and 'Shumer and Shem' (*Proceedings of the British Academy*, vol. vii, 1915) should certainly make themselves acquainted with them, in order that they may understand more clearly the principles of phonetic interchange and of the formation of triliteral roots which the theory presupposes. So far as I have been able, with my limited knowledge, to test and use the theory, I believe it to be fundamentally correct, and it is greatly to be hoped that the present volume will serve to bring this most important line of investigation to the notice of all serious Semitic philologists.

C. F. BURNEY.

OXFORD,
October, 1921.

CONTENTS

	PAGE
INTRODUCTION	1
REVISED TRANSLATION OF THE BOOK OF JOB	35
COMMENTARY, CRITICAL, PHILOLOGICAL, AND EXEGETICAL, ON THE HEBREW TEXT AND THE ANCIENT VERSIONS	95
APPENDIX.—ALTERNATIVE VERSION OF CHAP. 3	467
GENERAL INDEX	469
INDEX RERUM	470
INDEX TO NOTES ON HEBREW WORDS	471
SUMERIAN WITH SEMITIC GLOSSES	476

INTRODUCTION

IN this great poetical book, the highest achievement of the Hebrew Muse, which indeed our own Tennyson held to be the greatest poem in the world, we move in a different atmosphere from that of the generality of books which precede it in the Hebrew Canon. Amid all diversities of style and statement, one doctrine appears to have dominated the minds of legalists, historians, prophets, and psalmists alike: the doctrine that material prosperity depends upon, and is the reward of, obedience to the Divine Law, while misfortune of every kind, whether national or individual, is a direct and inevitable consequence and penalty of sin. With this dominant belief was associated a settled conviction that God was the immediate agent in all the phenomena of Nature, and in all the events and vicissitudes of human life and history; secondary causes were hardly recognized at all. And since God was perfectly impartial and absolutely just in dealing out good and evil according to men's deserts, it seemed to follow that there could be no such thing as unmerited suffering; that suffering was always an infallible indication of guilt. Job's three friends and would-be comforters are represented as obsessed by this doctrine; Job himself boldly and vehemently controverts it, as contrary to his own bitter experience and contradicting facts open to the observation of all men. The Prologue gives us what is clearly intended by the author to be the clue to the mystery of Job's unparalleled misfortunes. While affirming his perfect integrity, and tracing all his troubles to the Hand of God, as unquestioningly as both he and his friends do in their long controversy, it reveals a Divine purpose in his sufferings which neither he nor they suspect; a purpose not punitive, but designed to test his motives and to establish beyond all contradiction the sincerity of his goodness and the disinterested nature of his godliness, which had been questioned so persistently by the malevolent cynicism of the Accusing Angel.

The author evidently did not believe that suffering was always retributive. He held that Iahvah might afflict His servants upon other grounds than that of chastisement for sin. And he did not consider that this detracted from the perfect justice of the Divine Arbiter of all events. The infinitely wise and almighty Creator might do what He would with His creature man. It was His absolute right, and, as such, it involved no infringement of His attribute of Justice. *Shall the clay say to Him who mouldeth it, What makest Thou?* (Is 45⁹; cf also Ro 9¹⁴⁻²¹). The poet's outlook, moreover, did not extend beyond the present life (see notes on 19²⁵ ff.). To him, as to his contemporaries, this earth was the sole field of the Divine dealings with man. All the unmerited calamities of his hero were amply atoned for, and the justice of God was fully vindicated, when Iahvah made good all his losses, giving him 'twice as much as he had before'; a conception of justice which seems to depend on legal ideas of compensation such as we find in Ex 22⁴·⁷·⁹ (cf. also Is 40² 61⁷ Zc 9¹²), but which hardly satisfies the modern mind. No matter how great the wisdom and power of Deity is supposed to be, the picture presented to us in the Prologue of a blameless person surrendered, from whatever motive and under whatever restrictions, to the pitiless handling of an evil Angel by the Lord of All, shocks our sense of Justice, and almost suggests the despairing cry of Gloucester in the great tragedy of Lear:

> *As flies to wanton boys are we to the gods;*
> *They kill us for their sport.*

But the poet of Job had no such misgivings. He was apparently altogether satisfied with the *dénouement* of the story in which, after the Divine intervention, Job's fortunes are restored and all goes merrily as a marriage bell. The modern conscience will sympathize far more readily with the innocent sufferer's indignant protests and passionate outcries against the cruel injustice of Heaven than with the explanation of it which satisfied the poet, who seems to classify it with the earthquake and the storm as a lawful if terrible exhibition of irresponsible omnipotence in which the idea of justice is swallowed up and disappears, and about which it is futile to argue from the standpoint of human knowledge which falls hopelessly short of understanding either the works or the counsels of God. He seems to be satisfied with the solution *He reigns*; and the King can do no wrong.

The poetically splendid but scientifically obsolete parade of the wonders of the natural world, inanimate and animate, which constitutes the long-drawn and perhaps later-extended reply of Iahvah to Job's final appeal (31³⁵), may appear to us little better than a magnificent irrelevance, but was certainly intended by its author as a complete vindication of the ways of God which had proved so perplexing to Job. It says not a word of the Divine purpose in afflicting Job (see Prol.); and its sole effect upon the sufferer is that he confesses his utter ignorance and impotence in relation to God. It lies open to the obvious objection that, if a man believes himself wronged, the sense and smart of w... ... ... r ... ed by demonstration that the wrongdoer is incomparably stronger and wiser than he. At most, he may be reduced to the dull and dumb submission of the oriental fatalist by the conviction that resistance is futile; that he is a mere puppet in the hands of an Infinite Power.

Unlike so many thinkers of our own and former times, the poet of this immortal drama never loses faith in the being of God. The question of the existence of Iahvah, the supreme Arbiter of events, the absolute Lord of All ('the Sultan in the skies', as one has called Him), is never raised at all, never even approached or hinted at, within the whole compass of the book. Never, in the very extremity of his sufferings, does Job suggest a doubt that HE IS. Utterly baffled by the mystery of his own misfortunes, and steadfastly maintaining that he has not deserved them, he believes and affirms that the Divine Judge is fully aware of his righteousness, and repeatedly demands to be confronted with Him face to face; certain that he could then establish his contention, and satisfy his all-powerful Adversary. His confidence even reaches the point of solemnly declaring that his Avenger will one day appear on earth, and do him justice before his death ($19^{25\,\text{ff.}}$). This, accordingly, is what happens when Iahvah answers him 'out of the Stormwind' (38^1), rebukes and humiliates his uncharitable friends, and restores him to health, wealth, and peace.

In trying to find exact equivalents in modern speech for the ideas and phraseology of an ancient Hebrew thinker, it is necessary to bear in mind that our best results can only be approximately correct. To appreciate the breadth of the gulf which separates the common knowledge of our own time from the primitive standpoint of the poet and his contemporaries, we have only to glance at many of the questions about the ordinary phenomena of Nature, such as Light and Darkness, Dew and Rain and Hail, Frost, Ice and Snow, Clouds, Thunder and Lightning, which the Deity Himself propounds to Job as mysteries insoluble by human wisdom. In all such matters, thanks to the progress of Physical Science, the child of to-day may be far wiser than the sages of old. The ideas and terminology of the natural sciences are unknown to Biblical Hebrew. Everything is at the stage of the crudest beginnings. Light and Darkness, and other natural phenomena, e.g. the winds (Ps 135^7), snow and hail, are conceived as substantive and independent entities, existing in separate abodes or storehouses, out of which they are fetched at will by the sovran Disposer of All.

It must indeed be granted that Physical Science, which has thrown so much new light upon the laws and processes of Nature, is still silent upon the question of the Ultimate Cause (or Causes) of things. In numberless instances it has solved or is solving the question of the *How*, but it seems to be as far as ever from determining the *Whence* or the

Why. It has failed to divine the final secret; it is baffled when it tries to transcend material bounds, or even to reconcile the antinomies of reason. *Canst thou fathom the nature of God?* remains a question which admits of no answer but an unqualified negative.

Theories of the electrical constitution of matter, theories about the universal ether, chemical analysis pushed to its farthest, leave untouched the age-long and still-persistent problems of Life and Mind. Spiritual things are spiritually discerned. We cannot find them at the bottom of a crucible, or inspect them through a microscope, or lay them bare with a dissecting-knife, or exhibit them by help of radioscopy. God is Spirit; and we only recognize His Presence in the marvellous pageant of His works because we also are Spirits—an influx into material conditions of the eternal Spirit Whose offspring we are and in Whom we live and move and have our being.

It may seem strange, at first sight, that Iahvah makes no attempt to explain or justify His treatment of Job. He neither adopts nor even alludes to the edifying suggestions of Eliphaz (5^{17}) and Elihu. He simply humbles and silences the sufferer by bringing home to him the fact that he is as profoundly ignorant of God's ways and purposes in the world of Nature as in the moral world. The whole of Creation is a maze of wonders and mysteries: how then can an ephemeral being like Job dare to contend with the Majesty of the Universe, or presume to question the justice of the Divine dealings with the creatures of His Hand?

Thus the main, if not the only, motive of the writer would seem to be to discourage mankind from striving to penetrate the impenetrable secrets of God; to bid them recognize the limits of human understanding and abstain from all attempts to lay down rules for the Divine action even in the name of Justice and Right. Such inquiries are futile and lead nowhere. The subject is 'high as Heaven, deeper than She'ol'. Man must acquiesce in the dealings of Providence, assured that in the end everything will come right (cf. the story of Joseph).

The original work has evidently been much interpolated by later editors who were left unsatisfied by the poet's own solution of the moral difficulties raised by the story, and were doubtless as deeply shocked as many modern readers have been by the angry outcries and protests of Job against the apparent injustice of the Most High. How far the language of the poem has been modified under these influences, we cannot, of course, divine. Individual instances have been pointed out in the notes on particular passages. It is quite possible that ampler details of the Theophany were once given in the text ($37^{21\text{ff.}}$ may preserve some traces of them: see notes). However that may be, the somewhat long-winded and mock-modest harangues of Elihu, so unlike the authentic portions of the work, making, as they do, an awkward and unnatural break between Job's final appeal (31$^{38\,\text{ff.}}$) and the Divine response (38^1), and referred to nowhere else throughout the book, are a signal instance of an interpolated section, foreign to the original form of the book, as is now very generally recognized by most competent judges. Emendations, more or less probable, may be considered to have cleared the text of some part of its inconsequence and obscurity; and it seems possible that Elihu's pose as a younger man criticizing his elders is a sort of hint by the author that he himself belonged to a later period than that of the poet upon whose argument he seeks to improve, with no very striking success, at least as it appears to us. His laboured apology for intervention, running through a whole chapter and beyond it, may perhaps point in the same direction. If the great poem was already well known, it might be judged presumptuous to venture upon addition or criticism.

But when all due allowance has been made for manifest inferiority of genius, defects of style, repetition and attempted reinforcement of some of the arguments of the older work, apparent incoherences of thought occasioned or aggravated by corruptions of the text, for which the author is, of course, not responsible, the section as a whole is an interesting record of the criticism provoked by the original work at some date not long subsequent to its publication, and was well worthy of preservation as a fresh endeavour to rehandle the unsolved problem of the elder poet more successfully.

After solemnly affirming his own perfect impartiality (32$^{21\,\text{f.}}$), and challenging Job to meet his arguments as those of a fellow-mortal, before whom therefore he need not be cowed as he had professed to be before his Divine Adversary (9^{34} 13$^{21\,\text{f.}}$), Elihu proceeds to make objection against Job's assertions of innocence and complaints of God's hostile treatment of him and persistent deafness to his appeals (33$^{5-13}$). Elihu then declares that God does speak to man in several distinct ways; warning him by dreams (a reference to 4^{13}), or by the discipline of sickness, or by the voice of a 'Messenger' who interprets the providential meaning of his affliction (which is described in language intentionally recalling the sufferings of Job), and so leads him to repentance and salvation and joyful thanksgiving (33$^{14-28}$).

Here and elsewhere Elihu's exposition of 'the uses of Adversity' is far from valueless as a record of religious experience familiar to every Christian believer. But he travels considerably beyond the scope of the master-poet as defined by the Prologue and Epilogue.

After another rhetorical challenge to Job to answer his arguments, made in a tone which implies that they are unanswerable (Job and his three friends are supposed to be silent listeners throughout the section, in accordance with 31 32 7.), Elihu appeals to several

($34^{2.10.34 \text{ note}}$), the moral philosophers of the day, to weigh the force of his polemic against Job. He then returns to the subject of Job's self-justification and denial of the Divine justice ($34^{5 \text{ f.}}$; cf. 9^{21} $19^{6.7}$ 27^{2-6}), which he meets with an accusation of blasphemy and practical agreement with the godless ($34^{7.8.36 \text{ f.}}$), and with reiterated assertions that God is just, in that He rewards men according to their works, having absolute power of life and death, and dealing impartially with all, princes and people, rich and poor alike (34^{10-20}); seeing and judging all men, without need of holding a judicial inquiry in particular cases (as Job so eagerly desired in his own case); crushing mighty oppressors at the cry of their helpless victims, and putting down the impious king whom He has set up in His anger, and thus bringing him, it may be, to repentance (34^{21-32}). Does Job find fault with all this? can he suggest a better method for the administration of Divine Justice? (v. 33).

Elihu proceeds to combat the idea that righteousness is no advantage to a man (cf. $1^{9 \text{ f.}}$); ascribing this opinion to Job, doubtless on the ground of passages like $9^{22.28-31}$ 21^{7-15}, although Job has nowhere said it, and it contradicts what he does say, $31^{2 \text{ ff. }14-23}$, in reviewing the manner and motives of his past life. In opposition to this fallacious, though natural, deduction from some of Job's tortured utterances, Elihu declares that God in His Heaven is too far exalted above and remote from man to be personally affected by his conduct, good or evil. A man can only hurt or benefit his fellow creatures (35^{1-8}). Elihu seems to imply that, however righteous Job may have been, he could not have put the Deity under any obligation to reward him with the continuance of his prosperity. Righteousness establishes no claim upon God, as both he and his friends (v. 4) assumed (cf. Lk 17^{10}). God has received nothing from him, and therefore owes him nothing. Men naturally cry out under oppression; but their cries are not necessarily, as they should be, directed heavenwards; and therefore God may disregard them. Such cries are no more evidence of humble turning to God than the instinctive cries of animals. The proper attitude under suffering is not angry exclamation, like Job's, but supplication and patient waiting for God (cf. $33^{26 \text{ ff.}}$ $34^{31 \text{ ff.}}$). Such may perhaps be the general sense of this obscure and corrupt passage (35^{9-16}). As it is, however, Job is voluble against the Divine indifference or injustice, because He does not always pour out His wrath upon the godless (vv. 15, 16; cf. $21^{7 \text{ ff.}}$).

In what follows (chaps. 36, 37) Elihu varies his language, but adds little or nothing to what he has already urged in justification of God's dealings with Job. It is strange that, like the three friends, he nowhere makes any allusion to the clue afforded by the Prologue; viz. that affliction may be intended as a test of the genuine or disinterested character of a man's religion. He repeats that God is just, all-powerful,

INTRODUCTION 7

omniscient; and then he harks back to his favourite thesis of the warning and corrective intention of suffering and disaster (36^{7-15}; cf. 33^{14-30} 34^{24-32}); supposing the case of kings brought to repentance by captivity, and then restored to prosperity, like Manasseh (2 C 33^{11}, where the language coincides with that of 36^8: see the note there). (36^{11} may be an inference from 2 K 25^{29}; and vv. 13, 14, may refer to the untimely fate of Shallum-Jehoahaz, 2 K 23^{31} Je 22^{11}.) So far Elihu might seem to be more anxious to vindicate the justice of God than to prove that Job's calamities were the consequence of antecedent sin; but in the four verses 36^{18-21} he appears to hint (under cover of general precepts couched in proverbial form) that Job may have been guilty of certain sins common at the time among the rich and powerful, e.g. accepting bribes and indulgence in all-night carousals. In this, the author (or possibly an interpolator) not only ignores Job's own protestations of his integrity, but the Divine testimony thereto in the Prologue.

Elihu goes on to affirm that the Lord of All is accountable to none for His doings. His absolute power places Him as far beyond the sphere of human criticism, as the methods of His action in nature are beyond the range of human understanding, e.g. the formation of rain, clouds, thunder and lightning ($36^{22}-37^5$). (It goes without saying that had the author lived in our day, he would have expressed himself differently on the subject of the phenomena of the natural world. But his gain would have been our loss. Exact science is prosaic, and is apt to palsy the play of poetical imagination.) So also the snow and heavy rains of winter, the hurricane, frost, ice, and hailstorm, and, once more, that wonder of wonders the lightning, are all instruments by which He works His sovereign will on earth (vv. 6-13). The remainder of chap 37 has suffered much in transmission. It makes a final appeal to Job to 'consider the wonders of El', referring chiefly to the phenomena of cloud and sky; and at the close it seems to declare that the ground of religion is the union of Might with Right in the Supreme. (Vv. 21, 22 appear to prepare the way for the Theophany which follows, chap. 38. Indeed the author probably had his eye on chap 38 while composing the last section of his work, chaps. $36^{26}-37$; thinking perhaps to supplement that incomparable utterance of the original poet by the addition of edifying glosses and comments somewhat in the manner of a Targum or Midrash. He is, of course, not responsible for the manifold corruptions and possible interpolations of his text; but, after every allowance on that score, we cannot but feel that as a poet he is far inferior to his glorious model.)

Another manifest instance of later interpolation is the famous monologue in praise of the Divine Wisdom (chap. 28). In the present context this fine piece has no v.. t   with what follows it. It presents points of contact with the Divine reply (chap. 38) and with Proverbs (Pr 3^{11f.} 8^{10f. 22-31}), but, both in tone and substance, it is quite unlike the language ascribed to Job in the rest of the book. It reads more like a practical conclusion drawn from the Divine remonstrance (chaps. 38-41) than a possible utterance of the suffering hero. It denies to man the ultimate knowledge of things: *rerum cognoscere caussas* is the sole prerogative of the Creator who has bidden man to content himself with that practical wisdom which consists in *fearing God and departing from evil* (that very wisdom which is ascribed to Job by the Prologue, 1³, and which he steadily claims as his own throughout the controversy). If Job had already reached this attitude of complete resignation in the face of mysteries insoluble to him and his contemporaries, not a vestige of which is to be found in his subsequent and final soliloquy (chaps. 30-31), the Divine demonstration of his ignorance in those high matters (which, moreover, had not really been the subject of his complaints and protests) becomes superfluous and irrelevant.

A minor objection to regarding the chapter as a genuine part of the original work may be noticed here. The enumeration of precious stones, to our taste perhaps somewhat overdone, though it faithfully reflects the exaggerated fondness for jewellery characteristic of Orientals down to the present day, is a feature which does not agree with the patriarchal times in which Job was supposed to have flourished. Silver and gold, flocks and herds and slaves, are the only elements of wealth recognized in the rest of the book. (See also the introduction to the chapter, pp. 331 f.)

That the Book of Job is an original work in the highest sense of the word is self-evident to every discerning reader. We might as well expect to find Shakespeare as we know him in the pages of Holinshed or Plutarch, or in the plays of Plautus and Seneca, or in the dramas and romances of his Italian contemporaries, as to find the direct source of this extraordinary product of Israel's genius in Babylonian or any other older literature. To say this is not to say that the Hebrew poet invented either the persons or the plot of his drama, though he may be responsible for its religious colouring. The name of Job was known to the prophet Ezekiel as that of a personage famous for exceptional sanctity in the olden time ('Noah, Daniel, and Job,' Ez 14^{14,20}); a fact which, apart from other evidence, might suffice to prove that it is a real personal name, and not, as some have supposed, an artificial figment of the poet, significant of the character or fortunes of his hero. When the Talmud states 'Moses wrote his own book and the section concerning Balaam *and Job*' (Baba Bathra 14ᵃ), it merely means that the la n r ' the Patriarchal age (the author of Genesis) was credited

INTRODUCTION 9

with the book of Job whose story is laid in that period The name indeed may be regarded *pro tanto* as a mark of verisimilitude (although the Talmudic writer could hardly have been aware of the fact), inasmuch as the similar or identical A-a-bu ($Âbu = Ayabu$) and A-ia-bu (in the compound A-ia-bu-ia-qar = $Ayabu$-$yaqar$) occur in the lists of personal names of the Hammurabi-period (cf. Amraphel—$Ammurapi$, Gn 14). How far the story itself had its roots in Babylonian legend cannot at present be exactly determined. The cuneiform literature, as we know, has thrown much light upon the Biblical history of Noah; and the name of Daniel, who is also associated with Job by the prophet Ezekiel, and who was a traditional paragon of Wisdom (Ez 28[3]), may perhaps be compared with such names of the Hammurabi-period as Danya, Dan-Adad (?), Dan-URRA (cf *dannu*, 'strong ' > *dânu*, ' judge ').

It may be taken for granted that during the Exile, if not before, the Jewish literati became acquainted with much of the religious literature of their conquerors (see 26[12f.] notes); and the new knowledge doubtless exercised no small influence upon their ideas and subsequent writings (cf. Ez 1). It is now some twenty years since attention was first called to the remains of an old Babylonian poem in which many students have recognized a sort of parallel or prototype of the book of Job. The language is unusually difficult of interpretation; a difficulty aggravated for us by the more or less fragmentary condition of the tablets, especially the first, of which only a few lines have been preserved. These tablets, originally four in number and containing perhaps 120 verses apiece, are part of the treasure-trove from Assurbanipal's library at Nineveh; where also was found a commentary which supplies glosses on many of the more obscure words and phrases. Both text and commentary were copied by the royal scribes from originals in E-sag-ila, the great temple of Bel-Merodach at Babylon. The fact that a commentary was necessary to the understanding of the text even in the seventh century B.C. and before it, is significant of the great antiquity of the poem.

The purpose of this venerable relic of ancient piety is to glorify the god Merodach as a healer and saviour, and to attract sufferers to his temple in hope of deliverance. Unlike the book of Job, it is throughout a monologue (cf. Job's soliloquy 29–31), in which a king describes how, in spite of an exemplary attention to the claims of religious duty, by the agency of demons he was stricken with a terrible malady or accumulation of maladies, which baffled the wisdom of his magicians and soothsayers. God and goddess were deaf to his prayers, until at last Merodach relented, accepted his supplications, expelled the evil spirits, and freed the several members and organs of the patient from their manifold ailments, restoring his entire body to perfect health.

Below we give the text, so far as determinable, ... far as we have succeeded in the somewhat arduous attempt to make one). The reader will notice not only a general resemblance in the framework of the two stories, but also many points of coincidence in thought and language. The no less striking differences will also become apparent They are, for the most part, such as might be expected from the later period and higher theological standpoint of the Hebrew writer, who has the whole historical experience of Israel and the religious teaching of her prophets and psalmists behind him. Naturally there is no mention of a 'goddess' in the appeals and expostulations of Job (though Eliphaz does contemplate a possible appeal to the 'Holy Ones' or Angels— those 'Sons of God' who, in the evolution of Israel's faith, have taken the place of the older Babylonian Pantheon). The supreme Jahvah shares His sovranty with none; though He has a Court of lesser Powers, from which the sinister figure of the 'Satan', the Angel hostile to Man, is not excluded, since he also apparently is a 'Son of Elohim' (cf. 1 K 22 Zc 3¹²) The name of the afflicted Babylonian king, Shubshî-meshrê-Nergal, is no more like the Hebrew Job (Eyob) than the Uta-napishtim of the Babylonian story of the Flood is like the Hebrew Noah. But the outlook on life is much the same in the two poems. In each the present world is all; and, accordingly, in both the hero of the drama of suffering is restored to health and prosperity in the present life. In both, the world of the dead is a land of darkness from which there is no return; a shadowy realm of eternal night, where the souls of the departed abide in a feeble phantom existence. The Babylonian monarch's catalogue of the manifold symptoms of his mysterious malady which brought him to death's door (Tab. II) recalls Job's frequent insistence upon his bodily torments which appeared likely to have a speedy and fatal issue; but whereas the Babylonian poet repeats the long list of his hero's ailments *seriatim*, when he comes to describing their divine cure (Tab. III)—with a view perhaps to suggesting that Merodach knows how to heal every kind of disease—the poet of Job says not a word about his hero's recovery from his grievous plagues. In both works the restoration is wrought by a *Deus ex machina*; but the Babylonian describes the process, step by step; the Hebrew seems almost to imply that the change was an immediate result of the Voice and Vision of God (The fact that nothing is said of the disappearance of Job's disease may suggest that the author or editor, regarding Job's mysterious malady as a mere vehicle for his moralizings, did not think it worth while to say any more about it when its function in the drama was fulfilled Or has a reviser abridged the conclusion of the story?)

In both works worship by prayer and sacrifice is presupposed as the normal expression of religion. The purpose of the Hebrew poet is certainly not to traditional modes of worship. The burnt-offering is a special feature of Job's piety in the Prologue; and it is prescribed by Iahvah Himself in the Epilogue as an atonement for the guilt of the three friends. The Babylonian king also dwells at length upon his assiduous devotion: 'Prayer', he says, 'was my rule, Sacrifice my law.' Yet, although his life had been thus blameless, he has to complain (like Job) that Heaven has treated him as if he were a heinous evildoer. Good rulers and bad fare alike; and the unhappy king's misery inspires a momentary doubt whether religion is of any real advantage. Like Job, he makes no question of the existence of God and the supernatural world. His misgivings are only concerned with the customary worship which he had carefully observed and zealously enjoined upon his people. After a review of what he had done in this way, he exclaims: *I was sure that with God all this was acceptable*; and he goes on to draw the despairing inference *What seems good to a man's self is an offence to God; What in his own thought is suppressed is good before his god.* His sceptical mood culminates in the doubt whether an ephemeral creature like man, whose condition is one of perpetual change and instability, and whose life may be cut short at any moment, can arrive at any certainty about the Mind and Counsel of God. *Who*, he demands, *shall learn the Mind* (or Will · *têmu*) *of the gods in Heaven? Who shall comprehend the counsel of God, fraught with obscurity(?)? How did the communities* (or *mankind*) *learn the Way of God?* The reader will see that all this is in essential agreement with much that we find in the Book of Job, and may perhaps exhibit the germ of it. It should also be noted that, as in the case of Job, the poet offers no intellectual solution of the questions which perplexed the mind of his hero. Neither Merodach nor Iahvah deigns to propound any explanation of the anomalies of life, the apparent inequalities of the ways of Providence. The problem is left where it was, and both the older and the younger poet seem to think it enough that the sufferer was finally restored to his former prosperity.

Towards the end of Tab. III Obv., the poet-priest of Esagil, like Job's friends, appears to assume that the king's affliction was sent as a punishment for sin. He makes the king say that the anger of his Lord (Merodach) was appeased, so that He heard his prayers; and an isolated line adds. *My sins He caused the wind to carry away.* It would seem therefore that the demons acted as ministers of the wrath of Merodach. The evil Spirit, however, is permitted to afflict Job, not on account of any sins he might have committed (see 7^{21} 13^{26} 14^{17}), but, as we have seen, to make trial of the sincerity of his godliness.

THE BOOK OF JOB

TEXT AND TRANSLATION OF 'THE BABYLONIAN JOB'.

TABLET I.

The first half-line, which gives the title to the whole poem, is preserved in the Colophon of Tab. II. The rest of the Tablet is only known from the Commentary, which once contained some thirty-three lines relating to this Tablet. Unfortunately most of these are broken away; and of the remainder only about six or seven can be made to yield an adequate and connected sense. The commentator naturally cites only those lines which seemed to him to present some special difficulty. (See 5 R 47, where the remains of his work are lithographed.) We cannot, therefore, ascertain how many lines Tab. I of the poem originally contained. The opening words, *Ludlul bêl nîmeqi* . . . 'I will worship the Lord of Wisdom!' . . . , and a subsequent line, ingeniously restored by Jastrow, (*Qanî ilûtika*) *atammaḫ*, 'I grasp the Staff of Thy Godhead!', seem to indicate that the exordium was occupied with the grateful hero's praise of Bel-Merodach, his divine Deliverer. His relation of the calamities that befell him follows; but the beginning of this is lost, owing to the deplorable state of the document.

(*uznâa usakki*)*ka ḫašikkiš êmê*
'Mine ears He stopped, I became as one deaf.'

The first two words were restored from Tab. III. 51. But 5 R 47 gives ba-ra, not -ka. The glosses on the line are partly lost. Those which survive are ḫa-šik-ku suk-ku-ku ('stopped', 'blocked', 'deaf'; cf Arab. اَصَمّ), and e-mu-u ma-ʿa-lu ('to be or become like or equal to')

šarra kîma atur ana rêši
'A King, when I turned into a slave,'

rêšu, lit. 'a head', has the gloss LU URA, i.e. *wardu* or *ardu*, 'a slave'. But perhaps we should read šar-ra-ku-ma a-tur ana rêši, ' 'I was king and I became a slave'.

nalbubu lappê unamgarannî
'The fury of a comrade abuseth me'.

Such is the natural construction of the line. Cf. 'das Wuthen, Schnauben des Nächsten hat mich vernichtet (?)', suggested by *HWB*, s.v. *nakâru* We do not know whether, in the original text, the line was immediately consecutive to the last or not (Cf. 2 Sa 16⁵⁻¹³.) The gloss on *nalbubu* is *ši-gu-u*, 'to rage, be mad, to howl, lament', 'raging', 'mad'; e.g. *šumma sisû iššegûma lû tappâšu lû amêlûti unášak*, 'If a horse go mad and bite either his fellow or a human being' . . .; *šumma kalbu illenišeû* 'If a dog show madness' . . . (see *MA*, p. 1009). The line canno~ m an W; .n n Narr.n hab.n mich m.in/ G.f.hrt.n misshandelt

INTRODUCTION

(Landersdorfer). The verb, whatever its precise force may be, is sing., not plur. (*unamgarûnî* or *unamgarû'innî*; and the same is true of *eruranni* in the next line (L. *haben sie mich verflucht*). *unamgarannî* = unangarannî = unaggarannî; II. 1, Pres. 3 s. with Suff. of a root *nagâru*, נגר, or *nakâru* (*naqâru*), נקר, or even, as Jastrow supposes, *nakâru*, נכר (cf. Meissner, *Gram* § 15). In the first case, we might compare נִגְרָא, *bolt, bar,* and נָגַר, *to shut in, or up* (Jon 2⁷): 'The violence of a (my?) friend imprisoned me.' Then the following *eruranni* might perhaps be 'he bound me' (see *MA*). It is, however, perhaps more likely that our word involves the root נקר, which appears in Aramaic, Hebrew and Arabic with the meaning 'to bore', 'pierce', or 'hollow out'. The Arabic uses, in fact, appear to give the clue to the real meaning of our passage; for in that language the root (Med. *a*) is *perfodit, perforavit, excavavit*, and metaph. *fodicavit dicteriis vel contumeliis* ('to sting a man with reproaches'): cf. also the same root (Med. *e*) *iratus fuit*. Accordingly, we may render

'The rage of (my) familiar revileth me';

which agrees with the statement of the next line

ina ḫâš puḫri eruranni
'In the thronging of the assembly he cursed me.'

The gloss that once followed the line is almost entirely effaced

ana qâb SAL-SIG-ia pitâssu ḫâštum
'For him who spake well of me open for him was a pit.'

Or *for him who spake of favour for me*, i.e. from the gods. *qâb* is the St. Constr. of the Ptcp. *qâbû*. The Sumerian group should be read *damiqti* or perhaps *damqâti*, plur. (SIG-MEŠ): see 4 R 61, no. 2, 20 sq. I have taken *pitassu* as *pitât-su*; Pm., 3 fem. s. of *pitû*. For *ḫâštum*, see HWB *šuttu, šutiatu*, 'hole, pit, or pitfall'. The gloss is šu-u(t-tu?).

ûmu šutânuḫu mûšu girrâni
'Day was sighing, night was weeping',

- *ITU qita-a-a-ulu idirtu MU-AN-NA*
'The month was wailing, the year mourning.'

The gloss on qi-ta-a-a-u-lu is qu-u-(lu or lum), 'crying'.

TABLET II.

KUR-ud-ma ana balât adanna îtiq
'I had attained to a life which passed the limit' (?)

asaḫḫar-ma limun limun-ma
'I look around, all is evil';

ṣaburti(tum) utaṣ(ṣ)apa išarti(tum) ul uttû
'Tyranny increaseth, justice I see not.'

Gloss on ṣaburtum: ru-ub-tum (*ignotum per ignotius!*).

DINGIR alsîma ul iddina pânišu
'To the god I cried, He vouchsafed not His countenance';

usallî (DINGIR) Išta(tar)ri ul išaqqâ rîšiša
'I besought my goddess, she lifted not her head.'

i-šaq-qa-a: scribal error for u-šaq-qa-a. Cf. *Desc. of Ishtar*, Rev 18.

LU GAL îna bîr (bi-ri) arkât ul iprus
'The Seer by vision determined not the future'; (cf. II. 75.)

îna maššakka(ki) LU EN-ME-LI ul ušâpî dînî
'By drink-offering the Soothsayer revealed not my judgement.'

Lit. *caused not my judgement* or *right to come forth* or *appear*: cf. II. 74. ušâpî = ušêpî. III. 1 Pf. of (w)apû = יפע. The reading of B, *ina maššakka u LU EN-ME-LI*, violates both grammar and parallelism; and is obviously a mere scribal error. The Commentary gives the line as follows: *îna maššakki LU EN-ME-LI ul i-ša-me DI*, 'With a drink-offering the Soothsayer doth not settle judgement'. *išâme = išâm*, Pres. of *šâmu*, 'to settle', 'decide', 'decree'; and DI = *dînu, dênu*, 'judgement', S^b 185. The gloss on *maššakku* (from *šaqû*, 'to water', 'give to drink') is sur-ki-nu, i.e. *surqînu*, ša LU EN-ME-LI, 'libation (or drink-offering) of a Soothsayer'. The Sumerian designation LU EN-ME-LI means *man who is master of pure spells*; i.e. a wizard or magician or sorcerer.

za-ki-qu apulma ul upattî uznî
'The sorcerer I told, but he opened not mine ear';

zakiqu for *zaqîqu*; i.e. zâqiqu or else zaqîqu. According to Zimmern, a necromancer. For the root, cf. Aram. זקק, 'to bind'; with reference to incantations. 'He opened not mine ear' = revealed nothing to me. Is 50^5.

LU MAŠ-MAŠ îna kikiṭṭê kimiltî ul ipṭur
'The wizard with passes(?) the Wrath on me loosed not.'

For *kikiṭṭê* the *Comm.* gives AG-AG-ṭe-e; that is, the Sumerian ideogram AG, 'to do', repeated, with the Phonetic Determinative -tê added to remind the reader that the ideogram must be read *kikiṭṭê*. The gloss AG-AG-ṭu-ú ni-pi-ši, 'mode of action, proceedings, ceremonies' (*HWB*), or more simply 'manual acts', is added. *nîpišu* is, of course, 'act', 'something done' (AG, epêšu); *kikiṭṭû* may have sprung from a Sumerian KI-KID, KIKKID, KID-KID, 'handling', 'manipulating', or the like, from GAD, (G)ID, 'hand', or else from KID-KID (= SHID-SHID), 'ways' 'modes of action' (cf. ⸗ SHID, *alaktu*, and see ZA, i. 183).

a-a-i-te epšéti šanâti mâlitan
'What doings! 'tis an altered world!'
a-a-ı-te, A. a-a-it . . , elsewhere a-a-ta (*HWB*, p. 47), seems to be fem. pl. of a-a-u, quis? (so Zimmern, Dhorme, Ungnad). For *epšéti*, 'state', 'condition of things', see *HWB*, p. 118 *ad fin*. We might render: 'What a state of things! the whole world (or country) is changed!' *šanâti* = *šanâta*, *šanat*, Pm. 3 fem sing. of *šanû*.

amurma arkat rıdâti ippıru
'I looked back, Wrath *or* Misery was my pursuer.'
The line is difficult; but the general sense can hardly be very different from this. For the connexion of *arkat* (*Comm*. ar-ka-at, with the third sign almost effaced) with *rıdâti* (*Comm*. rı-ša-a-tum, 'rejoicings'; a mere scribal error for ri-da-a-tum), cf. the common phrases of the Assyr. historical inscription *arkîšu ardi*, *arkîšunu artedi*, 'I pursued him (them)'. *rıdâti* may be the Ptcp. fem. sing. I. Suff 1 pers. for *rédîti*, 'my pursuer' (cf. *bânât* = *bânît*); or, like *šanâti* in the preceding line, it may be a Permansive 3 sing. fem. (= *ridâta, rıdât*). *rıdâtum* is apparently the Ptcp. rather than an Abstractum pro Concreto, as Landersdorfer supposes. The gloss on *ippiru* is ıp-pı-ri: ma-na-aḫ-tum. GIG; see Tab. IV. 7. (The text of the previous line, as given 5 R 47, is ip-pi-e-ši, which if correctly copied, is a scribal error. But Assyr. e-ši is very like ri.) These glosses need not be exact equivalents of the obscure *ippıru*. If, as we suppose, *ippiri* meant 'my wrath', i. e. the (Divine) wrath against me (cf. l. 9 *supr*.), they are merely exegetical: 'He means his ailment or disease.' Cf. Syr. نَفَرَ 'to snort', which is used of a man snorting with anger. Then *ippîru* might be an If'âl form, *inpîru, like *ıkrîbu*. *ıplîru, eptennu* (Tab. IV. 2) = eptênu. On the other hand, the ideogram for *ippıru*, which consists of the symbol for *man* followed by the same symbol inverted (cf. my *Chinese and Sumerian*, p. 20), seems rather to suggest overthrow, prostration, or the like. See 2 R 16 30–33 b c, where we read.

DUG-MU AN-TA-TUM-TUM-MU
al-la-ka bir-ka-a-a
'nimble (are) my knees'
GIR-MU NU-KUŠ-ŠA
la a-ni-ḫa še-pa-a-a
'unresting my feet'
LU SAG DÚ DÚ NU-TUG-A
la ra-aš ta-šim-ti
'not having judgement'
LU-ΠƆ MU-UN-UŠ-E
ip-pi-ra r. ... ...
'falls (i. e. ..., ... m

16   THE BOOK OF JOB

This close parallel certainly seems to suggest the rendering 'I looked behind; Misfortune was the (my) Pursuer'; since *ippirû* might be plur., and *ridati* (= *rêdâti* = ri-da-a-tum) fem. plur. of the Ptcp. in concord therewith. The primary meaning of *ippiru*, however, might still be (the Divine) Wrath which, as the ideogram indicates, overthrows a man or casts him down. (If the ideogram existed in the linear period of the writing, it really represents the upright human figure inverted and reversed—a man 'upset', 'turned upside down', or 'topsy-turvy'.) With the Assyr. word we might further compare Syr. ܦܪܘܬܗܐ *pûrûthô*, 'rage', 'anger'; اِلْفِرْ *illephir*, 'to rage', 'be angry'; √ פור 'to boil'. (Assyr. *ippiru* may perhaps be a loan from a Sumerian IB-BIR; cf. IB *uggatu*, and BIR, *sarâṭu*, 'to rend', or BIR, *sapâḫu* (= *sapâḫu*); *saqqaštum*: as if 'tearing wrath' or 'destroying anger'.)

kî šâ tamkîtum ana DINGIR lâ uktînnu
'Like one who had appointed no offering for the god',

u ina mâkalê (DINGIR) Ištarri lâ zakru
'And at a meal made no mention of the goddess',

appi lâ ênû šukinni lâ amru
'(Whose) face was not bowed down, (whose) worship was not seen',

ina pîšu ipparkû suppê taslîti
'In whose mouth had ceased prayer (and) supplication',

ibṭilu UD-mu DINGIR i-nat-tû eššeši
'(Who) neglected the god's day, breaking the fasts (?)',

natû, Pres. *inatti*, 'to break in pieces', 'smash'. *eššešu*, a word of doubtful meaning; perhaps connected with *ašâšu*, 'to grieve', 'be sad', or with the Sumerian ISISH, 'lamentation', 'mourning', e.g. for the god Tammuz.

iddû aḫšu NU¹-mišunu imišu
'(Who) was remiss, (who) despised their image',

palâḫu û išudu lâ ušalmedû UN-MEŠ-šu
'(who) taught not his people to fear and praise (them)',

DINGIR-šu lâ izkur êkul akâlšu
'His god he named not, ate his food',

izib D. ištarta-šu maštim la ubla
'Forsook his goddess, brought no drink-offering';

ana šâ imḫû EN(bêla)šu imšû
'Unto him who was oppressive, who forgat his Lord'.

The Commentary quotes this line with be-la-šu for EN-šu; adding the gloss im-ḫu-ú ka-ba-tum ('to be heavy', 'burdensome', 'oppressive'; cf. 1 Sa 5¹¹; 1 K 12¹⁷).

INTRODUCTION 17

niš DINGIR-šu kabti qalliš isqur anâku amšal
'(Who) lightly sware by his mighty god I, even I, was made like!'
aḥsusma râmân suppû taslîti(tum)
'Yet I, for my part, was mindful of prayer (and) supplication';
taslîti(tum) tašîmat(mati, matum) niqû šakkûa
'Prayer was my rule, sacrifice my law';
Gloss: *šakkû parçi*.

UD-mu palâḥ DINGIR-MEŠ tûb ŠAB-bi-ia
'The day of the worship of the gods was my heart's delight';
UD-mu ridûti (D.) Ištar nimeli(la) tatturru (tattûru)
'The day of Procession of the goddess was gain (and) riches';
ridûtu, 'marching.' The gods were carried in procession on their festivals. *tatturru, tattûru*, a تَفْعُول form, from the √יתר, יתר; 'abundance', 'surplus', 'increase', and so 'wealth'.

ikribî LUGAL ší ḥidûtî
'Homage to the King that was my joy',
ù nigûtašu ana damiqtî šumma
'And His musical Service my delight was that.'

If *šummâ* were Pm. 3 fem. plur. of *šâmu*, II. 1, one would have expected a plur. *nigâtîšu*. But, further, the strict parallelism of the preceding and following couplets and the incomplete parallelism of this ('Prayer to the Divine King was my joy, And His music'—harping in His honour, or, 'His musical festival'— . . . . . .) almost demands here the conclusion 'that was my delight'. *šumma* = šû-ma, carelessly written instead of ši-ma (since *nigûtu* is fem.); and *damiqtu*, 'brightness', is here used in the sense of 'happiness'. Perhaps, however,

'The king's (appointed) worship was my joy,
And his psalmody became my pleasure.' Cf. Zimmern.

ušâr (ušârí) ana KUR-ia A-MEŠ DINGIR naçâri
'I taught my country the name of the god to keep';

ušar, apocopated form of *ušârí* (C), is Pf. III. 1, of *arû* = ירה, הורה, Heb. (so Dhorme). A-MEŠ (C. me-e) is an instance of the Phonetic use of a 'Borrowed Character', as the Chinese would call it (see my *Chinese and Sumerian*, p. 23). Mê, 'name', is here written with the Sumerian group denoting its homophone mê, 'water'.

šûmi (D.) ištar šûqur UN-MEŠ-ia ušlâḥiz
'The name of the goddess to honour, my people I instructed'.
tanâdâti LUGAL eliš (C. recte iliš) umaššil
'The majesty of the k.. . . . . I . i . .''

ù puluḫtu(ti) E-GAL umman ušalmid
'And awe of the Palace I made the multitude learn.'

lā îdî kî itti ili itamgur annâti
'I was sure that with God all this was acceptable.'
(*Lit.* there was accepting of these things.)

ša damqat râmânuš ana DINGIR qullultum
'What is pleasing to oneself is abomination to God';

ša ina ŠAB-bi-šu mussukat UGU DINGIR-šu damqat
'What in one's own heart is held back, to one's God is pleasing.'

a-a-u têm DINGIR-MEŠ kirib AN-ê ilammad
'Who the mind of the gods in Heaven can learn?'

milik ša DINGIR zanun zê[1] iḫakkim mannu
'The counsel of God full of subtlety who can comprehend?'

êkâma ilmadâ alakti DINGIR apâti
'How then have mortals learned the Way of God?'

ša ina amšat iblutu imût uddêš
'He who was alive yestereve died on the morrow.'

surriš uštadir zamâr iḫtamaš
'In a moment was he troubled, quickly was he crushed.'

ina çibit appi izammur elila
'At a seizure of the nose (a sneeze?) he sings a dirge',

ina pît purîdi uzarrab lallareš
'In opening the fork he wails like a mourner.'

L. renders the last two lines as follows: *In diesem Augenblick singt und spielt er noch, Im Nu schon heult er wie ein Klagemann*: 'This moment he is still singing and playing; In a trice he is already howling like a wailing-man.' This is excellent sense, if it can be got out of the Assyrian. That *izammur elêla* means he sings (or plays) some kind of music, joyous (cf. ina e-li-li, unter Gesang, Abp. x. 95) or mournful (cf. *Desc. of Ishtar, ad fin.*), is certain; and that *uzarrab lallareš* means 'he howls like a (professional) mourner' is virtually certain also (cf. *kî lallari qûbê ušazrab*, 'Like a wailing-man he made him utter shrieks'. 4 R² 54. 21 a). *zarâbu* must be cognate with *sarbu*, 'grief', 'mourning', 'lamentation' (NE IX. iv. 33–35 *ina sarbi*; cf. *id.* IX. i. 2 *zarbiš ibakki*). But whether *ina çibit appi, ina pît purîdi*, are phrases practically synonymous with *surriš* and *zamar*, is a question not so easy to decide.

---

[1] *Zû, zê* (zi-e), 'wisdom', 'craft', 'subtlety', or the like, may be a loan from Sumerian ZU, 'to know', 'wise', 'wisdom' (*idû, lê'û, nimequ*). Counsel and Wisdom are naturally associated: e. g. in the phrase *lā rāš têmê u milki*, 'destitute of wisdom and counsel' (Sn. v. 3). Cf. perhaps Br. 10557, 10561. (But Zimmern, *Du* ' . '.

INTRODUCTION

In 2 R 35. 44 c, d *çibit appi* renders the Sumerian UG-KIR ?-DIB, *slime* (mucus)-*nose-seize*; which might mean the attack of a cold or catarrh, or possibly, as HWB. suggests, 'a sneeze. 'In a sneeze' might perhaps be equivalent to 'suddenly'; and *ina pít purídi*, 'in the opening of the legs', 'in a (single) step', might be understood in a similar sense. 'Opening the legs' might mean stepping or walking (cf. passus from pando). See KB. vi 5).

kî pitê u katámi(*me*) *ténšina šitní*
'Like the opening and close (of day) their mood changeth.'

or 'With Dawn and Dusk their mood is changed'. Gloss : *kî pitê ù katáme*: UD-mu ù mu-ši, Day and Night.

immuçáma[1] *immá šalamtaš*
'When hungry, they are like a corpse';

išibbáma išannaná DINGIR-šun
'When full, they challenge their god!'

ina tábi itámá ilî šama'i
'In weal (gladness) they meditate (or talk of) ascending to heaven';

ulaššašáma[2] *idibbubá arád irkalla*
'In woe they speak (think) of descending to Hades.'

(Traces of another line appear in 4 R². The five lines following are preserved in the Commentary. How many intervening verses, not noticed by the Commentator, have been lost, we have no means of conjecturing.)

šúlum limnu ittaçá ina (*assukki*) *šu* (I. 2, Pf. gl. *šúlum ekimmu*)
'An evil Spirit issued from his lurking-place' (*vid.* Tab. iv 21).

illi urqit KI-tum ipiççá lu'útum (gloss: *lu'útum : murçu*)
'Like the verdure of the ground the sickness yelloweth (or blancheth).'

labani itíku urammú kišádu
'My nape they bruised, they relaxed the neck';

Cf. SA-TIG = *laban kišádi* (Br. 3099), and SA-TIG(GÚ) BAN-RAĠ = *labanšu itík*, 'his *laban* he crushed' (RAĠ, RA, *maḫáçu, rapásu*); *itík* Pf. of *táku* = *dáku* = *dakú*; cf. Targ. דוך ' to injure'; חובא ' injury '. (4 R 29, no. 3, 5 f) Since SA means *buánu, riksu*, 'joint', 'ligament', 'sinew', 'muscle', or the like, SA-TIG may be 'neck-joint', or 'neck-muscles'. The gloss on *itíku* is *ramú : šebiru*, 'to loosen', 'to break'; which would seem to be a hyperbole for the effects of disease. But we do not really know the context of the line, nor whether the verbs are sing. or plur.

---

[1] אמץ Pres. *immuc*, 'to stint', 'confine', (2) 'hunger.' Gloss *uncu* bu bu-tum
[2] II. 2. *ašášu*, 'be -ad or troubl...'.

gatī rapšatu' urbatiš ušnillum
'My ample form like a rush they threw prone';

(so HWB.) Gloss: ur-ba-tu, GIŠ ur-ba-nu, 'rush' (= אורבינא Syr. אַרְבְּנָא, juncus).

kī ulīltum annabik puppāniš annadī
'Like an *ulīltum* was I overturned (?); on my back (?) I was laid.'

Gloss: *ulīltum* su-un-kir-tum (which does not help us. Perhaps = sungir = šimmar in gi-šimmar, 'palm-tree'. Cf. Landesdorfer).

ašnan TAG-ma (illapit-ma) daddariš alahiš
'Bread was turned into stench, into corruption (sourness).'

Gloss: da-da-ru bu-u'-ša-nu.

appūnāma eterik silētum
'Mightily was the malady prolonged.'

Glosses: ap-pu-na-ma ma-'a-diš; si-li-e-tum GIG (i. e. *murçu*), 'sickness.'

ina lā (?) mākalē eṣ(bu ?) bu(būtī ?)
'For lack of food grass was my fare.'

(?) muha damī issu(-uh) . . . . .
'Die Kraft meines Blutes hat er mir entzogen (?) . . . . . .'

(L. nach Martin.) Rather perhaps read *it*-mu-ha, 'he took away', and is-su-ha (libbi-bi), 'wrenched away my understanding;' cf. 4 R 3. 19, 20 a.

e-çi ?-da ?-tum uz-zu-qat a-ri mad-bar . . . .
'Die Nahrung (Ernte) ward abgeschnitten, der Löwe der Wüste . . .'

(So Landesdorfer; but very doubtfully. The last two words might be a-tal-mad = *attalmad*, 'I was taught'.)

širānūa nuppuhu u-ri-ik-tum meš . . . .
'My joints (or nerves) were set on fire,' . . . .

ši-ir-a-nu-ú-a; cf. Syr. שרינא 'joint', 'nerve', 'membrane', 'vein', 'artery'. Lines 53–59, from the Sippara fragment, are very difficult and doubtful; partly owing to lacunae in the text and uncertainties of reading.

59. *ahuz iršu mestrū mūçē tanhu*[1]
'I took to (my) bed; Pain was a bar to going forth';

ana kišukkīa ītūra bētu
'The house (or chamber) became my prison.'

ta-ni-hu = *tniẓu*, 'rest.'

illurtum širta nadâ iddâ
'A clog on my body my hands were laid';

maškan ramnía muqqutu šépda
'A fetter of myself my feet were prostrate.'

nidâtîa šumruçâ miḫiçtu dan(nat)
'Mine overthrow was grievous; the wound was sore.'

qinazi iddanni malâ(+ti) çillâtum
'With a scourge he beat me down of many thongs (?)';

parušsu usaḫḫilanni ziqatum dannat
'With a staff (lance?) he pierced me whose point was hard.'

kâl ûmu rîdû iriddanni
'All day long the driver driveth me';

ina kašâd mûši ul unappašanni surriš
'When night cometh, he allows me not a moment's breath.

ina ttablakkûti[1] putturû riksûa
'With racking my joints (sinews) are loosened';

mešrítûa suppuḫâ itaddâ aḫîtum(ti)
'My members (or powers) are dissolved, thrown aside' (awry; distorted?).

ina rubçía abit kî alpi
'In my stable I fell down like an ox';

ubtallil kî immeri ina tabaštânía
'I wallowed like a sheep in my own dung.'

72. *sakikkía išḫutu LU MAŠ-MAŠ*
'The malady in my members distracted (?) the Enchanter',

u têrítía LU-ĠAL utaššî (II² ešû, verwirren)
'And the Seer confused my omens';

ul ušâpî âšipu šikin murçía
'The Sorcerer made not clear the nature of my sickness',

u adanna sili'tía[2] LU-ĠAL ul iddin
'And a term to mine infirmity the Seer assigned not.'

ul irûça ilu qâtî ul içbat
'The god helped not. my hand He took not';

ul irîmanni (D.) iš-ta-ri iddâ ul illik
'My goddess pitied me not, beside me walked not.'

---

[1] Lit. by being torn or wrenched asunder = convulsed; cf. Mk 9¹⁴.
[2] sili'tu, siletum nirru.

pitî KIMAG̊ (v. kimaḫi) iršû šukanûa
'Open(ed) was the Tomb; they took in hand my Burial';
adî lâ mîtûtima bikîti (v. tum) gamrat
'Ere my death my mourning was over';
kâl mâtîa kî ḫâbil¹ iqbûni
'My whole country said, "He is deceased!"'
išmêma ḫâdûa immerû pânûšû
'He that rejoiced over me heard of it; his countenance shone';
ḫâdîti ubassirû kabillašû (v. ša) ippirdu
'They told the good news to her that rejoiced over me; her spirits rose (*lit.* her liver brightened)'
idî ûmu ša gimir kimtîa
'I thought of the day when all my family'
ša kirib šêdê ilûtsûn irîm
'Within the Door-gods adored their deity.'

TABLET III.

kablat qâtsu ul ali'i našâša
'His hand was heavy; I cannot bear it.'

. . . .
. . . .

(mulmu)lli lutâmiḫ rit(tika? . .)
'Let thy hand . . grasp the javelin!'
(Tâbi-utul)-(D.)Bêl ašib Nippur (EN-LIL-KI)
'Ṭâbi-utul-Bêl who dwelleth in Nippur'
(ana du)ubbubîka išpurâ(ni)
'To report to thee hath sent me.'
(pa-a-)na ša êlî-ia id(din)²
'The face He himself hath shown to me'
(napa)-aš balâti iddâ umašši' ba ?(ka ?)
'Extension of life He hath pronounced; He hath taken away weeping.'
(ina mûši utul)ma šuttu anattal³
('In the night? I lay down) and saw a dream':

---

[1] Cf. חבל on Palmyrene gravestones
[2] *pânšu nadânu*, sich sehen lassen, sich zeigen; *pânšu la iddinšu*, zeigte sich ihm nicht
[3] . . . . *nu⁕i utu¹ma*, &c.

(šâ)lu šuttu attulu mûšíti
'This is the dream I saw in the night':
(êpiš) ardati bânû zi(kari)
'The Maker of the maid, the Creator of the man',
(mu-bil?)-la bi-ḫa-ti iliš maš(lat?)
'Who conferreth a realm (?) equal to (that of?) a god',
(Four lines missing.)

17. eqbíma aḫulâp (aḫulapi) dannis (*MA-GAL*) šunuḫ-ma
'Said I: "How long?" heavily sighing':
atumma ša ina šat mûši ûrû bi(i-ri)
'What was the vision which he saw in the night-time?'
ina *MÀ-MI* (D.) *UR-DINGIR-NIN-TIN-BÀGGA* šu(u-ma?)
'In the dream it was Ur-Bau himself'
idlu darru âpir agâšu *LU-MAŠ-MAŠ*-ma nâší li(e-ti?)
'The stalwart hero had donned his diadem, The Enchanter, Bringer of Victory.'
(D.) *Marduk*-ma išpuran(ni)
'Merodach hath sent me.'
ana (D.) *Šubší-mešrê-DINGIR-GIR* ubilla çi(im-ri?)[1]
'To Shubshi-meshrê-Nergal He hath brought happiness (?);'
ina *SHU-šu AZAG-MESH* ubilla çi(im-ri?)[1]
'With his pure hands He hath brought happiness (?).'
muttabbilía qatuššu ip(qid)[2]
'My Ruler to his hands He hath committed.'
(ina?) munattu išpurâ šipir(ta)
In the morning twilight He sent the message';
... damqâti[3] *UN-MESH*-ia uktal(lim)
'(the god?) favours to my people showed.'
(tes?)litu riku çir-it-( )
. . . .
( ) arḫiš ugamir iḫḫipi (duppi?)
'... quickly he finished, broken in pieces was (my bond?).
( ) ša bêlia libbašu i(nûḫ?)
'... of my Lord His heart was quieted',
( )-sint kabitta ip(šaḫ?)
'... the temper was appeased.'

---

[1] çi(ri-ta) = çirrita, 'the sceptre'?
[2] ip(qid-sa), 'he hath committed it'?
[3] L. *qâtâ*? but cf *šarru uktallim râmu*, 'the king has shown favour'; *uštaklima damqtu, id*

(u)*u unuinnî*(-*a išméma imḫuru supû'a?*)¹
'He heard my prayer and accepted my supplication.'
. . . . *tâbu* . . . .
'. . . . . good . . . .'

End of Tablet III. Obverse. A gap of unknown extent follows

êgâtia ušâbil šâru (*IM*)²
'My sins He caused the wind to carry away.'

. . . .
. . . .

(*iti*)*iḫḫamma idšu* (*ella?*) . . . .
'He drew near and (pronounced) his (pure) incantation';
(*išap*)*par imḫulla ana išid AN-e ana irat irçitim ubil*(*šu?*)
'He sendeth the ill wind to the foundation of Heaven; Into the bosom of Earth He brought it';
(*bî*)*rit apsîššu šâlu lim*(*nu utîr?*)
'Into the middle of the Abyss He made the evil spirit return.'
utukku lâ nîbu utîr E-kur-ri
'Demons without number He made return to Ekur';
GISH-KIB labartu šadâ ušéše(*ir*)
'With vervain the Labart He led to the mountain';
Agû tâmâtu šuruppâ ušamçi(*i?*)
'To the flood of Ocean He made the chill fever go forth.'
išid lu-u-tu³ ittasaḫ kîma šam(*mi*)
'The root of the disease He tore out like a plant's.'
šitti lâ tâbtu riḫâ⁴ salâ(*lia*)
'The slumber unhealthy that overflowed my downlying'—
kîma qutru immalû AN-e ušta(*ak-ta-mu*) (cf. Sanh. iv. 68)
'As with smoke were filled the heavens, they were covered'—
ina û-u-a-a a-a ni'u nišéš
'With a Ho! and a Ha! He drove back like a lion';
ušatbî imbariš Ki-tim uš(*mallî?*)
'He let it rise (come on?) like a hurricane (and) fill the earth.'
lazzu GIG-SAG-du ša ZU?-u išḫup(*pu*)⁵
'The clinging ailment, the headsickness, which had confounded the wise',—

---
¹ Cf Neb. II. 4.
² A line preserved in Comment. 5 R 47. (êgâti = ḫitâti. Comm.)
³ *lu'âtu : murçu* Gloss.   ⁴ Cf. NE xl. 209 *littum irḫâ elia*.
⁵ . . . .

INTRODUCTION 25

issuḫ(am?)ma nalši muši(?) UGU-ia ušlez(nun?)
'He tore out, and the cool shower of night upon me He rained down.'

te-'-a-ti SHI-aa ša uštašbiḫ šibiḫ mu-u(ši)
'As for mine eyeballs (?) which He had caused a cover of night to cover',—

ušatbî IM rašbu unammir ni(la-sin)[1]
'He brought on a mighty wind, He (or It) brightened their look.'

PI-aa ša ullammima (v me) ussakkika[2] *ḫašikkiš*
'Mine ears which were stopped and blocked like a deaf man's',—

ubal amîrašîn iptêtî(tê) nišmâ-a-a
'He took away their deafness, He opened Him their hearing.'

appa ša ina ridi ummi unappiqu ni(ipši-šu)[3]
'My nose whose breathing He had obstructed with a flow of mucus',—

nipšu is 'smell', 'scent', of a herb, in NE (xi. 272). *unappiqu* is difficult. The root cannot be identical with Aram. נפק 'to go out'. It may perhaps be another form of לפף which we see in Arab لفق 'to sew together', to join'; or we may compare it with Aram. לבך tenuit, retinuit; cf. the Syriac phrase לבכתא דנשמא *difficulty of breathing*. As to the phrase *ina ridi (ridî) ummi, ridû* 'to flow' is common enough; while *ummu*, which is neither *ummu*, 'mother', nor *ummu*, 'heat', may possibly be related to the Syriac ܐܡܐ *emmā*, 'pool', 'conduit', 'ditch', Ne 2¹⁴ (= ברכה), ܐܡܐ ܕܡܝܐ 'channel of water', Ecclus 24³⁴: cf. אַמָּה *'amma*, 'ditch', Bab. Kam. 50 b, Shab. 128 b. (*appu*, 'nose', plur. *appê*, is masc., like Heb. אַף.) My *niribšu* seems quite as probable as Thompson and Landersdorfer's *nipšišu* (l. 53), about the meaning of which the latter is not certain.

upaššiḫ miḫiçtašuma anappuš (anâku)
'He stilled its outpouring and I, I breathe again.'

šaptâa ša illabba ilqâ dan(nūtišina?)
'My lips which quivered, (whose) strength He had taken away',—

ikpur pulḫatsinâma qiçiršina ip(šur)
'He removed their fear, their knot He loosened';

pîa ša uktatimu çabâriš aš(kun?)
'My mouth which He had closed, which I set only to whispering',—

(im)suš kîma ki-e rušašu uš(nam-mir?)
'He refined (?) like bronze, its colour He made bright (?)';

[1] Or 'He cleared their sight'.

šinnâa ša ittaçbatâ išteniš inniqi(id-da)
'My teeth which were held, which were tied fast together',—
(ipte)tī biritsinâma irdasin uštam(ziz ?)
'He opened the space between them,[1] their foundation He secured';
(li)šânu ša innibṭa šutâbulu[2] lâ i(lîʾu ?)
'The tongue which was swollen, which could not articulate'—
(ip-šu-)uš ṭupuštašama iddad atmû(ša ?)
'He anointed its mass and its speech became clear(?)';
ur-ú-du ša innisru únappiqu lagabbiš[3]
'The throat which was bound, whose passage He had obstructed . . .',—
uštibba iratu(ti) ša malîliš iḫtalliššâ(la ?)
'He made good the chest which piped like a flute' (BPS 117).
(ru)'ti ša útappiqu lâ (i)maḫḫaru (. . .)
'My spittle which He had obstructed . . . . . .',—
lagâ'a ša isirma idiltaš iptī
'The bonds which He bound and its barred door He opened';

. (Three broken lines follow.)

TABLET IV.

šammaḫu ša ina unçi ittârû kima pir ân zal (çal? çil?) *li raksu*
'The stomach which quaked with want, which like a prisoner was bound',—

The difficulty of this line has been generally recognized. Landesdorfer renders: 'Dem Wohlhabenden, der dem Hungertode nahe gebracht war, gefesselt wie ein Schuldbeladener (?), (Brachte er Speise, versah ihn mit Getränk).' But we have not yet done with the list of bodily members which are consecutively restored to health and efficiency (cf. *kišâdi*, l. 3; *umâši*, l. 5; *birkâa*, l. 8); and it seems probable that *šammaḫu* denotes some other part or organ of the body. Since it 'quakes' (Hab 3[16]) or trembles 'with hunger' and receives food and drink (l. 2), it can hardly be anything else but the stomach (unless perhaps the gullet be intended). As for the etymology, *šammaḫu* need not be connected with the Assyrian √*šamâḫu*, 'to grow luxuriantly', 'to thrive', but is perhaps identical with *šamaḫḫu*, which is the name of a part of the body in 4 R 22 a, and is directly borrowed from the Sumerian SHA-MAG, 'lofty interior' (see 4 R 22. 34, 35).

[1] Lit. 'their middle' (*birtu*); or perhaps 'their bond' (*birtu, biritu*).
[2] *šutâpulu*, III, 2 Infin. of *apâlu*.
[3] *lu a . . . . . . LAGAB, uʾuʾtuʾʾ*; IMI I AGAB *a nṭum ša zumri*, Br. 10165; 1. 204. Vid. HWB. *ṭutṭi*.

INTRODUCTION 27

imaḫḫar iptenni ubbalá maškíta
'It receiveth food, He bringeth drink'
kišâdi ša irmû irnama[1] *ikkappu*
'My neck which was relaxed, bowed to the root',
upattin qi-ni-e amališ izqup
'He made firm (as) a young palm (?), like a cedar He set up';

The verb *patânu*, which here occurs in the Intensive form (Pael), is not apparently connected with its homophone *patânu*, 'to eat', whence comes *iptenni*, 'food', l. 2 (although the uses of סמך and סעד, 'to support', in the sense of sustaining or feeding, suggest a possible connexion). The √פתן in the sense here required may be a cognate of פתל 'to twist', and so 'tighten', 'make firm'; cf. Heb. קוה, strictly 'twist', whence קו 'cord', 'line' = Assyr. *qû*, and Arab. قَوِيَ 'to be strong', قُوَّة 'strength' and 'strand' (of a rope). The gloss on the next word qi-ni-e is qi-nu-u gin-ú. Probably the scribe inadvertently wrote qi-ni-e for qi-ni-e-eš or qi-ni-eš. For qi-nu, 'a young palm', see ZA xii. 410, 14.

The gloss on *amališ* is a-ma-lu GIŠ Ù-KU, which is elsewhere equated with *ašûḫu*, 'cedar' (5 R 65, 43; cf. *PSBA.*, 1887, p. 127). Is this Assyr. root *amal* (*awal*) identical with אול 'to be high', which appears to be the root of the Heb. tree-names אלון, אלה, איל?

ana gâmir abâri umâši umaššil
'To one perfect in strength He made my structure equal.'

On *abâru* the gloss is a-ba-ri e-mu-qu, the latter being a common word for 'strength'. The root is, of course, the same as that of the Heb. אביר 'abbîr, 'mighty'. For more obscure *úmâšu* the gloss is ú-ma-ši KAK-MU, or rather DÚ-MU; a Sumerian expression denoting 'my make' or 'build' or 'fabric' or 'structure' (DÚ, later RÚ, *banû*, *bînûtu*, *êpêšu*, *patâqu*; Br. 5248 ff.).

GIM nakimtum šûçî uçappira çupuraa
'Like (those of) a she-*nâkim* or a *šûçû*-demon He had made my finger-nails grow':

The demons called *nakmu* (masc.) and *nakimtu* (fem.), like other evil spirits, entered the bodies of men, so causing disease. See 4 R 28, No. 3, 11a: *lišêçî nakma û nakimti ša* SU(MU), 'Let him expel the *nâkim* and the *nâkimt* of my body!' The *nakmu* is described by the Sumerian epithet LU GISH-GI-KA-SAR, which perhaps means *amêl ḫîši*, 'Man of the Reedy Swamp' (חישת קנים, חִישָׁתָא); indicating his natural haunt or place of origin. (Cf. GISH-GI, *abu*, 'a reed-bed', and

---

[1] For ir-na-t. Gl.

GI-KA-SAR, *ḫíšu, id.;* Br. 2386; 2415 f.) An epithet of the *nakimtu,* his female counterpart, seems to indicate her baleful activity. She is called ID-KU(M) or A-KU(M), or A-RI(G). However the Sumerian group was read, the two signs of which it consists are *hand+pound* or *crush* (Br. 4710 f.; 6587); so that she grinds or crushes or pounds a man like corn (ḲUM, *ḫašâlu*), or completely crushes his strength. From the present passage it also appears that, like other demons, she possessed sharp nails or claws (see Handcock, *Mesopotamian Archaeology*, p. 262).

The rare word *šûçî* is explained by the following gloss: *amelu* šú-çu-ú *ša (ilu) Ištar ana IZI UD-DU-A,* which means 'whom Ishtar casts out into Fire'—a suitable destination for a maleficent demon. (We should have expected *GIM nâkimtum u šûçî,* 'like a *nakimtu* or a *šûçî*-demon'. The conjunction may have been omitted because it was absent in the Sumerian text, of which this is probably a translation.)

It will be evident to the reader that a special interest attaches to this line as illustrating the Biblical story of Nebuchadnezzar's madness; one feature of which was that his hair grew 'like eagles' feathers and his nails like birds' claws' (Dan 4[33]). In whatever relation the poem may stand to the book of Job, it seems clear, from the evidence of this and several previous lines, some of which have hitherto been misunderstood, that the familiar story of Daniel can hardly be altogether independent of this far older native Babylonian narration.

(As to the root *nakâmu,* I would compare it with the Arabic لَكَمَ *lakama,* pugno percussit, 'he smote with the fist' (l = n, as often).)

ilbuk manaḫtašun GAR(= šikin)-šun ušṭib

'He poured forth their ailment, He restored their condition.'

Glosses on this line are '*manaḫta*: GIG' (= *murçu*, 'sickness', elsewhere); and 'GAR-šu (*sic* !) : SAG-DU', which is a Sumerian group denoting 'head' (*qaqqâdu*), 'top', and here no doubt the 'top' or 'tip' of the nails, now restored to proper length and shape. It is thus an explanatory paraphrase rather than a strict equivalent or synonym of *šiknu.* That *manaḫtu* is *manâḫtu* from *nâḫu* (not from *anâḫu*) is made probable by 2 R 27, 36–38, where apparently three homophones are distinguished, viz. *nâḫu ša libbi,* 'to rest or be quieted, of the heart'— common phrase; *nâḫu ša murçi,* '*nâḫu,* of sickness', from which doubtless our *manâḫtu* springs; and *nâḫu ša šaḫê,* 'to be fat, of a swine'.

birkâa ša uktassâ bûçṣ . . . .

(Gl. bu-çi: *içsâr ḫurri,* 'bird of holes'.)

'My knees which were fettered like a falcon's (He unbound?)';

'uklulium ṭaẓ(ri)ia ištad(dâ çalam)šu

'The entire form of my body He heightened it- figure';

For *šuklultum* (?) *pagrîa*, see 4 R 57. 53 a; for *šadû*, 'to be high', *išiddi*, 'he made high', see Muss-Arnolt, s.v. Perhaps, however, the mutilated word was *ištaddal*, 'he enlarged, made fine or noble'. Cf. *çalam pagrišu*, NE. I. col ii. 2.

imšuš mammê rûšûš uzakkî
'He wiped away the rust, he purified its colour';

Glosses on this line are ma-šá-šu: ka-pa-ru: ma-am-mu-u · šú-uḫ-tu · ru-ši-iš: LU(DIB)-BI. With *kapâru*, cf. *dîmtaša ikappar*, 'he wipes away her tears' (Myth of Nergal and Ereškîgal, see ME. p 78, l 20). *Mammû* is probably a word of Sumerian origin (MAM, MAN?); its equivalent *šûḫtu* (= Syr. שׁוּחְתָא 'rust', 'verdigris', 'foulness') is one of the Assyrian values of the Sumerian character for copper (CT xii. 7); as is also *qû*, Tab. iii. 58 *supr.*, with which the present line must obviously be compared.

dûtum ummultum ittapirdî
'The enfeebled (?) form grew bright.'

Here we have the gloss du-ú-tu: bu-un-na-nu-u (i. e. 'form', 'appearance') With *ummulu*, f. *ummultu*, cf. Heb אמלל אמל 'weak', 'feeble'. The Assyr. *dûtu*, 'form', 'figure', may be from the √דמה 'to be like', and thus identical with Heb. דְּמוּת 'likeness'; cf *Dûzu*, from *Du'ûzu*, from *Dumûzu*, Tammûz

ina itê DINGIR-ID ašar dên UN-MEŠ ibbirru (I. 1. Pres)
'On the banks of the divine River where doom passeth on men',
Gloss on *itê DINGIR ID* (i. e. *itê ili Nâri*): ḫur-ša-an. *Huršân* was probably a local name ('eine heilige Landschaft', Hommel, *Grundriss*, 251).

multûtu ammarit abbultum appa (*te-ir*?)
'I had my long locks plucked, of the fetter I was freed'

The context points to some rite of lustration or purification, which completes the restoration of the sufferer; and this rite naturally has place on the bank of a sacred stream. Cf. the case of Naaman, 2 K 5[10–14]). With *multu*, plur. (?) *multûtu*, 'hair' of the temples (?), cf. Syr. מנא, מנתא, plur. מנין, מנא 'a hair', 'hair' = ביני בינתא, cf. Targ. and Talmud.

(Gap of four lines.)

. . . . *katru ina piširti ala'*
· . . . . 'in release I go up (?)'

ana E-SAG-ILA êgû¹ ina SHU-ia limur
'Unto Esagîla let the sinner through my guidance look!'

ina pî girra KU-ia iddî napsama (il) Mardug[1]
'In the mouth of the lion devouring me Merodach put a bit';
(il) Mardug ša mukaššidîa ikim aspašu assukkašu usaḫḫar[2]
'Merodach took away my pursuer's wily work by turning his ambush.'

The Story of Nebuchadnezzar's Humiliation and Reinstatement (Dan 4).

Tantalizing as we find the lacunas and obscurities of the text, this fragment of ancient Babylonian literature throws unexpected light upon another late portion of the Old Testament Canon besides the book of Job. The failure of the king's seers and soothsayers, sorcerers and enchanters, to relieve him of his perplexities (Tab. ii) and to reveal the cause and duration of his malady (Tab. iii) reminds us of the inability of the wise men, enchanters, sorcerers and astrologers, to reveal and interpret the dreams of Nebuchadnezzar (Dan 2 and 4); and it is by the dream of a seer of Nippur that Shubshî-meshrê-Nergal is warned of his approaching deliverance. But it is Nebuchadnezzar's personal narrative of another dream and its interpretation and issue (Dan 4) which presents the most striking points of contact with the personal narrative of Shubshî-meshrê-Nergal. The tall tree of the Bible story may have been suggested by the statement that the god made the bowed neck of the sick monarch as *firm as a young palm* and *erect as a cedar*; cf. also the earlier lines *My ample form like a reed they* (the demons) *prostrated; Like a palm was I overturned, on my back I was thrown*. The idea of Nebuchadnezzar's *heart* or sense being *changed* to that of a beast, so that he dwelt with the beasts of the field *and did eat grass like oxen*, may perhaps be based on the (more or less conjectural) lines *For lack of food grass* (*išpu*, 'sprouts'; or *içbu* or *išbu?*) *was my fare. He seized my blood, wrenched away my heart* (or *understanding*). *All the day the driver driveth me.... In my stable I fell down like an ox; I wallowed like a sheep in my own dung*. In the process of cure Merodach *tore out the clinging ailment and the head-sickness, and rained down upon me the cool showers of night*. So Nebuchadnezzar's *body was wet with the dew of heaven*. The lines *Like (those of) a she-swampfiend or a shûçû-*

---

[1] Glosses on this line: gir-ra: UR-MAG: nap-sa-mu: ma-ak-ça-ru ša KA ANŠU KUR-RA, 'bond of the mouth of a horse'.

[2] Glosses. as-suk-ku .... tu: aš-pu uš-bu, 'ambush': see HWB. s.v. *aspu*. Delitzsch explains *assukku* as 'a screen', 'stalking-fence', or 'cover for an ambuscade'. (The commentary preserves the fragments of five lines more; of which, however, little or nothing can be made.)

INTRODUCTION

demon He had sharpened my nails; He poured forth their ailment, He made good their state vividly remind us that Nebuchadnezzar's humiliation continued *until his hair had grown long as (that of) griffon-vultures, and his nails as (those of) birds* (Dan 4^{30}, AV^{33}). So, when Merodach heals him, the old king says: *Of my long hair I was plucked, Of the fetter I was freed.*

The Daniel-story makes pride the sin for which Nebuchadnezzar was so severely punished. This was perhaps an inference from the lines

*The Majesty of the King to that of a god I made equal;
And awe of the Palace I made the multitude learn.*

The Babylonian sovereign speaks only of his *sins* in general, which his Lord caused the wind to carry away.

The closing words of the Biblical account *Now I Nebuchadnezzar praise and extol and honour the King of heaven* read almost like a paraphrase of the opening words which constitute the title of the Babylonian poem *Ludlul Bêl nîmeqi*, 'I will worship the Lord of Wisdom'. The line *Šarrâkuma atûr ana rêši*, 'I am (was) king, and I became a thrall' (i.e. I was treated like one; I was abased from my royal dignity and humiliated to the utmost) might be regarded as the key-note to the story of Dan 4, which was written to demonstrate that *the Most High is sovran in the kingdom of men and gives it to whom He will, and appoints over it the lowliest of men* (Dan $4^{14(17)}$).

Lastly, it may be remarked that the line *In the mouth of the lion devouring me Merodach put a bit* supplies the *motif* of Dan 6.

Date of the Book of Job.

The date of the book can only be surmised with any degree of probability from internal evidence, part of which has already been submitted incidentally in the foregoing considerations. Not much stress can be laid upon the social characteristics and conditions of the time as they appear to be reflected in passages like chap. 24 or 29^{7-10}, 30^{1-8}, which might equally well indicate, so far as we know, any period of the history from the age of Abraham (First Babylonian Dynasty) down to the close of the Jewish monarchy. As we have seen, the moral questions raised by the book grew out of the painful experience of Jewish history. The prophets of the eighth century B.C. are unanimous in regarding the calamities of Israel and Judah as Iahvah's judgement upon the national sins. They are silent on the point which Job found so inconsistent with ordinary ideas of justice, 9^{22} ff., that the innocent may be involved in the fate of the guilty.

sweep away righteous and wicked alike? Shall not the Judge of all the Earth do justice? do not seem to have occurred to Hosea and Amos, Isaiah and Micah (see Gn 18²³⁻²³ J² circ. 650 B.C.?). It is not before the times of continual disaster, the age of Jeremiah and Ezekiel who witnessed the final tragedy of their country, that we hear voices of agonized entreaty and remonstrance with Iahvah such as meet us in the book of Job. *And I said, Alas, my Lord Iahvah! surely Thou hast altogether misled this people and Jerusalem with a promise of peace, whereas the sword reacheth to the life* (Je 4¹⁰): *Is there no balm in Gilead? is there no physician there?* (ib. 8²²). *Chastise me, Iahvah, but with justice; not in Thine anger, lest thou make me few* (ib. 10²⁴). *Righteous art Thou, Iahvah, though I complain of Thee: yet would I argue the case with Thee. Why does the way of the wicked prosper? why are all treacherous deceivers unmolested? Thou plantest them; they take root: they sprout* (leg. יחלפו? cf. Ps 90⁵,⁶, Ho 14⁷), *they bring forth fruit: Thou art nigh to their mouth, and far from their reins* (ib. 12¹,²). Cf. Jb 21⁷ ff. Jeremiah too is never weary of tracing the calamities of Judah to the national unfaithfulness to Iahvah in religion and breaches of the moral law in the dealings of everyday life. His contemporaries appear to have preferred to account for their misfortunes by the sins of their ancestors (cf. Ex 20⁵). In contradicting this popular view, which they expressed in a proverb current at the time, the prophet foretells happier days when people will no longer say, *The fathers have eaten sour grapes And the teeth of the sons are set on edge;* but a man will die for his own sin, and the eater of the sour grapes will have his own teeth set on edge (Je 31²⁹ f.): in other words, the innocent will not be involved in the fate of the guilty, but each will fare according to his personal deserts. As Ezekiel puts it, discussing the same proverb (Ez 18), *The soul that sinneth, it shall die. A son shall bear no part of the guilt of the father, and a father shall bear no part of the guilt of the son* (Ez 18²⁰). Ezekiel is combating the assertion that *The way of the Lord is not equitable* (יִתָּכֵן, measured out, scil. by the strict rule of right); which is precisely one of the contentions of Job. Zephaniah (1¹²) denounces coming judgement upon *the men who are settled upon their lees* (like wine left undisturbed to fine); *who think that Iahvah does neither good nor harm*—is indifferent to human conduct, intervening neither to rescue the righteous nor to punish the guilty great ones (*temp.* Josiah; before 621 B.C.).

But it is in Malachi,[1] the last of the OT prophetic writers (he belongs

---

[1] It is surely no real objection to the name Malachi = Malachiah that it belongs to no other person in the OT records. The same objection would lie against the name Hachaliah, f. of Nehemiah, or Jedidiah (2 S 12²⁵). If the full name was מַלְאָכִיָהוּ *Iahvah's Messenger*, it would quite naturally be abridged in colloquial use into מַלְאָכִי, ⟨. . .⟩ with the appellative מַלְאָכִי *my messenger*, which

to the Persian period; cf. 'thy pasha' 1⁸) that we have clear evidence of widespread unbelief in the practical value of the ancient faith and the traditional worship. *Ye have wearied Iahvah with your words and ye say, By what have we wearied Him? By your saying, Every one that doeth evil is pleasing in the eyes of Iahvah, and in them He delighteth: or else, Where is the God of Judgment?* (2¹⁷). *Your words have been strong against Me, said Iahvah, and ye say, What have we talked against Thee? Ye have said, It is vain to serve Elohim; and what profit is it that we have observed His observance, and that we have walked as mourners because of Iahvah Sabaoth? And now we call the presumptuous happy; yea, the doers of wickedness are built up; yea, they have tested Elohim and escaped hurt* (3¹³⁻¹⁵). Cf. Jb 21⁷⁻¹⁵ 34⁹ 35³. In view of the despairing mood of the pious and the scoffs of apostates, the prophet can only seek to reassure the one and alarm the other class in the community by announcing the intervention of Iahvah; after which they will *again see the difference between a righteous one and a wicked, between one who serveth Elohim and one who hath not served Him* (3¹⁷ᶠ 4¹ ᶠᶠ·).

If we are right in reading אִגָּר instead of אֶרֶז in 7⁶, as a royal post or mounted courier (= Gk. ἄγγαρος), cf. 9²⁵, the word will point us to the Persian period for the book of Job also. But however that may be, the appearance of 'The Satan' in the Prologue as an Angel hostile to man finds its only parallel in Zechariah who prophesied under Darius Hystaspis (520 B.C. onwards): see Zc 3¹·² where 'The Satan' plays the part of Adversary to Joshua the High Priest before the Angel of Iahvah.

There is certainly some evidence of progress in OT dealing with the problem. Ezekiel is content to deny that children suffer for the sins of their fathers, irrespective of the question of their own guilt or innocence.

---

occurs 3¹ as an allusive reference to the prophet's personal name (cf. 2 Esdr 1⁴⁰). That 𝔊 read מַלְאָכוֹ, *his messenger*, may only indicate that in the translator's time the existence of the prophet was already forgotten, if it was not due to a common confusion of the two similar letters Waw and Yod. To say that 'the name is not a likely one' (EB) is simply to beg the question. It is true that Malachiah or Malachi does not recur in the OT; neither does Habakkuk (cf also Jonah, Nahum). But rarity is no argument against the authenticity of a Proper Name, and as regards the meaning, a prophet might as fittingly be named *Iahvah's Messenger* as *Iahvah's Servant* (Obadiah), cf. the Sumerian LUG, *messenger* or *minister* (also read SHUKKAL, SUKKAL, Assyr. *sukkallu*), which may be in this sense a variation of LAG, *to go* (Caus. *to send*¹) = לָאךְ √ of מַלְאָךְ (cf Eth. *la'aka*, 'to send', *tal'ěka*, 'to be sent', 'wait on', 'minister'). The Sum. LUG (SHUKKAL) is used of subordinate deities who, like the classical Mercury and Iris, serve as ministers or messengers of the greater gods; and it occurs in personal names such as LUG (*Sukkal*)-*Rammân*, 'Rimmon's Messenger' or 'Minister'.

It seems possible that the word הַנָּבִיא, *the prophet*, has fallen out of the text before אָהַבְתִּי. If so, the original heading of Malachi was like those of Habakkuk and Haggai (Hab 1· Hg 1¹.

Iahvah is just; His way is equal; every man 'dies' for his own sins. If a sinner turn righteous, he 'lives'; if a righteous man turn sinner, he dies. A later generation was not satisfied with this simple solution which seemed to contradict experience. Malachi makes it clear that in his day many were throwing doubt on the value of the established religion, on the ground of its apparent inefficacy to ensure the prosperity of its adherents or to shield them from adversity. Their openly expressed conclusion was that *It is vain to serve Iahvah*, since *they who forget God prosper*. The prophet can only meet the difficulty by assuring his fellow-believers that it will not be so always: Iahvah will interpose in His approaching Day. Then the balance will be redressed; the godless will be swept away in fires of judgement, and will become ashes under the feet of the godly; and doubters and waverers will again discern the difference between righteous and wicked, between irreligious and religious. The difference in their fate will make it clear. The doubt, however, was not finally laid by this pronouncement. The Day of Iahvah was delayed. The vicissitudes of history, now favourable, now unfavourable, to the Jewish community, kept the question alive until, in the time of Christ, we hear the disciples asking whether congenital blindness was a punishment for the sufferer's own sins (committed, we must suppose, in a former life) or for those of his parents. Our Lord's answer contradicted both theories of suffering, by declaring (in the spirit of the Prologue of Job) that affliction is not necessarily punishment and, therefore, no presumption of antecedent sin. It may be designed to give scope for the play of Divine forces (Joh 9^3) and so to illustrate the Glory of God. This is surely the Final Cause and End of all permitted evil, as of all created existence—unless indeed we are to cry with the frank sensualist

'Thou, Nature, art my goddess!'

and surrender ourselves to a base idolatry of appetite, more degrading than the worship of stocks and stones with which, in other stages of human culture, it is usually associated.

Note on the prosody of the poem.

Some of the poetical portions of the book are translated into quatrains of triple-stressed lines after the original measures, which are not entirely obscured by the numerous interpolations of the text. Possible interpolations are enclosed in square brackets, thus [ ].

THE BOOK OF JOB IN ENGLISH

A TRANSLATION OF THE REVISED TEXT

CHAPTER 1.—1. A man there was in 'Ûç-land, Eyob by name. This man was moral and upright—godfearing and 2 averse from evil. So there were born to him seven sons 3 and three daughters; and his livestock came to seven thousand sheep and goats, and three thousand camels, and five hundred yoke of oxen, and five hundred she-asses, and an immense body of slaves: he became, in fact, the greatest of all the Eastern tribesmen.

4 Now his sons were wont to go and banquet in each others' houses in turn; and they would send and invite their three 5 sisters to eat and drink with them. But when the round of the banquets was complete, Eyob sent and purified them; and he would rise early and offer burnt-offerings in proportion to their number, for he thought 'Perhaps my sons have sinned by cursing God in thought!' so used Eyob to do all the year round.

6 But the day came when the Sons of God went in to stand in attendance on Iahvah; and the Satan too went in among 7 them. Said Iahvah to the Satan, 'Whence comest thou?' The Satan answered Iahvah, 'From roving on the earth and 8 roaming about in it.' Said Iahvah to the Satan, 'Hast thou noticed my servant Eyob? he has not his like on earth—a man moral and upright, godfearing and averse from evil.' 9 But the Satan answered Iahvah, 'Is it for nothing that Eyob 10 fears God? hast not Thou Thyself made a fence all round him and his houshold and everything that belongs to him? the work of his hands Thou hast blessed, and his livestock 11 has multiplied in the land. However, only stretch out Thine Hand and strike all that belongs to him, and he will assuredly 12 curse Thee to Thy Face!' Said Iahvah to the Satan, 'There! all that belongs to him is in thine hand, only against his

person stretch not out thine hand!' The Satan then withdrew from the presence of Iahvah.

13 And the day came when his sons and his daughters were eating bread and drinking wine in their eldest brother's house,
14 and a messenger went in to Eyob and said: 'The oxen were
15 ploughing, and the she-asses were grazing hard by, when the Sabeans attacked and seized them, but the young men they put to the sword; and only I scarce escaped alone to tell
16 thee!' He was still speaking when another came in and said: 'The Fire of God hath fallen from Heaven and set fire to the sheep and goats and the young men and devoured them;
17 and only I have scarce escaped alone to tell thee!' He was still speaking when another came in and said: 'The Chaldeans made three companies and dashed upon the camels and seized them, but the young men they put to the sword; and only
18 I scarce escaped alone to tell thee!' He was still speaking when another came in and said: 'Thy sons and daughters were eating bread and drinking wine in their eldest brother's
19 house, when lo, a hurricane blew from beyond the wilderness and struck the four corners of the house, and it fell upon the young men, and they perished; and only I have scarce escaped alone to tell thee!'
20 At that, Eyob started up and tore his mantle and shaved his head, and then threw himself upon the ground and did
21 reverence. Then he said:

'Bare came I forth from my Mother's womb,
And bare must I thither return!
'Twas Iahvah who gave, and Iahvah who took—
Let Iahvah's Name be blest!'

22 In all this Eyob sinned not, nor charged any faultiness to God.

CHAPTER 2.—1. But the day came when the Sons of God went in to stand in attendance on Iahvah; and the Satan too went in among them.
2 Said Iahvah to the Satan, 'Whence comest thou?' The Satan answered Iahvah, 'From roving on the earth and roam-
3 ing about in it.' Said Iahvah to the Satan, 'Hast thou noticed my servant Eyob? he has not his like on earth—a man moral and upright, god-fearing and averse from evil. He still maintains his virtue, though thou didst incite me against him,
4 that I might swallow him up without cause.' But the Satan

answered Iahvah, 'One skin for another! and all that the man hath will he give for himself. However, only stretch out Thine Hand and strike his bone and his flesh, and he will assuredly curse Thee to Thy Face!' Said Iahvah to the Satan, 'There! he is in thine hand! yet spare his life!'

The Satan then withdrew from the presence of Iahvah and smote Eyob with a malignant eczema from the sole of his foot to the crown of his head; and he took him a potsherd to scratch himself with. Now he was sitting among the ashes, when his wife demanded, 'Art thou still maintaining thy virtue? Curse God and die!' But he replied: 'Thou speakest like one of the silly wantons! Are we actually to accept what is good from God, and not to accept what is evil?' In all this Eyob sinned not with his lips.

And Eyob's Three Friends heard of all this evil which had come upon him; and they came from their respective places— Eliphaz the Temanite and Bildad the Shuhite and Zophar the Minean—and met by appointment, to come to condole with him and to comfort him. But when they caught sight of him from a distance and failed to recognize him, they burst into loud weeping and tore each of them his mantle and sprinkled dust upon their heads, throwing it up into the air. Then they sat down with him on the ground for seven days and seven nights, none of them speaking a word to him, because they saw that the pain was intolerable.

CHAPTER 3.—1. *Afterwards Eyob opened his mouth and cursed his day. And Eyob answered and said:*

3 Perish the Day I was born,
And the Night that said, 'Here is a Man!'
4 That Day become Darkness!
Light seek it not from Above,
Nor Sunlight beam upon it!
5 Darkness and Deathshade bedim it!
Cloud settle upon it!
Benightings of day affright it!
6 That Day—utter Gloom seize it!
Be it not one in the Days of the Year,
Nor be counted in the Days of the Month!
8 Day-enchanters ban it,
Adept in rousing the Dragon!

7 That Night become stone-barren!
No joyous birthshout enter it!
9 Darkened be the Stars of its Twilight!
Let it wait for the Light in vain,
Nor look on the Eyelids of Dawn!
10 Because it barred not my door(s),
Nor hid Trouble from mine eyes.

11 Why was I not born dying,—
Coming forth from the womb but to expire?
12 O why did knees receive me,
And breasts that I might suck?
13 For then had I lain down and were quiet;
I had slept; then peace were mine!
14 Like Kings and national Councillors,
Who rebuilded ruins for their pleasure;
15 And like Princes who had much gold,—
Who filled their houses with silver:
16 Or as a buried abortion I had been,—
As babes which never saw light.
17 There the wicked cease from raging;
And there the weary rest.
18 Together the prisoners repose;
They hear not the taskmaster's voice:
19 Small and great are there;
And the slave is free from his master.

20 Why is light given to the sufferer,
And life to them that are sorrowful,—
21 Who wait for Death in vain,
And dig for it rather than treasure,—
22 Who are glad beyond gladness,
And rejoice when they find the grave,—
23 To the Man whose path is hidden,
And whom Eloah hath fenced about?
24 He feedeth me with bread of sighs,
And I pour out my groans like water.
25 If I dread a thing, it cometh upon me,
And what I fear befalleth me.
26 I have neither ease nor quiet,—
No rest, and trouble cometh.

CHAPTER 4.—1: *In reply Eliphaz the Temanite said:*
2 Should one address discourse to the sick?
    Yet who can withhold speech?
3 Lo, thou hast put many right,
    And wouldst strengthen drooping hands:

4 Thy words would raise the stumbler,
    And thou madest bowed knees firm.
5 But now it cometh to thyself, thou art overcome,
    It reacheth thee, and thou art bewildered.

6 Is not thy piety thine assurance,
    And thine hope the perfectness of thy ways?
7 Think now, who that was guiltless ever perished?
    And where were the upright wiped out?

8 In my ken, 'tis the plowers of trouble
    And the sowers of misery, that reap it:
9 By the breath of Eloah they perish,—
    By the blast of His wrath are ended.

10 The fangs of the lion are shattered,
    And the teeth of the young lions broken out:
11 The old lion perisheth for lack of prey,
    And the she-lion's whelps are scattered.

12 But to me a word stole in,
    And mine ear caught a whisper of speech,
13 In thoughts woke by visions of night,
    When deep sleep falleth on men.

14 A fear came over me, and trembling,
    And every bone of me it shook with fear;
15 And a Breath o'er my face glideth on,—
    It raiseth the hairs of my head.

16 And behold, Shaddai is passing!
    He stoppeth, but I discern not His form;
    A Shape is before mine eyes;
    I hear a murmuring sound:

17 'Can a mortal be righteous with Eloah,
    Or a man be pure with his Maker?

18 Behold, in His Servants He trusteth not,
  And on His Angels He putteth no praise:

19 Much less in denizens of clay,
  Whose foundation is in the dust;
  Who are crushed at the turn of Dawn,—
20 Between Morning and Evening are shattered!'

  [For lack of Wit they perish for ever;
21 They die for want of Wisdom.]

CHAPTER 5.—1. Call then; is there any to answer thee
  And to which of the Holy Ones wilt turn?
2 Nay, impatience slayeth the fool,
  And passion killeth the simple.

3 I myself have seen the fool uprooted,
  And his home was suddenly plucked up.
4 His sons are far from welfare;
  They are crushed in the gate without help.

5 Whose harvest the hungry devoureth,
  And the thirsty ingathereth their fruitage.
6 For Affliction issueth not from the dust,
  And Trouble springeth not out of the ground:

7 [For Man is born to Trouble,
  As the vulture's brood to soaring.]
8 But I, I would appeal unto El,
  And would set my case before Elohim,
9 Who doeth great things and unsearchable,
  Wonders beyond all reckoning:

10 Who giveth rain on the ploughland,
  And sendeth water on the commons;
11 To set the lowly on high,
  And to raise mourners to wellbeing:

12 [Who thwarteth the schemes of the wily,
  That their hands achieve nothing real.]

13 Who catcheth the wise in their own craft,
   And the plan of the shifty befooleth;
14 So that by day they fumble with darkness,
   And grope at high noon as in the night.

15 So He saveth the humble from the sword,—
   The needy from the hand of the strong;
16 And hope is born for the poor,
   And Iniquity shutteth her mouth.

17 Happy whom Eloah correcteth!
   'Then refuse not Shaddai's chastisement!'
18 For 'tis His way to hurt and bind up,
   He smiteth, and His own hands heal.

19 In six straits He will rescue thee;
   Yea, in seven no harm shall strike thee;
20 In famine will He ransom thee from Death,
   And in war from the grip of the sword;

21 When the Pest is abroad, thou shalt be hidden,—
   Shalt be fearless of Havoc when it cometh;
22 At the lion and dragon thou shalt laugh,
   And of wild things have no fear;

23 [Having league with the children of the field,
   And the' wild things being made thy friends.]
24 And thou shalt know thy tent is safe,—
   Shalt go over thy fold and miss nothing.
25 Thou shalt know that thine offspring are many,—
   Thine issue as the grass of the earth.

26 Thou shalt come to the grave in thy vigour,
   As the corn is carried up in its season.
27 Lo this—we have searched it, thus it is;
   We have heard it; know it thou for thyself!

CHAPTER 6.—1. *In reply Eyob said:*
2 Would that my 'impatience' were weighed,
   And my misery balanced against it!
3 For 'tis heavier than the sand of seas;
   Therefore my words would go up.

4 For the arrows of Shaddai are in my flesh,
  Whose venom my spirit drinketh;
  Eloah's terrors trouble me,
  And the dread of El dismayeth me.

5 Doth a wild ass bray over grass,
  Or loweth an ox over fodder?
6 Is tasteless stuff eaten unsalted?
  Or is there flavour in the sap of mallows?

7 [My appetite declineth it;
  Loatheth it like vomit of my food.]
8 O that my boon might come,—
  That Eloah would grant my hope!
9 That Shaddai would will to crush me,—
  Would unloose His hand and cut me off!

11 What is my strength, that I should wait,
   And what my end, that I should endure?
12 Is my strength the strength of stones,
   Or my flesh—is it of bronze?

13 Behold, I have no aid,
   And help is driven away from me!
14 My friend hath cast off kindness,
   And forsaketh the fear of Shaddai.

15 My kin are faithless as a wâdy,—
   As a bed of transitory waters,
16 Which were dark with a pall of ice,
   And on which the snow lay piled:

17 In the dry season they disappear;
   When it is hot, they are extinct from their place.
19 The caravans of Tema looked forward,—
   The travelling companies of Sheba expected them;

20 They were ashamed for their confidence in them,—
   They reached them and were confounded.
18 They turn their way backward;
   They go up into the desert and perish.

21 Such now have ye proven to me;
   Ye see some scare, and are afraid.
22 Is it that I have said, 'Give me something,
   [And bribe with your means on my behalf;
23 And rescue me from an enemy,]
   And ransom me from robbers?'

24 Teach me, and I, I will be mum;
   Yea, give me to understand mine error!
25 Why are honest words grievous?
   And what doth your reproof reprove?

26 Mean ye to reprove mere words,
   And to answer windy speech?
27 Even upon the blameless will ye fall,
   And concoct words against your friend?

28 And now, so please you, face me!
   To your faces I surely shall not lie!
29 [Pray return; let there be no unfairness;
   But hear ye my straightforward pleadings!]
30 Is there really injustice in my tongue,
   Or cannot my palate distinguish truth?

CHAPTER 7.—11 I too will not gag my mouth,—
I will open my lips with Thee;
I will speak in the anguish of my spirit,—
Will complain in the bitterness of my soul:—

12 'Am I the Sea, or the Sea-Dragon,
   That Thou settest a guard over me?'
13 When I say, 'My couch will comfort me,—
   My bed ease in part my complaining';

14 Thou scarest me with dreams,
   And with visions dost affright me;
15 So that I choose strangling,
   And prefer death to my torments.

16 I said, I cannot always live;
   Let me alone, for my days are a breath!
17 What is a mortal that Thou shouldst make much of him,
   And shouldst set Thy mind upon him

18 That Thou shouldst visit him morn by morn,—
   Shouldst try him moment by moment?
19 How long wilt Thou not look away from me,
   Nor give me a moment's respite?

20 If I sin, what do I to Thee,
   Thou that keepest watch on man's heart?
   Why hast Thou made me a butt for Thee,
   So that I am become Thy target?

21 Why dost Thou not forgive my transgression,
   And let my sin pass?
   For soon in the dust I shall lie;
   And if Thou seek me, I shall be no more.

7.—1 Hath not Man a hard service on earth?
   Are not his days like those of a hireling?
2 Like the slave that panteth for the shade,
   And like the hireling who looketh forward to his wages,

3 So have I been assigned delusive days,
   And troubled nights have been allotted me.
4 Should I lie down on my bed, I say,
   'O that it were morning, that I might rise!'

   And if I rise, 'O that it were evening!'
   And I am full-fed with tossings until twilight.
5 My flesh is clothed with worms,
   My skin gathers and runs.

6 My time hath passed more swiftly than a post,—
   Hath hopelessly come to an end.
7 Remember then my life is but air;
   Mine eye will no more see good.

8 [The eye of my Beholder will not descry me;
   While Thine eyes are upon me, I shall vanish.]
9 The smoke dissolveth and disappeareth;
   So he who goeth down to Sheol cometh not up:
10 He returneth no more to his home,
   And his place knoweth him no more.

CHAPTER 8.—1 *In reply Bildad the Shuhite said:*
2 How long wilt thou utter such things,
 And shall thy mouth multiply windy words?
3 Would El wrest judgement,
 Or Shaddai pervert justice?
4 Though thy sons did sin against Him,
 And He threw them into the power of their transgression;
5 If thou thyself wilt seek El earnestly,
 And make thy prayer to Shaddai,
6 Surely now He will listen to thee,
 And repay thee after thy righteousness:
7 And thy first estate shall seem small,
 And thy last shall be very great.

8 For ask, I pray, of the first generation,
 And give heed to the findings of the Fathers;
9 [For ourselves are of yesterday, and we know not;
 And our time upon earth is like a shadow:]
10 Will not they teach thee and tell thee,
 And forth of their heart utter words?

11 Can papyrus grow tall without mire?
 Or the Nile-rush wax great without water?
12 Yet budding, if it have no moisture,
 Faster than any herb it withereth.
13 Such is the end of all who forget El,
 And the worldling's hope—it perisheth:
14 Whose confidence is but a cobweb,
 And his trust a spider's house:
15 [If he lean against his house, it standeth not;
 If he hold on thereby, it is not steady]
16 He is fresh and green before the sun,
 And his suckers spread over his garden;
17 About a cairn his roots he twineth,
 And a stony house he chooseth.
18 El swalloweth him up from his place,
 And it disowneth him—'I never saw thee!'
19 Thus HE plucketh up his abode,
 And from the ground cometh another to spring.

20 Lo El doth not spurn a perfect one,
Nor hold the hand of evildoers!
21 The mouth of the upright He filleth with laughter,
And the lips of the pure with shouting.

22 [They who hate Him are clothed with shame;
And the tent of the wicked is no more!]

CHAPTER 9.—1 *In reply Eyob said:*
2 Ah yes, I know it is so.
And how can frail man be right with El?
3 If he would fain dispute with Him,
He will not answer him one question in a thousand.

4 Allwise and Almighty—
Who hath ever opposed Him without hurt?
5 That removeth mountains, that they are not seen,
And from the roots overturneth them in His wrath;

6 That shaketh Earth out of her place,
And the pillars of Heaven—they tremble.
7 That forbiddeth Sol to rise,
And sealeth about the stars:

8 That spread the heavens, unhelped,
And treadeth the summits of the earth:
9 That made Kesîl and Kîmah,
And built the Chambers of the South

10 [That doeth great things beyond search,
And wondrous things beyond number.]
11 Lo, He passeth by me, but I see Him not,—
He glideth on, but I perceive Him not.
12 Should He break out, who can turn Him back?
Who say to Him, What doest Thou?

13 Eloah turneth not back His wrath;
Under Him bowed the Helpers of Rahab!
14 Much less could I answer Him,—
Could I choose my words with Him:

15 Whom, though I were right, I would not answer;
I would rather beg mine Adversary's mercy.

16 If I summoned Him, and He responded,
   I could not believe He would listen to my plea,

17 Who would snatch me away with a blast,
   And give me many wounds for no cause;—
18 Would not let me recover my breath,
   But would surfeit me with bitter griefs.

19 If I think of Might, He is strong;
   And if of Right—who is to arraign Him?
20 Though I were righteous, my own mouth would condemn me,—
   Though perfect, He would find me perverted!

21 I am perfect, but regard not my life,—
   Righteous, but loathe my existence;
22 Therefore say I, 'Tis all one!
   Perfect and godless alike He endeth!

23 [If the Scourge kill suddenly,
   He mocketh at the slaughter of the innocent!
24 The land He hath given to a Godless One;
   And the face of her judges He veileth:
   If not He, who else hath done it?]
25 My days have been swifter than a runner;
   They have fled without seeing any good;
26 They have sped like skiffs of papyrus,—
   Like a vulture that swoopeth on food.

27 If I say, 'I will forget my complaining,—
   Relax my looks and be cheerful';
28 I am fearful because of my sufferings;
   I know Thou dost not hold me innocent.

29 [If 'tis I who am in the wrong,
   Why should I labour in vain?]
30 Though I had washed me white as snow,—
   Had cleansed my hands with lye,
31 Thou wouldst plunge me then in filth,
   And my clothes would make me abhorred!

32 For He is not a man like me,
   That we should come to trial together.

33 Would there were an umpire between us,
To lay his hand upon us both!

34 Let Him move His Rod from off me,
And let not the awe of Him appal me!
35 I would speak, and would not fear Him:
For I, I know Him not right!

CHAPTER 10.—1 I have taken disgust at life;
I will give the rein to my complaining:
2 I will say to Eloah, Treat me not as guilty!
Let me know why Thou quarrellest with me!

3 Doth it please Thee to wrong the perfect,—
To spurn the creature of Thine Hands?
4 Hast Thou mere human eyes,
Or dost see as a mortal seeth?

5 [Are Thy days brief as a mortal's,
Or Thy years as the days of a man,]
6 That Thou seekest for my offence,
And searchest after my sin—
7 When Thou knowest I am not guilty,
And there is no wrong in my hands?

8 Thine own Hands framed me and fashioned me,
And wilt Thou turn round and swallow me up?
9 [O remember that Thou madest me of clay,
And to dust wilt make me return!]
10 Didst Thou not pour me out like milk,
And curdle me like cheese?

11 With skin and with flesh Thou didst clothe me,—
With bones and sinews didst enclose me.
12 Compassion and kindness Thou showedst me,
And Thine Oversight guarded my spirit.

13 But all this Thou didst hide in Thine heart.—
I know that this was in Thy thought:
14 Should I sin, Thou wouldst observe me,
And wouldst not absolve me from my fault;

15 Were I wicked, woe to me!
And were I righteous, I might not hold up my head.

16 Thou wouldst again deal wondrously with me,
17 And renew Thy blows upon me;

[Thou wouldst aggravate Thine anger with me,
And bring fresh thraldom upon me.]
18 But why out of the womb didst Thou bring me?
I might have died, and no eye have seen me:
19 As though I had never been, I should be,—
Borne from the belly to the tomb!

20 Are not the days of my life but few?
Let me alone, that I may cheer me awhile,
21 Before I depart, without return,
To the land of Darkness and Deathshade;

22 [The land of gloom sans light,
And daylight shineth not thereon.]

CHAPTER 11.—1 *In reply Zophar the Minaean said:*
2 Shall a master of words be unanswered,
Or a man of ready lips be justified?
3 At thy babble shall people be silent,
And thou scoff without rebuke?

4 [And say, 'I am pure,
And clean have I been before Him'?]
5 But Oh that He would speak,
And open His lips with thee,
6 And show thee the secrets of Wisdom—
For It is wonderful in substance!

7 [Canst thou fathom the nature of Eloah,
Or exhaust the being of Shaddai?]
8 'Tis higher than Heaven—what canst thou do?
Deeper than She'ol—what canst thou know?
9 Longer than Earth in measure,
And broader than the Sea.

11 For HE knoweth the wicked,
And seeth evil without effort.
12 But a witless wight will get wit,
When a wild-ass colt begetteth a man.

13 If even thou wilt prepare thine heart,
 And spread forth thine hands towards Him—
14 If Evil thou banish from thine hand,
 And harbour not Wrong in thy tent;

15 [Then indeed thou shalt hold up thy face,—
 Thou shalt become steadfast and fearless.]
16 Then thou, even thou, shalt forget Trouble,—
 Shalt remember it as a flood that is past:
17 And thy light shall be steady as noontide;
 Thou shalt shine forth, become like the Dawn.

18 And thou shalt know that there is indeed hope,
 And unafraid shalt lie down in safety:
19 Thou shalt couch, with none to alarm;
 And many shall pay thee court.

20 But the eyes of the godless shall fail,
 And refuge be lost to them;
 And their hope is a dying breath,
 For Eloah disdaineth their trust.

CHAPTER 12.—1 *In reply Eyob said:*
2 Doubtless ye are the Wise,
 And with you Wisdom will die!
3 I too have sense like you;
 And who hath not store of such talk?

4 Laughter to my friends I become;
 They laugh at the just and perfect:
5 Upon Ruin they pour contempt—
 Dishonour upon him whose foot slippeth.

6 [Robbers' tents are carefree,
 And provokers of El are secure.]
7 Ask now the beast, and it will teach thee,—
 The bird of the air, and it will tell thee;
8 Or contemplate Earth, and she will teach thee,
 And let the fish of the Sea inform thee!

9 Who knoweth not, by all these creatures,
 That Iahvah's Hand hath done this?
10 In Whose Hand is the soul of everything living,
 And the spirit of all human flesh

11 Doth not the ear test words,
   As the palate tasteth food?
12 Do not many years bring Wisdom,
   And length of days Understanding?

13 [With Him are Wisdom and Might;
   His are Strength and Understanding.]
14 Lo, He breaketh down, and there is no rebuilding,
   He prisoneth a man, and there is no release!
15 Lo, He stoppeth the waters, and they dry up;
   He letteth them go, and they whelm the land!

16 With Him are Might and exceeding Power;
   The misled and the misleader are His!
17 The counsel of Counsellors He maketh folly,
   And the Judges of the land He befooleth.

18 The raiment of kings He looseth,
   And removeth the girdle of their loins.
19 He marcheth Priests away disrobed;
   And the words of Prophets He maketh naught.

20 He depriveth the shrewd of speech,
   And the judgement of Elders He taketh away.
21 He poureth contempt upon nobles,
   And the girdle of magnates He looseth.

22 He revealeth deep things out of Darkness,
   And bringeth things hidden forth to Light.
23 He leadeth nations astray, and destroyeth them,
   He felleth peoples, and wipeth them out.

24 He distracteth the heads of a people,
   And maketh them wander in a pathless waste:
25 They grope in darkness void of light,
   And wander from the way like a drunkard.

   CHAPTER 13.—1 Lo, mine eye hath seen it all;
Mine ear hath heard and perceived it!
2 I too have knowledge like yours,
   And I fail not short of you.

3 Yet would I speak to Shaddai,
   And to El would fain present my case:
4 But ye, ye are quack-plasterers—
   Pseudo-physicians are ye all!

5 O that ye would keep strict silence!
   It might serve your turn as wisdom.
6 Hear ye now the reproof of my mouth,
   And listen to the pleading of my lips!

7 For El will ye speak unfairly,
   And for Him will ye utter deceit?
8 Will ye show favour to Shaddai,
   Or be special pleaders for El?

9 Will it be well when He searcheth you through?
   Or will ye trick Him like a mere mortal?
10 Assuredly He will punish you,
   If ye secretly show Him favour.

11 Should not the Fear of Him dismay you,
   And His Awe fall upon you?
12 Pray remember that ye dwell in the dust,
   And your houses are houses of clay!

13 Be silent, and I too will speak;
   And let Wrath pass over me!
14 I will take up my flesh in my teeth,
   And put my life in my hands:

15 Though He kill me, I will not wait,
   But my ways to His face will I prove!
16 Yea, HE must needs deliver me,
   For not before Him am I impious.

17 Hear ye still my discourse;
   And let me tell my knowledge in your ears!
18 Behold now, I have drawn up my case;
   I know it is I will be found right!

19 Who is there to contend with me?
   Were there any, I would be silent and die!

20 Grant Thou but two things in dealing with me;
   Then from Thy Face I will not hide!

21 Put far Thine Hand from off me,
   And let not Thy Terror intimidate me!
22 And call Thou, and I will reply;
   Or I will speak, and do Thou answer me!

23 How many misdeeds are mine?
   Let me know my transgression and my sin!
24 For what dost Thou hide Thy Face,
   And accountest me foe to Thyself?

25 Wouldst Thou scare a driven leaf,
   Or chase a withered stalk,
26 That Thou decreest bitter things for me,
   And bringest home to me the sins of my youth,

27 And puttest my feet in the stocks,
   And settest a bound to my steps?
28 (While they are like a fraying brocade—
   Like a garment the moth hath fretted)

CHAPTER 14.—1 Man, of woman born,
   Is shortlived, and full-fed with trouble.
2 Like the flowers he flowereth and fadeth,
   And fleeth like a shadow and stayeth not.

And he is like a decaying waterskin—
Like a garment the moth hath fretted.
5 Also his days are determined,
   And the number of his months is with Thee.

[His bound Thou hast set, and he passeth not]
3 Upon such a being dost Thou open Thine eye,
   And him dost Thou bring into Judgement?
4 [Who can purge himself from his uncleanness?
   Of all the sons of man not one.]
6 Look away from him and let him alone.
   Till his day, like a hireling's, be done.

7 For a tree indeed hath hope,
   If it have its boughs cut off;
   It may sprout again and bud,
   And the shoot of it may not fail.

8 If its root wax old in the earth,
   And its stock die in the soil;
9 At scent of water it may bud,
   And make wood like a sapling.

10 But a man dieth and is powerless—
   The human expireth and is no more!
11 [Waters have gone from a sea,
   And a river may parch and dry up;]
12 [And a wight lieth down and riseth not:]
   Till the heavens decay, he will not wake,
   Nor be roused out of his sleep.

13 O that Thou wouldst hide me in Hades—
   Wouldst conceal me till Thine Anger turn away,—
   Wouldst set me a term, and then remember me,
14 And from Death thereafter wouldst revive me!

   All the days of my hard service must I wait,
   Until my successor cometh.
15 Thou wilt call, but I shall not answer Thee;
   For the creature of Thine Hands Thou wilt yearn.

16 For now my very steps Thou countest,
   And passest over none of my sins;
17 Thou hast sealed my transgressions in a bag,
   And set a stamp upon all my misdeeds.

18 But the mountain falleth to ruin,
   And the rock removeth from its place;
19 Stones the waters wear away,
   [And a flood may wash away the soil,]
   And the hope of mortal man Thou destroyest.

20 [Thou overpowerest him, and for ever he departeth;
   Thou changest his face and sendest him off.]
21 His sons are honoured, but he doth not know,—
   Are reduced, but he doth not observe them:
22 Only, his flesh upon him is in pain,
   And his soul upon him mourneth.

CHAPTER 15.—1 *In reply Eliphaz the Temanite said:*
2 Should a wise man reply with wind,
　And charge himself full with the East?
3 Should he argue with speech that serveth not,
　And with words devoid of profit?

4 Thou, moreover, dost violate Reverence,
　And withdrawest prayer before El:
5 For thy guilt instructeth thy mouth,
　And thou choosest the tongue of the cunning.

6 [Thine own mouth condemneth thee, not I,
　And thine own lips testify against thee!]
7 Wast thou born first of mankind,
　And before the hills wast thou yeaned?
8 In the Council of Eloah didst thou listen,
　And was Wisdom revealed unto thee?

9 What dost thou know, and we know not,—
　Kennest thou, and it is not with us?
10 Both greybeard and withered age are among us,
　And one that is older than thy father.

11 Are El's consolations a little thing,
　And is Eloah's Word too little for thee?
12 [Why do thy feelings carry thee away,
　And why are thy glances haughty?]
13 That thou blowest thy breath at El,
　And lettest out words from thy mouth.

14 [What is a mortal that *he* should be pure,
　Or one born of woman be righteous?]
15 Behold, in His Holy Ones He trusteth not,
　And the Heavens are not pure in His eyes!
16 Much less a loathly and stinking one,
　That drinketh in wrong like water.

17 I will tell thee what I know; listen to me,
　And what I have seen I will relate!—
18 Facts which the Wise declare,
　And which their fathers concealed not from them.

19 [To whom alone the land was given,
   And no alien passed over amongst them.]
20 All his days the wicked is anxious;
   And but few years are the tyrant's:
21 Dreadful sounds ring in his ears;
   In peace-time the spoiler may assail him.

22 Unsure of return out of darkness,
   He expecteth the hands of the sword:
23 He is the destined food of kites;
   He knows that his ruin is ready.

24 [A day of darkness alarmeth him;
   Straits and distress encompass him.]
25 For he stretched forth his hand against El,
   And would match his might with Shaddai;
26 He would rush upon Him with a buckler,—
   With a warrior's helmet and shield.

24ᵇ [Like a king ready for the fray.]
27 For he covered his face with fat,
   And amassed brawn on his loins;
28 And settled in ruined cities,—
   In houses that none should inhabit.

29 Though he be rich, his wealth shall not last;
   Nor shall he strike his roots in the soil.
30 The sunglare shall wither his shoots,
   And his blossom shall be blown away by the wind.

31 [Let him not trust in a gadding vine,
   For naught will its produce be!]
32 His branch shall be lopped ere its time,
   And his palm-bough shall not be green.
33 He shall mar like a vine his unripe grapes,
   And will shed his bloom like an olive.

34 For the tribe of the impious is stone-barren;
   And fire hath devoured the tents of bribery:
35 They are big with mischief, and bring forth misery,
   And their womb harboureth delusion.

CHAPTER 16—1 *In reply Eyob said:*
2 I have heard many things like those;
Sorry comforters are ye all!
3 [Will windy words have an end?
Or what aggrieveth thee that thou must answer?]
4 I also could talk like you,
If yourselves were in my place;

Could compose speeches against you,
And shake my head over you;
5 Could hearten you with the issue of my mouth,
And with a word of my lips make you strong!

6 [Should I speak, my pain will not be checked;
And if I cease, what will go from me?]
7 But now El hath utterly wearied me,—
He hath wasted and worn out my skin;
8 And my ruin for witness riseth against me,
And my grief maketh answer to my face.

9 His wrath hath rent in pieces and slain me,
He hath gnashed His teeth over me.
[The shafts of His troops have fallen upon me,
My foes look daggers at me.
10 They have gaped at me with their mouth,—
In scorn they have smitten my cheeks;
With fury they are filled against me.]
11 El giveth me up to the unjust,
And into the hands of the wicked He hurleth me.

12 Whole was I, and He shattered me;
He seized me by the nape, and dashed me to pieces.
He setteth me up for His target;
13 His marksmen compass me around.

He cleaveth my kidneys mercilessly;
He poureth my gall to the ground.
14 He breacheth me, breach upon breach;
He rusheth upon me like a warrior.

15 [Sackcloth have I stitched upon my hide;
I have thrust my horn into the dust:]
16 Mine eyes, they are red with weeping,
And on mine eyelids is fallen darkness:

17 Although there is no violence in my hands,
    And the prayer of my lips is pure.

18 O Earth, cover not my blood,
    And let there be no place for my cry!
19 Lo, my Witness is in the Heavens,
    And e'en now my Voucher in the Heights!

20 My prayer, it reacheth Eloah,
    And before Him mine eye droppeth tears—
21 That He may judge for a man with Eloah,
    And between a son of man and his fellow!
22 [For, come but a few years more,
    And the way without return I must go.]

CHAPTER 17.—1 My mind is too disordered for speech;
    Words are extinct to me:
2 A pack of sophists is with me,
    And mine eye dwelleth on deceivers.

3 O appoint me a surety with Thyself!
    For who is he that will pledge himself for me?
4 For Thou hast hidden insight from their heart;
    Therefore Thou wilt not lift up their horn.

5 'Tis my lot to pour down tears,
    And mine eyes fail with weeping:
6 [And Thou hast made me a byword of peoples,—
    A portent to nations I become.]
7 And mine eye is dim with sorrow,
    And my frame is worn to a shadow.

8 [Upright men would be confounded at this,
    And an innocent be moved to impiety:
9 But the righteous will hold to his way,
    And the guiltless wax more resolute.]
10 [But pray you, come on again;
    And I shall not find a wise man among you.]

11 My days, they vanish like chaff;
    Snapt are the cords of my heart:
12 Night for day I put:
    And the light is dim for darkness.

13 Yea, I hope for She'ol as my home,—
   In the Darkness have I spread my couch;
14 To the Pit I cry, 'Thou art my father!',—
   'My Mother and Sister!' to the maggot.

15 And where then is there hope for me?
   And my good, who can descry it?
16 Will they descend with me into She'ol?
   Or shall we go down together into the Dust?

CHAPTER 18.—1 *In answer Bildad of Shuah said:*
2 How long wilt thou not restrain words?
  Hold! that we too may speak.
3 Why are we regarded as cattle,—
  Are we like to the brutes in thine eyes?

4 Shall the Earth be dispeopled for thy sake,
  And the rock remove from his place?
5 Yea, the light of the wicked goeth out,
  And the flame of his fire doth not shine.

6 [The light is darkened in his tent,
  And his lamp above him goeth out.]
7 His footsteps are cramped as he goeth,
  And his own counsel throweth him to the ground.
8 For he is rushed into the net by his own feet;
  And he walketh himself upon the toils.

9 The trap catcheth his heel;
  The gin layeth hold upon him:
10 His snare is hidden in the ground,
   And his springe upon the path.

11 All around Terrors alarm him,
   And Fearfulness dogs his heels.
12 Famine consumeth his strength,
   And Ruin is ready to swallow him.

4ᵃ He teareth himself in his rage,
13 For hunger he devoureth his own flesh.
14 His cords are broken away from his tent;
   Terrors hunt him like a lion.
15 [The Vampire haunteth his tent;
   Brimstone is sprinkled on his homestead.]¹

16 Beneath, his roots dry up;
   And above, his branches wither.
17 His memory perisheth from the land,
   And he hath no name in the street.

18 God thrusteth him out of light into darkness,
   And maketh him flee out of the world.
19 Nor chit nor child hath he among his people,
   And there is no survivor in his haunts.

20 At his Day his juniors are appalled,
   And his elders Horror seizeth.
21 So fareth the abode of the wrongdoer,
   And so the home of the ungodly.

CHAPTER 19.—1 *But Eyob answered as follows:*
2 How long will ye grieve my soul,
   And crush me with words without knowledge?
3 Ten times over ye insult me,
   And feel no shame in hurting me.

4 But even had I in sooth gone astray,
   With myself would my error abide:
5 But you against me talk big,
   And make my misery proof against me.

6 Know then, 'tis Eloah that hath bent me,
   And closed his net in upon me:
7 Lo, I cry 'Murder!', and am not answered;
   I shriek, but there is no justice!

8 My way He walled up, that I cannot pass;
   And on my paths He setteth darkness:
9 He hath stript me of my glory,
   And removed the coronal of my head.

10 He demolished me all round, and I am gone!
    And He pulled up my hope like a tree:
11 And His anger burned against me,
    And He reckoned me as a foe.

13 My clansmen He hath put far away from me,
    And my friends are wholly estranged from me:
14 My neighbours and my acquaintance have ceased (?);
    The guests of my house have forgotten me.

¹⁵ My bondmaids reckon me a stranger,—
A foreigner am I become in their eyes:
16 My slave I called, but he would not answer;
With my mouth I must needs entreat him.

17 My smell is odious to my wife;
And my stink to the sons of my body (?).
18 Even the boys despise me;
Would I rise, they remark upon me.

19 All the men of my circle abhor me,
And they whom I loved have turned against me:
20 To my skin my bone sticks fast,
And I escape with my flesh in my teeth.

21 Pity me, you my friends,
For the hand of Eloah hath stricken me!
22 Why like El run me down,
And not have enough of slander?

23 O that my sayings might be written,—
My words inscribed in a roll,—
24 That with stylus of iron and with lead
They might be graven in rock for ever!

25 For I, I know my Avenger,
At last He will come forward on earth!
26 I shall see, yet living, El's revenges,
And in my flesh gaze on Eloah!.

27 I myself shall behold Him, not Another,—
Mine eyes will look on Him and no Stranger!
My vitals are wasted with waiting
Until my hope shall come.

28 If ye muse, 'What shall we say to him,
That we may find in him the root of the thing?'
29 Fear ye a Sword for yourselves!
For Wrath will consume the unjust.

CHAPTER 20.—1 *In reply Zophar the Minaean said:*
2 Not so my thoughts reply to me,
And within me my heart is hot;
3 The monition of my reins I hear,
And my discerning spirit answereth me.

4 Knowest thou not from of old,—
  From the placing of Man upon Earth,—
5 That the joy of the wicked is soon over,
  And the mirth of the impious but momentary?

6 Though his height tower to heaven,
  And his head reach the clouds,
7 In his greatness he perisheth for ever—
  They who saw him ask, 'Where is he?'

8 Like a dream that vanisheth, he is not found,
  And he flitteth like a vision of night:
9 The eye that once glanced at him, doth it not again;
  And his place beholdeth him no more.

10 His palms oppress the poor,
   And his hands finger their substance:
11 His bones are full of perfidy,
   And with himself in the dust it lieth down.

12 Though evil be sweet in his mouth,—
   Though he hide it under his tongue;
13 Though he save it, nor let it go down,
   And hold it back in the middle of his palate;

14 Into venom in his bowels it turneth,—
   Into poison of asps within him:
15 He gorgeth riches, and throweth them up;
   El driveth them out of his belly.

16 Venom of asps he sucketh;
   The tongue of the viper killeth him:
17 He shall never look on streams of oil,—
   On rivers of honey and butter!

18 He toileth in vain, and profiteth not;
   He hopeth for his increase, and eateth not:
19 For he breaketh the neck of the poor;
   He seizeth a house that he built not.

20 No safety for him in his wealth,
   Nor doth he escape by his treasures.
21 There is no survivor in his tent:
   Therefore his name endureth not.

22 With a full fist, he is in straits;
   'Mid all his plenty, trouble assaileth him:
   Iahvah filleth his belly,
23 [Looseth against him His hot anger,]
   And raineth upon him snares.

24 If he flee from weapons of iron,
   The bow of bronze pierceth him through,
25 And the barb issueth from his back,
   And the flashing point from his gall.

26 All darkness is reserved for him;
   Fire unblown devoureth him:
   [And consumeth the survivor in his tent]
27 The Heavens expose his guilt,
   And the Earth upriseth against him.

28 The flood carrieth off his house,—
   Sweepeth it away in the day of his ruin.
29 Such is the lot of the wicked from Iahvah,
   And his portion assigned by El.

   CHAPTER 21.—1 *In reply Eyob said·*
2 Hear attentively my word,
   And be that your comfort to me!
3 Suffer me, and I too will speak;
   And after my speech ye may jeer!

4 For me, is my plaint of Man?
   Or why should I not be impatient?
5 Face ye me, and be appalled,
   And lay hand on mouth!

6 When I think of it, I am confounded;
   A shudder seizes my flesh:
7 Why do the godless live on,
   Grow old, yea, are mighty in power?

8 Their seed is established before them,
   And their issue before their eyes:
9 Their homes are safe from alarm—
   No rod of Eloah over them·

10 Their bull covers, nor fails;
　　Their cow calves, nor miscarries:
11 Their boys play about like the flock,
　　And their lads skip like the calf.

12 They sing to tabor and lyre,
　　And are merry at the sound of the pipe:
13 They end their days in happiness,
　　And in a moment go down to She'ol.

14 Yet they said unto El, 'Depart from us!
　　We want not knowledge of Thy ways!
15 What is Shaddai, that we should serve Him?
　　And what should we get by entreating Him?'

16 [Their weal was not in their own power;
　　The counsel of the godless is far from me.]

17 How often is the lamp of the godless put out,
　　And cometh their ruin upon them;—
18 Become they like chaff before wind,
　　And like stubble the storm carries off?

19 Doth He store his woe for his children?
　　Let Him recompense himself, that he may know!
20 Let his own eyes see his ruin,
　　And of Shaddai's burning anger let him drink!

21 For what hath he to do with his house after him,
　　When the sum of his months is cut short?
22 Shall not El teach knowledge,
　　When it is He that judgeth the Heights?

23 One man dieth in perfect felicity,
　　Entirely untroubled and at ease:
24 His belly is full of milk,
　　And the marrow of his bones is moist:

25 And another dieth in bitter mood,
　　Having never tasted happiness.
26 Together they lie down in the dust,
　　And worms cover them over.

27 Behold, I know your thoughts,
　　And the imaginings wherewith ye wrong me!

28 For ye say, 'Where is the Great Man's house?
   And where are the dwellings of the godless?'

29 Have ye not inquired of travellers,
   And their signs do ye not recognize,
30 That the bad man is kept from calamity,—
   That in the Day of Wrath he escapeth?

31 Who durst expose his way to his face?
   And what he hath done, who requiteth him,
32 When he to the tomb is borne,
   And above him a mound keepeth guard?

33 He is quiet 'mid the clods of the glen;
   And after him all men march.
34 How then would ye comfort me with breath,
   And answer me with profitless falsehood?

CHAPTER 22.—1 *In reply Eliphaz of Teman said:*
2 Can a man benefit El,
   That a learned and wise one should do it?
3 Is it Shaddai's concern that thou art just,
   Or His profit that thou perfectest thy ways?

4 Is it for thy godliness He chideth thee,—
   Entereth into judgement with thee?
5 Is not thy wickedness manifold,
   And are not thine iniquities endless?

6 Doubtless thou distrainest upon thy kin without cause,
   And strippest off the clothes of the naked,
7 Givest no water to the fainting,
   And from the hungry withholdest bread;

9 Widows thou hast sent away emptyhanded,
   And the arms of orphans thou crushest:
8 But the man of power thou favourest,
   And the person of rank thou treatest well.

10 Therefore snares are about thee,
   And a sudden scare alarmeth thee
11 Thy light is darkened. that thou seest not.
   And a deluge of waters whelmeth thee.

12 Look at the Heavens, and see,
   And behold the Stars far aloft!
13 And sayest thou, What doth El know?
   Through the mirk of clouds can He judge?
14 [The clouds are a cover to Him, that He seeth not,
   And upon the arch of Heaven He walketh.]

15 Wilt thou keep to the ancient way
   Which men of wickedness have trodden,
16 Who were snatched away untimely,—
   Whose foundation was washed away as by a stream?

17 Who said to El, 'Depart from us!
   What can Shaddai do for us?'
18 Yet 'twas He that filled their houses with good;
   And the counsel of the godless was unheeded by Him.

19 The righteous see and rejoice,
   And the innocent jeereth at them:
20 'Verily our adversaries are effaced,
   And their remnant fire hath devoured!'

21 O be reconciled with Him, and prosper!
   Truly thy gain shall be good!
22 O receive instruction from His mouth,
   And set His words in thine heart!

23 If thou repent, and turn unto Shaddai,—
   If thou banish injustice from thy tent;
24 Thou shalt make gold as dust,
   And Ophir ore as the rocks of the glen.
25 [And Shaddai will become thy Refiner;
   And will make thee shine as refined silver.]

26 For then thou wilt delight thyself in Shaddai;
   And wilt lift thy face toward Eloah:
27 Thou wilt pray unto Him, and He will hear thee;
   And thou wilt pay unto Him thy vows.

28 And He will raise thee thy righteous tent;
   And the light shall shine on thy paths:
29 For He abaseth the high and haughty;
   And the lowly-eyed He saveth.
30 [He letteth the innocent escape from ruin;
   And he escapeth thro' the purity of his palms.]

CHAPTER 23.—1 *In reply Eyob said:*
2 To-day too my plaint is of Shaddai;
His Hand, it lies heavy on my sighing.
3 O that I knew where to find Him,—
That I might come to His fixed Abode!
4 That I might marshal my case before Him,
And fill my mouth with proofs!
5 That I might know the words He would answer me,
And understand what He would say to me!
6 Would He strive with me in overwhelming strength?
Or would not HE listen to me?
7 There would He wrestle and reason with me,
And I should escape from my Judge for ever!

8 [Behold, I go east, but He is not there,
And west, but I discern Him not;
9 North I seek Him, but see Him not;
I turn south, and perceive Him not!]

10 For He knoweth my standing way;
If He test me, I shall come forth as gold.
11 My foot hath held fast to His steps;
His way have I kept without swerving.
12 From the commands of His lips I depart not;
In my bosom have I treasured His words.
13 But HE spoke, and who shall reverse it?
And what Himself pleased, He hath done:
14 I know that He will fulfil His decree,
And will finish His quarrel with me.
15 Therefore am I cowed before Him;
I consider, and stand in dread of Him:
16 Yea, 'tis El that hath softened my heart,
And Shaddai that hath cowed my soul:
17 For I am appalled by the darkness,
And my face the gloom hath covered.

CHAPTER 24.—1 Why are not oppressors annihilated,
And the wicked see not their own ruin?
2 They remove their neighbours' landmarks;
The flock they snatch and shepherd it:
3 The ass of orphans they drive off:
They distrain the widow's ox.

4 They thrust the poor aside from justice;
　The humble folk are hidden away together;
5 Like wild asses, into the steppe go forth,—
　Like ass-colts in quest of forage.
6 In the villain's field they reap,
　And the vineyard of the godless they glean.
7 They pass the night naked, for want of clothing,
　And their skin hath no covering in the cold.
8 They are drenched with the mountain storm,
　And for want of a refuge hug the rock.
9 [They snatch the orphan from the breast,
　And the poor man's babe they take in pledge.]
10 Naked they go about without raiment;
　And hungry, they carry the sheaf.
11 Between the twin rows they press oil;
　They tread the winepresses, and are thirsty.
12 [From the city the dying groan,
　And the soul of the deadly-wounded crieth for help;
　But Eloah heareth not their prayer.]
13 [These are rebels against daylight;
　They acknowledge not its ways,
　And abide not in its paths:]
14 [Ere dawn riseth the murderer;
　He slayeth the poor and needy:
　And at night prowleth the thief.]
15 [The adulterer's eye watcheth for dusk,—
　He thinks, 'Not an eye will see me!'
　And putteth a veil over his face.]
16 [They break into houses in the dark,
　And by day they seal up their doors:
　They know not to see the light.]
17 [For the morning scareth them all,
　But they are used to the terrors of darkness.]

18 [Accursed are they before Heaven;
　Their portion is accursed on earth:
　They turn not from the way of bloodshed.]
19 [Heat drieth up waters of snow;
　And She'ol snatcheth the sinner.]
20 [To-morrow his place will forget him,
　His name shall no more be remembered:

And Injustice is shattered like a tree]
21 [He hath wronged 'the barren that bare not';
And he doeth not good to the widow:
And he draggeth off the poor with his hook.]

22 [He standeth, 'but is uncertain of life',—
23 His trust whereon he leaneth, is not lasting:
And the eyes of El are on his ways.]
24 [He is exalted awhile, and is no more;
He is brought low, and is plucked like the mallow,
And cut off like the head of a corn-ear.]
25 But if not, then who shall prove me liar,
And reduce my word to nothing?

CHAPTER 25.—1 *In reply Bildad of Shuah said:*
2 An awful sovranty is with Him;
He maketh peace in His Heights.
3 Can his troops be numbered?
And against whom riseth not His ambush?
4 [How then can a man be righteous with El,
And the womanborn be pure?]
5 Lo, the Moon halteth and shineth not,
And the stars are not pure in His eyes!
6 Much less, a man—a maggot,
And a son of man—a worm!
26. 5 Do not the Dead tremble before Him,
Whose dwellings are beneath the waters?
6 She'ol is naked before Him,
And Abaddon hath no covering.
7 He stretcheth the North over the Void;
He hangeth the Earth over the Abyss.
8 He bindeth up water in His clouds,
And the bank bursteth not beneath it.
9 He hideth the face of the full moon,
By spreading His cloudbank over it.
10 He drew an arch over the face of the waters,
Unto the boundary of Light and Darkness.
11 The pillars of Heaven rock,
And are astounded at His rebuke.
12 By His power He stilled the Sea.
And by His craft He shattered Rahab.

13 By His Wind He cleared the skies;
His Hand pierced the Dragon.
14 Lo, these are the fringes of His Way,
[And what a whisper we hear in it!]
And the sum of His feats who perceiveth?

CHAPTER 26.—1 *In reply Eyob said:*
2 How hast thou helped the powerless,—
How aided the nerveless arm!
3 [How hast thou counselled the imprudent,
And plentifully declared sound wisdom!]
4 Whom hast thou told mere words?
And whose breath hath issued from thee?

CHAPTER 27.—1 *And Eyob resumed his* mashal *and said:*
2 As El liveth, Who hath set aside my right,
And Shaddai, Who hath embittered my soul—
3 [For 'my breath is still in me entire',
And Eloah's spirit in my nostrils—]
4 My lips do not speak wrong,
Nor my tongue murmur deceit!
5 Be it far from me to own you right!
Till I die, I will not disown my perfectness!
6 My righteousness I hold fast, nor let it go!
My conscience reproacheth me not.
11 I will instruct you in the Hand of El;
What is with Shaddai I will not hide.
12 Lo, ye all yourselves have seen!
And why do ye vapour in vain?

[*In reply Zophar the Minaean said:*]

7 Let mine enemy be as the godless,
And mine assailant as the wrongdoer!
8 For what is the hope of the impious,
When he lifteth his soul to Eloah?
9 Will El hear his cry,
When distress cometh upon him?
10 Will he take delight in Shaddai,
And call unto Him continually?
13 This is the award of the godless from El,
And the portion of the tyrant from Shaddai.

14 His sons grow up for the sword,
   And his offspring is not satisfied with bread.
15 [His survivors perish by the Plague,
   And his widows do not weep.]
16 Though he heap up silver like earth,
   And provide apparel like clay;
17 He may provide, but the just shall wear it,
   And the innocent share out the silver.
18 Like a spider he buildeth his house,
   And like a booth which a keeper maketh.
19 He lieth down, and riseth not again;
   He openeth his eyes, and is no more!
20 Terrors overtake him by day;
   In the night a storm carrieth him off.
21 The Sirocco taketh him up and goeth,—
   Yea, it whirleth him away from his place.
22 El shooteth at him unsparingly;
   From His Hand he fain would flee.
23 The passer-by clappeth his palms at him,
   And hisseth at his day of disaster.

CHAPTER 28.—[An interpolation.]

12 Wisdom, whence cometh it?
   And where is the place of Insight?
1 For silver hath a source,
   And the gold they refine hath a place;
2 Iron out of dust is taken,
   And ore is smelted into copper.
5 Out of the earth cometh the jacinth (?).
   And under her are carbuncle and jasper (?),
6 The place of sapphire are her stones,
   And the gleam of the emerald is theirs.
3 [A bound man setteth to darkness and deathshade,
   And the very end of gloom he exploreth
4 A foreign folk breaketh up the glens,
   Erst untrodden by the foot:
   Exiled from men and wanderers.]
12 But Wisdom, whence cometh it?
   And where is the place of Insight?
7 The path thereto no eagle knoweth,
   Nor hath eye of hawk descried·

8 The Sons of Pride have not trodden it;
   The Roarer hath not passed over it.
9 Against flint man stretches forth his hand;
   Overturneth mountains from the roots:
10 He divideth the depths of Nile-streams,
   And his eye seeth all things precious.
11 [The springs of the Rivers he searcheth,
   And bringeth to light what is hidden.]
12 But Wisdom, whence doth she come?
   And where is the place of Insight?
13 Man knoweth not the way to her,
   Nor is she found in the land of the living.
14 The Deep saith, She is not in me!
   And the Sea saith, She is not with me!
15 Fine gold cannot be given for her,
   Nor silver be weighed as her price.
16 She cannot be poised against Ophir-gold,
   Against precious onyx (?) and sapphire.
17 [Refined gold is not equal to her,
   Nor are things of beaten gold her worth.]
18 Coral (?) and Crystal are not to be named,
   And the price of Wisdom is above red coral.
19 One cannot compare with her the topaz of Cush;
   Against pure gold she cannot be balanced.
20 But Wisdom, whence doth she come?
   And where is the place of Insight?
21 It is hid from the eyes of all living,
   And concealed from the birds of the air.
22 Abaddon and Death declare,
   We have heard mere hearsay thereof.
23 Elohim, He discerneth the way to her,
   And 'tis He that knoweth her place;
24 For 'tis He that looketh to the ends of the Earth,—
   Seeth under the whole of Heaven.
25 When He made the weight for the Wind,
   And meted out the Waters by measure;—
26 [When He made a law for the Rain,
   And a way for the Thunderbolts,—]
27 Then He saw her and examined her,—
   He discerned her, yea, and proved her.
28 [*And He said to Mankind:*

Lo, the Fear of the Lord, that is Wisdom;
And turning away from Evil is Insight!]

CHAPTER 29.—1 [*And Eyob resumed his* mashal *and said:*]
2 Oh that I were as in months of old,
As in days when Eloah used to guard me;
3 When He made His lamp shine above my head,
And by its light I could walk amid darkness;—
4 As I was in the days of my health,
When Eloah protected my tent;
5 [When Shaddai was still with me,
And my young men stood around me;]
6 When my goings were bathed in curds,
And my footsteps ran with milk!
7 When I went forth to the gate by the city,—
In the square set up my seat,—
8 The young men saw me and retired,
And the aged arose and stood:
9 Princes did stop talking,
And would lay the palm to their mouth;
10 The voice of chiefs was silenced,
And their tongue clave to their palate
21 To me they listened and were silent,
And would tarry for my counsel.
22 After I spake, they would say no more,
And upon them my speech I would drop;
23 They tarried for me as for rain,
And opened wide their mouth as for the spring-rain.
24 If I smiled on them, they could not credit it,
The light of my face they durst not expect.
25 [I would try their way and examine them,
And I abode like a king in the host,
Like a captain of thousands in the camp.]
11 The ear heard, and called me happy;
The eye saw and bare me witness:
12 For I would save the poor from the opulent,
And the orphan who had no helper.
13 The blessing of the perishing would come on me,
And I made the widow's heart shout for joy.
14 I put on Righteousness, and it put me on,—
Justice, like mantle and turban.

15 Eyes I became to the blind,
   And feet to the lame was I.
16 A father was I to needy ones,
   And the cause I knew not I would search out;
17 And I broke the grinders of the wronger,
   And out of his teeth would draw the prey.
18 And methought, My stem will grow old,
   And like the palmtree I shall multiply days:
19 My root will sprout toward the water,
   And the dew will lie all night upon my boughs;
20 My palmbranch will renew its leafage,
   And my suckers will shoot forth again.

CHAPTER 30.—1 But now they laugh at me;
The sons of aliens insult me,
Whose fathers I had disdained
To set with the dogs of my flock!
2 [Yea, the strength of their hands is relaxed,—
With them vigour hath perished:
3 With want and with famine they are spent;]
They who gnaw the roots of the desert,
The growth of the desolate wild;—
4 Who pluck saltwort beside the bush,
And the root of the broom is their bread.
5 From sojourn in the city they are driven;
Men shout at them as at a thief.
6 The caves of the glens must they dwell in,—
Holes in the ground and the rocks.
7 Among the bushes they bray;
Under the scrub they huddle together:
8 Sons of the fool and sons of the nameless
Whose remembrance is lost from the land.
9 But now am I become their song,
And I serve them for a byword.
10 They loathe me, they stand aloof from me;
They refrain not to spit in my face:
11 [For their cord they have loosed, and humbled me,
And relaxed the bridle of their mouth.]
12 The young men arise behind me,
And raise their taunts at me:
13 They break up my path for my fall;

They engulf them that are helpless.
14 Like a broad outburst they come;
Like a terrible storm they roll on:
15 Mine honour fleeteth like the wind,
And like a cloud my welfare hath passed.
16 Upon me my soul is outpoured;
Days of affliction grip me:
17 By night my bones are racked.
And the gnawers of my skin are sleepless:
18 Like the wings of my raiment they enwrap me;
Like the neck of my tunic they encircle me.
19 *Thou* hast compared me with clay,
And I am made like dust and ashes.
20 I cry for help to Thee, and Thou answerest not;
I entreat, and Thou dost not heed me:
21 Thou turnest cruel to me;
With the strength of Thine Hand Thou assailest me.
22 Thou liftest me, dost mount me on the wind,
And like chaff the storm whirleth me away.
23 I know that to the Grave Thou wilt make me return,—
To the House of Assembly for all living.
24 [If I stretched not forth a hand against the poor,—
If in his calamity I would help him;
25 If I wept for him whose times were hard,—
If my soul was grieved for the needy:]
26 I hoped for good, and evil came;
I waited for light, and there came darkness.
27 My bowels boiled, and were not quiet;
Days of affliction met me.
28 A mourner I went about without a comforter;
I rose in the Moot, crying for help.
29 A brother became I to jackals,
And a comrade to ostriches.
30 My skin is blackened with disease,
And my bones are burnt up with fever;
31 So that my harp is become lamentation,
And my pipes the voice of weepers.

CHAPTER 31.—1 A covenant I made for mine eyes;
Never would I gaze on a virgin:
2 And what was Eloah's award from Above,

And Shaddai's allotment from on High?
3 Should not Ruin befall the unjust,
 And Misfortune evildoers?
4 Could not HE see my ways,
 And take account of all my steps?
5 If I walked with men of falsehood,
 And my foot hastened toward fraud,—
6 (Let Him weigh me in true balances,
 And Eloah will know my perfectness!)
7 If my footsteps would swerve from the way,
 And if my heart have gone after mine eyes;
8 Let me sow and let another eat,
 And let mine offspring be uprooted from the land!
9 If my heart have been enticed over a woman,
 And I have lurked at my neighbour's door;
10 Let my own wife grind for another,
 And over her let others incline!
11 [For that were wanton villainy;
 And that is a criminal offence:
12 'Tis a fire that devoureth unto Abaddon;
 And wherever it cometh, it burneth.]
13 If I slighted the cause of my thrall
 Or my bondmaid in their quarrel with me;
14 What should I do if El rose up,
 And if He visited what should I answer Him?
15 [Did not my own Maker make him in the belly,
 And form him in the selfsame womb?]
16 If I balked the poor of their desire,
 And let the eyes of the widow fail;
17 And would eat my morsel alone,
 And not feed the orphan therefrom—
18 [Nay, but from his childhood like a father I reared him
 And from his mother's womb I did guide him!]
19 If I saw one perishing for lack of clothing,
 And covered not the needy;
20 If his loins did not bless me,
 Nor was he warmed with the fleece of my lambs;—
21 If I shook my fist at the orphan,
 When I saw my abettors in the Gate;—
22 May my shoulder drop from its socket,
 And my arm break off from the joint!

23 [For the dread of El came over me,
 And before His Majesty I was powerless.]
24 If I ever made yellow gold my confidence,
 And called the red gold my stay,
25 If I joyed that my wealth was great,
 And my hand had come upon much;—
26 If I looked at the Sun as it shone,
 And the Moon marching in splendour,
27 And my heart was in secret seduced,
 And my hand kissed my mouth;—
28 [That also were a criminal offence,
 For I had been false to El above!]
29 If I rejoiced at the ruin of my foe,
 Elated when Misfortune found him;—
30 (Nay, I suffered not my palate to sin
 By imprecating his death:)
31 If the men of my tent have not said,
 'O that we might be satisfied with his flesh!'
32 [The stranger did not lodge in the street;
 I would open my doors to the traveller.
33 If I covered my transgressions as with a cloke,
 Concealing my guilt in my bosom;
34 Because I dreaded the great concourse,
 And the scorn of the clans alarmed me;—
 [So that I kept quiet, nor went out of doors;—]
38 If my land would cry out against me,
 And its furrows weep together,—
39 [If I have eaten its produce free,
 And sniffed at its owner's life;]
40 For wheat let the brier spring up,
 And noisome weeds for barley!

35 O that El would hear me,—
 That Shaddai would will to answer me;—
 That mine Adversary would write an indictment,
 And set out His case before me!
36 Verily, I would carry it on my shoulder,—
 I would bind it as a coronal on my brows:
37 The sum of my steps would I declare it,—
 As the words of a Prince would I present it!

The words of Job are ended.

CHAPTER 32.—1 And these three men ceased to answer
2 Eyob, because he was right in his own eyes. And the anger
of Elihu ben Baṛak'el, the Buzite of the clan of Râm, was
kindled; against Eyob was his anger kindled, on account of
his considering himself more righteous than Elohim.

3 Also against his (Eyob's) three friends was his anger kindled;
because they had found no answer, but let Elohim appear
unrighteous.

4 Now Elihu had waited while they were speaking with Eyob,
5 because they were his elders in years. And Elihu saw that
there was no answer in the mouth of the three men; so his
anger was kindled.

Then answered Elihu ben Barak'el, the Buzite, and said:

    Young am I in years,
    And ye are all of you aged;
    Therefore was I timid and afraid
    Of showing my knowledge to you.
7 Methought, 'Age should speak;
    And multitude of years should teach wisdom.'
8 But the Spirit of El is in Man;
    And the Breath of Shaddai informeth him.
9 'Tis not seniors that are wise,
    Nor the old that understand judgement:
10 Therefore say I, 'Hearken to me;
    And I too will declare what I know!'
11 Behold, I awaited your words,—
    I pondered, while ye sought what to say;
12 And lo, Eyob had none to confute him,
    To answer his words, among you.
13 But say not, 'We encountered wisdom;
    El may rout him, not a man!'
14 He marshalled no words against me;
    And with your arguments I will not answer him.
15 (Dismayed, they answered no longer;
    The power of speech forsook them:
16 And shall I wait, because they speak not,—
    Because they stopped, and answered no longer?)
17 I also will answer with my lore;
    I too will display my knowledge:
18 I will speak, for I am full of words;

The spirit in my bosom constraineth me.
19 Lo, my bosom is as wine unopened;
Like wineskins new it will burst.
20 I must speak to find relief,—
Must open my lips and answer!
21 I would show favour to none,
And to no man will I be indulgent:
22 For I know not showing favour—
Soon would my Maker away with me!

CHAPTER 33.—1 Hear now, O Eyob, my words;
And unto my sayings give ear!
2 Lo now, I have opened my mouth,—
My tongue in my palate hath spoken!
3 There are in my heart words of knowledge;
My lips shall speak sincerely.
4 'Twas the Spirit of El that made me;
And the Breath of Shaddai gave me life.
5 If thou canst, reply to me with words;
Marshal them before me, take thy stand!
6 Lo, I like thee am no god;
I too was nipt off from the clay!
7 Lo, my 'Terror shall not scare thee,
Nor my palm lie heavy upon thee'!
8 But this thou saidst in my hearing,
And the sound of thy words I heard·
9 'I am pure, and without transgression;
I am clean, and I have no guilt.
10 Behold, He findeth pretexts against me;
He accounteth me a foe to Himself:
11 He setteth my feet in the stocks;
He watcheth all my ways!'
12 How sayest thou, 'I cried and He answereth not?'
Should Eloah contend with a mortal?
13 Why complainest thou of Him,
That he answereth none of thy words?
14 For in one mode speaketh El,
And in a second He doth not reverse it
15 In a dream, in a vision of night,
In slumbers upon the bed:

16 Then He uncovereth the ear of men,
   And with ghostly Vision alarmeth them;
17 To make a mortal depart from wrong,
   And to clear a man of pride.
18 [To keep back his soul from the Pit,
   And his life from passing into She'ol.]
19 Or he chideth him with pain on the bed;
   And the pining of his bones is perpetual:
20 So that his soul loatheth bread,
   And his appetite dainty fare.
21 His flesh consumeth with sickness,
   And his bones are dried up for lack of moisture:
22 And his soul hath drawn nigh to the Pit,
   And his life to the Place of the Dead.
23 If there be beside him a Messenger,
   An Interpreter, One of a thousand,
   To declare to the man his fault,
   And to make known to him his sin;
24 And Eloah show him favour and say,
   'I will redeem him from descent to the Pit!
   [I have found a ransom for his life!]
25 Let his flesh wax plumper than childhood's,—
   Let him return to the days of his youth!'
26 Then he prayeth to Eloah, and He is pleased with him;
   And he seeth His Face with joy;
   And He restoreth to the man his wellbeing.
27 He singeth unto men, and saith:
   'I sinned and made crooked my way,
   And He requited me not my misdoing:
28 He ransomed my soul from the Pit,
   And my life gazeth on the Light.'
29 Lo, all this El is wont to do,
   Twice, yea thrice, with a man!
30 [To bring back his soul from the Pit,—
   To let him gaze on the light of life.]
31 Attend, Eyob! listen to me!
   Be silent, and I will speak!
32 If thou hast arguments, answer me;
   Speak; for I wish to find thee right!
33 If thou hast not, listen thou to me;
   Be silent, and I will teach thee wisdom!

CHAPTER 34.—1 *And Elihu answered and said:*
2 Hear, O ye wise, my words,
  And ye sages, give ear to me!
3 [For 'the ear, it trieth words,
  As the palate tasteth food.']
4 Choose we us what is right!
  Let us see between us what is good!
5 For Eyob hath said, 'I am just,
  And El hath set aside my right:
6 To me my Judge is false;
  Sore is my wound, sans fault!'
7 But indeed, what man is like Eyob,
  Who imbibeth scoffing like water;
8 And is for joining with workers of wickedness,
  And for walking with men of ungodliness?
9 (For he said, 'A man gaineth nothing
  By being on good terms with Elohim'.)
10 Therefore, ye wise, give ear!
  Men of mind, listen to me!
  Far be it from El to deal wickedly,
  And from Shaddai to pervert justice!
11 For after a man's work He rewardeth him,
  And according to one's way He causeth to befall him.
12 And indeed, El dealeth not wickedly;
  And Shaddai perverteth not right.
13 Who assigned Him the Earth as His charge?
  And who set Him over the whole world?
14 Should He recall His Spirit to Himself,
  And gather in His Breath to Him;
15 All Flesh would expire together,
  And Man would return to the dust.
16 But if thou hast wit, hear this;
  O give hear to the sound of my words!
17 Accountest thou El a foe of Right?
  Or impugnest thou the Justice of the Mighty One
18 Who calleth a king worthless,
  And nobles godless men?
19 He showeth no favour to princes,
  Nor preferreth a rich to a poor man:
  [For they all are the work of His Hands.]
20 Suddenly they die are cut off;

They perish like moths and pass away.
[And He removeth the magnates without hand.]
21 For His eyes are upon a man's ways,
And all his steps He beholdeth:
22 No darkness there is, no deathshade,
Where evildoers may hide:
23 For He setteth not a man a time
To go unto El in judgement.
24 He breaketh the mighty without trial,
And setteth up others in their stead:
25 He noteth well their doings,
And overthroweth them by night, that they are crushed.
26 Therefore He shattereth the godless;
He hurleth them down into the Place of the Dead:
27 Because they turned aside from following Him,
And considered not all His ways.
28 [To cause the cry of the poor to come to Him,
And that He might hear the shriek of the oppressed.
29 Should HE keep quiet, who shall rouse Him?
If He cover the face, who shall see Him?]
If His wrath be kindled at a nation,
30 And He make an infidel king:
Who hardeneth himself against Him,
And maketh his yoke heavy on the people:
31 When unto Eloah he saith,
'Forgive me! I will no more deal corruptly!
32 Do THOU show me the way;
And if I did wrong, I will not again!':
33 By *thy* standard should Eloah requite him,
That thou despisest the chastening of Shaddai?
For thou must choose, and not I;
So what thou knowest, speak!

34 Let men of sense give ear to me,
And the wise man listen to me!
35 Eyob speaketh not with knowledge,
And his words are void of insight:
36 I will prove Eyob to the end,
For answers like men of wickedness;
37 [For he addeth rebellion unto his sin;]
For against Shaddai he clappeth his hands,
And multiplieth his words against El.

CHAPTER 35.—1 *And Elihu answered and said:*
2 Dost reckon this for right,—
   Dost think it just with El,—
3 That thou sayest, 'What profit have I?
   What advantage have I above sinners?'
4 'Tis I that will answer thee with proofs,
   And thy three friends along with thee!
5 Look at the Heavens and behold,
   And see the Skies far above thee!
6 If thou sin, what workest thou against Him?
   If thy revolts be many, what doest thou to Him?
7 If thou art righteous, what dost thou give Him,
   Or what receiveth He from thine hand?
8 To a man like thyself is thy wickedness,
   And to a son of Adam thy righteousness.
9 At abounding oppressions men make outcry,—
   They shriek at the arm of the great ones:
10 But they say not, 'Where is Eloah our Maker,
    Who setteth watches in the night,—
11 Who teacheth us more than the beasts of the earth,
    And maketh us wiser than the birds of the air?'
12 There they cry, unanswered,
    Because of the pride of the wicked.
13 But an idle plaint El heareth not,
    And Shaddai hearkeneth not to vanity:
14 Much less when thou sayest thou seest Him not,
    The case is before Him and thou waitest for Him!

15 And now, because Eloah hath visited
    And hurt himself sorely for transgression,
16 Eyob vainly openeth his mouth,
    And without knowledge multiplieth words.

CHAPTER 36.—1 *And Elihu said besides:*
2 Wait me a while, and I will show thee;
   For Elihu hath yet more to say:
3 I will lift my thought to Him that is far off,
   And to my Maker ascribe Justice.
4 For indeed my words are no lie;
   The Perfect in all Knowledge is with me.
5 Lo, I! is mighty and tainteth not

Strong in Power and wise-hearted.
6 He letteth not the soul of the godless live,
　　And the cause of the oppressed He judgeth.
7 He letteth kings come to the throne,
　　And seateth them in state, that they wax haughty.
8 And if bound they walk in fetters,
　　Caught in the cords of distress,
9 And He hath shown them their behaviour
　　And their transgressions, that they played the tyrant,
10 And hath opened their ear to correction,
　　And bidden them return from wickedness:
11 If they obey Him and do Him service,
　　They fulfil their days in weal,
　　And their years in happiness;
12 But if not, they pass into She'ol,
　　And expire for lack of knowledge.
13 And the impious, in heart they lay up wrath;
　　And to El they cry not when He chasteneth them.
14 Their soul must die in childhood,
　　And their life pass away in youth.

15 He delivereth the oppressed from his oppression,
　　And redeemeth the needy from tyranny:
16 Yea, and He removeth him out of straits,
　　And broadeneth his goings under him.
　　[His table is filled with fatness.]
17 But the doom of the godless faileth not;
　　Judgement and Justice lay hold of them.

18 See that a bribe seduce thee not,
　　Nor let much ransom turn thee!
19 Is thy weal to be compared with gold,
　　Or with all the treasures of wealth?
20 Prolong not the night over wine,
　　Till the rising of day in its place.
21 Beware, turn not unto wickedness!
　　Because for this thou wast tried with affliction.

22 Lo, El is exalted in His Power;
　　And who is a teacher like Him?
23 Who imposed on Him His Way?
　　And who shall say, Thou hast done Injustice?

24 Remember that great is His Work
   Beyond what mortals have seen.
25 All mankind do gaze thereon,
   And a mortal beholdeth it afar off.
26 [Lo, El is great, beyond knowledge;
   The number of His years is unsearchable.]
27 For He collecteth the drops of water,
   And bindeth up the rain in His mist;
28 Wherewith the skies flow in its season,—
   They drop on the ground in showers.
29 Who understandeth the spread of the cloud,—
   The rise of the cloudbank, His covert?
30 Lo, He spreadeth the cloud over the light,
   And the sun with the cloudbank He shroudeth·
31 For through them He nourisheth the nations;
   He giveth food to all flesh.
32 With clouds He covereth the light,
   And chargeth it not to shine forth;
33 He draweth over it a curtain,—
   The place of the tent of the Storm.

   CHAPTER 37.—1 With terror my heart fluttereth,
   And springeth from its place within me.
2 Hark to the rumble of His Voice,
   And the mutter that issueth from His Mouth!
3 Under all Heaven He letteth it go,
   And His light unto the corners of Earth.
4 After it His Voice roareth;
   He thundereth with His Voice of Majesty:
   Nor doth He restrain the flood of waters,
   When His Voice of thunder is heard.

5 El performeth wonders;
   He doeth great things, we know not how.
6 For He saith to the snow, Be stored up!
   And to the torrent-rain, Overflow!
7 Every man He sealeth up,
   That mortals may know His work;
8 Wild beasts go into the lair,
   And abide in their dens.
9 Out of the Storechamber cometh the Cyclone
   And out of the Garner issueth Cold.

10 By the Breath of El it freezeth;
  And the broad water is like cast-iron.
11 Also the Flash putteth the Clouds to flight,—
  His Light scattereth the cloudmass;
12 And it—it compasseth Heaven,
  It turneth about by His guidance,
  To do whatsoever He biddeth
  All over His earthly world:
13 [Whether for a Rod of Wrath on the tyrant,
  Or for mercy to His land He send it forth.]
14 Give ear to this, O Eyob,
  And consider the Wonders of El!
16 Dost thou teach Him that spreadeth the clouds,
  And instruct the Perfectly Wise,
15 When He maketh the clouds His cloak,
  And the light of His thundercloud shineth out?
17 Thou whose garments are warm
  When the land is stilled from the South.
18 Couldst thou, like Him, beat out the skies
  Hard as a molten mirrour?
19 Teach us what we should say of Him;
  And from marshalling words we will refrain!
20 Will He be angry because I talk?
  Or will a man be swallowed up because he spoke?

21 And now the light is not seen,—
  Bedimmed it is in the skies;
  But the stormy wind cleareth them,
22 And out of the North a Brightness cometh.
  Upon Eloah appeareth Splendour;
23 But Shaddai is not found therein.
  He showeth great Might and Justice;
  And the cause of the righteous He wresteth not:
24 Therefore do men fear Him;
  But none of the Sages can see Him.

  CHAPTER 38.—1 *And Iahvah answered Eyob out of the Stormwind, and said:*
2 Who here obscureth counsel
  By words void of knowledge?
3 Pray gird up thy loins like a warrior;

I will ask thee, and do thou let me know!
4 Where wast thou, when I founded the Earth?
Declare, if thou knowest Insight!
5 Who determined her measures, since thou shouldst know;
Or who stretched the line upon her?
6 Upon what were her bases planted,—
Or who laid her cornerstone,—
7 When the Stars of Morning cheered together,
And all the Sons of Elohim shouted acclaim?
8 And who shut in the Sea with the sand,
When he burst forth, issuing from the womb?
9 When I made cloud his apparel,
And thick vapour his swathingband,
10 And imposed on him a decree,
And set a bar and doors
11 'Thus far thou mayst come, but no farther;
And here shall thy swell be broken!'
12 Didst thou order his outgoing to the Morning,
And appoint the Dawn his place,
13 To lay hold of the corners of Earth,
And to kindle flames out of her?
14 She changeth like clay under seal,
And standeth in the Light as (in) a garment.
15 [But their light shall be withheld from the wicked;
And the high arm shall be broken.]
16 Hast thou reached the springs of the Sea,
Or walked the bottom of the Deep?
17 Have the Gates of Death been discovered to thee,
And didst thou see the Doors of She'ol?
18 Hast thou considered the breadth of the Earth?
Tell, if thou knowest how great it is!
21 Thou knowest, for then thou wast born,
And the number of thy days is many.
19 Where dwelleth the Light,—
And Darkness, where is his place?
20 For thou takest him unto his bourn,
And perceivest the paths to his house.
22 Hast thou been into the Storechambers of Snow,
And the Storechambers of Hail canst thou see,
23 Which I reserved for the time of trouble.—
For the day of battle and warfare·

24 Where is the way to where Light forketh,
And scattereth flashes over Earth?
25 Who clave a conduit for the downpour,
And a way for the thunderbolts;
26 To rain on the land unpeopled,
On the wild where no man is;—
27 To sate the desert waste,
And to make grass spring from the dryness?

28 Hath the Rain a father?
Or who hath begotten the dewdrops?
29 Out of whose womb came the Ice?
And Heaven's Hoar-frost, who bare it?
30 [Like stone the waters stiffen,
And the face of the Deep groweth solid.]
31 Dost thou fasten the bonds of Kîmah,
Or loose the fetters of Kesîl?
32 Dost thou make Mazrô rise in his season,
And 'Aish with her Sons dost thou lead?
33 Didst thou impose the laws of Heaven,
Or appointest thou an ordinance for Earth?
34 Canst thou lift thy voice to the clouds,
That a deluge of water may cover thee?
35 Sendest thou the lightnings, that they go,
And say to thee, 'Here are we!'?
36 Who set thee such wisdom in the reins;
Or who gave insight to a fool?
37 Who telleth the clouds by Wisdom;
And who tilteth the waterskins of Heaven,
38 When the soil hardeneth into lumps,
And the clods cleave fast together?
39 Dost thou hunt the prey for the lioness,
And dost thou satisfy the young lions,
40 When they crouch low in their lairs,
And sit in their covert in ambush?
41 Who provideth the raven his fare,
And who bringeth him prey;
When his young ones cry to El,
And scream for want of food?

CHAPTER 39. 1 Carest thou for the rock-goats?
The travail of the hinds dost thou watch?

2 Dost thou reckon the months they fulfil,
   And fix their time of yeaning?
3 They bow, they liberate their young,—
   They shoot their burdens forth, and are well.
4 Their fawns grow up in the open;
   They go forth, and return not unto them.
5 Who let the wild ass go free,
   And who loosed the bonds of the onager,
6 Whose home I made the steppe,
   And his haunts the salty waste?
7 He laugheth at the uproar of the city;
   He heareth not the shouts of the driver:
8 He rangeth the mountains, his pasture;
   And seeketh after everything green.
9 Will the wild-ox be willing to serve thee,
   Or would he pass the night at thy manger?
10 Canst thou bind him with the cords of thy yoke;
   Or will he harrow the furrows of thy land?
11 Wilt thou trust him, because his strength is great,
   And leave to him thy labour?
12 Wilt thou rely on him to bring home thy seed,
   And to gather thy wheat into the threshingfloor?

13 Dost thou rejoice in the ostrich,
   Or love her that lacketh counsel?
14 For she leaveth her eggs to the earth,
   And layeth them on the ground,
15 And forgetteth that the foot may press it,
   And the wild beast tread upon it;
16 Dealing hardly with her young as not hers,
   For nought hath she toiled without care;
17 For Eloah made her forget wisdom,
   And gave her no share in sagacity.
18 When she worketh her wings in the race,
   She laugheth at the horse and his rider.

19 Givest thou strength to the horse?
   Dost thou clothe his neck with Terror?
20 Dost thou make him leap like the locust?
   Dost thou teach him his snort of thunder?
21 He paweth and exulteth in his strength;
   He goeth forth into the valley to battle.

22 He laugheth at the lance, and quaileth not;
  And recoileth not from the sword.
23 Upon him rattleth the quiver,
  The flame of spear and dart.
24 In his eagerness he scoopeth the ground,
  And standeth not at sound of trumpet.
25 At the sound of it he crieth 'Aha!',
  And afar he scenteth the fray;
  The cry of the warriors daunteth him not,—
  The thunder of the captains and the shouting.

26 [Through thy wit doth the hawk ply his wings,
  And spread his pinions southward?]
27 At thy hest doth the vulture soar,
  And for thee set high his nest?
28 On the crag he settleth and dwelleth,—
  On the tooth of the crag and the fastness;
29 And from there he searcheth for food;
  His eyes see far away.
30 His nestlings gorge them with blood,
  And are glutted with flesh of the slain.

  CHAPTER 40.—2 Is Shaddai's opponent corrected,
  And Eloah's critic answered?

3 *And Eyob answered Iahvah and said:*
4 Lo, I am little! what can I reply to thee?
  My hand have I laid to my mouth.
5 Once spake I, but I will not repeat it;
  And twice, but I will not again.

6 *And Iahvah answered Eyob out of the Stormwind and said:*
7 Pray gird up thy loins like a warrior;
  I will ask thee, and teach thou Me!
8 Wilt thou really abolish my Justice?
  Wilt condemn Me, that thou mayst be right?
9 Hast thou then an Arm like El's,
  And with a Voice like His canst thou thunder?
10 Pray deck thee with Majesty and Grandeur,
  And put on Glory and Greatness!
11 Scatter the overflowings of thy wrath,
  And bring every proud man low!

12 Look at every proud man and humble him;
   And crush the godless where they stand!
13 Hide them in the dust together,
   And their faces enshroud in clay!
14 For then I also will praise thee,
   Because thine own right hand can save thee.
15 Behold now Behemoth, My work!
   Grass like the cattle he eateth.
16 Behold now his strength is in his loins,—
   His force in the thews of his belly.
17 His tail is as rigid as a cedar;
   The muscles of his thighs are close-knit.
18 His bones are brazen pipes;
   His legs are iron bars.
19 He was the prime fruit of His Way;
   Eloah made him to sport withal.
20 The beasts of the hills stare at him;
   And all the live things of the field are astonished.
21 Under the deep water he lieth,
   In covert of reed and fen;
22 The lotus-trees screen him reclining;
   The willows of the wâdy environ him.
23 [Though the River overflow, he is not flurried;
   He is calm, though it burst into his mouth.]

25 Canst thou draw up Leviathan with a fish-hook,
   And bind cords on his teeth?
26 Canst thou put a rush-line through his nose,
   And pierce his jaw with a hook?
24 Canst thou take him alive in a trap,
   Or with bird-snares catch him by the snout?
31 Canst thou pack his hide with spikes,
   Or his head with fishing-spears?
27 Will he supplicate thee much,
   Or address thee in gentle speech?
28 Will he come to terms with thee,
   That thou take him as a lifelong thrall?
29 Wilt thou play with him like a pet sparrow,
   Or keep him as a sport for thy maidens?
30 Shall partners bargain about him?
   Shall they divide him between the traders?

32 If thou lay thine hand upon him,
  Thou wilt think of a battle no more!
CHAPTER 41.—1 Lo, the hope of his assailant proveth vain!
  Even at sight of him he will be thrown!
 2 He is fell; who durst arouse him?
  And who can stand up before him?
 3 Who hath ever faced him without hurt?
  Under all Heaven there is none!

 4 I will not be mute on his array,—
  His might and the strength of his outfit.
 5 Who can strip off the surface of his coat?
  Who can pierce his double mail?
 6 The doors of his mouth who can open?
  About his teeth is Terror.
 7 His back shields encompass;
  They shut it in as with wall of flint:
 8 One close upon another,
  No space cometh between them.
 9 [Each to his fellow clinging,
  They hold together inseparably.]
 10 His snorting flasheth light;
  And his eyes are like the lids of Dawn.
 11 Forth of his mouth go flames,
  And sparks of fire escape.
 12 From his nostrils issues a smoke,
  Like a pot blown hot and steaming.
 13 His breath kindleth coals,
  And a flare issueth from his mouth.
 14 [Behind him stalketh Fierceness,
  And before him boundeth Panic.]
 15 The folds of his flesh are solid;
  Firm-set upon him, it shaketh not.
 16 His heart is firm as a stone,
  And harder than the nether millstone.
 17 At his noise heroes are afraid;
  At his crashing the brave take to flight.
 18 If the sword reach him, it holdeth not;
  The spear starteth from his mail.
 19 He counteth iron as straw,—
  Bronze as worm-eaten wood.

20 The son of the bow cannot rout him;
   The stones of the sling become chaff to him.
21 The lance counteth to him as chaff;
   He laugheth at the hurtling of the javelin.
22 Under him are the sharpest of potsherds;
   He spreadeth a threshing sledge upon the mire.
23 He maketh the Deep boil like a pot;
   The broad stream he maketh like a caldron.
24 Behind him he whiteneth his track;
   The Deep might be thought hoar-haired.
25 There is not on earth his like,
   Who was made a lord of things living.
26 Him every high one feareth;
   He is King over all the things that creep.

CHAPTER 42.—1 *And Eyob answered Iahvah and said:*
2 I know that Thou art all-able,
  And nothing is unattainable to Thee:
3 Therefore hast Thou shown me what I discerned not,—
  Things too hard for me that I knew not
5 By mere hearsay had I heard of Thee,
  But now mine own eye hath seen Thee;
6 Therefore I melt where I stand,
  And become like dust and ashes.

CHAPTER 42. 7–17.—7 Now after speaking these words to Eyob, Iahvah said to Eliphaz of Teman: 'I am incensed against thee and thy two friends, because ye have not spoken 8 right of Me like my servant Eyob. But now take you seven bullocks and seven rams and go to my servant Eyob and offer a burnt-offering on behalf of yourselves, and let my servant Eyob intercede for you, for his intercession I will accept, that I may not wreak destruction upon you! because ye have not spoken what was right of Me, like my servant Eyob.' 9 Accordingly, Eliphaz of Teman, Bildad of Shuah, and Zophar of Ma'ân, went and did as Iahvah had bidden them; and 10 Iahvah accepted the intercession of Eyob. Iahvah restored Eyob's exile, when he interceded for his friends; and Iahvah 11 doubled all Eyob's possessions. Then came to him all his kinsmen and all his kinswomen and all his old acquaintance and feasted with him in his house, and they condoled with him and comforted him for all the evil which Iahvah had caused to come upon him, and each of them made him a present of an ingot and each a golden earring.

12 Now Iahvah blessed the end of Eyob more than his beginning; so that he had fourteen thousand sheep and goats, and six thousand camels, and a thousand yoke of oxen,
13 and a thousand she-asses. He had also seven sons and three
14 daughters. He named the first (of the latter) Yemîmah, the
15 second Keçî'ah, and the third Kèren-happûkh. No women were found in all the land as fair as Eyob's daughters; and
16 their father gave them an estate among their brothers. Eyob survived these events a hundred and forty years, and saw his sons and his sons' sons (and their sons?), four generations.
17 So Eyob died, an old man and sated with life.

A COMMENTARY

CRITICAL, PHILOLOGICAL, AND EXEGETICAL, ON THE HEBREW TEXT AND ANCIENT VERSIONS OF THE BOOK

Chapter 1.—*v. 1. A man there was.* The Prologue of the book thus begins in the traditional manner of the story-teller; as we might say, 'There was once a Man' or 'Once upon a time there was a Man'. There is no attempt to put the narrative into relation with history. The time of the events narrated is left quite vague and indefinite. The order of words at once concentrates the reader's attention upon the hero. (For the constr. cf. 2 Sa 12¹; Es 2⁵.) *In 'Ûç-land*; that is, the country of the tribe or tribal group called 'Ûç (Gn 22²¹). 𝔊 ἐν χώρᾳ τῇ Αὐσίτιδι, *in Ausitis*, which implies, as Duhm remarks, the pronunciation 'Ôç (עֹיץ) rather than 'Ûç (עוּץ). The exact locality is unknown; but the Biblical data seem to require a situation eastward of Palestine and not remote from the north-eastern border of Edom. *See Add. Note.*

Eyob by name. Lit. *Eyob* (was) *his name.* The hero's name is given in a way that seems to imply that it was well known in story, as one of the great names of old. Neither parentage nor pedigree is assigned him, as we should expect in an historical narrative—a significant omission. [The author of the Elihu-section proceeds differently (32²).] This name is not an artificial invention to suit the story, as has often been taken for granted because of its apparent derivation from אָיַב ('āyáb), 'to be hostile to' (Ex 23²²), whence the common word אוֹיֵב ('ôyéb), 'enemy', as though אִיּוֹב ('îyôb) meant 'object of enmity', 'one treated hostilely or persecuted', scil. by God, as Eyob appeared to be (*Ges. Thes.*). Ewald suggested a different origin, comparing the Arabic 'awwâb, 'penitent', strictly 'one who frequently returns', scil. to God from his sins (الاٴوّاب = אוּב).[1] This, however, hardly seems appropriate, for his need of penitence is precisely what Eyob refuses to admit all through the prolonged controversy with his friends. That the former derivation of the name is correct is virtually proven by the occurrence of such personal designations as Ayabu-waqar (CT vi. 23) and Aḫḫu-ayabî among proper names of the period of the First Babylonian Dynasty (*see* Ranke, *Early Babylonian Personal Names*, p. 221). Cf. also the abbreviated form

---

[1] In the Koran, Sûra 38, David, Solomon, and Eyob successively are so described (انا اوّاب).

A-a-bu, i.e. Âbu (Johns, *Doomsday Book*), which agrees with the usual spelling of the Assyrian *âbu*, 'enemy'; for which we also find the spellings a-ia-bu (i.e. *ayabu*), a-ia-a-bu (= *ayâbu*; 1 R 27, 68, No. 2), and ia-a-bu (ZA vi. 190, *rm* 10). Assuming that the Heb. 'Îyôb represents an older 'Ayyâb, as it may do, we can hardly help identifying it with the word so variously written in these Babylonian and Assyrian forms. 'Îyôb ('Ayyâb?) will thus be a shortened theophoric name, like Nathan for Elnathan or Nathanael; and the meaning may be conjectured by comparison with such names as Jacob (shortened from Jacobel = *Ya'qubilu*, a Bab. name) and Israel. The idea embodied in designations of this kind would seem to be, not so much that Deity was hostile to the person so designated (what parent would be likely to choose such a name?), as that the latter would triumph even over more than mortal opposition. Cf. Gn 32²⁹ Ho 12⁴·⁵. 'Îyôb-'êl might thus mean 'One who durst oppose God', and would overcome Him or bend Him to his will by superior force or cunning. Such ideas, of course, betoken a very early stage of religious thought.

If further proof be needed that Eyob is not an allegorical figment, although like all other Hebrew personal names it must have been originally significant of some definite idea, we may point to the mention of Eyob in Ez 14¹⁴·²⁰, where he figures along with Noah and Daniel as one whose name was a proverb of sanctity in the prophet's day.

And that man was good (or *moral*) *and upright* (or *straightforward*). The Heb. תָּם (8²⁰ 9²⁰·²¹·²²) does not predicate moral *perfection* of Eyob any more than does its cognate תָּמִים (12⁴) of Noah (Gn 6⁹). As Driver remarks, the corresponding substantives (תֻּמָּה 2³·⁹ 27⁵ 31⁶; תֹּם 4⁶) are rendered *integrity*; and it seems a pity that the Latin adjective *integer* has not been adopted into our language along with *integritas*. Horace's 'Integer vitae scelerisque purus' is about equivalent to the phrase of our text. The terms are those of popular estimation rather than theological precision. What the poet makes of Eyob's goodness may be seen in chaps. 29, 31 especially. It is clear from 7²¹ 13²⁶ al. that he does not suppose his hero absolutely free from sin. 𝔊 ἄμεμπτος, 'blameless'. 'Correct' or 'irreproachable' would be a better rendering of תָּם than 'perfect', although (in accordance with its etymology) the word also denotes *complete, whole, entire, sound, unblemished* (of sacrificial animals). The ἀληθινός added in 𝔊 is really an alternative rendering of יָשָׁר: *see* 2³ 4⁷ 8⁶ 17⁸.

Godfearing and avoiding evil. Omit the connective particle (ו) between this pair of epithets and the preceding one. So 𝔊; and 𝔐 v. 8, 2³ (Du). The first epithet here denotes, not so much 𝔊's θεοσεβής, *religious* or *pious*, in the sense of worship, as fearing God as the Avenger of all misdoing, and especially of injustice and oppression (cf. Gn 42¹⁸). The plur. אלהים is a vague expression, denoting originally all superhuman agents or spiritual beings; and seems to be used here quite generally, as we might speak of 'the Powers above'. But the author has no doubt of the supremacy of Iahvah over all other invisible potentates (cf. Ps 97⁷ 'Worship Him, all ye Gods!'; 136²), and, an Israelite himself, he naturally makes Eyob acknowledge the God of Israel (v. 21 al.).

vv. 2, 3. This good man was blessed with offspring—a great token of Divine favour (Ps 127³ ff. 128³). A still happier circumstance in Oriental estimation was that sons outnumbered daughters by more than two to one. The numbers seven and three, repeated in connexion with the sheep and camels (v. 3), are in themselves possible enough and might easily be paralleled in many families; but 42¹³, where Eyob is again the father of seven sons and three daughters, after these had perished, shows that we are not dealing with literal history in this particular feature of the story. These numbers may be got out of the name איוב, since א״ב $= 1+2 = 3$, and א״ו $= 1+6 = 7$; while the remaining letter י $= 10$, the sum of the two, the perfect number. (י is the numeral-letter for 10, the complete or perfect number, which was therefore assumed to have been the number of Eyob's children; cf. 1 Sa 1⁸ Ru 4¹⁵. But $10 = 7+3$, and א״ו $= 1+6 = 7$, while א״ב $= 1+2 = 3$.) It will be noticed that the legend or tradition was apparently ignorant of the names of Eyob's original family, or else that the author has not troubled to record them; whereas 42¹⁴ does specify the names of the second trio of daughters. Why are the sons nameless in both passages? The sacred and symbolical numbers are the most prominent feature of vv. 2, 3. Seven is the number of the Seven Heavenly Bodies (Sun, Moon, and Five Planets), while Three is that of the three realms of being, Heaven, Earth, the Deep (She'ol) and their presiding Spirits (the Babylonian Anu, Bel, Aê). Five is the number of the Five Planets and of the Five Intercalated or extra Days of the solar year (ἐπαγόμεναι ἡμέραι, Diod. 1. 50).

The primitive astro-mythological use would doubtless make these numbers popular in all sorts of applications. For the rest, it is obvious that the 7000, 3000, and twice 500 ($= 1000$) of Eyob's livestock are not likely to be other than 'round' numbers. There is no mention of he-asses (cf. Gn 12¹⁶), though of course their existence is implied in the mention of the more valuable sex (one female was worth three males). 𝔊 adds νομάδες $=$ רעות *grazing* (1 C 27²⁹); a gloss from v. 14 which may have stood in 𝔊's Heb. text. Eyob's very considerable flocks and herds imply command of extensive pastures. His possession of numerous camels indicates the neighbourhood of the Syro-Arabian desert. They would be used, as pack-horses were formerly used in England, for trading with distant markets.

pairs, just as they were used in ploughing and carting (v. 14). The asses were the ordinary beasts of burden about the fields. All this property in land and livestock was naturally served by 'an immense body of slaves' (lit. *a very great service*; cf. the Latin use of *servitium* for *servus* and *opera* for *operarius*). The phrase, which occurs Gn 26¹⁴, has a double rendering in 𝔊: καὶ ὑπηρεσία πολλὴ σφόδρα, which is quite correct, and καὶ ἔργα μεγάλα (ἦν αὐτῷ ἐπὶ τῆς γῆς), which implies the pointing עֲבֻדָּה (= ἔργα, Ex 1¹⁴) instead of the rare עֲבֻדָּה (Gn 26¹⁴).

The man was, in fact, the greatest of all the Benê Ḳèdem; i.e. the pastoral tribes of Arab and Aramean stock who lived E. and NE. of Palestine (Gn 29¹ Ju 6³·³³ 1 K 4³⁰ Is 11¹⁴ Ez 25⁴·¹⁰). Benê Ḳèdem, 'The Sons of the East', 'The Eastlanders', Kadmeans, Kadmites (or Kadmonites? Gn 15¹⁹), is a gentilic designation like Benê Yisrā'él, 'The Sons of Israel', Benê 'Ammôn, 'The Sons of Ammon', the Ammonites.

Eyob was the richest and most powerful chief (*amîr*) among all these various tribes of the eastern borderland. [𝔊 curiously: καὶ ἦν ὁ ἄνθρωπος ἐκεῖνος εὐγενὴς τῶν ἀφ' ἡλίου ἀνατολῶν, *and that man was noble* (=noblest?) *of them of the East*. Cf. Is 11¹⁴ τοὺς ἀφ' ἡλίου ἀνατολῶν = בְּנֵי קֶדֶם. The word εὐγενής is only an unusual rendering of גדול.]

vv. 4, 5. *An illustration of Eyob's alert and assiduous piety* (v. 1). His seven sons who, like royal princes (2 Sa 13⁷ 14³⁰·³¹), had each an 'establishment' of his own, led a joyous existence of continual feasting; entertaining each other and their three sisters in turn, day by day, until the seven days of the week had expired, when the round of revels would begin afresh. The Heb. verbs in v. 4 are all frequentative in sense, as rendered above; describing the customary proceedings of the family. Cf. 𝔊ᴬ ἐποίουν.

In each others' houses in turn. Lit. (*in*) *the house of a man* (*on*) *his day*. The first day of the week would naturally be 'the day' of the firstborn brother (cf. v. 13); and the others would take their turn in the order of age, so that the seventh day would fall to the youngest. (𝔊 paraphrases בית by πρὸς ἀλλήλους, connecting it with והלכו, and turns איש יומו by καθ' ἑκάστην ἡμέραν.) A tacit disapproval of these perpetual daylight (vv. 13, 14) revels is perhaps implied by the sequel of the story (cf. Ec 10¹⁶ Is 5¹¹ 1 Th 5⁷); and the sending home for the three sisters (unmarried, and therefore mere girls) seems also to be mentioned as an unusual if not improper proceeding. We are reminded somehow of Es 1¹⁰f·, and even of Lk 16¹⁹. (לִשְׁלֹשֶׁת אַף is a scribal error for לִשְׁלֹשׁ.)

v. 5. Lit. *And it was, when the days of feasting had gone the round* (or *made full circuit*). Cf. Is 29¹.

Eyob sent; scil. a message bidding them come to him to be purified (or bidding them purify themselves, Gn 35²) and to be present at the expiatory sacrifices, 1 Sa 16⁵. The 'hallowing' or 'purifying' was the

1. 5 NOTES ON THE TEXT 99

ritual qualification for assisting in an act of worship. As the first day began (according to Jewish reckoning) at six in the evening of the seventh day, the ceremonies of purification may then have been performed. Then, rising betimes, at daybreak the father, as spiritual as well as temporal head of the family, 'would offer burnt-offerings (the kind of victim is not stated) according to the number of them all'; i.e. of his sons, for whose possible sin the sacrifice was offered: cf. the words that immediately follow: *Perchance my sons have sinned*, &c. (The daughters, if thought of at all, are included with the sons; but the writer would hardly regard them as responsible.) Doubtless, therefore, the number was again the mystic seven (cf 4 2⁸; Nu 23¹·¹⁴·²⁹). 𝔊, after the quite adequate rendering καὶ προσέφερεν περὶ αὐτῶν θυσίαν (θυσίας אᶜᵃ A; θυσία = עולה Nu 23³) κατὰ τὸν ἀριθμὸν αὐτῶν, adds καὶ μόσχον ἕνα περὶ ἁμαρτίας περὶ τῶν ψυχῶν αὐτῶν = וּפַר חַטָּאת אֶחָד עַל־נַפְשׁוֹתָם: cf. Le 8². This gloss, intended to bring Eyob's worship into conformity with the Levitical law, may have stood in 𝔊's Hebrew text. It cannot be original. (The Israelite father appears to have officiated as his own priest from the earliest period down to the seventh century, when the Deuteronomic legislation began to be enforced.)

For Eyob said (or *thought*; *said in his heart*, i.e. to himself: Ps 10⁶), '*Perhaps my sons have sinned by cursing God in thought*' (lit. *and blessed God in their heart*). The context, both here and in the historical parallel, 1 K 21¹⁰·¹³, demands this sense, although in both instances the verb בֵּרַךְ 'to bless' has been substituted for קִלֵּל 'to curse' by some scribe or editor who shrank even from writing the original phrase, so repellent to his piety was the idea it conveyed. It is no objection to this assumption that such a phrase has been suffered to remain in Is 8²¹ (Du), where perhaps the meaning is rather *curse by his King and by his God* (cf. 1 Sa 17⁴³).. In other cases also the scribes have not been thorough in such matters; e.g. the איש־בשת of 2 Sa 2⁸ᶠᶠ· appears in the original and genuine form אשבעל in 1 C 8³³, and ירבעל survives in Judges (6³² al.) although ירבשת has taken its place in 2 Sa 11²¹ (but cf. 𝔊 ad loc.). Cursing God (קלל אלהים) is forbidden by the earlier (Ex 22²⁷) as well as the later legislation (Le 24¹⁵). In the latter the penalty is death, which is naturally absent here, although 2⁹ assumes that God would inflict it (cf. Ex 22²⁷). 𝔊 paraphrases חטאו וברכו אלהים by κακὰ ἐνενόησαν πρὸς θεόν, *thought evil things against God*; which at least lends no support to an original 'blessed'; while 𝔖 strongly confirms our view by rendering *have sinned and cursed* (or *reviled*) *God* (ܨܚܝܘ = קלל in 1 Sa 17⁴³ Is 8²¹ Le 24¹⁵ &c.). The qualifying addition בלבבם *in their heart* seems very improbable. If blasphemous thoughts occurred to a party of revellers, they would probably find an outlet in speech. We therefore suggest ברברם ÷ *their talk* (or perhaps ברבם *in their quarrelling*, a loan in a later sense of drinking-bouts). The stress laid on the heinousness of improper language about God (cf. v. 22, 2¹⁰, and especially 42⁷ᶠ·, where Eyob's three friends are bidden to offer a burnt-offering of seven bullocks and seven rams for this very offence) certainly lends colour to the former emendation.

A simpler and perhaps better way of eliminating the difficulty would be to suppose that בלבבם has been altered from בלבבו (Ps 15²), which originally followed איוב and got misplaced by some accident. Thus is restored the appropriate sense: *For Eyob said in his heart, 'Perhaps my sons have sinned by cursing God.'*

[The notion that בֵּרַךְ, which appears to be used in the senses of greeting and taking leave (Gn 47⁷·¹⁰ 2 K 4²⁹), might, like our own phrase 'bid farewell to', have come to mean *give up, renounce,* or *disown,* has no foundation in actual Hebrew usage. בֵּרַךְ, like the Assyrian כרב *karâbu,* is used of God blessing men and of men blessing God, but never of renouncing or disowning God; nor is it easy to see why Eyob should have entertained any fears on this score. It is evident also that such a sense is entirely inappropriate in the parallel passage 1 K 21¹⁰·¹³ ('Naboth hath *renounced* God and King!'—a very unlikely charge against a subject of Ahab). What our story really intends is rather some rash or petulant or even sportive utterance of inebriate folly. If there is 'a noteworthy εὐφημία ἀντιφραστική' (Du) in these passages, the euphemistic antiphrasis belongs to his editors, not to the author. Such a mode of speaking is unknown to the OT writers.]

So used Eyob to do all the year round; lit. *all the days,* i.e. *always,* or *continually,* as in Gn 43⁹ 44³² (AV 'for ever').

The Hebrew of vv. 4, 5 suggests several other questions. Might not the successive banquets be birthday celebrations? And in that case what is the precise meaning of *when the days of (the?) banquet had gone round?* Is it meant that the rejoicings on each occasion were prolonged over several days, after which the anxious father performed his atoning rites? or does the phrase *the days of banquet = the banquet-days* as a whole? and in that case does Eyob offer his expiatory sacrifice only once a year, viz. after the celebration of the seventh and last birthday? The idea of birthday celebrations brings the narrative nearer to the bounds of probability; but the picture of a continual round of careless gaiety harmonizes better with the character of the story as a whole. (Free potations appear to have been customary with the ancient Hebrews on occasions of rejoicing.)

vv. 6–12. The motive of Eyob's religion questioned by the Satan at the Court of Heaven. He receives permission to prove it by calamity. The scene that follows (repeated 2¹⁻⁶), upon which Goethe founded the splendid 'Prologue in Heaven' to his *Faust,* is not of course to be taken as literal history. Even the Talmud can relate that a certain Rabbi who sat before R. Samuel bar Nachmani said: 'Eyob never was, and was not created, but was a parable' (איוב לא היה ולא נברא אלא משל היה, Baba Bathra, 15 a). The narrative of the celestial levee is not poetry either in form or substance. It reflects the conceptions current in the time of the author, and is essentially similar to the vision of Micaiah ben Imlah, 1 K 22¹⁹ ff.: cf. also Ps 89⁵⁻⁷; and for the worship in the Temple-palace of Heaven, Is 6 Ps 29.

v. 6. But the day came when, &c. See Driver ad 1 Sa 1⁴. The phrase recurs 2¹ 2 K 4⁸,¹¹,¹⁸. Du prefers a different syntax: *And it happened (on) the day (cas. accus.)*; scil. on which it happened, the day so well known from the story—a common Hebrew construction.

The Sons of God. A very inadequate translation; with which, however, we must content ourselves, unless we choose simply to transcribe the Hebrew into *Běnê hā'ĕlôhîm*, or are bold enough to render 'gods' (cf. Ex 18¹¹ Ps 97⁷ 136²), which, after all, comes nearest to the original meaning. The Hebrew אלהים (*'Elôhîm*) is a vaguely used generic and collective expression, denoting all superhuman Agents or spiritual Intelligences (apparently including ghosts, 1 Sa 28¹³), as well as the Supreme Spirit, Who is 'the God of (the) gods' (Ps 136² Dan 2⁴⁷). As such, it is opposed to אָדָם 'Man', 'Mankind', 'human beings' (cf. Is 31³). And as בן אדם 'a son of Man', means simply a man (= בַּר אֱנָשׁ, Dan 7¹³), and the plur. בני אדם 'the Sons of Man', means either 'men', 'the human race' (Gn 11⁵), or 'human beings' as opposed to Iahvah (1 Sa 26¹⁹), so בן אלהים, which happens not to occur (cf. בַּר אֱלָהִין, Dan 3²⁵), would naturally mean 'a son of Godkind', i.e. a god, and the plur. בני (ה)אלהים is equivalent to '(the) celestial or divine beings', 'the gods'. Cf. Ps 82⁶,⁷. 'The Sons of (the) 'Elôhîm' are seldom mentioned elsewhere in the OT (Gn 6²,⁴ Jb 38⁷) Yet the story evidently assumes that the reader will know who they are without further explanation. In an ancient fragment of Hebrew folk-lore (Gn l.c.) they are represented as enamoured of the beautiful 'daughters of Man' (בנות האדם), who bore them giant offspring; while in the passage of Jb l.c. they, with the 'Stars of Morning', rejoice at the founding of Earth. The designation בני האלהים is probably a fossilized relic of primitive Semitic polytheism; and doubtless the name figured much more largely in popular (Canaanite?) myths of the olden time than would appear from the scanty references of Scripture. It is significant that although the poet of Job has admitted the Benê 'Elôhîm to participate, at least as interested spectators, in the great work of Creation (38⁷), yet they are not mentioned by name in either of the two accounts of Gn 1-3. Their presence, however, may well be implied in 1²⁶ 3²² ('one of Us'). In Ps 29¹ 89⁷ we have בני אלים as a (poetical) synonym of בני אלהים (which should perhaps be restored in both places).

The *Bĕnê 'Elôhîm* here 'came' or 'went in' (scil. into the throne-room of the celestial palace) 'to take their stand by (beside) Iahvah'; i.e. to stand in waiting or attendance on the heavenly King, as His ministers and servants, in readiness to receive His commands and 'do His pleasure' (Ps 103²¹; cf. Zc 6⁵); much as in Micaiah's vision Iahvah was 'seated upon His throne, with *all the Host of Heaven* standing beside Him at His right and at His left' (1 K 22¹⁹). In the equivalence Sons of Elohim = Host of Heaven = the Stars (38⁷ Dt 4¹⁹ Ne 9⁶ 'The Host of Heaven worshippeth Thee'; cf. Is 24²¹) we may discern how these ideas are blended in primitive Semitic mythology. Cf. the Babylonian Epic of Creation, Tab. VII. **15–17**, where the supreme God is acclaimed as 'ZI-UKKIN, Life of the Host of Heaven, Who established for the gods the shining heavens, Who chose their way and appointed their path'; also ib. **110**: 'Of the Stars of Heaven their way may He still uphold! Like sheep may He shepherd the gods all of them!' (cf. Is 40²⁶ Ps 147⁴). In the same cycle of legends the Assembly of the Gods fulfils an important function. They gather in a place which bears the Sumerian designation UB-SHU-GINA-KI, 'The Regions' Gatheringplace', and there hold council and feast together and determine destinies, appointing Merodach as their champion against Tiâmat, and (if victorious) their supreme Lord and King.

We note a difference of ideas between the picture of Heaven, as the Court of an Oriental monarch, in Jb and 1 K 22¹⁹, and the later and more spiritual representation of the prophet Isaiah, which conceives of Heaven as an august Temple, where the mystic Seraphim 'raise the Trisagion ever and aye' before the throne of Iahvah Sabaoth. The same general conception seems to be reflected in Ps 29.

As Iahvah's messengers and ministers in relation to man the celestial host are called מַלְאָכִים 'messengers' (= ἄγγελοι; cf. 𝔊 οἱ ἄγγελοι τοῦ θεοῦ = בני האלהים, Gn 6² and here); a designation which displaced all others in the ordinary use of the developed theology of the OT (cf. Ho 12⁴·⁵ אלהים = מלאך; Gn 32²⁸). In the poetical sections of our book (5¹ 15¹⁵) we meet with another title of these celestial beings, viz. קדשים 'Holy Ones' (cf. Ps 89⁶·⁸, where their assembly is called קהל קד׳ and סוד קד׳). The original implication of this term, derived from the primitive root *KAD* which we see in יקד 'to burn' and other cognates (*see Hilprecht Anniversary Volume*, p. 48) was *bright, pure*, physically (cf. 15¹⁵ᵇ); but, like its synonyms, the word soon came to include the ideas, first of ritual or ceremonial and then of moral and spiritual purity or 'holiness'.

Among the *Bĕnê hā'ĕlôhîm* there went in also one who is called השטן *The Adversary* or *Opposer*; who in the sequel justifies this designation by daring persistently to maintain his own contrary opinion against Iahvah Himself, and by his manifest malignity to Eyob. 𝔊, by its rendering ὁ διάβολος, seems to identify this 'Adversary' at once with the Arch-spirit of Evil, the Enemy of Mankind (cf. Mt 4^{1,3,8 10} ὁ διάβολος = Σαταναῖς). It is, however, evident that the Satan of our narrative, with his free access to the Throne of Heaven and direct intercourse with the Supreme, is a very different figure from the outcast and utterly fallen Spirit of the later theology, enemy alike of God and man; although his unfriendly insinuations against Eyob and the alacrity with which he sets about the ruin of an innocent person give us more than a hint of what was to become the salient feature of his character.

It is usual to remark that the presence of the Article in the Hebrew (השטן *the Satan*) shows that the phrase has not yet become a Proper Name. Possibly, however, we have here an instance of that peculiar use of the Article in Hebrew which must be rendered indefinitely in our language (*a Satan* or *an adversary* > *the S., the Adv.*); just as in the parallel passage (1 K 22^{21}) הרוח *the spirit* means the spirit who became known from his part in this vision and may be rendered more naturally by *a spirit* in our less vivid and picturesque idiom.

The equivalence שטן = διάβολος = ܐܟܠܩܪܨܐ (S Mt 4^1) *maligner, slanderer*—a conception of Satan which perhaps depends mainly upon the Prologue of Jb and Zc 3^1—may be justified by reference to Ezr 4^6, where the cognate שִׂטְנָה denotes *an accusation* or calumny.

v. 7. Iahvah's question, *Whence comest thou?* (as though the Omniscient required to be informed: Pr 15^3 Ps 139 Je 23^{24}) betrays the simplicity of the ancient myth. In the sense of the original legend the question may perhaps indicate surprise. Iahvah does not ask whence 'the Sons of God' in general have come. He knows the stations of the heavenly host. Perhaps also, although as a Spirit-being it is implied that the Satan is himself a *ben-hā'ělōhîm*, the statement *and the Satan too went in among them* implies that there was something unusual in his attendance at the Divine levee. it was an intrusion; he made his way in with the throng. At all events, his reply *From roving the earth and roaming about therein* may suggest that he was not altogether at home in the celestial sphere, the abode of the Host of Heaven; either he is an earthborn spirit, or at least (like the evil spirits of Babylonian sorcery) his haunt and home is the earth, with its deserts, and caves, and mountains (cf. Mt 4^1 12^{43}). The restlessness of a Babylonian demon, wandering about in search of a victim, may be said to characterize him (cf. also 1 Pe 5^8). The zest with which he falls to ruining the righteous Eyob bears this out. We can hardly say that, as God's instrument or minister, his 'own moral character does not come into question', or that he is neither a good nor a bad angel (Davidson). How can we conceive of a good spirit as inciting Iahvah to suspect a good man's integrity, and rejoicing in the infliction of unmerited miseries? He is, in fact, as his name indicates, already the Arch-enemy of man, sceptical of his goodness, disparaging his motives, eager to do him hurt. Why this should be so the story gives no hint. And since the author of the book has no further use for the Satan after the Prologue in Heaven, and neither Eyob nor any of the other speakers makes any reference to his instinctive hostility to man in general or to good men in particular as accounting for the calamities which befell the righteous hero, it is perhaps hardly worth while to lay much stress upon the details of an ancient popular legend, which the author chose for the setting of his great argument simply because it supplied a vivid and dramatic illustration of the truth which he desired to advocate: the truth, namely, that the same effects may be due to different causes, and that human suffering, so far from always being direct evidence of human sin, may sometimes be due to causes which have no relation at all to conduct. Had the author regarded Satan's malignity as the true solution of the riddle of the sufferings of the righteous, his closing Theodicy would hardly have omitted all reference to the fact (*see* 38-42⁶). It has often been pointed out that to press every detail of a parable is to imperil our perception of the lesson it was intended to convey; and it must be admitted that, from the standpoint of an absolute morality, it is as difficult to justify Iahvah's arbitrary dealing with one whose blamelessness He Himself emphatically affirms, as it is to account for the character and conduct of the Satan, if we confine our attention exclusively to OT sources. *Qui facit per alium facit per se*; and although Iahvah charges the Satan with urging Him on against Eyob (2³), the Epilogue plainly speaks of *all the evil which Iahvah had caused to come upon him* (Eyob): 42¹¹. After all, the story contains no suggestion that the Satan presented himself before Iahvah with the express purpose of disparaging Eyob's piety. It is Iahvah who first mentions the patriarch, challenging the judgement of the Satan upon his unique excellence, eliciting a sarcastic expression of doubt as to its disinterested nature, and then granting permission to the malign spirit to put it to the proof in his own pitiless way.

v. 8. *My servant*; i.e. my worshipper or votary. So in Gn of Abraham, Isaac, and Jacob: cf. 2 K 9⁷. Very common as an element in Semitic (Aram., Heb., Phoen., Arab.) Personal Names, e.g. Abdallah, *Servant of Allah*, Abdashtart, *Servant of Ashtoreth*, and the like. Cf. the cognate verb, 21¹⁵ Ex 3¹². Here, as in v. 21, the author seems to make Eyob a Iahvah-worshipper, that is, an Israelite. This may have been a feature of the popular story. In the speeches, however, he is careful to restrict Eyob and his friends, as non-Israelites, to the more general terms אל, אלוה, אלהים, and שדי.

He has not his like on earth. Eyob, like Noah, with whom Ezekiel mentions him as a paragon and proverb of righteousness (Ez 14¹⁴·²⁰), is the best man alive (Gn 6⁹), whether in the matter of *Cultus* or of conduct. The expression 'My servant' implies also that he is dear to Iahvah. The character of Eyob is repeated from v. 1, just as vv. 6-8 are repeated at 2¹⁻³. These and other similar recurrences of set phrases in the narrative are quite in the manner of the professional storyteller, and they remind us of the like repetitions of favourite lines and phrases in epic poetry, whether Semitic (e. g. the Babylonian Epic of Gilgamesh) or Aryan (Mahâbhârata; the Iliad and Odyssey). Our narrative, however, is not poetic in form, but rhythmic prose.

v. 9. Is it for nothing that Eyob fears God? A surprising question in an OT book. Eyob's religious consistency and constancy are admitted, but the question of motive is raised, and doubt is thrown on his disinterestedness. He expects and receives a *quid pro quo* for his piety. Let the recompense cease; and all this calculated goodness will disappear. Such a suggestion is certainly startling, in view of the fact that the moral teaching of the Law and the Prophets is everywhere recommended by the promise of such blessings as Eyob enjoyed. It is the whole burden of the fervid preaching of the Deuteronomist. The idea that an obedience consciously rendered with an eye to material benefits was morally worthless does not seem to have occurred to the authors of the older scriptures. The Satan suggests that Eyob is only apparently devoted to God; he loves the gifts, not the Giver, and his insincerity will be demonstrated the moment the gifts are withdrawn. In much the same way, modern adversaries of the faith have often objected to Christian piety that it really rests on a foundation of selfishness, viz. the hope of reward and the fear of punishment either here or hereafter, and cannot therefore claim to represent the highest ideal of moral excellence. In reply to such carping criticism it is surely enough to point to that lifelong yearning after the beauty of holiness, that hungering and thirsting after righteousness, that unquenchable aspiration to reflect the image of God, which has characterized the genuine saint in every age of the Church.

v. 10. Made a fence all round him (or *hedged him about all round*); like a choice vineyard (Is 5⁵ᵇ Mt 21³³), to protect it from thieves and wild beasts (Ps 80¹²,¹³ 89⁴⁰,⁴¹). Eyob's own person, his family, and all his belongings, are shielded by the Divine favour from all external attack. As Duhm observes, had there been any hole in the fence, the Satan would certainly have discovered it. We may remember how the evil spirits of old Babylonian myth penetrate everywhere, easily making their way through all obstacles and over all barriers. 'High walls (or fences, *ûrê*), broad walls, like a flood they surmount; From house to house they break thro'; Them the door shuts not out, the bolt turns not back! Thro' the door like a serpent they slip; Thro' the hinge (or by the pivot) like the wind they blow' (*T"u^hh. I·---d^i* Tab V -₁ --): see

Thompson, *Devils*, p. 52). And we have the repeated prayer of the exorcisms, 'Into my house may they not enter! Into my fence (or palisade, *úría*) may they not break through!' (4 R 1, col. 3, 55-8).

But not only were Eyob and his dependents secure from personal hurt and harm. Iahvah had also hitherto prospered *the work of his hands* (Dt 28¹² Ps 90¹⁷ 104²³ מעשה), his tillage and his trading enterprises; *and as for his livestock, it multiplied* (Gn 30³⁰ J) *in the land.* 𝔊: *and his cattle thou didst multiply*, &c. (πολλὰ ἐποίησας = פרצת; פָּרַצְתָּ?). Cf. Dt 28³ ff.

v. 11. Strike, as in *v. 19. And he will assuredly*, &c. The constr. is that of an oath. The Satan will take his oath that Eyob will break out into furious blasphemy, reviling Iahvah; much as barbarians have been known to abuse and even beat their idols for failing to avert disaster. (*To Thy Face* = 𝔊 εἰς πρόσωπόν σε εὐλογήσει = אל פניך ונ', as 2⁵. So אל should be read for על in v. 8, as in 2³, although 𝔊 has κατὰ in the former case.)

v. 12. Iahvah at once accepts the Satan's challenge, and by way of testing His blameless servant's constancy bids the Adversary work his will upon 'all that belongs to him', sparing only himself. The readiness with which Iahvah surrenders one whose innocence He has Himself asserted to such a merciless probation (cf. 2⁶) is certainly strange. Is it meant that the Satan had succeeded in instilling a doubt of Eyob's disinterestedness into the mind of Iahvah (which would imply that Iahvah did not Himself really know the true state of the case; cf. the question *Whence comest thou?* v. 7, and Gn 18²¹ 22¹²), and that He saw no other way of reassuring Himself than the drastic method suggested by the Satan? or is the idea rather that the Lord desires to vindicate His own judgement and the character of His servant in the sight of all the Sons of God (including the Satan) by submitting Eyob to the tests which the Satan proposes, knowing that His servant's loyalty will emerge triumphant from any possible trial? It must always be borne in mind that the manifest import of this parabolic legend is that misfortune does not necessarily presuppose guilt, but that a perfectly good man may become involved in it as a consequence of the activities of Powers above man, and, further, that he will continue steadfast under the most formidable shocks of calamity. But in spite of this lofty moral the hero appears too much like a mere pawn on the chessboard of Heaven; and we are somehow reminded of Gloucester's despairing cry in *Lear*: 'As flies to wanton boys are we to the gods: They kill us for their sport!'

The Satan then withdrew from the presence of Iahvah. Confident of success, he does not linger in the Court of Heaven, but hurries forth at once to execute his reluctantly conceded commission. (Iahvah's reluctance is apparently revealed in His anxious prohibition of any attack upon Eyob himself.) There is an evident reminiscence of the Satan's obtaining leave to make trial of Eyob's sincerity in the words which our Lord addressed to St. Peter respecting the Twelve and himself: 'Simon, Simon, behold the Satan did beg you (*plur.*) for sifting like wheat; but I, I prayed for thee that thy-faith fail not. And do thou, once thou hast returned, confirm thy brethren!' (Lk 22[31 32]). That misfortune is a touchstone of character is a fact of universal experience; but so also is prosperity.

vv. 13-22. *The first trial fails to shake Eyob's constancy.* The fixed phrases in which Eyob's successive misfortunes are related, belong, as already noted (v. 8), to the epic style of narration; and the breathless haste with which one messenger of evil tidings follows on the heels of another is profoundly impressive and dramatic. There are four strokes of calamity (cf. Ez 14[21]); and all is accomplished within the compass of a single day—the very day when, secure in the sense of solemn rites of expiation duly performed at dawn (*see* note on v. 5), and wholly unconscious of impending doom, his children were joyously feasting together in the house of the eldest-born. The curtain falls upon the patriarch mourning the loss of all, but bowing to the will of Iahvah in a spirit of pious resignation.

v. 13. *And the day came. See* note on v. 6. *his sons.* So 𝔐, it being obvious from the context that sons of the Satan could not be intended, although he is the nearest subject 𝔊 οἱ υἱοὶ Ἰώβ, to prevent misapprehension, which, however, was unlikely in a popular story.

Were eating bread and drinking wine לחם perhaps fell out after (אכלים), which 𝔊[B] om., giving simply ἔπινον οἶνον. (But 𝔊[A Rc a] pref. ἤσθιον καί, as 𝔐.) On account of the phrase *to eat and drink* in v. 4, Duhm would omit יין as probably added by a copyist.

vv. 14, 15. THE FIRST STROKE. The oxen, and she-asses raided by Bedawi marauders of Sabean stock (Heb. Sheba), who massacre the ploughmen and herdsmen. Taken by surprise, the latter, though probably armed, could make little resistance. The Sabeans (Σαβαῖοι of the Greek geographers) of Yemen in SW. Arabia were a famous nation in antiquity, whose offshoots may have extended as far north as the borders of Edom (Gn 10[7 28] 25[3]). Their caravans traded in gold, spices, and other costly merchandise (6[19] Is 60[8] Je 6[20] Ez 27[22] 1 K 10[1.10]). In Jo 3[8] (4[8]) they appear as trafficking in slaves. Of late years thousands of inscriptions in the so-called Himyaritic character have been recovered from the ruins of their ancient cities by Dr. Edward Glaser and others.

𝔊 καὶ ἐλθόντες οἱ αἰχμαλωτεύοντες (var. αἰχμαλωτεύσαντες) = ותבא שבה; cf Gn 14[14] 34[29]. The translator confused שבא, the Nom. Propr which he did not understand here, with שבה, Aram. שבא *to take captive*

v. 16. THE SECOND STROKE. The flocks and their shepherds blasted by lightning. That אש אלהים *Fire of God* or *Elohim's Fire* means the lightning is clear from 2 K 1¹²; cf. 1 K 18³⁸, where it is called אש יהוה *Iahvah's Fire*. Besides, *it falls from the Heavens*. Lightning is called simply Fire (so 𝔊 here) in Ex 9²³⁻²⁴ (cf. Ps 78⁴⁸). In 38³⁵ we have the ordinary word ברק (in *plur.*). Here the supernatural character of the phenomenon and its effect (it annihilated seven thousand small cattle and their attendants, seemingly with one flash!) are emphasized by the peculiar designation. The Satan appears in a different connexion with lightning, Lk 10¹⁸: 'I was gazing on the Satan as he fell like a flash of lightning out of Heaven!' Nowhere else in OT (or NT) does the Satan appear as wielding the Lightning, which is Iahvah's own special weapon of war (cf. 2 S 8²⁶ 38²⁵·³⁵ Ps 18¹⁴ 144⁶ Ez 1¹³ Hab 3¹¹ &c.). Having received a permission (which amounts to a commission) from Iahvah, he acts as His minister of evil in the present case.

> 'And since God suffers him to be,
> He too is God's minister,
> And labours for some good,
> By us not understood'

—nor by him intended. The overruling Power brings good out of evil. Gn 45⁸ 50²⁰ Is 10⁷.

v. 17. THE THIRD STROKE. *Three bands.* The same expression is found in Ju 7¹⁶ 9⁴³ al. The camels were attacked on three sides at once, as otherwise their swiftness would have given them a good chance of escape.

The 'Chaldeans' (Heb. *Kasdím*; Gn 11²⁸ 15⁷ 𝔊 Χαλδαίων), like the 'Sabeans', v. 15, may have been felt as a difficulty by the Greek translator, because of their distance from the supposed scene of action. 𝔊 gives οἱ ἱππεῖς, *the horsemen* (= פרשים Gn 50⁹ al.). But כשדים might have become פרשים by transposition of the second and third letters and the common confusion of ד with ר and כ with פ.

The Chaldeans were the people of the extreme south of Babylonia, in the neighbourhood of the Persian Gulf, the *mât Kaldu* of the Assyrian inscriptions (Ashurnâṣirpal, *Annals*, III, 24 al.). Always a thorn in the side of Assyria, and like Hereward's Saxons difficult of access in their jungle fastnesses, they finally succeeded in erecting the brilliant if short-lived neo-Babylonian monarchy on the ruins of the northern empire. At the earlier period when the story of Eyob may be supposed to have originated, roving bands of freebooters from the Chaldean marshes may have been in the habit of making plundering raids far and near, like the one briefly described in the text. (The language of the Hebrew reminds us of 1 Sa 23²⁷ 27⁸·¹⁰ 30¹: פשט *to make a dash or raid*. 𝔊 loosely καὶ ἐκύκλωσαν τὰς καμήλους, *and surrounded th. camels*.)

vv. 18, 19. THE FOURTH AND FINAL STROKE: the simultaneous death of Eyob's children. The introductory formula is the same as in vv. 16, 17; עד being merely *Scriptio Defectiva* for עוד *still*. The term *wine* (יין) does not appear in 𝔊; but *see* note on v. 12, and cf. 42¹¹ *eat bread*; Gn 43²⁵ Lk 14¹⁵ (eat bread = feast).

A hurricane (or *whirlwind*), &c. Lit. *a great wind came from the other side of the wilderness* (or *steppe*, 'veld'); i.e. it blew from the East, across the great Arabian desert (Ju 11²² Is 21¹), the western edge of which would be the eastern boundary of 'Ooçland; *and struck*; i.e. the hurricane struck. (ויגע is a scribal error for ותגע, as the subject רוח is feminine.)

vv. 20, 21, 22. *How Eyob took this rain of calamities.* Until the climax was reached with the death of his children, the old sheikh sat in dignified silence on his divan, giving audience to the scared messengers of woe. Now, still apparently without a word, he rises to his feet and performs the customary symbolical actions indicative of mourning, 'rending' or making a slit in his mantle (*mĕ'īl*), cf. 2 Sa 1¹¹ 3³¹ al., and then having his head shaved (doubtless by his usual attendant); the latter a foreign usage, forbidden to Israel, or at least to the priests (Le 19²⁷ 21⁵; cf. Is 15²), and not unknown to the Greeks, who covered the corpse of Patroklos with their shorn locks, as they bore it to the funeral pyre, where Achilleus himself also cut off his own 'yellow mane', and devoted it to his dead friend (Iliad 135–51; cf. also Hdt ii. 36; ix. 34). Cf. also Je 7²⁹ Mi 1¹⁶. After giving these outward signs of intense grief, Eyob 'fell', i.e. threw himself (נפל expressing a voluntary act, as in Gn 17³ 24⁶⁴) on the ground and did reverence (*abs.*); scil. before Iahvah, Whose Hand he recognized in these sudden disasters. It was an act of voiceless submission, all the more impressive because of its silence. Then, speaking to himself in soliloquy, or perhaps in the hearing of those about him, he gives utterance to his pious resignation in that poetical form which is the most natural vehicle of religious emotion, and which popular legend also employs occasionally for the expression of illustrative proverbs, riddles, and other pregnant sayings (cf. Ju 14¹⁴·¹⁸ 15¹⁶). The verse is a quatrain or tetra-stich in 𝔐; but between the third and fourth stichus 𝔊 interpolates ὡς τῷ κυρίῳ ἔδοξεν, οὕτως ἐγένετο, *As it seemed good to the Lord, so it befell* = יהוה כן היה (or על) בעיני כתוב (cf. Es 3⁸·¹¹ Jos 9²⁵ Gn 19⁸). Perhaps כן־היא 5²⁷; cf. Gn 44¹⁰.

We understand the statement *Naked came I out of my mother's womb*, which is obviously true of every human being. But what is the precise meaning of the second stichus *And naked shall* (or *must*) *I return thither*? We are reminded of the question of Nicodemus (Joh 3⁴). Clearly the womb to which a man returns at death is not the womb from which he emerges at birth. He returns to the dust (21²⁶ 34¹⁵ Ec 3²⁰) or the ground, out of which man was originally taken (Gn 2, or the earth

(Ec 12⁷): cf. 1 Co 15⁴⁷ ἐκ γῆς, said of the first man. The Earth, therefore, would seem to be here regarded as the common Mother of humanity, into whose womb or bosom it returns at death. This idea of the Earth as the Great Mother, common as it is in Aryan myth and poetry (παμμήτόρ τε Γῆ, Aesch. *Prom.* 90), is not found elsewhere in the OT (Ps 139¹⁵ is corrupt). In Babylonian religion, however, the Great Mother of Mankind (cf. NE xi. 123 f.), plays a principal part; and she is the goddess of the Underworld (Shĕ'ôl; Hades) which was regarded as the 'womb' or 'belly' of the earth (GARASH, *karašu*): cf. her title SHAG-TUR or SHA-SUR, 'Heart of the (great) Fold' (= *Inside of the earth*), and Radau's note, *Bab. Exp. Univ. Pennsylvania*, vol. xxx, Pt. 1, p. 52. (The שאול בטן or 'womb of Hades' is mentioned, Jon 2².)

'Twas Iahvah who gave, and Iahvah who took (away). Cf. 1 Sa 2⁷; Ps. 135⁶. The Divine Name is emphatic both times. God deals as He pleases with His creatures; and it is not for man to question His Will, but to acquiesce with all reverence and submission. This, as Duhm observes, might be called the creed and keynote of all Oriental piety. Eyob expresses no hope of restoration (42¹⁰ᶠᶠ·); at the moment he has none. But he remembers that he had nothing when life began, and that all his good things, enjoyed for many years, were the boon of Iahvah. And now that the Supreme has suddenly withdrawn His gifts, He has simply done what He would with His own. Thankful perhaps for the happy past, certainly awed by a vivid sense of the irresistible Power that controls the fortunes of man, he instinctively gives glory to God: *Let Iahvah's Name be blest!* This last word (מְבֹרָךְ *blessed*) shows that *he will bless thee* (יְבָרֲכֶךָ) cannot be the original reading in v. 11 (cf. v. 6). Eyob falsifies the Satan's prediction by doing the exact contrary, blessing instead of cursing God as the Author of his ruin. Of course he knows nothing of the Satan's part in the catastrophe. To him all is Iahvah's will and work; a point of view which makes his constancy at once more arduous and more admirable.

v. 22. *In all this*; scil. overwhelming trouble: cf. Is 5²⁵ 9¹¹·¹⁶·²⁰ 10⁴: *amid* or *in spite of* it all, *Eyob sinned not*; i.e. as the next clause and 2¹⁰ show, by rash or impious language: *he did not ascribe* תִּפְלָה *to God*. 𝔊 paraphrases well ἐν τούτοις πᾶσιν τοῖς συμβεβηκόσιν αὐτῷ, *In all these things that befell him* (= *In all this*), and continues οὐδὲν ἥμαρτεν Ἰὼβ ἐναντίον τοῦ κυρίου (= +לַיהוָֽה Gn 39⁹ Ex 10¹⁶: at least a correct gloss from the margin), καὶ οὐκ ἔδωκεν ἀφροσύνην τῷ θεῷ, *and ascribed not* folly *unto God*. The Heb. תִּפְלָה *tiflā* (4¹⁸) means the same as Lat. *insulsitas*, 'tastelessness, silliness, folly', from *insulsus*, 'unsalted, unseasoned, tasteless, insipid', of food (=Heb. תָּפֵל 6⁶; neo-Heb. *unsalted*, of fish; cf. שָׁוְא וְתָפֵל *falsehood and folly*. La 2¹⁴). In Ar. *tafala* is 'to spit', and *tufl, tafl, tifl*, 'spittle' (as being tasteless?). The primitive biliteral root TAP, DAB, appears in Talmudic תָּפַף *to spit*, Ethiopic *taféa*, id., and perhaps in תֹּפַח *spitting*, 17⁶ (√תוּף). The root-meaning is *to flow, to go.* cf. Aram. דוּב = Heb. זוּב *to flow*; דָּבַב *to glide, go slowly*, Heb. and Ar.

Duhm thinks that תִּפְלָה here, like בֵּרַךְ, vv. 5, 11, 2⁵ ⁹, and נָבָל נְבָלָה 2¹⁰, 42⁸, is a decent or euphemistic expression for some stronger term of blasphemy. This, however, is hardly necessary. To charge God with unreason in His moral government of man was surely offensive enough. (It seems possible, moreover, that תפלה may also imply fraud and delusion (cf. Je 23¹³ La 2¹⁴ Ez 22²⁸), as if events had proved God untrustworthy.) The phrase נתן תפלה לאל *to give folly to God* is a perfect parallel to יהב ליהוה כבוד ועז *to give* (i. e. ascribe or attribute) *glory and power to Iahvah* (Ps 29¹). 𝔊 | ܘ...ܠܐ ... ܕܐ ܠܐ*' nor blasphemed against God*, 𝔙 *neque stultum quid contra Deum locutus est*, seem to take נתן in the sense of *to utter* (cf. Jos 7¹⁹ Pr 2³); but this is less probable.

Duhm well remarks that the lesson of the chapter is that Misfortune is neither always the consequence of Sin, nor—in the case of a really pious man—is it any temptation to Sin.

Chapter 2 —*vv.* 1-10. *Failure of the Satan's second attempt to break down Eyob's constancy.*   *vv.* 11-13. *Eyob's Three Friends come to condole with him.* The scene in Heaven, vv. 1-7, is cast in the same mould as before (1⁶⁻¹²): *see* the notes on 1⁸ and the introductory remarks to 1¹³⁻²².

v. 1. 𝔐 adds להתיצב על־יהוה *to stand in attendance on Iahvah* at the end of the verse. 𝔊ᴺ* om., but 𝔊ᴮ 𝔖 𝔙 𝔗 have it, though it is probably dittography from the previous clause.

v. 2. *Where from?* אֵי מִזֶּה; the more prosaic expression = מֵאַיִן *Whence?* (1⁷), which is more poetical and rhetorical.

v. 3. The third clause adds something new in Iahvah's recognition of Eyob's splendid constancy and His implied reproach of the Satan's malevolent intervention. Perhaps, however, the words indicate neither reproach nor indignation; though the tone of a speaker's voice might cause them to convey either. In fact, Iahvah simply renews His challenge to the Satan, pointing out (surely with a feeling of satisfaction rather than of anger) that the latter has so far failed to justify his disparaging estimate of Eyob's piety. Lit. the last words run: *and thou eggedst Me on* (or *didst instigate Me*) *against him, to swallow him up* (metaph. = *to destroy him*) *for naught* (1⁹ 9¹⁷ 22⁶) or *without cause, wantonly.* The same verb הסית *to incite, egg on, instigate*, is used with the same construction, 1 C 21¹, also of 'Satan's' activity.

to swallow him up = in order that I might, &c. (cf. 1 C 21¹ 2 C 18²). Iahvah takes the responsibility for all that has happened. If Eyob were 'swallowed up', it would really be His doing no the Satan's.

[The Oxford Lexicon gives no cognates for the root בות, so that it appears to be peculiar to Biblical Hebrew. Perhaps it means *to prick* or *goad*, and may be akin to an obscure Assyrian word *situ* (spelt *si-i-tum*, 2 R 32, 11 gh), *point* or *pinnacle*; which is the meaning attached to a Sumerian word written SI-BAD, *horn* or projection *of a wall*. In that case, שִׂית *thorns* might be from a (dialectic) variation of the same root: סוּת = וּסוּת:, cf. Ju 12⁶.] It is possible that חִנָּם *without cause*, in spite of its position at the end of the verse, really belongs to the principal verb: *and thou eggedst Me on against him* (to destroy him) *for nothing*; that is, your suspicions and suggestions were entirely baseless, as is proved by the event. It does seem to be implied that if the issue had been otherwise, if Eyob had cast off all religious restraint and vented his miseries in blasphemies, his destruction would have been just: cursing God deserved and would entail death (v. 9ᵇ).

v. 4. The Satan is not yet convinced; the trial has not gone far enough to be conclusive. Eyob has lost his all, but not his life; touch him there, and he will give way. The familiar style of the Satan's reply, with its blunt application of a homely proverb, suggests no consciousness of indignation against himself on the part of Iahvah. He seems to match his own wits, though not his power, against the Lord of Heaven, and is confident of proving Him mistaken, if He will but grant him leave once more to deal with Eyob in his own way. *A skin for a skin* = 𝔊 Δέρμα ὑπὲρ δέρματος, *a hide* (pellis) or *skin* (cutis) *on behalf of a hide or skin*. The idea seems to be that of exchanging one thing in ransom for another; cf. 6²²ᵇ בַּעֲדִי *on my behalf*. The origin of the proverb, as Davidson observes, is obscure; and so is its precise application in the case before us. In barter like commodities are not always, nor even usually, exchanged for like. The phrase seems to be used like our *Quid pro quo*. 𝔗 renders אֲבָרָא אַמְטוּל אֲבָרָא *member for member*, meaning perhaps *one limb* (or *organ*) *for another*; as when a man sacrifices one part of his body to save another (an arm e.g. to save his head; so Driver). But the phrase is *Skin* (or *a skin*) *for skin* (or *a skin*); not *Skin for flesh* or some other portion of the body. And the word עוֹר is always either *skin, hide*, or *leather* (7⁵ 10¹¹ 18¹³ 19²⁰,²⁶ 30³⁰ 40³¹ 2 K 1⁸). Possibly the term in vulgar use might mean body or person; so that the Satan cries contemptuously, *Carcase for carcase!*, alluding to the death of Eyob's children, and implying that he might naturally be resigned to their loss so long as his own life was spared. We speak of 'saving one's own skin' in the sense of escaping personal harm. Cf. the explanation of St. Jerome: *pro corio suo coria obtulit filiorum, for his own hide he offered the sons' hides*. The Satan's low estimate of human nature is strikingly illustrated by such a suggestion. It is, of course, quite contrary to the common experience, in which men of only average goodness, and even bad men, have often been willing to sacrifice their own lives for their offspring. But the Satan's ill-grounded scepticism was necessary to the progress of the parabolic story.

The explanation of the phrase *Skin for skin* which makes it mean *The outer skin* (viz. his property, which Eyob has lost) *for the inner skin* (i.e. his real skin, which is still intact) is highly improbable. Where else is property compared with the skin? Duhm considers it most likely that the proverb originated in circles where skins were an important article of exchange and barter, and that its primary sense is, *For a skin people give* (or *receive*) *a skin's worth*. He then suggests various other applications; e.g. the Bedawi freebooter might thus have menaced the herdsman with hurt to his own skin, if he would not peaceably surrender a cow; the slave-hunter might have used the phrase in granting permission to a captive to secure his own release by the surrender of a slave or a child; the Avenger of Blood might utter it in attacking the kin of the homicide, &c. These examples, however, favour the interpretation *Skin for skin = One skin for another*, rather than Duhm's 'Fur eine Haut giebt (oder erhalt) man Hauteswert.'

the man; 𝔐 לָאִישׁ, meaning not any man in general, but Eyob in particular. This is the most natural view, as אִישׁ is the antecedent of the pronouns that follow in v. 5, although the statement might well be made of men generally (cf. Mt 16²⁶ Mk 8³⁶): so 𝔊ᴮ ὅσα ὑπάρχει ἀνθρώπῳ κτλ. (but 𝔊ᴬ τῷ ἀνθρώπῳ), and 𝔗 לְבַר נָשׁ (but 𝔖).

for himself; 𝔐 בְּעַד נַפְשׁוֹ. Or *for his life* (v. 6) = 𝔊 ὑπὲρ τῆς ψυχῆς αὐτοῦ. Cf. Mt 16²⁶. But נֶפֶשׁ *soul, life*, often corresponds to our reflexive pron. *self* (9²¹ 1 Sa 18¹ ³); and v. 5 *strike his bone and his flesh*, that is, himself or his person, indicates that meaning here. The Satan does not suggest the taking of Eyob's life, but only the extreme of bodily affliction.

v. 5. 𝔊 τῶν ὀστῶν αὐτοῦ καὶ τῶν σαρκῶν αὐτοῦ = אֶל־עֲצָמָיו וְאֶל־בְּשָׂרָיו (a difference of pointing only) For the plur. forms, cf. Gn 2²³ Pr 14³⁰. They are hardly correct here. 𝔊 stumbled at the collective use of עצמו *his bone*. Cf. ποδῶν instead of ποδός, v. 7, because a man has two feet!

he will curse thee; see notes on 1⁵,¹¹. 𝔊 σε εὐλογήσει. The general excellence of this version of Job suggests that the translator may have understood יברכך in an ironical sense (which it cannot have). Field gives βλασφημήσει σε (= יְנָרֶפְךָ; cf. 2 K 19⁶,²² or יְנָאֶצְךָ, Is 5²⁵).

v. 6. *yet* (or *only*) *spare his life*. To take it would be to defeat the object of these dealings with Eyob—the thorough testing of his godliness. Iahvah again yields to the force of the Satan's argument; as though it had not occurred to Himself.

𝔊's Ἰδοὺ παραδίδωμί σοι αὐτόν hardly denotes any difference of reading from 𝔐. It is merely an elegant paraphrase of a Hebraism.

114 THE BOOK OF JOB 2. 7

v. 7. *a malignant eczema* or *virulent eruption*; Heb. שְׁחִין רָע *a bad burning* or *inflammation*. The root is seen in the Assyrian šaḫânu, *to blaze up, burn, become hot* (Sumerian BI-BI, written *fire+fire*), šuḫnu, *daybreak*, as well as in Aram. שְׁחַן *to be* or *become warm, hot*, and Arab. سَخُن *be hot*, and then *to be inflamed* (of the eye). The same term שְׁחִין is used of Hezekiah's boil, 2 K 20⁷; and in Dt 28³⁵ we have the same phrase, with the same description of the spread of the disease; יכבה יהוה בשחין רע . . . . . מכף רגלך ועד קדקרך:, *Iahva will smite thee with a malignant eczema . . . from the sole of thy foot to the crown of thy head*. A שחין is one of the symptoms of incipient leprosy, according to Le 13¹⁸⁻²⁰,²³; and it is generally assumed, partly on this ground, which by itself is certainly far from conclusive, but more especially on the ground of the numerous descriptive allusions in the speeches of Eyob, that his malady was the worst form of leprosy (Elephantiasis, lepra tuberculosa, 'Black Leprosy'). But there seems no reason why, if leprosy were meant, a popular story which makes no pretence to poetical diction, should have preferred to describe this well-known scourge of the East by an ambiguous expression, instead of using the ordinary word (Dt 24⁸ Le 13⁹⁻¹¹ 2 K 5³ᶠᶠ. צָרַעַת). As we have seen, שְׁחִין is the name of Hezekiah's affection; it is also the designation of the sixth Plague of Egypt, Ex 9⁹⁻¹¹ (Bubonic or Oriental plague?). Perhaps the narrator need not have had any specific disease in his mind. In a moment, as it would seem, the Satan makes his victim a mass of ulcers from head to foot; whereas the supposed malady develops slowly at first, and spreads by degrees over the body. We might almost say that it is left to the imagination of the audience (or the reader) to recall the features of the most hideous disease known to it, whether plague or some form of leprosy.

from the sole of his foot; so that the disease, as it would seem, progressed from below upwards, as Elephantiasis is said to do, 'breaking out below the knees, and gradually spreading over the whole body' (Davidson). Cf. Dt 28³⁵, quoted above: *Iahvah will smite thee with a malignant eruption* upon the knees and upon the legs . . . . .

v. 8. An intolerable itching is the frequent accompaniment of skin-diseases. Eyob, in his misery, goes and sits down 'amid the ashes'; i.e. in all probability on the mound outside the village, the *mazbala* (مَزْبَلَة) or Mezbelè, 'the place of dung' (*zibl*), as it is called in modern Arabic: formed in the course of years by accumulations of the droppings of horses, camels, &c., and all the other rubbish of the place. From time to time the dung is burnt, and the ashes are left on the spot. Under the action of the winter rains the whole mass of mixed material is gradually welded into a solid hill of earth, the top of which serves as the village look out and a place of social intercourse in the sultry evenings.

Children play round it all day long; and there the poor outcasts of disease, expelled from the village, pass their days and nights (Wetzstein *ap.* Delitzsch). That 𝔊 took this view of the meaning is evident from its rendering καὶ ἐκάθητο ἐπὶ τῆς κοπρίας ἔξω τῆς πόλεως, *and he sat on the dunghill outside the town.* Cf. 1 Sa 2⁸ (where κοπρία = אַשְׁפֹּת, as in Ps 113⁷∥). 𝔙 in sterquilinio.

to scratch or *scrape himself with it.* 𝔐 להתגרד, a ἅπ λεγόμ. The sense is clear from the context, as well as from Aram. גְּרַד *to scratch* (𝔗 Ju 8¹⁶), Phoen. מגרדים *flesh-scrapers*, CIS 338. 4, Arab. جَرَدَ *peel* bark, &c. 𝔊ᴮ paraphrases ἵνα τὸν ἰχῶρα ξύῃ, *that he might scrape off the matter* (𝔊ᴬ ἵνα ἀποξέῃ τὸν ἰχῶρα αὐτοῦ).

v. 9. As in Gn 3⁶ the weaker sex succumbs first to the evil influence, and then tempts the stronger. Cf. also Gn 19²⁶. The natural effect of Eyob's fate upon a mind of the common sort is well suggested by the behaviour of Eyob's wife (Duhm). It is not supposed that she is a specially wicked or irreligious woman. Hers is simply a counsel of despair. She has no doubt that blasphemy involves instant death; and she holds that to be a less evil than to die by inches as her husband must—a death of lingering and ever-increasing pain.

Instead of the first member of this verse (*v.* 9 a) 𝔊 puts a speech of considerable length into the mouth of Eyob's wife. We may render the Greek as follows: *Now when much time had passed, his wife said to him, How long wilt thou be steadfast, saying, 'Lo, I will wait* (ἀναμενῶ?) *yet a little while, Expecting the hope of my salvation?' For lo, thy memorial hath been destroyed from the earth,* (*Thy*) *sons and daughters, pangs and throes of my womb, Whom in vain I travailed with in labour! And thou thyself sittest in wormy decay, passing the night out of doors; While I, a wanderer and a hireling,* (*Go about*) *from place to place and from house to house, Expecting* (i.e. *longing for*) *the sunset, That I may rest from my labours and the sorrows that now oppress me. But speak some word unto* (v. *against*) *Iahvah, and die!* The Greek of this curious and interesting interpolation leaves something to be desired in point of accuracy (e.g. the anarthrous nouns and the phrase οὕς ... ἐκοπίασα in 9 b and the lack of a finite verb in 9 d). Idioms and ideas alike suggest a writer who was far from being at home in Greek. They may indicate a Hebrew original. The brevity of 𝔐 is much more impressive; but the fuller text of 𝔊 may perhaps preserve an excerpt from a more diffuse recension of the story which anciently existed, and which the author of the book abridged to suit his purpose. The Hebrew may have run somewhat as follows: ויהי מרב ימים ותאמר לו אשתו עד אנה תחזק לאמור. הנני מקוה (7ᵃ) עוד מעט ויחלתי תקות ישעי: כי הנה זכרך אבד מן הארץ ו • ו • בניך יבנית חבל בטני ויניעי לריך יגעתי (39ʰ) בעמל:

ואתה ברטה (7ᵃ) תשב ובחוץ תלין ואני נודרה וּשְׂכִירָה (7¹) במקום ומקום
בבית ובית אשוט (1⁷) ויחלתי לשמש מתי יבוא (7⁹) לנוח מעמל וְיָנוֹן (עצב)
אשר יאחזני: ואולם רבר דבר ביהוה ומות:

v. 10. 𝔊 ὁ δὲ ἐμβλέψας εἶπεν αὐτῇ = וירא ויאמר אליה *and he looked* at *her and said to her*. In what follows we might correct the text of 𝔐 with Merx, Siegfried, Duhm, so as to get the sense *As one of the silly wantons would speak, wilt thou also speak? Shall we receive*, &c. (To extricate this sense, we must point תְּדַבְּרִי נַם־אָתְּ and assume that את the *Not. Accusat.* has fallen out after את *thou*, f.) Besides accounting for the otherwise difficult גם, we thus throw Eyob's reply into the metrical form of a tetrastich, as Duhm observes, comparing 1²¹. The metre, however, halts badly, and the diction is prosaic. In the third stichus we must at least read מיהוה for מאת האלהים to secure even a semblance of metre. Moreover, the stress laid on the pronoun—'*thou* also' or 'even thou'—as though Eyob expected his wife to be a paragon of piety, agrees better with modern and Western than with ancient Oriental sentiment in regard to women. Besides, Eyob's wife had spoken as directly and positively as possible: *Curse God and die!* and to such an open incentive to blasphemy a plain and positive rebuke was a far more natural reply (so all the versions) than the indirect remonstrance of a question. But an Interrogative Particle would be eminently in place before the indignant question that follows. We therefore propose אם *num?* instead of גם *etiam.* Cf. Gn 38¹⁷ Ju 5⁸ chap. 6¹². 𝔊 (εἰ τὰ ἀγαθὰ ἐδεξάμεθα κτλ.) 𝔙 (Si bona, suscepimus &c.) favour our view (εἰ = אם, ut saep.). 𝔖𝔄 omit גם (אם); but 𝔗 להוד ('auch', Levy), as in 28²⁷ 30².

the silly wantons. The *nabal* (נָבָל Ps 14¹: fem. נְבָלָה here only) is the fool who is wanting in moral and spiritual insight; a grossly selfish and sensual nature, insensible alike to human and religious obligations; the character of which Nabal (1 Sa 25) is the type, and which is sketched in its essential features by Isaiah (32⁶). Hence the cognate nouns נְבָלָה and נַבְלוּת came to be used of the most glaring instances of human 'folly'— offences against sexual righteousness, and of the dishonour and disgrace attending them (Gn 34⁷ Ju 19²³ 2 Sa 13¹² Ho 2¹²).

Are we actually to accept, &c. See the previous note. The text of 𝔐 cannot be rendered *we receive good . . . and shall we not also receive evil?* (Davidson), though such a rendering agrees well enough with the general meaning of the words, which seems to be expressed in the verse of Baxter's noble hymn:

> 'Take what He gives
> And praise Him still,
> Through good and ill,
> Who ever lives!'

Our text perhaps breathes more nearly the spirit of Eli's resignation: 'It is Iahvah: let Him do what seemeth Him good!' (1 Sa 3¹⁸). It is not for man to take exception to the Divine dealings, even when they run counter to his welfare and his wishes. Are we to honour God only in prosperity? (This was exactly what the Satan alleged to be the real character of Eyob's religion.)

In all this Eyob sinned not with his lips. 𝔊 *in all these things that had befallen him, Eyob sinned nothing with his lips before God* Cf. on 1²². It was one of the characteristics of the *nabal* 'to speak error of Iahvah' (Is 32⁶) · cf. on 1⁵; 42⁷. 𝔗 has the curious addition ברם ברעיוניה הרהר במלין *but in his mind he thought on words*; viz. those which he afterwards uttered in his speeches. According to Baba Bathra, 16 a, 'with his lips he sinned not; in his heart he sinned' (בלבו חטא). That, however, is not the meaning here, where the emphasis on בשפתיו *with his lips* is to be understood otherwise, as explained above, *notes* on 1⁵. The Targumist was no doubt shocked by the daring language of the speeches, which contrasts so conspicuously with the tone of complete resignation in the Prologue. Hence his harmonistic addition, as if the meaning were *So far Eyob sinned not with his lips, whatever he may have been meditating in his heart.*

vv. 11–13. EYOB'S THREE FRIENDS PAY HIM A VISIT OF CONDOLENCE. *Eliphaz the Temanite.* Eliphaz appears as a 'Son' of Esau, i.e. a tribal division or clan of Edom, Gn 36⁴; while Teman is in like manner a 'Son' or sept of Eliphaz, Gn 36¹¹, and the name also of its territory, Am 1¹² Ob⁹ Je 49⁷ Ez 25¹³. Evidently, therefore, this friend of Eyob's is an Edomite. The wisdom of the Temanites was proverbial; *see* Ob Je ll. cc.

The name of Eyob's wisest friend is thus seen not to have been coined for the purposes of the story Like Semitic personal names in general, it is of course significant; but it can hardly mean *God is fine gold* (OL doubtfully). *God crusheth* (cf. Assyr. îna qâtika tepéziz, *with thy hand thou didst crush*: MA s.v. pazâzu) is more probable (cf. also Gn 49²⁴ ויפזו זרעי ידיו), or *God leapeth* (Syr. use of the root), with possible reference to a Goat-god.

Bildad the Shuhite or Shuchite belonged to the tribe of Shuah (Shuach), which was of Qeturean stock, and was located somewhere to the east of Palestine (Gn 25²·⁶). The Sûḫu (mât Sûḫi, land of Sûḫu) of the Assyrian records (TP Cyl. v. 48), an Aramean district on the upper Euphrates, and the gentilic derivative Sûḫâia (Su-ḫa-a-a), Suchite, have been compared. The name Bildad probably involves that of the Storm-god, Hadad, various forms of which are supplied by the cuneiform inscriptions (Adad, Addu, Dadda, Dadi, &c.). It has been identified with Bir-Dadda, an Arab chief mentioned by Assurbanipal (KAT³ p. 450); but the first element, Bi, and the Bedad of Gn 36³⁵ ('Hadad ben Bedad', a king of Edom) certainly looks like Bildad with the *l* accidentally omitted.

Zophar the Naamathite (הנעמתי), the reading of 𝔐, can hardly be right. Naamah was a small town in SW. Judah (Jos 15⁴¹), whereas the other localities mentioned, Uz, Teman, and Shuah, were all situated beyond the eastern border of Palestine. 𝔊 Σωφὰρ ὁ Μειναίων βασιλεύς, *Zophar the king of the Minaeans* (Σωφὰρ ὁ Μειναῖος, 11¹ 20¹ 42⁹); whence Hommel acutely conjectured המעוני, so that Zophar would belong to the S. Arabian state of Ma'ân, which has become famous through Glaser's discoveries. Another attractive conjecture is that of Dozy, who read הרעמתי *the Raamathite*. Raamah (Ra'mat) was an Arabian trade-centre, which is mentioned along with Ma'ân in one of Glaser's Sabean inscriptions. Cf. 1 C 4⁴¹ 2 C 26⁷ (המעונים); Ez 27²²; Hommel AHT 240; 252. As for Zophar (צֹפַר, Σωφάρ), it may be the Hebrew transcription of a South Arabian name otherwise unknown; but not improbably it may be regarded as a scribal error for Zippor (צפור), which appears as a Moabite (Nu 22²) and, in the fem. form Zipporah (Ex 2²¹), a Midianite name. (Midian was a brother-tribe of Shuah, Gn 25².) In Gn 36¹¹·¹⁵ 𝔊 gives Σωφάρ for צפו, the third 'Son' of Eliphaz ben Esau. If that be the true reading there, Zophar also will have been of Edom.

Had come . . . came . . . to come. Not so much 'unbehilflich' (Du) as a trace of the natural simplicity of an oral narrative. *to condole with him* or *lament for him*, RV *bemoan him*, as if he were dead (Je 22¹⁰). Strictly, לנוד is *to move to and fro*, to shake the head or rock the body in token of grief, as mourners do. When we read (42¹¹) that, after the tide had turned, all Eyob's kinsfolk and acquaintance 'came . . . and condoled with him and comforted him', it certainly looks as if the popular story must have represented Eyob's second trial as of brief duration. (In 7³ the parallelism and entire context seem to require ימי *days* instead of ירחי *months*. Contr. Driver, *Introd.*, p. xiii.) The author of the book may have supposed a period of a lunar month from the arrival of the Friends to the close of the argument. (The seven days of silent mourning are followed by twenty-one speeches, each of which might be regarded as requiring a day for its delivery and subsequent consideration.)

v. 12. Lit. *And they lifted up their eyes afar off and recognized him not.* They could see him from some distance, because he was sitting on the mound, *v.* 8. They did not know him, because of the visible ravages of his malady.

They burst, &c. Lit. as AV *throwing it up into the air*; lit. *heavenward*. The idea underlying this symbolical action was perhaps that of darkening the air, since darkness is a natural symbol of sorrow and distress (Is 8²² al.). Cf. Jos 7⁸ 1 Sa 4¹² (*earth on his head*; so 2 Sa 1²) 2 Sa 13 (*ashes on her head*) Ne 9³ (*earth on them*). As a funeral custom, the primitive Semitic meaning may have been that of being buried with the dear departed.

v. 13. Sitting on the ground was a natural posture of humiliation and mourning (Is 3^{26} La 2^{10} Ez 26^{16}). Seven days was the usual time of mourning for the dead: see Gn 50^{10} 1 Sa 31^{13} Ecclus 22^{12}. The Friends mourn for Eyob as for a dead man, knowing that his disease is mortal.

Chapter 3 EYOB IS THE FIRST TO SPEAK. HE CURSES THE DAY OF HIS BIRTH. As others have noticed, Eyob speaks at the 'psychological' moment. He could answer his wife with dignified restraint, but the sympathy of his friends was more than he could bear. So he relieves his pent-up emotion by this passionate outcry (*see* Davidson). Whether this effect was intended by the author we can hardly say for certain. What does seem to be fairly certain is that he did not consider that, by such an utterance, Eyob was declining at all from the high level of his own piety. Christian sentiment may well be shocked by the violence of the language; but it must always be remembered that we are dealing with a pre-Christian writer. The historical instance of the prophet Jeremiah, who did not hesitate to express his despairing mood in precisely similar language (Je 20^{14-18}), proves that such a mode of bemoaning oneself was not regarded as at all reprehensible within the circle of Old Testament ideas. To us there may seem to be something irrational in cursing (imprecating evil on) a day, and that a day long past. How could a day be affected by either blessing or cursing? Was it supposed that the wish, good or evil, would affect the character of the particular day of the month, so that henceforth it would be either a lucky or an unlucky day, according to the nature of the wish? Whatever the original significance of the practice, in the olden times when magic was a dominant note in religion, we cannot suppose that either Jeremiah or the author of our book intended more than a lyrical expression of the wish, *Would that I had never been born!* (vv. 1-10). (The parallel in Je l c. is not strictly poetry, but prophetic prose, which is often more rhythmical in structure, because more emotional and elevated in substance, than ordinary prose. The mythical and magical allusions of v. 8 find no place in the prophet.)

An example of cursing a day, which demonstrates that it was a custom not unknown to the primitive ages of Semitic (and probably Sumerian) antiquity, may be recognized in the Babylonian Epic of Gilgamesh, in the famous episode of the Flood, where Ishtar, the Mother of Mankind, indignant at their destruction, exclaims: 'O that that day had perished (lit. *returned to dust*), when I in the Assembly of Gods decreed an evil thing!' (ûmu ullû ana ṭiṭṭi lû-itûr-ma aššû anâku ina puḫur ilâni aqbû limutta! NE xi. 119).

After the introductory formulas, vv 1-2, the chapter falls naturally into three divisions, which may be summarily styled the lament.

(1) *O that I had never been born!* (vv. 3–10);
(2) *O that I had died at birth!* (vv. 11–19);
(3) *Why do the wretches live on, who long only to die?* (vv. 20–26).

v. 1. *his day*; i.e. *the day of his birth*, rather than his birthday, which usually denotes the commemoration or anniversary of one's birth. Cf. on 1⁴. *Opened his mouth* = began to speak (Mt 5²). Cf. the equivalent phrase of the Babylonian Epics *pâšu êpuš-ma iqabbî, his mouth he opened and speaketh.*

v. 2. Lit. *And Eyob answered and said*; a frequent formula, from Gn 18²⁷ onwards. As no one had spoken, the vb. ענה (ויען) appears to be used here idiomatically in the sense of responded to the occasion, spoke in view of the circumstances (cf. Ju 18¹⁴ 1 Sa 9¹⁷ Is 14¹⁰). 𝔊ᴮ has simply λέγων for this verse, for the sake of style and to avoid what seemed a needless prolixity (but 𝔊ᴬ pr. καὶ ἀπεκρίθη Ἰώβ).

v. 3. The day is poetically regarded as a real being or substantive entity, which holds its place and always returns in the yearly cycle. Cf. Gn 1³⁻⁵ Ps 19³ chap. 38¹⁹. In what sense could it 'perish'? Only by being made the perpetual prey of clouds and darkness (Jo 2²), as the sequel indicates. Cf. also Am 4¹³ 5⁸. Henceforth, he cries, let it always be a day of sunless gloom, lost in eternal night! Nay more, as a *dies funestus*, a hopelessly unlucky day, let it find no place in the calendar (v. 6), but be erased from the list of the days of the month!

the day I was born = יוֹם אִוָּלֶד בּוֹ; with elliptical Relative Clause, as often in poetry. Je 20¹⁴ has the more prosaic construction הַיּוֹם אֲשֶׁר יֻלַּדְתִּי בּוֹ *the day* on which *I was born* (Pf.). Our אִוָּלֵד (Impf.) *I begin to be born, come to birth*, is much more lively. *and the Night (that) said* = וְהַלַּיְלָה אָמַר; again with Ellipsis of the Relative, as in the parallel stichus. (So 𝔗) וְהַלַּיִל הָאָמַר *and the Night which was saying* is not so likely, לילה being the form in Job passim (v. 7; 17¹² *et al. novies*), and לֵיל (Is 16³) being of very rare occurrence. הָאָמַר (late use of ה as Relat., cf. perhaps 2¹¹ Jos 10²⁴) is too prosy, though better than הָאֹמֵר. The cry 'Behold a Man!' would be momentary, not continuous. The Night speaks, because personified (cf. Ps 19²). According to 𝔐 it said הֹרָה נָבֶר = 𝔙 *Conceptus est homo!* הֹרָה being intended for Pual Pf. of הרה *to conceive* (so 𝔊 𝔗). But a reference to the time of conception, which would necessarily be unknown, seems out of place, and is a strange ὕστερον πρότερον here, where being born is the dominant idea (cf. v. 10). Otherwise we might read אִמִּי *my mother*, instead of אָמַר, and taking הֹרָה (= הוֹרָה) as Ptcp. Qal, render the whole stichus *And the Night* (when) *my Mother was conceiving a Man!* But 𝔊 Ἰδοὺ ἄρσεν, *Behold a Male!* (= הנה נבר) is decidedly preferable. The הנה may have been wrongly transferred from the margin here to v. 7, where it spoils the metre, and is not required by the sense. (הרה was perhaps rather a scribal corruption of this word than of the doubtful הֲרִי *Behold!*) There is no reason why גֶּבֶר should not have been used as a poetical equivalent of the purely prose-word זָכָר *male* (Je 20¹⁵).

(The Targum וְלֵילְיָא דִּי אֲמַר אִתְבְּרָא גְּבַר *and the Night which said, A man is created* clearly supports 𝔐. 𝔊ᴮ καὶ ἡ νὺξ ἐκείνη [om. ἐκ · 𝔊ᴺᴬᶜ] ᾗ [ἐν ᾗ 𝔊ᴺᴬᶜ] εἶπαν [εἶπον 𝔊ᴬ] *and that [the] Night in which they said* takes אָמַר as Impers and implies בּוֹ after it, which is probably wrong, though supplied by 𝔖 וְלֵילְיָא דְאִתְאֲמַר בֵּהּ *and the Night in which it was said*.)

v. 4. *That Day become Darkness!* Bickell omits, and Duhm prefers 𝔊 ἡ νὺξ ἐκείνη εἴη σκότος (so Beer). But surely darkness is already the essential characteristic of Night (Gn 1⁵). As I understand the first section, vv. 3–10, after an introductory couplet cursing the Day and the Night successively, we have first the development of the curse on the Day in three triplets followed by a closing couplet, and then that of the curse on the Night in a couplet followed by a triplet and a couplet. The stichus *That Day become Darkness!* (cf. Am 4¹³ 5⁸ Is 13¹⁰ Je 13¹⁶) corresponds in form to the opening stichus of the curse on the Night: *That Night become stone-barren!* (v. 7).

Light (or *the Dawn*) *seek it not from above!* reading אוֹר instead of 𝔐 אֱלוֹהַּ, 𝔊 ὁ κύριος, as in 4¹⁷ 5¹⁷ 6⁸ al. אוֹר agrees better with the ‖ נְהָרָה† = Aram. נְהוֹרָא *light* in the next stichus. Further, instead of יִדְרְשֵׁהוּ *seek it*, which does not seem very appropriate here, even if we keep 𝔐 and render *God regard it not* (or *care not for it*), Dt 11¹², we may perhaps restore יִפְרֹשׁ (cf 36³⁰) and make the stichus אַל־יִפְרֹשׂ אוֹר עָלָיו *Light spread not over it!*

v. 5. *Deathshade.* A compound like צַלְמָוֶת *shade of death*, in which the two elements are clearly discernible at sight (צֵל *shade* + מָוֶת *death*), is rare, if not unparalleled. How can מָוֶת *death*, that is, *the state* or *place of the dead* (28²² 38¹⁷), be supposed to cast a shadow, especially as צֵל is usually a metaphor of protection and grateful refreshment rather than darkness (cf. 7²)? The idea of Death as a dread angel (see on 18¹⁴), who casts a dark shadow on his victim, will not do. Death is not so personified in the OT, though the place (or city; cf. 38¹⁷) of the dead may be personified like any city or country of the living, e.g. Jerusalem or Babylon. The analysis of צַלְמָוֶת seems to depend, therefore, on popular etymology or perhaps on a mere fancy of the Massoretes; and the word should probably be pointed צַלְמוּת *blackness, pitch-darkness*, as Ewald long ago maintained. Cf. Assyr. çalmu (צלמו), *black*, and the corresponding Arab. root ظَلِمَ *to be dark*, whence ظُلْمَة *darkness*. (Cf. Am 5⁸ where צלמות, as here, has no reference to Death or She'ol, but means simply the darkness of night.)

for their own; a meaning which does not really harmonize with the context. AV *stain it* derives the word from גאל *to defile*. In that case we must point יְגָאֲלֻהוּ Pi. (cf. Is 63³): cf. 𝔗 יְטַנְּפוּן יָתֵיהּ *pollute it* = Aq. μολύναι αὐτήν. 𝔊 ἐκλάβοι(δὲ) αὐτήν, *seize it* (and carry it off), suggests a possible Aramaism יַקְבְּלֻהוּ *darken it* (Tg Am 5⁸ 8⁹), mispointed יַקְבְּלֻהוּ *take it*; cf. 𝔙 *Obscurent eum tenebrae*. 𝔖 נכסיוהי *cover it*. We might also conjecture an ἅπ. λεγόμ. יַאְפִּלֻהוּ *darken it*; cf. אֹפֶל, v. 6. (Of course, 𝔊 may have misread יקחהו = λάβοι here from v. 6.)

Benightings of day. Or *Eclipses of day*. Lit., as it would seem, *Blacknesses* or *Gloominesses*; ἅπ. λεγ. plur. tant. (כמר vb., La 5¹⁰†). Possibly an Intensive Plur. *Dunnest gloom*; otherwise the various causes of darkness in the daytime, such as eclipses, storms, &c., may be intended. The root is seen in Syr. ܟܡܪ *black, dark, gloomy*, of a cloud, a glen, night, the face. (𝔊 καταραθείη ἡ ἡμέρα, *Accursed be the Day!* as if מְאָרָר! הַיּוֹם! instead of כִּמְרִירֵי יוֹם, omitting יְבַעֲתֻהוּ. Text prob. imperfect. 𝔊 𝔄 𝔙 𝔗 wrongly connect with √מרר *bitter*; either neglecting the כ, or making it the Particle of Comparison; e.g. 𝔗 היך מרירי יומא.)

Affright it. יבעתהו. It is gratuitous to alter this to יתעבהו. The verb בעת occurs in Job eight times out of a total of sixteen in OT.

v. 6. The text of this and the following verses is disordered: see on v. 4. *That Day*. 𝔐 הלילה ההוא *That Night*; and so the Versions. Sense and context demand היום. It was his 'Day' that Eyob wished might be expunged from the calendar. *Be it not one in* or among *the Days*. Point יַחַד, fr. יָחַד *to be united* or *one* (*with*). So AV. The ‖ Gn 49⁶ (where both verbs אַל־תֵּחַד and אַל־תָּבֹא with בְּ occur as here) proves that this is correct. So 𝔊 𝔖 𝔗 𝔙. RV *Let it not rejoice among the days*, &c., pointing יִחַדְּ from חָדָה *to rejoice* (so OL); but this does not suit the parallel stichus, and, parallelism apart, where are days (or months or years) said to 'rejoice' elsewhere in OT?

Nor be counted in the Days of the Month; lit. *Into the number of the months let it not come!* (cf. Gn 49⁶ᵃ): i.e. Let it not be reckoned as a day of the month. We might read: במספר ימירח אל־יבא *Into the number of the month's days let it not come!* 𝔊 μηδὲ ἀριθμηθείη εἰς ἡμέρας μηνῶν = בִּימֵי יְרָחִים אַל־יִמָּנֶה gives the sense, and may even be original, or at least represent another recension of the Hebrew text.

v. 7. This verse evidently introduces the special curse on the Night, continued in vv. 9, 10; whereas v. 8 as evidently refers to the Day. We have therefore transposed vv. 7, 8. (Possibly v. 8 originally preceded v. 6ᵇᶜ, which might be considered a more appropriate climax to the curse on the Day.) *That Night be stone-barren*. The הנה *Lo* of 𝔐 overloads the line, giving four stresses for three, and must be omitted here with 𝔊 𝔖 𝔙 𝔄. See note on v. 3ᵇ. The quadriliteral גַּלְמוּד, which recurs at 15³⁴ (but prob. not at 30⁴: see the note there) and Is 49²¹ in the fem.

נַלְמוּדָה, is akin to Ar. جَلْمَد and جُلْمُود *rock*, جَلْمَد *stony*, of ground; which explains the metaphorical use in Hebrew, stony ground being naturally barren. Cf. the Chinese phrases shih nu, *stone* (= barren) *woman*; shih tai, *a stone* (= barren) *womb*. (𝔊 ὀδύνη *pain*; = 𝔗 צַעֲרָא id (also *disgrace*); but 𝔖 ܡܣܟܝܢ *deprived, bereaved, childless, lonely, barren* (of land); 𝔄 مَعْدُوم *lacking, wanting*; 𝔙 solitaria = μεμονωμένη al.; 𝔖 ἔκβλητος, *outcast*.

joyous birthshout; רִנָּה *a ringing cry* of joy or triumph (20⁵). The context gives the precise application; cf. also Je 20¹⁵. The gloss of 𝔗 is different: לָא תַעוּל רִנָּא דְתַרְנְגוֹל בָּרָא לְמַקְלְסָא בֵּיהּ *Let not the cry of the wild cock* (𝔗 39¹³) *enter it to praise!* (See 𝔗 38³⁶ also. The 'Cock of the Wild' is a fabulous bird; 𝔗 Ps 50¹¹: but תַּרְנְגוֹלָא, Syr. ܬܪܢܓܠܐ, is the Sumerian DAR-LUGÁLA, gallus, 'King of the Fowls')

v. 8. *Day-enchanters*; lit. *cursers of day*: i.e. sorcerers who by their spells professed to be able to darken the sky with storm and eclipse; who were always 'ready' (הָעֲתִידִים) to rouse from his slumber the great celestial dragon who causes darkness and tempest. Obviously we are here on mythological ground. The ideas, however, are not specially Babylonian, but belong to the circle of primitive Asiatic beliefs, which were the common heritage of the Semitic nations. There is no trace of the word or quasi-proper name (always anarthrous) לִוְיָתָן Leviathan ('ΑΣ Λευιαθάν here and 40²⁰) in Assyrio-Babylonian literature, where eclipses and obscurations of the moon and storms are ascribed to the agency of the Seven Evil Spirits. Of these the second is described as 'a Dragon open-mouthed' (USHUM-GAL, Great Worm, KA-GÁL, mouth-open), and the fourth as another kind of serpent, perhaps the fabled 'basilisk' (MUSH-MIR, serpent + crown or crest?); while the first is the South Wind, so destructive in Babylonia (IM-GALLU), the seventh another stormy wind or hurricane (IM-MIRRA IM-ĠULA), the third a fierce leopard, and the fifth and sixth other savage beasts at present undetermined.

> 'These Seven are Messengers of Anu the King;
> Town after town in twilight they put;
> Hurricanes, over Heaven madly they hunt;
> Thick clouds, over Heaven rain and darkness they put;
> Rushing blasts, bright Day darkness they make.'

(It is noteworthy that the Seven Evil Spirits are 'Messengers', LU KIN-GÁ, *már šipri*, of the King of Heaven. They are 'Evil Angels', מַלְאֲכִים רָעִים: cf. Ps 78⁴⁹). Further on in the same tablet we read: DUB-SAG-TA UD-SAR (D) EN-ZUNA SHUR-BI BAN-DIBBESH, 'Confronting the Crescent, (*the god*) Sîn they wrathfully surrounded' (*iltanauwú*; cf. Heb. *Liwyatan* fr. *lawah*). Then the god Enlil (Bêl) 'the hero Sîn's darkening in Heaven beh[eld], and [se]nt the [ev]il ne[w]s to En-ki

(Ea) in the Deep: 'My Son Sîn in Heaven his Darkness is sore!' (DU-MU D. EN-ZUNA ANNA SU-MUGGA-BI GIGGA). Ea, as usual, commissions his Son Mardug (Merodach) to intervene: 'Go, my Son Merodach! the Prince's Son, the New Moon, (*the god*) Sîn, in Heaven his Darkness is sore; His Darkness Heaven pervadeth!' (GINNA DU-MU *D*. ASARI DU-KU UD-SAR *D*. EN-ZUNA ANNA SU-MUGGA-BI GIGGA SU-MUGGA-BI ANNA DALLA-MUN-EA). Merodach, as usual, puts things to rights. Lastly, in a subsequent spell or exorcism, it is said of the same Evil Spirits: 'Sîn in Heaven's heart to Darkness they turned!' (D. EN-ZUNA ANNA-SHAB-TA SU-MUGGA GI-ESH). See *Utukki Limnûti*, Tab. XVI (CT xvi, Pl. 19); and cf. Thompson, *Devils*, p. 89 sqq.

The agents in these old Sumerian texts are, as we see, superhuman; but our verse as evidently contemplates human agency like that of the 'Lapland witches', famous in European folk-lore for raising winds and storms. The name Leviathan or Livyātān (H. לִוְיָתָן) is as pure Hebrew (Canaanite) as נְחֻשְׁתָּן Neḥuštan; another word which has elicited considerable difference of opinion. Formally, however, נְחֻשְׁתָּן may be a contracted dual = נְחֻשְׁתַּיִם (Ju 16²¹ al.), *brazen fetters* (2 Sa 3³⁴); cf. וֹתָן, דּתִינָה, Gn 37¹⁷. Hezekiah's contemptuous nickname for the Brazen Serpent (נְחַשׁ הַנְּחֹשֶׁת) might rest on a real or fanciful resemblance of the serpent coiled in two rings round its standard to a pair of bronze fetters (two rings with a cross-piece linking them together); such as we see in the Assyrian sculptures. Similarly, לויתן may be dual of לויה (archaic *livyat*), something round, e. g. a wreath (Pr 1⁹), from לָוָה = Assyr. *lamû (lawû), to go round, surround*; hence perhaps also a *ring*, or *coil*, so that Liyātān = *Double-Coil*, a suitable designation of a serpentine monster. But another interpretation suggests itself. Taking לִוְיָה in the sense in which it actually occurs twice in Proverbs, we may explain לִוְיָתָן *Two Wreaths* as denoting a Two-crested or Two-headed serpent or hydra; cf. Ps 74¹⁴, ''Twas Thou that didst crush Leviathan's heads', a reference to another myth about the Storm-serpent. From 26¹³, compared with Is 27¹, we learn that Livyathan was also known as 'the Fugitive or Fleeing Serpent', and the cause of darkness in the sky. It is the mythical aspect of the long trailing clouds that obscure the light before and during a storm. In the prophets (Is 27¹; cf. 51⁹ Ez 29³ 32²) such allusions are merely symbolical of the contemporary world-powers, and need not imply belief in the popular mythology; but our passage (3⁸) has a more original aspect, being a direct reference to the practices of contemporary magic, and apparently implying a belief in the primitive explanation of the phenomena of storm and eclipse. Iahvah, however, has the final control (26¹³). The Chinese say that, in an eclipse, the Moon is devoured by the Hia-ma (or Ha-ma) yu. 'The Toad-fish' (Morrison: Devil-fish).

Eclipse is shih, 'devour', written with the characters for *eating* and *serpent, reptile* (see my *Comp. Sign-list*, no. 91; ap. *Chinese and Sumerian*) In Ps 104²⁶ the Liwyatan figures as a monster of the Deep—perhaps the great 'Sea Serpent' (cf. 7¹²). Among the monsters created by Tiâmat (תְּהוֹם) to help her in her war against the gods of light were MUSH-MAG, *erect* (or *huge*) *serpents*, USHUM-GAL, *great worms* (vid. supr.), and several other kinds of snaky or dragon forms (Bab. Creation Epic) cf. 9¹³ 'Helpers of Rahab'. Since the Liwyatan is a water-monster, it is not very surprising to find the crocodile poetically described under this name, 40²⁵ ˢᵠᵠ (= 41¹ ˢᵠᵠ). Ophidians and Saurians were hardly distinguished with any exactness in ancient nomenclature; and Mythology has always displayed a strong predilection for blending the salient features of different classes of animals. And, in any case, a Hebrew poet might call a crocodile a 'Leviathan', much as a modern Englishman may call a strong man a Hercules, or a beautiful woman a Venus, without implying the identity of the objects compared or any belief in the mythical deities.

v. 9. Its twilight. נֶשֶׁף is usually the evening twilight (24¹⁵). Here that of morning (7⁴) agrees better with the parallelism, and the stars are those which usher in the dawn. Otherwise, we might think of both twilights (*crepusculum* as well as *diluculum*) and both evening and morning stars. (נשף is str. the *blowing*-time; i.e. the time when the evening or morning breeze springs up: Gn 3⁸. The root is shap, shab, seen also in נָשַׁב *to blow*, and שָׁאַף *to pant*. Cf. the Sumerian ZIB, ZIG, SUB, *evening, dusk, twilight*.) 𝔊 inexactly: τῆς νυκτὸς ἐκείνης.

the eyelids of dawn. 16¹⁶ 41¹⁰. A beautiful figure from the quivering and trembling of light on the arch of the horizon, which is as it were the Eye of Day. (In 16¹⁶ 𝔊 βλεφάροις recte. Here it paraphrases καὶ μὴ ἴδοι ἑωσφόρον ἀνατέλλοντα, *and may it not see Lucifer rising!* שַׁחַר = ἑωσφόρος, also 38¹² 41¹⁰.)

v. 10. כִּי לֹא סָגַר דַּלְתֵי בִטְנִי *Because it closed not the doors of my womb.* Apart from the strangeness of the expression *my womb* instead of *my mother's womb*, the line is metrically redundant (4 stresses for 3, the normal number). Pointing דְּלָתַי *my doors* and omitting בטני *my womb* as a marginal explanation (or variant?), we restore the metre and get a pregnant poetical phrase. 𝔊 πύλας γαστρὸς μητρός μου: so 𝔖𝔄𝔙 (ostia ventris qui portavit me). 𝔗 כרסי דְּשֵׁי *doors of my belly*, which it explains of Eyob's own organs, the navel, &c. (!)

The rhyme עֵינָי ⋯ דְּלָתַי suitably emphasizes the close of the first strophe. *hid*: וַיַּסְתֵּר. 𝔊 ἀπήλλαξεν = וַיָּסַר *removed*, as 9³⁴ 27⁵ al.

Strophe II. O THAT I HAD DIED AT OR BEFORE BIRTH! vv. 11–19. There does not seem to be any idea of a conscious existence, however feeble and shadowy, such as we find in Is 14 . expressed in these pathetic verses. The grave is a place of perfect rest and unbroken peace.

v. 11. ⑤ *For why died I not in the womb?* (ἐν κοιλίᾳ). Cf. v. 16. But this spoils the parallelism, and hardly agrees with the tense of the verb: lit. *Why not from the womb did I begin to die?* (*Why*) *did I* (*not*) *come forth* . . . *and begin to expire?* Duhm would transfer v. 16 to follow this, translating *Oder warum war ich nicht wie eine verscharrte Fehlgeburt, Wie Kinder, die das Licht nicht sahen?* But while this appears to be a gain in symmetry, it makes the Particle of Comparison seem superfluous and the Disjunctive 'Or' needless; whereas both are in place in the present position of the distich.

v. 12. *receive me*; lit. *meet* or *confront me*. The allusion seems to be to a custom like that which prevailed in ancient Rome. A newborn babe was laid by the nurse on the father's knees for his decision whether it was to be reared or exposed. Cf. Gn 50²³ (of Joseph recognizing the offspring of Machir) and Gn 30³ (of Rachel adopting her maid's progeny). Duhm pronounces the verse to be 'a younger addition'. It is, he observes, 'interesting enough, but does not suit the connexion, as according to it not God, to whom the "Wherefore" is addressed, but men would have been the cause of the premature death of Hiob.' But Eyob is not yet addressing God; he is only bewailing his unhappy lot with his Friends (cf. Je 20¹⁴ᶠᶠ·).

v. 13. The language is hardly appropriate, on Duhm's theory of the sense: *Denn dann* (wenn ich verscharrt wäre als Fehlgeburt) *läge ich*, &c. How could a babe that had never lived be said to 'lie down' and 'rest' and 'sleep', even by the farthest stretch of poetic license? Only a babe that had actually been born and nursed (v. 12) could do so. We therefore leave v. 16 where it is.

v. 14. *Like*; lit. *with* (עִם־). Cf. Ec 2¹⁶: *How dieth the Wise Man?* with (i. e. *like*) *the Fool.* Cf. also 9²⁶ 37¹⁸.

national counsellors: lit. *counsellors of the earth* or *land*. *Who rebuilded ruins for their pleasure* (lit. *for themselves*). The Heb. phrase בָּנָה חֳרָבוֹת occurs in the sense of rebuilding ruins, Is 58¹² 61⁴ Ez 36¹⁰·³³ Ma 1⁴. In the present context it reminds us of the numerous inscriptions of the kings of Assyria and Babylonia, recording their restoration of crumbling temples and palaces and decayed cities. Cf. Dan 4³⁰. The glory of these monarchs as builders must have been famous throughout the East. And if the author lived in Babylonia, he had many impressive examples of the glory of departed greatness before his eyes. A difficulty has been made of the line because commentators desiderated something more definite and specific, which the kings built 'for themselves', that is, for their own occupation, either palaces or tombs. Hence it has been proposed to read אַרְמְנוֹת *castles* or הֵיכָלוֹת *palaces* instead of חֳרָבוֹת. After what has been said above, there is no need to discuss either of these; but Duhm thinks there must have been mention of the rest of the grave in this line, and accepts Ewald's conjecture that חרבות is really a disguise or distortion of the Arabic 'hiram or ahram', the Pyramids. This is, to say the least, highly precarious. What evidence is there that the Arabs called the Pyramids أحْرَام in ancient times? Duhm, indeed, in answer to Dillmann, suggests that the Arabs chose this word (a common one in their language, denoting *forbidden ground, sanctuary*) because it came nearest to the sound of the Egyptian name; but the Egyptian for pyramid is *mer*.

The next couplet (v. 15), in construction and sense so closely connected with this one, almost demonstrates that the reference is not to the peace of the grave, but to the former greatness of those with whom, had Eyob died, he would have shared it, and at the same time it is implied that neither rank, nor renown, nor riches, exempt any from the common doom. Pallida Mors aequo pulsat pede pauperum tabernas, Regumque turres. Hor.

(𝔊 οἳ ἠγαυριῶντο ἐπὶ ξίφεσιν *who used to pride themselves on swords* = הָלִים עַל־חֲרָבוֹת; cf. 39²³. 𝔊 𝔗 𝔙 = 𝔐.)

v. 15. Duhm translates: *Or with Princes who* possess *Gold, Who filled their* (Grave-)*houses with Silver*. It is true that בית *house* has been supposed to mean *tomb* in Is 14¹⁸ and perhaps 53⁹, and we know that in Egypt especially the sepulchres of the great were constructed and decorated to resemble their former abodes. And, of course, זהב להם may mean either *who possess* or *who possessed gold*, according to the context. But it is questionable whether בית alone ever denotes a grave (see Box, *Isaiah*, p. 78, n. *e*, for the reading of Is 14¹⁸), although בית עולם *eternal house*, AV 'long home', Ec 12⁵ (cf. the Palmyr. בת עלמא), very naturally may. To say of the dead that 'they possess gold' is a curious way of suggesting that treasure was buried with them; and if it be objected that it was an Egyptian custom to do so in the case of kings and queens (as we know from recent discoveries, e.g. that of the jewellery of the great queen Hatshepsu), it must be observed that it was not the monarchs themselves, but their survivors, who honoured the departed in this way: not to insist on the fact that the couplet speaks of 'princes', not 'kings'. Silver and gold are mentioned merely as tokens of wealth (so in 22²⁴·²⁵; and cf. esp. 27¹⁶·¹⁷; 31²⁴·²⁷ 36¹⁹ Pr 1¹³ Is 2⁷ Gn 13²). The phrase *fill their houses* (מלא בתיהם) actually recurs, 22¹⁸, in much the same sense as here: cf. also Dt 6¹¹ Pr 1¹³.

v. 16. There seems to be something wrong with the first stichus The whole verse looks like an abridgement of 10¹⁸·¹⁹: *And why broughtest Thou me forth from th   n'   I h l'   '   '   ' ' As though I h n   l   (1)   v to the grave!* Ec 6³⁻⁵ moralizes quite in the tone of the present passage: *If a man beget a hundred, and live many years, and the days of his years be many, but his soul be not satisfied with good, and also he be left unburied; methinks the* nêfel *is better off than he. For into nothingness it came, and into the dark it departeth, and with darkness its name is covered. Also it hath not seen the sun nor been conscious: its rest is more perfect than the other's.* And Ec 4³ tells us that better off or in happier state than either dead or living is *he who hath never yet existed* (את אשר עדן לא היה); that is to say, non-being is better than being; which is about the deepest depth of Pessimism. (The reading לא הָיָה, suggested by Driver, is simple and attractive, as making a better parallel with the second stichus: *Or as a stillbirth, which never had being* . . .)

From 10¹⁹ we may infer that the לא in the first stichus is an insertion, perhaps due to the scribe's memory of the לא הייתי there; cf. 𝔊 ἡ ὥσπερ ἔκτρωμα ἐκπορευόμενον ἐκ μήτρας μητρός, which also omits the Neg. Particle and implies בטן instead of טמן; an easy confusion. No doubt 𝔊's Heb. copy was imperfect here, and טָמוּן *hidden* in the ground (cf. Ex 2¹²), *buried* out of sight at once, is right: cf. 10¹⁹ᵇ Ec 6³ (the *nêfel* at least has burial). The omission of לא gives a better connexion with the preceding verses, although 𝔊 𝔗 𝔙 retain it. (𝔊 makes the verse interrogative: *Or with buried abortions why have I not been, And as babes which have not seen the light?* 𝔗: *Or as the* niflā *that is hidden in its mother's womb* (cf. Je 20¹⁷), *I could not possibly exist,* &c. 𝔙: Aut sicut abortivum absconditum non subsisterem, &c.)

v. 17. *There*; where the dead, alike the most famous and the least regarded, are—in the grave; which is all the more vividly present to thought, because the poet does not expressly name it before the next strophe (v. 22). 'The wicked are the disturbers of peace, as contrasted with the good, the quiet in the land: cf. 9²⁴' (Duhm). The word רָשָׁע, rare before the Exile and found chiefly in Ezekiel, the Psalms, and the Wisdom-Literature, seems to include within its scope the ideas of irreligion, lawlessness, unscrupulous injustice, and violence. Cf. Is 14⁵. The root-idea seems to be that of breaking or crushing, the primitive root being RAŠ, RAṢ, RAS, which we see also in רָשַׁשׁ Po. *beat down* or *shatter*, Syr. *bray* or *pound*, *husk corn*, *crush*; רָצַץ *crush* = Ar. رضّ *bruise, bray, crush*; Aram. רְסַס *break, crush* = רָסַס in Heb. רָסִיס *fragment*; רָצַח *murder* = Ar. رضخ, رضّ *break, bruise, bray, crush*; and with Internal Triliteralization רְעַע *shatter* = Aram. רְעַע *smite, shatter*, &c., &c. (OL says 'cf. Ar. رسغ *be loose* of limbs, whence perhaps *disjointed, ill-regulated*', &c. But according to Lane رسغ,—not رسع, which is a *vox nihili*—means *to tether a camel by the forelegs*, and رسغ, is a *laxness in the legs of a camel*; which does not help us much.)

For רגן *excitement, disquiet, rage*, or *turbulence*, see 39²⁴ and the vb. Is 37²⁸·²⁹. With the meaning here cf. Is 57²⁰ᶠ·. All sorts and conditions of men are lulled in a common repose in the grave. 'Even the wicked there are no more agitated by the turbulence of their passions' (Da). There is here no hint of retribution in a life beyond the grave; nor indeed of any continued existence of the soul or spirit after death.

May these vivid allusions to the grandeur and lavish display (Is 2⁷) of kings and princes, to the ungovernable passions of the 'Wicked' (𝔊 ἀσεβεῖς; cf. the use of the word in 1 Macc), to the miseries of forced labour and bond-service, be taken to reflect the social conditions under which the poet lived? Their simplicity, directness, and deep feeling have all the air of truth and the colour of personal experience. They certainly do not suggest the idyllic peace of a patriarchal age. (חדלו רגן: 𝔊ᴮ, ἐξέκαυσαν θυμὸν ὀργῆς. The vb. must be a scribal error in the Greek for ἐξέπαυσαν: 𝔊ᴬ ἔπαυσαν *recte*.) *the weary*: lit *the weary in strength*; i.e. those worn out with bodily toil = 𝔊 κατάκοποι τῷ σώματι.

v. 18. *prisoners*: or *bondmen*. Prisoners of war and other captives, such as condemned criminals, debtors handed over to their creditors, refractory slaves, forced labourers in mines and quarries, and the like. See Gn 39²⁰·²² Ju 16²¹ (Samson grinding in the prison at Gaza) Ps 107¹⁰ Is 14¹⁷ 2 K 25²⁷ *taskmaster*: נגש, as in Ex 3¹¹: the overseers of forced labour, represented in the Egyptian and Assyrian monuments as flourishing whips and rods over their unhappy gangs of toilers. (𝔊 φορολόγου, *one who levies tribute*; also at 39⁷ = the meaning in Dan 11²⁰. For stichus i 𝔊 gives the extraordinary version or perversion ὁμοθυμαδὸν δὲ οἱ αἰώνιοι = עוֹלָם (עַם־) וְיַחַד אֲשֶׁר; which might have grown out of (וְ)יַחַד שַׁאֲנַנּוּ (אֲסִיר־)(ים) by the running together, partial effacement, and erroneous division of letters and words, such as occur not infrequently. עוֹלָם, however, might more easily have been corrupted from שלון or שָׁלֵיו (cf. חסיו and נטיו), as a badly written ן or יו might be mistaken for ם. Cf. שלותי, v. 26, ישׁלִיו 12⁶. Thus we recover an important possible variant = 𝔖 𝔄 שְׁלֵי 𝔊 ܡܠܟܝ.)

v. 19. *Small and great* = our 'High and low', as the ‖ stichus shows: cf. Dt 1¹⁷ 1 K 22³¹. Sometimes the Heb. phrase means *young and old*: Gn 19¹¹. *free*: חָפְשִׁי, as Ex 21²·⁵, where 𝔊 ἐλεύθερος *recte*. Here 𝔊 οὐ (א*ᶜ·ᵇ* A; but B om.) δεδοικώς, *not fearing*—a paraphrase not a different reading.

Strophe III WHY DO THE WRETCHES LIVE ON, WHO LONG BUT TO DIE?
vv. 20–26.

v. 20. *Why is light given* .. So 𝔊 𝔙 𝔖 𝔗 𝔄. 𝔐 יִתֵּן *giveth he*; or perhaps *giveth ·n*, Impers. Dt וְיֻתַּן Pass. There is no need to assume 'an indirect reference to God ... partly due to reverence'.

Eyob is speaking generally. *sorrowful*; lit. *bitter* (plur.) *of soul*; 1 Sa 1¹⁰ 22².

v. 21. *wait*: lit. so 2 K 7⁹ 9³; cf. chap. 32⁴. 𝔊 ὁμείρονται (=ἱμείρονται B³), *long for. in vain*: lit. *it is not*, or *there is naught of it* (sc. to them); *they have it not. rather than treasure*: מִמַּטְמוֹנִים, i.e. *hidden* (Gn 43²³ sing.) or *buried* (v. 16) *treasure*. 𝔊 (ἀνορύσσοντες) ὥσπερ θησαυρούς = בַּמַּטְמוֹנִים *like* (or *as for*) *treasure* (Pr 2⁴): so 𝔖 and 𝔙 (quasi effodientes thesaurum). The vb. *dig* (חָפַר) also means *search* (39²⁹).

v. 22. *beyond gladness*: lit. *unto exultation*. Cf. Ho 9¹ .. אֶל תִּשְׂמַח אֶל גִּיל. 𝔊 περιχαρεῖς δὲ ἐγένοντο gives the sense. So 𝔙 gaudentque vehementer. 𝔗 לְדִיצָא, = 𝔐. 𝔖 (*who are glad*) and come together (וּמִתְכַּנְּשִׁים) (?). Beer's גַּל *a heap* of stones (Gn 31⁴⁶), such as was raised over a corpse (Jos 7²⁶ 8²⁹ 2 Sa 18¹⁷), is frigid and improbable. Duhm, accepting it, explains that such unhappy ones are glad of a mere stone-heap, and exult if they find an ordinary (*ordentliches*) grave (קֶבֶר). But קֶבֶר is simply 'the grave', as in 10¹⁹; and 'finding a grave' = dying. The desperate do not trouble about the sort of interment that will be granted them. Besides, where גַּל means a stone-heap, אֲבָנִים always occurs in the context, even in 8¹⁷. A clear parallel to קֶבֶר would, however, not be amiss; and perhaps גִּיל preserves a vestige of נְדִישׁ *tomb*: see 21³². We might then render:

> *Who rejoice over the tomb,—*
> *Who are glad when they find the grave.*

For the second stichus 𝔊ᴮ has only ἐὰν καταтύχωσιν, *have succeeded* (𝔊ᴬ + θανάτου = קֶבֶר), omitting יָשִׂישׂוּ (*who*) *are glad*.

v. 23. Still subordinate to the question of v. 20: *Why is light given* ... Eyob now turns from the general case to his own special instance of it. He is not yet questioning the justice of God's dealings with him. He has so far admitted God's right to deal with him as He pleases (cf. 1²¹ 2¹⁰). He only wonders why he has not been permitted to die.

To the Man whose path is hidden; to whom all is dark, so that he cannot see his way, knows not what to do to escape from his present perplexities; cf. 19⁶⁻⁸. (𝔊 θάνατος ἀνδρὶ ἀνάπαυμα v. ἀνάπαυσις = קֶבֶר, שַׁחַת לְגֶבֶר נַחַת or לְגֶבֶר מְנוּחָה or something similar; which might be either a marginal note or a stichus omitted from 𝔐. 𝔊ᴬ adds ου ηδος απεκρυβη = אֲשֶׁר דַּרְכּוֹ נִסְתָּרָה, i.e. the part of 𝔐 wanting in 𝔊ᴮ. ηδος, of course, represents ἡ ὁδός. 𝔗 also felt the difficulty of going back so far as the beginning of v. 20 for the connexion of this verse, which it therefore begins thus: כָּל אִלֵּין מְרִירָתָא לְגֶבֶר דִּי וגו׳ *All these are bitter things* to the Man who, &c.)

hath hemmed in all round. The same vb. וַיָּסֶךְ recurs in 38⁸, 'And who shut in the Sea with doors?' It is spelt with שׂ instead of ס in 1¹

שך דרבה made *a fence all round him* for protection, and Ho 2⁸ שך דרבה
בסירים *fence off her way with thorns*. For the sense cf. 19⁸.

v. 24. 𝔐 כי לפני לחמי אנחתי תבא *For before* (= as, like 4¹⁹) *my bread
my sigh(ing) cometh*. Suspicious, in sense and redundant in metre
(four stresses). חבא, which does not seem to be very appropriate, may
be an intruder from the next verse (יבא; again in v. 26). 𝔙 Antequam
comedam suspiro = לפני לחמי אנחתי תבא, omitting the כי, which begins
the next verse also, giving the two verses an appearance of
being alternatives or duplicates. But 𝔊 𝔗 𝔖 = 𝔐. The idea of v. 24, which
Duhm and others regard as a marginal quotation, seems to be that sorrow
feeds on a diet of sighs and groans: cf. Ps 42⁴ 'My tears serve me for
bread day and night'; Ps 80⁶ 'Thou hast made them eat bread of
tears'; Ps 102¹⁰ 'For ashes like bread have I eaten'; also Ps 127²
Is 30²⁰. Centuries earlier the old Sumerian Psalmist wrote: U NU
MUN-KUE ER SHUG-MA-MU A NU MUN-NAGE ER U-A-MU
Food I ate not, Weeping was my fare (or *bread*); *Water I drank not, Weeping
was my diet* (lit. *food* and *water*).

Perhaps our כילפני has displaced an original האכילני *He has made me
eat*, and the whole line may have been האכילני לחם אנחות *He feeds me with
the bread of sighs* (plur. La 1²²); or the first word may have been אכלתי
or לחמתי (cf. Pr 4¹⁷), *I eat*. Another possible line would be כי לחמי
לחם אנחות *For my bread is bread of sighs. And I pour out my groans
like water*. Reading וָאַתֵּךְ (cf. 𝔊 and 10¹⁰) for 𝔐 ויתכו, since שַׁאֲגָתִי
is fem. We might also point שַׁאֲגָתִי (sing. ut Ps 22² 32³), and read
וָאַתֵּךְ· *And my groaning is poured out like water*. (𝔊 δακρύω δὲ ἐγὼ
συνεχόμενος φόβῳ. apparently not a paraphrase, but = וָאַתִּיךְ מַיִם בְּדְאָגָה
And I poured out water, i.e. shed tears, *in fear*. cf. Ez 12¹⁸f.)

v. 25. Or, 'For I fear a fear, and it cometh upon me, And that which
I dread cometh unto me', Driver. The Versions render the verbs in the
Past tense, but the Heb. Perfects and Imperfects with Strong Waw
possibly express the speaker's permanent condition. But see next
note.

v. 26. Dr: 'I have no ease, and no quiet, and no rest;
And yet turmoil cometh.'

Similarly Davidson, but this division of the stichi disregards the metre,
overweighting the first stichus, and giving a short line of two stresses for
the second. On the other hand, the symmetry of the grammatical
construction and the accentuation, and 𝔊 𝔙 among the Versions, distinctly favour this view. A word may have fallen out from the second
stichus, which sounds somewhat abrupt, and is, moreover, ambiguous
since רגן may mean either the personal *disquiet*, the agitation and 'tumult
of emotions' to which Eyob was subject, or the Divine anger which
was the supposed cause of it (cf. Hb 3 וברגז רחם תזכר. Here it may

cover both cause and consequence. 𝔊 ἦλθεν δέ μοι ὀργή, 𝔙 Et venit super me indignatio = ויבא עלי רגז; And Wrath attacks me: Gn 34⁷ (not quite the same as ויבא לי comes to me = 𝔊: see v. 25. Both constructions, Is 47⁹). This may be right; although a concluding stichus of two stresses, as in the Qînâh-measure (Elegiac metre), is conceivable here.

A more important question is whether these two concluding couplets really refer to the present or, as AV takes them, to the past. The Hebrew certainly admits of the rendering:

For a fear I feared, and it came to me,
And the thing I dreaded befell me:
Not careless, nor secure, nor at rest was I,
When the Wrath (or Trouble: 14¹) assailed (me).

(So the Versions. In stichus ii leg. בָּא pro יָבֹא; the י may be due to repetition of the preceding י. 𝔊 συνήντησέν μοι. 𝔗 alone has Impf.) Dramatically, this is far more impressive than the other interpretation, which makes Eyob complain that his affliction allows him no respite ('habe ich einen Augenblick Frieden, so kommt neue Unruhe,' Du), but no sooner has one paroxysm passed than another follows. This indeed seems rather far-fetched as an explanation of v. 25, however we understand the Heb. tenses. Davidson thinks that the reference cannot be to the real past, 'because it would be contrary to the idea of the poem to suppose that Job even in the days of his golden prime was haunted with indefinite fears of coming misfortune'. But the allusion appears to be to some definite anxiety; and that Eyob's consciousness of personal righteousness did not exempt him altogether from the fear of misfortune is evident from 1⁵. And the thing he dreaded actually befell him on a day about which he always felt the same anxiety (*Perhaps my sons have sinned* . . .)—the birthday of his eldest son (1¹⁸⁻¹⁹). He could never be certain that his sons had not sinned during the carousals of their birthdays (at which he was not himself present); and the thought of the sin would involve that of the penalty; so that on each birthday, as it recurred, the father's heart would be haunted, for a time at least, with fears of impending evil. On this view of the passage, v. 26 seems to make Eyob declare that he was not lulled in a false security (Ju 18⁷,¹⁰), but fully aware of possible dangers and alive to religious responsibility, when calamity suddenly overwhelmed him. There is nothing in chap. 29, or anywhere else, which really militates against this general construction of our passage. It certainly provides a finer climax to this opening monody than the other. 𝔗 makes v. 26 describe Eyob's demeanour on hearing the news of his successive misfortunes לא שליית מבסורתא דתורי ואתני וגו' *I was not gay at the news of oxen and asses, nor quiet at the news of the burning, nor did I rest at the news of the camels;* and *the anger* (רוגזא) *came, upon the news of the sons.* So Levy; but perhaps better interrogatively, with Walton (cf. 𝔙) : *Was I not still at the news of oxen and asses, and was I not quiet at the news of the burning, and did I not rest at the news of the camels, and did the anger come on the news of the sons?* Cf. 𝔙: Nonne dissimulavi? nonne silui? nonne quievi? et venit super me indignatio.

The First Round in the Disputation. Chaps. 4–14.

(i) The first speech of Eliphaz. Chaps. 4–5.

Chapter 4. *vv.* 1–5. *Strange that the comforter of others should himself despair!*

v. 2. There is something wrong with stichus 1. Not only is it metrically redundant with its four stresses, but the Hebrew as it stands is unmeaning. Driver suggests *If one attempt a word with thee, wilt thou be impatient?* (lit. *be weary*, i. e. wish it ended). But this would require at least נִסָּה דָבָר אֵלֶיךָ הֲתִלְאֶה; cf. Dt 28⁵⁶ and 4³⁴. נִסָּה דָבָר could hardly mean to *venture* a word (OL), but only to *test* or try it. We might read הֲיִנָּסֶה דָבָר אֵלֶיךָ נִלְאָה *Should one try to speak to the wearied* (*impatient*)?, or, since ה and ת are sometimes confused in manuscripts, we might restore חלה or נָחֲלָה *sick* for 𝔐's תִּלְאֶה. Cf. Je 12¹³ (נחלו 𝔐, נלאו 𝔊). Moreover, as we find נכה incorrectly written for נשא in Ps 4⁷, it is very tempting to suppose הנשא = הנכה here. For נָשָׂא דָבָר cf. Am 5¹. (So Duhm.) Eliphaz is reluctant to argue with a sick man, but feels bound to remonstrate with unreasonable despair. (תִּלְאֶה can hardly be an abridged Relative Clause, as Du asserts.) 𝔊 μὴ πολλάκις σοι λελάληται ἐν κόπῳ; = הֲהִרְבָּה דָבָר אֵלֶיךָ בִּתְלָאָה *Hath one spoken to thee much in weariness?*, which is obviously no improvement on 𝔐. 𝔖 *If I begin to speak with thee, thou wilt be weary.* 𝔙 Si coeperimus loqui tibi, forsitan moleste accipies.

St. ii. *withhold*: or *restrain*. עָצַר בְ as in 12¹⁵ 29⁹. *speech*: מִלִּין *words* (Aram. plur. = מִלִּים. Thirteen instances in Job.)

v. 3. *put right*: or *admonished*, *corrected*: יַסַּרְתָּ. The biliteral or primitive root is SAR, *bind*; cf. אָסַר *to bind* and Aram. יְסַר *to bind*. Thus we see that the Hebrew mind originally regarded moral discipline, training, and education as a sort of binding (cf. relligio).

drooping hands: i. e. the despondent and disheartened. Is 35³ 𝔊 εἰ γὰρ σὺ ἐνουθέτησας πολλούς, with הֲ (Aram.) = אִם instead of 𝔐 הִנֵּה. In st. ii χεῖρας ἀσθενοῦς (𝔊ᴬ ἀσθενούντων) does not indicate a difference of reading, but is a paraphrase giving the sense.

v. 4. *slumbler*: 𝔊 ἀσθενοῦντας. ἀσθενεῖν = כשׁל usually in 𝔊 (more than thirty times). *and to weak knees*. Is 35³. 𝔊 *powerless* (ἀδυνάτοισιν).

v. 5. Stichus i seems to be overloaded (כי עתה תבוא אליך ותלא עֵי), for it is difficult to give only one stress to תבוא אליך. Perhaps פִּי־עַתָּה תְבֹאֲךָ וַתֵּלֶא. For the vb. c suff. see 22²¹ Ez 32¹¹, and cf. chap. 15²¹ 20²².

overcome: lit. *weary*; i.e. spiritless, despondent.

bewildered: or *dismayed, confounded*.

𝔊 νῦν δὲ ἥκει ἐπὶ σὲ πόνος = תְלָאָה עליך תבוא ועתה. The first word may be right instead of עֵי כי עתה, the כ having been copied from בושל, the first word in the previous line, and the י being a misread ו, as often. In st. ii ἐσπούδασας = ותבהל; so 21⁶ 22¹⁰ 23¹⁶ Ec 8³.

vv. 6–11. Thy piety should inspire thee with hope; for it is not the righteous, but sinners, who are cut off by calamity.

thy piety: lit. *thy fear*, scil. of God = godliness, religion = יִרְאַת אֱלֹהִים Gn 20¹¹; יראת שדי 6¹⁴; יראת אדני 28²⁸; יראת יהוה Is 11³ Pr 10²⁷ al. In st. ii the conjunction ו must be transferred from the second word to the first. 𝔐 תקותך ותם דרכיך spoils the symmetry of the stichi, even if it could be taken as in AV. Siegfried and Duhm prefer וְתֹם דְּרָכֶיךָ תִּקְוָתֶךָ, which makes an intolerable jingle after כִּסְלָתֶךָ. 𝔊 ἐν ἀφροσύνῃ confuses two different meanings of the stem; cf. כֶּסֶל *confidence* 8¹⁴ and כֶּסֶל *folly* Ec 7²⁵ (a sense which does not occur in Job). 𝔊's ἡ κακία τῆς ὁδοῦ σου is obviously a scribal error for ἡ ἀκακία κτλ. (= תם Ps 7⁹; חמה chap. 2³ 27⁵).

v. 7. To scan aright מי־הוא־נקי must be read with a single stress. Perhaps מי־נקיא or even מי־הנקיא (*who was the innocent that perished*). 𝔊ᴬ ὅτι οὐδεὶς (οὐδείς, οὔτις) = בילוא pro מיחוא. Were there two variants אין־נקי and מי נקי? 𝔙 quis unquam innocens periit?

St. ii 𝔊 ἢ πότε ἀληθινοὶ ὁλόριζοι ἀπώλοντο = 𝔙 aut quando recti deleti sunt? But איפה is ubi? 38⁴. ישר = ἀληθινός, 2³ 8⁶ 17⁸. ὁλόριζοι ἀπώλοντο, radicitus perierunt; a good paraphrase of נכחדו *were hidden*, i.e. made unseen, destroyed, like ἠφανίσθησαν. Eliphaz does not deny that a really innocent man might suffer temporary affliction.

v. 8. Lit. *As I have seen, the plowers of trouble*, &c. An unsymmetrical distich with a prosaic beginning. The Versions do not help us here. If we emend with כְּשֻׁרִי *according to my seeing* or *when I noticed* (35¹³) for the prosy כַּאֲשֶׁר רָאִיתִי, we at least improve the metre and style of stichus i. שור = ראה is a favourite word in Job. It is confused with אשר again in 19²⁷. For the proverbial phraseology see Pr 22⁸ Ho 8⁷ 10¹³; and for a different figure, 15³³. Duhm thinks vv. 8, 9, 10, 11 may be spurious, because of their rude construction and want of pathos. To me vv. 8, 9 seem necessary to the argument; 10, 11 may perhaps be a marginal quotation. Merx and Siegfried reject the latter quatrain; though the abrupt change of metaphor need not startle us in Oriental poetry.

v. 9. For God's Breath as a destroying wind see Ps 18¹⁴ Is 40⁷. 𝔊 ἀπὸ προστάγματος κυρίου = יהוה משפט or משפט יהוה Ps 7⁷ or מצוות יהוה; against the parallelism.

v 10. The verse is (or has become) amorphous, and the apparent zeugma is improbable, a verb being necessary to the symmetry of the first stichus. We might correct שָׁאֲנַת אַרְיֵה נִשְׁבַּת (קוֹל) (*The sound of*) *the lion's roaring is stilled* (פָּחַת?; om. קוֹל?) or something similar. (𝔊 σθένος = ἰσχύς = גָּאוֹן or גָּאֹן for שְׁאָגַת.) But a better parallel would be gained by restoring שָׁחַל נִשְׁבְּרוּ מְתַלְּעוֹת *Broken are the fangs of the lion* cf 29¹⁷ Ps 58⁷, Jo 1⁶ (of lions) Pr 30¹⁴. In st. ii the supposed Aram. נָתָעוּ should be corrected נֶחְצוּ; see Ps 58⁷. (In Syriac ܢܬܥ is *outweigh*.) But cf. Assyr. *natû*, 'strike', 'crush', 'smash' (Pi), e. g. mountains. Lions are naturally a figure of fierce and violent oppressors, whether nations or individual tyrants (Is 5²⁹ Na 2¹²ff. Zp 3³ Pss 7² 10⁹ 17¹²). God's judgement on such is final and complete.

(There are four or five different words for lion in this quatrain. 𝔐 begins with אַרְיֵה, which occurs more than forty times in OT (while the shorter form אֲרִי is found only seventeen times), and which looks like an Aramaized pronunciation: cf. Syr. *'aryâ*. It is the Assyrian *arû*, lion, which may be the Semitized form of Sumerian UR, lion (*labbu*, *nêšu*) = UR, dog (*kalbu*). The second, שָׁחַל, might very well be a strengthened derivative from the same root as שׁוּעָל, Aram. תַעֲלָא fox or jackal; both animals being named from their cries, howling or roaring: cf. Assyr. *šaḫâlu* (שחל) to cry out, call, &c. The third, כְּפִיר a young lion, which has begun to hunt and roar over its prey, and is full of youthful vigour and strength (Is 5²⁹ 31⁴ Na 2¹⁴), is perhaps from a root כָּבַר = כפר and גָבַר to be strong (cf. also אבר in אָבִיר strong, mighty). The fourth, לַיִשׁ full-grown'(?) or mature lion, is Assyr. *nêšu*, lion, *nêštu*, lioness = Sumerian NIG, bitch, lioness; cf. LIG and DIŠ, values of the Sumerian character for dog, lion. The last word is לָבִיא lion, Gn 49⁹ Dt 33²⁰ = Assyr. *labbu*, lion (from *lab'u?*), perhaps meaning *growler*; from a root לבא = נבא Assyr. *nabû*, to call, cry aloud; cf. נבע Ps 59⁸, נָבְחָה, Ar. نَبَحَ to bark, and for the form לָבִיא, cf. נָבִיא mutterer, soothsayer, prophet. The Reflexives נִבָּא and הִתְנַבֵּא probably meant in the primitive period to mutter or talk in low tones to oneself, as is the way with the soothsayers of all ages and countries. Cf. 1 Sa 18¹⁰ 19²⁰⁻²⁴ Zc 13²⁻³.)

𝔊 σθένος for 𝔐 שַׁאֲגַת (σθένος = גְּבוּרָת 26¹⁴); perhaps due to a false reading שְׂנֵאַת, which 𝔊 connected with √שנא to be great. In st. ii γαυρίαμα δὲ δρακόντων ἐσβέσθη = : נִדְעַךְ (20¹⁵) פְּתָנִים ? וְשֵׁם; an unlikely guess at an illegible text. In v. 11 𝔊 renders לַיִשׁ by the curious μυρμηκολέων, ant-lion; cf. our term ant-bear.

vv. 12–21. Eliphaz relates a night-vision, in which he was taught the imperfection of all living beings, human as well as higher, relatively to

God. Eliphaz assumes the rôle of a Seer or Prophet, who has received a special revelation from a ghostly visitant.

v. 12. Lit. *And unto me* (emphatic by position; or *myself*) *a word* (or *thing*; דבר = ῥῆμα elsewhere) *was stolen* (יְגֻנַּב Gn 40¹⁵); here used in the sense *brought by stealth, stealthily* or *secretly brought*; cf. 2 K 11² Kal *she stealthily removed*; 2 Sa 19⁴ Hith. *to steal away, go off secretly*. We can say *A feeling* stole *over me*; *The truth gradually* stole *upon me*, and the like. 𝕲:

εἰ δέ τι ῥῆμα ἀληθινὸν ἐγεγόνει ἐν λόγοις σου,
οὐθὲν ἄν σοι (om. A) τούτων κακὸν (κακῶν· A) ἀπήντησεν,

But had there been a word of truth in thy speeches, Not one of these evils would have befallen thee! This strange perversion of the original text, for such it is, affords a good illustration of the pitfalls that lie in the way of the reader of an unpointed Hebrew codex. The translator naturally, but erroneously, pointed (or vocalized) the first word וְאִלּוּ *and if* (1⁸) instead of וְאֵלַי *and to me*; an error which necessitated further changes; e.g. יגנב was perhaps misread נכון *right* (cf. 42⁷·⁸ ἀληθές), and ותקח אזני שמץ מנהו became שמצ(א)הוה ותקר אין! (which, of course, is barbarous Hebrew; but 𝕲 failed to understand שמץ *whisper* both here and at 26¹⁴). Perhaps 𝕲 read or supposed merely קוֹרֵא אֵין שֶׁמַצָא מֶנְהוּ. It adds an alternative rendering of the second line: πότερον οὐ δέξεταί μου τὸ οὖς ἐξαίσια παρ' αὐτοῦ; *Shall* (should) *not my ear receive portentous things from Him?* = הלא תקח אזני שמץ מנהו. This really supports 𝔐, with another guess at the meaning of שמץ, whose only cognate in Hebrew is fem. form שִׁמְצָה *derisive whisper*, Ex 32²⁰. *a whisper of speech*: i.e. שֶׁמֶץ מִלָּה: cf. 26¹⁴ שֶׁמֶץ דָּבָר. The secrecy, suddenness, and unexpectedness of the revelation seem to be emphasized. Cf. 1 Th 5².

v. 13. Lit. *in thoughts* (20²) *from* or *out of visions of night*. This seems to say that Eliphaz had had a troubled dream, and was reflecting upon it, when the Visitation came to him. Dreams were regarded as a medium of intercourse between man and the spirit-world by all ancient peoples; and it was common to consult a god by sleeping in his sanctuary. Cf. Gn 15¹² 28¹¹ˢᵠᵠ· 32²⁴ˢᵠᵠ· 2 Sa 7⁴ 1 K 3⁵ Je 23²⁵ˢᵠᵠ· Zc 1⁸ Dan 2² 4⁵ 7⁷·¹³. The following verses, however, are to be understood as describing no merely subjective illusion, but an actual experience (perhaps of the poet himself). The 'thoughts' are apparently agitated, anxious or troubled and conflicting suggestions due to his dreams. The word שְׂעִפִּים, which recurs 20², and of which שַׂרְעַפִּים Ps 94¹⁹ 139²³ is a later and debased form, springs from a root שעף = סעף *to split, divide* (whence סְעִפִּים = שְׂעִפִּים *opinions*, 1 K 18²¹), which is formed by Internal Triliteralization from the primitive *SHAB* to split, to discern, see, &c. (Sumerian SHAB), and then to count, reckon, as in חשב ḥa-shab (cf.

perhaps √SAP in ספר sap̄-ar). Thinking and reckoning both involve division or separation of things from things, seeing them apart mentally.

𝔊 φόβῳ δὲ (A om.) καὶ ἤχῳ νυκτερινῇ = בְּשַׂעַר וּבֶהַמוֹן לָיְלָה; see 18²⁰ Am 5²³ 𝔊. This again suggests an illegible or corrupt Hebrew manuscript.

deep sleep: תַּרְדֵּמָה Gn 2²¹ 15¹² chap. 33¹⁵ (an echo of this passage). 𝔊 φόβος here and δεινὸς φόβος 33¹⁵; but ἔκστασις, *a trance*, Gn 2²¹ 15¹² (cf. Lk 10¹⁰), and strangely θάμβος, *astonishment, stupor*, 1 Sa 26¹²; κατάνυξις, *stupefaction, slumber*, Is 29¹⁰, and even ἀνδρόγυνος, Pr 19¹⁵. The word was generally misunderstood. The primitive biliteral root is *DAM* (*ṬAM, TAM*) *stop up, close, seal*, which is seen clearly in the Aramaic דמך *sleep* (*DAM + K, closed-like* = asleep); as also in אטם *shut* lips, *stop* ears, and Assyr. katâmu (כ־תם) *close* or *shut* mouth, lips, door, &c. A sleeper is as it were *closed* against the outer world; the organs of sense which are the avenues of perception are all stopped up or shut for the time being. Cf. Wordsworth's line, 'A slumber did my spirit seal.' (What is the significance of the ר by which the root is triliteralized into רדם? It may have replaced שׁ before ד, as is often the case in Assyrian, e.g. irdud = išdud, altu = aštu, &c. Thus שׁ־דם = ר־דם = *make stop up* or *close*. On Semitic Triliteralism see my paper in *Hilprecht Anniversary Volume*, Leipzig, 1906.)

In spite of the explanation suggested above I have always felt some doubt of the text בשׂעפים מחזיונות ל *In* (disquieting) *thoughts from night-visions*. It seems more natural to assume that the revelation (the apparition and its message) came to Eliphaz, as to other seers, *in* a vision of the night (cf. Gn 15¹²). בִּשְׁנוֹת בְּחֶזְיֹנוֹת ל *In slumbers* (Pr 6¹⁰; perhaps here = Assyr. šunâte, *dreams*), *in visions of night*, makes a better parallel, and agrees with the imitative 33¹⁵.

v. 14. *came over me*: lit as 𝔊 *met me*. St. ii, lit. *And the multitude of my bones it affrighted*. 𝔊 διέσεισεν, *it shook violently* probably gives the right sense, though it may represent a reading הֵחִיל (cf. Ps 29⁸) instead of הִפְחִיד (hîc tant.). The language is hyperbolical; as we might say 'My whole frame was convulsed with fear'. (The Hiphil might even be intrans. = *showed fear*.) Duhm's remark 'Wie das mit dem Tiefschlaf sich vereinigen lässt, weiss ich nicht' seems hypercritical.

v. 15. This narrative is unique in the OT—a fact worth noting for several reasons. Had the Jews been always the superstitious folk which writers hostile to faith in the Unseen would have us suppose, stories of similar apparitions would doubtless have abounded in their ancient records. As it is, the necromantic incident at Endor (1 Sa 28⁷ˢᵠᵠ·) and Elijah's experience in the sacred cave at Horeb (1 K 10⁹) are the only episodes which offer even a late parallel to the present narrative. Apparitions of 'Angels' (בְּנֵי הָאֱלֹהִים) belong, of course, to an entirely different category.

And: not *Then*; the consecution is close. *A wind*: or perhaps *A breath* of cold air. The word רוּחַ rûᵃḥ, like the Greek πνεῦμα (𝔊) is ambiguous, and may denote wind, breath, or spirit, according to the context (cf. Gn 1²). The Oxford Lex. (p. 322ª, s. v. חלף) suggests *wind* here; but elsewhere (p. 925ᵇ, s. v. רוח) *disembodied spirit*, though doubtfully, with the remark that Di Du prefer *breath* or *wind*. In his commentary, however, Du observes: 'v. 15 giebt nun die Ursache der Erschütterung an: *Ein Geist geht an mir vorüber*.' But (1) רוח is not found elsewhere in OT in the sense of a ghost or disembodied spirit, nor in that of such a spirit becoming visible (= an apparition). The apparition of Samuel at Endor is called אלהים, a *Divine* Being or *god* (1 Sa 28¹³; cf. Is 8¹⁹ אלהיו).

(2) The dead in Hades, mere shadows of their former selves, are called רפאים (26⁶); they are never called רוחות, spirits (Nu 16²²). We nowhere read that at death a man's רוח went down into She'ol; nor is it anywhere recorded that after a man's death his רוח reappeared in visible shape to the living.

(3) The verb יחלף *passes on swiftly, sweeps* or *rushes on*, a poetic syn. of עבר (see 𝔗), is used of wind, Is 21¹ Hb 1¹¹; and 𝔗 accordingly renders ויקא על אפי יעבר *And a blast passes on before me* (or *over my face*). Cf. 1 K 19¹¹, where, when Iahvah passes by, a violent wind (רוח) rages before Him, and it is said expressly that Iahvah was not in the רוּחַ. It was only a sign or accompaniment of His approach. So here, the mysterious wind betokens a supernatural Presence; and the vague sense of this makes the percipient's hair to stand on end with fear. It is a nice question whether על פני should be rendered *over my face* (so 𝔊), or, as is more usually the meaning of the phrase, *before me, in front of me*. Dr prefers the former: 'A mysterious breath, the symbol of a presence which he could not discern, seemed to pass over him.' But cf. Ex 33¹⁹ *I will make my Glory* (l. כבודי) *pass before thee* (על פניך).

(4) The Semitic root רוח is probably to be identified with the Sumerian RI (from RIG), *to blow* (záqu), *wind, blast* (ziqqu = 𝔗 וִיקָּא); and *wind* (*air, breath*), is doubtless the primary sense of the Hebrew רוח.

The hairs of my head = שַׂעֲרַת רֹאשִׁי (Ps 40¹³ 69⁵) instead of שַׂעֲרַת בְּשָׂרִי (ἅπ.) *a hair of my flesh*, which is a strange expression. A scribe may have modified the stichus from recollection of Ps 119¹²⁰ סָמַר מִפַּחְדְּךָ בְשָׂרִי *My flesh bristled up from fear of Thee*; where we might well read שְׂעָרִי *my hair*. Since the Kal is intrans., Piel should be trans.: *It lifts* or *makes to stand on end*. [We must read either יסמר, יחלף, or תסמר, תחלף; according to the gender of רוּחַ *wind*. This is fem. in 1¹⁹ 37²¹ 19¹⁷ (my *breath*? see note) but masc. in 41¹ (*th- air*) Hb 1¹¹, cf. 1 K 19¹¹. It is fem. in Is 40⁷ (*Elohim's Breath* = the wind). In the sense of the Divine Creative Breath 33⁴, which is the vital principle or 'spirit' in man, 6⁴ 17¹ 32⁸ (Gn 2⁷, cf. Ez 37⁹ ¹⁰), it is fem.; as also in the derived sense of a man's spirit or temper, 21⁴ 32¹⁸. In other passages of our book there is no indication of the gender of רוּחַ. (20³ is corrupt.)] Duhm asserts that רוּחַ here 'ist, weil masc., nicht der Wind, sondern ein Geist, vgl. I Reg 22 21; ein Wind wurde auch nicht zu dieser Erscheinung passen'. But the wind is sometimes masc., Ex 10¹³ Nu 11³¹ &c; and 1 K 22²¹ is hardly a secure foundation, for even if הָרוּחַ be original there, the passage is describing a vision of the celestial Court, not an earthly apparition inducing strong physical effects on the beholder, and causing his

> '... knotted and combined locks to part,
> And each particular hair to stand on end,
> Like quills upon the fretful porcupine.'
>
> *Hamlet*, Act i, Scene 5.

And lastly, as we have seen, the wind, as heralding the Divine Approach, does suit this apparition (or theophany), equally with the partially parallel passage, 1 K 19¹¹, on which it possibly depends.

v. 16**ᵃ** A tristich; a fact which suggests the loss of a line. Duhm thinks יעמד *It stops* ... may be the entire first stichus, which the poet cut short in order to deepen the impression of uneasiness, 'wie in einem Shakespeareschen Monolog' Such an abridged line is, however, without parallel in the book; and יעמד ולא־אכיר מראהו is a metrically perfect stichus as it stands. On the other hand, if the parallel with 1 K 19¹¹ ¹² hold good (cf. esp. the end of the verse), we can only suppose that some such stichus as והנה שדי עבר *And lo Shaddai went by !* has either been intentionally omitted, or has fallen out owing to similarity of letters (בשרי—שדי). The piece would thus become a theophany (cf. Ez 1²⁶).

He stops, but I discern not His form or looks, features: מַרְאֶה: cf. Joh 5³⁷ εἶδος = מראה Ez 1²⁶ (𝔊), Is 52¹⁴ (𝔊). Cf. also Ex 33²⁰.

A figure: or shape, likeness, form (𝔊 μορφή) Cf. Nu 12⁸ *And the form of Iahvah he beholds*: Dt 4¹² ¹⁵. Moses saw Iahvah's תמונה, but the people merely heard a Voice.

I hear a murmuring sound: lit. *A murmur* (or *whisper*) *and a voice I hear*. Cf. 1 K 19¹² *And after the fire* (lightning) *a sound of a low murmur*. דְּמָמָה *stillness, silence*, denotes a low voice or attenuated sound (קול דממה דקה); e.g. the light whisper or murmur of the wind when it dies away: *He husheth the storm to a murmur* (לדממה: Ps 107²⁹). Unwilling, as it would seem, to admit even a dim and indistinct vision of God, 𝔊 modifies the sense of vv. 15, 16 as follows: *And a wind came upon my face, But my hair and flesh bristled up. I stood up, and recognized not; I looked, and th a breeze and a voice.* This would require (v. 16) אֱמָר for אֱ יַעֲמֹד and אראה ותמונה לא נגד instead of אֱ מראהו תמונה לנגד. The changes are probably dogmatic, and obviously for the worse. (Of course allowance must also be made for the possibility of a partially illegible or otherwise corrupted Hebrew text.)

v. 17. אֱ מאלוה and מעשהו are most naturally taken as in AV *Shall a mortal be juster than Eloah, Or a man be purer than his Maker?* and perhaps the author of the Elihu-section understood it so (32²). But Eyob had said nothing so far to imply this absurdity. The context (vv. 18, 19) requires the meaning given above, *before God* (so Da Du Dr); i.e. in the judgement or estimation of God: so 𝔊 μὴ καθαρὸς ἔσται βροτὸς ἐναντίον τοῦ κυρίου; (the introductory Τί γάρ; is only a harmless rhetorical flourish). Cf. Nu 32²² והייתם נקים מיהוה = 𝔊 καὶ ἔσεσθε ἀθῷοι ἔναντι Κυρίου. There also, as here, a second 'מ = ἀπό; a fact which militates against Kittel's suggestion that 𝔊 read לפני 'י there. An ע may, however, have fallen out after ש (the two letters are often confused), and we may restore האנוש עם־אלוה יצדק; cf. 9² 25⁴, where the phrase עם צדק *to be just with* (= in the estimation of) (God) occurs in a similar connexion, 25⁵,⁶ constituting an exact parallel to 4¹⁸,¹⁹. In st. ii we must then restore וְעִם־מַעֲשֵׂהוּ for אֱ אִם־מֵעֹשֵׂהוּ. 𝔊 ἡ ἀπὸ τῶν ἔργων αὐτοῦ ἄμεμπτος ἀνήρ; = א(וֹ) מִמַּעֲשֵׂהוּ וגו׳, a difference mainly of pointing and division of letters.

v. 18. *Behold:* הֵן. 𝔊 εἰ = Aram. הֵן (Dan 2⁶+). *His servants* = the angels, as the ∥ st. indicates. Elsewhere only of human ministers of His will, patriarchs, prophets, &c. Cf. Am 3⁷ Is 44²⁶. (Cf. also σύνδουλος, Re 19¹⁰ 22⁹ of an angel.) Eliphaz repeats the same thought, 15¹⁵. God, apparently, is the Maker (v. 17) of Man, but not of the denizens of Heaven, who are altogether higher beings (בני האלהים) and, at least originally, minor gods grouped around the Supreme in the Court of Heaven. Hence Iahvah is the God of gods (*il iláni*), that is to say, the highest God, the Most High. Stripped of all mythological associations, the doctrine of Eliphaz is that no Being below the Highest can be absolutely free from relative imperfection. But imperfection involves liability to error; and error justifies the Divine censure.

The idea that the Supreme cannot altogether 'trust in' or depend upon the faithfulness and inerrancy of any lower beings, however exalted their nature, is perhaps implicit in the very notion of a hierarchy of heaven, arranged in ranks, one above another, in endless gradation. The conception of a 'Host of Heaven' involves the further conception of discipline and obedience, with the possibility of their opposites; and all such ideas, of course, have their physical basis in primitive observation of the regular and irregular movements of the heavenly bodies and other celestial phenomena—the daily course of the sun from east to west, the recurring changes of the moon, the apparent vagaries of the planets (πλάνητες ἀστέρες; cf. Jude¹³ ἀστέρες πλανῆται, 'wandering stars'), meteors, and shooting stars. In the Babylonian mythus of Creation Merodach takes measures to prevent the heavenly bodies from 'doing evil' or 'going astray' (Ana lâ êpêš annî ‖ lâ êgû manâma; Cr. Tab. V. 7); and he is praised as 'holding (v. appointing) the paths of the stars of heaven', and 'shepherding all the gods like sheep' (ša' kakkabâni šamâmê ‖ alkâtsûnu likillu! (v. likîn!) Kîma çêni lirtâ ‖ ilâni gimrašûn! Tab. VII. 110–111). The 'sin' of which these subordinate 'gods' might be guilty was deviation from their appointed paths (cf. Ju 5²⁰ Is 22²¹ 2 Pe 2⁴ Jude⁶ Re 12⁷)—deserting their stations and overstepping the boundaries which had been fixed by the Supreme. Such conceptions of the relation of the Angels to God are obviously primitive. Later speculation established a sharp distinction between evil angels and good, and in time even their names became known (cf. Is 40²⁶ Ps 147⁴).

The fault ascribed by the Supreme to His Angels is according to 𝔐 תהלה; an obscure and isolated word, which 𝔊 renders σκολιόν τι (= תהפכות Pr 16²⁸ al.), *something crooked* (unrighteous or amiss) = 𝔙 pravitatem; 𝔗 עִילָא *matter*, res (cf. 1 Sa 22¹⁵), *ground of accusation*, as in Dan 6⁵·⁶; 𝔖 ܬܡܗܐ (תמה) *stupor, amazement, awe*: all mere guesses from the context. It might conceivably mean *boasting, vain-glory, pride*, gloria (תהלה from הלל II, which is ultimately identical with הלל I), or *folly, witlessness, madness* (cf. Po'el, Po'al, Hithpo. of the same root, and הוֹלֵלוֹת, הוֹלֵלוּת *folly* or *madness*). The former sense agrees with Is 14¹²·¹³ (the Fall of Lucifer—הֵילֵל בֶּן שָׁחַר, the Morning Star); cf. also Lk 10¹⁸. 'By that sin fell the Angels.' The latter meaning, *folly*, which certainly suits the context, will also be the sense if we follow Hupfeld (Merx, &c.) in reading תִּפְלָה (1²² 24¹²·⁷); a very attractive conjecture, accepted by Budde, Siegfried, and others. The identical phrase, יָשִׂים תִּפְלָה (cf. נָתַן תִּפְלָה 1²²) actually recurs 24¹², if we may rely upon 𝔐 (but see the note ad loc.). Dillmann gets the meaning *error* by assuming that תהלה springs from a √תהל = Eth. ተሐለ፡ ተሓለ, which in Conj. III means *vagum oberrare* (Di Lex Aeth⁵⁵²). The sense is excellent (Jude⁶·¹³; vid. supr.); but the etymology doubtful. Others compare Arab. وَهَلَ *to make a mistake* in a matter, *to forget* [not in Lane]; as though תהלה were equivalent to תחלה from a √והל, which is hardly probable. [Does תְּהִלָּה represent a misunderstood תְּהִלָּה? *And to His Angels He attributeth* (not) *glory* (25⁵·⁶ Hb 3³)! *Much less*, &c., v. 19.]

v. 19. *Much more*: or *Much less*: see last note. The Heb. אַף (usually + כִּי) may be rendered either way, according to context. Perhaps we should read ב[שכני] for the following word.

𝔊ᴮ τοὺς δὲ καταλοίπους ... But 𝔊ᴬ ἐᾷ δὲ τοὺς κατοικ... the Heb. w... v. 1 אוי !h!

(Ez 24⁸). *Dwellers in houses* (constructed) *of clay*; i.e. poor humanity. The phrase seems to distinguish man himself from his material body, which is regarded as the house he lives in. It is built of clay (חֹמֶר), the fragile stuff of pottery (Je 18⁴): see chap. 10⁹. God is the Potter who fashions man out of this frail and brittle material: Is 45⁹ 64⁷. (The 'dust' or 'earth' of the next line is syn. here and Gn 2⁷.) In 33⁶ Elihu says: *Lo I, like thee, am no god; I too was nipped off from clay.* The old Babylonian Epic uses the same phrase of the creation of Engidu, the fellow of its hero Gilgamesh: 'The goddess Aruru washed her hands; clay she nipped off (*ṭîṭa iqtariṣ* = יקתרץ טיט), threw it on the plain (or desert: *ṣêri* = EDIN) . . . created Engidu' (NE viii. 34 sq.). The same goddess assists Merodach in the creation of man, according to the important bilingual text first published by Pinches (JRAS xxiii, NS, 393 sqq.; CT xiii. 35 sqq.), where we read:

NAM-LÙ-GÀLLU BA-RU
amelûti ibtani
D. ARURU NUMUN „ DINGIR-TA NEN-MA (?)
iltu „ zêr amelûti ittišu ibtanû

'Mankind He created; The goddess Aruru seed of Mankind with the god she made come forth' (Assyr. *with Him she created*). The allusion to Aruru here may be a harmonistic interpolation, as Marduk appears as sole Creator everywhere else in the piece, just as in the Seven Tablets of Creation.

Eliphaz argues that if celestial beings are not inerrant or impeccable in the sight of the Supreme, much less can terrestrial man be so. His ghostly visitant appears to ignore the story of the Fall, as Duhm has noted. Human frailty is traced to the imperfect material of the body: cf. Ps 103¹¹.

Whose foundation is in the dust (or *earth*). The Relative may refer either to the 'houses of clay' or to their inhabitants. The latter agrees better with what follows; but perhaps the two were not sharply distinguished in the mind of the poet. We might render: *Whose foundation* (יסוד; cf. cogn. סעד *stay support*; the foundation being that on which a building is supported) *consists in earth*, is earthen (*Beth Essentiae*), i.e. of clay.

Which (*Who*) *are crushed before a* (*the*) *moth*. Reading יְדֻכְּאוּ (5¹ 34²⁵) and מִלִּפְנֵי; as though the attack of the feeblest of insects might be fatal to a man. Cf. Is 50⁹ 51⁸. In these and other passages, however, where the moth (עָשׁ, Assyr. *ašašu*) is brought into relation with man, the reference is to the clothes-moths, of which there are various species, whose grubs fret or eat away garments of wool and fur: see 13²⁸. And as the punitive action of Iahvah is compared to this wearing and wasting work of the moth, Ps 39¹² Ho 5¹² (*And I was like the moth to*

Ephraim ‖ *And like a rot to the House of Israel*), we should naturally expect the same ground of reference here. This might be obtained by reading יְדַכְּאָם (or יַכֵּם = 𝔊 ἔπαισεν αὐτούς, *He smote them*) לְפִי עָשׁ (cf. הֻכָּה לְפִי חָרֶב), *Whom He* (Eloah) *demolishes by the mouth of the moth*. It is even possible that 𝔊 read or conjectured יֹאכְלֵם *Whom He eats*, instead of ידכאום, since ἔπαισεν may mean *He eat*, like ἐπάσατε (Hesych. παίειν, τύπτειν .. ἢ ἐσθίειν. Cf. Aristoph. Ach. 835). So 𝔙 Consumentur velut a tinea.

It must be admitted that the text is more or less uncertain from this point to the end of the chapter. The triplet instead of a couplet makes v. 19 suspicious at the outset, and it seems probable that the third line should begin the next distich. At all events, יְדֻכָּאוּ (or יְדֻכְּאוּ) is a synonym which makes a good parallel for יָבֹתוּ, and לִפְנֵי עָשׁ may conceal a note of time corresponding to מִבֹּקֶר לָעֶרֶב; e.g. לִפְנֵי עֲלוֹת־שַׁחַר referring to death in the night (cf Is 17¹⁴ 38¹²). This would give:

'Who are crushed ere the rise of Dawn,—
Between Morn and Eve are shattered.'

Or we might regard לִפְנֵי עָשׁ as a corruption of לִפְנוֹת שַׁחַר *at the approach of Dawn*: cf. Ex 14²⁷ Ps 46⁶. In any case, the point seems to be the brief duration of human life (cf. Ps 90³ ˢᑫᑫ); and, as we have seen, the moth is not elsewhere an emblem of ephemeral existence but of destructiveness. In the poem which has been called the 'Babylonian Job' we read:

Ša ina amšat iblutu imût uddeš
Surriš uštadir zamar iḫtamaš

'He who was alive yestereve died in the morning; In a moment was he troubled, quickly was he crushed.' Cf. our own popular saying 'Here to-day and gone to-morrow'; and the Chinese *Wei tsai tan sih*, 'The danger is between morning and evening' (= Death is only a question of hours) See Giles, *Dict.* 12589.

In the next clause of the Heb. the word מֵשִׂים is corrupt, the vb. שִׂים being unused in Hiphil. Even if משים (scil. לב) might mean *regarding* or *heeding*, מִבְּלִי מֵשִׂים לָנֶצַח יֹאבֵדוּ could only imply *For want of one* (or, *Without any*) *regarding they perish for ever* (cf. Ho 4⁶ and v. 11 supr., 24⁸ 31¹⁹). But Eliphaz does not mean that nobody troubles about the fate of men, because they are so unimportant, as Duhm puts it. See v. 8 sqq. 𝔊 βοηθῆσαι suggests מֹשִׁיעַ *helper, saviour*, as in Dt 28²⁹ ³¹ and a few other places But perhaps the word was תֻּשִׁיָּה which would give a better parallel to חָכְמָה (cf. 26³): see also 5¹² 6¹³ 11⁶. The phrase לָנֶצַח יֹאבֵדוּ is confirmed by 20⁷. The meaning is that, once dead, they never return from Sheol to the present life ; 7 10 14 . We get a good parallel sticks by a slight emende . . v. 21 b, reading בְּלֹא יָמוּתוּ

חכמה = 𝔊 ἀπώλοντο παρὰ τὸ μὴ ἔχειν αὐτοὺς σοφίαν. Thus the final couplet becomes :

 'Without Insight they perish for aye;
 They die in Ignorance (or, devoid of Wisdom).'

With this we may compare the lines which immediately precede the passage just quoted from the Babylonian poem :

 Aiu ṭếm DINGIR-MEŠ kirib AN-é ilammad
 Milik ša DINGIR zanûn zế iḫakkim mannu
 Êkáma ilmadá alakti DINGIR apáti

'Who shall learn the mind of the gods in heaven? Who shall comprehend the counsel of God which is full of subtlety? (*zú*; from Sum. ZU, *nimequ*). How have mortals learned the Way of God?'

v. 21 a, the text of which is very generally recognized as more or less corrupt, interrupts the sequence. It may be a marginal intrusion. Did הלא נסע originate in a mishearing of לנצח dictated? In that case יתרם בם (𝔊 𝔙 מהם יתרם), for which some would read יתרם מהם, may have grown out of יאבדו by successive perversions. 𝔊 ἐνεφύσησεν γὰρ αὐτοῖς καὶ ἐξηράνθησαν (𝔊ᴬ ἐτελεύτησαν = וימותו) = (or בם ויבשו (ויחרבו) or נשב (כי נפח; cf. Is 40⁷·²⁴ Ez 37⁹ Hg 1⁹. Strange as the fact may seem, this need not imply any other original text than that of 𝔐 : הלא נסע יתרם בם. It certainly favours בם or בהם rather than מהם, merely transposing it with יתרם misread as יחרב' (יחרבו). 𝔊 perhaps read הלא as הוא and guessed נשב or נפח for an almost obliterated נסע.

Chapter 5. The oracle has affirmed that all beings below God himself are imperfect and liable to error. If this is true in the superhuman or celestial sphere, much more is it true in the terrestrial world of man, whose corporeal nature, brief existence, and consequent ignorance, exclude and stultify all claim to be regarded and treated as blameless by the supreme Judge who alone is perfect. Eliphaz goes on to point out the folly of angry resentment against God's dealings and the wisdom of submission. The essential truth and beauty of his statement will always be evident to spiritual experience, in spite of the fallacy of his tacit assumption that only the guilty suffer and that extraordinary suffering is proof absolute of extraordinary guilt.

v. 1 is not a marginal quotation, intended originally to illustrate 4¹⁸, and wrongly inserted here by some scribe. Eliphaz demands, What is the use of all this outcry? To whom were Eyob's frantic appeals addressed? See 3¹¹·¹²·²⁰⁻²³. Does he expect any sympathy from the Angels in his rebellious complaints against the rule of their Lord? There are no rebels in Heaven now, however it may have been in the days of old. Rather, if he is wise, let him address his appeal to God (v. 8).

5. 1   NOTES ON THE TEXT   145

The holy ones are the Angels. cf. 4¹⁸ with 15¹⁵; Ps 89⁶·⁸ Zc 14⁵ Dan 4¹⁰ ¹⁴. As I have shown elsewhere, קדוש, קדשים, is properly *bright, shining*, and then *clear, pure, holy*; cf. Assyr. *quddušu, brilliant, pure*, a syn. of *ellu*, הלל, *namru*, נור. And since the Angels or Host of Heaven were originally the stars, we may infer that קדשים as a designation of the Angels primarily denoted the Shining Ones (cf. Dan 12³). The idea of what *we* mean by 'holiness', or moral and spiritual perfection, seems excluded by 4¹⁸.

Call (for help)*! is there one about to answer* (particip.) *thee? And unto whom of the Celestials wilt thou turn* (for aid: Le 19³¹ 20⁶)*?* The practice of the 'Invocation of Angels' seems to be implied by the question, and was probably not unknown in the author's day, although few traces of it survive in the OT. We know, however, that, in spite of the opposition of the Prophets, Necromancy was practised in Israel throughout the monarchical period (see my paper 'Shumer and Shem' in the *Proceedings of the British Academy*, vol VII); and if the spirits in She'ol below could be invoked in times of stress, why not also, and with more apparent reason, the mightier Powers of Heaven? Cf. perhaps Gn 48¹⁶ Ho 12⁴ and the direct address to the Angels, Ps 103²⁰·²¹ 148². Moreover, the Angels of God are so wise (חָכָם) that they know everything that happens here below (כחכמת מלאך האלהים לדעת את כל אשר בארץ: 2 Sa 14²⁰); a wisdom beyond the reach of mortal man (4²¹) If the 'spirit' (רוח) which brought the oracle to Eliphaz was angelic (cf. 1 K 22¹⁹ ²¹ ²⁴ Zc 1⁸ˢᑫᑫ)— and we can hardly suppose a ghost called up from She'ol to be intended— we understand why Eliphaz is so sure that it would be futile for Eyob to appeal to the Angels. The oracle has made him quite clear as to their point of view; precluding, as it does, for all created beings a case against the Creator. Why then, asks Eliphaz, persist in futile appeals or protests in the face of what we know of God's perfection and man's imperfection? why break in upon the silence of Heaven with outcries that are certainly vain and may prove hurtful to yourself? Only a fool would do it. v. 2. *For a fool resentment may slay, And a gull passion may kill*: that is, either You may die of rage, or else, Your blind insensate fury may provoke an aggravation of your sufferings. Cf. 2⁹ ¹⁰.

The term אויל *foolish, fool*, and its cognate יאל *to be foolish*, if related to Ar. آل *to return, to thicken, coagulate*, of fluids, might signify *thick, dense, crass, obtuse, thickhead*, or the like; but it seems more plausible to compare it with אמל *to be weak, feeble*. The √מל (= ול) reappears in נטלה *ant* (עם לא עז Pr 30²⁵) and perhaps in קמל *to languish* or *decay*. Cf. also Assyr. *ulālu, weak, weakling, weak-witted*; f *ulaltum*, of a woman, *weak* = become infertile = אמללה 1 Sa 2⁵ Je 15⁹; *ullu, ul, al*, Heb. אל, *non-existence, nothingness, naught, not*. The transition to the idea of moral evil usual in איל and other Heb words denoting foolish may be illustrated by our own ⸱⸱⸱⸱ ⸱⸱⸱⸱ ⸱ P⸱ ⸱ ⸱ I I⸱ √מל, ול may otherwise be the Sumerian MAL, GAL, *open*: cf. the syn. פָּתָה *open*, i.e. to all approaches, good or evil; *unreserved, unsuspecting, simple*, in the good, but chiefly in the bad sense; which comes from Sum. BAD, *pitû*, *to open*.)

Resentment; or *vexation, anger*, or *grief*, at unmerited treatment. Heb. כעש in Job (= כעס elsewhere and 22 codd. here). Cf. perhaps Sum. KASH, *impatient, furious*, of Ningirsu's chariot-horse.

Passion: or *heat*. קנאה can hardly be *jealousy* here. The word was originally a colour-term; cf. Ar. كَنَأَ *to become intensely red* (or *black*) from henna. In Syr. ܩܢܐ (קנא) is *pale, livid, colour of lead*. We may suppose that Sum. GIN, *çalmu, black, dark* (CT xii. 30) is related to the Sem. √קנא as Sum. GIN, GI, *qanû, reed*, to Sem. קָנֶה, קַנְיָא *reed*. Thus קנאה properly denotes the change of colour which betrays strong emotion, whether anger or jealousy.

v. 3. *I myself* (אני emphat.) *have seen a fool rooted out* (leg. מְשֹׁרָשׁ; cf. 31⁸: ⅏ ⑥ מַשְׁרִישׁ *striking root*; Ps 80¹⁰: which does not harmonize with the context). *And his homestead* (v. 24; 18¹⁵) *perished of a sudden*. Leg. ויאבד, or simply אבד instead of ⅏ ואקוב *And I cursed*. If this were genuine, it could only mean that the ruin of the fool's house was the consequence of the sudden curse of Eliphaz. Driver's 'I.e. his habitation having been suddenly ruined, I cursed it as the abode of one who had been a sinner' is remote from the plain sense of the Hebrew, and supplies a good instance of the shifts to which unwillingness to correct the text may reduce conservative scholars. ⑥ ἀλλ' εὐθέως ἐβρώθη αὐτῶν ἡ δίαιτα = פ' נָוֵהוּ וַיֹּאכַל: see 6⁶ 18¹³ Is 51⁸ for אכל = βιβρώσκω. Perhaps וַיֹּאכַל or וַיֹּאצַל is right here (*his habitation was devoured* or *consumed*; cf. Is 1⁷·²⁰); but אבד, a common word in Job, seems better. וירקב or רקב *rotted* (of timber, Is 40²⁰) does not suit נוהו. The ‖ suggests וַיְעַר *was uprooted*: Zp 2⁴. Usually δίαιτα = אֹהֶל *tent*, as in 8²² 11¹⁴ 18⁶·¹⁵ 22²³·²⁸. In 8⁶ it again = נוה (leg. נְוֵה pro נְוַת), which originally meant a place of *lying down*, a *resting-place* of flocks (2 Sa 7⁸ Is 65¹⁰). In Semitic the root seems to be peculiar to Hebrew and Sabean (see Driver's excellent note on 1 Sa 19¹⁸); but we need not suspect it on that account. On the contrary, we may regard it as an offshoot from the Sumerian NA, NU, for which we find the Assyr. equivalents *rabáçu*, to lie down (רבץ), *ṭarbaçu*, sheepfold, cattleshed; *narbaçu*, lair, abode; *šubtum*, dwelling-place, as well as *maialu, maialtum*, bed, &c., &c. It is surely more than a mere coincidence that in Hebrew נוה is associated with רבץ and its derivv. (the very root which in Assyr. is so freely used for the explication of the Sumerian NA, NU), and that the extension of meanings exhibited by the Hebrew נוה and its derivv. runs so far parallel to the uses of the Sumerian NA. See also Ez 25³⁴ Jr 33¹ Pr 24¹⁵ Ps 23².

⑥ generalizes with the plur. ἄφρονας ῥίζαν βάλλοντας ... αὐτῶν, but

Eliphaz appears to be alleging a particular instance from his own experience: *I myself once saw* ...

v. 4. The sins of the father are visited on the children; his ruin entails theirs. Left without their natural protector, whose death is implied in v. 3, they were far from secure or prosperous, and were always *crushed in the gateway* (so Pr 22²²)—robbed of their rights by the influence of powerful adversaries in the place of justice. Cf. 31²¹ Ps 127⁵ Am 5¹⁰. 𝕲 κολαβρισθείησαν δὲ ἐπὶ θύραις ἡσσόνων, *Let them be derided*(?) *at doors of inferiors*   κολαβρίζω = σκιρτᾶν (Hesych.). Perhaps corrupt for κολαφισθείησαν, *let them be buffeted*, or μαλακισθείησαν (cf. Is 53⁶ μεμαλάκισται = מְדֻכָּא: 𝕲ᴬ συνετρίβη) = ידכאו in all probability. So also 𝕲ᴬ ἐπιτριβήσονται 𝕲ᶿ κατεκλάσθησαν 𝕲ᶴ ταπεινωθήτωσαν imply same text as 𝔐.

v. 5. *Whose harvest* or crop: 𝔐 קְצִירוֹ: rather קְצִירָה. 𝕲 𝕾 imply קָצְרוּ, which some prefer. (ᴬ γὰρ ἐκεῖνοι συνήγαγον, 𝕲ᴬ ἐθέρισαν.) The noun gives a closer ∥ to what follows.

the hungry (emphat.) *eateth*: or *would eat* (freq.) every season. 𝕲 δίκαιοι ἔδονται, misreading ישר (1¹⁸) for רעב.

And all their sustenance he taketh: reading וכל מזונם for 𝔐 ואל מצנים, which is evidently corrupt. כל and אל are not seldom confused. מזון Gn 45²³; an Aramaism. The √זון may be compared with Sum. DUN, Ch. *tun, t'un*, to swallow, gobble up (DUN-DUN, to feast, *patânu ša amēli; naptanu, iptennu*, meal, feast. פתן = פ־תן = ב־רן!). 𝕲 αὐτοὶ δὲ ἐκ κακῶν οὐκ ἐξαίρετοι ἔσονται (= 𝕲ᴬ ἐξερεθήσονται = ἐξαιρεθήσονται) = וְאַל (וְלֹא) מֵרָעִים יָקְתוּ. This suggests מִרְעָם *their pasture*, or better perhaps עֲמִירָם *their sheaves*; cf. Am 2¹³ Mi 4¹².

The next line (also corrupt) makes the verse a tristich; so either this or that must be sacrificed. 𝔐 וְשָׁאַף צַמִּים חֵילָם, which some render *And a snare* (צַמִּים 18⁹ only) *snappeth at their wealth*, does not suit the context, even if the words could mean that. שאף (cognate with נשף and נשב and נשם, Is 42¹⁴, *breathe, blow, pant*) may mean *pant after, be eager for* ... as in 7², where the metre would be improved by adding the prep. אֶל (cf. Ec 1⁵); but hardly *snap after*. And why should a snare be so strongly personified in such a context? In 18⁹ 𝕲 gives διψῶντας = צְמֵ(א)ים *thirsty ones* for צַמִּים; and so 𝕲ᴬᶴ and 𝕾𝕭 here. This, or rather the sing. צָמֵא (∥ c רָעֵב in st. i) is prob. correct. But what of the verb? *And the thirsty is* (was) *eager for their wealth* is passable sense, but inadequate to the context. Duhm's ושאב צמא מנלם *And the thirsty draweth from their well* will not do, for גל *wave, heap*, never means a *well* (in Ct 4¹² גל must be read with many MSS and 𝕲 𝕾 𝕭). We prefer to transpose a letter and restore אסף = אשף (cf. בעס = בעש, v. 2); a harvesting term like קצר: se Ex 23¹⁰·¹⁶ Dt 11¹⁴ Is 62⁹·¹⁰ (of win and oil and fruit). *And the thirsty gathereth* (or the like) *their fruits* or *produce* (יְבֻלָם for חֵילָם). יְבוּל is ‖ c פְּרִי *fruit*, Lc 26⁴·²⁰ al., and in Hb 3¹⁷ denotes grapes. In Ez 34²⁷ 𝔊 actually gives τὴν ἰσχὺν αὐτῆς for יְבוּלָהּ, as though it read חֵילָהּ. On the other hand, Jo 2²² has חֵילָם (𝔊 τὴν ἰσχὺν αὐτῶν) of the fruit of the fig-tree and the vine and almost as a syn. of פְּרִי; and it seems not impossible that חֵילָם (𝔊 αὐτῶν ἡ ἰσχύς) may have been so intended here. (𝔊's verb ἐκσιφωνισθείη = וְשָׁאַב prob.) Cf. 24⁶·¹¹. The likeness of form between 𝔐 מִצְנִים and צְמִים and that of sense between יִקָּחֵהוּ and אַשָּׁף (אָסַף) suggest a suspicion that one or other of the two lines is a duplicate or variant.

vv. 6, 7. The ruin of the fool and his family was not due to mere ill luck or mischance; for affliction is not a spontaneous or accidental growth, springing up like a weed out of the ground. It is from above and is, in fact, an inevitable consequence of the congenital imperfection of man. Since Eyob was human, he was by nature liable to sin, and the greatness of his affliction indicated that he must have sinned greatly, though not past forgiveness, inasmuch as he had not himself perished like the fool whose destruction Eliphaz had witnessed. Every wise man will expect his share of trouble, greater or less according to his deserts. Thus there is no real contradiction of 4¹⁹ˢᵠᵠ·, and no good reason for banishing to the margin these two fine and perfectly relevant verses.

The כִּי of v. 6 rather overloads st. i, unless we pronounce כִּי־לֹא־יֵצֵא univocally. It may quite well be regarded as an accidental anticipation of v. 7.

v. 7. *is born.* Ketib Niph. Impf. יִוָּלֵד is preferable to Qere Pu. Pf. יֻלָּד on account of the ‖ יַגְבִּיהוּ. The phrase *is born to trouble* might mean *is a son of Trouble* (cf. 1² and the Nom. Prop. בֶּן־אוֹנִי), personifying עָמָל; but this is less likely. The verse is cast in a common proverbial type: lit. *For Man to Trouble is born; And Sons of the Vulture fly high* = 𝔊ᴮ ἀλλὰ ἄνθρωπος γεννᾶται κόπῳ (= לְאָדָם ut supr.?), νεοσσοὶ δὲ γυπὸς τὰ ὑψηλὰ πέτονται. *Sons of the Vulture*: leg. בְּנֵי נֶשֶׁר (Pr 30¹⁷ Hb 1⁸) instead of 𝔐 בְּנֵי רֶשֶׁף *Sons of Flame* = *sparks* (here only). The phrase of 𝔐 could not mean lightnings or fire-bolts (cf. Ps 78⁴⁸ Dt 32²⁴), for these do not 'soar high', but descend; and a similar objection lies against Cheyne's 'burning arrows' (cf. Ps. 76⁴). Even 'sparks' that shoot up can hardly be said to 'soar high'.

It is a mistake to expect scientific precision of statement in literature, especially in Oriental poetry. A spirit of pedantic and prosaic literalness has found many difficulties here in the connexion of thought; but what sensible reader will demand mathematical exactness in a proverb or a simile? The statement of the verse is simply that 'trouble' comes as naturally to man as soaring flight to young birds of prey. The causes of sin and suffering are inborn in man inherent in human nature.

vv. 16. If Eyob is wise, instead of continuing his angry outcries he will 'inquire of God' (דָּרַשׁ אֶל־ Is 8¹⁹ 19³ Dt 18¹¹), who is the author of all good both in the physical and in the moral sphere, and delights to show His power by humbling the mighty and exalting the weak and oppressed.

v. 8. my case. דִּבְרָה here only in this sense. עַל־דִּבְרַת *because of*, Ec 3¹⁸ al. 𝔊 paraphrases κύριον δὲ τὸν πάντων δεσπότην ἐπικαλέσομαι, possibly reading שׁדי for אלהים (𝔊^A παντοκράτορα).

In v. 9 ἔνδοξά τε καὶ ἐξαίσια, *both glorious and extraordinary things*, looks like a double rendering of נפלאות (= ἐξαίσια 37¹⁶; ἔνδοξα Ex 34¹⁰).

v. 10. הנתן is prob. a scribal error for נתן, as it is followed by שׁלח, and the ptcpp. of the other verses are anarthrous. The verse briefly indicates one department of God's wonder-working power. It is dwelt on at greater length, 38²⁵ ᶠᶠ. For the connexion of thought see Ps 107³³ ᶠᶠ God sends or withholds rain according to human desert. It is a feature of His moral government of mankind. Knowing nothing of the natural causes of atmospheric changes, the poet and his contemporaries regarded them as directly miraculous. For another view of their relation to conduct, see Mt 5⁴⁵. The verse is prob a (marginal?) quotation, since it is written in a different measure (four beats in each stichus).

the commons: or open country *outside* (חוּץ) the towns; 18¹⁷ (leg. plur., as here); Pr 8²⁶. The √ חוּץ = חצץ = חצה, &c., akin to קוץ = קצץ = קצה, &c., and the prob. more primitive (נח), גוז, גוה, &c. All these roots and their derivv. denote various kinds of *cutting, dividing, parting, separating, cutting off, ending*, and the original biliteral forms may be recognized in the Sumerian ĜAZ, ĜASH, GAZ, ḫaçâbu, ḫaçâçu, ḫipû, palâqu, dâku, &c. The street is the place where the houses are *cut off* or end abruptly, their end or boundary (קָצֶה, קצץ); the open field or country is the border or boundary of the town.

v. 11. the humble: or lowly; prob. in station, through poverty. God fertilizes their fields with His rain, and so raises them to wealth and prosperity. See Ps 107³⁵⁻³⁸

And to raise. יִשְׂגְּבוּ for שָׂגְבוּ, which cannot well continue the construction after the Infin. of Purpose לָשׂוּם. 𝔊 ἐξεγείροντα implies Pi.

them that mourn: scil. over the drought and barrenness of their land. קדרים: so קדרו, Je 14² (in a similar connexion. The whole chapter supplies an excellent illustration of our passage, clearly establishing the connexion between vv. 9–11, which some have needlessly doubted). 𝔊 ἀπολωλότας = אבדו; a misreading. *to wellbeing.* יֵשַׁע *accus. loci*; but restore לְיֵשַׁע or בישע (cf. למרום *ante*). Perhaps יֶשְׁגַּב יִשְׁעוֹ (cf. Ps 69³⁰), *His salvation setteth on high* or *raiseth*.

v. 12. As God exhibits His overruling Power by lifting up the humble, so He also displays it when He will by turning the wisdom of the worldly-wise into foolishness, causing them to overreach themselves and their own schemes to issue in their overthrow (2 Sa 15³¹ Ps 5¹¹ 18²⁶ᵇ). No mortal can hope to outwit the Allwise. Cf. 1 Co 1²⁰ 3¹⁹. We have here an implied contradiction of a primitive idea concerning the unseen Powers (see note on 1¹; and cf. the frauds practised upon Cronos, Silenus, and other gods in the Greek mythology).

thwarteth: or *frustrateth*: מפר: lit. *breaketh* or *shattereth*: of plans, *maketh to fail*. Ps 33¹⁰ Pr 15²² 2 Sa 15³⁴. (𝔊 διαλλάσσοντα = ממ(י)ר; a misreading of similar letters.)

achieve no success; or effect nothing real or solid. תושיה (from ישה like תוגה from ינה) strictly means *being, existence, fact, reality*, and so *solid or substantial counsel, practical wisdom*, and its result *success*. The √ישה, which in Heb. has been supplanted by the substantival יש, appears in Assyr. as išû, Pf. îšî, Pm. išâku, *to have, to exist, to be*. Thus 𝔊 ἀληθές, (anything) *real* or *substantial*, any solid result, is apt enough. Perhaps, however, we should read תשועה *deliverance*, as 𝔊 does (wrongly) in 30²²: *So that their hands effect no deliverance.*

v. 13. *catcheth* or *snareth*, as in a trap: Je 5²⁶ Pr 5²² Am 3⁵.

in their own craft or *cunning* or *shrewdness* or *prudence* (Pr 1⁴ 8⁵·¹²): (𝔊 ἐν τῇ φρονήσει (but 𝔊ᴬ + αὐτῶν), perhaps reading בְּעָרְמָה זוּ בְּעָרְמָם (from עָרֵם, which is not otherwise found) is improb. Leg. בְּעָרְמָתָם (cf. Pr *ll. cc.*), and see S. Paul's quotation from memory, 1 Co 3¹⁹ (ὁ δρασ-σόμενος τοὺς σοφοὺς ἐν τῇ πανουργίᾳ αὐτῶν). For the idea, see also Ps 7¹⁵f. 9¹⁵f. Pr 26²⁷. Ec 10⁸, &c. What seemed a faultless plan may fail, and even involve its authors in ruin. בְּאָרְבָּם *in their treachery* (Je 9⁷) is unsuitable. The irony of Fortune, or rather of Providence, may defeat the schemes of the wisest. Cf. Pr 21³⁰.

the shifty; or *tortuous*: lit. those who *twist* and *writhe*, as in wrestling (נפתלים; cf. Gn 30⁸ Ps 18²⁶ᵇ Pr 8⁸). 𝔊 πολυπλόκων, *much-tangled* or *twisting*; cf. πολυπλοκία, *craftiness* (but Σ σκολιά).

maketh vain: יְהַבְלָה for נמהרה. 𝔊 ἐξέστησεν, *he deranged* or *distracted* = יְהֹלֵל, *maketh foolish* (12¹⁷), which is possibly right (יהוללה or מהוללה, as Ec 2²): cf. Is 44²⁵. Otherwise we might restore יהפכה *he changeth* or *overthroweth* or *perverteth it* (v. 5); or even יַהְבִּלֶנָּה *he maketh it vain* or *futile*. An Impf. seems to be required by the context; and in any case נמהר, which is only used of persons elsewhere (Is 32⁴ 35⁴ Hb 1⁶; all), is unsatisfactory here. It cannot mean 'is carried headlong' (to ruin?), as RV, but only 'is hurried, hasty, impetuous, anxious', or the like: an inadequate sense in the context.

v. 14. Quem Deus vult perdere prius dementat, 12¹⁶ Je 4¹⁰ 20⁷ 1 K 22²⁰ Ez 14⁹ Ro 1²¹ f. 2 Th 2¹¹. Judicial blindness obscures even the obvious. Their clever schemes having failed, the worldly-wise are lost in bewilderment. We may remember that the zealous propagandists of Negation have not yet found any better substitute for the Light of the

World (Joh 8¹² 12³⁵ᶠ·) than a dark and dreary pessimism, whose ultimate outcome can only be the paralysis of moral endeavour and despair of the future of the race. Cf. Is 58¹⁰ 59¹⁰ (and perhaps read ינשעו after the latter passage).

v. 15. אָז ויֹשע מחרב מפיהם *and he hath saved from the sword from their mouth* is clearly corrupt, as the transitive verb requires an object in place of the meaningless מפיהם which, moreover, violates the parallelism. It may be regarded as a gloss on מחרב which has displaced the original עָנִי *poor, humble*, a common ‖ to אביון 24⁴ Pr 31²⁰. The *ductus litterarum* might also suggest יתום *the orphan* (Je 5²⁸). Duhm strangely alters וישע into וִישַׁע! 'aber er wird retten', as if Eliphaz were making a special promise to Eyob, instead of a general statement of the Divine procedure. (The Impf. c Waw Conv., in continuation of the Ptcpp. מפר לבד, affirms what God has always done in the past and therefore will do in the future) 𝔊 ἀπόλοι(ν)το δὲ ἐν πολέμῳ implies וישם or וישד for וישע. In st. ii ἐξέλθοι may represent a guess of (Aram.) מפיק for מפיהם.

v. 16. Lit. *And there became to the weak a hope; And Injustice, she shut her mouth.* False accusations, insults, and injurious menaces to the weak and helpless are shamed or scared into silence by the signal interposition of Heaven. St. ii recurs in Ps 107⁴² (an echo of this passage). Cf. also Is 52¹⁵. For עולה *injustice* or iniquity, in the special sense of untruthful language, see 13⁷ 27⁴.

vv. 17-24. Affliction is a blessing in disguise; and, if humbly accepted as such, can only issue in greater good than ever.

v. 17. The emphatic exclamation אשרי should naturally head its own sentence, as in Ps 1¹ *al. saep*. The intrusive הנה (om. 5 codd.; 𝔊 𝔙 𝔖) is prob. from the hand of a copyist who, ignoring the rhythm, desired to call special attention to what follows. Om. also אלוה metr. grat. For the sentiment see Pr 3¹¹·¹² (where in v. 12 we must read ויכאיב *and he hurteth*, as here, instead of וכאב *and like a father*). See also Heb 12⁵⁻¹¹. Elihu amplifies the idea of the remedial intention of sickness, 33¹⁷⁻³⁰.

v. 18. Or, *For 'tis He that hurteth*, &c. Sickness and health, weal and woe, are both from God, as Eyob, of course, admitted equally with his would-be monitor. It was the ground of his perplexity. For the thought see Ho 6¹ Dt 32³⁹ Ps 147³. *bind up*. 𝔊 πάλιν ἀποκαθίστησιν = ישיב for יחבש. But 𝔊ˢ ἐπιθήσει = ישים, 𝔊ᴬ μοτώσει *will bandage* (= יחבש Ho 6¹ 𝔊). Ad fin. v. תרפינה = תרפאנה (י for א, by attraction of preceding *e*-vowel; or perhaps a mere scribal error).

v. 19. *In six* . . . *And in seven* . . . This shows that בשש is right, not משש (wrongly inferred from 𝔊 ἑξάκις ἐξαναγκῶν κτλ.). The sense is: In all successive troubles, no matter how many, He will deliver thee. For the mode of speaking, cf. Pr 6¹⁶⁻¹⁹: *These six things hateth IAHVAH, And seven are an abomination of His soul. The seven are* then enumerated. Cf. also Pr 30¹⁵ᶠᶠ·. Accordingly, we should expect a similar enumeration here, if the text be sound; and, in fact, vv. 20–22 supply it even in the traditional text.

v. 20. The first two 'straits'—War and Famine. *he will ransom thee*: Heb פדך: a Pf. of Future Certainty. 𝔊 rightly ῥύσεταί σε. The Common-Semitic √פדה, Assyr. *padû, to release, set free*, prob. goes back to the Sum. BAD, *to open*, as do also *pitû*, פתח, פתה, &c. 𝔐 מידי dual. Leg. מיר sing., c 𝔊 ἐκ χειρός, and Ho 13¹⁴; Ps 22²¹ al.

v. 21. *from the lash* (or *scourge*) *of the tongue* = 𝔊 ἀπὸ μάστιγὸς γλώσσης. מָשׁוֹט for בְּשׁוֹט. Cf. Ps 31²¹. But all the other evils mentioned are physical calamities; and it is strange to find slander in such company. Moreover, God's four sore judgements had become almost a proverb (Famine, Wild Beasts, Pestilence, and Sword: Ez 15¹⁷ 14¹⁸ ᵃˡ; cf. Le 26¹⁶⁻²⁶ Dt 32²⁴ᶠ·); and after the 'Famine' and 'Sword' of v. 20, Wild Beasts and Pestilence would naturally follow. And as the former are specified in v. 22 (חית הארץ), mention of the latter might well be expected in the intervening verse. Now שׁוֹט *whip* (Na 3²) seems to occur in 9²³ fig. = Divine Scourge, Plague, or some other calamity (cf. Is 10²⁶; not 28¹⁵: see Box ad loc.), but is not so found elsewhere in Job. On the other hand, we have שׁוּט, 1⁷ 2², of Satan's roaming and roving about the earth. We may therefore point בְּשֻׁוט, and reading רֶשֶׁף *pestilence* (Hb 3⁵ Dt 32²⁴) for לְשׁוֹן *tongue* (with Duhm), we get the sense *When the Pest is abroad, thou shalt be hidden*. With שׁוט here cf. יהלך, Ps 91⁶; a passage which also suggests בְּשׁוּד קָטָב *when Plague wasteth* (or *killeth*, Ju 5²⁷ Je 5⁸). For קטב as a syn. of רשׁף pestis, cf. Dt 32²⁴ (Ho 13¹⁴ = דֶּבֶר id.). We might get the same general sense by reading the whole verse thus:

מִשּׁוֹד יָשׁוּד תֵּחָבֵא
ולא תירא רשׁף כי תבוא =

From the Scourge that killeth thou shalt be hidden (cf. Ps 91⁴),
And thou shalt not fear the Pest when it cometh.

ישׁוד for לשׁון; רשׁף = משׁד reversed! But שׁוד almost certainly echoes ישׁוד in Ps 91 l. c. (note the Med. ן); and there are other points of connexion with the psalm, as we shall see presently.

v. 22. 'dl (dupl)' is Kittel's curt and positive note. It is true that we have לא תירא and משׁוד in v. 21 and אל תירא and לשׁד in v. 22; while כפן *famine*, v. 22 (also 30³) is an Aramaism = רעב, v. 20. If, however, v. 22 was originally a mere duplicate of the previous verse, the poet's catalogue of Seven Evils cannot satisfactorily be made out. But שׁד may represent a partly effaced שׁחל, and כפן may be a disguise of פתן, the letters כפת being subject to frequent confusion in Hebrew manuscripts. We therefore restore לשׁחל ילפתן תשׂחק (cf. 11) *At the lion and the cobra thou shalt laugh, And of the beasts of the earth thou shalt not* (leg. ולא) *be afraid.* Cf. Ps 91¹⁴. A cross-division, no doubt; but the poet is enumerating objects of terror, after his literary precedents, and is not attempting a zoological classification.

𝔊ᴮ ἀπὸ κακῶν ἐρχομένων hardly implies טרע for משׁ(ו)ד, but merely paraphrases 𝔐. 𝔊ᴬ ἀπὸ ταλαιπωρίας = משׁד; see Hb 1³ 2¹⁷. Instead of לשׁד ולכפן 𝔐 𝔊 gives ἀδίκων καὶ ἀνόμων = לְעָוֶל וּלְחָנֵף (see 18²¹ 29¹⁷ 31³ and Is 9¹⁶⁽¹⁷⁾), which may lend some support to לשׁחל ולפתן עו = שׁ; ה = ת, as often). 'Die Lesung der LXX: שׁדד und כפר,' aramäisch, kommt nicht ernstlich in Betracht' (Duhm). But that is not the reading of 𝔊, which never renders שׁדד by ἀδικεῖν or ἄδικος.

v. 23. Lit. *For with the sons* (בני) *of the field is thy covenant.* 𝔐 אבני *stones.* Rashi's conjecture of an older reading אַרְגֵי *lords,* in the sense of the mythical satyrs and the like, is less probable. The passage is a reminiscence of Ho 2²⁰⁽ᴬⱽ ¹⁸⁾; and בני השׂדה is a poetic variation of חית השׂדה. These, the wild boar, the fox, &c (Ps 80¹⁴ Ct 2¹⁵ Ho 2¹⁴⁽¹²⁾), will no longer ravage the fields and vineyards. 𝔊 om., not understanding the st., or by mere oversight.

Was אבני suggested by Ps 91¹²ᵇ פן תגוף באבן רגלך *Lest thou strike thy foot on the stone?* Driver thinks of a 'poet figure, implying that stones will not accumulate to mar his fields'. But how could this happen, except on a hill-side, or through human agency (2 K 3¹⁹), which is hardly implied here?

v. 24. *Shalt go over thy fold* or *muster thy flock.* For פקד see 1 Sa 11⁸ al. For נוה *sheepfold*(s) or *pastures,* see notes on *v.* 3. 𝔊ᴮ ἡ δὲ δίαιτα τῆς σκηνῆς σου οὐ μὴ ἁμάρτῃ, *The abode* (or *maintenance?*) *of thy tent shall not fail,* is curious. It looks as if 𝔊 read וּנְוֵה אָהֳלְךָ לֹא תֶחֱטָא (נוה = δίαιτα in vv. 3 and 8⁶). 𝔊ᴬ gives καὶ ἐπισκοπὴ τῆς εὐπρεπείας σου καὶ οὐ μὴ ἁμάρτῃς, pointing וּפָקַרְתָּ against the sense and mistaking נוה for נאוה.

v. 25. *And thou shalt know,* as before, *v.* 24. 'Dass beide Verse mit וְיָדַעְתָּ beginnen, ist nicht grade schon und wohl auch nicht ursprunglich.' The repetitions in vv. 21-25, however, may be regarded as rhetorical. They give the impression of eager urgency on the part of the speaker, as though he were making an extemporaneous appeal. It would have been as easy for the poet to vary his phrases as it is for a modern critic to find fault with a sameness which so effectively mimics the manner of unpremeditated speech. 8 codd. and 𝔊 𝔗 השׂדה *the field* pro 𝔐 הארץ *the earth*; but cf. Am 7².

v. 26. *with powers unimpaired:* or *in thy full vigour:* lit. *in thy moisture* or *freshness.* Thou shalt never become dry and sapless, like a withered tree; but shalt retain all thy faculties to the last, like Moses, Dt 34⁷, whose 'eye was not dim nor his natural force (לֵחַ) abated' at the age of 120. Leg. בְּלֵחֲךָ pro 𝔐 בְּכֶלַח here, and in 30² (the only other place where the doubtful word כֶּלַח occurs), עֲלֵימוֹ אָבַד לָחַם *such whose sap has perished.* (The Ar. كلّ *to show the teeth, grin,* lends no support to כָּלַח in the sense required by the context.) Cf. also Je 11¹⁹ (בלחמו>בלחו). 𝔊 om. hic; 30² legit, ut videtur, כָּלָה συντέλεια.

As the corn (lit. *heap* or *shock* of sheaves: Ex 22⁶ Ju 15⁵) *goeth up*; scil. to the high place where it was threshed and winnowed, the גֹּרֶן or threshing-floor. 𝔊ᴮ has a double or conflate version of the st., the alternative being the more accurate rendering (θιμωνιά = θημωνιά = classical θημών, *a heap*).

We cannot suppose a direct reference to the complete restoration of Eyob's fortunes in the Epilogue (42¹⁰ ff.), although Eliphaz perhaps poses as a Seer, 4¹² ff.. Nor has the poet for the moment forgotten (vv. 20, 24, 25) that Eyob has already lost his all—slaves, flocks and herds, and children alike. But neither can we suppose 'a gentle irony' (eine leise Ironie) to be intended by making Eliphaz develop his doctrine at such length in contradiction of the obvious facts of the case before him, and close with an emphatic assertion that things are really so unless indeed the same irony is to be traced in every reiteration of the same doctrine in the speeches of the Three Friends and even in those of Elihu. The section vv. 17–27 (*Happy the man,* &c., ... *in its season*), which reads almost like a psalm (cf. Pss 1, 91, 92, 112, 128, &c.), might conceivably be a quotation of a then well-known piece; in which case the poet would not feel free to make any material alteration in its phraseology. But that assumption is not essential to a right conception of the argument. The opening 'Happy is the man,' &c., is quite general; and the repeated 'thou's' and 'thee's' of the following verses are no more personal to Eyob than those of Ps 92. The poet, of course, knows the issue, but Eliphaz does not. The dénouement when it comes is a great surprise to the three friends who had been so certain of Eyob's guilt that they felt small sympathy for his miseries (cf. 6¹⁴ ff.). Vv. 19–26 cannot be a prophecy of Eyob's future, if only because of v. 27 which declares that what precedes is a statement of the results of the friends' personal observation and experience, which Eyob would do well to lay to heart. Eliphaz does not forget. The painful facts are before his eyes. He shows an appalling want of sympathy when he deliberately draws an idyllic picture of the good old man enjoying to the last those marks of the Divine favour—health, wealth, and numerous offspring—of which Eyob had so suddenly been bereft. He implies that if Eyob's life had always been governed by the rule of patient submission to the Divine Hand, alike in weal and woe, he would not have been brought to this pass, and his fortunes would have been far otherwise. Even now there is room for penitence and mercy; and Eyob may live to see brighter days. Eyob replies (7¹ ff) that it is too late; his sickness is fatal, and his sufferings will soon end in death.

6.4 NOTES ON THE TEXT 155

So far from ignoring or forgetting Eyob's ruined state, Eliphaz has it always present to his mind as proof absolute of that guilt which, according to him and his friends, such ruin must always imply. The section, as a whole, purports to set forth how God usually deals with the man who admits his fault and takes whatever ill befalls him as a Divine chastisement intended for his good. Had this always been Eyob's attitude, the blessedness described would have been his happy lot. But, as things were, his actual condition was crying evidence of the sin that caused it, and angry rebellion was an aggravation of the original offence. The only hope for him lies in acknowledgment and submission. In bitter contrast with the woful present, Eliphaz draws a picture of what might have been. In the long run it goes well with the good man who owns his faults and is patient under the Divine chastisement. His health, his crops, his cattle, his children, thrive, and his end is happy. Eyob's unparalleled calamities, the opposite of all this, are conclusive evidence of unacknowledged guilt; but if he will submit and humbly confess his fault, he may yet find mercy.

v. 27. *We have heard it*: שְׁמַעֲנָה; cf. ⓖ ταῦτά ἐστιν ἃ ἀκηκόαμεν. שִׁמְעָנָה 𝔐 *hear it!* The other pointing gives a better parallel, and is almost required with the emphatic אַתָּה which follows. ✓

Chapters 6, 7. Eyob's First Answer to Eliphaz.

Chapter 6. My affliction far outweighs my 'resentment', as you call it (בעש, 5²). I do not cry out without cause, any more than a wild ass or an ox would be noisy if he were not hungry. Complaining is the salt which helps me to stomach my sufferings. I long to die; for, worn out with disease, I am helpless and hopeless (vv. 1–13).

v. 2. *my misery* or *trouble* (אָנְיִי = ⓖ τὰς δὲ ὀδύνας μου· cf. 20¹⁰ Gn 35¹⁸). Or leg. אֵידִי *my calamity* or *distress*. Both words are common in Wisdom-Lit. 𝔐 (Q) הַוָּתִי *my ruin*; fem. sing. But in this sense the plur. is usual, Ps 91³ al. Pr 19¹³ v. 30 (30¹³ is corrupt). Moreover, a masc. subject is required for יכבד, v. ƒ. ל.

St. ii, lit. *And that they would lift* (Impers.=*were lifted*): ⓖ ἄραι, sing. *he* (or *one*) *would lift.* 'To lift' is also the etymological meaning of שקל, Assyr. *šaqâlu, to weigh* (cf. the Sum. GAL, *našû* = אָשָׂא, *lift, carry*); and our own 'weigh' = A. S. wegan, *lift, carry.* See Skeat.

v. 3. 𝔐 כי עתה *For now* (= then), as in 3¹³. The עתה overloads the st., and is superfluous. With the simile cf. Pr 27³.

wild: incoherent and disordered, like the babble of delirium. 𝔐 לָעוּ, Pf. of לוע or לעה. ⓖ τὰ ῥήματά μού ἐστιν φαῦλα, perhaps reading לָעֲוּ (?לְעָנוּ). cf. ⓖ Is 28¹¹ 33¹⁹ (of unintelligible foreign speech); Ho 7¹⁶. But see also Pr 20²⁵ Ob¹⁶. יַעֲלוּ *go up* (in the balance Ps 62¹⁰) gives a better parallel.

v. 4. *in my flesh*: בִּבְשָׂרִי 𝔊 𝔐 עֲשָׂרַי ... the act. tr. means 'ever present to my consciousness'. בְּעוֹרִי *in my skin* or בבשרי *in my flesh* = 𝕲 ἐν τῷ σώματί μου, is simpler, and yields a better ‖ to '*my spirit*'. Eyob's skin was the visible seat of his malady: see 7^5 19^{29} 30^{30}. For בשר = σῶμα, see 41^{15}. With the 'arrows of Shaddai', tipped with the poison of disease, we may compare the shafts of death which Apollo Smintheus shot at the Achaean host, Il. i. 44 ff. See also Ps $91^{5\,f.}$ Dt 28^{22} $32^{23\,f.}$ Ps 18^{15} Ez 5^{16} Ps 38^2 La $3^{12\,f.}$ al.

Whose venom my spirit drinketh. Om: אשר as superfluous and prosaic. It spoils the rhythm, unless we read שְׁחֻמתם. 𝕲 ὧν ὁ θυμὸς αὐτῶν ἐκπίνει μου τὸ αἷμα (θυμός = חֵמָה as in Dt 32^{33}) reads דמי for רוחי (רוּחִי).

Eloah's terrors array themselves against me = בְּעוּתֵי אלוה יערכוני. A questionable text. The first word recurs, Ps 88^{17} only; and 𝕲 gives ὅταν ἄρξωμαι λαλεῖν (= בִּפְצֹה אָמְרִי) κεντοῦσί με (= ידקרוני: cf. Nu 25^8 ἀπεκέντησεν = וידקר; Ju 9^{34} ἐξεκέντησεν αὐτόν = וידקרהו; κατακεντ Je 51^4), *Whenever I begin to speak, they stab me.*

Kittel's note 'l c 𝕲 יַעַבְרוּנִי cf I R 18, 18' is therefore incorrect as regards 𝕲 (עבר = διαστρέφειν in l. c., 1 K $18^{17\,f.}$). Otherwise Dillmann's יעברוני *trouble me* is a good suggestion, and perhaps better than יערקוני *gnaw me* (cf. 30^{17}). Duhm completes the tetrastich by transference of v. 7^a *My soul refuseth to rest*, which is certainly ingenious; see, however, the notes on that verse. Possibly a line like וְאֵימַת אֵל תְּבַעֲתַּנִי (33^7 9^{34} 3^5 $13^{11.21}$ 15^{24} Ps $88^{16\,f.}$) *And the dread of El affrighteth me* has fallen out owing to its resemblance to בעותי אלוה.

v. 5. As animals cry out for hunger, so I cry out for pain.

fodder: בְּלִיל (24^6): str. *moistened food, maslin*. See Is 30^{24} בְּלִיל חָמִיץ *fodder seasoned* with rock salt or with salt herbs, which would bring out the sap. The √בלל = Assyr. *balâlu, to pour, pour out* or *over, to moisten, wet*, and (of metals) *melt*. The primitive root is seen in the Sumerian BAL, *tabâku, to pour out*. (Om. Suff. c 𝕲𝔙𝔖.)

v. 6. *Is* tafıl *eaten without salt?* The name of some succulent vegetable, eaten as salad, seems to be required by the parallelism. In Arabic *tufl* means spittle (which is a slimy and, in health, a tasteless fluid), and *tafala* is *to spit* or *spirt saliva*. In the Talmud תָּפֵל = *unsalted, fresh*, of בָּשָׂר *flesh* and דָּג *fish*, as opp. to מָלִיחַ *salted* (Shab. 128^a), prob. as retaining the slimy and sticky juices which salt draws out. In Ez $13^{10\,ff.}$ תָּפֵל = the *plaster* of a wall (a slimy sticky substance, smeared over the surface) = Assyr. *tapalu*. In this last sense Heb. and Aram. have also טפל (13^4), *to plaster, stick on*, with the intermediate *t*, from the root D-B preserved in דבק *to stick* or *cling to*.

𝔖 ܠܡܕܡ *the thing that has lost its flavour* or *savour*, insulsum, insipidum (cf. Mt 5^{13}); a term used, like Heb. תָּפֵל (La 2^{14}) and תִּפְלָה *folly, unreason* (1^{22} Je 23^1), fig. in the sense of *foolish, silly*.

without salt: 𝔖 ولا سحمد is prob. a scribal error, due to reading

مُلَح *salt* backwards. 𝔗 תבשילא מדלית מלחא *cooked stuff in which is no salt.*

sap of bugloss (Anchusa officinalis). or *slimy juice of purslane* (Portulaca oleracea). Heb. בריר חלמות *in the slime of* ḥallāmūth. רִיר is *spittle* in 1 Sa 21¹⁴ (= Aram. רִירָא). As vb. it means *to flow, let flow* (Le 15³), and may be compared with Sum. RI, *to go, to flow, to beget* (also A-RI, *water—let flow* = beget; cf. Nu 24⁷); UG-RIA, *witchcraft, bewitching, enchantment* (*spittle—let flow*). The importance of spittle in Babylonian magic is well known. (RIR = RI-RI? The Arab. *rawwala, slaver, emit semen, rála, to slaver, riyál, slaver*, are younger forms. The same root R-L = R-R may perhaps be recognized in ערל *uncircumcised*; cf. Arab. أَغْرَل and أَغْرَل (רעל = רל triliteralized internally). The primary sense would be *fluxui obnoxius*.

חלמות: 𝔗 חלבון ביעתא וחלמונא *the white of an egg and the yolk*; combining two opposite interpretations. It adds: 'Another Targum. As no greenstuff (בשׂי = Syr. ܒܫܠܐ *wild rue!*) is eaten without salt, so there is no taste in the slime of the yolk (בריראּ דחלמונא).' The 'slime of the yolk' seems an odd way of signifying the 'white' of an egg. 𝔖 *Or is there taste* ܐܣܟܚܐܠ حيّ او ـــــه *in the slime of the* Anchusa *herb* (a kind of borage)? Saad., however, renders *fī rīqi'l ḥamqā'i*, in succo portulacae, *in the juice of purslane*; a leguminous plant which exudes mucilage (see Lane, s. v. حمق).

𝔊, which gives a good paraphrase of the last verse, has ἄρτος (לחם) for תפל (owing to confusion and transposition of similar letters); while instead of בריר חלמות it presents ἐν ῥήμασιν κενοῖς, reading בדברי (Ex 5⁹) and perhaps pointing חֲלֹמוֹת (= *in words of dreams*).

v. 7. In v. 7 a we find παύσασθαι = לרגיע (cf. Dt 28⁶⁵ תרגיע = ἀναπαύσει) and ἡ ὀργή μου = כעשׂי (v. 2) instead of נפשׁי. *For mine 'impatience' refuseth to rest* is at least a good variant, if not the original reading. Eyob's indignant outcries were the salt of his sufferings. For 7 b we have βρόμον (= βρῶμον) γὰρ ὁρῶ τὰ σῖτά μου (3²⁴) ὥσπερ ὀσμὴν λέοντος *For I perceive my food as rank as the reek of a lion*; a possible paraphrase of וְהֵמָּה כָּאֲרִי לַחְמִי. *It maketh my bread stink like the lion*. (Cf. 33²⁰: Bateson Wright.) Rejecting the improbable allusion to the smell of a lion, and reading כְּקִיא (= בקיא), we get the sense *It loathes it as vomit of my food* or *It makes my food loathsome* (lit. *stinking*) *as vomit*. הֵמָּה כְּדְוֵי לַחְמִי *They are like the sickness of my food*, which is clearly nonsense. It is quite likely, considering that in the ‖ passage 33²⁰ חיה is the subject of וזהמת and ‖ to נפש in the sense of *appetite* (38³⁰), that the true text here is זהמה חיתי לחמי *My Life loatheth my food*.

Duhm, after completing the quota to v. 4 [...] *My soul refuseth to r...* [...] דויר ברי לחמי [...]

to the margin as the perversion of an Aramaic gloss on חלמות, viz. הָמוֹ כַּדוּ חַלָמוֹן *They are*(?) *now egg-yolk*. Further, out of this gloss, already embodied in the text, 𝔊 made (א)המה כריח לבי *They are like the stink of a lion*. Duhm adds that, as Bickell notes, the Syrians call leprosy 'Lion-stench', because of the foul smell of the ulcers. Ingenious as all this may be, it leaves out half of 𝔊's rendering (βρόμον ὁρῶ τὰ σῖτά μου = לָחְמִי (?) וְהָמַת). Moreover, the plur. המה—המו cannot refer only to חלמות.

𝔊 *My soul is weary of its striking, Or my battle shouteth like a drunken man*, absurd as it sounds, agrees with 𝔐 in st. i, merely taking לנוע in its other sense, *to strike*; while in st. ii it points הָמָה *shouted* instead of הַמָּה *they* and לְחָמִי *my fighting* instead of לַחְמִי *my food*, and substitutes כְּרַוֶּה *ut ebrius* for the unintelligible כְּדְוֵי. The verse may be a marginal intrusion. Cf. Bickell.

v. 8. *My hope*. Apparently a reference to the words of Eliphaz, 4⁶ 5¹⁶. Eyob repudiates the suggestions of his mentor. His only hope and prayer is to die. תַּאֲוָתִי *my wish* (Hupfeld) would yield a closer ∥, but is hardly necessary. Ps 21³.

v. 9. *Eloah*; 𝔊 ὁ κύριος (also in v. 8, where 𝔊ᴬ θ͞c, i.e. θεός). Leg. שדי *Shaddai* here (= Κύριος, vv. 4, 14).

would will: or *be pleased*: or *undertake* (= 𝔊 ἀρξάμενος). The √יאל, ואל, may be compared with Sum. UL, *joy, pleasure* (*ullu, elṣu*), and MUL (= WUL), *shine, be bright*, whence also springs אל *God*.

crush: 4¹⁹ 19² al. 𝔊 τρωσάτω με. Prob. not a different reading. The translator uses τιτρώσκω loosely for various Heb. verbs: see 16⁶ 20²⁴ 41²⁰. Instead of *Would let loose* (יַתֵּר Hi. Impf. of נתר 37¹; Ps 105²⁵ Is 58⁶) *his hand and cut me off* (scil. like threads from the warp: Is 38¹²), 𝔊 writes εἰς τέλος δὲ μή με ἀνελέτω, *But let him not take me away utterly* (or *for ever*)!—a deliberate alteration. The daring language of the original shocked the translator's sense of reverence. It is possible, of course, that his text was illegible here, and that he read וְיֶתֶר לֹא יְבַצְּעֵנִי; but such a contradiction of the previous line is unlikely. 𝔊 perhaps remembered Je 10²⁴. (𝔊ᴬˣ ἐπιβαλὼν τὴν χεῖρα κτλ. more correctly. (For a similar prayer, cf. Nu 11¹⁵ 1 K 19⁴.)

v. 10 (a triplet) looks like a doctrinal gloss based upon Ps 119⁴⁹·⁵⁰. נֶחָמָתִי *my comfort*, occurs only there and here. קדוש *The Holy One* (Is 40²⁵ Hb 3³) is not a name of God elsewhere in Job. In fact, the word does not occur at all in the sing., and only twice in the plur. (as a designation of the Angels). Further, the Heb. text is very doubtful. The form וּתְהִי (Weak Waw c Juss.) naturally continues the previous construction: *And that my comfort might still exist*: which is almost meaningless. Reading וְאֵת, with three codd., 𝔈 (דֵּי), 𝔙, and, above all, with the archetypal passage Ps 119⁵⁰, and taking ותהי as beginning the Apodosis, we get the sense: *Then this should become my comfort* (𝕲 εἴη δέ μου πόλις τάφος = וּתְהִי עִיר קְבוּרָתִי); a misreading of similar letters, which really confirms 𝔐. For τάφος 𝕲^{AΘ} παράκλησις *recte*.

And I would exult. 𝔐 וַאֲסַלְּדָה; almost certainly corrupt. The *semel dict.* סלד, which in the Talmud = *aduri, retrahi*, does not suit here, and is prob. a disguise of עלם = עלז *to rejoice, exult,* which we find elsewhere only in Job (20^{18} 39^{13}), and in Pr 7^{18}†. The ἅπ. λεγ. חִילָה, again, should at least be the not uncommon חִיל (Ex 15^{14} and five other places; but not elsewhere in Job). לֹא יַחְמוֹל, however, which follows, can only refer to a person—in this case, God (cf. 16^{13} 27^{22}). We therefore restore בְּהָחִיל *when he tortureth* (Hi. Infin.—cf. Ps 29^{3}), or we might perhaps merely point בְּחִילוֹ = בְּחִילָה in the same sense. For לֹא leg. וְלֹא c 26 codd. The st. thus says · *And I would exult when He tortured and spared not!* 𝕲 ἐφ' ἧς ἐπὶ τειχέων ἡλλόμην ἐπ' αὐτῆς = וָאֶעֶלְסָה בְחִיקָהּ (or וָאֲדַלְּגָה; cf. Ps 18^{30}). St. in is not very clear. *For I have not hidden* (put out of sight) *the words* (moral precepts) *of the Holy One.* In 23^{12} he protests that he has treasured them in his bosom. For כחד Pi. *to hide* principles or facts of moral observation, cf. 15^{18} 27^{11}. If it be meant that Eyob has never disregarded the Commandments, and that 'no accusing conscience would therefore impair his comfort in death' (Dr), the verse would seem to hint at redress in the life beyond the grave. As we shall see, however, nothing of that kind is to be found anywhere in the rest of the book Eyob expected and obtained complete vindication in the present life. A more suitable statement would be something of this kind: 'It should still be my comfort and joy, amid the extremest agonies, that (כִּי; Ps 119^{50}) I have spoken nothing but the truth.' *That I have not hidden* = that I have openly declared; a meiosis. קָדוֹשׁ, which overweights the st. with a fourth stress, may be replaced by קֹדֶשׁ (cf. 𝕲 ῥήματα ἅγια) or even יָשָׁר (v. 25). What I said (3^{20}ff.) about God's dealings with man was not impious, as you suggest, but *holy* (i. e. blameless) or *right* (i.e. correct). Cf. 42^{7.8}. 𝕲 οὐ γὰρ ἐψευσάμην ῥήματα ἅγια Θεοῦ μου, *For I belied not holy words* (= broke not holy commandments?) *of my God* (𝕲^{A} ἐν ῥήματι θεοῦ). But כחד is not *negare, mentiri*, anywhere else in Job (where it occurs six times besides) or the OT, though the root has that meaning in Ethiopic (cf. also Ar. جحد negavit).

v. 11. *wait*: the attitude of hope is implied. יחל is used thus abs., 13^{15} 14^{14}. It is trans. in Ps 119^{49}; but cf. vv. 74, 81. 𝕲 ὑπομένω, cf. Ja 5^{11} τὴν ὑπομονὴν Ἰώβ. Add עוֹד *metri gratia*.

end: i. e. of life: its appointed limit: Ps 39^{5} Gn 6^{13} It seems implied that the end is near. *endure*: or *be patient*: lit. *prolong* or *lengthen my soul.* In Heb. length and shortness of soul or spirit mean patience and impatience respectively. So we speak of a 'short temper'.

v. 12. The second st. is metrically too short. Prob אִם (הֲיֵשׁ) has fallen out at the end before the following הא, v. 13. Also a Waw cop. (leg. ואם) has fallen out after Yod (י) *ad init.* st. ii.

of bronze. The anomalous and isolated adj. נחוש should probably be replaced by the subst. נחושה *copper, bronze* (28⁷ 40¹⁸ 41¹⁹; 20²⁴); the poetic equivalent of נְחֻשָׁה, the root of which has nothing to do with נחש *serpent* (from נחש = לחש *to hiss, whisper,* &c.), but prob. means *shining, brilliant*, and may be affiliated to the Sumerian GUSH, ĠUS, ĠUSH, and ĠASH, in the like sense (נ-חש = NI + ĠUŠ, *what is bright*; cf. Assyr. loan-word ḫuššû, *red-gleaming*, said of gold and other metals). Copper or bronze is a standard image of brightness in the similes of old Babylonian religious poetry (the incantations, exorcisms, &c.): e.g. IM-SUB-TA ĠEN-TA-SUB = *kîma kê mašši limmašiš,* 'Like glistening bronze let him *glisten*!' The obscure נחשת of Ez 16³⁶ may be compared with Assyr. *nuḫšu, overflow, luxury.*

v. 13. 𝔐 is again evidently corrupt. RV would require הלא instead of האם. The אם may have been repeated from the last verse, or have grown out of repetition of the following אין. Leg. הֵן *Lo!* a common word in Job (4¹⁸ 9¹¹ᶠ· 13¹⁵, &c.), c 𝔊𝔙, and עזרתה instead of עזרתי (Ps 60¹³ 63⁸): *Lo, there is no help in me;* no power of resistance, to bear up against my sufferings. But perhaps we should read לי for בי, in closer agreement with st. ii: *Behold, there is no help for me* (or *I have no help!*). In st. ii we must restore תשועה *aid, deliverance, salvation* (= 𝔊 βοήθεια), the ‖ to עזרת in Ps 60¹³. Cf. 5¹². [In st. i 𝔊's ἡ οὐκ ἐπ' αὐτῷ ἐπεποίθειν; implies no difference from 𝔐 except בו *in Him* for בי *in me.* The reading proposed by Duhm, הא מאין, which merely divides the letters differently, *Lo, whence is my help in me (myself?)?* = I have no inward strength at all, though yielding a tolerable sense, does not harmonize well with the form of st. ii, and finds but doubtful support in Is 40²⁴, where also the text is questionable. הֵא (Gn 47²³ Ez 16⁴³ ?) is not a Job-word.] ✓

v. 14. 𝔐 למס מרעהו חסד is meaningless. Nothing plausible can be made of לָמָּס; and a verb is demanded both for sense and parallelism. Now, in the section beginning with this verse (vv. 14-23) Eyob is very naturally upbraiding his friends for that lack of sympathy which makes them so ready to suspect him, and to reproach instead of consoling him. 𝔊 ἀπείπατο suggests מאס (cf. 10³ ἀπείπω = תמאס) or למאס for למס. The verb may be recognized in חסד (point חִסֵּר!), *he has reproached*; an Aramaism, as in Pr 25¹⁰. For מרעהו *his friend(s)*, see Pr 19⁷ Gn 26²⁶. Thus we recover the sense *Him that is dissolving his friend hath reproached; And the fear of Shaddai he* (the friend) *forsaketh.* ' is dissolving ' = is in the throes of dissolution, is already melting away or going to pieces (cf. 7¹ Ps 58 both Niph.). Since, however, מָאַס *to reject, despise,* is common in Job (5¹⁷ 8· 19ᵛ·al.), and since חֶסֶד *kindness, mercy, sympathy* is a good ‖ to ירְאַת שׁ׳ (Ho 6⁶ Mi 6⁸), it may perhaps seem preferable to restore מאס מרעי (ב)חסר *My friend hath refused mercy*. (Cf. 𝔊 *Mercy renounced me*.) 𝔊 oddly renders יראת by ἐπισκοπή, as if the root were ירא > ראה. The sentiment of RV is doubtless implicit in the modern doctrine of Toleration, but quite contrary to the spirit of the OT, which nowhere expresses forbearance towards the man 'who forsaketh the Fear of Shaddai'. And it is without parallel in the book of Job.

v. 15. *My own kinsmen have proved faithless as a Wâdy*; a winter torrent, which gradually dries up in summer, cheating the hopes of wayfarers who expect to find water there. 𝔊 χειμάρρους ἐκλείπων

transitory waters. Lit. *waters that pass away*: leg. מים יעברו: cf. 11¹⁶ בטים עברו. 𝔐 נחלים improb. repeats נחל from st. i. 𝔊 ἡ ὥσπερ κῦμα παρῆλθόν με: cf. 11¹⁶ ὥσπερ κῦμα παρελθόν. (𝔊 𝔖 omit אפיק)

v. 16. *with a pall of ice*: lit. *from ice*. 𝔊 curiously misrenders οἵτινές με διευλαβοῦντο, νῦν ἐπιπεπτώκασίν μοι ὥσπερ χιών ἢ κρύσταλλος πεπηγώς (cf. Ex 15⁸ 𝔊) = הינורים מני עתה נפלו עלי משלג וקרח. For גָּר = διευλαβ. see Dt 28⁶⁰ Je 22²⁵. It is a Job word, 3²⁵ 9²³. 𝔖 also gives דחלין *who fear*.

lay piled: or *pileth itself*: reading יִתְעָרֶם for 𝔐 יתעלם *hideth itself*. Cf. נֶעֶרְמוּ Niph., Ex 15⁸, and the Syriac use of the same root.

v. 17. *In the dry season*. reading חרב *scorching heat* for יורב(ו). Cf. Gn 31⁴⁰ Is 4⁶ *In the time of summer heat* (חֹרֶב) opp to קָרַח) is a much more natural expression than *In the time when they are burnt* (Du, versenkt werden), and חֹרֶב recurs, 30³⁰. We might also read שָׁרָב, Is 49¹⁰. The Waw belongs to the following word.

they disappear: ונצמתו: str. they are *silenced*, and so *destroyed* or *annihilated*. צמת (in Heb. a poetic word: Pss Job La 3⁵³) may be compared with the synonymous שמם, שמד (1. *silenced, struck dumb, astonished*; 2. *ravaged, destroyed*), and with דמם *become silent, perish* (SH = earlier D). Thus צמת = Ar. صمت to be or become *silent, mute*, or *speechless*.

when it is hot: or *when it becometh warm*. בְּחֻמּוֹ > בְּחֹם. There is no reference for the masc. suff., and the Waw belongs to the following verb (Waw Conv.). דָּעֲךָ *go out, be douted*, of a light (Aram.; poet. in Heb.), 18⁶ 21¹⁷ Pr 13⁹ Is 43¹⁷. Niph. here only (pass qs. 'are douted'). The word is an Internal Triliteralization of a root *DAG* = Sum. DAG, *go away, yield, give place, cease* (*naparkû*).

vv. 18–20 explain why the winter torrents have become 'a proverb of faithlessness. They disappoint the hopes of travellers who turn out of their way, expecting to find water in them, and perish in the desert. But there is something strange in the Hebrew of v. 18; and the difficulty does not altogether disappear with the reading אָרְחֹות (with one MS) for אָרְחוֹת etc. See Gn 37⁰ Is 21⁰. The same cl. m. evidently necessary to the sense in the next verse (point אָרְחוֹת!). RV *The caravans that travel by the way of them turn aside* makes the best of a bad case; but אורחות דרכם is a curious phrase, and st. ii *They go up into the Waste and perish* is surely the climax which should follow, not precede, vv. 19, 20. (The statement obviously cannot refer to 'the course of the streams being diverted and lost in the desert'. Water does not 'go up'.) First we have the caravans, v. 19, looking eagerly (3⁹) for the vanished waters; then their mortification at finding their confidence misplaced, v. 20; and finally their ascending by the dry bed of the wâdy into the desert again, to perish miserably (v. 18). Instead of ארחות in v. 18 we propose לאחור *backward*: cf. Ps 114⁸. The Niph. ילפתו should be pointed Pi., in the sense of *they bend* or *turn round*. So one cod. Cf. Ar. لفت *to twist, wring, or turn a thing about; to turn a man aside*. Cf. Niph. in Ru 3⁸. In Assyr. *lapâtu*, Pret. *ilput*, means *to turn, revolve* (of doors), *to overturn or overthrow*, and *to touch, handle*, or *take hold of* (cf. Ju 16²⁹). In v. 20 sense and metre require בָּטְחוּ בָם *they trusted in them* instead of the meaningless בָּטָח of 𝔐. 𝔊 𝔗 read the plur. In st. ii read עדיהם (referring to מים v. 15; cf. 16, 17) for עדיה.

In v. 17 𝔊 appears to have read לעמת שרב ובחמו לא נדע מקומו *According as it melted and when it became warm, its place* (or *existence* Aram.?) *was not known* (or נכר?). But in v. 18 it seems to depart entirely from the text of 𝔐 with the paraphrase: *So was I also forsaken by all; Yea I perished and became an outcast*. Yet this might be a loose rendering of יַפְּתוּ דרכם מעלי ומביתי אובד *They turn aside their way from me, And from my home I perish*, or something very similar; which hardly presupposes anything more than corruption of the text of 𝔐.

In v. 19 𝔊 mispoints הַבִּיטוּ and misreads לוי for קוּי; in v. 20 באו עדיהם has been mistaken for באן ועָרים (= ἐπὶ πόλεσιν καὶ χρήμασιν). 𝔊 turns the verse into a proverb: *And they will incur shame Who trust in cities and riches*.

v. 21. *Such ... to me*. Lit. *So now have ye become to me*: restoring כֵּן ... לִי for 𝔐 כִּי ... לוֹ. Instead of לוֹ *to him*, which is quite unsuitable here (if the statement were *For now ye are His*), the Ketib is לֹא *not*, which RV assumes may mean *nothing* (*For now ye are nothing*); but that is never the case. 𝔊 ἄταρ δὲ καὶ ὑμεῖς ἐπέβητέ μοι ἀνελεημόνως = כי אתם נהפכתם לאבור־לי: see 30²¹. Perhaps we should read כי אתם הייתם לאבזר־לי *For ye have become cruel to me*. לאבזר, moreover, might be 𝔊's misreading of לאכזב *a deceptive stream* (Je 15¹⁸).

In st. ii leg. וַתֵּרְאוּ. Waw has fallen out after Waw (or Yod). Cf. 𝔊 ὥστε ἰδόντες τὸ ἐμὸν τραῦμα φοβήθητε = וְתִרְאוּ כְּאֵבִי וּתִירָאוּ (τραῦμα = כאב, 16⁶; cf. the verb. 14²². כאבי *my pain* may be right here, instead of the ἅπ. λεγ. חֲתַת *a terror*. See also 2¹: *They saw that the pain was very great*). Eyob says: I had expected a refreshing draught of sympathy

6. 25   NOTES ON THE TEXT   163

from you, my old friends, to cool the heat of my torments; but at the sight of them you take alarm, and fear is apt to be cruel. They were afraid that unqualified sympathy might be construed as approval of Eyob's protestations and bring similar calamities upon themselves. In the next two verses (22, 23) Eyob takes an ironical tone. 'You need not be so alarmed. You are as cold and hard as if I had asked you for money. I have asked no material succour of you. Sympathy is cheap; and kind words cost nothing.' Eyob had asked no complimentary presents, such as are customary in the East (cf. 1 K 10$^{2.10\ 13.25}$), nor bribes to win the favour of a judge (cf. Mi 3^{11}), nor intervention (in the shape of propitiatory gifts?) between himself and powerful enemies, nor payment of ransom to brigands (? עריצים *terrible ones*), or figuratively, as in Je 15^{21}, deliverance from formidable foes. Perhaps עריץ sing. *the tyrant*, would be better; cf. the ||, and 15^{20} 27^{13} note (all the occurrences of עריץ in Job).

In v. 22 ⅁ paraphrases st. i, and ἐπιδέομαι in st. ii suggests שִׁחַרְתִּי *have I sought?* or perhaps חָשַׂרְתִּי (= חסרתי), *do I need?* (Dt 15^{8}), instead of שחדו.

vv. 24–26. Cease your dark hints, and speak out! tell me my sin plainly, and I will say no more. Or are you merely blaming the wild words of despair? Words are but wind.

v. 24. *Teach me*. like priests giving oracular responses (Mi 3^{11}).

mine error. Heb. מה שגיתי *how I have gone astray*; not so much wilfully (Eliphaz had not charged him with any wilful sin), as through the infirmity natural to man, 4^{19}. Yet see 4^{78}. But st. i ('I will be silent') and v. 25 f. indicate that it is rather the objection taken to the violence of his language and his questionings of Providence that Eyob intends. He maintains the practical innocence of his complaints, irreverent and presumptuous as they may seem to us.

v. 25 *Why are honest words* (lit. *words of uprightness*) *grievous* (*hard, difficult, intolerable*)? נמרצו: see 16^{3} Hi. *aggrieveth thee* (but leg. phps. יפריצך); 1 K 2^{8} and Burney's note ad loc.; Mi 2^{10} (?). The root מרץ is common in Assyr. in the senses *hard, difficult, troublesome, grievous, sick, painful* (of disease), *sorrowful*, and the like: e.g. ḫarânam namraça, *a road of difficulty*, Neb. ii. 21; Ša Ahuramazda utâmâ ina muḫḫika la imarruç, *What Ahuramazda commandeth, let it not be troublesome to thee!* Inscr. of Darius, Naksh-i-Rustam, 36. Eyob asks why his 'honest' (or truthful) words should annoy his friends so seriously. Cf. ⅁'s elegant paraphrase: 'But, as it seems, a truthful one's words are amiss.' We might also render the Heb. stichus as a sarcastic exclamation: *How painful* (or *grievous*) *are honest words!* There is therefore no need to substitute נמלצו (Ps 119^{103}) for נמרצו. c 1 MS and 𝔗.

And what . . . . Contemptuous irony. *Repr* . . . . . is more emphatic than y . . . . (הריחכם),

laying, as it does, a bitter stress on the pronoun. The expression is, however, isolated; and the Versions failed to understand it. ⅏ 'For not from you (מִכֶּם) do I beg strength (פֹּחַ)' virtually repeats v. 22.

v. 26. Lit. *Is it to reprove words that ye think?* ⅏ παύσει = תשבית for תחשבו. In st. ii the Heb. ולרוח אמרי נואש might perhaps mean *And (But) for the wind are the words of a despairing one!* if the context were different. But ולרוח prob. disguises a form ∥ to להוכח, perhaps ולניח (= ולהניח) *And to quiet*, > ולדיח *And to wash away*, Is 4⁴ (Dr), which, though nearer in form, is remoter in sense. וליסר *And to correct* (4³ al.), is also possible (Heth and Samech being sometimes confused in manuscripts: see Dr, *Mosheh ben Shesheth*, p. ix), or even וּלְחָרִישׁ *to silence* (11³†). ⅏ οὐδὲ γὰρ (⅏ᴬ om.) ὑμῶν φθέγμα ῥήματος ἀνέξομαι = ולא רוח אמרכם אשא. (For ἀνέχομαι = נשא see ⅏ˣ 21⁵). This suggests an illegible text rather than arbitrary alteration. Assuming dislocation of the original order of the Heb. words, and comparing 16⁸ (see also 8²), we might be inclined to more drastic emendation and read ולענות אמרי רוח *And to answer words of wind?* Cf. also 32¹² 33¹⁸.

v. 27. This verse, as it stands, is correctly rendered in RV. It seems to accuse the friends of a degree of hardheartedness that would stop at nothing where sordid gain was in view. Eyob, however, was not an unprotected 'orphan'; nor was there any question of 'bargaining' (40³⁰) over his person. The language looks proverbial, but is inappropriate to the context. Reading (by a different division of the letters) עלי תם for על יח(ו)ם, and (with ⅏ 𝔙) תָּפֹּלוּ instead of תַּפִּילוּ, and in st. ii (which is metrically short) וְתַחְבִּירוּ בְמִלִּים עַל־רֵעֲכֶם, we get the satisfactory couplet

> Even upon the blameless (1¹ 8²⁰ 9²⁰) *will ye fall*,
> *And join words together against your friend?*

Cf. ⅏, which gives ἐνάλλεσθε δέ for ותכרו here, and in 16⁴ renders אחבירה עליכם במלים by ἐναλοῦμαι ὑμῖν ῥήμασιν.

v. 28. *Look at me*: lit. *turn* or *face round*; as if they had averted their faces from him, in indignation or shame at his reproaches. Cf. 21⁸; and for פָּנָה בְ Ec 2¹¹. Look me in the face, he cries; eye to eye can I lie to you? (אִם Interrog. = *Num?* cf. v. 12.) ⅏ *But now, looking into your faces, I will not lie!* taking אִם (perhaps rightly) as the Particle of solemn asseveration common in oaths. As the st. is metr. short (2 beats), insert אני which may have fallen out before אם: *And to your face I* (emph.) *will not lie!*

v. 29. Go back on your hasty presumption of my guilt; and do me not the injustice of refusing to hear me out. The repeated שֻׁב is suspicious: ⅏ (καθίσατε δή) points the first שְׁבוּ *Be seated!* (as though the friends had risen to depart in disgust), and omits the second. For st. ii it gives καὶ πάλιν τῷ δικαίῳ συνέρχεσθε = ועוד עם־צדיק באו (cf. 22¹ καὶ συνελεύσεταί σοι εἰς κρίσιν = במשפט עמך יבוא, and 9³²). Now, as 𝔊^{Nca} and 𝔊^A add ἐν κρίσει at the end of st. i, some such reading as ובמשפט עוד צדקי יבוא: (*And let my righteousness again be tried!*) would appear to be indicated, or (lit as 𝔊): ובמשפט עוד עם־צדיק באו (*And into judgement again with a righteous one enter!*), or simply ובמשפט עוד־עמדי (ת)באו: (*And again with me enter into judgement!*). Other emendations might be suggested, e. g. והשבו עוד צדקי לי *And give me back my righteousness!* or, again, *Yea, return! my righteousness is still in me!* (בי for בה, which 𝔊𝔙 appear to omit). 𝔖 *Return now, and justify!* (= צדקי 32²) It would be better to point צְדָקִי *be just!* sc. in your judgement of me (?בי *in me* = in my case): cf. 10¹⁵ Ps 51⁶. ועוֹד צדק יבא *And again let Justice come!* is a plausible, if not a convincing conjecture (Kittel); but when Duhm retains the text of 𝔐, and renders *Yea return; my right is still therein*; i.e. I am justified in speaking as I do; we can hardly suppress the objection that there is no possible antecedent to בָה in the verse except עולה, with which, as he says, no reasonable man would think of connecting it. After all this, we shall perhaps be pardoned if we venture to make another suggestion, which has at least the merit of simplicity. Read ושמעו דברי צדקי *And hear my righteous words.*

v. 30. Is there really 'Injustice' (5¹⁶)—anything morally wrong—in what I have said? have I lost the faculty of discernment between truth and falsehood? Dr rendered st. ii: *Cannot my taste* (lit. *palate*) *discriminate calamities* (30¹³)? explaining, 'i.e. whether they are deserved or not'. But the Heb. seems rather to ask: *Or my palate—doth it not sense* (or *perceive*) '*calamities*' (if that be the meaning of הַוּוֹת)? The verb בין is used of sense-perception, 9¹¹ 14²¹ 13¹ al. (all c ל of Direct Obj., but Pr 7⁷ al. c Accus. as here). If Eyob's misfortunes be intended by הוות, the meaning will be: Does not my palate know calamity by its nauseous taste? i.e. My sufferings are not imaginary; I do not cry out for nothing (cf. 6⁶). This, however, is a bad ‖ to st. i, which demands to be informed whether there is any 'injustice' (of statement, untruth: 13⁷) in his 'tongue'; i.e. perhaps as an inherent incapacity for speaking aright or truly. If הוות might mean *deceit, falsehood* (cf. 13⁷ 27⁴ where the ‖ to עולה is רמיה), we might well adopt that meaning here. Now in Ps 5¹⁰ 38¹³ 52³ 55¹² Pr 17⁴ the word is associated with crafty speech and lying. Moreover, the Arabic uses of the root هوى (הוה) seem to indicate *hole, pit, hollow*, as the primitive meaning, from which the transition is easy and natural to the idea of *emptiness*, on the one hand, and to that of *falling down, inclining to*, &c, on the other See Lane. Thus הַוּוֹת *emptiness, hollowness, falsity, villainy*, whether of words or opinions, would be a synonym of שָׁוְא *emptiness, nothingness, falsity, worthlessness* (7³ 11¹¹ 15³¹ 31⁵ al. .

(It is, o. cour… possible that the ר of רמיה c… was i…identally omitted, and that מיה was then read backwards as הות, since ו and י, מ and ח, are often mistaken for each other in Hebrew manuscripts.)

(𝔊 ἢ ὁ λάρυγξ μου οὐχὶ σύνεσιν μελετᾷ; = ; אם חכי לא בינה יהנה (cf. 27⁴ Is 59³ Ps 35²⁸ = 𝔊 34³²); an interesting but hardly correct substitute for 𝔐, which 𝔖𝔙𝔗 also failed to understand. (𝔊 perhaps read אמת *truth* for הות.) Cf. also Ma 2⁶.

Chapter 7. After a brief pause, as it would seem, Eyob resumes his pleadings, which appear to be aimed at God rather than the three friends. It is a passage which reads like an exquisitely plaintive and pathetic elegy, lamenting the general hardness of man's lot, but more especially his own hopeless misery which has no prospect but speedy death. Therefore he is bold to remonstrate with his Maker, and to demand why He cares to persecute to the death a being so infinitely beneath Himself as mortal Man.

vv. 11–21. In 6²⁸⁻³⁰ Eyob has begged a further hearing, on the ground that his tongue and his palate, his powers of speech and his moral sense, are still unimpaired. In 7¹¹ he continues: *I also will not restrain* (16⁶) *my mouth*: I will speak as freely as you have done. (RV *Therefore I will not,* &c.; but גם אני means *I also, I too*, with emphatic Pron.) This statement follows naturally on 6³⁰. We have therefore transposed the section to the beginning of the chapter. The division of the chapters is evidently, as often, quite arbitrary.

v. 11. The verse, as it stands, is a triplet. A stichus like אפתחה שפתי עמך *I will open my lips with Thee* (cf. 11⁵ 32²⁰), or שפתי לא אֶכְלָא *My lips I will not shut* (cf. Ps 40¹⁰) may be supplied to complete the quatrain. The former seems preferable. 𝔊 opens st. iii with ἀνοίξω (= אפתחה: 3¹ al.), and עמך supplies a reference for 'Thou' (vv. 12, 14). Otherwise we might be tempted to think that stt. ii, iii were variant forms of the same line derived from different editions or recensions of the Heb. text; 'doublets' such as we find, for instance, in the old Babylonian Epic of Nimrod (Gilgamesh). Cf. 10¹ אדברה במר נפשי *I will speak in the bitterness of my soul*, which Bickell and Duhm consider to be the true reading here (after 'die ursprüngliche LXX' [?]), interpolated there.

v. 12. An allusion to the ancient Babylonian mythus of Creation, which told how Bel-Merodach, the great god of Light, after his supreme conflict with Tiâmat (חהום), the mighty Dragon of the primeval chaos of waters, divided her vast carcase between heaven and earth, spreading half of it over heaven ('the waters above the firmament': Gn 1); after which 'He drew bolt(s), he posted a watch, He charged them not to suffer her waters to come forth' (*mišlušša iškunamma šamāma uçallil; išdud parkū maççarū ušaçbit; mēša la ŝûçâ šunuti imta'ir*. Creation Tab. IV. 138–40). The naked brevity of the reference here proves that the poet assumed that the allusion would be familiar to his readers. See also 26¹²

38⁸⁻¹⁰; Is 27¹ 51⁹. The word תַּנִּין *serpent, dragon*, used in Heb. of aquatic monsters, and in these passages of the legendary Monster of the Deep, may be derived from the √תנן = Assyr. *danânu*, דנן *to be strong* (cf. *nadânu* = נתן, and conversely *abâtu, kabâtu* = אבד, כבד; also TA *tanniš* = *danniš*, &c.), and would thus mean, strictly speaking, *strong, mighty, forceful* one. The Heb. *tannín* is, in that case, etymologically and formally identical with the Assyrio-Babylonian *dannínu*, a syn. of *irçitu, the Earth* (Creation Tab. VII. 115; 5 R 21. 59); and the Earth, as fashioned out of the other half of Tiâmat, may have been mythically conceived as a huge dragon lying in the Deep and rising above it (cf. 2 Pe 3⁵ · 'Earth, consolidated out of Water and amid Water').

v. 13. *When I say.* Or *If I think* (= *say* in my heart. בלבב may be either expressed, as in Ps 10⁶ ¹¹ ¹³, or omitted).

will take away part of my complaining. שיחי for 𝔐 בשיחי. If we keep 𝔐, we must render *My bed will help me bear*, &c., supplying אתי *with me*, which is expressed in the same construction, Nu 11¹⁷. 𝔊 ἀνοίσω δὲ πρὸς ἐμαυτὸν ἰδίᾳ λόγον (A διάλογον ἰδίᾳ) τῇ κοίτῃ μου = אשא שיחי במשכבי, taking שיח in the sense of *talk*, and changing the Pers. of the Verb. (Prob. not a different reading, but a misinterpretation of the text.)

v. 14. *with visions.* 'בחז for 'מחז, which is a reminiscence of 4¹³. 𝔊 ἐν ὁράμασιν *recte*. Fearful dreams were believed to be divine portents of imminent evil. They are said to be characteristic of Eyob's malady (Elephantiasis). Both stichi of this verse are metrically defective, unless we admit that a long word may have two stresses. Of course we might suppose that a word has fallen out of each member, e. g. לילה and ראשי respectively: *Thou scarest me with dreams of the night, And with the visions of my head* (Dan 2²⁸ 7¹ ¹⁵ Aram.) *affrightest me*, cf. 4¹³ 20⁸ 33¹⁵. It is also possible that Eyob dwelt upon the fact that even his bed, instead of giving him some respite, only aggravated his miseries. Accordingly, על־ערשי, על־משכבי, may once have stood in the verse: *Thou scarest me with dreams on my couch, And with visions on my bed Thou affrightest me.*

v. 15. As pointed, 𝔐 can only mean: *And Thou hast chosen the strangling of my soul.* Point מַחֲנָק instead of the Stat. Constr. מַחֲנַק. The word occurs here only; but see 2 Sa 17²³ for the related verb (חנק). This root is cognate with ענק, Ar *onq*, Aram. עוּנְקָא *neck*, which look like worn forms of the Sumerian GU(N), *neck*, with nasalized final sound (cf. Chinese *king, kêng, neck, throat,* and *hiang, hong, ngoñg, nape of neck*).

𝔊 ἀπαλλάξεις ἀπὸ πνεύματός μου (𝔊ᴬ om. μου) τὴν ψυχήν (𝔊ᴬ ζωήν) μου = נפשי)׳ מרוחי) תסיר חיתי (𝔊ᴬ, ut 33²²) *Thou removest* (9³⁴ 27⁵ 34⁸) *from* (my) *spirit my soul* (life). This seems to depend on misreading of similar and partially effaced Heb. letters. For it. ii, which like both members of v. 14 (q. v.) appears to have lost a third accented word,

𝔊ᴮ gives ἀπὸ δὲ θανάτου τὰ ὀστᾶ μου = וּמִמּוֹת עַצְמוֹתִי (= 𝔐, slightly modified to suit 𝔊's version of st. i). (𝔊ᴬ τὴν δὲ ψυχήν μου ἀπὸ τοῦ σώματός μου = וְנַפְשִׁי מֵעַצְמִי. Cf. Ps 139¹⁵ (עָצְמִי). This does not help us much, although מות *And death* is prob. right > מוח (ו having fallen out after י as often). Reading מַעְצְבוֹתִי (9²⁸) in place of מַעְצְמוֹתִי, we get the passable sense *And death rather than my pains.* (RV *And death rather than* these *my bones* = *rather than* this *skeleton* will not do; if only for the reason that the indispensable pronoun is wanting in the Heb.). We may further reinstate some verb denoting desire after מות; e. g. אִוְּתָה, the Subject of which is usually נפש (23¹³), or חֻפְּתָה c לְ (3²¹). The spirit of the suggestion (Reiske and others) that מאסתי, the (corrupt?) word which now begins v. 16, should really end v. 15, is too modern. Duhm translates: *Den Tod verachte ich vor meinen Schmerzen.* But Eyob never speaks of *despising* death. He longs for it, as the sure end of his miseries (chap. 3 throughout). There is pathos and an intense melancholy in the tone of 7⁹·¹⁰·²¹ 9²⁵ f. 10¹⁸⁻²² 14 (throughout), but never a word of contempt. In fact, nowhere in the OT is death so regarded. Moreover, if we detach מאסתי from it, st. i of v. 16 becomes metrically too short. We may read נמאסתי *I flow, dissolve, melt* or *waste away*, sc. with my malady (v. 5 ad fin.); cf. the cognate roots מסס Niph. *to melt, flow away* (Ps 58⁸) and מסה id.: or better perhaps אמרתי *I have said* (*Methinks*), as in v. 13. 𝔊 om.¹ (These words are prob. akin to Assyr. *misû, wash, purify*, and *mašâšu* Niph. *become bright*; the ultimate primary root being the Sumerian MASH, *bright, shining, to purify*. The other and much commoner מָאַס *reject, despise*, springs from a root MAS = BAS, BAZ, preserved in בּוּז, בָּזָה *despise*, and בּוּס *trample on*, which last perhaps contains the original idea.)

v. 16. *I cannot always live*: lit. *Not for ever shall I live.* It seems hardly worth while for the Eternal to persecute His ephemeral creature, or to pay so much attention to mortal man. Cf. Is 2²². Vv. 17, 18 apply the thought of Ps 8⁴ in a bitterly ironical sense.

v. 17. *set thy mind upon him*: or *give thy thought to him*; *heed* or *notice him*, 1⁸.

v. 18. *visit*: or *observe*. Cf. 10¹² 31¹⁴ 35¹⁵. Rather perhaps: *visit his faults with* punishment (cf. v. 21). לִבְקָרִים, as in Ps 73¹⁴ Is 33² al. (not לְבֹקֶר ut 𝔐). לִרְגָעִים *at moments*; *momently*. Is 27³ Ez 26¹⁶ al. *try*: *test* or *examine* his moral condition. (Point וְתִפְקֹד, not וַתִּפְקֹד. Cf. 𝔊, which, however, misunderstands the Adverbial expressions with its ἕως τὸ πρωί and καὶ εἰς ἀνάπαυσιν = וְלָרְגִיעַ: cf. Dt 28⁶⁵ Is 34¹⁴: perhaps וְלַמַּרְגּוֹעַ: cf. Je 6¹⁶). From the metrical point of view, the remarks on v. 14 apply to this verse also. Possibly the Adv. expression was originally repeated in each stichus, to indicate the systematic regularity of the visitations

¹ [... ἵνα μακροθυμήσῃς ' מאסתי ' כי א א ריך · misread are transposed?).

(cf יוֹם יוֹם *day by day*) A scribe may have omitted the repeated words as needless, or by sheer inadvertence.

v. 19. *How long?* בַּמָּה: so also in Ps 35¹⁷. In 13²³ Ps 119⁸⁴ it means *How many?*; in 21¹⁷ *How often?* Cf. Ps 78⁴⁰. *look away from me.* See Ps 39¹⁴. *Nor give me a moment's respite?* lit. *Wilt not drop me until I swallow my spittle?* (30¹⁰. רֹק *saliva*, רָקַק, יָרַק *to spit*; cf. Sum. UĠ, *id.* The other ירק = Sum. RIG, *green*.) 𝔊 adds ἐν ὀδύνῃ; a gloss implying (wrongly) that he 'swallowed his spittle', or gulped, for pain.

v. 20. Restore אִם before חטאתי: see the echo of this question, 35⁶, which also proves that the meaning cannot be: *If I have sinned, what shall I do for Thee* (sc. by way of satisfaction), but *If I have sinned, what do I to Thy detriment?* (Dr: 'how can I injure Thee?'). How can anything I do affect God, one way or the other? Cf. also the like implications of Eliphaz, 22²·³. 'Die unpoetische Form macht aber v. 20ᵃ verdächtig,' says Duhm. The form is, however, practically identical with that of 35⁶. נֹצֵר הָאָדָם *Thou Guard* (or *Keeper*) *of Man!* which would usually imply protection (cf the syn. שֹׁמֵר, 14¹⁶ Ps 121), has here the unfavourable sense of keeper or guard of prisoners and the like. The metre might be completed by inserting עָלַי *over* after נֹצֵר (cf. Ps 141³) or better לֵב *heart* (𝔊 τὸν νοῦν = לֵב, as in v. 17); but perhaps the first half of the verse should follow the second The transposition would give us three couplets in Qînah-measure for the close of the chapter.

> If I sin, what do I to Thee,
>   Thou Keeper of Man?
> And why not pardon my fault,
>   And let my guilt pass?
> For soon in the dust I must lie,
>   And Thou seek me when gone!

Wherefore hast Thou set me for a butt to Thee? מִפְגָּע something to aim at, hit or attack; a *butt* or *mark*; syn. (ἅπ·) of מטרה which follows. (𝔊 κατεντευκτήν σου, 'thine assailant', pointing מַפְגִּיעַ. Cf. 36³².) *So that I am become Thy target?* = ואהיה לך למטרא: cf. 16¹² La 3¹². This at least provides a better parallel than 𝔐: ואהיה עלי למשא *So that I am become a burden on me* (i.e. *myself*). Cf. 2 Sa 15³³. עָלַי *on me* is one of the eighteen changes of reading made by the Scribes, according to Jewish tradition (תקוני סופרים), on the ground of religious reverence, עָלֶיךָ *on Thee* having been the original text (cf. 𝔊 εἰμὶ δὲ ἐπὶ σοὶ φορτίον). The change, as in other instances, cannot but seem childish, in view of the many far more daring expressions which have been left unaltered in the speeches of Eyob.

v. 21. *And why*. Leg. וּלָמָּה (𝔊 καὶ διὰ τί), as in v. 20. The question *And why dost Thou not take away* (or *forgive*) *my transgression*, &c. implies the prec line אם חטאתי (*. .*) and supplies the obvious genuineness. Instead of תִשָּׂא (𝔊 pass. תִּשָּׂא or תִשֶּׁה (*/ . ./*, or rather Hi, תָשִׁיא)

cause to forget (οὐκ ἐποιήσω τῆς ἀνομίας μοι λήθην). In st. ii the insertion of מֵעָלַי after וְתַעֲבִיר (cf. Zc 3⁴) would restore the normal measure: *And let my sin pass from me?*

For now. As it is, my punishment is fatal; and pardon will come too late after the inevitable end. For 𝔐 לֶעָפָר read עַל־עָפָר with the verb שָׁכַב, as in 20¹¹ 21²⁶. *To lie down on the ground* = to die.

v. 1. *a hard service*: or *a term of warfare*. The word צָבָא is used of the work done by the Levites in the Sanctuary, Nu 4^{3.23 al.}, which was certainly arduous enough; and the context here requires the meaning *service*, as in 14¹⁴. [There can be little doubt of the identity of Heb. צבא *army, warfare, service*, (and the Denom. צבא *to war*), with Assyr. çâbu (from çab'u), *man, warrior*, the common ideogram of which is, in the primitive Sumerian script, the outline of a bow (see *Chinese and Sumerian*, p. 20; Sign-list, no. 43); indicating that the original meaning of the symbol (read ERIM, ERIN, ZAB) was *bowman, archer, warrior*. Cf. the Egyptian hieroglyph for *menfit*, 'soldier', 'army', viz. a man kneeling on one knee and grasping a strung bow.] Cf. the Latin *militia*, in the sense of a civil service or office, esp. a laborious one.

A man's life at best is a weary time of continual toil, allotted by the Divine Taskmaster (Gn 3¹⁷⁻¹⁹ Ec 1¹³). Read עָלֵי c Qrî > עַל Ktîb.

Are not his days like those of a hireling? i.e. jealously measured out and exactly determined, not bating a single hour of labour and sorrow. Cf. 14⁶. See also Is 16¹⁴ 21¹⁶, where we have the similar phrase כִּשְׁנֵי שָׂכִיר *like the years of a hireling*; i.e. full or exact years. 𝔊, taking צבא in the military sense, curiously renders it πειρατήριον, *piratical expedition* or *enterprise*, perhaps *raid*; prop. *nest* or *gang of pirates* (so again, 10¹⁷). In 19¹² the same word = גְּדוּד *troop of raiders* (so Gn 49¹⁹), cf. 25³ (πειραταί).

v. 2. *pants for shade*; prob. of evening, Je 6⁴ Ct 2¹⁷. (שאף *pant, breathe hard, gasp, desire*, springs from the same root as נשב, נשף, נשם *blow, breathe*; and אבה, ארה *desire, want,* &c., are of the same origin, since AB, AW, may be regarded as worn forms of SHAB. Further, the perplexing נאף, which like שאף takes the simple Accus., may be explained as the N-form of the latter, since breathing hard is associated with desire and the sexual nisus, Je 2²⁴ 5⁷⁻⁸. See *Proc. Brit. Acad.*, vol. vii, 'Shumer and Shem', p. 29 ff. for these variations of sound.)

𝔊 ἢ ὥσπερ θεράπων δεδοικὼς τὸν κύριον αὐτῶν καὶ τετευχὼς σκιᾶς is app. a combination of two renderings. In 3¹⁹ καὶ θεράπων δεδοικὼς (א^{c.b} A οὐ δεδ.) τὸν κύριον αὐτοῦ represents Heb. וְעֶבֶד חָפְשִׁי מֵאֲדֹנָיו. It would seem therefore that ישאף was misread חפשי here; the three letters common to both words being read backwards, as in other instances. 𝔊 uses δέδοικα six times in Job for as many different Heb. words! It seems to be a favourite word with the translator. It is correctly used, 3²¹ 38⁴⁰; cf. Is 60¹⁴, but is strangely as here. 26¹· 41⁵. τετευχώς (Λ τετυχηκώς) = ימצא; another perversion of ישאף.

v. 3. *I have been endowed with*: or *made to possess* (Heb. הִנְחַלְתִּי) But 𝔊 ὑπέμεινα = הוֹחַלְתִּי (32¹¹·¹⁶) *I have waited*, or יִחַלְתִּי (6¹¹ 14¹⁴), id. 𝔐 agrees better with st. ii. *Months* (ירחי): an unlikely ∥ to *nights* (לילות). *Days* (ימי) would be more natural; esp. as, both in what precedes and in what follows, Eyob is complaining about his 'days'. In fact, the point of the simile, vv. 1, 2, is obscured by the reading 'months'; the point being that Eyob, like the hired labourer or the toiling slave, ardently longs for the end of every day. And since he is hopeless of recovery, he desires above all the end of his 'hard service', which can only be death.

delusive: or *disappointing*, or *void* of all good, *futile*, *vain* and *profitless*. שוא *emptiness*, *nothingness*, *falsity*, and more positively *evil*, like און. 11¹¹ 15³¹ 31⁵ 35¹³; Ps 60¹³; Ex 20⁷·¹⁶. In Arabic, where سوء and its derivatives are largely represented, the last appears to be the predominant meaning, and there is no trace of the idea of emptiness. Two of the native authorities compare it with بأس = באש; and it seems not impossible that the Sem. root was שו = שב, a softened form of חב = Sumerian ĠAB, *bišu, stinking, foul, bad*.

In st. i 𝔊𝔙 (but not 𝔖) om. לְ, which, however, may really belong to the following word, if we read the whole line thus: כן הוחלתי לימי שוא *So have I waited in evil days* (perhaps בימי; but cf. Ez 22¹⁴ al. for לְ of Time). St. ii may then be rendered . *And* (in) *the troublous nights allotted me* (pointing מֻנּוּ־לִי; a Relat. clause).

v. 4. As it stands in 𝔐, this verse is both grammatically and metrically defective. וּמִדַּד עֶרֶב cannot mean *but the night is long* (RV), but only *and evening measure*, which is nonsense. Pr 7⁹ (OL) is no real instance of ערב = *night*. Moreover, the original quatrain has become a triplet. The ∥ passage Dt 28⁶⁷ suggests the tentative restoration: אם־שכבתי מריתן בקר ואקום (על־משכבי) ואמרתי *If I lie down* (on my bed) *I say*, *Would that it were morning that I might rise!* ואם־קמתי מי־יתן ערב *And if I rise, Would that it were evening!* ושבעתי וגו׳ *And I am sated with unrest* (flutterings, agitations) *until twilight*. 𝔊, however, gives: ἐὰν κοιμηθῶ, λέγω Πότε ἡμέρα; ὡς δ᾽ ἂν ἀναστῶ, πάλιν Πότε ἑσπέρα, = אם־שכבתי ואמרתי מתי יום ואם־אקום מתי ערב. Thus, by supplying יום *day* or בקר *morning* (= ἡμέρα 1 Sa 14³⁸) after מתי in st. i, and reading מתי for מדד in st. ii, 𝔊 mends the sense but not the metre of the verse. Some phrase like על משכבי *on my bed*, or לישן *to sleep*, improves both in st. i. נשף is never the *morning*, but always the *evening, twilight*, even in Ps 119¹⁴⁷. Otherwise, rejecting (מתי) ערב ומדד as an intrusion from the margin, we might reduce the verse to a distich, *If I lie down, I say, When shall I rise?* (מתיראקום, perhaps spoken as one word *māthāqūm*, or the like); *And I am surfeited with r̄ ue m ‥ ‥ nt un 'th m rn.ng grey*. Cf. 𝔊 (ἀπὸ ἑσπέρας ἕως πρωί. (𝔙 ἀληαις . מְרִידֹת f̱o̱r נדדים: cf. 3²⁰ Ez 21⁶.)

v. 5. 𝕲 paraphrases st. i: φύρεται δέ μου τὸ σῶμα ἐν σαπρίᾳ σκωλήκων, *My body is mixed* (wetted) *with wormy rot.* רמה *worm* is str. σκώληξ. Ex 16²⁴ (= syn. תולעת 25ᵉ); but is rendered σαπρία, *rottenness* (of which worms are a symptom) in 17¹⁴ 21²⁶ 25⁶. In Pr 12⁴, on the other hand, רקב *rottenness* is rendered σκώληξ. What we have here, therefore, is app. a 'conflate' equivalent of רמה.

The two next words, וְגִישׁ עָפָר (Qrî וְגוּשׁ), traditionally interpreted *and clods of earth* (= 𝕲 βώλακας γῆς, cf. Ecclus 22¹⁶), are metrically redundant, and may have crept in from the margin. In many codd. the ג is a minuscule, which may imply that it is not original, but was added conjecturally. In that case, גיש עפר may perhaps be a relic of 21²⁶ על עפר ישכבו ורמה וג׳ once cited here in the margin. The last three words, עורי רגע וימאס *My skin* (a frequent ∥ to *flesh*) *hardens and dissolves* (i.e. in turn), suffice both in sense and metre for the second stichus. רגע may perhaps bear the same sense here as Ethiop. ረግዐ: concrescere, coagulari, spissari, congelari (see Di): *thickens,* or as we say, *gathers,* of ulcers and sores: but the use is unique in OT. [The Sumerian RA, which is prob. from RAG—cf. LAG̃, in the like meanings—and signifies both *alâku*, 'walk', 'go', and *kânu*, 'be fixed', 'firm', will be seen to account for the various applications of the root *RAG* in Semitic. The primitive character is an outline of *the foot,* the organ alike of *moving* or *going* and *standing* or *stopping.* Hence we can explain רֶגֶל *foot,* str. the *walker* and *stander,* רָגַז *quiver, shiver, shake,* with fear, anger, or other emotions, רָנֵעַ *move to and fro* or *up and down, stir up, disturb, agitate,* Is 51¹⁵, רֶגַע *a brief space of time, a moment,* v. 18, 20⁵ 21¹³, cf. Is 54⁷ בְּרֶגַע קָטֹן *for a brief while,* str. perhaps a *stand* or *stop,* cf. Lat. *statim,* or else a quick movement, a *shake,* cf. our phrase 'in two shakes', ארגיע *id.,* Pr. 12¹⁹, and רגע Niph. *to stand, stop, become fixed* or *set, to rest,* Hiph. trans. *fix, set, appoint,* like הניח, Is 51⁴. The Arab. رَجُل *a man* is prob. not connected with this root, but may be equated with the Sumerian LÙGÀL, *amêlu, a man,* since R and L interchange; much as Aram. תַּרְנְגֹלָא *a cock* = Sum. DAR-LUGÁLU, id., lit. 'the Fowl King', with interchange of L and N.]

For st. ii 𝕲 gives: τήκω δὲ βώλακας γῆς ἀπὸ ἰχῶρος ξύων, *While I melt clods of earth with matter as I scrape* = וְגִישׁ עָפָר מִתְגָּרֵד אֶמְסֶה: . See 2⁸, where להתגרד *to scrape himself* (i.e. to scrape off the pus and scurf from his ulcers) is rendered ἵνα τὸν ἰχῶρα ξύῃ. Here the translator supposes that the dropping pus dissolves the clods at the sufferer's feet. For τήκω = המסה, cf. Ps 147¹⁸. Others interpret גוש עפר as denoting 'the hard earthy-like crust of his sores'. But, apart from other objections, עפר in Job is always the *ground* (soil, dirt, earth): 4¹⁹ 5⁶ 7²¹ 8¹⁹ 10⁹ 14¹⁹ 16¹⁵ 17¹⁶ 19²⁵ 20¹¹ 21²⁶ 22²⁴ 27¹⁶ 28²·⁶ 30⁶·¹⁹ 34¹⁵ 38³⁸ 39¹⁴ 40¹³ 42⁶. It is not hard but soft earth, 38³⁸. such as humus, dirt, and dust.

v. 6. שַׁלּוּ lit. *My days are swifter than a loom* (Ju 16¹⁴), which can hardly be right. The loom is fixed; it is the shuttle that 'goes flashing through the loom'. Hence AV, RV. In 9²⁵ we have: *My days are swifter than* a runner; cf. 2 C 30⁶: the 'runner' being a royal post or messenger. ארג might be a corruption of ציר *messenger*, Pr 13¹⁷; but it seems quite possible that it represents a lost word אגר (אִגָּר) ἄγγαρος, *a royal post* or messenger, such as bore the king's dispatches (אִגְּרוֹת) in the Persian empire. 𝔊 λαλία = אֹמֶר *speech*. This slightly confirms our conjecture, so far as the order of the letters is concerned. For the rest, ὁ βίος μου is a good paraphrase of ימי *my days* (cf. v. 1 𝔊). St. ii, lit. *And are finished* (or *ended*) *without hope*. He expects a speedy death: cf. 17¹¹·¹⁵. 𝔊 ἐν κενῇ ἐλπίδι, *in delusive hope* does not quite express the meaning.

v. 7. *Remember then.* Insert אֵפוֹ = 𝔊 οὖν, 17¹⁵ 19⁶.
but air: or *mere breath*: or *wind*. רוּחַ is *wind, air, breath, spirit*, acc. to the context. See on 4¹⁵.

v. 8. *Him that seeth me*; i.e. God, the Allseeing, cf. st. ii, and אֵל רֳאִי Gn 16¹⁷.
descry: or *behold*: 𝔊 περιβλέψεταί με, *look round at* or *look about for me*. שׁוּר is a favourite word in Job (see on 19²⁷); in origin perhaps akin to שָׁמַר (= shawar), *watch, guard, observe*, and תּוּר *seek out, spy out, explore*. Cf. Sum. SIR, SHER, *light, shine*, &c. (*nûru, namâru*).
With Thine eyes upon me, I shall be no more: or *I shall disappear under Thine eyes*. Lit. *Thine eyes (will be) on me, and I am not.* In the moment of death Thy victim will escape Thee for ever. The Heb. is terse and vivid. For the construction see Ps 101⁶ Pr 23⁵ Ru 2⁹.

v. 9. *Smoke*: reading עָשָׁן c 𝔗 (וְתָנָנָא) for עָנָן *cloud(s)*; 𝔊 νέφος. The verb כָּלָה (v. 6) suits this: cf Ps 102⁴ *For my days are consumed* (כלו) *like smoke* (בעשן). Cf. also Is 51⁶ To read עלה *goeth up* (Ps 18⁹ al) instead of כלה would produce a false antithesis with לא יעלה at the end of the verse. 𝔊's loose paraphrase connects st. i with v. 8 (*And I am no more, As a cloud cleared off from heaven*).

What is denied is the possibility of a bodily return from the grave. 'Coming up' from Hades (Heb. She'ol) as a ghost or apparition (1 Sa 28¹⁴) is not questioned. The assertion is that, once a man is dead, there is no renewal of his earthly life.

Chapter 8. FIRST SPEECH OF BILDAD THE SHUHITE.

v. 2. There is some error in st. ii. ורוח כביר אמרי פיך שַׁ cannot mean RV, but only *And a strong wind be the words of thy mouth?* Besides רוח *wind* is fem. in Job (1¹⁹): see on 4¹⁵. We might restore ורוחך תכביר מלין וגו' *And thy temper multiply the words of thy mouth?* (רוח = *anger*). cf. 15². See also 21 רוח ... וג' has יכביר מלין, 35. Reading the phrase דברי רוח ... ד (וה'),

we may further suggest ופיך יכביר אמרי־רוח *And thy mouth multiply windy words?* 𝔊 πνεῦμα πολυρῆμον τοῦ στόματός σου = 𝔐.

v. 3 *wrest:* or *crook:* or *distort.* יְעַקֵּל pro 𝔐 יְעַוֵּת, which recurs in st. ii. A scribe overlooked the rare word. Cf. Hb 1⁴. מִשְׁפָּט מְעֻקָּל *wrested* or *crooked judgement* (the same noun as here). 34¹², however, favours יְעַוֶּה; and the emphatic repetition of the word may have been intentional. (Neither יְעַוֶּה, 33²⁷; nor יְעַקֵּשׁ, Mi 3⁹, is found with Obj. מִשְׁפָּט elsewhere. 𝔊 ἀδικήσει κρίνων = יְעַוֵּת בְּשָׁפֹט: cf. 10³ for the verb. In st. ii, ταράξει = יְעַוֵּת: cf. 19⁶ עותני = ἐστιν ὁ ταράξας με.)

v. 4. *Though* or *If.* אִם, which also introduces the next two verses. With RV marg. we might regard st. ii as the apodosis: *If thy sons sinned against Him, He threw them* (cf. באש שלח *throw into fire*) *into the hand* (*power*) *of their offence.* So 𝔊. Bildad assumes that they had sinned. From his point of view, their destruction was proof of it. Or we might omit אִם here and, noting the emphatic position of בָּנֶיךָ, translate: *Thy sons, they sinned against Him; And* (the inevitable consequence) *He threw them,* &c. Bildad does not refer to the death of Eyob's children as the chief of his calamities, but as a signal instance of the truth of the doctrine that, as sin issues in suffering, so suffering presupposes guilt.

v. 5. *If thou thyself.* אִם־אַתָּה The Pers. Pron. is emphatic. *Thou* wilt not share the fate of thy sons, if only thou wilt now seek grace. It seems to be implied that Eyob had also sinned, though not in the same degree, since his life had been spared hitherto. (If we adopt either of the alternative renderings of v. 4 suggested in the note on that verse, we should read וְאִם־אַתָּה *But if thou thyself,* &c. Cf. 𝔊 : σὺ δὲ ὄρθριζε. *seek El earnestly:* תְּשַׁחֵר אֶל־אֵל. As שִׁחֵר usually takes an Accusative of the Object, it has been proposed to omit אל *unto.* 'Nicht sehr schön ist . . . in v. 5 das אל ואל אל,' remarks Duhm; adding 'die LXX hat die beiden ersten אל nicht'. The latter statement is erroneous; for πρὸς κύριον = אֶל־אֵל, acc. to the usage of 𝔊 in Job, where אֵל = κύριος (or ὁ κύριος) some forty times. 𝔊 omits the following וְאֶל־, so as to connect שַׁדַּי = παντοκράτορα (so fifteen times in Job) with the preceding אֵל; thinking, no doubt, of אֵל שַׁדַּי El Shaddai, but disregarding the metrical division of the stichi. For the rest, the construction שִׁחֵר אֶל־ may be compared with שִׁחֵר לְ, 24⁵ (both are doubtless late constructions). To omit the first אֶל־, in fact, would spoil the symmetry of the stichi. cf. 5⁸. So much for the matter of 'Schönheit'. As to the suggested אֶת־אֵל (Kittel), that phrase would be unique in Job and, indeed, in the OT.

v. 6 A tristich: so also in 𝔊. Most critics relegate st. ii to the margin. But כִּי־עַתָּה forms a good introduction for the Apodosis of v. 5; and אִם־זַךְ וְיָשָׁר אַתָּה, st. i, looks like a variant of אִם־אַתָּה תְּשַׁחֵר (v. 5 a); while it certainly interrupts the syntax rather awkwardly, following, as it does, on the compound protasis of v. 5. *Surely, now He would* awake (Ps 35²³) over (= for; late use of עַל) thee, And would requite thee according to thy righteousness. The text is questionable in both stichi. 𝔊 omits כי עתה, and gives δεήσεως ἐπακούσεταί σου (= (or עָלֶיךָ 2 K 20¹²) יִשְׁמַע־לָךְ He will listen to thee (or perhaps יֵעָתֶר־לָךְ He will become propitious to thee; cf. 2 Sa 21¹⁴. But ἐπακούω = שמע more than twenty times; נעתר only about six), instead of יָעִיר עָלֶיךָ (for which יָעוּר would be more usual: Ju 5⁹ Is 51¹²). Then, again, st. ii, ושלם נות צדקך And make safe (?) thy righteous abode has a strange appearance. שִׁלַּם is not so used elsewhere. The common meanings are to requite, recompense, reward, compensate, pay a vow, 21¹⁹·³¹ 34¹¹·³³ 22²⁷. The probable sense here is that God will make up everything, will make everything good to His suppliant. נָוֶה (Ps 68¹³ †) should at least be נְוֵה Ex 15¹³ Je 31²³ נוה צדק: see on 5³·²⁴ 18¹⁵. But read כְּמוֹ: And He will make good (or compensate, sc thee) according to thy righteousness: or else ושלם לך כצדקך And He will repay thee according to thy righteousness. The similar passage 22²⁷ may, however, suggest the more radical emendation: ושלמת לו נדריך And thou shalt pay Him thy vows. Ps 50¹⁴ 66¹³.

v. 7. Lit. And thy beginning (Gn 1¹) shall be smallness (Gn 19²⁰), And thine end or after-state (42¹²) shall grow greatly (Ps 92¹²). 𝔊 Thy first things, then, shall be few, But thy last untold (ἀμύθητα = רב much, many, 36²⁸) The gender is neglected in both clauses. There is therefore no reason to follow 𝔊 in pointing ישגה as Hiph. He will increase (Ols, Siegfr, Du), or to read שְׁגִיאָה instead of it (on the ground of 𝔊, which really supports 𝔐). A more strictly literal rendering might be: And it shall be, thy beginning was fewness ; And thine end (shall be)—it (i. e. the fewness) shall increase greatly.

vv. 8–19. Bildad appeals to the Wisdom of the Fathers, the experience of the past which proves, as he thinks, that they who forget God suddenly perish. He wishes Eyob to apply the moral to himself.

v. 8. the first (not former) age or generation; i. e. the primitive and patriarchal times (אבות), when men lived longer (cf. v. 9), and therefore attained to fuller knowledge and riper experience than their degenerate descendants. The wisdom of the Ancients has always and everywhere been proverbial, until comparatively modern times.

St. ii. Reading בונן consider attentively (Dt 32¹⁰) or give heed to. 𝔐 כונן fix (scil. thine heart) on . . . ; but this verb is not so used elsewhere. See 1 Sa 23²² for a similar error. 𝔊 ܘܣܟܠ and understand = ובונן. the findings (lit. search; thing sought out) or quest of the Fathers. 𝔐 אבותם of their fathers The 3 Pers. Pron., which could only refer to the 'First Generation', may be due to reminiscence of 15¹⁸. Or the ם may be a misreading of נו our. 𝔊 curiously: ἐξιχνίασον δὲ κατὰ γένος πατέρων = יל(אמני) (חקרי) אבות: Gn 1" ?'. ... ... = חָקַר. ־" al.

v. 9. Of ۱ ۰٬ ،٬ ،٬ : מתמול : . . ݰ ۱. 𝔐 . m. ו٬٬۰. ܫ. חֲמוֹל, Aram.

אֶתְמוֹלִי ,אֶתְמוֹל, Mand. עתמאל, Assyr. timâli, itimâli, inatimâli, supplies an instance of the weakening of ע to א; being derived from עת *time* and מול *before*, *ante*, and thus meaning the *day before* to-day. With the first element in the compound cf. Assyr. inu, enu, f. ittu, ettu, *time*, Sumerian EN, ENE, *id.*)

like a shadow: as transitory, and soon vanishing away. בְּצֵל, as in the quotation 1 C 29¹⁵ 'בצל ימינו על הא. Cf. also 17⁷. So 𝕲𝕾𝕿. Perhaps וְכַצֵּל (not וּכְצֵל). The verse is parenthetic, if genuine.

v. 10. *Will not* they (emphatic Pron.) *teach thee and* (restoring ו, c codd. et 𝕲𝕾𝕿) *tell thee*? That is, the Ancients who lived long enough to find out the truth, and whose lore has come down to us by hallowed tradition.

from their heart's wisdom: lit. *out of their heart*: cf. 15¹³ *from thy mouth*. Heart here = intelligence, thought, or insight and understanding as resulting from thought and reflexion. 36⁵.

v. 11. Insert אִם *or* to introduce st. ii and improve both construction and rhythm. So 𝕲 𝕾. For the *papyrus* or paper-reed (גֹּמֶא), see Ex 2³ Is 18². 𝕾 confuses the word with Heb. אֲגַם *marsh*, which, however, is also used in the sense of אַגְמוֹן *bulrush*, Je 51³². בִּצָּה *biççâ mire*, mud, moist earth, 40²¹, and בִּץ *id.*, Je 38²², correspond to Assyr. *baççu*; e. g. in the phrase *baçça u turuba šipik epirû rabûtim*, 'mud and dust (ترب), a heap of much earth'.

Nile-rush: or *sedge*: אָחוּ, Gn 41².¹⁸ (app. an Egyptian word). 𝕲 βούτομον, perhaps *butomus*, the flowering rush. The poet appears to have had some knowledge of Egypt (cf. the description of the crocodile, chap. 41. Macgregor of the 'Rob Roy', however, encountered a crocodile among the reeds of lake Hûleh in N. Syria.)

The verse appears to cite the Wisdom of the Ancients in appropriate gnomic or proverbial form; reminding us of the traditional saws of the Seven Sages of Hellas.

v. 12. Lit. *It is still in growth and* (but) *is not moist* (or *sappy*). We read ירטבו: cf. v. 16 רָטֹב עוֹדֶנּוּ אִבּוֹ וְלֹא יִקָּטֵף *wet, moist, sappy*; 24⁸ *they are wet, soaked*, by showers. אִם קטף עודנו באבו לא *It is still in its freshness* (or *first growth*); *it is not plucked off* (or up): קטף 30⁴ Dt 23²⁶ Ez 17⁴. The point is that the marsh-plant, if deprived of the water which supplies its vital sap, withers rapidly and fails to attain full growth.

With the ἅπ. λεγόμ. אֵבֶב, cf. Aram. מָאַבֵּב, 𝕿 Ho 9¹⁰, and Assyr. *abâbu*, to be *bright, fresh*, e.g. *kîma irçitim libib*, 'Like the earth let him flourish!'; *ababa = qistu*, *wood, forest*, Aram. אַבָּא *id.*

v. 13. *the end*: the hereafter or future, the latter end: reading אחרית (𝕲 τὰ ἔσχατα: v. 7, 42¹²) instead of ארחות *the paths*.

the wicked: 𝕲 ἀσεβοῖς, *impious, ungodly*. So again 8¹³ 15³⁴ 27⁸. In twenty-two other places ἀσεβής = רָשָׁע in Job, as in Proverbs (sixty-five

8. 16   NOTES ON THE TEXT   177

times) and gen. in OT. The sense here is defined by the preceding phrase, 'those who forget God'; i.e. the irreligious or worldly, in whose thought and life there is no recognition of God, and who are ἄθεοι ἐν τῷ κόσμῳ (Eph 2¹²). The root חנף has usually been compared with Ar. حنف to incline to, or decline from, a thing, and حنف or حنف to have a wry or crooked foot or leg. It would then be one of the numerous offshoots of the primitive GAM, GAN, KAM, KAN, ḤAM, ḤAN, to bend, bow, &c. (Proc. Brit. Acad., vol. vii, 'Shumer and Shem', p 23). It is, however, perhaps better to connect it with Assyr. ḥanâbu or ḥanâpu, to sprout or grow luxuriantly, of hair and vegetation; since words denoting luxuriant growth are metaphorically used to express wantonness and rebellion against moral restraints   Cf. also the phrase ḥanâpu šâ tâmtim, app. meaning the swell of the sea (Sum. SIG-DU DU, to be wool-heaped or wool-covered; alluding to the white wool-like crests of the waves 5 R 19 7a), and גָּאָה to grow up, v. 11, used of the rising of a torrent, Ez 47⁵, גֵּאֶה proud, גַּאֲוָה swelling of the sea, Ps 46⁴, and other derivv. The pride which refuses to acknowledge dependence upon God and issues in many kinds of rebellion, is perhaps the most deadly sin from the point of view of spiritual religion. 'By that sin fell the Angels.' (Cf. Is 14¹³,¹⁴; Mt 11²⁹,³⁰). The legends of the Titanic rebels who of old fought against Heaven fitly symbolize their impious pride by their monstrous growth and stature.

v. 14. 𝔐 יָקוֹט a word otherwise unknown; RV *shall break in sunder*, marg. *be cut off*, as if from a supposed קטט = Ar. قطّ *to cut*. So Saad. يَنْقَطِع *cut off*. But a noun is required, as in the ‖ st. and 31²⁴. קַוִּים will not do; קַו is always a measuring-line (38⁵), and the plur. does not occur. קוּרֵי עַכָּבִישׁ *spider-threads*, Is 59⁵, suggests קוּרִים (spider-)*threads, a cobweb*; perhaps *a gossamer* (Dr) or spider's *film* floating in the air. קַוֵּי קַיִץ *summer-threads* (?) is pretty but improbable. כַחוּט *like a thread* (Ju 16¹²; simile for a thing easily broken), or בְחוּט *in a thread*, may be further suggested. We say, 'His life hangs on a thread.'

𝔊, not understanding יקוט and misled by בית in st. ii, gives an infelicitous paraphrase: *For his house shall be uninhabited, But his tent shall turn out a spider* (!). Cf. 𝔊 27¹⁸.

v. 15. Or, *He leaneth upon his house, and it standeth not; He clutcheth it, and it remains not upright* (gives way)

v. 16. 𝔐 על גנתו *over his garden* does not seem quite satisfactory. 𝔊 ἐκ σαπρίας αὐτοῦ, *out of his decay* (= רִמָּה in three other places, 17¹⁴ al.). Ps 80¹² חשלח קצירה עד ים ואל נהר יונק' suggests עלי נהר *beside* (or אלי *unto*) *the river*; or אל פלג *unto the canal* (29⁶, cf. 38²⁵).

על־גנות ai . . . . f. n. the root at the . . . . es from the soil. After all, 𝔐 may be right: *Sappy is he before the sun* (he can face the summer heats without fear of being dried up); *And on his garden his suckers spring forth.* A last suggestion, however, may not be deemed superfluous. Since 'suckers' shoot forth about and beside a trunk, it seems plausible to read נועו for נגתו (see 14⁸ Is 11¹ 40²⁴): *And by his stock his sucker cometh forth.*

v. 17. *About a cairn his roots he twineth ; And a house of stones* (stony house) *he chooseth.* For גל *a heap of stones,* see 15²⁸ (ruins), Jos 7²⁶ (over a grave). RV marg. *beside the spring*; but גל never has this meaning (in Ct 4¹² גן must be read c 𝔊𝔖𝔙). The tree which symbolizes the ungodly in prosperity has a firm grip of the ground, being founded as it were upon rock instead of loose soil. 𝔐 יְסֻבָּכוּ *are entwined*; but 𝔊 takes the verb as a Sing. and connects the ו with st. ii, which agrees better with the context. Read therefore יְסַבֵּךְ or יְשַׂבֵּךְ (𝔊 κοιμᾶται = ישכב; cf. also שבכה 18ᵃ). συναγωγὴν λίθων is a quaint but not inaccurate explanation of גל.

a house of stones. The stone heap out of which its stem rises is regarded as the tree's 'house', chosen for its strength and security against wind and storm. A man's house is his castle; as was more especially the case in ancient times. Under different figures the seeming security and real insecurity of the godless is insisted upon in vv. 14 ff.; and the occurrence of בית in 14, 15 favours its recurrence here. 𝔊 ἐν δὲ μέσῳ χαλίκων ζήσεται = ובין אבנים יחיה *And between stones he liveth.* The verb יחזה has troubled later translators than 𝔊, and various substitutes have been proposed, of which the most ingenious is Hoffmann's יֶחֱוֵה (= יֹאחֲוֶה) *he graspeth it.* But there seems no reason why יֶחֱזֶה should not mean *he looketh out* or *chooseth* (cf. Ex 18²¹) = יראה, the action of the tree being poetically regarded as personal.

v. 18. *El swalloweth him up out of his place.* Leg. אֵל, the necessary Subj., pro 𝔐 אִם־ *If*, which leaves the Verb Act. without a definite Subj. Cf. 27²¹. Moreover, the hypothetical form is quite inappropriate here, where the sudden end of the godless man's seeming security is stated. The cause is, of course, according to Bildad's doctrine, the intervention of God. For בָּלַע *to swallow,* akin to לוע *id.,* see 7¹⁹ 20¹⁵.¹⁸; Pi. fig. *swallow* up, *destroy,* 2³ 10⁸; Pu 37²⁰ *be destroyed.* *His place* (מקום) or *stead* confirms בית > בין in the previous verse: see 7¹⁰ where בית and מקום are associated as here. The same passage throws light on st. ii: *And it* (his place) *disowneth him with ' I know thee not!'* (lit. *I have not seen thee*; or, as we might say, 'I never saw thee before'). His home knows him no more. He becomes a stranger to the familiar spot. It soon forgets him. Cf. also 20⁹; and 20⁷ ראיו = ירעיו *his acquaintance,* they who knew him). 𝔊 (wrongly): οὐχ ἑόρακας τοιαῦτα = : לא ראיתה כן.

v. 19. St. i. proves that the metaphor of the tree is maintained; but in the present text of st. 1 it appears to be dropped 'Lo, that is the joy of his way' is a strange statement to be made of a stationary object like a tree, and further is out of all clear relation to the context, even if the word 'joy' be 'meant ironically' (Dr). 𝔊 gives something quite different: ὅτι καταστροφὴ (15^{21}) ἀσεβοῦς τοιαύτη. We propose דורו (מסיע) משיע הוא כן, and in st. ii יַצְמִיהַ: *Thus He* (emphatic pron.; viz. El) *plucketh away his abode ; And causeth another to spring from the ground.* The phrase הסיע דור is from Is 38^{12}. Otherwise, we might suggest משרש for משוש: *Thus He uprooteth his abode*: cf Ps 52^7.

v. 20. *Nor hold* (or *grasp*) *the hand of evildoers*: either to support or to lead them. 𝔊 πᾶν δὲ δῶρον ἀσεβοῦς οὐ δέξεται = ולא יקח מיד מרע. 𝔐 is preferable; though the affirmation that El is an incorruptible Judge is not unsuitable to the context.

vv. 21, 22. 𝔐's continuation *Until* (עַד) *He fill thy mouth with laughing, And thy lips with shouting* (a metrically short st.) does not really continue the previous sense; and the pointing עֹד *yet, still, again*, only gives us a prophecy in the air. The change from the third to the second Pers. Pron. in these two verses breaks the connexion with what precedes. 𝔊 ἀληθινῶν δὲ στόμα ἐμπλήσει γέλωτος, Τὰ δὲ χείλη αὐτῶν ἐξομολογήσεως· (22) Οἱ δὲ ἐχθροὶ αὐτῶν κτλ. yields a more consecutive and natural close to Bildad's argument. In accordance with this, we read:

פי ישר ימלא שחוק
ושפתי זך תרועה:
שנאיו ילבשו בשת
ואהל רשעים איננו:

Thus Bildad implies that Eyob was *not* תם וישר איש (2^3 1^1), inasmuch as his 'tent' was certainly 'no more'.

(In v. 20 𝔊 ἄκακον = תָם; and in 2^3 ἄκακος ἀληθινός = תם וישר. For ἀληθινός = ישר, see also 4^7 8^6 17^8. We may regard 𝔐 עד as a disguised relic of ישר, since ע and שׁ are sometimes, and ד, ר very often, confused with each other. In שפתיך one letter (י) has fallen out before the ך. Bildad has already (v. 6) coupled together זך *pure* and ישר *upright*. 𝔐 would thus appear to be an infelicitous restoration of a mutilated text.)

Chapter 9. Eyob ironically grants that God is never unjust (8^3). He is, in fact, so far exalted above man, as to be beyond the reach of argument or remonstrance. He does what He wills, and is a law to Himself.

v. 2. *And how shall a mortal be just with God?* See the note on 4^{17}; and cf. 25^4 where this question is repeated. The implication is that frail humanity can never be wholly without fault in the eyes of the Divine Judge (cf. 𝔊 πῶς γὰρ ἔσται δίκαιος βροτὸς παρὰ Κυρίῳ;). This at least is Bildad's meaning. The following verse, however, seem to involve a new construction of the question in the mouth of Eyob, viz. How is a mere man *to be justified* with God? how is he to compel God to admit his righteousness?

v. 3. *If he would fain argue his case with Him* (13⁸), *He will not answer him one* point *of a thousand*: He will not vouchsafe even the least reply to his questionings; He will give him no answer at all. Again and again Eyob complains that he cannot come at his Divine Persecutor (he, like his Friends, believes that his calamities are directly due to God, though the Prologue teaches us otherwise); that God eludes all his approaches, holding Himself aloof from His creature in inaccessible Majesty, apparently indifferent alike to the protests and the sufferings of His victim. Cf. v. 11 and 23³⁻⁹. (The reference of the Pers. Pronouns in this verse is ambiguous; and in a different context the meaning might be, as Dr gives it: 'If one were to desire to dispute with Him, he could not answer Him one of the innumerable questions which, in His infinite superiority to man, He would put to him.' Cf. the 'innumerable questions' of 38–41. But Eyob would not be likely to recognize evidence of his own guilt in mere ignorance of the constitution of Nature. Indeed, after making him realize that ignorance to the full by the long series of questions in chaps. 38 sqq., God Himself is represented as expressly confirming the justice of his argument (42⁷).)

v. 4. Lit. *Wise of heart and firm* (or *stout*) *of strength, Who hath resisted Him* (הקשה *hardened*, scil. *his neck*, Je 7²⁰, or *his heart*, Pr 28¹⁴) *and remained whole?* (וישלם = 𝔊 ὑπέμεινεν: so 22²¹ 41³).

v. 5. *Who removeth mountains unperceived*: reading (!) וְלֹא יָדַע instead of וְלֹא יָדְעוּ *and they know not*. The unconsciousness of the mountains hardly called for remark; but the Divine Agent acts, without letting Himself be seen. For ידע Niph. cf. Gn 41²¹ and esp. Ps 77¹⁹. (𝔊 *without knowing it*; lit. *and does not know*, meaning perhaps *without heeding* or *caring*; but the ascription of unconscious or heedless action to God is unlikely here. Indeed st. ii makes the action intentional.) We may also suggest וְלֹא יֵוָדֵעַ, or even Pu. Pf. יֻדָּע, *and they are no more perceived* = and they disappear; cf. Assyr. *idû*, *to see*, *to know*, Pa. Permans. *ld uddá uçurâti*, 'the sculptures were not visible', Neb. *Senkereh* Cyl. (The root דע may be compared with שע in שעה *to gaze at*.) In st. ii the prosaic אשר is obviously corrupt. But וְהֹפְכָם בְּאַפּוֹ is both unmetrical and bad Hebrew. A slight change would give וְאָשְׁדָם הָפַךְ בְּאַפּוֹ *And their foundation He overturneth in His wrath*: cf. Assyr. *išdu, foundation*, and אשר Nu 21¹⁵. It seems preferable, however, to see in אשר a vestige of (וּ)מִשָּׁרְשׁ (*And*) *from the roots He overturneth them in His wrath*: cf. 28⁹.

The great disturbances of Nature, wrought by volcanic agency, earthquakes, and storms on land or sea, are ascribed, as usually in the OT, to the immediate action of God. They are cited as evidence of Power, with which it were both vain and presumptuous for man to contend. Ⓖ ὁ παλαιῶν ὄρη, *Who ageth the mountains*: not a different reading, but misinterpreting עתק in the Aram. sense of *growing old*, which occurs 21⁷, instead of *moving* (14¹⁸ 18⁴).

v. 6 *out of her place*: Ⓖ ἐκ θεμελίων. The same paraphrase in 18⁴, Is 13¹³. The 2nd stichus ועמודיה יתפלצון *And her pillars shudder* seems metrically short, and is, perhaps, otherwise doubtful. We have ארץ and עמודיה again in Ps 75⁴, but meaning, as it would seem, 'the country' and 'its nobles'—a metaphorical use of 'pillars'. The word rendered 'pillars' in 1 Sa 2⁸ is not the same. Moreover, 26⁷ᵇ does not suggest that the poet believed the earth to be supported on pillars; but 26¹¹ does speak of 'the pillars of Heaven' (עמודי שמים). If the earth were shaken, these pillars (conceived as resting upon it) would certainly sway and tremble. Otherwise, we might read עמודי תבל *the pillars of the world*. (With the vb. יתפלצון ἅπ. λεγόμ. cf. n. פלצות *horror*, 21⁶. פלץ is app. cogn. with Assyr. פלח *to fear*, and נלד, נלח, *id*. Cf. Sum. LUG, Ch. li, lit, lik, *id.*, Giles 6976.)

v. 7. *Sol*. The Heb. is the rare חֶרֶס (see Ju 1³⁵ 2⁹ 8¹³ 14¹⁸), not the ordinary term שמש. It may mean the young or rising sun, and, as a Semitic etymology is wanting, we may compare the Egyptian 𓅃 Har, Horus, in the like sense; a name which also appears in חרנפר Harnefer, 1 C 7³⁶, 'the beauteous Horus' (see my note in Ellicott's Comm. ad loc., London, 1883) (In 3 R 68, 64 we find mention of a Sumerian God חר GAR, who is called KIN-GEA DINGIR MAŠ-TABBA, 'The Messenger of the Twin God(s)'. His name is written 𒀭𒄞 *god + bullock*; which might indicate either a sun or a river deity.) The verb חרה *to rise*, of the sun, is cognate with Ar. شرق and Aram. דנח; and the biliteral root of these and other kindred Semitic words may be recognized in the Sumerian LAG, LAĜ, RA (from RAG, RAĜ), and ZA-LAG, all values of the Sun-character, and all meaning *light, shine*, &c. (See CT xii. 6.)

The allusion is not only to eclipses, which are rare, but to the darkness of clouded and stormy skies (3⁵), when neither sun nor stars are visible. *sealeth* (37⁷?) *about the stars*: so that they cannot move on in their 'courses' (Ju 5²⁰) or appointed paths across the heavens. They are shut behind sealed doors in their celestial abodes. Cf. the Babylonian Epic of Creation, Tab. V for the fixed paths of the heavenly bodies in the solid vault of the firmament.

Ⓖᴮ adds: κατὰ δὲ ἀγγέλων αὐτοῦ σκολιόν τι ἐπενόησεν = ובמלאכיו ישים תהלה; app. a marginal citation of 4¹⁸, and a very clear instance of inept interpolation. It is quite possible that vv. 8–10 are also to be regarded as inauthentic additions to the Heb. text by some scribe who failed to notice that the context (vv. 5, 7) deals only with the seemingly arbitrary and capricious activity of God, and not with His beneficent creative work.

v. 8. *That spread the heavens*: Je 10¹² Is 40²² Ps 104² ('like a curtain'). Cf. 26⁷. Should לבדו *alóne* be (ע)ל־בהו) *over the Void?* Or ברק, Is 40²²? *And treadeth upon the heights of the Earth.* 𝔐 has יָם *sea* instead of אֶרֶץ *earth*. But the phrase במתי ים *high places of the sea* is unparalleled as an expression for the swelling waves of the sea. במות always means either *mountains*, like its original the Assyrio-Bab. *bâmâtê*, or as a t. t. of religion the *high places*, natural or artificial, which served as the sanctuaries of Canaan. (*Bâmah*, from √בום ; perhaps a labialized form of קום *stand up, rise*, with which cf. GIN, a value of the Sumerian Mountain-character, Ch. k'in, *high peaks*, G 2113, and also GIN, *kânu*, כן. In Assyr. *bâmâtê šă šadê* is *the tops* or *peaks of the mountains*.) The st. seems to be borrowed from Am 4¹³, word for word (cf. also Mi 1³). Otherwise, we might read עָב *clouds* instead of יָם, with 3 Heb. codd., and compare Is 14¹⁴ Na 1³. But the clouds are usually God's chariot, Is 19¹ Ps 104³.

v. 9. The three stellar groups עש (עיש), כסיל, and כימה, are mentioned again, in reverse order, 38³¹·³². The same order obtains in Am 5⁸ (עֹשֵׂה כִימָה וּכְסִיל); a passage of which the present may be a reminiscence. 𝔊 ὁ ποιῶν Πλειάδα καὶ Ἕσπερον καὶ Ἀρκτοῦρον = עשה כימה וכסיל וע(י)ש; but 𝔖 עשה עש כסיל 𝔐 . עשה כימה ועיש וכסיל = הו דעבד כימא ועיותא וגנברא is strange. The Asyndeton may be corrected by reading וכסיל, c 𝔊 𝔖 𝔙; and עש should doubtless be עיש, as in 38³², and as is indicated by the Syriac equivalent ܥܝܘܬܐ, on the ground of which it has been proposed to point the Heb. word עַיִשׁ 'iyyûsh (perhaps rather עָיִשׁ 'iyyôsh or עַיָּ 'ayyôsh). עשה עש כסיל, however, looks as if עש were a scribe's inadvertent repetition of the first two letters of עשה. This would account both for the spelling עש (instead of עיש) and for the Asyndeton כסיל instead of וכסיל. Then the first st. would be עשה כסיל וכימה *That made Kesîl and Kîmah* (cf. Am 5⁸). The second st., which is too short, might be completed by supposing that בֹּנֶה has fallen out after the somewhat similar כימה: *That built the Chambers of the South*: cf. Am 9⁶ᵃ. *Inner Chambers of the Southern Sky* is not a probable name for a single constellation, like the other names of the verse. It must rather denote the whole southern quarter of the heavens, regarded as containing the fixed abodes or stations (Assyr. *manzalê*: cf. v. 7; 37⁹) of certain brilliant stars or groups of stars which become visible as one journeys to the South, e. g. the Southern Cross, of which the poet might have heard from travellers. The other names can hardly be identified with certainty. See Burney, EB s. v. STARS. But this no more affects the general sense than the absence of the names of particular stars in Is 40²⁶.

The Syr. 'iyyûthâ (= עיש) seems to be either Aldebaran, i. e. α Tauri, or Capella Aurigae; but 𝔊 gives Arcturus, and 𝔄 'al-'Ayyûqa, i. e.

the star Capella, which follows the Pleiades ('al-Thurayyā = כימה here). If כימה be really the Pleiades (𝔊 Saad.) or Hyades (𝔙), the name may be compared with Assyrio-Bab. *kîmu*, f. *kîmtu*, 'family', from *kamû*, 'to bind', cf. our popular name 'The Seven Sisters'. According to classical myth the Pleiades were the seven daughters of Atlas, and sisters of the Hyades; who were pursued by the giant hunter Orion, until Zeus in compassion changed them and their pursuer into neighbouring constellations. It agrees with this that כסיל is rendered 'The Giant' by 𝔊 and 𝔄 ('*al-gabbāra*) and *Oriona* by 𝔙. So also 𝔗 נְפִילָא (cf. הנפלים Gn 6⁴). In 38³¹ 𝔊 Ὠρίωνος = כסיל; but here, strangely enough, Ἕσπερον, *the Evening Star* or Venus, which in 38³² does duty for עיש ! (on the ground of עש־תר Ishtar?).

v. 10. Repeated from 5⁹, and prob. a marginal intrusion here. (5⁹ ואין חקר *and unsearchable*: cf. 𝔊 καὶ ἀνεξιχνίαστα 𝔙 *et incomprehensibilia: how* He does them, man cannot find out. עד אין חקר seems rather to emphasize their number; and the עד is due to the influence of st. ii.) Cf. Ps 136⁴.—The anarthrous Ptcpp. in vv. 8-10 should perhaps be pointed as Constr. States: cf. vv. 5-7.

v. 11. *Behold*: הֵן; 𝔊 ἐάν, *If* (Aram. use): cf. 40²³ Ex 4¹ al. So 𝔖𝔙. Perhaps a better sense: *If He pass along by me* (Gn 18⁵: or *over me*, Ps 42⁸), *I see Him not* (the following ו belongs to אראה: leg. אראהו, c 𝔖𝔄𝔙); *If He glide by, I perceive Him not* חלף (v. 26 4¹⁵ 11¹⁰), as v. 26 shows, implies swift passage. It is a poet. syn. of עבר, *pass over, through, by, onward*, the root of which may well be Sum. BAR, 'side' (*aḫâtu, pâdu*), so that it str. means *to go to the other side*; while חל־ף may be compared with ĜAL (ח), *split, part, divide, run swiftly*, of water, (*zâzu, garâru ša mê*), also *to open* (*pitû*), just as BAR is also *split, divide, open*, and *half* (*parâsu, pitû, mišlu, zûzu*). The *sides* are the *dividers* and *boundaries* or *bounds* (*kamâtu*) of things. Moreover, since BA means *rend, divide, half* (*našâru, zâzu, mišlu*), חל־ף (= חל־ב) may perhaps = ĜAL-BA. For the connexion of ideas in חלף *pass on, away, through* (= *pierce*, 20²⁴ Ju 5²⁶), *change, alter, substitute*, cf. also Sum. BAL (= BAR?), *axe, break through, pass over, change, alter* (a god's command; a temple-site), &c. (*pilaqqu, nabalkutu, ebêru, enû*).

God eludes human sight, even when His overwhelming Power is displayed in the more violent phenomena of Nature. Cf. 1 K 19¹¹·¹². In 23⁸·⁹ this complaint of the elusiveness of God is repeated and amplified.

v 12. *If He glide by* (or *fleet past, speed onward*), *who can turn Him back?* Leg. יחלף, as in v. 11, instead of 𝔐 יחתף (ἄπ·), which is usually taken to mean *seizeth* prey (= יחטף); but this does not agree with ישיבנו (which, in that case, would naturally mean *Who can restore it?* cf. Is 42²²). Besides, the Obj. of the vb. is indispensable. Cf. 11¹⁰ מי ישיבנו ... אם יחלף (prob. an echo of this verse).

𝔊 ἐὰν ἀπαλλάξῃ τίς ἀποστρέψει *If H. ı m·.* or *d·η·. u h shall turn back?* (חתף in Syr. is *to break in pieces*: and 𝔖 here renders בל,

which shows that it read יַחְתֹּף, pointing prob. as Pi.). Leg. fort. יִפְרִיץ *break forth*: cf. 𝔊 Ex 19²²; vel יחריב *lay waste*, vel יחרים *destroy* (Is 34²).

v. 13. *Eloah turneth not back His wrath*: cf. v. 12 a. (The repetitions of vv. 9–13 throw some suspicion on the text.) Nothing can arrest the course of Divine activity. His Anger is an all-subduing force. *Under It* (or *Him*) *were bowed* of old *the Helpers of Rahab*. That Rahab is a personification of the sea is evident from the similar allusions, probably to the same ancient myth, in 26¹¹, Ps 89⁹·¹⁰. Rahab (the *wrathful, raging, passionate,* or *violent*; str. phps. *noisy, clamorous*, like the cogn. ריב: cf. Assyr. *ra'âbu, to be enraged, become furious, behave furiously*) appears, in fact, to be the Canaanite or Hebrew name of the primal Deep, the chaotic mass of dark waters which existed before Heaven and Earth, out of which first the gods and afterwards all other things emerged or were created, and which in Assyrio-Bab. was usually called Tiâmat (= תהום, Gn 1²), i.e. the Sea (= *tiamtu, tamtu, tamdu,* pl. *tâmâte,* &c.). In the Babylonian Epic of Creation, which relates how Tiâmat warred against the gods, and was vanquished by Merodach, who built heaven and earth out of the two halves of her cloven carcase, she is also called 'the Mother ĜUBUR' (*um-mu ḫu-bur, um-ma ḫu-bu-ur*: Tab. II. 19, III. 81 al.), as well as *um-ma Ti-amat,* 'the Mother Tiâmat' (III. 73); a title in which a trace of the original Sumerian text of the poem is preserved, ĜU-BUR being a Sum. word meaning *hole, pit, bottom, beneath* (*šapliš.* BUR is *hole, well, pit,* &c.). Cf. Is 51¹ מקבת בור. The *nâri* ĜUBUR was the River of the Underworld; i.e. 'the waters under the earth', the subterranean portion of Tiâmat, whom Berosus, in a well-known passage, calls Ὀμορωκα = Sum. UMU-ĜUBÚRA (cf. Μολοβοβαρ = MULU-BABAR, for the first element. As regards the second, Ĝ or n̄ = K, as sometimes in LXX; B = W, as in כוב from כבב, and UWU = Ô; while the Metathesis of the K and R, if not accidental, may be paralleled by Heb. רחל = Assyr. *laḫru,* 'ewe'; Sum. ADAGUR, *adaguru,* Heb. אגרטל, &c.).

Such a line as 'Under Him bowed the Helpers of Rahab' seems to show that the poet was acquainted with the Bab. Epic of Creation almost in the form in which we have it; and the brevity of his allusions implies that his readers were equally familiar with the ancient story. Cf. Tab. IV. 105 ff. where we read:

> 'After he had smitten the leader, Tiamat,
> Her strength was crushed, her army broken up:
> And the gods, her helpers, marching beside her,
> Quaked, were terrified, turned their backs.
>   .   .   .   .   .
> He took them prisoners, and shattered their weapons.
> In the net they lay, in the meshes they sate:
> The Four Regions they filled with wailing.'

(See *Light from the East*, p. 10.)

The root שחח *bow down, crouch* (38), cogn. c שוח *sink down*, whence שַׁחַת a *sinking* in the ground, *pit*, may be connected with נוח *lie down, rest* (N = S). Cf. also נוה (= רבץ), and שוה *lie flat, be level*, and Sum. NA, NU, *lie down, rest* (p. 146 supr).

⅁ κήτη τὰ ὑπ' οὐρανόν, *the subcelestial sea-monsters*, appears to show knowledge of the primitive myth. So τὸ κῆτος = רהב 26¹². Contrast the euhemeristic paraphrase of ⅁ᴢ οἱ ἐρειδόμενοι ἀλαζονείᾳ.

v. 14. Answering and arguing are a kind of opposition; and all opposition to the Omnipotent is futile. If superhuman beings failed (v. 13), the certain failure of a human opponent may be taken for granted. No distinction is drawn between physical and moral opposition. *With Him*: i. e. in argument with Him or, perhaps, in His presence. Awed and overwhelmed by the sense of God's Omnipotence, Eyob would be silenced if not convinced. ⅁, missing the point, alters the Pers. of the verbs (ὑπακούσεται = יענה) and, further, reads יבחן (διακρινεῖ: 12¹¹) instead of אבחר' (cf. 15⁵). So also in v. 15 εἰσακούσεταί μου = יעננו instead of אענה.

v. 15. Perhaps a marginal variant or interpolation. *Choosing words* might have been understood in the sense of careful entreaty or *supplication*. (אעננו would be clearer than אענה: cf. ⅁, where γὰρ = אשר). St. ii is short. Perhaps אף כי למשפטי את' *Yea, rather, I would entreat*, &c., or, better, במו־פי למ' את' *With my mouth would I entreat*, &c. (19¹⁶), instead of arguing his case against Him. (⅁ τοῦ κρίματος αὐτοῦ, pointing לְמִשְׁפָּטוֹ for לְמִשְׁפָּטִי, is no improvement, even if it were possible Hebrew. 𝔖𝔗 *my judge*, as if לְשֹׁפְטִי; but the meaning required is rather *antagonist* or plaintiff in the case. מְשַׁפֵּט seems to occur in this sense, Zp 3¹⁵, if not also in Ps 109³¹.)

v. 16. The 'calling' and 'answering' seem to imply a citation or summons and the acceptance of it by the 'adversary', to trial of the case in a court of law. ⅁ᴮ inserts a 'not' in st. 1. 'And if I have called, and He hath not answered me, I do not believe that He listened to me.' This hardly betters the sense; and ⅁ᴺᴬ omit the μή.

v. 17. Or *Who with a storm would sweep* (or *whirl*) *me away*: cf. 27²¹. שְׂעָרָה = סְעָרָה is prob. right. The שַׂעֲרָה *a* (single) *hair* of 𝔖𝔗, which reminds us of Gabriel carrying Mahomet by a single hair (cf. Ez 8³), is merely curious (𝔖 *Who on every hair of my head with force hath smitten me!*). The verb יְשׁוּפֵנִי *would bruise me* (Aram. שוף), Gn 3¹⁵, does not suit (= ⅁ ἐκτρίψῃ, *rub out*, 𝔙 *conteret me*), nor does it agree with the ‖ passages, 27²⁰·²¹ 30²². We might point ישופני = יסופני, and regard the verb as a Denom. from סוּפָה *stormwind* (like שֵׂעָר 27²¹ Ps 58¹⁰)—a favourite word in Job (21¹⁸ 27²⁰), which is coupled with שְׂעָרָה, Na 1³. (⅁ μὴ γνόφῳ με ἐκτρίψῃ; cf. 27²⁰ γνόφος = סוּפָה !). The objection to יְסִיפֵנִי *make an end of me*, from סיף Am 3 . . . . in the context . . . . ing is not intended, but only such hurts as might be suffered by one caught up and dashed about by a sudden blast or hurricane: cf. st. ii. The same objection lies against the root אשף = אסף, Zp 1² Je 8¹³. The phrase of st. ii *would multiply my wounds* (or *bruises*) *for no cause* aptly describes the result of being blown about by the stormwind. And if we understand שׁוּף in the Aram. sense of *rubbing* and *grinding*, יְשׁוּפֵנִי may, after all, be the authentic reading, as indicating abrasions and contusions. Cf. 𝔗 14¹⁹ אבניא שָׁיְפֵי מיא.

v. 18. One would naturally be breathless, after being blown about by the wind. In st. ii בַּמְּרֹרִים (La 3¹⁵) is prob. to be restored, instead of the anomalous מַמְּרֹרִים. Elsewhere in Job the *fem.* plur. occurs: 13²⁶. Cf. the sing. 20¹⁴,²⁵.

v. 19. The simplest emendation of the impossible Heb. of st. i is to read הוּא (so 𝔊) for the meaningless הִנֵּה. A scribe may have mistaken הָא *He* for הֲא *Lo!* in the unpointed text. Then, as a verb is wanting, we may suppose that אָמַרְתִּי *I speak* or *think* (vv. 22, 27), governing לְכֹחַ (Gn 20¹³), has fallen out before אַמִּיץ. (𝔊 also read הוא אמיץ = κρατεῖ: cf. 𝔊^Σ κραταιός ἐστιν. 𝔊^B ὅτι μὲν γὰρ ἰσχύει, κρατεῖ, *For because He is strong He prevaileth*; but 𝔊^{אA} ἰσχύι = לְכֹחַ of 𝔐.)

The idea of the verse seems to be that God is an antagonist too strong to be vanquished, whether by main force or by process of law. St. ii. *Right*: or *Judgement* or trial by legal process.

arraign: or *summon*. Quis diem ei dicet? Read יוֹעִידֶנּוּ, c Suff. 3 Pers. (𝔖), instead of 1 Pers., which might be due to a scribe's remembrance of Je 49¹⁹ 50⁴⁴, where Iahvah demands מי יועידני *Who will arraign Me?* i.e. appoint Me a time and place for trial. But the reading יְעִידֵנִי *bear witness for me* (29¹¹) is perhaps preferable. So 𝔙 nemo audet pro me testimonium dicere: 𝔗: מן יסהיד עלי. Another possibility is יְעִידֵנוּ *bear witness against Him* (1 K 21¹⁰,¹³), which, however, comes to much the same thing. No man would dare to give evidence for Eyob against Iahvah. (𝔊 τίς οὖν κρίματι αὐτοῦ ἀντιστήσεται; cf. Je 49¹⁹ 50⁴⁴ καὶ τίς ἀντιστήσεταί μοι;)

v. 20. *His mouth*: פִיו. 𝔐 פִי *my* (own) *mouth*; as though terror might confuse Eyob's evidence, and turn it against himself. The emphatic position perhaps favours this. Moreover, *mouth* in Job always has a human reference, except in 22²² 23¹²; and the words of Eliphaz ירשיעך פיך ולא אני *Thine own mouth condemneth thee, not I* (15⁶)—an apparent reminiscence of this passage—clinches the argument for פִי, which has the support of all the Versions.

It (or *He*) *would make* (prove) *me perverted* (or *crooked*). Read וִיעַקְּשֵׁנִי Pi. c. Weak Waw, or better, as parallel to ירשיעני, וְיַעַקְּשֵׁנִי Hiph. (The ו may be om. as due to preceding י.)

v. 21. Eyob affirms his own innocence, regardless of consequences.

9. 23

The distich is metrically defective (st. ii); and, so far from deleting תם־אני as an inadvertent repetition from v. 20^b, we must satisfy metre and parallelism by supplying צָדִיק or אֶצְדָּק *I am righteous* in st. ii. Thus we restore as follows: תם־אני ולא־ארע נפשי אצדק ואמאס חיי. Cf. 7¹⁵ 10¹ 13^{14.15}. 𝔊 εἴτε γὰρ ἠσέβησα, οὐκ οἶδα τῇ ψυχῇ, Πλὴν (ὅτι) ἀφαιρεῖταί μου ἡ ζωή = נפשי לא־ארע אם־רשעתי (v. 20, 10⁷), phps a corruption of פִּשְׁעִי · *If I am guilty, I know not my fault*; אך יאספו חיי *But my life is being taken away* (cf. Ps 26⁹) This is at least good sense, and may approximate to the original text more nearly than 𝔐. But 𝔊 *I am perfect and know (it) not; My soul hath despised my life*, and 𝔙 Etiamsi simplex fuero, hoc ipsum ignorabit anima mea, et taedebit me vitae meae, make Eyob deny what he is always affirming, viz. his consciousness of entire innocence, while they do not imply any substantial difference from the text of 𝔐.

v. 22. We have transposed the two halves of st. i. *Therefore I say* (or *think*) naturally introduces Eyob's conclusion from the facts; and '*Tis all one* (or *It is the same thing*) is explained by *perfect and wicked He destroyeth* (treating all alike, without difference or discrimination).

𝔊 om. אחת היא, and app. reads רב וריץ for תם ורשע, by confusion and transposition of similar letters, while for the Pron. היא it reads (or substitutes) אף = ὀργή *anger* (? הָיָּה); thus getting for the whole verse *Wherefore I said, Great man and lordling anger destroyeth*, and going far astray from the sense of the context. 𝔗 has a good paraphrase of חדא מכילתא היא ליה, viz. אחת היא *He* (God) *hath but one measure*.

v. 23. a Scourge; or *Plague*. 𝔊 *his Rod* or *Plague* (שָׁבְטוֹ). שׁוֹט is a horsewhip, Pr 26³. Any general calamity, such as plague or famine, was held to be a Scourge of God. Is 10²⁶; cf. Ez 14²¹ 2 Sa 24^{13 ff.} 2 K 19³⁵. A sudden outbreak of some epidemic, such as at all times has been frequent in Eastern countries, cutting off good and bad alike, seems to be intended here. And Eyob daringly asserts, not merely that God 'looks on unconcernedly' (Dr), but that He actually *derides* or mocks at the slaughter of the innocent.

slaughter: reading לְמַכַּת (see Is 10²⁶, where כְּמַכַּת follows שׁוֹט). The word is also used of *plagues*, Dt 28⁵⁹ al. 𝔐 לְמַסַּת *at the trial* or *testing* (√נסה) Others derive the word from √מסס *melt* intr., Niph. *faint, grow fearful*, and render *despair* (see on 6¹⁴), which hardly agrees with the context, not to mention philological objections. Not the feelings, but the destruction, of the righteous, is the object of the Divine Destroyer's mirth. And although the explanation of calamity as a *trial* or *test* of the righteous is revealed to us in the Prologue, it is altogether absent from the utterances of Eyob; the main ground of his complaints being that God's dealings with him are an inscrutable mystery. (נסה occurs in Job only once, 4²; and then only in the sense of *attempting*, not *tempting* or *trying*.)

⑤ *Because worthless men* are *in an extraordinary death, But righteous are derided*: prob. not due to theological prejudice, but to misreading of a more or less illegible Heb. text (= רשעים במות מפלאות: cf. 22¹⁰, where ἐξαίσιος = פתאם, as here: 37¹⁶ ἐξαίσια = מפלאות: st. ii : וּלְמוֹ נקיים ילענו; cf. 27¹⁴ 29²¹ for the Prep., which suggests לָמוֹ = לָמוּת for למסת).

v. 24. Lit. *The land* (or *earth*)—*He hath given it to a Wicked* (or *Godless*) *One; The face of its Judges He covereth* (so that they fail to discern Right from Wrong and Truth from Falsehood. Cf. 12¹⁷ 22¹³·¹⁴ Pr 8¹⁵·¹⁶ Is 11²⁻⁴). Point נְתָנָהּ *He hath given her* (with ⑤) for 𝔐 נִתְּנָה *She hath been given*. The Perf., after all the preceding Impff., is remarkable; and, taken along with the Sing. רשע *a Villain*, appears to present an historical datum, indicative of the actual state of things at the time. ⑤ παραδέδονται γὰρ εἰς χεῖρας ἀσεβοῦς. Jason, the Hellenizing High Priest, is called ὁ ἀσεβής, 2 Macc 4¹³, and οἱ ἀσεβεῖς (= הרשעים) denotes the Hellenizing faction in Judea, 1 Macc 3⁶·¹⁵ 6²¹ 9⁷³.

(The verse is a triplet, and may be a later insertion, as may also v. 23, where the 'Scourge' might refer to one of the Syrian raids of the Maccabean period. It would, of course, be easy to supply a line, e.g. ולא יבינו דעת *So that they discern not knowledge*: cf. Pr 26⁷. But the two vv. 23, 24 do not hang together very well with the context on either side of them, in which the speaker considers his own case only. Eyob's previous words find a suitable conclusion in v. 22.)

If not He, who else? i.e. inflicts calamity, regardless of the deserts of its victims. Reading: אִם־לֹא הוּא מִי־אֵפוֹא. So ⑤ εἰ δὲ μὴ αὐτός ἐστιν, τίς ἐστιν; and 𝔙𝔗. But ⑤ follows order of 𝔐, and points אַפּוֹ *His anger*, reading or guessing יְשָׁא for הוּא, and rendering *But His anger who endureth?* Cf. also 24²⁵ Gn 27³³.

v. 25. Resumes the personal note. *My days.* Om. introd. *And* (RV *Now*), c 2 MSS, ⑤𝔗𝔙. The ו is only dupl. of the following י, as often. *A runner*: i.e. a courier, or King's Messenger. See on 7⁸. Es 3¹³·¹⁵. *without seeing*: lit. *and have not seen good* (leg. ולא c ⑤ ⑤𝔙. Waw has fallen out of 𝔐 after preceding Waw). *To see good* is to experience happiness or prosperity: cf. Ps 4⁷. The statement is strange, in view of the Prologue, with its account of Eyob's former great prosperity. See also 7⁶·⁷, which this verse briefly repeats (esp. 7⁷ᵇ *Mine eye will no more see good*). Perhaps יראו should be read for ראו: *and will not see good.* We might also render 𝔐: *My days, they are swifter than a runner; They fly, they see not good.* But the Perff. seem more appropriate to a review of the past (cf. Gn 47⁹); and Eyob would hardly insist on the swift passage of the long' hours of his hopeless misery (cf. 7²⁻⁴). ⑤ om. טובה: *They ran away unawares* (lit. *and knew not*: cf. v. 5); but this cannot be right.

v. 26. *papyrus*: אֵבֶה here only. The Assyr. a-bu, a-pu, means *bed of reeds* or *jungle*; e.g. *qanê api*, 'reeds of the jungle' in Anp. al.; but we cannot be sure of the connexion. One would have expected to find an Egyptian source for the word. Freytag's اَبٌ *arundines* does not appear in Lane. 𝕲 app. substitutes עקב *footprint* or *track* (ἴχνος ὁδοῦ) for אבה; remembering Ps 77²⁰ (𝕲 76¹⁹) and Wisd 5¹⁰·¹¹, 𝔗 אלפיא דטינין מנדיא *ships laden with choice fruits* (cf. Dt 33¹³ Ct 4¹³ 7¹⁴) and 𝔙 naves poma portantes, both equate אבה with Aram. אב *fruit* (Dan 4⁹); while 𝔖, with its *great ships of enemies*, equates the word with איבה *enmity*!

It is evident from the context that light swift boats, like the old Nile-craft of papyrus, are intended, not heavy freight-boats. Cf. Is 18².

Like an eagle: or *vulture*. *Swoopeth*: or *flieth down*. The ἅπ. טוש = Aram. טוס *to fly* (𝔗 Je 5⁷) may be akin to Heb. סוס *a* (swift) *horse*, Aram. סוסיא, Assyr. *sîsû*, and the homonym סוס, סוסיא, a *swift* or *swallow*. (𝕲 st. ii. see Wisd 5¹¹.)

v. 27. I say or (*have said*) or *think*: אָמַרְתִּי: so 1 MS, 𝕲𝔙 pr 𝔐 אֹמְרִי. Cf. 𝔗 אִין אֵימַר *If I shall say*. *I will relax* אֶעֶזְבָה. lit. *let loose*. cf. 10¹ 20¹³. We should rather have expected *I will lift up*, אשא, or perhaps אזבלה (cf. Gn 30²⁰ metaph. *lift up* = honour). 𝔗 has אשבק רוגזי = אעזבה אפי *I will let go my wrath* (אפי pro פני), which may be right (Ps 37⁸). 𝕲 συγκύψας τῷ προσώπῳ στενάξω, *With the face bowed down, I will groan*, gives the very opposite of the required sense. (στενάξω = אאבלה instead of אבלינה: cf. Is 19⁸. But the rare בלג Hiph. *shine, brighten up, smile*, or the like, which recurs 10²⁰ Ps 39¹⁴, is doubtless right. It may be compared with ש־לג *snow*, so called as *glistening* white, ד־לק *burn*, שָׁלַק *scorched* by the sun, Sum ZA-LAG *shine, light* of fire, LAG *shine, light*. ב־לג = *to be a-shine* or *in shining*.)

v. 28. 𝔐 lit. *I dread all my pains*; i.e. app. he fears their return, and therefore dares not be cheerful. Instead of עצבתי (7¹⁵) 𝕲 seems to have read עצמתי *my limbs* (20¹¹ 21²⁴), which is no improvement here. But 𝔙 opera mea = עצבתי (cf. Pr 5¹⁰ עצביך *thy labours*). 𝔗 צַעֲרַי *my pains* (cf. Gn 3¹⁶), and 𝔖 'And if I am quiet, I am afraid of all torment': a correct paraphrase. (𝔗 gives כנשית *I gathered* = אגרתי for יגרתי *I dread*.) Read perhaps מפני *because of* pro 𝔐 כל *all*: cf. 7¹⁵ Dt 28⁶⁰ (but also 3²⁵).

v. 29. St. i is too short in 𝔐. An introductory אם *If*, or הן *Lo!* or perhaps both (so 𝔖), may be restored: (*Lo,*) *if I* (emph.) *am to be found guilty* (or *condemned*), as is certain beforehand, *Wherefore should I labour in vain* to establish my innocence? Cf. 𝔙 Si autem et sic impius sum, &c. 𝕲 ἐπειδὴ (δέ) εἰμι ἀσεβής, Διὰ τί οὐκ ἀπέθανον, (= למה זה בל אגוע:), *But since I am guilty, Why did I not die* without further question? A good sense in itself, but not in harmony with the context. Read perhaps אם־אמנם אנכי וגו' *If indeed I am to be guilty*.

v. 30. Sn... is a natural em..'em of p...t p...ty (Is... Ps 51): but people do not wash *with snow* (Kt בְּמוֹ שָׁלֶג 𝔊), nor *with snow water* (בְּמֵי שָׁלֶג; 𝔄𝔖𝔙 RV) to secure it. Read therefore כְּמוֹ *like* for בְּמוֹ *with*, in the sense *as white as*, and render: *Though I had washed me snow-white*.

St. ii. בֹּר בְּפַּיִם is *purity of hands* in 22³⁰; cf. Ps 18²¹·²⁵. Here בַּפַּי must be the Obj. of the Trans. verb, and בֹּר is not *cleanness* (so 𝔊𝔖𝔙), but an alkaline substance used for cleansing, viz. *lye* (*Lauge*); a mixture of potash and water: cf. Is 1²⁵. A syn. is בֹּרִית, Je 2²². The common root is ברר Assyr. *barâru*, *be bright, shine*, the Prim. Root of which is seen in Sum. BAR, *shine* (*namâru*), *light* (*nûru*), *the sun* (*šamšu*), PAR, *bright* (*namru*), &c., whence also כפר *sunlike, bright, pure*, Trans. *wash, cleanse, purify*, &c. In the same way דָּכָה, Aram. דְּכָא, Assyr. *zakû, be clean, pure*, and זָכַךְ *be bright, shining, pure*, זַךְ *pure*, may be traced back to Sum. DAG, *bright, shining, pure*, SHAG, *bright, purify* metals, ZA(G), *bright*, ZAG, *flame*, &c. (all akin to LAG, LAG, *bright*; ZA-LAG, *shining, light of fire*). The idea of moral purity thus found its original expression through the natural and beautiful metaphor of light.

v. 31. The Apodosis to v. 30.—𝔐 בשחת *in the pit*; cf. 17¹⁴ 33²² al. (of She'ol). *A pitfall*, Ps 7¹⁶ 9¹⁶ al. Nowhere app. *a ditch* (גֵּב, 2 K 3¹⁶). בשחוותא 𝔗 = 𝔐. 𝔊 ἐν ῥύπῳ, *in filth* (ῥύπος = צֹאָה, *foul*, 14⁴; צֹאָה *filth*, Is 4⁴. Cf. Zc 3³·⁴ ἱμάτια ῥυπαρά = בגדים צואים) = 𝔙 sordibus. But 𝔖 נוטמא = שחת *pit*, Pr 26²⁷ al. There is no need to read בְּסֻתָּה (Is 5²⁵). 𝔊𝔙 render acc. to the sense. A cesspit or hole for refuse is meant.

And my clothes would make me abhorred (or *offensive*). People would turn away from him in disgust, as foul to sight and smell and, moreover, ceremonially 'unclean'. Cf. Ez 16²⁵ (for this use of תעב Pi.); Zc 3³·⁴. It has been proposed to read שַׂלְמַי or שַׂלְמָי (?), in the sense of *my friends* (*And my friends would abhor me*); but neither word occurs elsewhere in the book. See also 19¹⁷·¹⁹. (תעב = TA Formative + ĠAB: cf. Sum. ĠAB, *bi'šu, stinking, foul, bad*. Perhaps Tg. סאיב *pollute* = SA Formative, Saphel + ĠAB = *make foul*.)

v. 32. Something has gone wrong with 𝔐. The first st. seems too long, though כי־לא־איש—note the Maqqephs—might perhaps be spoken with a single stress (cf. כי־לא־כן, v. 35); and a barely possible rendering of the whole verse might be: *For One that is not Man, like me—can I answer Him? Shall we enter into Judgement together?* But we must at least restore ו before אעננו (Nu 23¹⁹ al.) and prob. before נבוא also (𝔖; cf. 𝔙 nec), which has fallen out, as often, after י and ו. Perhaps ואעננו is an insertion: *For He is not human, like me, That we should enter*, &c. But the Pron. הוא (for which 𝔊 supplies אתה, misled by vv. 28 31) is wanted after כי־לא־איש; cf. 𝔖. The change to 3 Pers. marks the beginning of a new paragraph, and agrees with what follows,

vv. 34, 35. (𝔙 neque enim viro qui similis mei est, respondebo, answers to 𝔐 word for word.) For איש לא, cf. 12¹⁰ 32¹³ Nu 23¹⁹ Is 31⁸.

v. 33. Pointing לֹא (2 Sa 18¹²) = לוּא, לוּ, Opt. Pt. *Would that...*, *O that...*, c 13 MSS, 𝔊 (εἴθε or εἰ γάρ) 𝔖. But 𝔗𝔙 = 𝔐: *There is not an umpire*, &c. (𝔊's rendering: *O that our Mediator were both arguing And hearing between both !* = 'ש׳ לוּ אִישׁ־בֵּינֵינוּ מוֹכִיחַ וְשֹׁמֵעַ בֵּין: cf. Dt 1¹⁶ for שׁמע בֵּין of judges. אִישׁ בֵּינֵינוּ, *our between-man* = ὁ μεσίτης ἡμῶν, Ga 3¹⁹ ²⁰ Heb 8⁶. Cf. also 1 Sa 17⁴⁻²³ אִישׁ הַבֵּינַיִם. Μεσίτης, *mediator, arbitrator, umpire*, does not occur elsewhere in 𝔊.)

That he might lay his hand upon the twain of us! as imposing his decision on both alike, and perhaps as reconciling them to each other.

v. 34. *His Rod*: 𝔐 שִׁבְטוֹ, c ם majore So 𝔊 ῥάβδον, 𝔙 virgam, 𝔖 שבטה; but 𝔗 מחתיה *His stroke* or *plague* = שׁוֹטוֹ v. 23: cf. Na 3² Is 10²⁶. This may be right.

appal me: 𝔊 με στροβείτω, *whirl about, distract me*; a word which recurs 13¹¹ 15²³ 33⁷ (not elsewhere in 𝔊). בעת, Ar. نغت *fall upon a man suddenly, take him by surprise* or *unawares*, is prob. cogn. with פחד *be afraid*.

v. 35. 𝔊 transposes the two members of st. i: *And I will not be afraid, but will speak.* St. ii. 𝔐 כִּי לֹא כֵן אָנֹכִי עִמָּדִי: 'For not so (i.e. in a position to be in fear of Him) *am I with myself* (i.e. in my conscience). 'With' is in Heb. used idiomatically (cf. 10¹³ 23¹⁴ 27¹¹) to express *in the mind* or *knowledge of*' (Dr) In the three reff. עם appears to express intention or design rather than conscience or knowledge; and not one of those passages, nor any other that I know of, presents a real parallel to the strange *Not so am I with me*. The Pron. אנכי seems to require a verb, such as is, in fact, supplied by 𝔊 οὐ γὰρ οὕτω συνεπίσταμαι = כִּי לֹא־כֵן אָנֹכִי יוֹדֵעַ: *For Unright* (or *Injustice*) *I know*; i.e. I know the difference between Right and Wrong (6³⁰), Justice and Injustice. (יודע pro 𝔐 עמדי). The rare συνεπίσταμαι = אחוה, 19²⁷.) For לֹא־כֵן *not right*, see 2 K 7⁹ Je 8⁶ al. The rendering of 𝔊^{A N.c.a} οὐ γὰρ (οὕτω om. A) συνεπίστ. ἐμαυτῷ ἄδικον, *For I am not conscious of wrongdoing*, is good sense, and seems to support our interpretation of לֹא־כֵן. Perhaps, however, we should read יְדַעְתִּי, in place of עמדי: *For Unjust I* (emph.) *know Him*; i.e. God is not just in dealing as He has done with me; I know, if you do not, that my miseries are altogether unmerited. Cf. vv. 21, 22, 10⁷.

Chapter 10. *v.* 1. Lit. *My soul feels loathing* (or *sickens*) *at my life*.

I will give the rein to: or *let loose*: אֶעֶזְבָה, 9²⁷. So 𝔊 ἐπαφήσω; 𝔙 dimittam; 𝔗 אשבוק. But perhaps אשפכה *I will pour out* (c עָלַי: Ps 42⁵) *upon me my complaining* (𝔊 *groaning* = שִׂיחִי), *I will loose against Him* (עָלָיו) instead of (עָלַי) *my words*. But 𝔐 is preferable (Ps 42⁵), since *I will* … … *El*… … v. 2. The redundant third line

I will speak in the bitterness of my soul looks like a gloss (from 7¹¹) on st. ii.

v. 2. Treat me not as guilty: or *Do not condemn me*: 9²⁰ 15⁸ al. 𝔊 Μή με ἀσεβεῖν δίδασκε, *Teach me not to be wicked!* app. reading הרשע and connecting with it הודיעני (= δίδασκε, 13²³ al.) from st. ii.

v. 3. Doth it please: or *profit* Thee: Is it any good to Thee? Cui bono? As הטוב-לך has but one stress, and as תעשק usu. has an Obj., we suppose that תם *blameless* has fallen out before תמאס. But 𝔊: ἢ καλόν σοι ἐὰν ἀδικήσω; (= רשעת for תעשק; app. read backwards!). Perhaps due to theological offence. St. iii is prob. an interpolation. Apart from the metrical objection, it is irrelevant to the argument here, though it agrees with 9²⁴: see the note there.

smiled: lit. *shone*: 3⁴ v. 22 37¹⁵ Ps 50² 80² Dt 33². The √יפע, used only in Hiph. as here, is in Heb. poetic, and found only in Job, Pss, and Dt l. c. The corresponding Assyr. root is common both in poetry and in elevated prose, esp. in Shaph. (= Heb. Hiph.) and pass. Ishtaphal, in the sense of *causing to come or shine forth, making splendid or glorious, creating or bringing into existence*, and the corresp. passive meanings (ušēpī, ušāpā; uštāpū, uštēpā, &c.). The original idea was prob. that of *springing out and up, rising into light and sight* (cf. *napāḫu*). The Assyr. *šūpū* (III 1. 2.) is the usual equivalent of the Sumerian PA-Ê, *shining + come forth*. This PA may be compared with PAR, *shining* (*namru*) and with PA, *a shoot* or *sprout* (*aru*), and with BAR, BA, *shine*. It may very well be the Primitive Root of יפע, ופע, and its weaker cognate יפה, as also of Ar. يَافِع *adultus, grown up, grown tall*, of a boy, and Sab. יפע, *raise, heighten*. (𝔊 προσέσχες = הקשבת for הופעת: 13⁶: perperam.)

v. 4. Lit. *Hast Thou eyes of Flesh? Or like a Mortal's seeing seest Thou?* Cf. 1 Sa 16⁷. Art Thou liable to human errors of judgement? Hast Thou no more insight than my friends, that Thou treatest me so?

v. 5. Lit. *Are Thy days like a mortal's days*, &c. Cf. Ps 90 102²⁴⁻²⁶ for the contrast between God's eternity and Man's mortality. But the connexion of thought between vv. 5, 6 is hardly obvious. The suggestion, however, may be that it is hardly worthy of an Eternal Being to pay so much attention to the behaviour of an ephemeral creature like man. A similar sequence of thought is observable in 7¹⁷ ᶠᶠ. In fact, chap. 10 may almost be called a mere expansion of 7¹⁶⁻²¹. Driver's paraphrase 'Art Thou short-lived, that Thou hastenest (vv. 6, 7) to find out my sin, even before it is committed, lest it should escape punishment?' seems improbable. The verses say nothing about 'haste' or search for sin 'before it is committed'.

v. 6. Both stt. seem metr. short. In st. i insert אתה *Thou* emph.; in st. ii we might read ואחר חט, as 39⁸. For דרש c different construction, see 3⁵. (ברש, √. i, only here in Job.)

10.9 NOTES ON THE TEXT

v. 7. *When* (or *Although*) *Thou knowest* (lit. *Upon Thy knowing*: 16¹⁷ Is 53⁹) *that I am . . . And* (that) *there is not*, &c But st. ii is no parallel to st i. 𝔊 ἀλλὰ τίς ἐστιν ὁ ἐκ τῶν χειρῶν σου ἐξαιρούμενος; = ומי מידיך מציל is no better. The emendation בִּידֵי מָעַל (וְאֵין) *And* (that) *there is no perfidy in my hand* makes a good parallel, but מָעַל does not occur elsewhere in Job (21³⁴ is corrupt). Perhaps בִּידַי מָעוֹל *And that there is no wrong in my hands.* (For מן, cf. OL, p. 580, 3 c.; for עול, 34¹⁰·³² Ps 7⁴). The verse, however, is not necessary to the sense (see note on v. 5) and may be an exegetic interpolation.

v. 8. *Thine own Hands*: or *'Twas Thy Hands that framed*, &c. The word is emphatic. עצבוני *framed* or *fashioned* me. עצב Pi., Je 44¹⁹ (?), compared by Buhl with Ar. عَصَبَ *cut off*, e. g. a limb, perhaps means to *cut out* or *carve* (cf. ברא) Possibly, however, it may be to *bind, put together, combine, construct,* or *build* (cf. perhaps Ar. عَصَبَ *bind* or *tie round*); if we may judge by the analogy of Assyr. vbb. of binding, like *rakâsu* and *k(q)açâru*, which are often used of building. Cf. also Assyr. *eçêpu* (עצף), *combine, put together, add.* (The rare Heb. עצב Pi. as here used may be disguised under the meaningless form בעצמים, Ec 11⁵, where it seems plausible to restore בָּעָצֵב גֹּלֶם as *it fashioneth the embryo* (Ps 139¹⁶) in the pregnant womb.) 𝔊 ἔπλασάν με = יצרוני (יצר = πλάττω, Gn 27⁸ ¹⁹ et al.), *moulded me.* Cf Ps 119⁷³.

St. ii. *And afterwards* (𝔊𝔖) *wilt Thou turn round and swallow me?* reading וְאַחַר תּסוֹב וּתְבַלְּעֵנִי instead of 𝔐's impossible יַחַד סָבִיב וַתְּבַלְּעֵנִי *Together around; and Thou hast swallowed me up.* (אחר סבות ותבלעני *Afterwards Thou didst turn round and swallow me up* is of course equally possible, but has a prosaic sound, and does not agree so well with the pleading tone of the next verse.) In fact, Eyob had not yet been 'swallowed up' or annihilated (8¹⁸), though the Satan desired it (2³).

𝔊 μετὰ (+ δὲ 𝔊ᴬ) ταῦτα (= וְאַחַר) μεταβαλών (= תָּסוֹב; or וַתָּשָׁב, v. 16) ἔπαισας The vb. ἔπαισας, Thou *struckest*, is remarkable. This vb. usu. renders הִכָּה, as in 2⁷. We might suppose a rg. וַתַּכֵּנִי for וַתְּבַלְּעֵנִי; but it seems possible that ἔπαισας represents ἔπισας, *drankest up* (a false formation from πίνω), or even πιέσαι, *wilt drink up* (Lk 17⁸), or perhaps ἐπάσω, *didst eat.*

v. 9. *O remember that Thou madest me of clay!* 𝔊𝔖 om. נא Part. of Entreaty, *O* or *Pray!* 𝔙 *quaeso. of clay* = חֹמֶר, Accus. of Material · Gn 2⁷ Ex 25¹⁸ al. 𝔐 כַחֹמֶר *like the clay.* St. ii. *And (that) unto (the) dust* (or *earth*) *Thou wilt make me return*: a ref. to Gn 3¹⁹ : ואל־עפר תשוב. RV *And wilt Thou bring me into dust again?* as though it were unreasonable in God, after making him of 'clay', to resolve him again into his constituent material. ('Clay' and 'dust' are synonymous, both meaning earth (4ᶠ notes)) This will not do. Eyob implores God to desist from further persecution of a being who is not, like Himself, eternal, but of earthly origin and mortal nature. He does not complain of the inevitable. He knows that, in any case, he must soon die: vv. 20, 21; 7⁶·⁷ 9²³.

v. 10. *pour me out*: Hiph. of נתך (see on 3²⁴) *pour out*, intrans., str. *flow* = Assyr. *natâku*, and then *melt* (Ez 22²⁰⁻²²). The root is prob. *tak*, which may be compared with *zak* in זכה, זכך, &c., and with Sum. DAG, *shining, pure*, SHAG and SIG, *bright, pure, purify, smelt*, or *refine* metals.

Whatever the legendary lore of his race had to tell of the origin of Man on the earth (v. 9; cf. notes on 4¹⁹) the poet knew well enough that it was only in a figurative sense that he himself could be said to have been moulded out of clay. The present verse obviously refers to the processes of natural generation; first, the emission of the milky semen, and then its coagulation in the womb, as milk thickens into curd or 'cheese' (גְּבִינָה; ἅπ· in OT). And all these gradual processes of the growth and shaping of the body, which we call 'natural', he regards as due to the direct personal activity of the Eternal Creator (v. 11). Cf. Ps 139¹³⁻¹⁶. Nor can it be pretended that a more exact knowledge of protoplasmic matter and the evolution of germ and cell has solved for the modern world the ultimate mystery of life.

(The Versions miss the ref. to Generation; e.g. 𝔗 for תתיכני gives יתי סננתא *purifiedst me*. Cf. Sum. SHEN, *ebbu, ellu, bright*, or *pure*.)

v. 11. We do not, of course, expect anatomical precision, but only a statement in poetic form of things open to ordinary observation. If the skin and the flesh, the outer and inner integuments of our mortal frame, may be called its 'clothing', what function is fulfilled by the bones and sinews or muscles? Clearly they are the strength and support of the whole structure. Accordingly, 𝔊 gives שררתני *Thou didst strengthen me* or *make me firm* (cf. שְׁרִירֵי *muscles*, 40¹⁶; Sum. SHER, *bind, bond*) for תשככני; and it is quite conceivable that this old Aram. vb. stood in the original text. 𝔊, however, has ἔνειρας, *entwinedst, intertwinedst*, or *didst string me together*, and 𝔗 אשתיתני *wovest me* = תְּסֹכְכֵנִי Ps 139¹³; whence it is usually supposed that the ἅπ· שׂכך = the ἅπ· סכך *to weave* or *weave together*: cf. שׂרג Pu. *intertwined*, of the sinews of the river-horse, 40¹⁷. On the other hand, שׂכך = סכך may perhaps be Poel of סוך = שׂוך *hedge* or *fence in*, 1¹⁰ 3²³ 38⁸ (the bones and sinews being regarded as the third line of the Self or Soul's defence). So Ps 139¹³ *didst enclose me in my mother's womb*.

v. 12. *Compassion*: רחמים (Ho 2²¹) for חיים *life*; or perhaps it should be חֵן (incorrectly written חין, and then mistaken for חיים = חיין) *favour*. It hardly suits the context to read חיים וָחֶלֶד *life and duration* or *continuance*, even if we accept שֶׁת (𝔊 ἴσον vt. 14) for עָשִׂיתָ; for such a phrase would most naturally refer to the life after birth (Ps 39⁵·⁶ 89⁴⁸), and the ref. here is to Eyob's antenatal experience, viz. God's loving care of him as a babe in the womb: cf. v. 18. Besides, *Thou didst put life with me* (instead of *Thou gavest me life*) would be a strange expression; and חלד is not a Job-word (see on 11¹¹). On the other hand, עשה חסד עם *deal kindly with, show kindness to* is a common phrase (Gn 19¹⁹ al.). The st. has four beats, unless there is a crasis of vb. and prep. (we might perhaps read לִי enclitic pro עמדי: cf. Ps. 18⁵¹).

v. 13. *And* (all the time of this assiduous care) *Thou wast cherishing these* intentions (in regard to Thy future dealing with me; viz. those described in vv. 14–16). Lit. *And these things Thou didst hide* (or *hoard*, or *treasure up*: צפן 15²⁰ 21¹⁹ 23¹²; 14¹³ Hi. 24¹ Ni.) *in Thy heart*. Malice lurked under the fair show of Divine favour. The Pronouns אלה and זאת thus refer to what immediately follows. But why are both used? It looks as if the meaning might be *These calamities—This, my present condition*. 𝔊 ταῦτα ἔχων ἐν σεαυτῷ (= בלבבך), οἶδα ὅτι πάντα δύνασαι = יָדַעְתִּי כִּי־כֹל תּוּכַל = 42²ᵃ (𝔊 adds the rest of that verse here). 𝔖 *I knew that this was in thy mind* (בְּרַעֲיָנָךְ = 𝔐 עִמָּךְ *with Thee*). But 𝔙 Licet haec celes in corde tuo, tamen scio quia universorum memineris(!), which suggests: ידעתי כי כל זאת עמך (cf. 𝔊).

v. 14. *absolve me: treat me as pure* or *innocent, acquit me*: נקה Pi. Ps 19¹³. The Prim. Root may be NAG = Sum. SHAG, *bright, pure, purify*, DAG, *shining* (see note on 9²⁰). And since there is a close connexion between the ideas of *brightening* and *cleansing* or *purifying*, while purification is commonly effected by *pouring* water on the thing to be purified, we may further recognize a relation to the Sum. NAG, *drink, drench, water* land (A.-S. *drincan, drencan*), drinking being a kind of *pouring*, viz. into the mouth or down the throat (figured as a bottle in the linear script). Hence Assyr. *naqû*, *pour out* water for the dead (*náq mê*, the man who does it), wine in libation to the gods, and met. sighing. Cf. Syr. ܢܩܦ II. *pour a libation*, and Ar. نقى II. *cleanse* or *purify*.

v. 15. *woe to me!* אללי לי. So Mi 7¹. Cf. Gk. ἀλαλή, ἀλαλά, *loud cry*, ἐλελεῦ, *war-cry, cry of pain*; Assyr. *elêlu, to play* (and *sing*), *elêlu, woful strain, lament, alâlu, joyous shouting*, Sum. ELALU, ILU, *shriek, howl, sing*, ELLU, *joyous cry*, &c. UL, ULU, *rejoicing* (*ullu, ulçu* = עליץ); Heb. הלל, ילל, &c. (Mostly, perhaps, onomatopoetic, like Eng. *yell*. But Sum. UL looks like a sec. form of GUL, *ḫidûtu, rejoicing*.)

St. iii is a self-evident marginal intrusion, violating the metre of the verse, and in itself unmetrical with its two or four stresses. Moreover, the second member וראה עניי *and see Thou my affliction!* (𝔊 om.) is clearly corrupt, as out of construction with the preceding phrase. Lagarde's רְוֵה עֳנִי *drenched* (lit. *watered*) *with affliction* agrees perfectly with שְׂבַע קָלוֹן *full-f*·*d w*·*th d*·*sh*·*n*·*u*·· and must be right. Cf. Is 51¹⁷, La 3¹⁶. Shame and humiliation are ··· ab·un·li··, food and drink,

Ps 42⁴ 80⁶. (Of course, רְאֵה might be a later or Aramaized pronunciation of רְוֵה; cf. נָאת = נוּת, Ps 23² al.) These marginal notes, consisting of more or less apposite quotations, exegetical glosses and various readings, may be taken as evidence of the popularity of the book from ancient times. In the instance before us, the annotator gives a reason (wrongly based on Eyob's present misery) why he would not 'lift up his head', i.e. dare to exhibit the confident bearing of security. Ju 8²⁸ Ps 83³.

v. 16. In immediate connexion with לא אשא ראשי *I might not* or *durst not hold up my head* in the fearless confidence of conscious innocence (v. 15). *Were I elated,* lifted up in spirit; reading אם גאה(1) pro 𝔐 ויגאה (cf. 𝔊 ܡܶܬܓܰܐܶܐ, 𐌾𐍉). 𝔐 is usu. rendered *And if it* (my head) *should lift itself up* (cf. RV); but the change of Obj. to Subj. is improb. תנאה *Thou wouldst exalt Thyself,* exhibit Thy superior Power, or 'triumph' (see Ex 15¹·⁷·¹²), would be better. This verse, indeed, with its גאה and פלא (st. ii), may be partly due to reminiscence of Ex. l.c., with its גאה גאון, and עשה פלא. *like a lion* (שחל 4¹⁰ 28⁸) *Thou wouldst hunt me.* Is the lion here the hunted, or the Divine hunter Himself? 𝔊 supposes the former (ἀγρεύομαι γὰρ ὥσπερ λέων εἰς σφαγήν = להרוג pro ¹ויגאה); and so 𝔙 *Et propter superbiam quasi leaenam capies me* (*superbiam* = my defiant bearing in 'lifting up my head'). Hunting the lion (the frequent boast of Assyrian kings) is, however, unknown to the OT writers, with whom the king of beasts is always a symbol of surpassing strength and terror. On the other hand, Iahvah is 'like a lion' (כמו שחל, כשחל) in His destructive aspect (Ho 5¹⁴ 13⁷). Perhaps we should emend תצדני *wouldst lie in wait for me* (cf. Ps 10⁹ La 3¹⁰), from צדה, 1 Sa 24¹²; a term which seems more appropriate to the activity of beasts of prey than צוד (cf., however, 38³⁹). The st. may be an intrusion.

St. ii. *Thou* [leg. אתה pro ו] *wouldst again shew Thyself marvellous* (i.e. act strangely, mysteriously, or uniquely) *against me.* Cf. Is 29¹⁴. The √פלא (Hithpa. here only) occurs most freq. in Niph. Ptcp. fem. plur. (of God's wonderful works, regarded as beyond human understanding, 42³), 5³ 37⁵·¹⁴, and is most common in the Pss (about thirty times). The Prim. Root is prob. identical with Sum. BAL, *split, break through* or *into, divide,* &c. (cf. BAL, *axe, pilaqqu*), which ramifies in the series פלה, פל־ג, פל־ח, פלל, &c. Thus פֶּלֶא *a wonder* is, strictly speaking, something *separate* and *apart from* other and ordinary things. 𝔊 δεινῶς με ὀλέκεις is a paraphrase which does not imply any difference of reading (cf. 𝔊^{AΘ} ἐθαυμάστωσας).

v. 17. Suspicious, as a tristich. *Thou wouldst renew Thy witnesses before me* is, indeed, grammatical, but the meaning is uncertain. The

---

¹ It εἰς σφαγήν לשחט, the latter may be a variant of כשחל; and then it will be true to say that 𝔊 omits ויגאה.

'witnesses' are said to be Eyob's 'sufferings', which were held by all to be glaring evidence of guilt. But Eyob himself stoutly denied this inference; how then can *before me* (נֶגְדִּי) be right? 𝔊 ἐπανακαινίζων ἐπ' ἐμὲ τὴν ἐτασίν μου (𝔊^A σου) = (תְּנַגֵּשׁ) תְּחַדֵּשׁ עָלַי נִגְעִי *Thou wouldst renew upon me Thy stroke* (? נִגְעֶיךָ) *Thy strokes*: Gn 12¹⁷); cf. Ps 38¹² 39¹¹. For ἔτασις, *trial, examination*, as a paraphrastic rendering of נגע *stroke, plague,* see Gn 12¹⁷ (נגעים ... ויגגע = καὶ ἤτασεν ... ἐτασμοῖς). This simpler and more natural reading agrees better with the preceding line (*Thou wouldst again deal strangely with me*), of which it appears to be explicative (and with which it may form a distich, if 16ᵃ be an interpolation), while it also affords a better parallel to what follows: *And Thou wouldst increase Thine anger* (בעש = בעם) *with me* (cf. Ps 85⁵ בעסך עמנו).

St. iii עִמִּי: חֲלִיפוֹת וְצָבָא עִמִּי *Changes* or *reliefs*, *relays* (1 K 5²⁸) *and a host or warfare are with me*, is obviously corrupt, whatever way we take it. The author does not use the fig. Hendiadys; and if he did, it would not help us here, for how could 'a host in relays' be 'with' Eyob? In 7¹ צבא denotes a (time of) *hard service*; cf. 14¹⁴. *All the days of my service* (צבאי) *will I wait, Until my relief* (חליפתי) *cometh*. In the sense of *army* or *warfare*, צָבָא does not occur in Job. (These three are the only reff.) At the end of the verse, עמי, after עמדי, cannot be right. Read therefore חֲלִיפַת צְבָאִי עָמָד: *The relief of my service tarrieth* (עָמַד, Gn 45⁹: pro עמי), which may be a marginal intrusion. 𝔊 ἐπήγαγες δὲ ἐπ' ἐμὲ πειρατήρια = ; ותחליף צבא עלי *And wouldst bring fresh thraldom upon me*. For חלף see 4¹⁵ 9¹¹·²⁰; and for צבא = πειρατήριον, 7¹. If the line is original, this (or something like it) may be right. Cf. 𝔖 ܐܢܐ ܚܝܠܬܟ ܡܫܢܝܬ *And hosts Thou changest* (or *renewest*) *against me*; taking צבא (c 𝔊) in the sense of *an army* of assailing troubles.

v. 18. *I might have died*: or *should* (or *ought to*) *have expired* (3¹¹). For the Prim. Root, cf. perhaps Sum 𒄷𒌋 UG (GUG), *dead* > Ar. جاع *be hungry* (though Eng. *starve* orig. meant *die*). Or is גוע (Heb. only) = נמע, *gasp for breath?* cf. Aram. נמע *to swallow*. There is no need to insert וְלֹא c 𝔊 καὶ οὐκ ἀπέθανον. See 𝔖𝔗, which give it rightly. We might perhaps render *Died I, no eye would have seen me*.

v. 20. Ketîb: *Are not my days few? let Him cease!* (יֶחְדַּל) *Let Him set* (His heart, 7¹⁷, or His face, Nu 24¹) *away from me, that I may brighten up a little!* Qerî: *Are not my days few? then cease Thou* (וַחֲדָל); *And set* (Thy heart) *away from me*, &c. Both are ill-knit and barely grammatical. It has been proposed to read יְמֵי חָלְדִי or (!) יְמֵי יֶחְלְדִי, on the ground of 𝔊 𝔖 and Ps 39⁶; but חֶלֶד does not seem to be a Job-word (see on v. 12 and 11¹⁷, where 𝔊 gives ζωή for the corrupt חלד, while 𝔊's word here is βίος). In the four other places where the word חֶלֶד (P. occurs in the present Heb. text, 𝔐 nowhere renders it βίος or ζωή

(Ps 17¹⁴ מֵחֶלֶד = ἀπὸ γῆς, Ps 49² יֹשְׁבֵי חָלֶד = οἱ κατοικοῦντες τὴν οἰκουμένην; Ps 39⁶ חֶלְדִּי = ἡ ὑπόστασίς μου = תּוֹחַלְתִּי Ps 39⁸; Ps 89⁴⁸ זְכָר־אֲנִי מֶה־חָלֶד = μνήσθητι τίς μου ἡ ὑπόστασις, i. e. my ground of hope, my confidence, He 11¹). ⅏ ὁ βίος τοῦ χρόνου μου, *the life of my time*, a curious expression for which ⅏^A gives the more natural ὁ χρόνος τοῦ βίου μου, *the time of my life*. Ὁ βίος μου = יָמַי, 7⁶⁻¹⁶ 8⁹ 9²⁵; but יָמִים is rendered χρόνος some sixteen times, e.g. 32⁸·⁷ Gn 26¹ (בִּימֵי א׳ = ἐν τῷ χρόνῳ τοῦ 'Α.). Perhaps ⅏^A = יְמֵי חַיַּי *the days of my life*: so ⅖ (cf Pr 31¹² πάντα τὸν βίον = כָּל יְמֵי חַיֶּיהָ). Thus, reading שְׁעֵה (cf. 7¹⁹ 14⁶ Ps 39¹⁴) for יָשִׁית, st. ii, we get *Are not the days of my life few? Look away from me, that I may brighten up* (*a little*, or *a while*: omit? cf. 9²⁷). Perhaps, however, we should restore שְׁנֹתַי *my years* for יָשִׁית (cf. Pr 5⁹ σὸν βίον = שְׁנוֹתֶיךָ), and transpose it with חֲדַל, pointing יְמֵי instead of יָמַי: *Are not the days of my years few? Let me alone, that I may brighten up* (*a while*: מְעָט: ? dittogr.). For the phrase חֲדַל מִמֶּנִּי see 7¹⁶ ἀπόστα ἀπ' ἐμοῦ. (But ⅏ ἔασόν με, cf. 7¹⁹ οὐκ ἐᾷς με = לֹא תִשְׁעֶה מִמֶּנִּי; yet 14⁶ שְׁעֵה מֵעָלָיו = ἀπόστα ἀπ' αὐτοῦ, and Ps 39¹⁴ שְׁעֵה מִמֶּנִּי = ἄνες μοι.)

v. 21. Cf. Ps 39¹⁴, of which vv. 20, 21, are an apparent echo.

v. 22. As a triplet, the verse is suspicious; and the repetition of צַלְמָוֶת is improb., and still more so the duplicated כְּמוֹ אֹפֶל. The sense of the quatrain being complete with v. 21, this one must be rejected as an interpolation. ⅏ εἰς γῆν σκότους αἰωνίου = אֶל־אֶרֶץ אֹפֶל עוֹלָם (σκότος = אֹפֶל, as in 3⁶, although in eighteen other places in Job, as usu. elsewhere, σκότος = חֹשֶׁךְ; and עוֹלָם instead of צַלְמָוֶת); οὗ οὐκ ἔστιν φέγγος = וְלֹא־אוֹר or בְּלֹא־אוֹר (φέγγος = אוֹר, 41¹⁰) or וְלֹא־נְהָרָה (φέγγος = נְהָרָה, 3⁴); οὐδὲ ὁρᾶν ζωὴν βροτῶν = וְלֹא רְאוֹת חַיֵּי אָדָם (!). This at least gives us a distich instead of a tristich; while st. ii is good evidence that the text was already corrupt. וַתֹּפַע כְּמוֹ אֹפֶל looks like a dupl. of עֵיפָתָה כְּמוֹ אֹפֶל, the ἅπ· עֵיפָתָה (usu. referred to עֵיפָה, Am 4¹³) originating in וַתֹּפַע written backwards. The prosaic word סְדָרִים, *ranks* or *rows*, *series* (= שְׂדֵרוֹת, 2 K 11⁸), for which ⅏ has φέγγος, *light*, finds no support in OT conceptions of She'ol, the dark and dreary, but not disordered, world of the dead, where kings still have their thrones (Is 14⁹), and doubtless the classes below them retain their relative positions. Every spirit has 'his own place' (cf. Acts 1²⁵). Neither the ancient Hebrews, nor the Babylonians from whom they derived so many of their cosmic ideas, conceived of the Underworld as a chaos. Lastly, we may note that וַתֹּפַע כְּמוֹ אֹפֶל *And it* (i.e. *the land* of the dead) *shineth* (v. 3 3⁴) *like darkness* is sheer nonsense. The land cannot be said to 'shine'. *And where the light is as darkness* (RV) could not be so expressed in Hebrew. We might read וַתָּעַף *And it is dim* or *murky* (cf. Is 8²²·²³, but not 11¹²) instead נ וַתֹּפַע. The whole distich might have run somewhat thus:

11.3

אֶרֶץ עֵיפָתָה וְלֹא־אוֹר
וַתֹּעַף כְּמוֹ אֹפֶל :

Or st. ii וְלֹא תוֹפִיעַ עָלֶיהָ נְהָרָה (cf. 3⁴).

The land of gloom and no light; Yea, gloomy it is as night (or, *And daylight shineth not on it*). See 12²⁵ for וְלֹא־אוֹר. 𝔊's οὐδὲ ὁρᾶν ζωὴν βροτῶν is as interesting as it is perplexing. וְלֹא רָאוֹת may have grown out of וְלֹא אוֹר (אֹרוֹת? אוֹרִים?) in the previous line; but ζωὴν βροτῶν = חַיֵּי אָדָם (or חַיַּת אָדָם) suggests a possible misunderstanding of חַיֵּי *kindreds, tribes* (1 Sa 18¹⁸) or of חַיַּת *communities* of man (2 Sa 23¹³). Cf. 𝔖: *The land which is waste* (ܐܪܥܐ) as the Pit (ܓܘܒܐ = בְּאֵר for אֹפֶל in both places: Ps 69¹⁶) *and the Shades of Death; And wherein there are no rows of homesteads* (סְדָרִין דְּדָרִין; explan. of סְדָרִים), *But it is wasted* (ܡܚܒܠܐ) *like the Pit*; also 𝔗: *The land whose eyelids* (תִּימוֹרָהָא = עַפְעַפֶּיהָ! = עֵיפָתָה!) *are like the darkness of the Shades of Death, without rows of human habitations* (וְלָא סִדְרֵי יָתֵב בְּנֵי נָשָׁא), *And glooming* (מַפְעֲפַעָא; cf. 11¹⁷) *like darkness*. Both think of דּוּר *to dwell* (cf. דּוֹר, Is 38¹²) in connexion with סְדָרִים; and neither refers וַתֹּעַף to √יפע *shine forth*.

Chapter 11. First Remonstrance of Zophar the Minaean.

v. 2. *A master of words:* or *one abounding in words:* pointing רַב pr. רֹב: cf. 𝔊 𝔖 𝔗. A better parallel to *a man of lips*. (Did 𝔊 read הֲדָבַר רַבִּים, dividing the letters differently?)

St. ii. *A man of lips:* i. e. of fluent speech; here implying insincerity or want of conviction. Cf. Ex 4¹⁰ *a man of words* = an orator or ready speaker, and Is 29¹³ (the contrast of lip-worship with heart-worship). 𝔊 εὔλαλος = 𝔗 in Ex 4¹⁰, where, however, there is no implication of insincerity.

v. 3. At thy babble: (הֲ)לְבַדֶּיךָ: cf. 𝔙 Tibi soli (analysing the word wrongly, as if it were from לְבַד *alone*). For לְ cf. Nu 30⁵,⁶. The Ptc. Interrog. הֲ derives some support from 𝔊 הָא *Lo!* בַּדֶּיךָ is not, however, indefensible: see 41⁴, where הֶחֱרִישׁ is *to be silent about, to pass over in silence*, as here. The verb is never 'Causative'. 𝔙 Tibi soli tacebunt homines? 𝔊 *Lo, on thy words* the dead *will be silent* (mispointing מְתִים *men*, v. 11 al., as מֵתִים *dead*. With מְתִים *men*, str. *males*, cf. not only Assyr. *mutu*, *husband*, but also Sum. MESH, MUSH, MU, MISH, MEZ, ME, *male, man*). 𝔊, after misreading בָּדֶיךָ (*thy babble, idle talk*: ἅπ. in Job: cf. Is 16⁶ 44²⁵) as בָּרוּךְ εὐλογημένος, continues with γεννητὸς γυναικὸς ὀλιγόβιος = יְלִיד אִשָּׁה קְצַר יָמִים, cf. 14¹; a queer perversion, or perhaps rather an interpolation, since it is followed by a distich which may be partly accounted for by misreading of 𝔐 (confusion of similar letters): μὴ πολὺς ἐν ῥήμασιν γίνου, Οὐ γάρ ἐστιν ὁ ἀντικρινόμενός σοι = אַל רַב מִלִּים, cf. 14²¹ 𝔊; or even אַל תְּחַבֵּד בְּמִלִּים, 34³⁷ (or אַל תֶּרֶב מִלִּים = וַיַּעַן אִיּוֹב וַיֹּאמַר עָלָיו: יהוה כִּי אִי מֵשִׁיב מִלִּים: (בְּאָמְרִים תִּהְיֶה The אַל may indicate אֶל (or עַל; so 𝔊) as the true reading at the beginning of the verse (אל־בדיך).

St. ii. Lit. *And thou scoff* (pointing וְתִלְעַג), *and there be none shaming* (or *no reprover*), הבלים, which only recurs once in Job (19³), means *to shame* or *mortify*, *confound* utterly (cf. 2 Sa 10⁵). The prim. mg. may be to *cut* and *wound*, as we speak of 'cutting words'; cf. Aram. פֻּם, to *cut* and to *threaten*, and נרף Pi. NH *cut, wound, revile*, and חרף *taunt, reproach*, which also perhaps orig. meant *cut* or *pierce* (cf. סייפא חריפא, the sword that *cuts, the sharp sword*; Syr. חרפא, *sword*), all of which may be cogn. with כלם and Ar. كَلَبَ *cut, wound* (not in Lane). Possibly חרם *to ban, devote*, was orig. to *cut off, separate*, and so *consecrate*. It seems needless to adopt 𝔊 דְּכָלֵא לָךְ *who restraineth thee* or 𝔊¹ מַכִיחָךְ *who refuteth thee*. 𝔙 מבלים = דְּמַכְסֵף.

v. 4. עַל וַתֹּאמֶר. Point וְתֹאמֶר *And thou say* (?). In any case, the question is continued.

I am pure: זַךְ אָנֹכִי: cf. 8⁶ 33⁹: זַךְ לִקְחִי *my lore* or *teaching is pure*. But Eyob never speaks of his 'teaching' or doctrine, as if he were a Rabbi sitting in a group of disciples. Nor is לקח (9 occ.) usu. qualified by an epithet (ל׳ טוב once, Pr 4²). Moreover, זך describes persons and conduct (Pr 20¹¹; 16¹⁷ תפלתי, cf. Ps 66¹⁸) > matter of instruction. We might also read זַךְ פָּעֳלִי *my conduct is pure*: cf. 𝔊 μὴ γὰρ λέγε ὅτι καθαρός εἰμι τοῖς ἔργοις = פעלי (אל תאמר זך פעל = ἔργα 36⁹ Pr 21⁸ al.). Other possible readings are זך דרכי or זך ארחי *my way is pure* (ἔργα 13²⁷ 34²¹ 36²³), but not לָכְתִּי (34⁸ only; לכתי 1 K 2⁸ only), which finds no support in 𝔊.

in His sight: so 𝔊 ἐναντίον αὐτοῦ (= בעיניו: 15¹⁵ 25⁵ 32¹). Cf. 10⁷. But the conjecture בעיני *in my own eyes* is favoured by 32¹, and by the fact that Zophar has not yet mentioned God.

v. 5. St. i is too long (four stresses). Omit אלוה and read ידבר instead of Infin. דבר (6⁸ 14¹³ 31²¹) or וידבר (19²³). The י was perhaps mistaken for ׳י (יהוה) and אלוה substituted.

with thee: i.e. in converse with thee. The עמך belongs in sense to both members, since דִּבֶּר עִם is to *speak with*, Ex 19⁹ (Subj. usu. God). Not *against thee* (RV).

v. 6. A tristich with a more or less corrupted text. St. ii seems too short, and st. iii is certainly too long, besides being mere prose.

tell or *declare to* (Gn 3¹¹) *thee the hidden* things (concr., as 28¹¹ of what is hidden in the ground; Ps 44²² in the heart, secret sins) *of Divine Wisdom*; esp. its infallible means of detecting sin, whether conscious or unknown. Cf. Ps 19¹³ 90⁸. Perhaps תעלמות חכמה = *the hidden things* (i.e. thy 'secret sins') *known to Wisdom* (cf. עלומינו Ps 90⁸).

For It (the Divine Wisdom) *is marvellous in resource* (or *insight*: see on 5). כִּי F׳ (It is) d׳ull in r׳sur׳: = כפלים d ubl (Is 40²). The statement admits of no satisfactory explanation. The suggested כְּפִלְאִים *like marvels* is objectionable on the grounds that the Subj. is not indicated, and that פֶּלֶא is not a Job-word (ἅπ· פִּלְאִים adv., La 1⁹) Read therefore (הִיא) נִפְלָאת (Dt 30¹¹) or נפלאתה (2 Sa 1²⁶). The allusions to Heaven and the sea, vv. 8, 9, may be further reminiscences of Dt 30¹¹⁻¹⁴. The line may be a marg. gloss on תעלמות חכמה, unless st. iii be considered an interpolation, as may very well be the case.

St. iii, as it stands, is doubtful Heb. Lit. *And know thou that Eloah maketh forget for thee* (some) *of thy iniquity*. Whom does He 'make forget'? cf. 39¹⁷, for the Hiph. of נשה c Accus. Pers. et Rei. (Hiph. not elsewhere in OT, nor does the Root recur in any form in Job.) As to the exegesis, it is gen. assumed that Zophar here asserts that 'God is really not punishing him as much as he deserves' (Dr); that his guilt is so heinous as to merit far worse calamities than those which have befallen him. This, however, is not borne out by the rest of the chapter (cf. v. 14). Indeed, there is no other trace of such an extreme assertion in any of the speeches of the Friends. They merely try to wring from the sufferer an admission that his woes are the penalty of past misdoing: δράσαντι παθεῖν.

As regards the Versions, 𝔊 δύναμιν σοφίας = תעלמות חכמה; and so תעלמה = δύναμιν, 28¹¹, wrongly connecting the word with Aram. עלם *to be strong*. Ὅτι διπλοῦς ἔσται (𝔊ᴬ ἐστιν) τῶν (אַ* τῷ) κατὰ σέ = כי כפלים לעמתך *that* (He is) *double as compared with thee* (or לפי שלך?) = misreading of 𝔐's מטול ראית כה קפלא and 𝔖 ארום כופלא לחובמתא (But 𝔗. לתושיה = 𝔐. לחבמתא. 𝔙 *et quod multiplex esset lex eius*: a rabbinical paraphrase of 𝔐. כפלים *duplex* is explained by *multiplex*, manifold; and the Law is the embodiment of the Divine Wisdom.)

For st. iii, 𝔊 gives καὶ τότε γνώσῃ ὅτι ἄξιά σοι ἀπέβη ἀπὸ Κυρίου ὧν ἡμάρτηκας = ותדע כי שוה לך יהוה בעוֹנך: הִשְׁוָה or שָׁוָה, or Impf. יְשַׁוֶּה or יְשַׁוֶּה, pro מַשֶּׁה וְשָׁה, and בַּעֲוֹנָך pro מ. Cf. esp. 33²⁷ 𝔊, where καὶ οὐκ ἄξια ἤτασέ με ὧν ἥμαρτον = מ. שוה לי (ו)לא העויתי וישר (?וַיֹּאשֶׁר). See note on that passage, and on 30¹. The meaning of שָׁוָה (cogn. c נָוָה *he down flat?*) is *to be* or *become flat, level*, aequus, c בְּ *equal with*, Pr 3¹⁵ 8¹¹; and so *to be like*, Is 40²⁵, Caus. *to liken*, Is 46⁵ Hiph. (Pi. *to level* or *flatten out* the soil for sowing, Is 28²⁵.) The word is not used of recompense or requital (שָׁלַם), nor is it found in Job outside the Elihu-section, where also it is prob. spurious. The orig. st. here may have been ותדע כי שלם לך אלוה בעוֹנך: *And that thou mightiest know that God hath requited thee acc. to thy iniquity* (cf. Ps 62¹³), or reading פעל for מעונך *hath requited thee thy doing* (34¹¹). (The author of the Elihu-section may be responsible for this and other apparent interpolations of the original text.)

v. 7. Lit. *The limit of Eloah findest thou, Or unto the end of Shaddai arrivest thou?* חָקֶר Act. = n hm., Ju 5 ch. 5 to v. xf r... to ning *and finding, end* or *limit of search*, 34²¹ 36²⁶ Is 40²⁸ Ps 145³ and so *Object of search* or investigation, 8⁸. [Our Eng. 'search' = chercher = Lat. circare, *go round* or *about*, which may perhaps be the prim. sense of חֵקֶר (and the labialized בִּקֵּשׁ, בָּקַשׁ); cf. Ju 18² (|| רֶגֶל). The Sum. GAR is *to surround*; GAR is also *a fetter*, as surrounding; IN-GAR is a surrounding *wall* (cf. KAR, *wall*); GAR is *enclose*, *confine*, and GISH-GAR *bounds*, *limits* (e. g. of Heaven and Earth). Cf. also קִיר *wall*, כָּרַר *go round*, and other kindred words.]

the end, תַּכְלִית, i.e. the boundary or limit, 26¹⁰ 28³. God is boundless or infinite: 'Pater immensus' (*Ath. Creed*). Ad fin. we must read הָבוֹא *come* (cf. ⑨ ἀφίκου, and Pr 1²⁷⑨) or תָּאַחֶה (3²⁵ 16²² al.) instead of the second תִּמְצָא. The verse may be an interpolation, since it seems to interrupt the connexion between v. 6 and v. 8.

v. 8. *It is higher than Heaven*: נְבֹהָה מִשָּׁמַיִם pro 𝔐 גָּבְהֵי שָׁמַיִם *Heights of Heaven!* (so Da); an unparalleled expression. Besides, the plur. of גֹּבַהּ is found nowhere else (cf. 22¹²), and the || עֲמֻקָּה מִשְּׁאוֹל demands the change (cf. 𝔙 Excelsior caelo est). What is it that is 'higher than Heaven and deeper than She'ol'? Apparently, the Wisdom of God (v. 6), upon which both depend. Grammatically, of course, these fem. predicates might refer to the תַּכְלִית שַׁדַּי (v. 7).

v. 9. Lit. *Longer than the Earth in measure* (pointing מִדָּה Accus. pro 𝔐 מִדָּהּ *its measure*, which should rather be מִדָּתָהּ). The Earth was conceived as rectangular, its globular shape being unknown to antiquity. It rested upon pillars (9⁶? 38⁶; cf. also 1 Sa 2⁸ Ps 75³), as, acc. to the Hindu myth, it rests upon an elephant, and the elephant upon the back of a tortoise. In like manner, the solid firmament or arch of Heaven was upheld by pillars (26¹¹) rising from the ends of the Earth.

v. 10. Corrupt, unmetrical, and prob. spurious. Cf. ⑨, which recalls 9¹². Lit. *If He glide past* (4¹⁵ 9¹¹) *and deliver up* (16¹¹) or *shut up*, *confine* (12¹⁴ Le 13⁵,¹¹) *and assemble* (vb. קהל not elsewhere in Job: קָהָל *assembly* once, 30²⁸) *and who shall turn Him back?* In whatever sense we take this, it is neither lucid, nor coherent with the context, nor poetical, even if the Obj. required by the vbb. יַסְגִּיר and יַקְהִיל could be supplied. ⑨ ἐὰν δὲ καταστρέψῃ τὰ πάντα, τίς ἐρεῖ αὐτῷ τί ἐποίησας;

This omits יַחֲלֹף and prob. reads וַיֹּאמֶר or וַיֹּמַר (Ps 89⁴⁵; Ezr 6¹² Aram. = καταστρέψαι) pro וְיַסְגִּיר, while substituting הַקָּהָל (as if it could mean *the multitude*) or perhaps rather הַכֹּל = τὰ πάντα for וְיַקְהִיל. Possibly also καταστρέψῃ = יְסַלֵּף (12¹⁹⑨) *overthrow*. In any case, a more tolerable couplet results, if we read אִם־יֹאמַר(יְסַלֵּף)־כֹּל מִי־יְשִׁיבֶנּוּ וּמִי־יֹאמַר אֵלָיו מַה־תַּעֲשֶׂה: *If He hurl down* (*overthrow*) *All, who can turn Him back? Or who can say unto Him, What doest Thou?* (9¹²).

v. 11. *For HE*. The Pron. is emphatic: He knows, whoever else may fail to know. *The wicked*: lit. *men of naught* (שָׁוְא); see note on 7³.

without effort: lit. *and attendeth not closely*. He needs no scrutiny to discover sin; He discerns it at sight. But 𝔊 ἰδὼν δὲ ἄτοπα οὐ παρόψεται = : וְלֹא יתבונן and *it He heedeth*; doth not let it pass unnoticed and unpunished.

v. 12. The form of the verse suggests a popular proverb. The sense is obscure, as is often the case with proverbs. The phrase אִישׁ נָבוּב occurs nowhere else in OT. It appears to mean *a hollow man*; i. e. one who is empty or devoid of intelligence (לֵב, לֵבָב); one who 'has nothing in him', as we say; an *inane* fellow. The word נָבוּב *hollowed, hollow* (not solid), is used of the altar, Ex 27⁸ 38⁷, and of the two 'pillars' before the temple, Je 52²¹. It is natural to compare it with Assyr. *imbûbu* (*inbubu*), *flute* (a *hollow* reed) = Aram. אַבּוּבָא (*anbûba*), and Horace's Ambubaiarum collegia, 'gilds of flute-girls', as well as Ar. *'unbûb, 'unbûba*, part of a *reed* between the knots (which is hollow), a *pipe* or *tube*. The Pred. יִלָּבֵב (note the Assonance with נָבוּב), as a Denom. from לֵבָב *heart, mind, intelligence*, cannot possibly mean *is* void of *understanding* (RV), but rather *will become wise* (cf. AV) or *show himself intelligent*: cf. Ar. لَبَّ *he was*, or *became, possessed of understanding* or *intelligence*. (Since לֵבָב *heart* is also *courage*, the Denom. לֵבֵב Pi. may mean *to encourage, inspirit, comfort*, as in Syriac; cf. Ct 4⁹; but that use is unsuitable here, although 𝔖 adopts it in rendering *And the man who is pure* (*void* scil. of evil) *taketh heart*. Nor does the Assyr. *labâbu, nalbubu, to be heart-stirred, spirited, full of courage and ferocity, to rage and fume*, or the like, help us further than by adding another illustration of the manifold but perfectly natural extensions of the simple primitive idea involved in all these various idioms, viz *the heart*, regarded as the seat of both thought and feeling.)

𝔊 ἄνθρωπος δὲ ἄλλως νήχεται λόγοις *But a man in vain* (taking נָבוּב as Adv. *emptily*) *swimmeth with reasonings* (= יְלַבֵּב; qs *reflects* or *reasons*); but 𝔊ˣ θρασύνεται, *is courageous* or *speaks boldly* = 𝔐.

In st. ii עַיִר פֶּרֶא should prob. be pointed עַיִר־פֶּרֶא (cf. עִירֹה *his ass-colt*, Gn 49¹¹), c 𝔗 עִילָא דְמוּרדָא and 𝔙 *pullum onagri*. For יִוָּלֵד point יוֹלִיד (יֹלִיד), if we may thus far sacrifice symmetry to sense. Then we may translate the verse: *But a witless wight will get wit, When a wild ass's colt begets a man*: i.e. never. Zophar sarcastically suggests that Eyob's blindness to commonly recognized truth is congenital and hopeless. With this he drops the subject of Divine and human intelligence, assuming a more friendly tone in the next paragraph.

If we keep to the traditional pointing, st. ii will be · *When a wild ass's colt is born a man* (RV marg; cf. 15⁷ Ec 4¹⁴ Pr 17¹⁷).

Others would connect the verse with what precedes it by rendering: *And so* (or *Thus*) *an empty man gets* (or *may get*) *understanding, And a wild ass's colt is* (or *may be*) *born* (*anew as*) *man*: that is to say, the Divine chastisements are potent to subdue headstrong untameable natures like that of the wild ass (39^{5-8} Gn 16^{12})—and Eyob himself, and to bring them to reason and submission. But the idea of *regeneration* is thus read into the Heb. In view of the possible meanings of לֵבָב, אִישׁ perhaps admits of the rendering: *An empty fellow will be daring* (or *defiant*), *And man is born* (i.e. is by nature) *a wild ass colt* (i.e. ungovernable by reason). Cf. 𝔙 Vir vanus in superbiam erigitur, et tanquam pullum onagri se liberum natum putat. (For st. ii, 𝔊 gives: *And He Who is Mighty helpeth a man*; app. reading שְׂדֵי פֶרֶק pro עִיר פֶּרֶא and omitting וָעִיר = ! יִוָּלֵד (𝔊 βροτὸς δὲ γεννητὸς γυναικὸς ἴσα (𝔊^A om.) ὄνῳ ἐρημίτῃ = פֶּרֶא אָדָם יִוָּלֵד אִשָּׁה: See 14^1.)

v. 13. The Pron. *thou* is emphatic; as though the speaker were turning from generalities to the particular case of Eyob. This would seem to favour the last view of v. 12. Or the implication may rather be: *If thou* (guilty as thou art); *if thou* (with all the proofs of thy sin upon thee) *shalt have prepared* (*ordered aright*, Ps 78^8; or *directed*, 1 Sa 7^2 c אֶל cf. st. ii) *thine heart, And outspread thy palms* (פֵּרַשׂ כַּפִּים Ex 9^{29} 1 K 8^{38}) *towards Him*; scil. in prayer, in which it was customary to *lift up the hands* (נָשָׂא יָדַיִם Ps 28^2 63^5 141^2), with the palms spread out towards the Deity. (𝔊 καθαρὰν ἔθου = הֲכִנֹתָ *shalt have purified* (9^{30}) pro הֲכִינוֹתָ which, however, seems preferable.)

v. 14. *Evil* (אָוֶן v. 11) perhaps meaning idolatry (Ho 4^{15} בֵּית אָוֶן 12^2 al.), while *Wrong* (עַוְלָה) is injustice towards man. It is questionable whether אִם אָוֶן בְּיָדְךָ can mean *If evil be in thy hand* (= אִם־יֵשׁ־אָוֶן בְּיָדְךָ or אִם יֵשׁ עָוֶל בְּכַפַּי). The יֵשׁ may have fallen out; cf. Ps 7^4 (אִם הָיָה בְיָדִי אָוֶן). *If there be wrong in my palms*; Ps 66^{18} אָוֶן אִם רָאִיתִי בְלִבִּי; also Ps 26^{10}.

away with it! or *put it far off; banish it!* The Hiph. of the vb. רָחַק *to be or become distant, far from*, c מִן (5^4 21^{16} 22^{18} 30^{10}) occurs four times in Job, always in the Trans. sense of *removing* or *putting far away*: viz. 11^{14} 13^{21} בְּכַפְּךָ מֵעָלַי הַרְחֵק *Thy Hand from upon me remove Thou!* 22^{23} תַּרְחִיק עַוְלָה מֵאָהֳלֶיךָ (*if*) *thou remove wrong from thy tents*, and 19^{13} (see the note there). It would improve the connexion to read here אִם אָוֶן מִיָּדְךָ הִרְחַקְתָּה וְלֹא תִשְׁכֹּן בְּאֹהָלֶךָ עַוְלָה: *If thou banish Evil from thine hand, And give Wrong no place in thy tent.* (Instead of the Caus. תַּשְׁכֵּן 𝔊 𝔙 point תִּשְׁכֹּן a needless change. Otherwise 𝔙 is good: Si iniquitatem, quae est in manu tua, abstuleris a te et non manserit in tabernaculo tuo iniustitia.)

in thy tent: בְּאָהֳלֶךָ c 41 codd. and 𝔊 𝔙 𝔖 𝔗 pro בְּאֹהָלֶיךָ *in thy tents*. Cf. 22^{23} and 5^{24}. The word is always Sing. in Job when it means the abode of an individual: see further 8^{22} $18^{6.14.15}$ 20^{26} 21^{28} 19^{12} 29^4 31^{31}: cf. plur. 12^6 15^{34} (all). On the other hand, אִישׁ לְאֹהָלָיו *a man to his tents*, Ju 7^8 1 Sa 4^{10} means *each to the tents of his army or company*.

v. 15. St. i is metr. redundant. For כִּי אָז *Surely then*, see 22^{26} 2 Sa 2^{27} 19^7 (in Hypoth. Clauses). To *lift up th fo* is to hold up the head fearlessly; the sign of a good conscience (2 Sa 2²²): cf. also 10¹⁵. A *fallen*, lowering, or downcast face is also a sign of mortification, while *lifting the face* may denote the recovery of cheerfulness: cf. Gn 4⁵·⁶·⁷. This last may be the meaning here: cf. 𝔊 *For so shall thy face shine again* (ἀναλάμψει) = יאורו for תשא (cf Ec 8¹). But 𝔖 *And then thou shalt lift up thine hands* (!). The addition in 𝔐 מומ *from blemish*, 𝔗 דלא מום *without blemish*, stain, or sign of shame (cf. Le 21¹⁷ ᵃˡ Pr 9⁷), 𝔙 absque macula, may be om. c 𝔖. 𝔊 ὥσπερ ὕδωρ καθαρόν = במים. This word, originally due to the scribe's eye having wandered to the next verse, was afterwards altered in 𝔐 to מומ, in order to secure a tolerable sense, instead of being expelled from the text, as would have been done had ancient revisers understood their business. (מום = מאום 31⁷ Dn 1⁴, a later double Triliteralization of the Root, Aram. מומא, is prob. cogn c מאומה *a thing, anything*, Assyr. *mamma, mimma, mumma, any one or thing*, Sum. NIG (NING), NIN, MIM, ÀM, IM, res, quidquid, &c. From meaning *anything whatever*, מום, מאום, naturally came to mean *anything amiss*. When we say 'If anything happens', we gen. hint at unfavourable contingencies.)

steadfast: 𝔐 מֻצָק *molten* or *cast*, str. of metal (37¹⁸ 1 K 7¹⁶ ²³ ³³; cf. 𝔙 et eris *stabilis*, et non timebis. Possibly *refined* or *purified* would be more accordant with analogy (so 𝔗 סנין מחבולא *purified from the hurtful*: סניא is *molten*, cast, in 37¹⁸). Perhaps מֻצָק = מוּצָק (Ps 12⁷) was written מצק owing to an error of dictation. In Qal יָצַק is *to pour out*, e.g. water, oil, blood, melted ore (= *to cast*), and the Pass. Ptcp. יָצוּק means *cast*, and then met. *solid, firm, hard* (e.g. crocodile's skin and heart, 41¹⁵ ¹⁶), as though made of cast metal; as we say 'a cast-iron man', which is perhaps the import of the Hoph. Ptcp. here, although מֻצָק is not so used where it recurs in Job (31¹⁸ *cast*, of a metal mirror; 38³⁸ app. *lump* or *clod* or *solidified mass* of earth), nor elsewhere in OT. The Impf. יִצַּק (22¹⁶), usu rendered *is poured out*, may bear that meaning, but the context is doubtful.

Some would replace מָצַק in 11¹⁵ by the questionable מִצַּק *far from distress* (Dn 9²⁵), following 𝔖 ומן עקא לא תדחל *And of distress thou shalt not be afraid* The word should at least be מְצָקָה or מְצוּקָה (15²⁴). 𝔊 paraphrases. ἐκδύσῃ δὲ ῥύπον (9³¹ 14¹) καὶ οὐ μὴ φοβηθῇς, *while thou shalt doff impurity, and shalt not fear*; taking מצק in the sense of *purified*. Upon the whole, if we do not read ἀπ' מָצַק or מוּצָק, it may be better to restore מֻצָּב *set up* or *stablished* (Gn 28¹²). At Na 2⁸ pro הצב leg. הער *urbs*).

v. 16. *For thou, even thou*: כי אתה. · Or read simply ואתה *And thou* (wretched as thou art at present). The Pron. is emph. 𝔖 *And then* (as in v. 15) *thou shalt forget thy trouble*. 𝔊 καὶ τὸν κόπον ἐπιλήσῃ = ועמל 'ת make the st. to o slen . I . . . . ἤσῃ, *and thou shalt not be scared* (cf. v. 15 ad fin.); wrongly connecting כמים עברו (*like waters which have passed away*) with st. i, and spoiling the metre, perhaps because תזכר *thou wilt remember* was misread תרגז *wilt quake*.

v. 17. Text corrupt in more than one respect. 𝔊 transposes the two stt. *While thy prayer* (*shall be*) *as the Morning-star, And out of midday life shall arise for thee.* This implies תפלה (= εὐχή 16^{17}) for תעפה, renders כבקר (*like the Dawn*) by ὥσπερ Ἑωσφόρος (a favourite term with the translator = שחר 3^9 38^{12} 41^{10}; cf. Is 14^{12}), and חלד by ζωή (? חלדך = σοι ζωή; see note on 10^{20}). But nowhere else in Job does ζωή = חלד. In fact, it represents חיים in seven places and חיה in two others; while in 147 other cases in OT⁽𝔊⁾ it stands for one or another derivative of the complementary Roots חיי, חיה. It cannot therefore be safely assumed that 𝔊 had חלדך before it here. 𝔗, which makes the verse a direct reference to the Resurrection of the Dead, certainly read ומצהרים וטטהר (ומן טהרא 𝔊; cf. ומטיהר?), and appears to have read חָלָדְךָ) גשמך דחליד בגרגושתא *thy body which is rusting with the clod* or *burrows into the clod, is buried*: see Levy CHWB¹), may be corrected by a later hand from the Heb., since רָהָלַךְ *which has gone into the clod* is the ordinary text. 𝔙, as in some other instances, approaches nearest to what must be regarded as the original sense of the passage: *Et quasi meridianus fulgor consurget tibi ad vesperam: et cum te consumptum putaveris, orieris ut Lucifer.* As contrasted with Dawn (כבקר; so all Versions), Noon (צהרים) is the time of fullest and steadiest light (5^{14} Am 8^9); and the כבקר of st. ii makes כצהרים prob. in st. i (so 𝔙). Moreover, *light* (אוֹר) may be said to *rise* (יקום); but where shall we find *duration of life* (חָלֶד) or *life* (חַיִּים), much less *noonday* (צהרים), spoken of as *rising*? If we restore וכצהרים יקום אוֹרֶךָ *And like noonday* (= bright as noon) *thy light shall arise* we get a good || to st. ii, and a met. which finds support in Is 58^{10b} $60^{1.3}$ Ps 37^6.

In st. ii, if we point the anomalous תָּעֻפָה (RV *though it be dark*) תְּעֻפָּה *Darkness*, c 3 codd., we shall be in accord with 𝔊: *And cloudiness* (ערפלא) *shall be as the morning*, and 𝔗: היך צפרא תהוי, דפיעפוע דקבלא *Because the gloom of darkness shall be as the morning.* (𝔙 fort. תעיפה *thou mayst faint.*) Possibly the word was עֲ(יְ)פָתָה *dimness* or *murk* (see on 10^{22}). But parallelism seems to demand *thy dimness*: עיפתך כבקר תהיה. We prefer to read תֹפִיעַ *thou shalt shine forth, shalt become like the Dawn.* (We may perhaps compare the common invocation of the priest over his patient in the old Babylonian exorcisms: *amêlu mâr ilišu lilil libib limmir*, May the man, the son of his god, brighten, glisten, shine! i.e. become free of the possessing demon, and so purified and restored to health.)

---

¹ Cf. 𝔊: '*And from* (= Higher than) *noon the grave* (חפרא) *shall arise*' (taking חלד as from חָלַד *to creep, to burrow*.

v. 18. *thou shalt feel secure*: or *be confident*, 6²⁰ Ju 18⁷. Perhaps וידעת *And thou shalt know* > ובטחת, on account of כי יש (not בהיות) and the following לבטח, which a scribe may have anticipated here. *And thou shalt know that there is indeed ground of hope*. Light is associated with hope, Is 8²⁰ 9¹ 59⁹ All the Verss. reproduce 𝔐 in st. i. With st. ii textual doubts meet us again. 𝔐 וחפרת לבטח תשכב *And thou shalt dig* (or *search for*, 3²¹ 39²⁹)—no Obj. expressed!—*in security shalt lie down*. It is clear that וחפרת will not do. If it means *look carefully* about thee before going to rest (OL; RV), it is in ludicrous contrast with the promise of complete confidence with which the verse opens. Accordingly, the Verss exhibit a curious variety of interpretations. 𝔗 *And thou shalt prepare a burial-place* (an impossible expansion of 𝔐's וחפרת *and thou shalt dig*); *in security shalt thou lie down*. So 𝔙 et *defossus securus dormies* (qs reading וְחָפַר or וְחָפַרְתָּ). cf. Syr. ܩܒܪܐ *a grave* cited above. 𝔊 omits וחפרת לבטח, and renders: *And thou shalt sleep and rest without one waking thee* (v. 19). 𝔊 ἐκ δὲ μερίμνης καὶ φροντίδος ἀναφανεῖταί σοι εἰρήνη. The opening phrase is almost certainly a paraphrastic equivalent of ומפחד *And from dread* (ומפחד = וחפרת; ד = ר, מ = ת, as often): cf. 3²⁵ ἐφρόντισα = פחדתי, and 21⁹ בתיהם שלום מפחד *Their homes are safe from alarm*. And since ἀναφαίνομαι (Job only), which recurs 13¹⁸ 40⁸, is used by the translator as a complementary verb in both passages (δίκαιος ἀναφανοῦμαι = אצדק, δίκαιος ἀναφανής = תצדק), it is not unlikely that ἀναφανεῖταί σοι εἰρήνη = תשלם (pro 𝔐 תשכב) *Thou shalt be safe* (8⁶ 9¹). It may, of course, be merely a loose paraphrase of לבטח תשכב *thou shalt lie down in security*: see Is 14³⁰, where לבטח ירבצו = ἐπ' εἰρήνης ἀναπαύσονται (for the Heb. phrase, cf Ho 2²⁰ Ps 4⁹): or possibly it represents another reading, e.g. לך יזרח שלם *for thee shall peace arise* (cf. Ma 3²⁰). Upon the whole, ומפחד לבטח תשכב was prob. the orig. text of 𝔐. Cf. also Pr 3²⁴ אם תשכב לא תפחד *If thou lie down, thou shalt not dread*.

v. 19. St. i is a virtual repetition of 18ᵇ, and some would omit it as a gloss. Allowing for the change of Pers., it is identical with Is 17²ᵇ ורבצו ואין מחריד. Cf. also Le 26⁶ ושכבתם ואין מחריד. - But the st. supplies a link with what follows. Not only shalt thou dwell in peace, with none to molest thee, but many will court thy favour: cf. 𝔊 μεταβαλόμενοι δὲ πολλοί σου δεηθήσονται.

St. ii. Pr 19⁶. The phrase חלה פני פ׳, usu. explained *to sweeten or make pleasant the face of any being*, Divine or human, by comparison with Aram. חֲלִי *to be sweet* (of taste) and Ar. حلو *be sweet*, met. *pleasing*, opp. to مر *bitter*, may perhaps rather be connected with Assyr. *ḫalû, be bright, shining*, a syn. of *namâru* (Shamash, e. g., is called *mušaḫlâ ûmu*, Brightener of Day). This agrees with the analogy of בלג (9²⁷ 10²⁰) and esp. the phrase האיר פני׳ *to make the face shine* upon one (Nu 6²⁵, cf. Ec 8¹). Cf. also Ps 104'.

v. 20. A triplet, where we might have expected a quatrain. The text is still uncertain: see 𝔊, which connects st. ii in sense with 19^b, and concludes with st. i. Thus: (19^b) *But changing sides* (μεταβαλόμενοι: or *turning round*: cf. 10^8),'*many will beg help of thee*; (20) *But deliverance will forsake them: For their hope is perdition* (ἀπώλεια), *But eyes of impious ones will melt.* 𝔊^A adds a 4th st., viz. (*For*) *with Him are Wisdom and Might,* = 12^{13} (כי עמו חכמה ונבורה). Cf. also 12^{16}. This gloss, app. intended to sum up Zophar's argument by insisting upon his two main points, viz. that by His omniscience God is always aware of sin wherever it is present (v. 11), and by His omnipotence is always able to punish it, has a very abrupt effect and can hardly be original. Nor does the transposition of its members really improve the verse. Some such line as באפס כסלה ינועו *Without hope will they die,* or כי מאס אלוה מבטחם *For Eloah disdaineth their trust* (8$^{14.20}$ 10^3 18^{14} 31^{24} Je 2^{37}), may have fallen out after ומנוס אבד מנהם. Cf. Pr 14^{26} for the connexion of thought.

St. i. *the eyes of the godless shall fail*: or *waste, pine away,* with looking in vain for help. The same phrase, 17^5: cf. Ps 69^4 La 4^{17}. The √ כלה Assyr. *kalû* is *to stop, end, finish, cease,* Trans. and Intrans. = Sum. GUL (*kalû, ahâtu*); cf. GAL, GIL, GUL, *destroy*. (𝔊 נחשבן *shall be darkened*; qs תבלינה for תכמהנה.) St. ii. *refuge*: or *place of refuge,* or simply *flight, escape.* Same phrase, Am. 2^{14} Je 25^{35}. 𝔗 שיזבותא = 𝔊 σωτηρία. 𝔗 uses the same word in Nu 35$^{6.11}$ (Cities of *Refuge*). 𝔊 תוקפהון *their strength* (= מעוז *place of refuge* pro מנוס). St. iii. Fort. leg. כמו ante מפח: *And their trust is as an expiring breath* or *last gasp;* lit. *breathing out of soul* (here only; cf. Je 15^9 ch 31^{39}); which 𝔙 explains *abominatio animae*, as if the idea were *blowing* or *sniffing at* in token of contempt (cf. Ma 1^{13}). 𝔊 has only *And the hope of their souls*, omitting מפח.

Chapter 12. Eyob's Answer to Zophar.

v. 2. *ye are knowing*: ידעים *clever,* or *the wise* (Ec 9^{11} Pr 1^2 17^{27}). אתם עם could only mean *ye are common people*; and חכמה in the || st. requires some term denoting the possession of wisdom. (𝔊^A ἄνθρωποι μόνοι (the) *only men* is an attempt to meet the difficulty. So 𝔙 ergo vos estis soli homines. Others have suggested ערומים *crafty* (5^{12} 15^5 only), which seems less suitable, as too restricted in scope. Cf. v. 9 and 13^2. (𝔗 חַבְרַיָא *companions* = רעים 2^{11}, perhaps ידעים here?).

v. 3. *sense*: or *intelligence*: lit. *a heart.* The verse has 3 stt., of which 𝔊 omits both the second (rightly; = 13^{2b}) and the third.

St. iii. Lit. *And with whom are there not* (things) *like these?* viz. which thou hast been saying; his commonplaces about the Wisdom and Power of God. Cf. 15^{9b}. 𝔊 לטן הוי איך הלין (om. אין), *To whom have things like these happened?* but 𝔗 correctly ועם מן לית רבמה אלין *And with whom are there not things like these?* 𝔙 paraph. Quis enim haec quae nostis ignorat?

v. 4. Again a triplet, and otherwise corrupt. ⅏ δίκαιος γὰρ ἀνὴρ καὶ ἄμεμπτος ἐγενήθη (⅏^A ἐγενόμην = 𝔐) εἰς χλεύασμα (-όν) = כִּי אִישׁ צַדִּיק וְתָמִים יִהְיֶה לִשְׂחוֹק, omitting st. ii. קֹרֵא לֶאֱלוֹהַּ וַיַּעֲנֵהוּ *One that called unto Eloah, and He answered him*; which may be either a gloss upon אִישׁ צַדִּיק וְתָמִים *a man just and blameless*, or intended as a specimen of the mocking words addressed to the sufferer: *He called* (קָרָא?) *upon Eloah*, &c., cf. Ps 22⁸ ⁹. ⅏ also om. לְרֵעֵהוּ *to his friend*, and app. read אִישׁ *a man* instead of the 2nd שְׂחוֹק *a derision* (La 3¹⁴ Je 20⁷), besides supplying the necessary Conj. with תָּמִים, and transposing the stichi (1, 3). 𝔖 *To whom have happened such things, and he hath become a derision to his friends and called upon God and He answered him, Who hath pleasure in just men without blame?* שְׂחֹק לְרֵעֵהוּ אֶהְיֶה *A derision-to-his-friend* (= one that is a laughing-stock) *I become*; but the change of Pers. is really intolerable. If we keep אֶהְיֶה, we must read לְרֵעִי *to my friend* (31⁹) or לְרֵעַי (16²⁰ 19²¹) *to my friends*. If we retain לְרֵעֵהוּ (𝔖 לְחַבְרוֹהִי) לְרֵעָיו plur. 32³, 16²¹ sic leg. et 42¹⁰), we should also adopt יִהְיֶה (⅏^B 𝔖). It is difficult to choose between these alternatives. Perhaps we should read: שְׂחֹק לְרֵעַי אֶהְיֶה שָׂחֲקוּ עַל צַדִּיק וְתָמִים *I become a derision to my friends* (cf. 30¹); *They deride the just and blameless* (or in st. ii: וַאֲנִי צַדִּיק וְתָמִים *Though I be a man just and blameless*). שְׂחֹק לְרֵעֵהוּ יִהְיֶה | אִישׁ עֲדָיו וְתָמִים does not afford a quite satisfactory couplet, even if (with ⅏) we invert the two members. Nor is it quite clear how Eyob considers that he has become a jest to his friends. Certainly neither Zophar nor the others have expressed contempt for his misfortunes. Zophar, however, has suggested that he is a mere empty-headed babbler, blind to notorious truth, and as obstinate as a wild ass.

v. 5. לַפִּיד בּוּז לְעַשְׁתּוּת שַׁאֲנָן נָכוֹן, which RV boldly renders *In the thought of him that is at ease there is contempt for misfortune*, can only mean *A torch of contempt hath the thought of one at ease*. So 𝔙 Lampas contempta apud cogitationes (עַשְׁתּוּת) divitum, and 𝔗 *A torch* (אוּדָא) *which is despised hath the godless one from thought secure*. Nonsense as this may be, it shows that the corrupt text of 𝔐 lay before the translators. There can be little doubt that we should point לַפִּיד (RV?) or rather restore עַל־פִּיד *Upon ruin* or *calamity* (30²⁴ 31²⁹; see on v. 6) And if, further, we read יִשְׁפּוֹךְ *poureth*, or the Plur., after v. 21 (שֹׁפֵךְ בּוּז עַל נְדִיבִים) instead of the very questionable ἅπ. λεγ. לְעַשְׁתּוּת, the sentence will take a more prob. form and gain in coherence and clearness of expression *Upon Ruin* (the ruined) *the prosperous* (שַׁאֲנָן; perhaps a gloss) *poureth contempt*. (פִּיד is compared with Ar. فَادَ, يَفِيدُ *die, pass away, depart*, also used of property. The Prim. Root may be cogn. with Sum. ⊢⊣ BAD, *far, be or go far, depart, dead*.) In st. ii, 𝔐 נָכוֹן לְמוֹעֲדֵי רָגֶל *It* (i.e. contempt) *is ready for them whose foot slippeth*, כָּלוֹן *dishonour* (for נָכוֹן *ready*) would give a better parallel: קָלוֹן עַל מוֹעֵד רָגֶל (He poureth) *dishonour upon the fallen*. (Leg. fort. לְמוֹעֲדֵי poet. form in cst. like אַשְׁרֵי in 49⁰.) (ⱽ treating the verse as a single stichus, and making 6ᵃ the 2nd st., translates εἰς χρόνον (γὰρ) τακτὸν ἡτοίμαστο πεσεῖν ὑπὸ ἄλλων (-ους, -οις), Οἴκους τε αὐτοῦ (μου) ἐκπορθεῖσθαι ὑπὸ ἀνόμων. Here ἡτοίμαστο πεσεῖν ὑπὸ ἄλλων evidently implies (?נָכוֹן לְמוֹעֵד לְרֶגֶל), and οἴκους τε ... ἀνόμων as clearly represents אהלים לשדדים (?ישׁלּוּ). So far, with the exception of the misreading ישׁלּוּ (or ישׁלוּ; both non-existent forms of שׁלל *spoil, pillage*) for שׁליו, 𝔊 presents no material difference from 𝔐. As regards εἰς χρόνον τακτὸν, which is all there is to represent (שׁאנן) לפיד בוז לעשתות, comparison of 14ᵇ חקו עשית = εἰς χρόνον ἔθου (where 𝔊 app. read שׁת pro עשׁית) and 14¹³ תשׁית לי חק = καὶ τάξῃ μοι χρόνον, it seems prob. that εἰς χρόνον τακτὸν here stands for (לְ)חֹק שְׁתוּת, *for an appointed time*. Thus פיד was misread חק and עשתות became שׁתות, while בוז and perhaps שׁאנן were omitted. We cannot therefore say that 𝔊 read לעתות for לעשתות. Possibly ὑπὸ ἄλλων (-ους, -οις) = שׁאנן, pointed שֹׁאֲנָן = שׁוֹנִים *different ones, others* (!); cf. Es 17 3⁹. For ἡτοίμαστο πεσεῖν = נָכוֹן לְמוֹעֵד רֶגֶל, cf. also 18¹² πτῶμα δὲ (αὐτῷ) ἡτοίμασται = וְאֵיד נָכוֹן. 𝔙 renders 5ᵇ parata ad tempus statutum, (a torch) *prepared for an appointed time*; and so 𝔗 מְכַוַּן לְהִתַּרְפָּקְתֵּי זִמְנָא *prepared for the misfortunes of the time*. Both app. read לַמּוֹעֵד pro לְמוֹעֲדֵי. 𝔖 takes לפיד as Hiph. Infin. (לְהָפִיד) = Syr. فلّ *to turn aside*, translating the verse: *to drive away folly and wrong* (לְפִיד בֶּסֶל וְעִקְשׁוּת = למפרקי שטיותא ועולא); *and to make firm the tottering foot* (= 𝔐).

v. 6. *are free from care*: or *are at ease, secure*: יִשְׁלָיוּ: Ps 122⁶: an uncontracted (archaic) form = שָׁלוּ, from שָׁלָה = שָׁלוּ. If, however, this were right, we should expect אהלי שׁדדים > אהלים לשׁדדים. And if st. ii is sound, parallelism requires שׁלום אהלים *Peace of tents* (is *to robbers*). St. ii lit. *And (perfect) safety* or *security* (is) *to enragers of El*. The Intens. Plur. ἅπ· בַּטֻּחוֹת may be comp. with the Ptcp. Pass. בָּטוּחַ Is 26³ Ps 112⁷. But if we retain 𝔐 ישליו in st. i, we may read here וּבַטְחוּ כל מר׳ אל *And all provokers of God are secure*. (שׁדד = Assyr. *šadâdu*, drag, draw, or pull along, cars or captives, is a syn. of שׁלל, *šalâlu*, lead or drive off captives, spoil, &c., and perhaps cogn. with it.) St. iii לאשׁר הביא אלוה בידו *To those whom God hath brought into His hand* (or *put in his power*) is meaningless and prob. a corrupt gloss. It cannot mean *That bring their god in their hand* (RV marg.); i.e. Whose only god is their own strong arm (Dr, quoting Virgil's *Dextra mihi Deus*, and Hab 1¹¹). לאשר is suspicious and unpoetical; הביא is unsuitable; אלוה cannot = אלהיהם; and בידו (not בידם) naturally belongs to Eloah. The line is prob. a gloss on 5ᵃ: *To (Upon) him whom Eloah hath brought into his (the שׁאנן's) power*. Or reading פידו instead of בידו, we get a gloss on לפיד: *To whom Eloah hath brought his ruin*.

𝔊 which, as we saw, connects 6ᵃ with 5, curiously renders (or paraphrases) 6^bc as follows οὐ μὴν δὲ ἀλλὰ μηδεὶς πεποιθέτω πονηρὸς ὢν ἀθῷος ἔσεσθαι, | ὅσοι παροργίζουσιν τὸν κύριον, | ὡς οὐχὶ καὶ ἔτασις αὐτῶν ἔσται. ואולם (v. 7) אל יבטח איש רע להיות נקי (להנקות) | כל מרניזי אדני | כאשר = לוא יבוא גם פידם: See 10^17 for note on ἔτασις = נֻגַע *plague*; here perhaps פיד (= שַׁד ביד). (ביד שַׁד =) מַתְתָא בידיה אֵיךְ פרעה דאיתי אלוה עלוהי *Like Pharaoh, upon whom God brought the plague with His hand*. But 𝔊 *Because* (= בַּאֲשֶׁר) *God was not in their heart* (= בלבם pro פידם). 𝔙 cum (= כאשר) Ipse dederit omnia in manus eorum: כאשר הביא כל בידם.

v. 7. St. i has four stresses. All Verss. agree. ואולם ad init. seems superfluous (see note on v 6^(3)). Others would om. ותורך (𝔊 ἐάν σοι εἴπωσιν יָמֹרוּךָ app. cf. Ps. 139^20), which recurs in v. 8, and is perhaps not abs. necessary here. For בְהֵמוֹת plur. (40^15, cf. Ps 73^22) we must read the sing. בְהֵמָה *the beasts* (18^3 Gn 1^24 al.), *cattle*, which is coll. as usual. 𝔊 לחיותא pointed as Sing

v. 8. *Contemplate Earth*. השניח אל ארץ (Is 14^16 Ps 33^14): or *Gaze on the Earth*. 𝔐 או שיח לארץ *Or speak to the Earth* (RV); but this use of שיח *muse, complain* (7^11; cf. the noun, 7^13 9^27 10^1 21^4 23^2 15^4 fem.) is doubtful. שעה אל ארץ (7^19 14^6) or שית לב אל ארץ (7^17) are also possible. Simpler and perhaps more prob. would be או שמע לארץ *Or listen to Earth* (ח = ט). In spite of resemblance of letters, the suggestion וזחלי ארץ *crawlers of the earth*, reptiles (Mi 7^17) is improb. The context requires a verb (esp. after או), and שְׁאַל (v. 7) is too far away; while the proposed emendation involves the further change of ותרך into וידך. Similar objections lie against שרץ *crawling things* and חית *animalia*. Besides, the animal creation is summed up in beasts, birds, and fishes, as in Ps 8^8, and in the same order. (𝔊 ἐκδιήγησαι γῇ = 𝔖 אשתעא לארעא = 𝔗 מלל לארעא = 𝔙 loquere terrae.)

v. 9. St. ii 𝔗: *That the stroke* (or *plague*: מחת) *of the Lord's Hand hath done this*. 'Who cannot learn, by the simple observation of nature, that the hand of God *doeth this* (xi. 10, 11)—rules over all living creatures of the earth (cf. v. 10)' (Driver). The meaning of vv. 7 sqq seems rather to be that, inasmuch as God created the world and its denizens, and maintains them all in being, it goes without saying that whatever befalls any of them, whether good or ill (e. g. Eyob's present calamities), is due to the direct and sole action of the Creator Himself, upon Whom they all depend (v. 10). On this head there was no difference between Eyob and his friends; and he is indignant with them for supposing that he is so dull and blind to the obvious as not to see it (vv. 2, 3).

Iahvah's hand. The Divine Name, which occurs some twenty-five times in the prose portions of the book (Prologue and Epilogue, and introd. sentences, 40^1,3,6 42^1), occurs only here in the speeches themselves. Seven codd. substitute אלוה in the text and one in marg. But all the Verss. rightly give equivalents of יהוה (𝕲 χεὶρ κυρίου). It is surely significant that the poet, whose hero is a non-Israelite, and who makes Eyob and his friends designate the Supreme by more general names common to the other Semitic peoples, such as El (Assyr., Phoen., Aram.), usu. explained 'the Mighty One', but perhaps rather 'the bright' or 'shining One' (cf. Sum. EL, *bright, pure,* UL, *to glitter,* of stars, MUL (WUL), id., *a star*); Eloah (Ar., Aram.), 'the Awful' or 'Fearful One', orig. perhaps denoting *ghost, spirit* (plur. Elohim, 5^8 28^{23} 34^9 38^7 only); and Shaddai, 'the Mountain' (Assyr. *šadû, šaddé,* Sum. SHAD? SAD? SATI, *bâmâtu*), should here, and here only, introduce the special name of the God of Israel. In so doing, he not only betrays his own nationality. He also reveals his purpose of comforting his people during a period of national calamity, by assuring them that their affliction is the work of no hostile heathen deity, but of the God of their fathers, Whose Hand both smites and heals.

v. 10. *human flesh*: lit. *flesh of man* (איש, as opp. to the brutes, Ex 11^7, and to God, 9^{32} 32^{13}). If all living are in His Hand, whatever happens to them must be His doing. (The verse, with its prosaic אשר בירו, may be an interpolation.)

v. 11. *test* or *try* the quality of *words*; whether they are true or false, wise or foolish, sense or nonsense: just as the palate discriminates between various kinds of food by their taste, whether they are pleasant or nauseous, wholesome or hurtful. The meaning seems to be: As you cannot deny that I possess the same organs of perception and discrimination as yourselves, how can you pretend to be so much wiser than I? (cf. v. 3, which this verse might very well follow.) Instead of οὖς *ear* 𝕲 has νοῦς *mind, intelligence* (= לֵב 7^{17} al; רוּחַ Is 40^{13}). Cf. 13^1 and Assyr. *uznu, ear, sense, intelligence.*

v. 12. St. i seems too short with two stresses. Some word or words may have fallen out; as we may also conclude from the difficulty of discerning the relevance of the words in Eyob's mouth. Acc. to Dr 'the experience of the aged is mentioned by Job as a second source of the knowledge of God's rule of the world'. But see note on v. 9. Eyob does not admit that wisdom is an invariable attribute of age (v. 20). Eliphaz, on the other hand, claims the support of the aged for his own views (15^{10}). Bildad's appeal to tradition (8^{8-10}) does not seem to be quite the same thing. Nor is the RV marg. 'With aged men,' *ye say*, 'is wisdom' satisfactory, as Dr points out. None of the friends had said so.

𝕲 ἐν πολλῷ χρόνῳ σοφία | ἐν δὲ πολλῷ βίῳ ἐπιστήμη. Cf. 32^7, where ἐν πολλοῖς δὲ ἔτεσιν = וְרֹב שָׁנִים *And a multitude of years.* This suggests the reading ורב שנים for בישישים here, in better agreement with the parallel ארך ימים *length of days.* If Eyob says *And many years are* (i. e. bring or imply) *wisdom. And a long life is discernment,* he may mean: I not only possess the same faculties as you (v. 11), but like you I can boast the wisdom acquired by years of experience. It is also possible that הֲלֹא should be restored at the beginning of the verse, as question after question is quite in the author's manner; and רב־שׁנים gives but a single stress (32⁷). הלא רב־שנים חכמה ונו׳ *Do not many years bring wisdom?* &c. Am I not old enough to know as well as you? Less probably, but still possibly, the question might be a sarcasm: Have not years brought you wisdom or common sense? = You are old enough to know better.

v. 13. May be an interpolation suggested by the previous verse: *wisdom* and *discernment* occur in both, and in the same relative positions. Moreover, this verse is hardly suitable as an introd. to the long illustration of God's apparently capricious use of His omnipotence in the world of man (vv. 14–25). The passage suggests the arbitrary exercise of irresponsible and irresistible power rather than government by wisdom and justice. (In st. ii leg. עָצְמָה *strength*, Is 40²⁹, instead of עֵצָה *counsel*, for the sake of parallelism. Throughout the book, even in 38², the latter is always used of human, never of Divine, wisdom.)

v. 14. We have to go back to v. 9 for the subject of the verb, viz. Iahvah; a fact which confirms our suspicion that v. 13 is spurious, and that the quatrain vv. 11, 12, originally followed v. 3.

He (Iahvah) *breaketh down*; הָרַס · of walls and cities, met. of men; opp. to בָּנָה *build* or *rebuild*, acc. to context. Je 1¹⁰ Ps 28⁵ Ex 15⁷. As Obj. עִיר *a city* or בַּיִת *a house* might be supplied, since ה+verb makes but a single stress in v. 15. (ה־רס is cogn. with II רס־ם Aram. רְסַם and prob. √ ס־רס of סרים, רצץ ,רצ־ח, رفص , &c.) *and there is no rebuilding*. וְלֹא יִבָּנֶה lit. *and he is not rebuilt*. This can hardly be right. RV *and it*, &c., implies תִבָּנֶה 3 fem. It is better to point יִבְנֶה 'Lo, He breaketh down, and (re)buildeth not' Cf. Ps 28⁵. 𝔊 *if He have thrown down, who shall build?* taking הֵן as Hypoth. = אִם (23⁸ 40²⁹), which may be right, and reading מִי יִבְנֶה. Cf. 𝔊 הָא אִן סָחַף מַנוּ בָּנָא *Lo, if he pull down, who rebuildeth?* So 𝔊𝔖 in st ii also. *He prisoneth a man*: or *closeth in upon a man.* cf. Ex 14³ Perhaps *closeth* (doors) *against a man* = 𝔊 ἐὰν κλείσῃ κατὰ ἀνθρώπων. *there is no release*: lit. *and he is not opened*, i. e. *loosed*: Is 51¹⁴. Perhaps we should point יִפְתַח c 𝔊𝔖𝔙: *and openeth not*. All the havoc and ruin wrought by man, e. g. the razing of Samaria and Jerusalem and the imprisonment of their kings (2 K 17¹·⁵ 24¹⁵ 25⁶⁻¹⁰) are ascribed to the personal action of Iahvah (cf. 2 K 17¹⁸ ᵐ 21¹²·¹³ 24²⁻⁴).

v. 15. *stoppeth*: *holdeth in* or *back*. עָצַר, cogn. c צוּר *besiege*, and צָרַר *bind* (the Prim. sense of all three: cf. Sum. SAR, *bind, bond*). Cf. Dt 11¹⁷ 1 K 8³⁵. When 'waters' or floods (Gn 8³) dry up (Gn 8⁷), it is due (not to absorption by the soil or evaporation) but to the *binding* or *restraining* Hand of Iahvah. 𝔊 incorrectly: ἐὰν κωλύσῃ τὸ ὕδωρ ξηρανεῖ τὴν γῆν, *He will dry u*... ... : pointing וּבָשׁ Hiph. and Sing., and addm. אֲרִי

from st. ii, which it renders: *But if He have let loose* (ἐπαφῇ: scil. *upon it*), *He destroyed it by overturning*; app. pointing וַיְשַׁלְחֵם וַיַּהֲפָךְ אָרֶץ. Torrential rains and floods 'overturning' the land are characteristic of Babylonia rather than of Palestine. But the allusion of the verse may be, as Dr says, to destructive droughts and floods generally.

v. 16. In st. i 𝔐 gives עִמּוֹ עֹז וְתוּשִׁיָּה *With Him are Strength and Sound Wisdom* (or *Insight*, *Sagacity*). Cf. v. 13. 𝔊, however, παρ' αὐτῷ κράτος καὶ ἰσχύς, which is really more suitable to the context, since the whole passage, vv. 13-25, demonstrates not the Wisdom but the Omnipotence of Iahvah. Moreover, תּוּשִׁיָּה, which occurs twelve times in OT acc. to 𝔐, is nowhere ascribed to God (see on 11⁶) in Job, if indeed elsewhere, though He may endow man with it (Is 28²⁹). Leg. fort. עֹז וְתַעֲצֻמוֹת *Strength and exceeding Might* (Intens. Plur., see the same phrase Ps 68³⁶) = Omnipotence. St. ii *Misled and misleader*: שֹׁגֵג וּמַשְׁגֶּה: lit. *he who goes astray and he who causes to go astray*. The two closely kindred Roots are used of sinning unwittingly (Le 4¹³ 5¹⁸); here app. of erring in judgement. They do not imply deceit. (Driver neatly suggests לוֹ שֹׁגֶה וּמַשְׁגֵּהוּ *To him* belong *the erring one and he who causeth him to err*.) In this and the following verses the ruin of nations (meaning prob. Israel and Judah), and the political mistakes and delusions which were the cause of it, are described as the work of Iahvah, in the exercise of His sovran will or caprice. Both the blind guides and their misguided followers are alike 'His'—pawns in His stupendous game, and absolutely subject to His control. If there is any deceiver in question, it is Iahvah Who deceives both: cf. Je 4¹⁰ 20⁷ Ez 14⁹ Is 19¹²⁻¹⁴ 29⁹,¹⁰. 𝔊 quite differently: αὐτῷ ἐπιστήμη καὶ σύνεσις = (?) לוֹ שֵׂכֶל וְהַשְׂכֵּל: cf. vv. 12, 13, 34³³. 𝔊 *His are strength and redemption* (!). (The Prim. sense of שׁג״ג, שׁג״ה, and שׁג״ע, Assyr. *šêgû*, *mad, frenzied*, is prob. *drunken*; cf. שׁגה Is 28⁷ Pr 20¹ and Sum. NAG = SHAG, שקה *drink*.) It is, however, possible that the Neg. Ptc. לֹא *not* has been confused here, as elsewhere (Is 9³ Ps 100²), with לוֹ *to Him*. St. ii might then be: *He erreth not, nor is made to err* (pointing מָשְׁגֶּה for מַשְׁגֶּה); His judgement is unerring, infallible, and cannot be blinded or hoodwinked by human dissimulation or hypocrisy. This would favour תּוּשִׁיָּה in st. i. Lastly, since what follows obviously relates to national catastrophes, we may perhaps further suggest לוֹ שֹׁדֵד וּמְשֻׁדָּד *His are both waster and wasted*. Je 4²⁰ 6²⁶.

v. 17. 𝔐 *marcheth away*: or *leadeth off*; scil. into exile (Je 32⁵ 2 K 24¹⁵). *disrobed*: שׁוֹלָל: Mi 1⁸. The phrase recurs, v. 19. 𝔊 renders שׁוֹלָל (only found in these three locc.) αἰχμαλώτους, *captives*, *prisoners-of-war*, here, correctly giving the general sense, and doubtless deriving the word from שׁלל *to drive off captives, to spoil*; but in Mi 1⁸ ἀνυπόδετος, *unshod*: cf. Is 20²⁻⁴: as captives appear in the sculptures of

Assyrian conquerors   The term seems to be more general than יָחֵף *barefoot* (Is 20²); meaning *stripped* of all but a loincloth. Cf 24¹⁰ Is 20⁴. 𝔗 משתלשלין *enchained*, qs from שלשלתא *chain*. 𝔊 (בתמהא *in amazement*) and 𝔙 (in stultum finem) seem to have read or guessed שומם for שׁולל. It must be admitted that 𝔐 is not satisfactory; st. i is a poor parallel to st. ii. מוליך may be due to the scribe's eye having wandered to v. 19, and this word may have displaced עֵצָה; just as 𝔊 gives *kings* (from v. 18) instead of *counsellors* in this line. It might even be that the Aramaic equivalent of עצת, viz. מלך or מלכת (see 38² מילבא *counsel*), orig. stood here, and the unrecognized Aramaism was purposely altered. Now, if the verse began thus, a verb is needed in place of שׁולל. This may well have been שׂכל (= סכל, 2 Sa 15³¹ Is 44²⁵ ‖ יהולל as here); with שׂ = ס, as in שכלות = סכלות, Ec 1¹⁷ cf. 2³. *The counsel of the Counsellors* (of State) *He maketh folly* (or *stullifieth*) is a good parallel to *And the Judges of the Land He befooleth* (or as 𝔊 *crazeth*). For the Perf. שִׁבֵּל cf. v. 18 פִּתֵּחַ. In st. ii, which is metr. curtailed, read c 𝔊 (κριτὰς γῆς) שפטי ארץ pro 𝔐 שפטים.

v. 18. 𝔐 מוּסַר מְלָכִים *chastisement* or *discipline* (5¹² 20³ al.) *of kings* can hardly be right. 𝔗 שׁוֹשִׁילְתָּא דְמַלְכַּיָא *the chain* or *bond of kings*, pointing מוֹסֵר; but Plur. required as in 39⁵ (c פִּתֵּחַ as here ; Is 52² Ps 2³ 116¹⁶): Sing. not found. 𝔙 Balteum (swordbelt) regum dissolvit (= 𝔗). We might read מוֹסְרֵי (Is 52²) and render . *The bonds of kings He looseth*; but this will not suit st. ii, whether we understand *bonds laid on kings* by their conquerors (cf. 2 K 25²⁷), or *bonds imposed by kings* on their captives (Ps 2³). Since, however, פִּתַּח is used of *putting off* clothing (Is 20² Ps 30¹² שַׂק), harness, armour (1 K 20¹¹), as well as bonds (38³¹ 39⁵ Is 58⁶), some term for clothing may have stood here, e.g. כסות (Sam. Gn 49¹¹ ch 24⁷ 31¹⁹ ‖ לבוש in all 3 locc. Dt 22¹²) or even the rare and easily mistaken syn. מכסה (Is 14¹¹ 23¹⁸). The letters כ and ר, ט and ת, are sometimes confused with each other (כסות read backwards = מוסך !). The verse might thus have been: *The clothing of kings he removeth, And bindeth a waistcloth on their loins*: scil. as prisoners-of-war (cf. 3²⁴). 𝔊 καθιζάνων βασιλεῖς ἐπὶ θρόνους (𝔊^A καθίζων 𝔊^א θρόνων) = משיב מלכים על כסא. see 36⁷ 𝔊 Hg 2²² 1 K 2²⁴; or מֵנִיחַ מלכים על בסא *Who* placeth *kings on the throne* (or כסאות *thrones*)· see Pr 18¹⁶ ינחנו = καθιζάνει αὐτόν Gn 8⁴ ותנח = καὶ ἐκάθισεν 2 K 17⁶ 13¹¹ הניח syn. of הושיב). 'The word כסות or מכסה might easily be confused with בסא, כסה (Plur. כסאות) *throne* (cf. Pr 12²³ כסה = θρόνος !). 𝔊 points פָּתַח *He maketh kings go down to the gate* (מחת = מנחת 21¹³), which may confirm מניח.

(𝔐) מוסר may have been influenced by מסיר, v. 20. It is also perhaps possible that 𝔊 read the word מיסר Pi. *Who appointeth*, 1 C 9²², and like 𝔊 pointed פֶּתַח or Paus. פָּתַח *Who appointeth kings in the gate*; a good sense, of which their rendering might be regarded as a paraphrase.

Cf. 2 Sa 19⁹. 𝕲 might even have read מסיר and understood מֹשֵׁיר qs *Who maketh kings reign*: cf. Ho 8⁴. The second st. also is not free from difficulty. 'The waistcloth,' says Driver, 'is named as the badge of a captive.' אֵזוֹר is always associated with words denoting the loins (מתנים, חלצים), as here; a fact which renders the suggested rg. אֵסוּר from Ju 15¹⁴ abortive. In 2 K 1⁸ it is Elijah's leathern girdle; in Is 5²⁷ Ez 23¹⁵ the girdle of Assyr. and Chaldean warriors; in Is 11⁵ a king's girdle; and in Je 13¹·⁴·⁶·⁷·¹⁰·¹¹ a linen girdle worn by the prophet-priest. The captive women of Is 3²⁴ are to wear a *rope* (נקפה) instead of the usual girdle (חגורה): cf. 1 K 20³¹. Since the אזור was a recognized part of the king's apparel (Is 11⁵), 𝕲 καὶ περιέδησεν ζώνῃ ὀσφύας αὐτῶν prob. means that Iahvah invested him therewith; which agrees with 𝕲's version of st. i. But the pessimistic tone of the whole context is against this interpretation. 𝔙 Balteum regum dissolvit, et praecingit fune renes eorum, seems much more natural. Perhaps we should read ויסר for ויאסר and om. ב before מתנ׳: *The raiment* (perhaps סריון *armour*) *of kings He looseth, And removeth the girdle of their loins* (so that they become powerless for action: cf. 38³).

v. 19. St. i: see notes on v. 17. 𝕲 מוליך ἐξαποστέλλων = מְשַׁלֵּחַ (14³⁰ 22⁹ 30¹¹ 39⁸: so usu. in OT). An ancient various reading.

St. ii. 𝔐 ואיתנים יסלף RV *And overthroweth the mighty*: Dr 'Rather, *them that are firmly established*—men holding long-established, hereditary dignities.' 𝕲 ולעשינא משפל *And bringeth low the strong* (warriors). 𝔗 ותקיפיא מקלקל *And maketh naught of the mighty ones*. 𝔙 et optimates supplantat. But איתנים does not recur with such a meaning. In Mi 6² האזינו *Give ear!* must be read for האתנים, which in 1 K 8² appears as the Heb. name of the seventh month (Tisri); which is not certainly identical with our word, although it is usually assumed to be so, and explained 'month of *steady flowings*', or month when water is found only in *everflowing wâdys*: an unlikely designation of a dry month, when the harvest was gathered in (Le 23³⁹). The word may have a mythological reference. (In spite of the trad. vocalization, which app. connects אֵתָנִים with אִיתָן—note, however, the absence of י—it is conceivable that אתנים is related to אתן asina, Assyr. *atânu*, Sum. ANSHU, ὄσνος, ὄνος, as the ass was a theanthropic animal, and sacred to the Sun. Cf. Smythe Palmer, *Samson Saga*, pp. 123 sqq. A Sum. syn. of ANSHU is SHAKAN, written with the Det. of Deity, which I have elsewhere compared with the name of Shekem ben Hamor.) The present, then, is the only certain occurrence in 𝔐 of the Plur. איתנים; and we may perhaps see further reason to regard it as questionable here. The Sing. איתן (doubtful in Gn 49²⁴, and cert. corrupt in Pr 13¹⁵) occurs in 8 or 9 other locc. as a Subst., mostly in the Genit. Case. (The phrase נחל איתן *torrens perennitatis*, Dt 21⁴ Am 5²⁴, should be comp. with נהרות איתן *amnes* perennitatis = amnes perennes, Ps 74¹⁵. So גוי איתן gens perennitatis = gens perennis = גוי עולמים, Je 5¹⁵, 'an immemorial people'; נְוֵה אֵיתָן pascuum perennitatis, Je 49¹⁹ = 50⁴⁴, 'an unfailing pasture'; and the sea returns לְאֵיתָנוֹ ad perennitatem eius, Ex 14²⁷, 'to his everlasting flow' or continual state.) In Nu 14²¹ איתן מושבך Perennitas sedes tua = sedes tua perennis est, 'Thine abode is eternal' or imperishable (as hewn out in the cliffs, Je 49¹⁶). אֵתָן, 33¹⁹, is doubtful: see the notes there. Apart from the very dubious existence of the Plur., we should not have expected איתנים, perennitates, as a designation of a class of men, without some qualifying term (cf. Perennitas tua, as a form of address to the later Roman emperors). 𝔊 δυνάστας δὲ γῆς κατέστρεψεν (= הפך 9⁸ חלף 11¹⁰). Perhaps אַדִּירֵי עָם (Ju 5²⁵ Ps 16³ app. of priests) or אֵילֵי ארץ (2 K 24¹⁵); which would give the stichus the normal 3 stresses. 𝔊 poss. read יַחֲלֹף *He causeth to pass away* (ח and ס may be confused). וִיסַלֵּף is of uncertain meaning. In Aram. Tg. סְלֵף is *twist, wrest, distort, turn awry*. The word appears to be an S-form of the Root לף, seen also in לפ־ת *twist, turn*, 6¹⁸; cf. Ar. لَفَت *he twisted* or *wrung his neck; he turned him aside*, to right or left; Assyr. *lapâtu, turn, overturn* or *destroy*; Ar. لَفَّ *he rolled* or *wrapped up* one thing in another. In Ar. (סלף) سَلَف is *it* or *he passed*, or *passed away, came to an end or to naught; he or it went before, preceded*; but also *he turned over* the ground for sowing. For the Heb. use, cf. Ex 23⁸ Dt 16¹⁹ *The bribe blindeth the eyes of wise men*, וִיסַלֵּף דִּבְרֵי צַדִּיק *and* twisteth *the words* (or *subverteth the cause*) *of just men*; or *maketh naught of the pleas of just men*; either distorteth their evidence, or garbleth their case. But 'צדיק, like חכמים, may refer to the judges: a bribe distorts the *decisions* or *sentences* of men who would otherwise be just. Cf. Pr 22¹² where it is said that *the Eyes of Iahvah* (unblinded by bribes) *keep knowledge* (keep to truth and fact), *And He bringeth to naught* (defeateth) *the words of the treacherous*. Cf. also Pr 19³: *A man's folly twisteth* or *maketh devious* or *overturneth his way* (Ps 1⁶); and the more or less corrupt Pr 13⁶ 21¹².

It is evident from the use of איתן in other passages that איתנים is no more likely than עולמים (Je 5¹⁵) as an epithet descriptive of a class of men, although acc. to Ex 29⁹ the office of priest was eternal (cf. Ps 110⁴); nor acc. to Heb. usage would סלף be appropriate in such a connexion. And since priests and prophets are commonly associated, and the Obj. of סלף is דברי in 3 of the 6 other locc. where the word is found, we may perhaps restore the short stichus to normal rhythm and sense by reading ודברי נביאם יסלף *And the words of the Prophets He bringeth to naught* (1 K 22²² Ez 14⁹ cf. Je 20⁷ 2²⁶ 5³¹ La 2¹⁴ al.). נביא' was misread נתיא', by the common confusion of ב, ת, and then the meaningless word was read backwards as איתנ', i.e. איתנים. Cf. Is 10¹⁸, where 𝔊 (ἀ)σεδεκ = (ה)סדה (היחרם —), the true reading of the Heb., cf. ת ב, Gn 22¹⁴

טבח = ταβεκ). This agrees well with what follows, v. 20 (cf. also Is 28⁷ 29¹⁰).

v. 20. Lit. *He removeth the lip* (= language, power of speech) *to faithful ones* or *the trusty*; i.e. makes them speechless. For נאמנים *faithful, trustworthy*, see Nu 12⁷ Sing. (poet. fragm. contrasting ordinary prophets with Moses); Ne 13¹³ Plur. (of storekeepers); נאמני ארץ Ps 101⁶ *men of integrity*; ערים נאמנים *trustworthy witnesses*, Is 8². Plur. of men not elsewhere. 'Eloquent and trusted ministers find their powers fail them' (Driver). But does eloquence imply trustiness, or trustiness eloquence? 𝕲 indeed χείλη πιστῶν: but perhaps we should read נבונים *the intelligent* for נאמנים. Cf. Pr 10¹³ 16²¹ 17²⁸; and for Iahvah's part, Ex 4¹¹. Is 29¹⁴. Instead of יקח *He taketh away*, st. ii, 𝕲 ἔγνω = ידע.

v. 21. St. i is identical with Ps 107⁴⁰. *the girdle*: or *belt*: 𝔐 מֵזִיחַ, which should perhaps be מֵזִיחַ = מֵזַח, Ps 109¹⁹ only. Cf. Assyr. *mezaḥ*, syn. of *mesirru, strap, thong*. Iahvah *letteth down* or *causeth to drop* (רפה), a stronger word than פתח, v. 18: see note on Repha'îm, 26⁵) the belt of *mighty ones* (אבירים, 24²² 34²⁰, pro 𝔐 אפיקים; al. חקים *the strong*, an Aramaism). 𝕊 וחליצוחהון דתקיפא הו מרפא *And the strength of mighty ones He weakeneth*; 𝔗 וּתְקוֹף מלכיא מחליש *And the strength of the kings He weakeneth*. But 𝕲 ταπεινοὺς δὲ ἰάσατο = רפא ואביונים (om. מזח, rg. אביונים pro אפיקים, and confusing רפה *let drop* with רפא *heal*).

v. 22. The nobles are app. disgraced by exposure. (But vv. 22, 23 may both be add. to the orig. text.) The *deep* things appear to be political intrigues and machinations, which are naturally kept close by their authors until their success is known. Cf. Is 29¹⁵ 30¹; Ps 64⁷. St. ii. Fort. leg. נעלמות pro 𝔐 צלמות *And bringeth forth secrets (hidden things) to light*. Cf. Mi 7⁹. Or תעלמות: 11⁶ 28¹¹·²¹. Pr 26⁴ נעלמים *dissemblers*.

v. 23. 𝔐 מַשְׂגִּיא *He maketh grow* or *increaseth, maketh great*: an Aramaism (Qal 8¹¹ Hiph. *magnify*, 36²⁴). So 𝔙 𝔗; but 𝕲^{Bab A} πλανῶν ἔθνη (καὶ ἀπολλύων αὐτά), which 𝕲^B accid. om., and 𝕊 לעממא מטעא = מַשְׁגֵּי וגו', Aramaism = מַשְׁגֶּה *Who misleadeth nations*, or *causeth them to go astray* (Qal 6²⁶ 19⁴ see on v. 16). So 7 codd. and Aq. Theod. This perhaps harmonizes better with the general tone of the section, which is one of unrelieved gloom: cf. what follows. Iahvah purposely misleads the nations with a view to destroying them. Cf. however, v. 15. 𝔐 *He increaseth the nations and* (then) *destroyeth them* (so RV) would amount to the somewhat milder charge of caprice or fickleness. (Perhaps משיע לגוים *He saveth nations*. For constr. cf. Ju 10¹⁴.)

St. ii. 𝕲 καταστρωννύων ἔθνη καὶ καθοδηγῶν αὐτά = 𝔐 שטח לגוים וַיַּנְחֵם (pointing ל pro לְ, which is preferable in both stt.). 𝔗, not understanding שטח, inserts מצודתא *the net*: *He spreadeth* the net *for the nations* (אומיא var. עממיא, as in st. i), *and leadeth* or *driveth them away*

(ודברנון). ⅁ שטח לאמוותא ושבק להן He spreadeth out the peoples (Heb. perhaps ללאמים) and leaveth them, pointing וַיַּנִּחֵם (cf. 1 Sa 22⁴ Je 14⁹ Ps 119¹²¹). In all other locc. נחה Hiph. is used of friendly leading or guidance (31¹⁸ Ps 23³ et saep.). Here, on the analogy of מוֹלִיךְ, v 19, it might perhaps mean leadeth them away, scil. into exile. Otherwise, pointing וַיַּנְחֵם, we may render (c ⅁) and forsaketh them, or and layeth them low (a classical mg. of καταστρωννύων): cf. Am 5⁷. The vb. שטח is not altogether beyond suspicion. It is nowhere else used of the expansion of nations, but always of spreading things out in a lit. sense (on the ground, Nu 11³² Je 8²; on a well-cover, 2 Sa 17¹⁹; once of spreading out the palms in prayer, Ps 88¹⁰). Perhaps שׂחֵט לְאֻמִּים וַיִּמְחֵם He slaughtereth peoples and wipeth them out (cf. Nu 14¹⁶ וַיִּשְׁחָטֵם = ⅁ καὶ κατέστρωσεν αὐτούς); or משחת He felleth, ruineth, &c. (Pi. or Hiph. Ho 11⁹ 2 K 19¹². c לְ Obj. Nu 32¹⁵. שחת prim. mg. to fall = Assyr. šaḫâtu: cf. Ju 20²¹, and Burney ad loc. ם om. after ם.)

v. 24. There is something wrong with the metrically redundant st. i: He taketh away the heart (i.e. either sense or courage) of the heads (chiefs) of the people of the land. 'The people of the land', i.e. the common people, 2 K 25¹⁹, might well be mentioned here after the various classes of their rulers. Deprived of their natural leaders, they wander about in hopeless bewilderment. If we interpret so, we must omit ראשי heads. ⅁ διαλλάσσων καρδίας ἀρχόντων γῆς app. om. עם people; but 1 Sa 9² העם = τὴν γῆν Is 63¹¹ [מעם] מים = ἐκ τῆς γῆς, and it is possible that ἀρχόντων γῆς (not τῆς γῆς = הארץ) represents ראשי עָם, for which phrase see Nu 25⁴ Dt 33⁵ ²¹.

St. ii is identical with Ps 107⁴⁰ᵇ. (⅁ gives διαλλάσσων, changing, for מסיר in v. 20 also; but in 5¹² for מפר. ⅌ משטא besotteth or crazeth, 𝔙 immutans, refer the 'changing' to madness: cf. 1 Sa 21¹³.)

v. 25. Lit. They feel darkness: cf. Ex 10²¹. Perhaps בחשך in darkness: cf. 5¹⁴ בצהרים: Dt 28²⁹. Read לא־אור lightless, as epithet of חשך, om. וְ; cf. לא־דרך pathless, v. 24.

St. ii is metr. short. For ויתעם (rep. from v. 24) read וַיִּתְעוּ מִדַּרְכָּם And they wander from the way. (⅁ πλανηθείησαν = וְיִתְעוּ Niph.) Cf. Is 19¹⁴ 28⁷ Pr 21¹⁶.

With the rhetorical form of vv. 17–24 cf. Is 44²⁴⁻²⁸, which the passage appears to imitate. How far it is genuine, we do not venture to pronounce.

Chapter 13. After thus demonstrating by salient examples Iahvah's absolute Power in the world of man, Eyob continues his speech without a break.

v. 1. it all: lit. all these things: כל־אלה (12⁹) pro כל 𝔐. So 12 codd., ⅁ 𝔙. perceived it: or understood it. ⅁ om. ⅌ om. לה (for ל see 9¹¹ 14²¹), which is hardly necessary to the sense.

v. 2. *I fall not below* or *away from you.* 𝔙 nec inferior vestri sum; 𝔖 *and I am not less than you* (בְּצִיר אֲנָא מִנְכוֹן 𝔗); ולית פריש אנא מנכון *and I am not separated from you.* The use of נפל *to fall* seems to be unique in Heb. and must be pronounced doubtful. (𝔊 ἀσύνετος = נבל *foolish*, Dt 32²¹ (cf. fem. 2¹⁹) may be right: *And I am no more a fool than you.* (The ו of ולא has fallen out after י, as often.)

v. 3. Lit. *But I* (emph.), *to Shaddai would I speak.* The emph. Pron. אני overweights the stichus, is not really wanted, and may be an inadvertent rep. from v. 2ᵃ. Eyob says in effect: 'For all that—for all you have said, which is common knowledge—I am still fain to speak directly to Shaddai, the All-powerful Author of my ruin; to justify myself to Him, not to you.' St. ii. והוכח אל־אל אחפץ. For the vb. and constr. cf. v. 15 15³. The root יכח, cogn. c נכח, prob. means *be in front* or *before*; Factitive, *to put in front* or *before*, and so *to argue*, and (its consequence) *convince, convict* (of error in thought or conduct), or, in a milder sense, *to chide, reprove*, and *correct*, which involve setting a sinner's faults before him. Cf. Ar. وجه *face*; واجه *face* or *confront a man, face* or *encounter him with speech or words*. (ונה cogn. c יכח. Cf. perhaps Sum. KA, *mouth, face*.)

𝔙 bene ut saep. Sed tamen ad Omnipotentem loquar, et disputare cum Deo cupio. 𝔊 (perhaps objecting to the idea of 'reproving' God) ἐλέγξω δὲ ἐναντίον αὐτοῦ ἐὰν βούληται = ואוכח (והוכחתי) לו אם יחפץ.

v. 4. Om. אולם (scribe's rep. from v. 3), c 𝔊 ὑμεῖς δέ ἐστε ἰατροὶ ἄδικοι: an interesting trans., as giving a better ‖ to st. ii than the usual interpretation. 'Plasters' (ἔμπλαστρα, Galen) are known to medicine as well as building (cf. Le 14⁴²·⁴³); and 𝔊 seems to have taken טפלי שקר in the sense of pseudo-physicians, applying worthless plasters to Eyob's wounds. טפל *to plaster* (cf. תִּפֵּל Ez 13¹⁰ 22²⁸) or *daub on* or *over* (Ps 119⁶⁹), is, no doubt, the Assyr. *ṭapâlu*, which is used fig. of *slander*, in Sargon's phrase *amât tašqirti ṭápilti Ullusunu ana Daiaukku idbub*, 'A word of slander (שקר) besmirching (*beplastering*) Ullusun to Deioces he spoke' (Sarg. Ann. 76); cf. the gloss on תִּפֵל, Dt 1¹, in 𝔗𝔍 I ומפלתון עלוי מילי שקרא *and ye bedaubed him with words of slander.* Our phrase טפלי שקר, *quack-plasterers* or *slander-plasterers*, may allude to both meanings. (In 5 R 21 19, 20 Sum. EME-SIG, *destroying tongue*, is explained *qarṣu, slander*, and coupled with .. AN-GAR taš-gi-ir-tu, i.e. *tašqirtu*, as a syn. With √GAR, QAR, cf. perhaps Chinese ka, kia, *false, unreal, to pretend*, Giles 1160.)

worthless physicians: רֹפְאֵי אֱלִל *healers of naught* or *no worth.* אֱלִיל is perhaps akin to Assyr. *alâlu, to be feeble, ulâlu, weakling, feebleminded,* 'a poor creature', syn. *enšu* (אנש); or (and?) to אל, Assyr. *ul, not*; cf. our 'naught', 'naughty' (= good-for-nothing; Pr 6¹² AV), 'not'. But (𝔊 καὶ ἰατροὶ κακῶν πάντες, i.e. לְפֹאֵי אָוֶן (i.t. 𝔊 Pr 6¹· 10¹⁹), or רֹ' אֱוֶלֶת

foolish physicians (cf. ⅏ Pr 14²⁸ 15²·¹⁵), either of which might be right. 𝔖 *healers* בלא מרם *without anything are ye* (= 𝔐).

v. 5. St. 2· lit. *And that it might become* (or *And let it be for*) '*wisdom*' *to you*. Silence often passes for wisdom. ⅏ καὶ ἀποβήσεται ὑμῖν σοφία, *And it would turn out in your case to be wisdom*. Cf. RV.

v. 6. *the reproof of my mouth*: rg. תּוֹכַחַת פִּי = ⅏ ἔλεγχον τοῦ στόματός μου: 𝔐 תּוֹכַחְתִּי *my reproof* (or *argument*). Metre and parallelism justify the addition. *contention*· or *pleading* or *remonstrance*. רִיבַת = ⅏ κρίσιν 9 codd., and 𝔖𝔗𝔙 also Sing., 𝔐 Plur. The reproof or remonstrance follows, vv. 7–12.

v. 7. ⅏ *Are ye not speaking before Iahvah?* App הלא לעיני יהוה תדברו; עיני pro 𝔐 עולה *injustice?* *utter*: or *pour out·* תביעו (Ps 94⁴) = ⅏ φθέγγεσθε: 𝔐 rep. תדברו *will ye speak?*

v. 8. St. i is too short metr. 𝔐 פניו *His face* may represent orig. 'פני, i.e. פני יהוה *the face of Iahvah* (or שדי *of Shaddai*, as in v. 3). Lit. *The face of I. will ye lift up?* 32²¹ 34¹⁹; i.e. treat him with personal favour or partiality, as an unjust judge might do. Cf. Dt 10¹⁷. ⅏ᶿ πρόσωπον λαμβάνετε; cf. Ma 1⁸·⁹ 2⁹ ⅏, and NT προσωπολημπτεῖν, προσωπολήμπτης, προσωποληψία (not in ⅏), 'respect of persons'. ⅏ ἦ ὑποστελεῖσθε; *Will ye dissemble* (or *prevaricate*)? cloaking your real thoughts from fear. It seems, however, prob. that πρόσωπον αὐτοῦ has fallen out of the Gk. text, and that we must render *Will ye shrink from His Face?* Cf. Dt 1⁷ Wisd 6⁷ and Goodrick's excellent note. St. ii in 𝔐 is also too short metr. אתם *you*, emph., may have fallen out after אם (ואם?). Cf. Ju 6³¹ האתם תריבון לבעל '*Will you plead for the Baal?*' So here: *Will you plead for El?* ⅏ ὑμεῖς δὲ αὐτοὶ (⅏ᴬ αὐτοὶ ὑμεῖς) κριταὶ γένεσθε = ואתם תריבון (cf. Is 3¹³ 63⁷) רב טוב = κριτὴς ἀγαθός!). ⅏ᴬ adds a gloss καλῶς γε λαλοῦντες ('as you are such fine speakers') = מְטִיבִים דבר. Perhaps we should read ריב תריבון, *will you really plead?*

v. 9. You are exposing yourselves to the peril of a Divine exposure. God sees through you, and knows your real motives. RV may be right: *Is it good that He should search you out?* St. ii. *like a mere mortal*: lit. *like mocking at a* (mortal) *man*. For the vb. הָתֵל, see Gn 31⁷ Ju 16¹⁰ 1 K 18²⁷ וַיְהָתֵל? וַיְהַתֵּל; cf. on 17²) Je 9⁴. Like Lat. *illudere* it seems to mean *playing* or *sporting with* a thing, and then *making sport or game of, mocking or jeering at* a pers. or thing (c dat. or *in aliquem* or *aliquo*); cf. also *deludere, mock, deceive, delude* (e.g. *amantem*). ⅏'s curious rend. seems partly due to an illegible text εἰ γὰρ (⅏ˢ καὶ) τὰ πάντα ποιοῦντες προστεθήσεσθε αὐτῷ (⅏ᴬ ὁδῷ αὐτοῦ), οὐθὲν ἧττον ἐλέγξει ὑμᾶς = הוכח ונו' (Dt 13⁵ ⅏). אם הכל עשים תרבקו בו. This makes v. 10ᵃ the apodosis to 9ᵇ. Here, as often, ⅏ betrays complete unconsciousness of the metrical arrangement. 𝔖 substitutes (ב) אתתדין *go to law with* for התל *to mock*. (The Pnm. Rᵗ may be r......

taltallum, a part of the palm-tree, *gišimmaru*, viz. the *hanging* spathes or flower-sheaths, Heb. תלתלים, and in the derivv. תלה, דלה, תלל, דלל, גֹּל, גַּל, &c. The prim. idea seems to be that of hanging or dangling, swaying or swinging about; whence letting down or lowering, e.g. a bucket into a well, and so throwing down or prostrating, whence *dalâlu, humble, worship*, דַּל *poor*. The Sum. DAL is *to fly*, because flying birds are as it were *suspended* in the air, or because flight is a swinging and swaying motion. So Ar. دلّ is used of the amorous play or dalliance of a woman, her swaying movements and gestures, talking and jesting in a pleasing manner; and התל is to play or trifle with, and then to mock, delude, and the like.)

v. 10. *punish*: or *reprove* or *convict* (הוכיח; v. 3). Cf. 42⁷·⁸.

partial: so 𝔊 πρόσωπα θαυμάσεσθε. But 𝔊ˣ𝔖𝔗𝔙 *accept His face*; פני pro 𝔐 פנים. See note on v. 8. Burney thinks the couplet weak and unoriginal.

v. 11. *His Terror*: אימתו (v. 21) or יראתו 𝔊 *His fear*. So דחלתה, and perhaps 𝔊 δεινά [ΔΕΙΝΑ], scrib. error for δεῖμα [ΔΕΙΜΑ]? αὐτοῦ. But 𝔗 *when He is raised on the throne of judgement, will not His terror* (רתיתה) *dismay you, And His terror* &c. seems to be conflate. 𝔙 Statim ut se commoverit = 𝔐 שאתו *His uplifting* or *uprising*. Cf. 31²³; 41¹⁷. If 𝔐 is right, it may mean either *His uprising* or *His loftiness, majesty*. The proposed שְׁאֵתוֹ (30³·¹⁴ Pr 3²⁵), *His devastation*, does not seem likely, though involving only a change of points. (Δεινός is very rare in 𝔊. In 2 Sa 1⁹ the ἅπ. השבץ, qs 'the horrors', is rend. σκότος δεινόν, 𝔗 רתיתא, ut hîc. ? הֲשָׁבֵּץ *twisting, writhing, terror*, like חיל Ex 15¹⁴ joined with אחז Is 13⁸ al. So פלצות 21⁶.)

v. 12. *your saws*: or *aphorisms*: str. perhaps *memorized sayings, reminders*: זכרניכם. So here only. 𝔙 Memoria vestra, as if Sing. So 𝔗. 𝔊 τὸ ἀγαυρίαμα ὑμῶν, *your insolence* (Ba 4³⁴) = זרונכם. 𝔊𝔗 confounds משלי *proverbs* with מְשָׁל *likeness* (41²⁶): ἴσα (v. ἴσον) σποδῷ: 𝔖 with מֹשֵׁל *ruler*.

St. ii. 𝔐 לגבי־חמר גביכם *For bosses of clay are your bosses*; or *Your bosses become* (or *prove*) *bosses of clay*. But 𝔊 τὸ δὲ σῶμα πήλινον, *while your body is of clay*, or *And your body will prove to be* (ἀποβήσεται) *clay* = וְגֵפְכֶם חו' (Aram.). The word גַּב *back* appears to be used for the *boss* of a shield in 15²⁶. The Heb. text, however, is not above suspicion. 'Bosses' is not a good parallel to the doubtful 'memories'; לגבי is strange; and משלי *maxims* or *similitudes* is not elsewhere found with a qualifying Genitive, except to denote the author of the sayings. 𝔊 *Remember that your sultan is of dust, And beside the clay is your dwelling-place*. Cf. 4¹⁹ 10⁹. It is quite probable that the verse began with זכרנא *Pray you remember* ... It may have continued with כי תשכנו ובתי חמר *that ye dwell in dust* (or שכני עפר *ye dwellers in the dust!*), עפר

בתיכם *And your houses are houses of clay!'* (or כי בתי *That your houses*, &c.), or something similar, as an ironical reference to 4^{19}. (𝔊 𝔗 𝔚 suggest rather ‏וכרינא כר־מׇשלכם אפר *Remember that your likeness is ashes*: cf. 30^{19} 41^{25}; ועל־נב חמר *And hard by the clay*, &c). Such a reference to human frailty makes a better connexion with the sense of the last verse.

v. 13. *Be silent that I too may speak*: or *and I too will speak*. Emph. Pron. 𝔊 bene אף אנא. 𝔐 החרישו ממני *Be silent from me*: i.e. leave off talking to me: so Je 38^{27}, where, as here, 𝔊 om. ממני. Cf. also 1 Sa 7^8. Here it seems to overload the stichus, while st. ii is perhaps too short.

St. ii. Lit. *And let aught pass over me!* Cf. 2 Sa $18^{22\,23}$ Ps 42^8. I.e. Let what will befall me! scil. in the way of Divine Wrath. But מה *What?* ($34^{2,33}$), *How?* is not so used elsewhere in the book; and 𝔊 has καὶ ἀναπαύσωμαι θυμοῦ, *and that I may desist* or *rest* from anger = ואבליגה מחמה: see 2^{26} 10^{20} 6^4 19^{29}. Perhaps: ותעבר עלי חמה *And let Wrath pass over* (Ps 42^8 al.) *me!* or ויַעֲבר עלי חמה *And let Him cause Wrath to pass over me!* Let Him deluge (or overwhelm) me with His Wrath! Burney suggests מאומה *anything* pro מה.

v. 14. 𝔐 prefixes על־מה *Upon what* or *Wherefore?* which is, however, only a scribe's erroneous rep of מה (עלי) from the end of the last verse, spoiling the metre (4 stresses for 3) Eyob says that he will run all risks in affirming his own innocence to the face of the Divine Judge. *I will take up* (or *carry*) *my flesh* (my body or myself) *in my teeth*; as a wild beast (or even a cat) at bay will snatch up its young and, so hampered, face its enemy. See on 19^{20}. This vivid metaphor occurs here only. That of st. ii recurs Ju 12^3 1 Sa 19^5 c כף Sing. ut hîc. 𝔊ᴮ ἐν χειρί 𝔊ᴺ ἐν χερσίν. 𝔊ᴬ ἐν χερσίν μου : so a few codd., 𝔖 𝔗 𝔚. Cf. 16^{17}.

v. 15. *If* (or *Though*. הֵן 40^{23} Is 54^{15}) *He slay me* in His Wrath at my daring, *I will not wait* (14^{14}, cf. 6^{11} Mi 5^6) any longer; but will at once proceed to prove (אוכיח st. ii: see on v. 3) 'my ways'—my manner of life—*to His face* or before Him. The Ketîb לא *not* is prob. right here. Qerî לו *for Him* I (will) wait 𝔊 ἐάν με χειρώσηται (38 only) ὁ δυνάστης, ἐπεὶ καὶ ἦρκται, ἢ μὴν λαλήσω καὶ ἐλέγξω ἐναντίον αὐτοῦ = הן יקטלני | אל כי החל | אך־ארבר אל־פניו ואוכיח *If El slay me* (*for He hath begun*) | *Yet will I speak to His face and argue* scil. my case. Here אל evidently springs from לא; so that 𝔊 must not be adduced as supporting the Qerî.

𝔖 *If He kill me, for Himself alone am I waiting* or *looking* (לה הו מסכאַאנא); *Because my ways are before Him*. 𝔗 *Behold, if He kill me, before Him* (לו) *will I pray; But my ways before Him will I argue* (= 𝔐). 𝔙 *Etiamsi occiderit me, in ipso sperabo*: verumtamen vias meas in conspectu eius arguam. For the confusion between לא and לו see on 12^{16}. The render ng *I. H . . . , I . . . . n . . .* also possible, so far as the mere words are concerned; but, apart from the unusual division of the stichus into two independent sentences, it does not agree so well with the context.

Eyob is not insisting here on his expectation of speedy death, but on his determination to speak out, even if it provoke Iahvah to kill him for his presumption (as his friends, no doubt, assumed and as he himself feared would be the consequence).

[The rare קטל *to kill* (Jb 13^{15} 24^{14} Ps 139^{19} קָטֶל n. Ob 1^9 all), which in Ar., Old Aram., Eth., and Sab. has ח Rad. Med., is cogn. c קטן *small*, str. *cut short*, cf. Assyr. *qatnu, short*, e.g. *sûqu qatnu, a short street, qattan, cut short*, of hair; קָטַב *cut off*; קרץ, קצב, קצה, קצץ, קצר, &c. נזר, גזל, גזז, גזה, &c., all denoting various kinds of cutting. Cf. Sum. GAZ, *kill*, ĜAŠ, *cut off, kill, smash*; KUD, *cut, cut off*.] The √יחל (Heb. only), used mostly in Pi. (some twenty-five times) and about twelve times in Hiph. (Niph. app. twice; Gn 8^{12} leg. וַיְיַחֶל or וַיֹּחֶל; cf. 1 Sa 13^8; Ez 19^5 corrupt), always means *to wait, continue expectant*, and is usu. joined with לְ indicating the Pers. or Thing waited *for* (about twenty times; אֶל thrice). In eight or nine instances it is used Abs. The Temporal implication comes out clearly in 6^{11} 14^{14} 29^{23} 30^{26} 32^{11,16} Mi 5^6 Gn 8^{12} 1 Sa 10^8 13^8. It may be cogn. c חול, חיל *to be strong, firm*, and so (20^{21}) *enduring, lasting, abiding*. Cf. perhaps Sum. GAL, *ašâbu, kânu, bašû*. Possibly, after all, since Eyob really longed for death (3^{21} 6^{8,9} 7^{15}), the verse should be rendered: *Behold, He will slay me and for Him* (וְלוֹ; ו exc. post י) *I wait* (expecting His blow); *Only my ways to His face I will argue* (or *before Him I will lay*).

v. 16. *Also He* (emph.; cf. 7^{11} 12^3 16^4) *must be my salvation* (or *will become my salvation* or *deliverance*; lit. *to me will be for s.*, as Ex 15^2). Here and elsewhere Eyob expresses confidence that Iahvah, who knows the truth and is well aware of his innocence, will one day vindicate him (16^{19} 19^{25}). If only He would grant him an audience, and listen to his pleas, He could not deny the justice of his arguments, but must needs pronounce him guiltless (23$^{6-7}$). 𝔊 καὶ τοῦτό μοι ἀποβήσεται εἰς σωτηρίαν which would require וְהָיָה at least (rather וְזֹאת). 𝔙 *recte Et ipse erit salvator meus*; 𝔖 ואף הו נהוא לי פרוקא *And also He himself will become to me a saviour*; 𝔗 לחוד הוא לי לפורקנא *But He will be to me for salvation* (= 𝔐).

For an apostate (or *dissembler*: חנף: see on 8^{13}) *would not come before Him*. Lit. *For not before Him will* (or *can* or *doth*) *an apostate come*. The reference may be general (cf. Ps 5^5), or particular: *For it would not be an apostate that came before Him*; i.e. I am no חנף, but a man sincerely pious and upright, and therefore He is bound to save me. For חנף 𝔊 gives δόλος (= רמיה, v. 7; כרמה, 15", where 'A𝔊 ὑποκριτής, as also 20^5 and ? 𝔊 34 36^1) 𝔖 ܣܟܠܐ is an error for ܠܐ ܒܪ = 𝔐. 𝔙 *omnis* hypocrita. 𝔗 דילטור = delator; so 15³⁴ al. Perhaps we should read חנף־אנכי or חנף־אני; thus gaining the more direct and less ambiguous sense: *For not before Him* (emph.) *am I a renegade* (?). [יבוא may be a disguise of אנכי written backwards!] This would be quite in the manner of Eyob's frequent assertions of his own integrity (9²¹, cf. 11⁴).

v. 17. St. ii is short, and אחותי *my declaration* (Aram. Aph. Infin of חוי *to tell, declare*) is almost certainly corrupt. 𝔊 ἀναγγελῶ γάρ = וָאֲחַוֶּה. The missing word after this may be either דַּעְתִּי (Ps 19³) or דעי *my knowledge* (32¹⁰·¹⁷) or the Pers. Obj. אתכם *you* (emph. 32⁶; cf. 15¹⁷ 36²). These are the only occurrences of this Aram. rt. חוה in Heb. Cf. Dn 2¹¹. 𝔖 ותחויתי אמר קדמיכון And my declaration *I will speak before you.* The translators felt that all was not right with the text. (The verse looks like an insertion of the Elihu-editor.)

v. 18. *my case* or *cause*, to be presented for judgement. משפטי c Suff. pro משפט אל. So 1 cod., 𝔊𝔖. Cf. 23⁴ 1 K 3¹¹. Eyob's arrangement of his case, or marshalling of his main points, is briefly stated in vv. 23 ff. For ערכתי struxi, e.g. verba, copias, etc., 𝔊 seems to have read קרבתי ἐγγύς εἰμι (τοῦ κρίματός μου). Cf. 17¹².

v. 19. Is any one ready to meet and confute my statements? for if that be so כי עתה *For now* = for then, for in that case), I will say no more, but resign myself to death.

v. 20. Lit. *Only, two things do not Thou unto me!* This is in strictly logical connexion with v. 21ᵇ (*And Thy Terror, let it not scare me!*), but not with 21ᵃ (*Thy palm from off me remove!*), at least according to our idiom. But the sense is clear enough: Let not Thy heavy Hand remain upon me! For the mode of expression, cf. Pr 30⁷·⁸. *Then from Thy Face I will not hide*; I will not shrink from facing Thee, as a guilty man might: Gn 3⁸⁻¹⁰. With vv. 21, 22, cf. 9³¹·³⁵.

v. 22, st. ii. 𝔊 *Or Thou shalt speak, but I to Thee will give an answer* Prob. not a different reading; but substituted on the ground of reverence. Insert אַתָּה *Thou*, emph before השיבני metr. grat. Cf. also the parallel st. i.

v. 23. Lit. *How many have I errors* (v. 26) *and failures*; i.e. in conduct and behaviour. 𝔊 reverses the order: αἱ ἁμαρτίαι μου καὶ αἱ ἀνομίαι μου. Usually, though by no means uniformly, עון = ἀνομία and חטאת = ἁμαρτία (e.g. 10⁶⁻¹⁴ 14¹⁶). Cf. 1 Jn 3⁴ ἡ ἁμαρτία ἐστὶν ἡ ἀνομία. Etymologically, עון is an *erring* or *straying from the* right *way* (עוה = Ar. غوى *he erred*; *deviated from the right way or course,* or *from that which was right*; *was disappointed, failed of attaining his desire*; Lane). Cf. perhaps Sum. NAM, *annu, arnu*, 'sin' or 'misdeed' (ngam = GAM, GAV, *bend*). חטאת *a missing of one's aim* or *mark. goal* or *way*. fr. חטא *to miss the mark* (Ju 20¹ Hi.: Qal? Pr 19), *i mi th p*... *k' t' fau in suly*, *to sin* against God or man. is well repres nted by the Greek word ἁμαρτία.

the idea of *miss, mistake, error, failure, loss* (cf. Gn 31³⁹), being predominant. Cf. Assyr. *ḫiṭêtu*, pl. *ḫiṭâti*, *a sin*, against a god or a king. It will be seen that, in their original sense, חטא, עון, and שגגה or משנה are not far apart; all three denoting error or mistake rather than guilt or wickedness.

The two plurs. here are obviously supplementary to each other; although we might well om. וחטאות as overloading the st., and since וחטאתי follows in st. ii. The rg. עון ופשע suggested for st. i is bad Heb. (We could hardly say במה לי עון ופשע: cf. Gn 47⁸ 1 K 22¹⁶); and to omit פשעי in st. ii would make the line metr. defective. In the first member Eyob asks what is the total number of his sins; in the second, he demands to know what special or particular sin is laid to his charge.

v. 24. St. i; cf. 34²⁹ Ps 10¹¹ al.

St. ii. *foe*: אויב: an apparent play or pun on his own name איוב: see note on 1¹. Cf. 1 Sa 25²⁵. The same thought recurs 19¹¹.

v. 25. *scare*: or *dread*, Trans., as 31³⁴ c accus. Heb. תערוץ *to awe* or *overawe*, Is 2¹⁹·²¹. Cf. adj. עריץ 6²³ 15²⁰. If the root be that which we see in רצ״ח, רצ״ץ *break, crush* we may compare the transition of ideas in חתת *shattered, broken, dismayed*. Possibly, however, ערץ is akin to Aram. ערק *flee, flee away* (a natural effect of fear). Then עריץ will be a man who puts others to flight or from whom they flee; one who *scares* them away. *driven*: נדף: scil. by the wind: Ps 1⁴ Is 19⁷ Le 26³⁶ Is 41².—St. ii. *Or*: rg. ואם, for which קש presents the scribal error את. *a stalk*: קש Coll *stubble*, or the like: Ex 5¹² Is 40²⁴. Cf. Syr. קשא *stubble, dry stalks, grass or leaves*. [The √קש = בש *dry*; cf. קום = בום *high*. The transition from *dry* to *hard, firm, strong*, is easy: cf. קשה *hard, fierce*; ܩܫܐ *endured it*; *struggled against troubles or difficulties*; Assyr. *kaššu, strong, kašūšu, mighty one, kiššūtu, power, might*, &c., with which Aram. קשיש *old, elder*, orig. *full-grown, grown up* (Syr.) > *dried up*, may be connected (cf. our 'old', *altus*, i.e. grown up). Cf. perhaps also Syr. ܩܬ ܡܐ *firm, fixed*, Pa. *cause to wither* (Lexx); and עזא (Syr.) *endure*, עז, עזז *powerful, forceful, strong, fierce*, Assyr. *ezêzu, ezzu*. קשת = قوس *bow*, however, may be str. a *strung* bow: cf. Sum. KESH, *to bind*; unless קש = קמיש from GAM, *to bend, to bow*, in which case קשת = thing for *bending*; c Sum. Postpos. SHU, *for*.]

v. 26. Lit. *For* (or *That*) *Thou writest upon me bitter things*. Possibly an allusion to the visible marks and scars of his disease, graven upon him by 'the Finger of God', and read by his friends as Divine testimony to his guilt. 𝔊 *That Thou didst write down* (or *record*) *against me evils*; perhaps meaning didst register the 'sins of my youth', st. ii. If כתב *to write* means *to decree* in this passage, כתבת *Thou hast decreed* would seem more suitable than תכתב: cf. the Ptcp. pass. Ps 40⁸. But כתב על is usu. *to writ upon* a tablet or the like. The word מרה, 20¹⁴, denotes venom, poison (of serpents), and in 20²³ a man's *gall* or gall-bladder (cf. מְרֵרָה 16¹³). The plur. מְרֹרֹת recurs Dt 32³² (unless we should point מְרֹרַת: cf. the parallel עִנְּבֵי רוֹשׁ), where *clusters of poisons* = poisonous clusters. Comparing Is 44⁵, it is conceivable that we should render: *For Thou writest on me 'Poison'* (Plur. intens.) or (rg. מרדות, cf. 24¹³ 1 Sa 20²⁰) 'Rebellion' (so 𝔖). Or should we point תִּכְתָּב and render: *Thou makest harsh decrees for me* (Is 10¹)?

St. ii. Lit. *And makest me possess the errors* (or *faults*) *of my youth.* 𝔖 *And rememberest against me*, &c. Cf. Ps 25⁷. 𝔙 *And willest to consume me with*, &c. וְתוֹרִישֵׁנִי does not seem quite satisfactory; but the meaning may perhaps be: Thou treatest the forgotten faults of a time long past as though they still belonged to me, characterized my present conduct. 𝔊 περιέθηκας δέ μοι νεότητος ἁμαρτίας. Cf. 39²⁰ περιέθηκας αὐτῷ pro וְתַרְעִישֵׁנִי (!). Perhaps we should read וְתוֹדִיעֵנִי *And makest me know the sins of my youth*; recognize them as sins now, if I failed to do so then; or וְתִזְכּר עָלַי *and rememberest against me* (𝔖). In any case, it is evident that Eyob does not claim absolute sinlessness; but only that his conduct, since he had arrived at years of discretion, had not been such as to merit the calamities which had befallen him.

v. 27. *the stocks*: † סַד = Syr. סָדָא (so 𝔖). Prob. a sort of heavy wooden clog which the prisoner might drag about a little; not like our old English stocks, which confined the offender to a sitting posture. Akin to Assyr. *šadâdu, to drag* or *draw*? or Ar. سدّ *close up, block, obstruct*? This line and the next are quoted for comment, 33¹¹. 𝔊 κώλυμα, *impediment*, 𝔊ᴬ εὑλοπέδη, 𝔊ᵃˡ ποδοκάκη; but in 33¹¹ the classical ξύλον. 𝔙 in nervo, *recte*. 𝔗 בְּשִׁיעַ *in cement* (as if the Heb. word were סִיד = שִׂיד *lime*!).

St. ii. Leg. עַל *on* pro כָּל־עָז *all* (also at 33¹¹): cf. 14¹⁶. But the Verss. are against this. As the verse is a triplet, and as watching his 'ways' would be needless if his feet were in the 'stocks', this st. may be omitted (interpolated from 33¹¹).

St. iii (2). עַל־שָׁרְשֵׁי רַגְלַי תִּתְחַקֶּה *On the roots of my feet Thou gravest Thyself*. Besides the solitary instance of Hithpa. here, only the Pu. Ptcp. מְחֻקֶּה occurs (1 K 6³⁵ Ez 8¹⁰ 23¹⁴), in the sense of *carved, graven, carved work*. If the strange phrase 'roots of my feet' might, as is usually supposed, mean 'soles' (lit. *bottoms*? cf. 28⁵; 36³⁰ is corrupt), and if, as is prob., תִּתְחַקֶּה is a scribal error for תְּחַקֶּה *Thou gravest* (Pi. here only); *On the soles* (כַּפּוֹת elsewhere) *of my feet Thou gravest* might be a metaph. allusion to the galls and even wounds conceivably caused by wearing the *Sad*. (For the constr., see Ez 11. cc. מְחֻקֶּה עַל־הַקִּיר *carven on the wall*). But since the √חק suggests also drawing, marking out, or setting bounds or *limits* (Pr 8²⁷ : חֹק 26¹⁰ ;…), our st. has been rendered: 'Thou grav..' Th… …rav… … markest a lin… f..t (r..ab..ut) th …les *of my feet*, fixest limits for them' (OL). Apart, however, from other objections, the meaning assumed for שרש is very questionable; and the repetition of רגלי from st. î may also be a mere dittography. We should expect something like חק תשת ועל־אשורי *And upon my steps Thou settest a bound* (cf. 23¹¹ 31⁷ 38¹⁰). 𝔙 Et vestigia (= אשורו 23¹¹) pedum meorum considerasti = ועל־אשורי רגלי תחזה. 𝔖 ועל תוקפא דרגלי תחוא *And on the strength* (app. rg. שרירי for שרש: cf. 40¹⁶ and Syr. שריר firmus, solidus, durus) *of my feet Thou lookest* (cf. 𝔙 considerasti). תחזה might represent תחזק (18⁹): *On the steps of my feet Thou keepest hold*: as the Sad would do. 𝔗 על סמיוני רינלי תרשום *On the traces* (= vestigia; עקבות (?)) *of my feet Thou makest marks or gravest*. Neither 𝔖 nor 𝔗 nor 𝔙 appears to have read (or been satisfied with) שרשי. 𝔊, however, has it: εἰς δὲ ῥίζας τῶν ποδῶν μου ἀφίκου = ואל־שרשי רגלי תגיע (or 'ועד־שר) *And (even) unto the roots of my feet Thou reachest* (cf. 4⁵ 15⁸ Gn 28¹²). Perhaps 𝔊 read תחקר *Thou searchest* (v. 9) instead of the dubious תתחקה. Possibly the orig. stichus ran וכל־שרירי רגלי תנתק *And all the sinews of my feet Thou snappest* (cf. 𝔖 and 40¹⁸); i.e. with the weight and strain of the *Sad* or cangue. But, something may also be said for ועלי שרשרותיך תחזק *And upon me Thou makest firm Thy fetters* (cf. Ju 3¹² Is 22²¹): for although שרשרה happens to occur elsewhere in OT only in the sense of decorative chains (Ex 28¹⁴ 1 K 7¹⁷ al.), the Assyr. *šaršarratu*, which exactly corresponds to it, is used of a penal chain or fetter (Sum. SAR-SAR, c Det. Pr. URUDU, *Copper*; i.e. made of copper: cf. Ju 16²¹ La 3⁷).

v. 28. RV: *Though I am like a rotten thing that consumeth, Like a garment that is moth-eaten* connects the verse with what precedes (cf. 𝔙), but is not justified by the Heb. which, as the marg. states, lit. runs: *And he* (emph.) *is like*, &c. We may well ask, Who? The only obvious way out of the difficulty is to suppose that הוא (or הֵם?) or הֵנָּה) refers to Eyob's feet, as affected by his disease and gradually wasting away (cf. 1 K 15²³): *And they are like*, &c. (So 𝔊^A οἱ παλαιοῦνται ἴσα ἀσκῷ, Which grow old like a wine-skin.) Further, כרקב *like rottenness or decay* (of bones, Pr 12⁴ 14³⁰ Ha 3¹⁶; cf. רָקָב *to rot*, of wood, Is 40²⁰; met. Pr 10⁷; רִקָּבוֹן *rottenness*, of wood, Jb 41¹²) is somewhat dubious, on account of the Pred. יבלה *which weareth out* (Is 51⁶): cf. Ho 5¹², the only ref. for רָקָב: *And I will be like the moth to Ephraim, And like* the rot *to Judah*, i.e. the rot caused by the moth: where, indeed, some syn. of *moth*, e.g. סָס (Is 51⁸) would yield a closer parallel. Here, possibly, we have an Aramaism, and רקב = Syr. רַקְבָּא *a skin* or *leathern bottle* (so 𝔖 רקבא דבלא *uterculus marcidus*, and 𝔊 ἴσα ἀσκῷ).

Otherwise, we might suggest רֶקֶם (= רִקְמָה, Ju 5³⁰) *a broidered or figured cloth or robe*. *And they, they are like a brocade that frayeth* is a good parallel to *Like a garment the moth hath fretted*. The verse may have been transposed from an original position after 14⁴, as some suppose; but this assumption is hardly necessary, if we make the slight change indicated above and virtually supported by 𝔊 𝔖.

Chapter 14. After a pause, Eyob resumes his remonstrance with God, basing his appeal on the brief and troubled course of man's life and the hopeless finality of death (vv. 1–12).

v. 1. Lit. *short of days* only here. Cf. קְצַר אַפַּיִם *short of temper*, Pr 14⁷. *trouble*: or *unrest, disquiet*: רֹגֶז: cf. 3¹⁷·²⁶ 37² 39²⁴. The root is cogn. with רגש, רעש *shake, tremble* and prob. also ראש, from which comes רֹאשׁ *head*, the *shaker*, as קרקר, *qaqqádu*, is the *bower* or *nodder*.

v. 2. *he cometh forth·* not elsewhere Abs. Cf. Dt 14²² הַיֹּצֵא הַשָּׂדֶה *what cometh forth of the field*; Ju 13¹⁴; ch. 28⁵. יִצְמָח *he shoots, sprouts*, or *springs up* (usu. of plants and trees) has been proposed; but יָצִיץ *he flowers* or *blossoms* (Ps 90⁶ 103¹⁵ בְּצִיץ הַשָּׂדֶה כֵּן יָצִיץ) seems better. Cf. 𝔊 ὥσπερ ἄνθος ἀνθήσαν, *as a flower after flowering*. But 𝔖𝔙𝔗 read יָצָא *and fadeth*: pointing וַיִּמָּל. For the vb. cf. 18¹⁶ and Ps 37²: *For like grass they quickly fade* (יִמָּלוּ); *And like green herbage they fall away* or *wither and fall* (יִבּוֹלוּן). Cf. also Ps 90⁶ יְמוֹלֵל Pol. [The Prim. root of this מלל is prob. the same as that of אמל, אמלל, *droop, languish, become weak and powerless*. And since MAL = BAL, PAL, נפל, נבל, may also be regarded as cogn. Cf Sum. MAL in KA-ŠU-MAL = KA-ŠU-GAL, *labánu appi*, 'to throw down the face', i.e. prostrate oneself, face downwards in prayer; KI-AN-BAL (place+high+low), *šapiltum u elîtum*, 'upper and lower side'; IM-BAL, a *wind* that *downs* things, a hurricane (*nabbaltu*); *nabâlu*, also written *napâlu*, *to 'down', throw down, destroy*, cities; *nabultum*, a *prostrate* body, a *corpse*, Heb. נְבֵלָה; perhaps *nabâlu*, *land*, as opp. to *tâmtu*, the sea, str. the *low*, the *bottom, ground*, fundus >the *dry*, which would connect it with *nablu* = Sum. BIL, BAL, *fire*, a different word. The Assyr. *labánu, to 'down'*, may be a phonetic variation of *nabâlu, throw down*. (So מלל *to say, speak*, is akin to Sum. BAL, *to speak, say, tamú, dabâbu*.)] 𝔊 ἐξέπεσεν; cf. Is 40⁷·⁸ נָבֵל צִיץ = τὸ ἄνθος ἐξέπεσεν, Is 28¹ צִיץ נֹבֵל = τὸ ἄνθος τὸ ἐκπεσόν: but Ps 37² shows that we need not substitute יבול for its syn. ימל here. 𝔖 וְחָמָא וְיָבֵשׁ *and withers and dries up*.

St. ii. *fleeth like a shadow*. So 𝔊 ἀπέδρα (*runneth away*) ὥσπερ σκιά. usu. compared with Ct 2¹⁷ וְנָסוּ הַצְּלָלִים, where, however, 𝔊 𝔙 𝔖 ונטו (*and the shadows*) *stretch out* or *lengthen*—as they do towards evening, when the sun sinks lower and lower in the heavens. Since the shadows only lengthen slowly, ברח *fugit* does not seem very appropriate as a description of their motion. (It is prob. akin to Aram. פרח *to fly*; Syr. פרחתא *bird, insect*). But the ref. may be to the quick play of the shadows thrown by moving objects (e.g. clouds and foliage on a windy day), which appear and vanish from moment to moment. Cf. א Ps 102¹ 109 and esp. 144⁴

כְּצֵל עוֹבֵר *like a* passing *shadow.* (An וִיפְרַח כְּעֵץ וְלֹא־יַ *And sprouteth like a tree, and endureth not?* פרח ‖ צִיץ, Is 27⁶ al.)

v. 3. Leg. אִם Interrog., pro אַף (cf. v. 5, which should precede this vs.). Lit. *Upon this (being) hast Thou opened Thine eye?* scil. to watch and judge him. Cf. 𝔊 *taken account of him;* 7¹⁷ff· Ps 8⁵.

St. ii. Lit. *And him dost* (or *wilt*) *Thou bring into Judgement?* Reading וְאֹתוֹ c 𝔊𝔙𝔖 pro וְאֹתִי *And me,* and om. עִמָּךְ *with Thee* ad fin., as overloading the stichus, and as opposed to the speaker's meaning, which is not the sentiment of Ps 143². Eyob earnestly desired to come before God, and argue out his case with Him, face to face (13³⁻²²). He considers that he has been judged and punished without trial, by One against whose Power there is no appeal. Otherwise we might read וְאִתּוֹ תָבוֹא *And with him wilt Thou enter . . . ?*

v. 4. The verse is incomplete, and otherwise dubious. One cod. om. The phrase מִי יִתֵּן is a common formula of wishing, v. 13, 6⁸ 11⁵ 19²³ al.; and st. i ought to mean: *Oh that a pure might come out of an unclean one!* lit. *Who will give* (*yield* or *make*) *a pure one out of an unclean* (or *defiled, tainted*) *one?* Cf. Nu 11²⁹. The Adjj. are both masc. (RV marg. *Oh that a clean thing could come out of an unclean! not one* is incoherent and incorrect.) 𝔙 Quis potest facere mundum de immundo *conceptum semine* (an exeget. gloss)? nonne tu qui solus es? So 𝔗: *Who will give a pure one out of a man who is defiled with sins, if not God who is One, Who forgiveth him?* 𝔊 *For who shall be pure from uncleanness* (ῥύπος, *filth,* 9³¹ 11¹⁵)? *why, none, If his life on the earth* (*be*) *even one day;* connecting with v. 5. This = מִי יִטְהַר מִטֻּמְאָה לֹא אֶחָד יוֹם בָּאָרֶץ יָמָיו. The words לֹא אֶחָד would seem to have been written twice in 𝔊's MS.; and the translator pointed the second לֹא as לֻא *if.* Further, חֲרוּצִים was misread בָּאָרֶץ, and יָמִים *days* is often βίος, *life* in 𝔊 (v. 6, 7⁶·¹⁶ 8⁹ al.). The verse, which is prob. an interpolated comment on v. 3, may be restored somewhat as follows: מִי יַטְהֵר מִטֻּמְאָתוֹ *Who can become pure from his uncleanness?* cf. 𝔊 (app. a reminiscence of Ez 24¹³ 36²⁵ where the same phrase occurs); מִבְּנֵי־אָדָם לֹא אֶחָד *Of the sons of man not one.* Cf. Ps 14²⁻³ 53⁴ Ex 9⁶·⁷. (For st. ii, 𝔙 Nonne tu qui solus es? suggests הֲלֹא אַתָּה אֶחָד: cf. אֶחָד in Is 51²ᵇ.)

v. 5. *Also:* or *Yea:* אַף pro אִם, which belongs to v. 3. *determined:* or *decided.* Verbs of *cutting* or *cutting off,* like חָרַץ (cf. Le 22²²), גזר Aram. (cf. 22²⁰), are met. used in the sense of deciding, decreeing, &c. *his days,* i.e. the term of his life. *with Thee,* i.e. in Thy mind. (The Conj. ו must be restored before מִסְפַּר *the number.* It was om., as often, after the ו preceding it.) The exact length of a man's life is predetermined by His Maker. (𝔊 παρ' αὐτοῦ = אִתּוֹ *with Him.*)

St. iii. *His boundary* or *limit* (Ketib חֻקּוֹ recte) *Thou hast set* (שַׁתָּ pro וְ) עָשִׂיתָ *Thou hast made.* See v. 13, 26¹⁰ 38¹⁰. So 𝔊 ἔθου and 𝔙 constituistu, but cf. 28²⁹), *and he passeth not.* ⑤ εἰς χρόνον ἔθου So χρόνος = חק, v. 13. ⑤ נמוסא *a law*. The stichus adds nothing to the sense of the previous distich, and violates the metrical scheme. It is prob. an addition.

v. 6. *And let him alone*: חֲדַל־מֶנְהוּ (מִמֶּנּוּ) *cease from him*, pro 𝔐 ויחדל *and let him cease*, which would give a diff. mg. (e.g. v. 7). So one cod. Cf. 7¹⁶. 𝔗 *and let* his plague *cease*. ⑤ וַנְפוּשׁ *and let him stay* or *cease* (= 𝔐). ⑤ ἵνα ἡσυχάσῃ = 𝔙 ut quiescat = 𝔐. But חדל does not mean *to rest* (שבת, נוח 3¹⁷·²⁶). *Take Thine eye off him*, or *Look away from him*, 7¹⁹. *Until he make good* (pointing יִרְצֶה Hiph. pro 𝔐 Qal), *like a hireling, his day* (of toil, i.e. his allotted term of life). Cf. 7¹, acc. to which man's life is a time of hard service, like that of a hired labourer who has to work from morning to night under the eye of a jealous master, and longs for the evening hour which will end his toil. For the meaning of ירצה, cf. Le 26³⁴ ⁴¹ ⁴³ and Is 40² (where נרצה עונו *her guilt is made good* or satisfactory to the Deity, scil. by the expiation of suffering, is parallel to מלא צבאה *her hard service is completed*) עַד יִרְצֶה יוֹמוֹ cannot mean lit. *Till he shall accomplish his day* (RV), qs יְכַלֶּה, 21¹³ 36¹¹. It could only signify *Till he be pleased* or *satisfied with his day*. Hence Driver: '*Till he can enjoy, as a hireling, his* (finished) *day* (cf. 7²), i.e., here, the evening of his life.' This ingenious interpretation reads too much into the text. There is no suggestion about enjoying the evening of life, either here, or in 7². The general sense is simply, Let him alone until his brief day is done. In the case of a hireling's task it is the master, not the man, who has to be pleased or satisfied with the work. We might point יָרְצֶה (cf. Is 40²), which would yield the sense. *Till his day, like that of a hireling, be accepted*, or *made good*, or *satisfactorily accomplished*. ⑤ *Until he run* (נרהטן), *like a hireling, his days*, i.e. the course of his life: reading ירוץ for ירצה (cf. Ps 19⁶ 119³²) This may be right; for the hireling (in desire) hastens to the end of his task. 𝔗 *Until he receive his wages, like the h, in his day*. Possibly יומו = his day's work, i.e. the reward of it (פעלו, 7², which might even be the orig. text here also); although any idea of satisfaction seems to jar with the context, the tone of which is one of unrelieved melancholy.

(The word רצה *to be pleased* or *satisfied with* a person or offering, *to regard with favour, accept favourably* (33²⁶), like other Heb. words of similar meaning, orig. denoted pleasure as evinced by the *brightness* of the face: cf. האיר פנים Nu 6²⁵; חרה Assyr. *ḥadû, to be glad*, str. *to shine, be* or *look bright*, from Sum. GAD, *bright, shining*. The Sum. KA-ZAL, *face-shine* is explained *tašîltu, pleasure*. So the Prim. Root of רצה may be recognized in Sum. RAZ, RUZ, SHU-RUZ, *kabâbu, kubbubu, sparkle, glitter, shine* whence *kakkabu, star,* כּוֹכָב.)

v. 7. A tistich in 𝔐 and Vers. Some such word as we have

ventured to supply may have fallen out. For קָצִיר *boughs*, *branches* (|| יוֹנֶקֶת Ps 80¹²) cf. v. 9, 18¹⁶ 29¹⁰ Is 27¹¹; for יִפְרִיחַ or יִפְרַח v. 9, Ps 92¹⁴·¹³. Thus we get קְצִירוֹ יָכֶרֶת לוֹ אִם־יִפְרַח | עוֹד יַחֲלִיף וִיפְרַח. (The ו prefixed to עוֹד in 𝔐 is really the Suff. of קָצִיר or some word of like meaning, which, with its Suff., has fallen out of the text followed by 𝔊𝔖𝔗𝔙.)

v. 8. *in the soil*: בֶּעָפָר *in the dust*. 𝔊 ἐὰν (ἐν recte Bᵃᵇ⁽ˢᵘᵖʳᵃˢ⁾ 𝔄) δὲ πέτρα· cf. 30⁸ πετρῶν = עָפָר וּכְפִים; 39¹·²⁸ πέτρας = סֶלַע. 𝔊 θερισμόν confounds קָצִיר *boughs* with קָצִיר *harvest* (5⁵).

v. 10. *a man* (emph.). Str. a *strong* one; vir: mostly poet. in Heb., but common in Aram. (גְּבַר, גַּבְרָא). The word is not directly derived from Assyr. *gabrû*, *opponent*, *equal*, *a copy*, *an answer* (from the Sum. compound GAB-RI), but is prob. cogn. c Heb. אבר and כבר *strong*, *great* or *mighty*. The Prim. Root of all three words, however, may perhaps be Sum. GAB, *breast*; since to 'breast' a thing is to meet, encounter, or oppose it (= GAB-RI, *maḫâru*), which is the natural function of the male.

and becometh powerless: וַיֶּחֱלָשׁ. Cf. Is 14¹⁰ '*Art thou made weak— like us?*'; said of the dead in She'ol. Cf. also Jo 4¹⁰ '*Let the weak* (הַחַלָּשׁ) say, "*I am* a mighty man" (גִּבּוֹר)'; Is 14¹² '*Weakener of all the nations*'. An Aramaism: שׁ חֲלַשׁ *be slackened*, *weakened*; Pa 12²¹ = רָפָה. 𝔗 אתמקמק *dissolveth* or *falleth away*; 𝔖 בלא *weareth* or *wasteth away*. But 𝔊 ᾤχετο = וַיֵּלֶךְ v. 20; cf. 19¹⁰ וָאֵלַךְ = καὶ ᾠχόμην; 30¹⁵ ᾤχετο = תַּחֲלֹף (or עָבְרָה). Either וְיַחֲלֹף (9²⁶ Is 2¹⁸) or וַיֵּלֶךְ would suit here.

where is he? וְאַיּוֹ. So 𝔙𝔗; but 𝔊 οὐκέτι ἐστίν, *he is no more*: 𝔖 וליתוהי *and he is not* = וְאֵינֶנּוּ Gn 37³⁰ 42³⁶. This is prob. right. Eyob had no doubt *where* the dead were; viz. in She'ol (v. 13, 7⁹ 10²¹ 11⁸ 26⁵·⁶). One cod. וְאַיִן.

v. 11. App. a marginal note, based on Is 19⁵ which refers to the drying up of the Nile, there called a 'sea' (יָם; cf. also Is 27¹ Ez 32² Plur. of Nile-arms; Je 51³⁶ Sing. of Euphrates). Water hardly fails the sea proper; but a very low Nile is not unknown. Of course יָם might denote a lake (ים כנרת; cf. NT use of θαλάσση); but that is not the mg. in Is 19⁵ with which this vs. almost coincides (st. ii is identical in both). The vb. אזל *go, go away, be gone* ('all gone', 1 Sa 9⁷), is Aram. rather than Heb. (Sam., Syr., Tg.). Cf. Ar. آزل; *he passed along quickly, he ran, slipped along or away*, &c., and perhaps Sum. SIL, SUL, ESIR, *road, street*, SIR, *depart* = סור, Tg. זור (R = L).

parcheth: or is *scorched up*: יֶחֱרָב. Ps 106⁹ Is 37²⁵ 50². חָרַב (Heb. and Aram.) is cogn. c חָרָה, חֲרִי, *burn, kindle, be hot* with anger, חֶרֶס *the sun*, חָרַר *burn* (30³⁰), *be scorched, parched*, Assyr. *arâru*, *become burnt, scorched, dried up*, of crops, *arratu*, *drought*, *arûrtu*, id. (Cf. perhaps Sum. GISH, *fire*; D. GISH, *the Sun*: Assyr. *Girru*, the Fire-god; NIM-GÍR, 'Heaven's Fire', *lightning*. GISH = GIR, GAR?)

v. 12. A tristich. The third st. may be an addition, as the sense is complete without it. Others would transfer st. 1 to follow v. 19, which also is a tristich, as it stands.

till the Heavens wear out or *decay*: rg. בְּלוֹת (or pointing בִּלְתִּי, as a poet. form of the same word) instead of בְּלְתִּי not. So 𝔊ᴬˣᶿ𝔖𝔙. Cf. Ps 102²⁷. 𝔊ᴮ ἕως ἂν ὁ οὐρανός, *whilst Heaven* (endureth); the vb. being accidentally omitted. οὐ μὴ συρραφῇ, *he will not be stitched together* (cf. 16¹⁵ ἔραψαν = תפרתי!) 𝔊 seems to have misread בלתי as יתפר, partly reversing the order of the letters, and to have transferred it to the place of (ו)יקיץ, which 𝔊ᴬ καὶ οὐ μὴ ἐξεγερθῇ connects with st. 1, and then more correctly replaces συρραφῇ by παλαιωθῇ which is evidence for בלתי: see 13²⁸ παλαιοῦται = יבלה.

he will not wake: rg. יקיץ Sing. pro יקיצו Plur So 𝔊ᴬ𝔙; but in st. iii only 𝔙 supports the Sing. It renders the two stt. thus: donec atteratur caelum, non evigilabit, nec consurget de somno suo. If the two lines are genuine, not a marginal intrusion, this must be correct.

be roused out of his sleep: יֵעֹר מִשְּׁנָתוֹ. So Zc 4¹.

The phrase *until the Heavens wear away*, in this context, prob. means *for ever*. Cf. Ps 89³⁰: *I will establish . . . his* (David's) *throne as the days of the Heavens*: i.e. it shall endure for ever. There is no hint in the entire book that 'Heaven and Earth will pass away', as in Ps 102²⁶⁻²⁸ Is 34⁴ 51⁶, and that a new world 'wherein dwelleth righteousness' will be created in their stead (Is 65¹⁷). There is no trace of Apocalypse or Eschatology in the book of Job. Eyob expects and receives his complete vindication in the present life (see the Epilogue).

v. 13, 14ᵃ. *O that in Hades Thou wouldst hide me,—Wouldst screen me till Thy wrath turn away! Wouldst set me a term, then to remember me,— If a man may die and come to life* (חיה 2 K 13²¹; Is 26¹⁴). The tristich is made a tetrastich, and the metrical balance restored, by help of the first st. of v. 14 which, as it stands, is also a tristich. *O that in Sheʾol* (Hades) *Thou wouldst hide* (צפן Hiph. Ex 2³; Ps 27⁵ ‖ יסתירני as here: cf. ספן *cover* = Assyr. *sapânu, šapânu, cover*) *me!* Eyob longed for death as the end of his sufferings (3²⁰ᶠ 6⁸ᶠ 7¹⁻²); but here he seems to wish to be allowed a temporary refuge in Hades from the Wrath which now pursues him, until it 'turn away' (Gn 27⁴⁵ of Esau's resentment): and then, when the period of danger is over, to be recalled to the land of the living. But, since that cannot be, he will resign himself to waiting for the inevitable end (v. 14): *All the days of my hard service* (7¹ = man's earthly life) *will I wait* (13¹⁵), *Until my relief* (חליפה 10¹⁷; or *successor*, cf. 8¹⁹) *cometh*. Then it will be too late to pity me (7⁶·²¹); I shall be beyond the reach of help (v. 15): *Thou wilt call, but I* (emph.) *shall not* (לֹא from v. 16ᵇ where it is needless) *answer Thee; Thou wilt regret* (חכסף miss and yearn for: Gn 31 Ps 84…

In v. 13 *that Thou wouldst set me a term* or *limit* of time (חֹק) *and remember me* implies that he wishes to be out of God's mind for a time, to be forgotten in the obscurity of Hades (cf. Ps 31¹⁵), in 'the land of forgetfulness' (Ps 88¹¹⁻¹²); and then, when the Divine anger is appeased and the prescribed time has expired, to be thought of again (Gn 8¹) and recalled to the light of day. (Ps 139⁷˙⁸ might almost be an answer to this strange aspiration.) 𝔙 *bene*: Et constituas mihi tempus in quo recorderis mei. In v. 14 𝔐 היחיה may be right, instead of ויחיה, the suggestion adopted above. *If a man die* (or *were to die*), *can* (or *might* or *could*) *he revive* (or *come to life again*)? A negative answer is expected (𝔊𝔙𝔗). 𝔊 ἐὰν γὰρ ἀποθάνῃ ἄνθρωπος, ζήσεται, συντελέσας ἡμέρας τοῦ βίου αὐτοῦ· ὑπομενῶ ἕως πάλιν γένωμαι = כי אם ימות גבר (וּ?) יחיה ויכל (21¹³ 36¹¹) מי צבאו איחל עד בוא חליפתי. The paraphrase ἕως πάλιν γένωμαι, *Until again I come into being*, shows that 𝔊 interpreted חליפה in the light of יחליף (v. 7), as if it meant *sprouting again*, like a tree, *renewal of life*; but the express contrast between the tree and man, vv. 7-10, proves that this view is erroneous. The idea of the word חליפה seems rather to be that of a person or thing which takes the place of a preceding pers. or thing as substitute or successor (cf. Ar. خَلِيف *successor*, Khalif or 'Caliph', with which in form it exactly corresponds. That the √חלף was so used in Heb. is proved by MI. 6 ויחלפה בנה *and his son succeeded him*. Cf. also Is 9⁹ *substitute*). Thus it denotes a *change* of clothing (i.e. a dress worn as substitute for another or in succession to it), and a *relay* or body of relief-troops, succeeding to the post of others (see on 10¹⁷). The clue to the mg. here is given by 8¹⁹. Death makes no gap in human life. The coming of the new generation is the signal for the departure of the old (cf. Ec 1⁴). Eyob will patiently wait till his turn comes and his successor appears.

The question (v. 14ᵃ or 13ᵈ?) *If a man die, shall he live again?* looks like a marg. note on v. 13. The principle of parallelism is conspicuous by its absence, whether we connect it with the previous or the following lines. And if we read ויחיה (וחיה?) and render *If a man may die and survive*, the passion of the previous utterance is weakened by this prosaic condition which really goes without saying. Besides, the speaker believed in a continuance of life in Hades. What he longed for was a return to the present life after temporary seclusion in Hades. Corruption of the text may have gone farther than is generally supposed. ימות גבר may be due to גבר ימות (v. 10). We might secure a parallel to the preceding line by restoring (תְּחַיֵּנִי?) וּמִמָּוֶת אַחַר תְּחַיֵּנִי *And from Death thereafter wouldst revive me!* or even כִּי אַתָּ תָּמִית וּתְחַיֵּה [𝔊] *For it is Thou that killest and makest live!* (1 Sa 2⁶ Ps 71²⁰ Dt 32³⁹).

The objection to RV and Driver's version of vv. 14ᵇᶜ 15 is that *my warfare* can only refer to the present life (7¹ 14¹). There is no 'warfare' in She'ol. And חליפה can hardly mean 'change' or 'release' from 'the weary darkness of the grave to a new life'. Eyob longs for the grave as a place of perfect rest from earth's weariness ($3^{13\,17}$); and when he speaks of 'waiting' (אֲיַחֵל 13^{15}) he means waiting for death. Verse 15 is clearly (like 7^8) a suggestion that his Creator may hereafter miss his faithful servant and, when it is too late, regret having persecuted him to the death.

v. 16. *For*: the ordinary meaning of כִּי. The 'But' of RV was necessitated by its interpretation of the previous verses. Eyob longed to escape from God's anger, because his present life of inquisitorial supervision had become intolerable. His every movement was watched, and every fault noted and treasured up for punishment. St. ii cannot be a question, as RV; while taken affirmatively it contradicts st. i. (𝔊 inserts a Neg. Ptc. in st. i also.) If we keep the Neg. here, we must read חַעֲבוּר = 𝔊 παρέλθῃ (so 6^{15} al) pro תִּשְׁמוֹר 𝔐; and prob. עַל־כָּל־חַטָּאתִי; cf. 𝔊 καὶ οὐ μὴ παρέλθῃ σε οὐδὲν τῶν ἁμαρτιῶν μου, *and none of my sins escaped Thee*; but the mg. of the corresp. Heb. is *And Thou passest over none of my sins*: cf. Mi 7^{18} Pr 19^{11}. (𝔊𝔖𝔙 point חַטֹּאתִי as Plur. parallel to צְעָדַי st. i.) We might also read תִּשְׁמוֹר עָלַי כָּל־חַטֹּאתַי *Thou keepest watch over all my sins*. Cf. 10^{14} 13^{27} 33^{11}.

v. 17. *Thou hast sealed up*: חתמת pro 𝔐 חָתָם Pass. Ptcp. (is) *sealed up*. (ת om. between the two sim. letters מ, ב, with both of which it is often confused in codd.) So 𝔊 ἐσφράγισας and 𝔙. (𝔖 Imper. in both stt.)

in a bag: בִּצְרוֹר. 𝔊 ἐν βαλαντίῳ = class. βαλλαντίῳ, *in a bag* or *purse*. 𝔙 in sacculo. Or *bundle*. צְרוֹר from צרר I. *to bind* (cf. Sum. SAR id.). But 𝔗 *in a book of memoranda!* The idea of both stt. is that Eyob's offences are carefully preserved or treasured up as evidence against him. Ho 13^{12}. The Sing. nouns in both stt. should prob. be Plur. as 𝔖. Read פְּשָׁעַי and עֲוֹנֹתַי. Cf. $13^{23\,26}$. 𝔗 Plur. in st. ii; 𝔊𝔙 in st. i. (Point perhaps עֲוֹנִי). *set a stamp*: leg. וּתְטַבַּע (Arabism? cf. طَبَع *to stamp* or *seal*) pro 𝔐 וַתִּטְפֹּל *and hast plastered over* (13^4). Cf. also Heb טַבַּעַת *signet-ring*. 𝔊 *recte* ἐπεσημήνω δέ. Since, however, the st. is metr. short, and 𝔐 וַתִּטְפֹּל requires an Object, we might insert חֹמֶר (seal-) *clay And plastered clay over my misdeeds*. Cf. 38^{14}.

v. 18. Lit. *But a mountain may utterly fall*, or *fall to pieces*. leg. c 𝔊 (πίπτον διαπεσεῖται) נָפוֹל יִפּוֹל pro 𝔐 הַר יִבּוֹל, which is nonsense (*A falling mountain may fade!*). *be removed*: יֵעָתַק: 9^5 18^4

v. 19. *And* (+ו quod exc. p. 1) *water hath worn away* (or *powdered*, pulverized, reduced to dust) *even stones* (emph.). 𝔊ᴬ *recte* ἐλέανεν, levigavit. Ps 18^{43}. With שחק Heb. Aram. Ar. cf. Sum. SAGAR, *dust* (*epru*, עפר).

St. ii For סְפִיחֶיהָ read †סְפִיחָה a *downpour* or *outpouring* of water, either heavy rain or a river-flood; a *deluge*. Cf. Ar سَفَح *to pour out*, of water, Trans. and Intrans. But as √ספח or שפח is not elsewhere so used in OT (cf., however, משטף Is 5²), we may prefer to read סְחִיפָה, and compare the common Assyr. *saḫâpu* (also written *šaḫâpu*), *to throw down*; e.g. *kîma til abûbi ašḫup*, 'like a storm-heap I overthrew', *kîma tib mêḫê azîq-ma kîma imbari asḫupšu*, 'like the onset of the south wind I blew, and like a hurricane overthrew him'. Thus †סְחִיפָה may be supposed to mean a *tempest* or *stormflood*, which *washes* or *sweeps away* (תשטף Is 28¹⁷, cf. שֶׁטֶף 38²⁵, root not elsewhere in Job) the soil. Cf. Pr 28³ מטר סחף *a rain that lays* or *prostrates* the grain. Ⓖ καὶ κατέκλυσεν ὕδατα ὕπτια τοῦ χώματος τῆς γῆς *And washed down* (or *away* Je 47²) *sloping* parts of *the dike* (χῶμα = עפר five times in Job; 17¹⁶ al.) *of the land* (ὕδατα = מים dittogr. from st. i). Ὕπτιος (ἅπ᾽ in Ⓖ; cf. ὑπτιάζεις = ! פָּרַשְׂתָּ 11¹³) *supinus, turned downside up, bottom uppermost*, perhaps favours סחיפה > ספיחה. Ⓖ might also be rendered: *And waters upturned have washed away* of *the soil* of *the earth* (Partit. Gen.). 𝔙 *et alluvione paulatim terra consumitur*. 𝔐 תִּשְׁטֹף סְפִיחֶיהָ, which could only mean *She inundates* or *Thou inundatest* or *washest away her self-growths* (Le 25¹¹), cannot possibly be right in this context. There is no visible ref. for vb. or suff., and וַתִּשְׁטֹף (cf. Ⓖ) is almost necessary after שחקו. Ⓖ may represent 'וישטף מים סחוף/(מ)עפר הארץ. The st. may be a marg. intrusion, as it makes a tristich of the verse. (The √ספח or שפח *to pour* is obv. cogn. c שפח = ‫سفح‬, and שָׁפַך, Assyr. *šapâku*, *tabâku*, id., *labâku*, Aram. נְבַג, Heb. נָבַג 38¹⁶, נבע, בוע, בקק, &c. It is a Shaph. or Saph. formation from a Prim. BAG, akin to Sum. BAL, *pour out*. Cf. also נבה.)

v. 20. This verse also is prob. an interpolation. The sense is complete without it; and it violates the strophic arrangement.

St. i. 𝔐 תתקפהו לנצח *Thou overpowerest him for ever, and he hath gone*. The Aramaism תקף (cf. Ec 4¹²), found in Dan, Ec, Es, only recurs once in Job (15²⁴ also dubious). The 'for ever' would go better with ויהלך (cf. 23⁷). Does it here mean 'victoriously' (Aram.)? Ⓖ ὤσας αὐτὸν εἰς τέλος, καὶ ᾤχετο, *Thou hast thrust him away for ever* &c. = וַתֶּהְדְּפֵהוּ (18¹⁸), which may be right. For לנצח we might read לחוץ *to the outside, out*: see again 18¹⁸. St. ii. 𝔐 משנה פניו = 𝔙 *immutans faciem eius*: referring to the pallor of death. Ⓖ seems to have read בבשת פניו *with the shame of his face*. Ⓖ ἐπέστησας αὐτῷ τὸ πρόσωπον, reading מָשִׂים (4²⁰) or ותשם (Ⓖᴬ καὶ ἐπεστ') pro משנה, *altering*. (? leg. תשנה *Thou alterest*.)

v. 21. Cf. Ec 9⁵ 'The dead know not anything'; scil. that passes in the world above them. It will be remembered that Dante is eagerly questioned by the spirits in the Inferno for news of the living, of whom they know nothing, although partly able to foresee their future.

> 'His sons grow up that bear his name,
> Some grow to honour, some to shame,—
> But he is chill to praise or blame.'—*Tennyson*.

יִכְבְּדוּ. 𝔐 יִכְבָּרוּ. Point יִכְבְּדוּ (so also in Ez 27²⁵ Is 66¹). Q¹ is *to be heavy*, lit. and met. Cf. Is 43⁴ al. 𝔊 takes this word and its parallel to mean *become numerous* and *few*, respectively.

v. 22. Only his flesh upon him (𝔊ᴮ om. contra metr.: 𝔊ᴬ ἐπ' αὐτῷ) *is in pain* (יִכְאָב Pr 14¹³; physical, Gn 34²⁵, Hiph. 5¹⁸; cf. subst. 2¹³ 16⁶). Prim. Rt. perhaps Sum. GIB, dialectic form of GIG, *sick, painful* (cf. NU-GIG = MU-GIB, *qadištum*); cf. GIG-BA (i.e. GIBBA?), *kibtu, pain, grief.*

The verse seems to say that the departed spirit, while cut off from all knowledge of the world it has left, is conscious of pain in its decomposing body (its 'flesh', lying in the grave), and of mourning in its 'soul' which still haunts the body, or is in some way still associated with it. Cf. note on 4¹⁵. Is 66²⁴ Judith 16¹⁷ Ecclus 7¹⁷ Mk 9⁴⁸. In Egypt, as we know, the utmost care was taken for the preservation of the body after death; and various forms or elements of the composite soul were believed to visit it or abide with it at pleasure. (See Budge, *Book of the Dead*, Introd., p. lix sqq. on the *ka*, the *ba*, the *khu* or *iḥ*, &c) Cf. 𝔗¹ *But his flesh from the worms upon him smarteth* (בָּאֵב), *And his soul in the House of Judgement upon him mourneth.* 𝔗² *But his flesh, before the gravestone is closed* (עַד לָא גוֹלְלָא מְסַתְּתִם), *during the seven days of mourning, upon him mourneth in the tomb* (בבית קבורתא).

Chapter 15 opens the second round of discourses, the speakers following each other in the same order as before. And first Eliphaz reproaches Eyob with impious irreverence of language, which is itself sufficient evidence of inward corruption (vv 1–6).

v. 2. If you were 'wise', as we are, and as you also claim to be (12³ ¹² 13¹·²), you would not vent such windy ideas and heated replies. Your wisdom is as unsubstantial as wind (cf. 7⁷ 8²), without solid content. In fact, you 'feed on wind' (Ho 12² Pr 15¹⁴ Ec 1¹⁴ 4⁵ al.), and that (st. ii) the burning blast of the desert (the Sirocco): an allusion to the indignation which had blazed out in some of Eyob's protests against their injurious assumptions (6¹⁵ ²⁷ 13⁴ᶠ·⁷⁻¹²). St. i has four stresses. Perhaps דעת should be omitted.

St. ii. Lit. *And fill his belly* (or *womb*· cf. v. 35) *with the east wind?* Cf. 𝔙 et implebit *ardore* stomachum suum? 𝔖 *And fill his belly* with wrath (חמתא). 𝔊 πόνον = עָמָל *trouble* (3¹⁰ 5⁶).

v. 3. Arguing: 𝔐 הוֹכֵחַ Infin. Mod. An leg. הֲיֹכַח *Should he argue?* 𝔊 ἐλέγχων (= 𝔐, ut saep.?); cf. 𝔗 דמכסין = מוֹכִיחַ; at 𝔖 לְמִכַּסוּ = לְהוֹכִיחַ, *to argue·* so 𝔄. 𝔙 Arguis. *with speech:* בדבר. 𝔊 ἐν ῥήμασιν = 'בדבר (*i.e.* ברברים).

serves: benefits or *is of use* or *profitable:* יִסְכָּן 22² 34⁹ 35³: Hiph. 22²¹. Cf. TA *u liskin šarru ana mātišu,* 'and let the King be helpful to or have care for his land.' Its occurrence in TA shows that סכן is an old Canaanite word. It is prob. a doublet of שכן. Assyr. *'ašinu, fi v. put, place, make*, and a Saph. (= Shaph.) formation from כן, Assyr. *kânu, be fixed, firm, right*, &c., so that סכן is str. *to make or put right, arrange, prepare or provide for*, and so *to serve a man's purpose*. The Prim. Rt. will thus be Sum. GIN, *kânu, kunnu.* St. ii. *with words*: leg. ובמלים. שׁוע om. ב. 𝔊 ἐν λόγοις.

devoid of profit. Lit. *with which he profits not*: לא יועיל: 21¹⁵ (30¹³ is corrupt) 35². 𝔗 דלית משׁשׁא בהון *in which there is nothing tangible* or *real*; 𝔖 *in which there is no profit* (יתרן); 𝔊 οἷς οὐδὲν ὄφελος. יועיל favours היוכיח ad init., but in any case we need not read הועיל (Infin.).

v. 4. *Thou, indeed*: אף אתה (emph. Pron.). *dost violate*: or *breakest up, makest naught of*: תפר 5¹² 40⁸, cf. 16¹². *reverence* or *fear*: i.e. Fear of God or 'religion' (6¹⁴ 28²⁸ Gn 20¹¹). Cf. 4⁶ *thy piety*; 22⁴. Abs. only here.

dost away with: תגרע. Perhaps lit. *clippest, cuttest off* (cf. Is 15² Je 48³⁷); cf. Aram. גְּרַע *shave* head (cogn. c גְּלַב, גְּלַח). Not Ar. جرع which is akin to בלע. The trans. to idea of *taking away, withdrawing*, 36⁷·²⁷, is not difficult. But 𝔊 συντελέσω δὲ ῥήματα τοιαῦτα κτλ. = יתגמר (Ps 77⁹), *and hast put an end to* . . .

prayer: or *complaint*, or *musing, meditation*: שיחה fr. שיח, which in Aram. and NH is *to speak*. Cf. שיח *complaint*, 7¹³ 9²⁷ 10¹ and vb. 7¹¹ 12¹; and שיחה Ps 119⁹⁷·⁹⁹. (With this somewhat baffling root שיח the Ar. شحا *to open the mouth* may be cogn. Thus *to speak* might be the orig. meaning in Heb. The Prim. source is perhaps Sum. ZAG, *tamêtu*, 'wording' of an inscr., 'address' to a god, and the 'oracle' in reply; SAG, *mâmîtu*, 'exorcism', i.e. spoken charm; cf. also SA = SA-G, SIM = SING, 'call', 'name'; DUG, 'speak'; and, for the other meaning of שיח, SA, SIG, SI, 'to be troubled', 'grieve', 'to mourn'. Moreover, since SAG may spring from NAG, cf. also Assyr. *nagû*, and *nagâgu*, 'to cry or call to a god'.)

v. 5. Sin inspires your sinful words and shifty evasions (cf. 5¹² Gn 3¹). *instructeth*: יאלף. 33³³ 35¹¹. Pr 22²³ Qal (*to learn*). Aramaism (not found al. in OT).

𝔊 quite differently: ἔνοχος εἶ ῥήμασιν στόματός σου, *Thou art liable* (ἄπ· in Job) *for the words of thy mouth*. Perhaps a loose paraphr. of *For thy mouth teacheth thy guilt* (another way of taking the Heb.—so 𝔖𝔗). Οὐδὲ διέκρινας ῥήματα δυναστῶν = לא תבחן לשׁון עריצים (cf. v. 20, 12¹¹ 6²⁸ 15²⁰ al.), *And thou discernedst not the tongue of tyrants!* (Confusion of sim. letters.)

v. 6. Thy language supplies unconscious evidence of thy wickedness. The verse should perhaps follow v. 12.

vv. 7-8 make the ironical suggestion that Eyob must have derived his novel and startling opinions, which contradict the traditional doctrines, directly from the first age, before tradition began. How else could he be so much wiser than his elders?

v. 7. Cf. ⅏ τί γάρ; μὴ πρῶτος ἀνθρώπων ἐγενήθης; Or, *As first* (Secondary Pred.; cf. 11¹² Pr 17¹⁷ Ec 4¹⁴) *wast thou born man?* (ראישׁן does not occur as *Constr.*)   *before the hills.* The st. is either a reminiscence of Pr 8²⁵ᵇ ולפני גבעות חוללתי (said by Wisdom of herself), or founded on a popular proverbial phrase. To read נבהים (Ec 5⁷) seems curiously erratic; for even acc. to Gn 2⁷⁸ Iahvah made Man before preparing his place of abode, and in the old Babylonian bilingual story of Creation, Man is made before the beasts, the two great rivers, vegetation, the mountains (KUR-KURA, rendered *matâti, countries,* by the tablet, but also meaning *šadê, mountains*), marshes &c (*Light from the East*, p. 19)

⅏ ἡ πρὸ θινῶν ἐπάγης; *or before the dunes wast thou compacted* (or *put together*)? For θῖνες, *sandhills,* or *sandbanks* = גבעות, *hills*, see Dt 12²; and for πήγνυμι, which renders various words in Job, see 10¹⁰ 38⁶ 41¹⁸.

v. 8. *In the Council* (or *Conclave*) *of Eloah didst thou listen?* viz. at the Creation: cf. 38⁴⁻⁷. 'Or, *dost thou listen?* art thou admitted to the intimacy of the Most High? But this does not agree so well with the context. ⅏ ⅏ 𝔙 recte. The סוד of Eloah is the Court of Heaven— the *circle* or *society* of the 'Sons of Elohim' (1⁶) who attend His dîwân or audience and wait on His will (cf. Je 23¹⁸·²² Ps 89⁸ c Jb 5¹ 1 K 22¹⁹ ff·). Of a man's circle of intimates, 19¹⁹. From *intimate converse* סוד gets the mg. of *secret counsel* or *purpose* (Am 3⁷) and a *secret* in gen. (Pr 11¹³ al.). It is difficult to decide whether the Prim. mg. was that of *sitting in conclave* (cf. the vb. יסד Niph. Ps 2² 31¹⁴)—which would hardly suit the סוד יהוה—or of *speaking* and *talking.* The Syr. ܣܘܕܐ, a *rug* or *divan-cushion,* more usu. means *converse, speech*; and the vb. (Pa, Ethpa.) is *to talk* or *converse* (cf. Ecclus 42¹² הסתיד) Cf. perhaps Sum. SHID, *atmû, speech*, and Chinese shut, shot, shwo, *speak, talk.*

⅏ σύνταγμα (ἅπ· in OT) = σύνταξις, perhaps חק (Ex 5¹⁴), or *covenant* (cf. Ps 25¹⁴ ‖ ברית); but ⅏ᴬ ἀπόρρητα, *secrets* (so 𝔖 רזי, ראו), ⅏ᵉ μυστήριον, ⅏ˣ ὁμιλίαν, *familiar intercourse, converse.*

and did wisdom come unto thee? תניע = ⅏ ἀφίκετο pro תגרע (v. 4). Or ⅏ אתגלית = תגלה (*was Wisdom revealed unto thee?*) may seem preferable.

vv. 9, 10. Cf. 12³ 13² Ps 50¹¹, 8⁸ ff·. 𝔗² paraphrases v. 10 as follows: *But Eliphaz who is grey, and Bildad who is aged is with us, and Zophar who is older than thy father.* The ref. is, of course, more general; leg. היא pro הוא, v. 9 end.

v. 11. *Ar El· ·n ·lah n· (21) to ·mal'* (or *·l··ʼl· f u*) *f r thee* (cf. Is 7¹³)? St. 11 seems to require a vb. Lat. *And z ·· ·d (·· t· ·ch)*, *gently* (לְאַט) *in* or *acc. to gentleness*: cf. Gn 33¹⁴ Is 8⁶ 1 K 21²⁷) *with thee?* An elliptic expression is more natural in the brief charge, 2 Sa 18⁵. In the other 3 locc. אט or לאט qualifies a vb. of motion. Cf. Pr 25¹¹ דבר דבר *a word spoken*; but this would overload our line. A possible st. would be וּדְבַר אֱלֹ' מְעַט מִמֶּךָ: *And is Eloah's Word too little for thee?* ('לאט עמ =) אל מעט *read backwards*; and the ך is a relic of מִמך, which is not necessary in st. i: cf. Gn 30¹³).

𝔗 למהוי נכח חוי (Levy, *HWB*) וּמללא בניח חוי *And speaking in quiet is proper to be with thee* = 𝔐. 𝔊 (*Restrain from thee the threatenings of God,*) *And speak in quietness with thy soul* = 𝔐 in st. ii, at punct. וְדַבֵּר pro וְדָבָר, et suppl. verbum desideratum. (In st. i, autem, 𝔊 punctavit הַמְעַט *diminue!*, et legit תלחומות = לוחמוהי *minas eius*.) It is evident that 𝔊𝔗 both had ודבר לאט עמך before them. Not so 𝔙 *Numquid grande est ut consoletur te Deus? Sed verba tua prava hoc prohibent* (st. i paraphrase of 𝔐: st. ii = (?) וְדִבֶּר עֲוֺנְךָ יַכְלֶא). 𝔊 differs from all: ὀλίγα ὧν ἡμάρτηκας μεμαστίγωσαι. Μεγάλως ὑπερβαλλόντως λελάληκας, *For few of the sins thou hast committed hast thou been scourged* (Ex 5¹⁴⋅¹⁶ Ps 73⁵⋅¹⁴); *Greatly, excessively* (ὑπερβ· ἀπ· in OT) *hast thou spoken*. But the first words here may represent מְעַט מִמְּךָ (cf. 11¹⁵ 31⁷); μεμαστίγ· perhaps stands for נחמת or התנחמת *thou hast rued* (c אל ut Praep. ad init. translatum!) = אל תנחומות, so that even 𝔊 may confirm 𝔐; while st. ii = עֲבֹר מְאֹד דִּבַּרְתָּ (reversing the order of the words: עמך = עבר; לאט = מאד!).

v. 12. carry thee away. Ez 3¹⁴. 𝔊 τί ἐτόλμησεν; cf. Es 7⁵, which suggests ימלאך *fill thee*. 𝔗 *teach thee* (cf. לַמֵּד *teaching*); 𝔙 te elevat; 𝔖 *Why is thy heart lifted up?*

St. ii. *And why are thy glances haughty?* (lit. *eyes uplifted?*): rg. ירומו c cod. Kenn. 89, pro ἀπ· ירזמון, for which 5 codd. and 𝔊𝔗 read ירמזון *wink*; an Aramaism (רְמַז *wink, make signs, with eyes or fingers*); a sense which hardly agrees with what follows, for which reason Dr suggests that the strange word in 𝔐 means *gleam* with passion. This is better; but Eliphaz is accusing Eyob of pride or arrogance; an attitude hateful to God (Ps 131¹ Pr 6¹⁷ 30¹³). 𝔊 ἢ τί (𝔊ᴬ σοι) ἐπήνεγκαν οἱ ὀφθαλμοί σου, *Or what* (*upon thee*) *brought thine eyes* (that thou didst break out in a rage against Iahvah? v. 13) &c. cannot be alleged in favour of this rg. (Both stt. appear metr. short. Is the verse an intruder?)

v. 13. That thou blowest thy breath at El. Rg. תָּשִׁיב (Ps 147¹⁸) pro תָּשִׁיב *turnest*. השיב רוח means *to draw in* or *recover thee breath*, 9¹⁸. Words are but breath or wind (v. 2; 8²). 𝔊 ὅτι θυμὸν ἔρρηξας ἔναντι κυρίου. רוח is sometimes *temper, passion*, e. g. 21⁴ Pr 16³²; but not here. ἔναντι = לְ 13⁷ 19²⁸. 𝔐 אל. 𝔖 app. read תשׂגב *thou exaltest* (thy spirit). St. ii, cf. 8¹⁰, and esp. Ec 5¹. There is no need to read מְרִי *rebellion* pro מִלִּין *words* (6ᵃ al.). 𝔊 ῥήματα τοιαῦτα, paraphr. correctly. It was addressing such free, not to say daring, language to the Supreme that scandalized Eliphaz.

v. 14. Eliphaz repeats his former argument, with merely verbal variations, 4¹⁷ᶠᶠ. Insert הוא before יֻלַּד metr. grat. *born of a woman*: 14¹ 25⁴ (all). Poet. syn. of *man*. In Chinese the clan-name or surname (*sing*) of an individual is written 姓 *woman-born*; and *wan sing*, 'the myriad clan-names', means mankind.

v. 15. *His Holy Ones*: His Angels: see note on 5¹.

v. 16. *a foul and tainted thing*: lit. *one abhorred and corrupted* or *stinking*. The √תעב appears to be a ת-formation from the Prim. Bilit. which we see in the Sum. GAB, *bad foulsmelling* or *offensive* (Assyr. *bîšu*). It is prob. akin to Tg. סאיב *to defile*, or *make foul* (Sum G = ע saep) Thus the Pi. lit. means *to regard as foulsmelling, to loathe as stinking or offensive*, and to make so, 9³¹. The rare √אלח (Pss 14³ 53⁴ only) is a syn. Lane does not give Ar. ‏الج with which it has usu. been compared. In Assyr., however, we have *alaḫiš*, 'into stench'; a syn. of *daddariš*, id. Both words, in fact, occur in a line of the Babylonian parallel to our book: *Ašnan TAG-ma daddariš alaḫiš*, 'Corn (or bread) turned to reek and stench' (5 R 47. 53 a: where the gloss *bu'šânu* = באש is added to da-da-ru, i. e. *daddaru*). A disease is called *muruç daddari*, 'the ill-smelling malady' (4 R 3. 30 b). There may be a brutal allusion to Eyob's malady as well as to his assumed moral corruption: cf. st. ii, which seems to be a direct accusation (34⁷). (Addit. note on אלח. The Sum. IN-IN explained *ulluḫu* is perhaps akin to IM *to dye, stain*, *šanû*; cf. Chinese ím, jan, *dye, taint, infect, vitiate*, Giles 5562 ; and *alâ ulluḫu qarradûtu* may mean *a demon infecting valour*.)

𝔊 ἔα δὲ ἐβδελυγμένος καὶ ἀκάθαρτος, *Let alone* (= *Not to mention*) *a loathed and unclean one!* (St. ii om. איש ad init. metr. grat.?)

v. 17. Metrically defective. We might read אחוך ושמע־נא אלי *I will tell thee; and pray listen unto me!* The vb. חוה, an Aramaism which occurs four times in the Elihu-section (32⁶ ¹⁰,¹⁷ 36²), and besides only in Ps 19³, and thus not elsewhere in the original part of Job, reflects some suspicion on the verse. It might well be followed by ידעי = *what I know*, here as in 32⁶ ¹⁰,¹⁷ (or דעתי id., as in Ps. 19³), by way of parallel to *what I have seen* in st ii. We might thus restore the balance of st. i by reading אחוך דעי שמע־לי *I will tell thee what I know, hearken to me!* (The Aram. √חוה fr. חו may be compared with Sum. GU, *šasû*, *qibû*, 'to speak' &c.) In st. ii om. ו ante אספרה c 𝔊𝔙.)

v. 18. *Facts which ...* or *That which ...* But the Rel. Pron. אשר refers to the זה *what* of v. 17, which may be Plur. in sense (as a Rel. Indecl): cf. 19¹⁹ where it is equivalent to *those whom*. St. ii כחדום אבותם (c 𝔐 as Suff. to vb.; masc. pro fem.) instead of כהדו מאבותם. 𝔐 can only mean: *And they one at i* [them] n* fi i t r*t, rs.

RV is impossible, unless we transpose the order of the Heb. words, and violate the natural division of the stichi. Possibly בחדום = *concealed from them*; the Suff. including a Prep., as is the case with some other verbs. Cf. 27¹¹ Is 3⁹ for כחד sine Praep., and 8⁸ for the gen. sense of the verse. 𝕲ᴮ οὐκ ἔκρυψαν πατέρας αὐτῶν contains an obvious scribal error, corrected by the πρες, i.e. πατέρες of 𝕲ᴬᶜ. 𝕾 recte : *And their fathers have not concealed*. 𝖁 om. אשר ad init. Sapientes confitentur, et non abscondunt patres suos (cf. 𝕲ᴮ): an excellent sentiment, but quite irrelevant to the context.

v. 19. St. i is overloaded with four stresses, as in the English equivalent *To thém* (or *To whom*) *alóne the lánd was gíven*. This app. means *to the* 'Fathers'; but whose 'Fathers'? It seems most natural to understand the Fathers of Israel (cf. Gn 12⁷ al. Ex 13⁵), and to translate st. ii *And no foreigner passed over amongst them* ; i. e. no alien passed over the Jordan with the Chosen People into the Promised Land: the Fathers from whom the traditional wisdom was transmitted were a pure race, uncontaminated by admixture with foreign elements, and so their doctrine was pure and undefiled. The sense is not materially altered if we render, as we might, *And no foreigner passed through their midst*. (Is לבדם a var. lect. for להם?) This may seem a strange reference in the mouth of a Temanite; but if Eyob is really 'a type of the godly suffering Israelite' of some period of trial and trouble after the Return from Babylon, we can understand it. The distich may, however, be an interpolation.

v. 20. ff. purport to state the Wisdom of the Ancients which has been handed down from the beginning. *torments himself*: i. e. is a prey to anxious fears: or simply *is anxious*. So 𝕲 *All the life of an impious* (man) *is in anxiety* (ἐν φροντίδι· rare in 𝕲: cf. vb. ἐφρόντισα = פחדתי *I dreaded*, 3¹⁸) = 𝕲ᴬ ἐν ὀδύνῃ, *in pain*. Cf. Polel, *wait anxiously for* . . . 35¹⁴. This agrees better with the context than 𝕲ˣ ἀλαζονεύεται, *makes false pretensions* or *plays the braggart* = 𝕲ᶿ ματαιοῦται, *deals foolishly* (cf. 1 Sa 26²¹), 𝖁 superbit, 𝕾 מתרורב *magnifies himself, behaves arrogantly*, all of which seem to imply מתחולל pro 𝔐 מתחלל.

St. ii. Lit. *And* (during) *the few years* (cf. Ec 2³, ch. 16²²) that *are reserved for the tyrant* (עריץ : see on 13²⁵). If this is right, the introd. ו *And* seems needless. (RV *Even*; a convenient but doubtful rendering.) It is more natural to render *And but few years are reserved for the tyrant*. Both stt. have four stresses. Leg. fort. כל-ימיו רשע מתחולל *All his days the wicked is anxious*; and om. נצפנו in st. ii.

v. 21. His uneasy conscience takes alarm at every sound (cf. Is 24¹⁸ Pr 28¹ Ps 53⁵). *When all is well*: lit. *in the peace*, i. e. in time of peace (cf. 1 K 2⁵ anarthrous, בְּשָׁלוֹם): *the destroyer* or *spoiler* (שׁוֹדֵד) *comes upon* or *assails him*; i. e. in his distempered fancy. שָׁדַד is perhaps str. *to drag away* spoils and captives; cf. Assyr. *šadâdu*, 'drag', 'draw', a cart, timber, &c. 𝔊 ἡ καταστροφή (= איד, 21¹⁷; or perhaps שׂוֹר plenè); but al. σκύλευσις = שׁר. 𝔙 benè. Et cum pax sit, ille semper insidias suspicatur.

v. 22. *He is not sure of return out of darkness.* For constr. cf. Ps 27¹³. This may mean either that the wicked oppressor has no hope of recovery from the ruin he anticipates (so Dr); or that, when darkness falls, he has no confidence of surviving till the return of day. Cf. 24²². He is afraid of being cut off in the night. St. ii. 𝔐 צָפוּ or צָפוּי (some codd and Qerī), 'watched', is corrupt. OL's '*spied out* (and brought) *to the sword*' is improb. Read צֹפֶה (Ps 37³²) or מְצַפֶּה (Ps 5⁴ La 4¹⁷): *And he looketh out for* or *expecteth* the hands of the sword (after 𝔊 ἐντέταλται γὰρ ἤδη εἰς χεῖρας σιδήρου). For the curious expression אֱלֵי־יְדֵי חרב cf. Ps 63¹¹, and the freq. פי החרב *mouth of the sword*. Ἐντέταλται implies a rg מְצֻוָּה (cf. 36³² 37¹²), *given in charge unto* the hands &c. Cf. Am 9⁴. Ewald's ingenious צָפוּן (*And he is reserved for the sword*) finds no support in 𝔊, and is less suitable than (מ)צפה in a description of imaginary terrors. Cf. 𝔙 circumspectans undique gladium. 𝔖 חָזֵא לְחַרְבָּא *looking to the sword* also confirms our view.

v 23 𝔐 lit. *He wanders* or *is wandering* (i.e. in his dream of coming evil) *about for the bread*—'*Where?*'; *He knows that ready at his hand* (side) *is a* (the) *day of darkness.* The incoherence of st. i, and the metrical overweight of st. ii, must be corrected from 𝔊, which has preserved the true text of the verse. κατατέτακται δὲ εἰς σῖτα γυψίν, *and he hath been appointed for food to vultures*, prob. Heb. נִתַּן הוּא לְלֶחֶם לְאַיָּה. Cf. Ez 35¹². For καταταάσσω = נתן see 35¹⁰. (In 7¹² = שׂים.) The suggested rg וְנַעַר is improb. (2¹¹). איה prob. means *kites*

St. ii. οἶδεν δὲ ἐν ἑαυτῷ ὅτι μένει εἰς πτῶμα = (? קֵץ, cf. v. 29) יָדַע כִּי־נָכוֹן לְאֵיד *he knows that he is ready for calamity* (איד 18¹² 21¹⁷ ³⁰ 31³). But פִּידוֹ *his ruin* more nearly resembles 𝔐 בְּיָדוֹ *in his hand*, and is more suitable here as a stronger term than אֵיד *overburdening, distress* (see ٲيد| in Lane): 12⁵·⁶ 21²⁰ 30²⁴ 31²⁹. יום חשך *a day of darkness*, which overloads the stichus, might perhaps be a gloss on פיד, but is better connected with v. 24, as in 𝔊 *A dark day dismayeth him* (though this makes a tristich of the verse). Point יְבַעֲתָהוּ; or read יְבַעֲתֻנּוּ For בעת *fall upon, startle, terrify*, see 3⁵ 9³⁴ 13¹¹ ²¹ al. In st. ii leg. צָרָה (27⁹ Zp 1¹⁵). The 'darkness' is prob. physical. He is terrified by a gloomy sunless day, regarding it as a portent of evil. *Straits and distress overpower him*: point תִּתְקְפֵהוּ (yet 𝔊 καθέξει) He is paralysed with fear. For the Aramaism תקף see on 14²⁰. 𝔙 vallabit eum = תַּקְפֵהוּ; so 𝔗. This may point to תַּקְפֵהוּ as the authentic text. 𝔊 καθέξει = תחזיקהו *seize him* (Je 6²⁴): so 𝔖.

v. 24 St. iii. *Like a king ready for the fray*: בְּמֶלֶךְ עָתִיד לִכִידוֹר. The third word here is an obscure ἅπ., rendered by 𝔊 לְקָרָבָא — לִקְרָב (אל ³), which is perhaps the orig. tg. (? misread as כידר — ר for ב) both [...] errors;

ר = ב). So 𝔙 ad praelium; and 𝔄 للقتال. But 𝔗 (*They surround him like a king who is ready*—ἑτοιμος) לְנִלוֹנְדָּךְ *for a litter* (or *footstool*: Levy, HWB, suggests *a bier*). It is, of course, possible that בידור was an ancient or archaic term for *battle*, although its complete isolation renders it suspicious. 𝔊 ὥσπερ στρατηγὸς πρωτοστάτης πίπτων (or πεπτωκώς). The word πρωτοστάτης is found here only in 𝔊 (cf. Acts 24⁵). 'Standing first' or 'in front' may represent עמד לקדם, which is an easy perversion of עתיד לקרב *ready for the battle*. The πίπτων may be merely a gloss due to a scribe of 𝔊. The stichus prob. does not belong here, but is to be regarded as a marg. gloss on v. 25. *at*: אֶל. But perhaps עַל *against* should be read in both stt. The two Preps. are often confused with each other by copyists. vv. 25, 26 contain a hardly veiled allusion to the daring language of Eyob. *stretched out*: נטה. 𝔊 ἦρκεν, *lifted* = נשא (נשה?): 6² 21³. Cf. sim. error in Je 43¹⁰.

v. 25. would match his might: lit. *show his might*: יתגבר: 36⁹ Is 42¹³ (על). 𝔊 ἐτραχηλίασεν, *arched his neck proudly*, like a horse (ἄπ· in 𝔊).

v. 26. with his buckler: reading בצנתו (Ps 35²) pro 𝔐 בצואר *with neck* (which perhaps suggested 𝔊's ἐτραχηλίασεν in 25 b). The צִנָּה, a large shield covering the whole body, is a better parallel to מגן, st. ii, than בגבור *like a warrior* (16¹⁴). 𝔊 ὕβρει = בגאון (35¹² 37⁴); unless the translator thought of בצואר עתק, Ps 75⁶ (so RV).

St. ii. Lit. *with the thickness of the backs* (supposed to mean *bosses*) *of his shields*. So 𝔊 (with Sing. for Plur.) ἐν πάχει νώτου ἀσπίδος αὐτοῦ = בעבי גב מגנו. But עֲבִי *thickness* (2 C 4¹⁷ only), cf. עָבְיִ (1 K 7²⁶), seems rather dubious in this connexion; and the גב of a shield is not mentioned anywhere else in OT. בְּכוֹבַע *with helmet* is an attractive correction of בעבי (cf. Ez 23²⁴ 27¹⁰ 38⁴·⁵), and נבי may be גִּבֹּר *warrior*, if it be not a Heb. equivalent of Assyr. gababu (also qababu), *shield* (of wood, covered with leather). Thus, reading (𝔊) בְּכוֹבַע גִּבֹּר וּמָגִנּוֹ, we get the good sense *With a warrior's helmet and shield*. The whole verse might be read more simply: ידוץ עליו בצנא | ובכובע גבור ומגן.

v. 27. Rg. חלב pro חלבו his *fat*. The ו seems to be an anticipation of the following ו. For the figure, see Dt 32¹⁵ Ps 17¹⁰ 73⁷ 119⁷⁰.

St. ii. 'Made (i.e. produced, e.g. Gn 1¹¹ Ho 8⁷) flesh' is a common English phrase; but the ἄπ· פִּימָה appears to be a syn. of חלב *fat*. 𝔙 arvina, 'grease', 'fat', 'lard'; 𝔗 רוּטְבָּא 'sap', 'marrow', 'suet', 'fat'. (𝔖 went astray through misreading פימה as בימה, and pointing בְּסָל instead of כְּסָל: see 9⁹.) The word seems to be an offshoot of the √פום; cf. Aram. פים *mouth* = Ar. fam, fum, fim, *id*. = Assyr. pû, Heb. פה, פי. The ideas of *feeding* and *fattening* are naturally associated with the mouth, and expressed by words which are offshoots of the same root. Hence, with Internal Triliteralization, Ar. فَأَمَ fa'ama, 'fill the mouth with food or drink', 4. 'fill a vessel', 'widen a waterskin', مُفْأَم muf'am, 'fat, and wide within', &c.; Eth. fa'em, 'mouth or hole of a tunic' (περιστόμιον so 𝔊 here; '30¹⁸ = פִי), and 'a morsel', 'small mouthful'; 'af'ama, 'to feed', 'give food to a beggar'. The Sum. PE-SH, PI, 'widen' or 'broaden', 'extend', 'increase', 'fat', 'plump', 'stout', 'strong', 'pregnant' (= filled out or enlarged, 'big with child'), and the Ch. fei, p'i, bi, 'fat', 'plump', 'robust', 'fertile'; pi, pwi, 'pregnant', may belong to the same Bilit. Root. (Cf. also the Aryan √PI, 'to swell', Gk. πῖος, πίων, πῖαρ, πιαρός, πιμελή—so 𝔊ˣ here—Sanskr. pīvan, and Engl. *fat*.)

v. 28. *ruined*: נבחרות. 4¹ 22²⁰. Str. *hidden, covered up*, scil. with rubbish and soil. The √בחר, cogn. c כחש *deceive, deny* (cf. 6¹⁰ c Ho 9²), is a K(G)-form of בגד, which also denotes both *covering* and *deceiving* (cf. Sum. GAD, *kitû*, 'cloth' or 'linen').

which none should inhabit. understanding ישבו in sens. indef. But the Sing. ישב (*he should not inhabit* = he ought not to have inhabited) would seem better. For לָמוֹ cf. 2¹³ לָאָרֶץ. The idea might be sitting or settling *on to* the ruined site. Cf. Is 13²⁰, where the same two verbs occur; a passage which, however, suggests the mg. *which should not be inhabited*, and the substitution of לנצח (or לעולם or לעד) *for ever* pro לָמוֹ (𝔊 app. יבוא = εἰσέλθοι, *May he enter!* 𝔊's Optatives in both stt. are due to pointing וְיִשְׁבֹּן instead of וְיֵשׁ &c.). Ruined sites lay under the eternal ban of Heaven; and to rebuild or inhabit them entailed the curse of God (Jos 6²⁶ 1 K 16³⁴). Cf. 3¹⁴.

St. iii. *which were* (had been) *made ready* (התעתדו), i. e. destined, *for heaps* (Plur. of גַל, 8¹⁷); i e. to become and remain ruinous mounds. Prob. a gloss on the genuine verse. 𝔊 ἃ δὲ ἐκεῖνοι ἡτοίμασαν (𝔊ᴺᶜᵃ 𝔊ᴬ Sing.) ἄλλοι ἀποίσονται, *But what they* (or *he*) *prepared, others will carry off*; taking the ἅπ· (ו) התעתדו in the Reflexive sense (*sibi paravit*), and rg. לזרים *for strangers* (*it shall be*) pro 𝔐 לְגַלִּים *for heaps*. Ἄλλος = זָר, 19²⁷; but perhaps 𝔊 really means לנרים. It is possible that vv. 27–8 are an interpolation or, as some think, even vv. 25–8. Certainly v. 29 might very well follow immediately on v. 24.

v. 29. 𝔐 lit. *He shall not be(come) rich, and his wealth shall not stand*. Might the verse continue the representation of the godless man's fears (vv. 20 ff.)? *He will not be rich, nor can his wealth endure*. Read perhaps לֹא (לוֹ 16³) *If he be* (or *become*) *rich, his wealth* &c.

St. ii. 𝔐 מִנְלָם; a vox nihili. RV *their produce*; marg. *their possessions*. The Plur. Suff. alone would make the word dubious. We should expect מנלו parallel to חילו. 𝔖 *words* = מלים or מלץ (not מלתם, as OL); Ar. *kalāman*, id. 𝔗 מִנְּהוֹן = לָם מַן (aught) *of theirs*; merely dividing the word. 𝔙 is more sensible: Nec mittet in terra radicem suam, 'Nor shall he take root in the earth'. This is quite congruous with what precedes, as it expresses the idea of instability under a different figure. It is also favoured by the association of שָׁרְשׁוֹ *his root* with יוֹנַקְתּוֹ *his sucker* or *shoot* (v. 30) in 8¹⁶·¹⁷ 14⁷·⁸ Is 53² Ho 14⁶·⁷ (cf. also Ps 80¹⁰⁻¹²). The word שָׁרְשׁוֹ or שָׁרְשָׁה does not look much like מִנְלָם; but if we suppose that the scribal error is very ancient, originating in the old writing in which מ (ᛘ) and שׁ (W) do resemble each other, the difficulty practically disappears. A more obvious solution is to suppose that the three κέραιαι, Mt 5¹⁸, of מג, the מ being partly effaced and broken (נוג), suggested to 𝔙 that the two letters were one, viz. שׁ. 𝔊, however, has οὐ μὴ βάλῃ ἐπὶ τὴν γῆν σκιάν = phps. (40²²) עֲלֵי־אָרֶץ (יַטִּיל) וְלֹא־יַטֶּה (cf. 𝔊?) צְלָלָה *And he shall not cast his* (protecting) *shadow over the land*. Here again we may note that, while צ and שׁ are distinct enough in the modern character, they might perhaps be confused in the ancient script, and ל is sometimes mistaken for נ. For the figure cf. Ez 31⁶.

The רָשָׁע, whose fortunes the poet is describing, is not a person of no social importance, but a tribal chief (cf. v. 34) or prince, whose fate involves that of his dependents. Hence we might read שָׁלוֹם for מִנְלָם, and the whole st. would be וְלֹא־יִטֶּה לָאָרֶץ שָׁלֵם *And he shall not extend prosperity to the land*—as he would, if he were a good man and, consequently, Heaven blest his rule. For the phrase cf. Is 66¹² (נֹטֶה אֵל׳ שָׁלוֹם). In any case, שִׁבֳּלִים *ears of corn* (Dillmann; 24²⁴) or מְלִילֹת id. (Dt 23²⁶) and Driver's '*Neither shall his ears bend to the earth*,—his fields will bear no heavily-laden crops', seem very unlikely. Eyob's wealth consisted of cattle and slaves (1³), and nothing is said of cornfields. Some reject the verse, along with v. 30 a. (וְלֹא־יִטַּע בָּאָרֶץ נִצְרוֹ seems also possible: *Nor shall he plant his scion in the soil* = establish his offspring in the land. Cf. Is 60²¹.) But we get a better parallel to st. i by reading וְלֹא־יִטּוֹר אֹצָרוֹ לְעוֹלָם *nor shall he keep his treasure for ever*.

v. 30. A tristich. Prob. st. i is spurious. *He shall not depart out of darkness* looks like a gloss on v. 22. The sense offers no parallel to either of the following stichi. The line is at least out of place here.

Flame: i.e. sun-glare. Cf. Ez 21³ (20⁴⁷) שַׁלְהֶבֶת, an Aramaism; here and Ez l. c. and Ct 8⁶ only. Another kindred form is Tg. צְלָהֵב *to burn* (Ps 50³), and Heb. זַלְעָפָה, pl. זַלְעָפוֹת, *burning heat* of the sirocco, Ps 11⁶, or famine, La 5¹⁰, may also be cogn. If 𝔙 is right in v. 29ᵇ (*Nor shall he strike his roots*—יַכֶּה שָׁרָשָׁיו?, cf. Ho 14⁶ or יְשַׁלַּח שׁ׳ Je 17⁸ = 𝔊 βαλεῖ τὰς ῥίζας αὐτοῦ in both locc.—*in the soil*), the metaph. of the tree is continued from the last verse. For שַׁלְהֶבֶת 𝔊 gives ἄνεμος, i.e. the hot wind of the desert, the sirocco. (But it om. בְּרוּחַ in st. ii.)

st. ii. Rg. וְיָבוֹל בְּרוּחַ פִּרְחוֹ pro וְנֵז בְּרוּחַ פִּיו יָסוּר *And he shall depart by the breath of His mouth*. Cf. Is 40⁷·⁸ 28¹ נֹבֵל parallel to יָבֵשׁ. 𝔊 ἐκπέσοι δὲ αὐτοῦ τὸ ἄνθος: cf. v. 33ᵇ, and see note on 14². Perhaps וְיִשַּׁל בְּרוּחַ פִּרְיוֹ *And his fruit shall drop off in the wind* would be better: cf. Dt 19⁵ 𝔊 28⁴⁰. ἐκπέσοι = יִשַּׁל v. 33. (ל = סו; ר = שׁ.) But וְיֹעַר (cf. Ho 13³) comes nearer to ויסור : *And his flower* (leg. פרחו c 𝔊) *shall be stormed away by the wind* Cf וישׂערהוּ, 27²¹ 1¹⁹.

v. 31. As it stands in 𝔐, this verse can only be regarded as an awkward interpolation, interrupting, as it does, the connexion of v. 30 with 32 ff. which continue the metaph. of the tree. What it says is. *Let him not trust in Vanity being misled* (?); *For Vanity shall his exchange be !* This has an air of proverbial wisdom, but is far from lucid in the context. The verse, however, becomes quite relevant, if we read אל־יאמן בְּעֵת נשׂא כריסאה תהיה זמורתו *Let him not be confident in the time of bearing, For his vine-twigs will become a wreck.* Cf. Is 17¹⁰·¹¹ 18⁵. Or perhaps אל־יאמן בְּלֹשֶׁר (בסר) נִטְעוֹ *Let him not trust in his plant's unripe fruit* (v. 33), &c (See Duhm. But בשוב, cf. v. 22, will not do; and בשוא Ps 89¹⁰† pro אל־יֶאֱמֵן בְּשׁוֹן[רָק] is dub.), or better תִּהְיֶה (בְּאִישִׁים) תעה | כי־שׁוא בנשוא תְבוּאָתו *Let him not trust in a gadding vine* (Is 5² 16⁸); *For naught* (*ill grapes ?*) *will his produce be*(*come*) *!* Cf. also Je 2²¹. Or read נִצּוֹ *his blossom* instead of *his produce* (cf. 𝔊).

v. 32. St i is too short תִּמֹּרוֹ *his palm tree* exc. post תמורתו (31. זמורתו), cf. כפתו *his palm branch* in the parallel st. ii. Or supply זמורתו *his bough* (18¹⁶). 𝔊 ἡ τομὴ αὐτοῦ πρὸ ὥρας φθαρήσεται = קְצִירוֹ בלא־יומ׳ תב(י)ל *His vine-branch, ere his day* (cf. 22¹⁶), *falls off* (see note on 14²) In Ct 2¹² τομή appears to mean *pruning* = זָמִיר. For the vb. see also Is 24⁴ and 𝔊. We must, of course, read תִּפֹּל (or יִמָּל) instead of תִמָּלֵא; cf. 18¹⁶. 𝔊 יבשׁ *dry, wither*.

St. ii *flourish*: or *be fresh, green*. רַעֲנַן as vb (?) here only. Cf. Ct 1¹⁶. As adj epithet of trees, twelve times. Of oil, *fresh* or *rich*, Ps. 92¹¹. Of persons, *flourishing, healthy*, Ps 92¹⁵ Dan 4¹ (Aram.). Not identified in the other Semitic languages. (Ar. رَعِنَ is *to be foolish, stupid, lax*; and רענן Dan 4¹ is prob. a Hebraism.) In Sum. we have RIG (RING) *green*, in U-RIG, *urqitu*, 'greens', and RIN, RIM, 'bright' (*ellu*), cf. Chinese luk, Jap. ryoku, *green*. This brings רענן into apparent connexion with ירק Assyr. *arqu*, 'green'.

v. 33. Cf La 2ᵈ Is 18⁵. ℨ יַתֵּר הֵיךְ גוּפְנָא בוּסְרֵיהּ *He shall let fall, like a vine, his unripe grapes.* It is said that the vine does not cast its abortive fruit, as the olive does (Dt 28⁴⁰); but perhaps absolute accuracy is hardly to be expected in a poetical simile. Cf. Ma 3¹¹. (The √חמס *treat hardly or with violence* is perhaps akin to חמץ Ps 71⁴ Is 1¹⁷ Assyr. *ḫamâçu*, 'oppress', Shaph. *šuḫmuçu*, 'violate', e. g. women. Cf. also Assyr. *ḫamâšu, ḫummušu*, 'crush', 'grind', e. g. corn, Sum. ĜUM, LUM, Chinese lung, 'grind', 'a mill', yen, ngien, 'grind'. ĜUM = GUM in ŠE GUM-GUM *ḫummušu*, 'grind corn'; cf. GUM, *ḫašâlu ša šeim*, 'pound corn'. The connexion of ideas between 'crushing' or 'grinding' and 'oppressing' i evident in Is 3¹⁵, with which we may perhaps compare Sum. GIGUR-ĜU MGUM. *ḫuršu ša pini*, 'smash or 'grind the face').)

Possibly חמס in connexion with the vine should be compared with חמץ *sour*, Aram. חֲמַע; so that the meaning will rather be *He will sour his immature grape, like the vine*.

will cast: Heb. *let him cast*; Jussive Mood of vb. perhaps due to preceding אל־יאמן. Point תַּשְׁלֵךְ? But the Juss. may express the strong assent of the speaker to the event described. (The √שׁלך *throw*, 18⁷ 27¹² 29¹⁷ (?), is str. *cause to go*, and is akin to the weaker שׁלח *let go, send, shoot*. Ar. سَرَح *drive* to pasture, *send*, Aram. שְׁלַק *throw*, קִלְקֵל = לְקַלְקֵל id., as well as הלך *go, walk*, Assyr. *aláku*, id., and Ar. سلك *go along* a road, *go into* a place, also Causative in both senses; سلى *throw supine*, and other Semitic words. It is a Shaph. formation from the Prim. Bilit. preserved in Sum. LAG, *lead, lead off, drive* to pasture, *bring*, &c. = *cause to go or come*, RA [from RAG], *aláku*, &c.)

his bloom: נִצָּתוֹ. 𝔖 ܡܕ̈ܒܠܗ *his plant*. 𝔖 has the same equivalent for תמרתו, v. 31 ad fin.; and this may perhaps be regarded as a vestige of the original reference of that enigmatical verse.

v. 34. *company*: cf. Nu 26⁹ *the c. of Korah*; i.e. the whole body of his clients or tribal dependents and retainers, including his 'family' or kindred of all degrees. (𝔊 infeliciter μαρτύριον = עֵדָה de עוּד; nostr. עֵדָה ex יעד oritur; 𝔙 𝔖 𝔗 𝔄 recte.) *barren*: or *stone-barren*: 3⁷ 30³ (?) Is 49²¹ (all). An Arabism. (𝔊 θάνατος = מות = גלמוד half-effaced. 𝔙 recte *sterilis*; 𝔖 𝔄 *a desert*.) The st. alludes not obscurely to the greatest of Eyob's misfortunes, the sudden destruction of all his children (1¹⁹). St. ii may refer to 1¹⁶. v. 34 may almost be called an interpretation of the metaphors of vv. 30–33. Cf. 18¹⁵⁻²¹ 21²⁸. The suggestion that he has corrupted justice by giving or accepting bribes ('the tents of bribery'; 𝔖 *the dwellings of the unjust*) is implicitly contradicted by Eyob in 29¹¹⁻¹⁷ and repeated by Elihu, 36¹⁸. Perhaps שֹׁחֵר Ptcp. *the briber* or *bribegiver* 6²² Ez 16³³. The word seems to be of Aram. origin; שְׁחַר *to bribe*, which may be compared with אֲחַד *to take in the hand* (Sum. GAD, *hand*), so that שׁ־חד = *cause to take or accept*. (The Sum. IGI-SA, 'gift', is suggestively written ⟨⊢ ⟨⊨ *eye-judgement!*)

v. 35. *Big with mischief, and bringing forth misery.* For the Infin. Abs. cf. Ho 4²; but the idiom is doubtful in Job. We should rather expect וַיֵּלֶד . . . . הָרָה *He hath conceived . . . and brought forth.* 𝔊 *He will conceive . . . And vain things will issue for him* (= 31ᵇ ap. 𝔊!) = וַיֵּלֶד אָוֶן or וַיֵּלֶד א׳ (Points). St. ii. *And his* (so 𝔊 𝔙; 𝔐 *their*) *womb* (cf. st. i and v. 2) *prepareth guile* (or *treachery*: Ps 17¹). 𝔊 ὑποίσει = תכיל *containeth*: see on 4²; Am 7¹⁰ 𝔊. So prob. 𝔖 (*And their bellies are filled with guile*). If מִרְמָה has its usual mg. of crafty or deceitful dealing with others (cf שׁקר in Ps 7¹⁵, which is a perfect parallel to this verse), the speech is brought to a rather lame conclusion. But if 'deceit' may mean *disappointment* for the wicked schemer himself, as Driver takes it, the idea will be that the machinations of the godless issue in their own destruction. Cf. 4⁸ Is 33¹¹. But the angry speaker may be merely intending an insinuation that Eyob has habitually perverted justice by wiles and hypocrisy.

Chapter 16. Eyob replies to the foregoing.

v. 2. Lit. *I have heard many things like those.* The phrase מְנַחֲמֵי עָמָל, taking up a word (עָמָל *toil, trouble,* 'mischief') which Eliphaz has just used, might be rendered *mischievous* or *harmful comforters.* He means, Your comforting hurts, and is no comfort; is 'sorry' comfort.

v. 3. *words of wind:* an allusion to 15²: a *Tu quoque* for Eliphaz. (𝔊 has τάξις = קֵץ again, 28³.) *aileth thee:* or *aggrieveth* or *annoyeth thee:* יַמְרִיצֶךָ. See note on 6²⁵. 𝔊 ἢ τί παρενοχλήσει σοι, *Or what will annoy thee greatly,* &c. Cf. 𝔊 Ju 16¹⁷ Ps 35¹³. Cf. also Mi 2¹⁰ Je 14¹⁷ Heb. (for connexion of the ideas of *sick* and *sore* or grievous). *Urgeth* would seem more suitable here: cf. Ju l. c. (= יְאַמְּצֶךָ). Possibly יַפְרִיצֶךָ *maketh thee break out* (not found elsewhere). 𝔗 יַבְסְמִינָךְ *pleaseth thee* = יַמְלִיצֶךָ (cf. Ps 119¹⁰³).

v. 4. st. ii. Lit. *If your soul were in the place of my soul.* נפש *soul* = self, as often *compose speeches:* or *join words together.* Cf. 'shake *with* my head' = shake my head, *infr.*; 'gnash *with* my teeth' = gnash my teeth, v. 9 (Ps 22⁷ 35¹⁶). חבר Hiph. here only (but cf. on 6²⁷). The constr. with בְּ might denote either instrument *or* accompaniment. make a *joining* or *alliance* or *union* with words. The word most commonly signifies alliance or association. The Root-mg. seems to be to *bind.* 𝔊 ἐναλοῦμαι ὑμῖν ῥήμασιν, *leap on* or *attack you with w.* (= הוֹבִיתַ 19⁵ לָמָשׁ 16¹⁰). 𝔙 *consolarer vos;* 𝔖 *proved you* (with words); not understanding the phrase.

v. 5. 𝔐 *I would* (or *could*) *strengthen* (or *encourage, comfort*) *you with my mouth.* But as במרפי has but one stress, we may complete the st. by restoring בְּמוֹצָא פִי *with the utterance of my mouth* (Je 17¹⁶ Ps 89³⁵); which also affords a better parallel to *solace of my lips.* (The letters צא exc. p. 'אאמצ'.) Or we might read במלי פי *with the words of my mouth.* In st. ii 𝔐 is evidently corrupt. וניד שפתי יחשך cannot possibly mean *And the solace of my lips should assuage* your grief (RV). 𝔊 κίνησιν δὲ χειλέων οὐ φείσομαι. *And the motion of* (my) *lips I will not spare* involves only the change of one letter (אחשך pro יחשך) with the add of the Neg לא. The latter feature, however, and the dubious ἅπ ניד *motion* or *comfort,* lead us to prefer ובדבר שפתי אחזקכם *And with a word of my lips would I sustain* (or *strengthen*) *you;* a closer parallel to st. i. Cf. 4³ Dt 3²⁸ Is 36⁵. Leg. fort. נוד *consoling; sympathizing* or *condolence:* cf. 2¹¹ Ps 69²¹ Is 51¹⁹.

v. 6. The verse seems superfluous. It interrupts the connexion between vv 4 5, and 7: *If y u v · · · · · · f! · · · . Pi·· · · · ·* &c. 𝔊 οὐκ ἀλγήσει τὸ τραῦμα (μω.) = אבאב לא (i. 14); -ן · m. יחשר, as belonging to v. 5 b. St. ii. שׁוּ יהלך; מה מני יהלך; but 𝕲 τί ἔλασσον τρωθήσομαι = מה מעט אחלה (Ct 2⁵) or מה מעט אחלל מה מעט (cf. Pr 7²⁶). Cf. also 20²⁴. 𝕲 מנו = מרוּחַ לִי *who will enlarge* (i.e. relieve) *me?* (𝔐 preferable, but not above suspicion.)

v. 7. Both stt. are metr. short. In st. i the Subj. אֵל *El* (𝔐 כאבי) *dolor meus*) exc. post הלאני: *But now* (= as it is) *El hath exhausted me*. לאה (4²·⁵) *be weary* or *overcome, faint*; akin to להה, Aram. לְהִי, and perhaps Assyr. *lā'û, lâû*, 'small', 'weak'. Cf. Sum. LAL, LA, 'weak' (*enšu*), 'decrease', 'become less' or 'weak' (*maṭû*). (𝕲 *But now He hath made me* κατάκοπον, *very weary*; 3¹⁷.)

st. ii. Reading הֵשַׁם וַיְבַל עוֹרִי, after La 3 בִּלָּה בְשָׂרִי וְעוֹרִי, instead of שַׁו הִשִׁמוֹת כל עדתי. [𝕲 pro עדתי כל השׁם' gives μῶρον, σεσηπότα. μῶρος = נָבַל Is 32⁵·⁶ σαπῶσι = יבל 33²¹ = יבל? The second Gk. word may be a gloss or variant of the first.] The use of השׁם in such a sense is, however, questionable; see 17⁸ 18²⁰ 21⁵ acc. to which locc. we might propose הֵשַׁם עלי את־כל־עדתי *He hath confounded* (or *appalled, astonied*) *all my company at me*. For 'company' see 15³⁴. Cf. also 19¹³·¹⁴.

v. 8. 𝔐 ותקמטני לעד היה: lit. *And Thou didst grasp me; he became a witness*. This, to say the least, hardly justifies RV. The first word (Aram. קמט *lay hold of, grip, contract* or *shrink*: see 22¹⁶) is obviously corrupt, and renders the st. incoherent; while st. ii is overloaded and metr. redundant. The phrase ויקם־בי, st. ii, appears to be a marg. variant or correction of ותקמטני. Accordingly, st. i might be וַיְקָם־בִּי לְעֵד הָיָה *And He hath raised up for a witness against me* (my) *Ruin* (for היה = הוה, see note on 6²). Then st. ii בפני יענה (וְבַעֲשִׂי) ובחשי *And my Sorrow to my face replieth*, follows quite naturally. In Aram. בחשא, no doubt, is *leanness* (cf. Ps 109²⁴?); but that word does not seem to be a specially happy description of Eyob's disease, and, moreover, in 6² כעש is the parallel to (הוה) היה, as here.—It would perhaps be better, in view of st. ii, as a closer parallel, to restore st. i thus: ותקם בי לעד הותי *And my Ruin rose up against me as a witness* (Ps 27¹²).—𝕲 gives a lit. trans. of 𝔐: καὶ ἐπελάβου μου· εἰς μαρτύριον ἐγενήθη· καὶ ἀνέστη ἐν ἐμοὶ τὸ ψεῦδός μου, κατὰ πρόσωπόν μου ἀνταπεκρίθη.

v. 9. *and slain me* (i.e. in intention): rg. ויקטלני (cf. 𝕲 κατέβαλέν με = ויטילני) pro שׁוּ וַיִּשְׂטְמֵנִי (30²¹) *and bore a grudge against me* (Gn 27⁴¹) or assailed me (30²¹ Ps 55⁴). 𝕲 also uses καταβάλλω for שָׁחַת *let fall, throw down* (Ex 26⁴), which would suit here. 𝔖 פשחני *rent me* (cf. 2 K 9³³ פשׁח = 𝕲 שׁמט! whence some would read וַיִּשְׁמְטֵנִי *and dropped me* or *threw me down* here). שׂטם, שׂטן, str. *bind, shackle, shut up, close* = Syr. ܫܛܡ, cogn. c סָתַם and אָטַם, is a Shaph. or Saph. formation form √TAM, TAN, with which cf. Sum. DIM, *bind fast, close, a rope* or *cable*, &c.

Satan is the 'Binder' (cf. Lk 13¹).

gnashed or *ground his teeth*: in rage or hatred. Ps 35¹⁶ 37¹² 112¹⁰

La 2¹⁶. As it stands, the verse is a tristich; but 𝔊 restores the balance by add. here the st. βέλη (6⁴) πειρατῶν (25³) αὐτοῦ ἐπ' ἐμοὶ ἔπεσεν = חצי גדודיו נפלו עלי *His raiders' arrows have fallen upon me* There is no trace of this in the other versions, but 𝔊's Heb. text must have had it.

St. iii (iv). 𝔐 lit. *My Foe sharpens His eyes at me*. An isolated use of לטש *whet* or *sharpen* implements (1 Sa 13²⁰) and weapons (Ps 7¹³). Cf. our metaph. 'whetting the appetite'. As, however, שניו might easily have been misread עיניו, the st. was perhaps orig. a variant or gloss on st. ii, *He grinds upon me with His teeth*. עלי for לי (𝔊 *My enemies fixed their eyes* upon me) 𝔊 also points צָרַי *my foes*, with following plurals; connecting the st with v. 10, where the plur. comes in very abruptly, but would be quite natural, if the st. added by 𝔊 were authentic, as a reference to גדודיו *His raiding bands* (cf. 1¹⁰ ¹⁷). 𝔊 ἀκίσιν ὀφθαλμῶν ἐνήλατο, *With the barbs* (or *arrows*) *of* (*His*) *eyes He struck* (or *attacked*)= צְרֵי עֵינָיו יִלְטוֹשׁ *The blades of His eyes* (i. e. His cutting looks) *He sharpens*. For צר cf. Ex 4²⁵ Ps 89⁴¹ (flint knife). (ἐνήλατο is perhaps a scribal error in 𝔊 for ἐνηλάσατο.) There is much reason to regard vv. 9–14 as considerably interpolated, although it is no longer easy to distinguish the original from the later elements.

v. 10. Another tristich. St. i may be a marg intrusion. As the vb. פער *open wide* (only of the mouth) is trans. everywhere else (29²³ Is 5¹⁴ Ps 119¹³¹), leg. פיהם sine ב c 9 codd. et 𝔊𝔗𝔙. Cf. the sim. phrase Ps 22¹⁴ La 2¹⁶ al. (ב = פ rep.? or is the unus. constr. a mark of the interpolator's hand? Cf., however, note on v. 4 c.) St. ii. *In scorn*: בחרפה: or *with a taunt*. See La 3³⁰: *He will offer the cheek to the Smiter,—Will be full-fed with scorn*. Cf. also Ps 3⁸ for the constr. (Mi 4¹⁴ 1 K 22²⁴ c עַל). 𝔊, however, read אל (εἰς) or על (ἐπὶ 𝔊ᴬ) here also. For the whole st. it gives: ὀξεῖ ἔπαισέν με εἰς τὰ γόνατα (𝔊ᴬ* γονατας. A scribal error for γέννας or γένεια, neither of which is a 𝔊 word, or more prob. σιαγόνα, 1 K 22²⁴). ὀξεῖ = בְּחַדָּה: see Is 49² Ez 5¹ Ps 57⁵ (all חֶרֶב חַדָּה *a sharp sword*: it is not prob. that חרפה here is an Aramaism = Syr. חרפא *ḥarpā* or *ḥerpā*, 'blade' or 'sword').

St. iii. 𝔐 יחד עלי יתמלאון is unsatisfactory. יתמל' *they gather themselves together* (RV), or *mass themselves*, denom. fr. מָלֹא *multitude* (OL), is improb. It should mean *they fill themselves* or *are filled*. It is most likely that יחד (which 𝔊𝔗 seem to have read חרי) conceals the Obj. of the vb., viz. *burning anger* or fury (La 2³). Leg חרי־אף, 𝔊 חמתא, 𝔗 בנסא (var. כנסא).

v. 11. *giveth me up to* . . ., Dt 23¹⁶ (a slave to his owner). 11¹⁰.

the unjust. Leg. עַוָּלִים (18²¹ 27⁷) pro 𝔐 עֲוִיל which should mean *a boy* (19¹⁸ 21¹¹). Plur. as parallel to רשעים, st. ii (assuming the distich to be original. If, as seems prob., it be an interpolation, the Sing. might be a ref. to an unjust ruler of the period to which it belongs). 𝔊 δὲ κου

Sing. (𝔊𝔖); 𝔗 Plur.   *hurleth me*: מ ירטני, a doubtful word in Heb. Recurs app. Nu 22³² יָרַט, where, however, רַע or יָרֵע is almost certainly the true rg. The Ar. ورط (Pj.!), usu. compared, has the usual reek of the camel in it, and does not help us much. It is said to mean *He made him fall into* ورطة, *warta*, i.e. *thin mud* or *slime* (also *a deep hollow* or *pit*), *from which he could not extricate himself* (see Lane). 𝔊 ἔρριψέν με (𝔊ˣ ἔβαλε) suggests יִרְמֵנִי (Ex 15¹·²¹) or יָרֵנִי (30¹⁹). Possibly יִטְלֵנִי (see note on v. 9; cf. Je 16¹³ 22²⁸), or even יִפְלֵנִי *lifts* (and lays) *me* (La 3²⁸). 𝔖 gives אשלם *delivered up to . . .* in both stt.

v. 12. Another tristich; but st. iii may really belong to v. 13 as its first stichus.   *At ease was I.* 3²⁶ 12⁶ Je 12¹ La 1⁵ Ps 122⁶ (all). Perhaps rather שָׁלֵם *whole* (cf. Josh 8³¹), which agrees better with the violent ויפרפרני *and He shattered me* (Pilp. here only) and ויפצפצני *and He dashed me in pieces.* 𝔊 εἰρηνεύοντα (cf. 5²⁴ 15²¹ = שָׁלוֹם).

St. ii. Leg. אָחַז om. ו (due to prec. י). So 𝔊𝔙𝔖. *He seized me by the nape* or back of the neck (עֹרֶף). 𝔊 τῆς κόμης, *by the hair* = פֶּרַע (Ez 44²⁰) = ערף read backwards! Cf. also Nu 6⁵. (Therefore not due to thinking of Ar. عرف *a mane*.) St. iii. Cf. La 3¹²; 1 Sa 20²⁰. The statement is obv. connected with what follows, as beginning a different simile from that of the preceding distich. *He setteth me up*: om. ו (due to prec. י) c 𝔊𝔖.

v. 13. *His marksmen* or *archers*; רַבָּיו. So Je 50²⁹ רַבִּים (cf. Gn 21²⁰ רֹבֶה, 49²³ ורבו, Ps 18¹⁵ רָב). Since רבב, רבה, *to shoot*, are really *voces nihili*, leg. רֹמָיו (cf. Je 4²⁹ Ps 78⁹). 𝔊 λόγχαις = רֹמַח (Ez 39⁹ Ne 4¹⁰), partially confirming רמיו.

cleaveth: i.e. with His arrows (יפלח): Pr 7²³. All verbs in vv. 13, 14 are plur. in 𝔊. With st. i cf. La 3¹³, and with st. ii נשפך לארץ כבדי *My liver is poured out on the ground*, La 2¹¹. See also note on 20²⁵.

v. 14. עַל פְּנֵי פָרֶץ *upon* the face of *breach*. The superfluous פני is simply an erroneous anticipation or misreading of the following פרץ; or perhaps a mistaken substitute for it (pointing פָּנַי *my face*), as the third letter ץ is a minuscule (written small as if it were conjectural). Cf. 2 Sa 5²⁰ 6⁸. 𝔊 *They threw me down* (Pr. 25²⁸ עִיר פְּרוּצָה) πτῶμα ἐπὶ πτώματι, *fall upon fall.* The figure represents Eyob as an assaulted fortress.

v. 15. *my hide.* גֶלֶד here only. Prob. an Aramaism; cf. Syr. ܓܠܕܐ *skin, hide*; ܓܠܕܘܢܐ *a little skin*; ܓܠܕܢܝܐ *leathery.* Cf. also Assyr. *gilâdu*, *a hide* (c Det. of *leather*); Ar. جلد the *skin* of any animal (and plur. the *body and limbs* of a man). So 𝔊 ἐπὶ βύρσης μου, 𝔖 על משכי *on my skin* (= Assyr. *mašku*).

(*and*) *I have thrust.* The ו may be om., as due to prec. י. The vb. עֹלַלְתִּי *I have made to enter, put into*, is another Aramaism only found here; cf. Old Aram. עלל. Syr. ܥܠ *entr* = בֹּא. *my horn*: a natural symbol of pride and strength: cf. Dt 33¹⁷ Ps 75⁵·¹⁰. 𝕲 τὸ σθένος μου (For the verb 𝕲 gives ἐσβέσθη *was quenched* = תנתע, cf. 4¹⁰, or תכנע, cf. 40¹², either of which might = עללה' misread backwards. The more usual equivalent of ἐσβέσθη is, of course, תדעך: 18⁵·⁶ 21¹⁷: but apart from the question of the *ductus litterarum*, 'quenched' does not suit the sense here. We may suspect a corruption in 𝕲, ἐσβέσθη having perhaps arisen out of ἐσεβιβάσθη or some similar form.)

v. 16. 𝕲 ἡ γαστήρ μου συνκέκαυται ἀπὸ κλαυθμοῦ, *My belly is burnt up from weeping*: rg. בטני (γαστήρ = בטן eleven times in Job) for פני; no doubt under the influence of La 1²⁰ 2¹¹, מעי חמרמרו *My bowels are in a ferment* or 'work': see חמר I = Ar. خمر. Here, however, the Root seems to be חמר·IV = Ar. حمر 9 *it became* أحمر *red* (ἅπ· in OT). It looks as if the poet had misunderstood La ll. cc. עיני *my eye* (or *eyes?*) would give a better parallel to 'eyelids'; and if pointed as Sing., would account for Ketib חמרמרה: cf v. 20, La 3⁴⁹ Ps 6⁸ 88¹⁰. The eyes do redden with weeping; and in seven of the ten locc. where עפעפים *eyelids* occurs עינים the *eyes* are also mentioned (the exceptions are 3⁹ and Pr 6²⁵). Leg. therefore עֵינַי חֳמַרְמָרוּ *Mine eyes are red with weeping* (vb. as Qerî).

St. ii is metr. short, as the first two words (the Prep. and its Noun) involve only one stress. Add נָפְלָה before צלמות: *And upon mine eyelids Darkness is fallen*: cf. Gn 15¹², and see note on 3⁵. There is no reference here, nor in 12²² 24¹⁷ 28³ 34²², nor in any of the eighteen locc. where צלמות occurs, to the shadow that falls on the face of the dying. The word simply means *intense darkness*, and is a stronger syn. of חשך, in combination with which it is naturally used to describe the gloom of She'ol, the dark world of the Dead, 10²¹.

v. 17. Perhaps should follow v 14. St. i על לא חמס בכפי For the constr cf. Is 53⁹ על לא חמס עשה *Although he had done no violence*. Cf. also for על 10⁷ 34⁶. (1 C 12¹⁷ בלא חמס בכפי: בלא = על לא.)

St. ii is metr. too short. After ותפלתי we might insert the somewhat similar לפניו *before Him* (*And my prayer before Him was pure*); cf. Ps 18⁷ or we might read ותפלת שפתי זכה *And the Prayer* of my lips *was pure* (i. e. sincere); cf. Ps 17¹ 40¹⁰ 51¹⁷. The latter expedient provides a parallel to בכפי, st. i.

v. 18. *O Earth, cover not my blood!* Perhaps דָּמַי plur as in Gn 4¹⁰. *Hark! thy brother's outpourings of blood are crying to Me out of the ground!* (𝕲 *the blood* of my flesh: add. בשרי.) Even the blood of wild animals snared or shot for food had to be poured on the ground and covered with soil (Le 17¹³), since the blood was the life, alike of man and beast, and, as such, a sacred or forbidden thing (*tapū*). If left uncovered, the blood of a murdered man was believed to call down the vengeance of Heaven on the murderer. The pray·Ind. . . n ·   ·/   (6¹⁷) *for my cry!* is an entreaty that the appeal of his blood for vengeance may not be stifled by imprisonment underground (covered in, as it were, on the spot where it had been shed), but may rise unhindered to the ear of God. מקום *a standing-place, station, a place of stay* or *abode* (2¹¹ 7¹⁰ 6¹⁷ 9⁶ 8¹⁹ 27²¹ 28¹² al.), means, not so much a '*resting* place' (RV), as a place of fixed abode (= Ar. مَقام *maqâm*). Cf. the *maqâms* of buried Moslem saints. Such a home in the earth was supposed to appease and silence the 'crying' or protesting blood.

The addition ap. 𝔊 τῆς σαρκός μου makes the st. too long. If it were authentic, the allusion would not be to Eyob's death, as that of a man unjustly slain, but rather to the bloody ooze of his sores (7⁵), which drops from his tortured body on the ground. V. 22 ('a few years') shows that he is not expecting immediate death.

v. 19. The Heb. is in partial disorder. Consequently, st. i is too long, and st. ii too short metr. Either נם־עתה or הנה must be transferred to st. ii. The former seems preferable: *Behold, my Witness is in Heaven; And even now my Testifier is in the Heights!* The Aramaism שָׂהֵד (ἅπ'), is merely a poet. syn. of עֵד (st. i). Cf. שָׂהֲדוּתָא *Testimony*, Gn 31⁴⁷. 𝔖 ܣܗܕܝ *my witnesses* in st. i; ܣܗܕܝ *my acquaintance*, st. ii. Cf. 𝔊 ὁ δὲ συνίστωρ μου ἐν ὑψίστοις = 𝔅 Et conscius meus in excelsis. Soph. Philoct. 1293, ὡς θεοὶ συνίστορες, 'As the gods are witnesses!'

v. 20. St. i metr. short, prosaic, and ill-coherent with st. ii. Lit. *My scorners* (or *interpreters*, 33²³) *are my friends; Unto Eloah mine eye hath dropped* or *dripped* (RV supplet *tears*). 𝔊 ἀφίκοιτό μου ἡ δέησις πρὸς Κύριον | ἔναντι δὲ αὐτοῦ στάζοι μου ὁ ὀφθαλμός = צלותי תגע אל־יהוה | ולפניו דלפה עיני: *My prayer* (Aramaism = צלותא), *it cometh unto Iahvah* (cf. 4⁵ Jon 3⁶); *And before Him mine eye droppeth tears.* This may be right.

v. 21. Lit. *That He may argue* (or *reason*) *for a man with Eloah* (i.e. with Himself), *And between* (leg. בין pro בן c 5 codd.) *a mortal and his fellow.* Perhaps ובין בן־אדם *And between a son of man.* The likeness of the two words might have easily led to the omission of one of them. It will be seen that the verse thus represents the thing prayed for (v. 20). 𝔖 takes ויוכח as an Optative (of 𝔊), and so breaks the connexion with the previous verse: *But would that a son of man might convince* (or *confute*) *God, as a man his fellow!* = ויכח בן אדם עם אלוה כגבר לרעהו: 𝔗 (app. transposing the two synn. for *man*). 𝔗 *Is it possible that a son of man argue with God, even as* (והיך) *a man with his fellow?* Cf. also 𝔅.

v. 22. Eyob still expects a few years of life (though only a few) before the inevitable end, according to the normal course of his malady. The words are not those of one 'feeling that he is about to die', as Driver supposed.

Chapter 17. The opening verses are extremely corrupt, if not hopelessly so. V. 1, to begin with, is incoherent, unmetrical, and expressed in dubious if not impossible Hebrew. Lit. it runs, or rather halts: *My spirit is broken* (Is 10²⁷? or *destroyed, ruined*)—*my days are quenched—graves for me!* Forcible as this may sound to an English reader, it is too disjointed both in form and sense. Moreover, חבל is never used of the spirit, which comes from God (Gn 2⁷ 6³ 7²² Job 10¹² 27³ 32⁸ 34¹⁴ Ps 104²⁹·³⁰) and at death 'goeth upward' (Ec 3²¹), that is, app., returns to God. The idea of 'destroying' רוח is quite alien to Heb. thought. In Assyr. *ḥabâlu* Pa. is to *destroy* buildings. Cf. also the word חבל app. *dead*, common at the end of the Palmyrene epitaphs. In Ar. we have جَلَّ *be*, or *become, corrupted, unsound, vitiated*, or *disordered*, abs. (cf. Ne 1⁷ ch. 34³¹), and esp. in mind, *deranged* or *insane*, and Trans. جَلَّ *corrupt* or *render unsound*, &c., also *restrain, withhold*, or *debar* a man from doing something. 𝔊 ὀλέκομαι (cf. 32¹⁸) πνεύματι φερόμενος | Δέομαι δὲ ταφῆς καὶ οὐ τυγχάνω, *I am perishing, carried away by the wind, While I beg a grave and obtain it not* = נדף) חָבַלְתִּי בְרוּחַ נִדָּף 13³² Le 26³⁶ 𝔊); or, since φέρω usu. renders הביא (over 130 times), φερόμενος may indicate מוּבָא instead of נדף: וְזָעַקְתִּי קֶבֶר וָאַיִן לִי. But although this brings us nearer to a normal distich, apart from objections to the implied Heb., it does not agree with Eyob's anticipation of a few more years of life expressed in the preceding verse (16²²). Duhm's רוּחִי חֻבְּלָה יָמַי *His spirit* (i.e. *temper, animosity*, Ju 8³) *hath destroyed my days*, נָעֲזְבוּ קְבָרִים לִי *The graves are left to me*, though attractive, is far from certain. He assumes a non-existent נָזֻע = φερόμενος and supposes that δέομαι = בִּי a Particle of Entreaty, as in the Hexateuch; and then combines the two into נעזבו, referring to Is 18⁶. But that passage hardly justifies the required mg. of נעזבו. Eyob does not mean *The graves are abandoned* or *wholly given up to me*. And there is an obvious rhetorical pause at 16²², which is violated by connecting this distich closely with that verse, as Duhm finds himself obliged to do. Besides, the δὲ = וּ must not be ignored ('וּבִי does not seem possible). We suggest רוּחִי חֻבְּלָה מֵאֹמֶר *My mind is too disordered for speech* (אֹמֶר Ps 19⁴ or אָמַר Infin.), cf the Ar. use of the root חבל: *Words* (דברים pro קברים) *are abhorrent* (נתעבו pro נעזבו) *to me*. Or we might read נדעכו c 10 codd. and 𝔖𝔗 for the otherwise unknown נעזבו: *Words are extinct to me* (6¹⁷ 18⁵·⁶ 21¹⁷) He feels too ill and weary to continue a futile argument.

v. 2. RV is enough to suggest a suspicion of corruption here. What is the mg. of 'mine eye abideth in their provocation'? It is difficult to attain to even a relative certainty of text. 𝔊's Heb. appears to have been very defective here. Instead of אִם לֹא הֲתֻלִּים עִמָּדִי it presents us with λίσσομαι κάμνων, καὶ τί ποιήσας (-σω); as if remembering Is 16¹² לְהִתְפַּלֵּל .. נִלְאָה and reading or guessing אֶתְפַּלֵּל נִלְאֵיתִי וּמֶה אֶעֱשֶׂה from a coll[ation] n[ot] ill-written [a]nd part[ly effaced] ? . . This hardly helps us; but it is instructive to note the confusion of letters involved in עשה = עמדי (W pro ⟨?⟩; ה = די conjunct.), and the letters of לאה occurring in that order in 𝔐 ('ה לא).

For st. ii instead of 𝔐's highly problematical עיני תלן ובהמרותם *And mine eye must rest on their display of rebellion* (?), 𝔊 gives us ἔκλεψαν δέ μου τὰ ὑπάρχοντα ἀλλότριοι = אוני נגבו וזרים *And strangers have stolen my goods*. Here אוני clearly corresponds to 𝔐 עיני; while וזרים (or ונכרים?) suggests a possible orig. ובכזבים *And on lies*, which would be a suitable parallel to התולים *deceptions, mockeries*.

But since נגב may mean *to deceive* or *delude* as well as *to steal* (Gn 31²⁷ al.), it seems possible that it stood in the original text here and that 𝔊, misunderstanding this use of it and desiderating an object of the supposed theft, misread or altered עיני into אוני = τὰ ὑπάρχοντά μου. As a tentative restoration of the Heb. text we may therefore suggest: עמדי מהתלים מלא | עיני תלן ובמנגבים *A mob of sophists is with me;* | *And mine eye resteth on* (19⁴) *deceivers*. For מלא *a multitude* or *crowd*, see Gn 48¹⁹ Is 31⁴. But perhaps we should retain אם-לא *Verily* (1¹¹, cf. 6²⁸). (In my old notes I find ובמרלות for ובהמרותם, with a reference to chap. 13²⁰. I mention the fact because Duhm reads בתמרורים on the basis of the same passage. Leaving the rest of the distich as it stands in 𝔐, we thus get the sense: *Verily deceptions or mock-arguments, mockeries, are with me; And mine eye dwelleth on bitternesses*. This, however, does not agree so well with the preceding distich; and for the sake of the parallelism it would be better to read ובמרמות *and on deceits, wiles*; 15³⁵ Gn 27³⁵ 34¹³ Ps 10⁷ 35²⁹.)

v. 3. *Appoint, I pray, a surety for me with Thyself, For* (כי omitted after ך?) *who is he that will pledge himself for me?* Here, with Reiske, we point עָרְבֵנִי *my pledge* = *surety* or *bail for me*, instead of 𝔐 עָרְבֵנִי *go surety for me* (Is 38¹⁴). The elliptic use of שימה *Appoint* (a pledge) is hardly probable. In what follows, st. ii, the expression is unusual: lit. *Who is he that will strike himself* (i.e. his own hand) *for my hand?* But read מי־הוא־לי יְתַקַּע יָדוֹ. Cf. Pr 6¹ 17¹⁸ (𝔊 apparently יַקֵּשׁ = συνδέ- θήτω for יְתַקַּע. It omits the first stichus of the verse altogether. What does Duhm mean by טָמְנוּ?)

v. 4. 𝔐 lit. *For their heart* (i.e. the heart of his friends) *Thou hast hidden from insight* (cf. Ps 31²¹). OL strangely: '*Thou* (God) *hast treasured up* their heart *away from* understanding, kept it therefrom.' If we transpose the Prep. (the usual const. Ps. 31²¹) we get the more natural sense *For Thou hast hidden insight from their heart*. St. ii has only two stresses (the *Qînah*-measure, of which we have had so many apparent examples). Moreover, if the points of 𝔐 are correct (תְּרֹמֵם), the trans. vb. lacks an O¹·j. This might be קרנם *their horn* (1 Sa 2¹⁰ Ps 75¹¹ 89¹⁸ 92¹¹), and תרמם may be the remains of תְּרֹמֵם(קַרְנָם) which would complete the distich. Cf. also 16¹⁵. (ראשׁם *their head* is also possible: Pr 3⁴ 27⁵. The couplet reads like a psalm-verse, and may be an interpolation.)

v. 5. 𝔐 is really meaningless. לְחֵלֶק יַגִּיד רֵעִים *For a share* (of the feast or booty?) *he reporteth* (*informeth agst.*? cf. Je 20¹⁰) *friends* is an unlikely statement in this context, even if the Heb. could signify so much, which is more than doubtful. 𝔊 varies the vowels of רעים: τῇ μερίδι ἀναγγελεῖ κακίας (i.e. רָעִים): while in st. ii it gives ἐφ᾽ υἱοῖς = עַל־בְּנֵי for בניו. For ἐτάκησαν = תבלינה see 11²⁰. The distich may possibly be a mere variation of 6²⁷ (*They cast the lot over their friend, And over the orphan they bargain*, or the like). The *ductus litt.* will, however, be followed more closely if we emend יַחֲלְקוּ לַגֵּר רָעָה *They apportion evil to the stranger* (31³²); leaving st. ii almost or altogether as it stands in 𝔐: *And the eyes of his* (the *gêr's*) *children fail*. It is true that such an indictment of Eyob's friends does not seem specially appropriate here; and the verse may be a marginal quotation which has intruded into the text. Duhm, regarding it as such, hazards the following version of 𝔐: 'Whoso informs against a friend on account of a pledge, His children's eyes do pine'; a proverbial saying (משל) which he compares with 6¹⁴, referring to 2 Sa 20²⁽¹⁾ for the sense of חלק and paraphrasing our verse: 'He who causes an insolvent friend to be distrained upon at law, his children will rue it!' Ingenious as this interpretation may be, it is questionable whether להלק can bear the mg. put upon it. A better connexion of thought with the sequel would be gained by reading חלקי להגיר דמעה | ועיני בבכי תבלינה *'Tis my lot to pour down tears, And mine eyes fail with weeping* (cf. 𝔊ᴬᶜ ὀφθαλμοὶ δέ μου = ועיני). This would also obviate rejection of the verse.

v. 6. 𝔐 וְהִצִּיגַנִי. Either omit the ו or, as seems better, read c 𝔊 (ἔθου δέ με), וַתַּצִּיגֵנִי *And Thou hast set me for* (= made me) *a byword of peoples* (point לְמָשָׁל instead of the ἅπ.—למשל—an old scribal error), or perhaps *of the tribes* in Eyob's neighbourhood. In st. ii תֹּפֶת *spittle* (?) is very doubtful ᴧ *Gehenna*; identifying the word with 'the Tophet' in the valley of ben Hinnom (2 K 23¹⁰ Je 7³¹ al.); 𝔖 תחפיתא a *veil* or *covering*; 𝔙 *exemplum* (= מֹפֵת?); 𝔊 γέλως an object of *mirth*, a *laughing-stock* (connecting the word with תֹּף *timbrel*, 21¹²). In the similar passage, 30⁹ ¹⁰, the term for spittle is רֹק, as also in Is 50⁶. The existence of a √תף or תפף or תוף *to spit* may perhaps be inferred from תָּפֵל and Ar. تَفَلَ *to spit a little saliva*, as well as from Eth. *tafĕa*, spuit, exspuit, inspuit; but if our stichus means *And I become one in whose face they spit* (Duhm: 'Ein Spei-ihn-an, a Spit-in-his-face'), ולתפת פנים אהיה would be a more natural way of expressing it than ותפת פנים אהיה: cf. במסתר פנים Is 53³. Instead of לפנים, however, 𝔊𝔙 suggest לפניהם *before them*; and 𝔙's version of the stichus *Et exemplum* ⸻ perhaps supports the apt conjecu.ᵉ מפת in pla e of תפת. *An I* ⸻ (or ⸻ , or wonder) *before them*. 𝔊 αὐτοῖς = לָהֶם *unto them*; the more usual constr. (see Ez 12⁶ 24²⁴·²⁷ Ps 71⁷). As affording a better parallel to עַמִּים we may suggest לִלְאֻמִּים (cf. Assyr. li-i-mu, syn. of *kimtu*, 'family') *to nations* instead of לִפְנִים: *And I become a sign* (*portent* or *wonder*; cf. v. 8 Ps 71⁷) *to nations*. The verse, in any case, seems more appropriate to Israel in exile than to a suffering individual (cf. מְשֹׁל עַמִּים and Dt 28⁴⁶) and may not have belonged here originally. It interrupts the connexion between vv. 5, 7, and should perhaps follow the latter verse. The words מֹפֵת and לְאֻמִּים (Pss Pr) are not found elsewhere in Job.

v. 7. כַּעַשׂ (5² 6² 10¹⁷) *vexation, anger*, here means *grief, sorrow*, as כַּעַס in Ps 6⁸ 31¹⁰. The eyes are dimmed (Gn 27¹) by weeping. Cf. v. 5.

St. 2. 𝔙 *et membra mea quasi in nihilum redacta sunt*. Hence the usual rendering: *And my limbs are all like a shadow*. But יְצֻרַי *my limbs* is a dubious ἅπ· We might read צָרִי (= צוּרִי) after Ps 49¹⁵ Q. *my form*; thus vindicating another occurrence for a rare word; or we might point יְצָרַי *my frame*, Ps 103¹⁴ (cf. 𝔊 *my thoughts*, pointing יְצָרַי *my* 'frames of mind', *purposes*). 𝔊's πεπολιόρκημαι μεγάλως ὑπὸ πάντων, *I have been besieged greatly by all* (confusing צוּר *to fashion* or *draw*, Ez 43¹¹, with צוּר *to besiege*) seems to favour צָרַי. (In 30⁸⁰ μεγάλως = מֵעָלַי! Here it stands for כְּצֵל, perhaps misread מַעַל. Thus 𝔊's version of the st. may represent וְצָרִים עָלַי כֻּלָּם.) For כֻּלָּם read כָּלָה *is wasted* (7⁹ 33²¹). Another possible and perhaps probable emendation of the st. is וּשְׁאֵרִי כְּצֵל כָּלָה (the first word perhaps written defectively וִצְרִי = וְשֵׁרִי) *And my flesh is as worn as a shadow* (cf. Pr 5¹¹ Ps 73²⁶).

vv. 8-10 interrupt the connexion of vv. 7, 11 sqq. We might render v. 8ᵃ *Upright men would be confounded at this*; understanding the words as an insinuation that the Friends were not honest and sincere; had they been so, they must have been confounded at the sight of Eyob's unmerited sufferings. The second stichus, as it stands, cannot be translated so as to agree with this. But a slight correction gives the sense: *And an innocent one might be moved to impiety* or *apostasy* (reading לַחֹנֵף Is 32⁶, or לַחֲנֻפָּה Je 23¹⁵, or Infin. לַחֲנֹף; cf. Is 64⁶ מִתְעוֹרֵר לְהַחֲזִיק בָּךְ *bestirring himself to lay hold on Thee*). Then v. 9 will be: *But the righteous* (i. e. I myself) *will hold fast his way, And the guiltless become more resolute* (lit. *And the clean-handed adds* or *will add strength*: אֹמֶץ? אַמֵּץ Infin.). The greater his sufferings, the stronger Eyob's determination to affirm and to abide by his own innocence (cf. 2³ᵇ 27⁶ᵃ). At best, however, the verses remain an interruption; and v. 11, which resumes the tone and tenor of v. 7, is hardly a natural continuation of them. On the other hand, Bildad's echo of them, 18²⁰, goes to prove vv. 8, 9, authentic. Possibly, therefore, vv. 8-10 should be transferred to the end of the chapter, to which they would form a not unsuitable close. After avowing his own despair, Eyob defies his friends to produce any argument that can shake his inflexible consciousness of innocence. (Duhm thinks that vv. 8–10 express the point of view of Eyob's friends rather than his own, and may have been transferred hither from chap. 18.)

v. 8. If with 𝔊^A we transpose the two nouns in st. ii, we get for the verse the excellent sense· *Upright men are confounded at this* (i. e. the spectacle of his sufferings), *And the impious triumpheth over the innocent* (cf. 31²⁹ for this mg. of the vb.); as is quite natural, and often happens. To this v. 9 adds that, however baffling to reason the dealings of Providence may prove to be in individual cases, they will never cause the good man to swerve from the way of righteousness.

v. 9. For צדיק *righteous* 𝔊 gives πιστός (𝔊^Θ δίκαιος), the usual equivalent of נאמן *trusty* (12²⁰); perhaps a variant in the Heb. text. In st. ii 𝔊 misread app. יובל (ἀναλάβοι θάρσος· cf. Is 46¹) for יסיף.

v. 10. St. i is metr. too long and more or less corrupt. The line will still be unmetr., if (c 5 codd. et 𝔊𝔚) we read כלכם *all of you* for 𝔐's ungrammatical כלם *all of them.* The var. יבאו (K^(or)) for ובאו indicates perception of the difficulty, but only half remedies it (!תשבו). The simplest way of restoring both sense and metre is to omit כלם as dittogr (from v. 7 end) or as having grown out of אלם repet., and to read ואלם שובו בארנא *But, pray you, come on again!* Cf. Is 21¹³. See further at 18⁴. (𝔊 ἐρείδετε = תפשו pro תשבו! Cf. Pr 30²⁸.)

v. 11. This and the following verse are again extremely corrupt. AV and its margin fairly render 𝔐's text of v. 11; but the triple division of the words sets the metre at naught. 𝔊 at least gives us a distich: 'My days did pass in uproar; And the joints of my heart were broken.' Ἐν βρόμῳ, *in din*, or *fury*, suggests a storm; as if 𝔊 read or guessed בְּרַעַם (24⁸; cf Ps 90⁵), which might represent an original כְּרַעַם *like the rainstorm.* Possibly, however, ἐν βρόμῳ = בזעם or בועף *in fury* or *raging.* 𝔊^A ἐν δρόμῳ, *at a run* = בִּמְרֻצָה. Βρόμος may, however, stand for βρῶμος, *foul smell, stink*, as in 6⁷. Possibly, therefore, 𝔊 connected ימתי (or whatever corresponded to it in 𝔊's exemplar) with the √זהם (Heb, Aram., Ar.) *to be foul* or *stinking* (33²⁰). 'My days pass in noisomeness' gives an adequate sense (בזהמות?). But inasmuch as the √זמם in Aramaic (Syriac) may signify *sound* and *noise*, 𝔊 may, after all, have had זמתי in its Heb. text. We would restore נצמתו *are ended*, after 6¹⁷ 23¹⁷, La 3⁵³. (Duhm: צָמָתוּ.) Those who desiderate a simile in stichus i, may prefer to read כְּמֹץ or כְּמוֹץ *like chaff*; comparing כמץ עבר יום, Zp 2² Is 29⁵: see also 21¹⁸ Ho 13³. וזמתי *my purposes* might have been orig. a marginal gloss on מורשי לבבי, which Buhl and Duhm explain *the wishes of my heart*, deriving מורש from √ארש, Assyr. *êrêšu, to wish, ask for.* With such a verb as נתץ, however, one would expect something more concrete and physi---'. e.x. my h ar! s/r.n---(מיתרי לבבי); and we may even perhaps suspect the presence of an A.amaism. and interpret th—v. λε/ηp. מורשי

in the sense of *beams* (Aram. מרישא *a beam*, 1 K 6³⁶). The phrase מ' לבבי may thus be analogous to, and perhaps a later equivalent of Jeremiah's קירות לבי *the walls of my heart* (Je 4¹⁹), which might very well be corrected into קורות ל׳ *the beams of my heart*. Our distich would thus become

> *My days pass away* (6¹⁶ 11¹⁶) *like chaff;*
> *The beams* (or strings?) *of my heart are snapped asunder.*

For the meaning *strings* or *cords*, we might compare another Aram. term, viz. the Syriac ܚܒܠܐ, ܚܒܠܐ, *hempen rope, cable*. In either case, the second stichus is preserved without alteration. But I cannot refrain from mentioning another expedient which I find in my old notes, viz. to read שרשי for מורשי (ש = ש֖), and to render *Torn up are the roots of my heart*.

v. 12. There is great diversity in the attempts to explain or emend this verse. The general sense appears to be that God turns Eyob's day into night.

> *Night for day I* (or *He*, i.e. Eloah: vss. 3, 4, 6) *put* (*putteth*);
> *And my* (*the*) *light* (or *dawn*) *is dim* (murky) *with darkness*.

The first stichus recalls Isaiah's שמים חשך לאור, and is probably a reminiscence of that passage (5²⁰). For ישימו אור read (א)י(שים ואור. Instead of קרוב מפני we suggest קדר מני, as in 6¹⁶, although מפני might mean *because of, through*. Cf. also וקדר עליהם היום (Mi 3⁶). 𝕲 supports 𝔐: νύκτα εἰς ἡμέραν ἔθηκα(v: A), Φῶς ἐγγὺς ἀπὸ προσώπου σκότους. We can say in English, *And the light is* wellnigh *darkness*; but it is doubtful whether קרוב מפני could be so used in Hebrew. We might also emend: ואור יקריב במרחשך *And the light He* joineth to *darkness* (*makes them one*: cf. Is 5⁸ שדה בשדה יקריב). Duhm reads לילה ליום אשים מפני חשך | ואור and translates 'Die Nacht mache ich zum Tage, | Und Licht ist vor mir Finsternis.' But is not the poet's meaning rather that Eyob's day is turned into night (cf. the parallel stichus)? and can מפני express 'vor mir', *before me* (לפני)? Would not מפני rather mean 'from my presence', or else 'because of me'? Moreover, the metre of Duhm's second stichus is rather halting, and the disyllable קרוב, which he rejects as a distortion of קראתי, a supposed gloss on אשים, is not metrically redundant. It is probably a disguise of some word (e. g. קדר or בוקר) in the original text. But אשים, the first pers., may be preferred to ישים, which I conjectured independently many years ago. We might then read אורי *my light* instead of ואור. Lastly, in view of 7⁴, we may suggest the distich לילה ליום אשים | אור־בקר ואפן לחשך *Night for day I put; Dawn shineth, and I look for darkness*. Gn 44 Hg 1⁶.

v. 13.   *Yea, I hope for She'ol as my home,*
           In (the) Darkness I (have) spread my couch;
v. 14.   *To the Pit I cry, 'Thou art my father!'—*
           'My mother and sister!' to the maggot.

In v. 13ᵃ 𝔐 has אִם *if* (𝔊 ἐάν), for which אַף *yea, also, besides* seems better. Duhm: 'If I hope, She'ol is my house' &c. But the verb קוה requires an Object (7² 30²⁶): and here Eyob is looking forward to death as the end of his sufferings. V. 14 *end* 𝔊 paraphrases רמה, the corpse-devouring *maggot*, by σαπρίαν, *rottenness* (so 21²⁶ 25⁶) in curious agreement with the √רמם = Ar. رَمَّ *to rot, decay*, whence רמה *maggot* is derived.

v 15.   *And where, then, is there* (other) *hope for me?*
          And my good, who can descry it?

תקותי *my hope* = hope for me. In st. ii 𝔐 ותקותי is obviously a scribe's erroneous repetition. Read טובתי *my good* (22²¹) = 𝔊 τὰ ἀγαθά μου, with Merx, Bickell, Duhm. 𝔊's ὄψομαι is a reminiscence of 7⁷.

v. 16.   *Will they descend with me into She'ol?*
           Or shall we go down together into the Dust?

So 𝔊· ἦ μετ' ἐμοῦ εἰς ᾅδην καταβήσονται, ἢ ὁμοθυμαδὸν ἐπὶ χώματος καταβησόμεθα; = ואם־יחד על־עפר נחת | העפרי שאל תרדנה. 𝔐 has: *To the bars* (str. *poles* or *staves*) *of She'ol will they descend; Or together on the Dust (will there be) rest?* But the particle הֲ is almost necessary to the construction (a Disjunctive Interrogation) at the beginning of stichus 1; and it might easily have fallen out after the preceding ה. When the ע also had disappeared, the meaningless מדי became בדי (Ho 11⁶). But the usual expression is not *bars*, but *gates* of She'ol (Is 38¹⁰ Ps 9¹³; cf. chap. 38¹⁷). The difference between נַחַת (Pausal form נָחַת) *rest* and נֵחַת *shall we go down*, in stichus ii, is merely a matter of points; and the verse as a whole affords an excellent instance of the preservation of the authentic text by 𝔊. (𝔙's In profundissimum infernum = בְּדִי שׁאֹל.)

Chapter 18.   *In answer Bildad of Shuah said:*
              How long wilt thou not make an end?
              Hold! that we too may speak.

So 𝔊: Μέχρι τίνος οὐ παύσῃ; Ἐπίσχες, ἵνα καὶ αὐτοὶ λαλήσωμεν. The original text may have been—

עד אנה לא תָשֵׂם קֵץ
תָּכֶל ואנחנו נדבר:

שים קץ *set or put an end*; sc. to words, as implied by the context. Cf. 16³. תכל *finish!* or *have done!* Cf. כִּלָּה לְדַבֵּר, Gn 18³³ Je 26⁸. We might also point תָּכֹל *hold in!* cf. Je 6¹¹ 20⁹; or read תֶּחְדַּל *cease!* (= ἐπίσχες. cf. 1 K 22). Better perhaps עד־אנה לא־תעצר במלין *How long wilt thou not refrain words* (1. 29 𝔊; 4·12ᵃ)

The text of 𝔐 cannot be original, for it violates both sense and metre. It is usually rendered: 'How long will ye set snares for words? Attend (*or* Understand) ye, and afterwards we will speak.' But the plur. verbs in addressing Eyob are manifestly inappropriate; the meaning *snares* for the once-occurring קנצי has no better basis than comparison of the Ar. vb. قنص *catch, ensnare*; the grammar of st. i is bad (קנץ should be קנצים), and st. ii is really nonsensical. As Duhm observes, Bildad was not going to speak 'afterwards', but immediately. It is evident that st. i is overloaded, and that something must be sacrificed for the sake of the metre. Duhm rejects עד אנה, as added from 19¹ after the verse had already become corrupt, and reads simply תשם קץ למלין *Put an end to words!*, which barely satisfies rhythm and metre, besides diverging too far from both 𝔊 and 𝔐, and making too abrupt a beginning.

v. 3.   *Why are we regarded as cattle—*
         As the beasts that perish—in thine eyes?

In st. ii 𝔐 gives: נטמינו בעיניכם, usually taken to mean, (*Why*) *are we treated as unclean* (נטמאנו = נטמינו) *in thine eyes?* But the Niphal of טמא is not so used elsewhere, and hardly makes good sense here. 𝔊 perhaps read נדמנו (= σεσιωπήκαμεν); see 29²¹; 41⁴ for דמם = σιωπάω. [It reproduces only one of the two verbs of the verse. Possibly it misread נחשבנו in st. i as החרשנו (= σεσιωπήκαμεν: see 41⁴ 𝔊).] In any case, it is clear that the stichus, with its two words, is metrically too short. בער might easily have fallen out after its syn. בהמה. I have therefore ventured on כבעיר נדמו בעיניך (cf. Ps 49¹³·²¹); or we might read נמשלנו לבעיר בעיניך (Ps 49, l. c.), thus getting the sense:

         Why are we regarded as cattle—
         Are we like to the beasts in thine eyes?

𝔊 rightly implies the sing. suffix with its ἐναντίον σου (cf. note on v. 2).

v. 4.   [*O render of himself in wrath!*] Cf. 16⁹. 𝔊 renders vb. by χράομαι, as in 16⁹. (κέχρηταί σοι ὀργή, *anger possesses*(?) *thee.*) This line being only half a distich, it is evident that (if it be genuine) another line at least has been accidentally omitted either before or after it. Accordingly Duhm transfers the five stichi, ch. 17⁸⁻¹⁰ᵃ, to this place; remarking that they form two complete tetrastichs when thus prefixed to the three stichi of 18⁴. He rejects 17¹⁰ᵇ as added, possibly, by the same hand as 17⁴, in order to complete the distich in its new position. Then he links 17¹⁰ᵃ, which he reads ואלם תשב ובא נא, with 18⁴ᵃ; thus getting the distich:

         But come back hither, I pray,
         O man that rendeth himself in his wrath!

It must, however, be admitted that the statement *Upright men are dumbfounded at such talk* (as thine: על זאת; cf. 8⁸, על אלה). *And the pure* rises up against the unholy, And the righteous holds fast his way, And the pure-handed becomes all the firmer! does not seem to follow naturally on the indignant question *Why are we regarded as cattle, As the beasts that perish, in thine eyes?* (18³). The unaccommodating passage, in fact, interrupts the context here almost as violently as in ch. 17; and style, tone, and spirit are quite different. Moreover, if טרף נפשו באפו were directly addressed to Eyob, it would prob. have been otherwise expressed; viz. טרף נפשך באפך, c suff. 2 Pers. > 3 Pers. The line may be a marginal comment on Bildad's angry bearing. But more prob. it belongs to v. 13: see the note there.

    Shall the earth be dispeopled for thy sake,   (Is 6¹² 7¹⁶)
    And the rock remove from its place (site)?   (Cf. Jb 9⁵ 14¹⁸.)

𝔊 paraphrases st. i · τί γάρ; ἐὰν σὺ ἀποθάνῃς, ἀοίκητος ἡ ὑπ' οὐρανόν; *What! if thou die, will all under heaven be uninhabited?* (Perhaps reading הלמותך for הלמענך)

In st ii 𝔊 gives: ἡ καταστραφήσεται ὄρη (A: ἡ γῆ) ἐκ θεμελίων; *Or will mountains (the earth) be overturned from foundations?* = יֵהָפֵךְ 9⁵ 12¹⁵ 28⁹, הפך = καταστρέφω) צוּר מְמוֹסָדָיו (Dt 32²² Ps 18⁸ מוסדי הרים; מוסדי ארץ, Ps 82⁵ al) צור = ὄρη, as here, 29⁶; cf. Nu 23⁹. Duhm reads יִנָּתֵק מִמּוֹסְדָיו, because of the previous occurrence (14¹⁸) of the stichus in 𝔐, which seems an insufficient reason; and the use of נתק is questionable. 𝔊 possibly read ויעתק צ' ממוסדיו.

v. 5.   *Yea (or Yet) the light of the wicked goeth out,*
          And the flame of his fire doth not shine

In st. i read רָשָׁע sing., c 𝔙, as implied by אשׁ in st. ii, and by the Sing. of the following verses. For the statement, see 21⁷, Pr 13⁹. In st. ii שָׁבִיב = Aram. שְׁבִיבָא; Ecclus 8¹⁰ 45¹⁹. Cf. also Assyr. *šabbu*, 'shining' (syn. *namru*); *šabâbu*, 'to blaze', 'burn'. 𝔊 καὶ οὐκ ἀποβήσεται (𝔊ᴬ ἀναβήσεται, *go up*) αὐτῶν (𝔊ᴬ αὐτοῦ rectè!) ἡ φλόξ, *And their flame shall not go off (succeed?* but 𝔊ᴬ *go up*). Perhaps an error for ἀπο(ἀνα)φανήσεται.

v. 6.   *The light is darkened in his tent,*
          And his lamp over him (29³) *goeth out.*

For *tent* (אהל) 𝔊 gives the curious word δίαιτα, which means *way of living*, and then *dwelling, abode, room*. So again in v. 15, as also in 8²² 11¹⁴ 22²³. (As D passes into Z, the roots of δίαιτα and ζάω, *live*, may be related.) The verse looks like a variant of v. 5, perhaps taken in from the margin. Such variants from different recensions or editions abound in ancient poetry; e. g. in the Babylonian Epic of Nimrod.

v. 7.   *His footsteps are cramped in his way* (or *as he goeth*);
          And his own counsel throweth him to the ground.

𝔐 צעדי אונו t. *f h.* all (20) or *f h. m. ur* (Gn 49), as Duhm takes it (die Schritte seiner Manneskraft). But in any case the phrase is a strange one. Moreover, צעד (sing. or plur.) usually has a suffix, Ps 18³⁷ (14¹⁸ 31⁴,³⁷ 34²¹); and the constr. plur. is found nowhere else in OT. Read בארחו *in his going* (34⁸) = בלכתו in Pr 4¹²ᵃ, of which this stichus might be called a variation. Leg. prob. (צְעָרוֹ) צְעָרָיו (יצר) יררו בְּאָרְחוֹ.

Throweth him (*down*): a late use of השליך; Dan 8⁷ (adds ארצה *to the ground*). In st. i 𝔊 misread יָרֻרוּ צְעָרָיו֯ /אוֹנוֹ = θηρεύσωσιν ἐλάχιστοι τὰ ὑπάρχοντα αὐτοῦ. St. ii is too short. Perhaps we should read וּבְלִכְתּוֹ (ובדרכו) תַּכְשִׁילֵהוּ עצתו *And when he walketh, his own counsel maketh him stumble.* Cf. 𝔊 σφάλαι δὲ αὐτοῦ ἡ βουλή. 4⁴ כושל = σφαλέντας. Or ותבשיל כחו עצתו *And his counsel weakeneth his strength.*

v. 8.   For he is rushed into the net by his own feet;
          And he walketh himself into (upon) the toils.

v. 9.   The trap catcheth him by the heel;
          The gin (hunting-net?) layeth hold upon him. (Ne 10³⁰.)

v. 10.   His snare is hidden in the ground,
          And his springe upon the path.

He is rushed or *hurried* or *sped*; שֻׁלַּח, as in Ju 5¹⁵. But ברגליו here is used in a different sense apparently (*instrumental*). Hence Du reads ... רגלו שֻׁלְּחָה *For his foot rusheth into the net* = 𝔊 ἐμβέβληται δὲ ὁ ποὺς αὐτοῦ ἐν παγίδι. (𝔙𝔖 make the verb active: שִׁלַּח.) 𝔊 renders יתהלך by ἐλιχθείη. This does not necessarily imply the different reading יתגלל (Kittel; cf. Is 34⁴ 𝔊), as ἐλίσσομαι may mean *to turn hither and thither, to go about*, like התהלך : see II. xii. 49.

In v. 9 read עקבו *his heel*, 𝔊𝔙; Ki. Cf. Gn 25²⁶; ch. 16¹². In st. ii 𝔊𝔖𝔙 confuse the isolated צמים, which 𝔊 renders διψῶντας, with צְמֵאִים *thirsty* (plur.). In 5⁵, as we have seen, צמא *the thirsty one* is right, although 𝔐 has צמים as here. Perhaps מָצוֹר, as in 19⁶.

v. 11.   All around (Je 6²⁵ 20³) Terrors alarm him,
          And Fearfulness dogs his heels (behind him).

Reading in st. ii וּפְלָצוֹת בָּאָה (הָלְכָה) לְרַגְלָיו; cf. 𝔊 and Is 21⁴ פלצות בעתתני; Ps 55⁶. The line is too short in 𝔐, some word having fallen out. Or we may suppose the loss of a single letter from והפצהו *and scatter him*, a verb which demands a plur. obj., and read וְהִפְלִיצָהוּ אֵימִים וגו' *and Fears* (20²⁵) *affright him behind*: cf. 9⁶ 21⁵ for √פלץ, which certainly agrees better with the context than פוץ. 𝔊 has πολλοὶ δὲ περὶ πόδα αὐτοῦ ἔλθοισαν = ורבים באו לרגלו (or ל' בא המון). Cf. Hab 3⁵. For לרגלי *after him*, cf. Gn 30³⁰ (contrasted with לפני); Is 41² (see Box *ad loc.*).

v. 12.   𝔐: יהי רעב אנו *Let his* (*manly*) *strength become hungry* (i.e. *fail*: OL; but this is hardly satisfactory, although 𝔙 so understood the line: Attenuetur fame robur eius. 𝔊: ἔλθοι(σαν) ἐν λιμῷ στενῷ =

יבא(ו) ברָעָב צר. 𝔖 *And hunger shall be his sorrow* = יהיה רָעָב אונו, which is possibly right:

Famine becometh his trouble;
And Ruin is ready to swallow him up.

𝔐 לצלעו, *for his limping* or *stumbling*; Ps 38^{18}, כי אֲני לְצֶלַע נָכוֹן *For I am ready for stumbling*; cf. Ps 35^{15} Je 20^{10}. But *Ruin is ready for his stumbling* seems an unnatural phrase; and לבלעו *to swallow him* is an easy and natural correction, the term being a favourite with the poet (2^{3} 8^{18} 10^{8}; cf. 7^{19} 20^{15} &c.). St. i may perhaps be restored, יְכַלֶּה רָעָב אֹנוֹ *Famine consumeth his strength* (9^{22} 31^{16} Gn 41^{30}). 𝔊 read the second line apparently, ואיד נכון לו פתאם *And Ruin is ready for him suddenly* (ἐξαίσιον, *violent, extraordinary* = פתאם 𝔊, 9^{23} 22^{10}: see also 4^{12} 20^{7}, where the Heb. words are different). Duhm restores st. i, יהיה רָעֵב אָוֶן לו *Mischief is hungry for him* (cf. Je 42^{14}, לַלֶּחֶם *for bread*). But why not ירעב (cf. Je l. c.)? Cf. also Am 8^{11} (רָעָב . . . לִשְׁמֹעַ). (𝔊 runs v. 11^{b} and v. 12^{a} together, perhaps reading or guessing ונפוצים לְרַגְלָו יָבֹאוּ בְרָעָב צַר)

v. 13. *He teareth himself in his rage;* (4^{a} trans hither!)
For famine he devoureth his own flesh.

We have replaced טֹרֵף נַפְשׁוֹ בְּאַפּוֹ here from v. 4^{a}. The starving wretch gnaws his own flesh for food, as if he were a wild beast and his own body his prey. Cf. Is 49^{26}. As the verse stands in 𝔐 it evidently consists of two variants of a single stichus:

יאכל בדי עורו
יאכל בדיו בכור (מ)ו(ת):

He devoureth the limbs (41^{4}) *of his skin* (!);
Devoureth his limbs the Firstborn of Death.

בכור מות, which occurs nowhere else, is usually taken to mean the deadliest of diseases, and is compared with 'the firstborn of the poor', i. e. the poorest, in Is 14^{30}, which, however, itself is rejected by the best critics (see Box *ad loc.*). Probably בכור is a disguise of some synonym of עור, possibly בשר *flesh*; and מות may be a marginal note. K^{Or} gives בדוי *in sickness* for בדיו *his limbs*, perhaps a reminiscence of 6^{7}. We suggest יאכל בכפן בשרו *He devoureth through famine his own flesh*, which harmonizes well enough with the supposed parallel, v. 4^{a}. 𝔊 βρωθείησαν αὐτοῦ κλῶνες ποδῶν, | κατέδεται τὰ ὡραῖα αὐτοῦ θάνατος = יאכַל שַׁפִּרוֹ מָוֶת רגליו :יֵאָכְלוּ בַדֵּי רַגְלָיו. בַדֵּי is rendered *twigs* or *shoots* (Ez 17^{6}), and רגליו is evidently due to the translator's eye having wandered back to the end of v. 11 In the second stichus 𝔊 omits the repeated בדיו, and gives τὰ ὡραῖα αὐτοῦ, *his beauties*, for בכור. Perhaps the translator misread בשרו *his flesh* as Aram. שפרו (i. e. שַׁפִּיר = ὡραῖα; of leaves, Dan 4^{9}).

v. 14. [illegible]
[illegible]

For 𝔐 מבטחו *his confidence* read מיתריו *his cords*, Je 10²⁰, or חבליו, *id.*, Is 33²⁰, of course with plur. ינתקו. (𝔊 ἴασις = מַרְפֵּא *healing*. In st. ii for 𝔐 תצעדהו I have substituted תצורהו, cf. 10¹⁶. A similar statement occurs 27²⁰ ותשינהו כמים בלהות *And Terrors overtake him like a flood.* Perhaps, indeed, this is the true reading here (כמים = במלך).

At all events, כמלך *like a king* (𝔙 quasi rex) is more probable than 𝔐's למלך: cf. 15²⁴. One is reluctant to sacrifice a phrase which has passed into general literature; but מלך בלהות *the King of Terrors* (= Death personified), however familiar to the modern ear, is isolated in Hebrew, although בלהות occurs five times in our book ; and besides, the entire statement of 𝔐 *It makes him march to the King of Terrors*, whether 'It' be a vague reference to 'an unseen Power' (Di al.) or 'Destiny' (Buhl), or to Eyob's disease, which is assumed to be leprosy (Duhm), is a strange way of saying *It* (the 'Firstborn of Death' = the most malignant of maladies) *kills him*. Moreover, those who interpret thus are obliged to cancel 14ᵃ as a gloss possibly on 15ᵃ. 𝔙 gives Et calcet super eum, quasi rex, Interitus! *And let Ruin trample upon him, like a King!* pointing וְיִצְעָדֵהוּ and app. reading כמלך. The figure is that of a conqueror setting his foot on his enemy; a well-known subject of Assyrian sculpture. The curious version of 𝔊 σχοίη δὲ αὐτὸν ἀνάγκη αἰτίᾳ βασιλικῇ = (!) וְתֵצֶר לוֹ בְּעֶצֶב(הַ)מֶּלֶךְ (v. 7 Ju 10⁹; see 15²⁴ צר = ἀνάγκη, and Dan 6⁵,⁶ for Aram. עלה = αἰτία) shows that 𝔊 read the verb without ע and confused ד with ר, as often. Cf. La 4¹⁸, where 𝔐 has צדו instead of צרו. The rest of 𝔊's text is plainly a distortion of כמלך בלהות. (A comparison of 10¹⁶ 19²² suggests the possibility that למלך originated in כמו לבי or כלביא(א) *like a lioness*. Indeed the כשאל תצודני of 10¹⁶ favours something similar here; as ם and ש, i.e. ם and ש, are liable to confusion, and מחל might have become מלך by way of correction.)

v. 15. *The Vampire* (Is 34¹⁴) *haunteth his tent;*
    Brimstone is sprinkled (leg. 'תזר) *upon his habitation*
(5³,²⁴ 8⁶ Is 34⁹,¹⁸). 'The Vampire', Heb. לילית as I conjectured from the ἐν νυκτὶ αὐτοῦ (= בלילו) of 𝔊 many years ago. 𝔐 מִבְּלִי־לוֹ is really impossible as the subject of תשכון ; and is, besides, very prosaic, whether translated *something of that which is not his, what is naught of his* (Hitz OL)—such a perfectly problematical and indefinite reference to the new denizen of Eyob's dwelling being wholly unparalleled— or *It* (terror) *shall dwell in his tent, so that it is no more his* (Ges). The language of the verse is obviously coloured by reminiscence of Is 34 (נפרית Is 34⁹; נוה Is 34¹³; לילית Is 34¹⁴). In accordance with his theory that the whole passage, vv. 13–15, contains a brutally direct reference to Eyob's malady, Duhm reads בליעל, which he takes to mean *incurableness* ('wörtlich : das Nichtaufkommen' = not getting well), and explains as the malignant kind of house-leprosy, which made a house uninhabitable (L⁶ 14⁴⁴). But

our passage speaks of an אהל, a *tent*, not a *house* (בית) of stone and plaster; and the meaning assumed for בליעל is very doubtful (see the note on 34¹⁸ *infra*). Omitting 13ᵃ and 14ᵃ as spurious for the reasons assigned, Duhm renders vv. 13–15 as follows :—

'There fretteth his limbs the Firstborn of Death
And maketh him walk to the King of Terror,
There dwelleth in his tent Incurableness,
Strewn upon his dwelling-place is brimstone.'

(𝔊 τὰ εὐπρεπῆ αὐτοῦ confuses נוה *abode* with נאוה *comely*; cf. Je 6².) But the following verses show that Bildad is harping on the fate of the wicked in general, not the affliction of Eyob in particular.

vv. 16–17.   *Beneath—his roots dry up*, (Am 2⁹.)
             And above—his branches wither. (14² 24²⁴ 14⁹ 29¹⁹.)
             His memory perisheth from the land,
             And he hath no name in the street.

His branches wither. 𝔊 ἐπιπεσεῖται θερισμὸς αὐτοῦ = יפל קצירו (מ confused with פ as often). *in the streets* or *in* (over) *the open country*; reading the plur. חוצות 5¹⁰ Pr 8²⁰. But Pr 24²⁷ בחוץ ‖ with בשדה.

v. 18.   *God thrusteth him out of light into darkness*,
           And maketh him flee out of the world. (20⁸.)

There might seem to be no need to alter the indefinite plur. of the two verbs, as is done by Du Ki following the Kethb. If we do so, we must suppose the Subject of the verbs to be God, not men. And this perhaps agrees better with the matter of the verse; cf. 19⁸ 30²⁶, and with st. ii especially (Gn 4¹²,¹⁴). 𝔊 has the sing. (ἀπώσειεν cf. 2 K 4²⁷) in st. i It omits st ii. 𝔙 gives sing. in both; 𝔗𝔖 plur. in both. (Since st. ii is metr. short, אלוה *God*, the Subj. of both stt, might be restored at the end after יְנִדֻּהוּ.)

v. 19.   *Nor chit nor child hath he among his people*,
           And there is no survivor in his place of sojourn. (Ps 55¹⁶.)

נין ... ונכד, an alliterative phrase, used in traditional formulas, e.g. the oath of friendship, Gn 21²³, and the Divine ban, Is 14²² (שם וּשְׁאָר נִין וָנֶכֶד). We might imitate with *son or scion, offshoot or offspring* (Var. Bibl.), *chick or child* Cf. also our *kith and kin*. If √ נון means *propagate, increase*, of offspring (Ps 72¹⁷), נין may very well be represented by our 'chit', an old word for *shoot, sprout, child*. Cf. also the Sumerian NUNU, 'sprout', 'offspring', 'child' (*bâbu ; lipu*), CT xii 19b. 𝔊 οὐκ ἔσται ἐπίγνωστος ἐν λαῷ αὐτοῦ, app. misreading נכר ...בין for נכד ...נין (see 𝔊 Pr 14⁶ ἐπιγνώσεται = הָבִין: La 4⁸ ἐπεγνώσθησαν = וְנִכְרוּ). For st. ii 𝔊 gives: οὐδὲ σεσωσμένος ἐν τῇ ὑπ' οὐρανοὺ ὁ οἶκος αὐτοῦ. ἡ ὑπ' οὐρανόν = ארץ *the land*, in v. 4, and ἐν τῇ ὑπ' οὐρανόν =. בכל־הארץ in 42 . 𝔊 therefore seems to have read בְּאֶרֶץ מְגוּרָיו *in the land of his sojournings* (Gn 17⁸ 28⁴ &c.), which looks as if it might be right. (שָׂרִיד = σεσωσμένος, Jos 8²².)

v. 20. *At his Day* (𝕲 *At him*) *his juniors are appalled,*
And his elders horror seizeth.

At his Day; the day of his doom or retribution. (𝕲 may perhaps be right with ἐπ' αὐτῷ = עָלֵימוֹ = עָלָיו as I conjectured before looking at 𝕲. Cf. 17⁸.) נָשַׁמּוּ *were appalled* or *confounded*, is doubtless correct; see 17⁸, to which this passage evidently refers. 𝕲 ἐστέναξαν, app. pointing נָשְׁמוּ *panted*.

His juniors or those who come after; lit. *after ones*: cf. 19²⁵? Ec 1¹¹ 4¹⁶. 𝕲 ἔσχατοι, *the last* or *latest* generation. 𝔙 In die eius stupebunt novissimi, et primos invadet horror. 𝔐 קַדְמֹנִים *former ones*; i.e. Eyob's elders; the previous generation. Cf. 1 Sa 24¹⁴. Eyob is not yet reckoned as an old man himself. The theory of his friends involved the idea of premature death for the wicked. Eliphaz at least was his senior. 𝕲 recte πρώτους δὲ ἔσχεν θαῦμα (rg. אָחַז Sing.; so 𝔙 *prob.* 𝔖 𝔗; cf. Ex 15¹⁵ יֹאחֲזֵמוֹ רַעַד). Ewald suggested that אַחֲרֹנִים and קַדְמֹנִים meant *western* and *eastern* people. So Duhm: 'die im Westen ... die im Osten.' But there seems no reason why eastern and western folk should be specified rather than northerners and southerners, and the Heb. terms are not so used elsewhere.

v. 21. '*Surely this was the abode of a wrongdoer,*
And this the place of one that knew not El!'

The reflection or exclamation of all who gaze upon the signal desolation of the evildoer's ruined homestead. 𝔗 introduces the verse with *And they will say*. We might, however, also render the words as expressing the conclusion of Bildad himself: *Surely* (or *Only*) *such are the dwellings of the unjust; And such is the place of the godless.*

Chapter 19. *But Eyob answered as follows:*
How long will ye weary my soul,
And crush me with mere words?
Ten times over ye insult me;
And are not ashamed of giving me pain (or *wronging me*).

v. 2. *Weary me.* So 𝕲 ἔγκοπον ποιήσετε = תּוֹגִיעוּ; Is 43²³; cf. Ec 1⁸. 𝔐 תּוֹגְיוּן *make me to sorrow* (Is 51²³ Ec 1¹² 3³²·³³) seems less appropriate here, and is not found with an independent object elsewhere, nor at all in Job. The √יגע occurs 10³ 20¹⁸ 39¹¹·¹⁶. In st. ii καθαιρεῖτε, *ye pull down* or *destroy* (= הָרַס), is merely an inexact rendering and hardly implies a different reading. The stichus seems too short. בְּלִי־דַעַת *without knowledge* may have been omitted after בְמִלִּים (which בְּלִי resembles).

v. 3. 𝔐 זֶה עֶשֶׂר פְּעָמִים תַּכְלִימוּנִי has four stresses and is metrically redundant, unless we suppose a Crasis of the first two words and pronounce *zèser* for *zĕ 'ĕser*. 𝔊 γνῶτε μόνον ὅτι ὁ κύριος ἐποίησέν με οὕτως apparently makes matters worse; but really it only represents זה עשׂה עמי *this He did with me*; an evident corruption of זה עשׂר פעמי 'עמי *these ten times*. (The γνῶτε μόνον ὅτι ὁ κύριος is due to the scribe's eye having wandered to v. 6.) For the doubtful Heb. תהכרו לי (3 codd. תחברו; 4 codd. Kennicott בי pro לי) 𝔊 gives ἐπίκεισθέ μοι, *ye press upon me*, i.e. either with entreaty or attack (Hdt 5 104; ib. 81). In 21²⁷ ἐπίκεισθέ μοι = עָלַי תַּחְמֹסוּ *ye are hard upon me* or *do me wrong*; and such a sense would suit the present passage. Olshausen's conjecture תְּחָרְפוּ לִי *taunt me* gives a good parallel; but the constr. is doubtful (see 27⁶). Adopting the reading of 3 codd. תחברו we might (with Ewald, Duhm, al.) compare Ar. خَبَرَ *he wronged* (him), *behaved injuriously towards* (him), or *with bad fellowship impugned his character*, &c. (Lane). 𝔊 ܡܟܐܒܝܢ ܐܢܬܘܢ *ye make me sad, grieve me*, suggests an Aramaism = תַכְרוּ Hiph of כרה = כְרָא. Possibly also תהכרו is an error of pronunciation (dictation?) for תעכרו *trouble me*

v. 4. *But even had I in sooth gone astray* (really erred), *With myself would my error abide.*

So 𝔊𝔙. Read וְאִם or rather וְאַף אִם (or וְאַף אָנֹכִי וְאִם metr. grat.) instead of 𝔐's וְאַף. Cf. OL, which renders 𝔐 *And even indeed* (if) *I have erred* ... 𝔊 ναὶ δή = 𝔐. Its version is Ναὶ δὴ ἐπ' ἀληθείας ἐγὼ ἐπλανήθην, Παρ' ἐμοὶ δὲ αὐλίζεται πλάνος, *Yea, in truth, I did err, And with me lodgeth error*; to which it adds the explanatory distich Λαλῆσαι ῥήματα ἃ οὐκ ἔδει, Τὰ δὲ ῥήματά μου πλανᾶται καὶ οὐκ ἐπὶ καιροῦ, *by speaking words which one ought not, And my words err and* (are) *not in season*. This is probably an old gloss which 𝔊 found in its Heb. text.

לֵאמֹר דָּבָר לֹא יִסָּכֵן
וּמִלַּי תָעוּ וְאֵין־בָּעֵת׃

Cf. 15⁸ Pr 15²³. As v. 4 appeared to contain an admission of guilt on the part of Eyob, and thus to be altogether inconsistent with his attitude throughout the poem, this gloss was added to put a different construction upon his words

v 5. 𝔐 אם אמנם can hardly be right. אמנם is repeated from v. 4. 𝔊 does not repeat ἐπ' ἀληθείας, and seems to have read וְאִם (ἔα δὲ ὅτι ἐπ' ἐμοὶ μεγαλύνεσθε). As it gives no good sense to connect the verse immediately with the next (so AV, RV), we emend וְאַתֶּם *But ye* (emphatic Pron.), or perhaps rather וְאוּלָם *But*, which occurs at least ten times in the book:

But ye deal arrogantly with me (take the high hand with me), (Ez 35¹³.)
And make my misery (reproachful state) *proof against me.*

Cf. 𝔙 At vos contra me erigimini Et arguitis me opprobriis meis.

In st. ii 𝔊 ἐνάλλεσθε δέ μοι ὀνείδει, *And ye leap* (or *rush*) *on me with reproach*; as if reading וְתִכְרוּ עָלַי בְּחֶרְפָּה (see 6¹⁷ ἐνάλλομαι = כרה על). 𝔐 is preferable. חרפתי *my reproach* = that with which I am reproached, viz. my ruin, which is regarded as retributive of secret sin, and therefore made a matter of reproach instead of sympathy.

vv. 4–5. *But even if I really have erred* (אם exc. inter אף et אמנם), *Mine error abideth with myself* (i. e. it does not affect you). *But you* (leg. ואתם: 𝔙 At vos) *against me talk big, And urge against me my reproach* (as though by sin I had caused my own misery). Duhm renders as follows: 'And have I then really erred, With me must error abide? Or will ye against me deal arrogantly (*gegen mich grossthun*) And against me argue with abuse?' He reads מְשׁוּגָה at the end of v. 4 (cf. 𝔊), and then ואם עלי תגדילו, which is barely adequate for the rhythm, with בְּחֶרְפָּה at the end of the verse, after 𝔊. Besides, such a version would require the readings ואתי... והאף in v. 4 and ואם v. 5.

v. 6. *Know then that it is Eloah who hath bent me,*
  And hath closed his net in upon me! (2 K 6¹⁴ La 3⁵ OL.)

𝔊 ὁ ταράξας (με) = עותני, as in 8³ 34¹² La 3⁹. Instead of מצודו הקיף 𝔊 read מצורו הקים *hath raised his rampart* or *siegework* (Zc 9³ Pr 12¹²). ὀχύρωμα δὲ αὐτοῦ ἐπ' ἐμὲ ὕψωσεν. My ruin is not self-caused, but a direct (and arbitrary) infliction of God, against whose omnipotence protest is unavailing. Cf. v. 21.

v. 7. *Lo, I cry 'Wrong!', and am not answered;*
  I shriek for help, but there is no justice!

𝔊's variations, though incorrect, are critically instructive. ἰδοὺ γελῶ ὀνείδει καὶ οὐ λαλήσω, *Lo, I laugh at reproach and will not speak.* γελῶ = אצחק pro אצעק; a confusion of sound (not form) apparently between ע and ח. (This so far favours עכר for חכר in v. 2; see note *ad loc.*). ὀνείδει is prob. due to the scribe's eye having wandered to the end of v. 5. λαλήσω implies only a difference of pointing: אֶעֱנֶה for אֶעָנֶה.

vv. 8–9. *My way he hath walled up, so that I cannot pass;* (La 3⁹.)
  And on my paths he setteth darkness.

In st. ii 𝔊 ἐπὶ πρόσωπόν μου = על פני *on my face.* (Variant text? But 𝔊ᴬ ἀτραπούς.)

  He hath stripped me of my glory, (22⁸.)
  And removed the circlet of my head. (La 5¹⁶.)

v. 10. *He demolished me all round, and I am gone;*
  And he (hath) pulled up my hope like a tree.

𝔐 יתצני. Read ויתצני, with Waw Conversive. The ו fell out after י. Cf. 𝔊 διέσπασέν (א᾿⁻ᴬ δέ) με.

v. 11   *And his anger burned against me,*   (c עָל ; usu. c בְּ.)
           And he reckoned me as a foe.

In st. i וַיַּחַר is merely a scribal error for the common וַיִּחַר: 𝔙 𝔊. In st. ii 𝔐 כְּצָרָיו *as his foes.* 𝔊𝔖 כְּצָר, which is best after לֹ. So Du. 𝔙 כְּצָרוֹ, *quasi hostem suum, as his foe.*

v. 12 is an interpolation, or intrusion from marg.

   Together come his troops,
   And have cast up their way (approach) *against me,*
   And have encamped around my tent.

A line of the tetrastich is missing. 𝔊, reading וְיָסֹלּוּ for וַיָּסֹלּוּ (Is 57¹⁴) and apparently omitting the strange לְאָהֳלִי (would forces of any kind lay regular siege to a 'tent'?), presents a distich:

   ὁμοθυμαδὸν δὲ ἦλθον τὰ πειρατήρια αὐτοῦ ἐπ' ἐμοί,
   ταῖς ὁδοῖς μου ἐκύκλωσαν ἐγκάθετοι.
   ויחד באו גדודיו עלי
   ויסבו דרכי בארב:

   And together came his troops against me,
   And beset my ways with an ambush (31⁹).

Better though this may be, it still suggests an excrescence which has grown out of the expression כְּצָר *like an enemy,* as if צָר *foe* (from צרר) meant צָר *besieger* (from צור). 𝔊 has πειρατήριον for גְּדוּד in Gn 49¹⁹ (but πειρατής 25³) and for צָבָא, 7¹ 10¹⁷. Here it uses ἐγκάθετος, *suborned,* as equivalent to ἐγκαθημένος, *lying in ambush* (אֹרֵב). So also 31⁹; cf. Ps 9³⁰ 𝔊.

v. 13. *My fellow-tribesmen he hath put far away from me.* הִרְחִיק is so used, Ps 88⁹·¹⁹, and is trans. in the three other places where it occurs in our book (11¹⁴ 13²¹ 22²³). So 𝔙. Cod. K³⁰ 𝔊'A∑𝔖 connect with the following וְ and read הִרְחִיקוּ intrans., as in Gn 44⁴. *My f. have gone far away from me.* (So Du Ki al.) The second stichus is doubtful. 𝔐 וְיֹדְעַי אַךְ־זָרוּ מִמֶּנִּי is usually rendered *And my acquaintance are wholly estranged from me.* But יֹדְעַי (Ps 87⁴) is unlikely, if only because of מְיֻדָּעַי in the next verse; and אַךְ־זָרוּ is a suspicious collocation, if only because of its resemblance to אַכְזָר (30²¹), *cruel, fierce* (41²), אַכְזָרִי, *id.* Indecl. (Je 30¹⁴ 50⁴² Pr 12¹⁰ c plur. subj.). Read perhaps וְרֵעַי אַכְזָרִי לִי *And my friends are cruel to me;* or נִכְזְבוּ לִי *have proven false to me* (cf. 41¹). Possibly, however, זָרוּ = סָרוּ; *And my friends have wholly departed from me.* The מִמֶּנִּי seems to belong to the next verse, 14, the first stichus of which is too short in 𝔐: מִמֶּנִּי חָדְלוּ קְרוֹבָי *My neighbours have left me to myself* (cf. 7¹⁶ᵇ), *And my acquaintance have forgotten me.* 𝔊 has a double version of v. 13: ἔγνωσάν με ἀλλότριοί ἦ ἐμέ · יָדְעוּ זָרִים סְמָנִי They regar[d] [me as st]ran[gers], whi[c]h apa[rt] from the c[o]ntusions of

ו and י, differs from the letters of 𝔐 only in omitting אך; and φίλοι δέ μου ἀνελεήμονες γεγόνασιν = (לְ)אַכְזָר לִי (הָיוּ) וְרֵעַי (2^{11} 6^{27} v. 21; 30^{21}; Pr 5^9 12^{10}), or ורעי אכזרי לי, which may be the authentic reading. (V. 14^b prob. supplies the correct reading of Ps 88^{19b}, viz.: כְּיָדַע שְׁכֵחָנִי *my acquaintance have forgotten me*. The final ני run together was misread מ, and then the letters rearranged into מחשך.)

v. 14 is too short in both members. With חדלו *have ceased*, ממני *from me* is certainly required; and if not taken from v. 13, may be repeated after חדלו. In st. ii כלם *all of them* may be inserted: *And my acquaintance have all forgotten me.*

v. 15. St. i is much overloaded in 𝔐. 𝔊 presents a stichus of normal length: γείτονες οἰκίας θεράπαιναί τε μου = שכני ביתי ואמהתי (γείτων, *neighbour* = שָׁכֵן, 26^8; שָׁכֵן, שְׁכֵנָה, Ex 3^{22}, מִשְׁכַּנְתָּהּ וּמִגָּרַת בֵּיתָהּ *fr. her neighbour and the guest of her house*: שֹׁכְנֵי *dwellers* may have been a variant of גָּרֵי *guests* in this passage) This omits לְזָר תַּחְשְׁבֵנִי, which might conceivably be a phrase based on vv. 11^b, 13^b, and introduced here to get rid of the anacoluthon: *The dwellers (sojourners) in my house and my bondmaids— A stranger am I become in their eyes* (= 𝔊's ἀλλογενής ἤμην or ἐγενόμην ἐναντίων αὐτῶν). But the association of guests with bondmaids seems odd; and זר and נכרי are parallel (cf. Ps 69^9 Is 28^{21}). Upon the whole, therefore, it may be better to divide vv. 14, 15 differently, making גָּרֵי בֵיתִי the close of v. 14 instead of the beginning of v. 15:

My neighbours (Ps 38^{12}) *and mine acquaintance have ceased;*
The guests of my house have forgotten me.

Duhm ingeniously suggests מֹדְעַי for וּמְיֻדָּעַי, thus getting the sense *My neighbours have ceased from knowing me*; an excellent parallel to st. ii. But דַּע is not so used elsewhere (in $32^{6.10.17}$ 36^3 it means *opinion*, and the plur. דֵּעִים is *knowledge*, 37^{16}, Elihu-speeches); while דֵּעָה (Is 11^9) and דַּעַת Je 22^{16}) are both found with a personal object.

My bondmaids reckon me (take me for) *a stranger,*
A foreigner am I become in their eyes.

If we adopt this arrangement of the text, we must also give the preference to the reading of v. 13^b which finds support in 𝔊¹: וידעי זרו ממני *and they who knew me have turned away from me* (זרו = סרו; ? Aramaism). This is 𝔐, merely omitting אך, with 𝔊.

v. 16.   *My slave I called, but he would not answer;*
           With my mouth I must needs beseech him.

v. 17. *My breath is repulsive to my wife* (*foul, loathly, hateful*: contrast Ct 7^9). Cf. the old Sumerio-Babylonian Family-law V: *Šumma aššatu mussu izîr-ma ul mutî atta iqtabi, ana nâru inaddušu*, 'If a wife hate her husband and say, Thou art not my husband, they shall cast her into the river.' See Haupt, SFG: Hommel SL, p. 110. (Sum. ĜUL =

limnu, bi'šu, zíru, 'bad', 'hostile', 'foul', 'hateful'.) 𝔊 omits רוּחִי זָרָה, connecting v. 16 ᵇ with לאשתי thus: στόμα δέ μου ἐδέετο, καὶ ἱκέτευον τὴν γυναῖκά μου, *but my mouth was begging, and I was supplicating my wife* = בעה פי ואתחנן לאשתי; cf. Dan 6¹² בָּעֵה וּמִתְחַנַּן.

I am offensive to my homeborn slaves.

𝔐 חַנּוֹתִי *I stink*; √ חנן = Arab. خَنّ x. *foetorem emisit* (puteus); so Freytag, but Lane does not give this meaning, which is accepted by OL, after Ew De Di, but *to snuffle*, and to have خُنَان *a kind of disease of the nose*. OL compares also Syr. ܚܰܢܺܝܢܳܐ ḥannīnā, *rancid*. The existence of a √ḤAN, *smell, stink*, is established by the Heb. word צַחֲנָה *stench*, Jo 2²⁰ (hence Du would read צָחַנְתִּי in the present passage), which implies a √צחן, i.e. צ־חן = ס־חן or ש־חן *to make or emit odour*; and this ḤAN (KHAN) is probably a weakened form of the primitive Asiatic root KAN(GAN), which we seem to see in the Sumerian GIN, *sweet, pleasant* (*tâbu*; cf. קנה הטוב Je 6²⁰), KU(N), *sweet*, and in the Chinese kan, kam, keñ kö, *sweet*, which Edkins regarded as the source of hong, Jap. kyō, kom, *incense, sweet-smelling* (*Rad.* 186). We might read וְצָחַנְתִּי *and my stink* (cf. Jo 2²⁰).

In st. i perhaps רֵיחִי *my smell* or odour > *my breath* : cf. Gn 27²⁷ Ct 7⁹. In st. ii 𝔐 בני בטני might perhaps mean *sons of my mother*: cf. 3¹⁰ דלתי בטני *doors of my womb* = doors of the womb that bare me. In Mi 6⁷, however, we have the expression פרי בטני *fruit of my body* (*belly*) as parallel to בכורי *my firstborn*; so that we might perhaps prefer to render *the sons of my body*. The Prologue tells of the sudden death of Eyob's sons, i.e. the sons of his principal wife; but 'the sons of the concubines' or secondary wives (cf. Gn 25⁶) might be intended, although these are not otherwise mentioned Eyob still had אמהות (Gn 20¹⁷ 21¹⁰ ¹² 30³ al.). It is thus that 𝔊 understands the phrase: προσεκαλούμην δὲ κολακεύων υἱοὺς παλλακίδων μου, *but I would entreat with flatteries sons of my concubines* = וְחִלִּיתִי פְּנֵי בְנֵי בְטָנִי: cf. 11¹⁹ ᵇ. In 20¹⁵ 𝔊 reads ביתי for בטני; and it seems possible that בני ביתי *the sons of my house* (cf. ילידי ביתו Gn 14¹⁴) was the original reading here.

v. 18. *Even boys* (עוילים; so 21¹¹) *despise me;*
    Would I rise, they speak against me (Ps 50²⁰).

(Or *Let me but rise* (stir, move), *and they pass remarks on me*.)

אקומה. *if I rise up*, i.e. set about something; cf. Ps 139². Others think he refers to his struggles to rise from his seat on the ash-heap. Cf. also 2 K 2²³ for the mockery of the young lads. (Du, who explains 'if he goes out, or goes about'.) 𝔊 οἱ δὲ εἰς τὸν αἰῶνα = להם לעולם pro (ו)גם עוילים! The same queer blunder appears again, 21¹¹. The translator did not know the rare word עויל. He renders s.. ii οταν ἀναστῶ κατ' ἐμοῦ λαλοῦσιν an excellent translation

v. 19. *All the men of my circle* (my intimates) *abhor me* (cf. Ps 88⁸),
    And they whom I loved have turned against me.

For כָּל־מְתֵי סוֹדִי *all the men of my counsel* or *converse*, 𝔊 has οἱ ἰδόντες με, *they who saw me* (𝔊ᴬ ἴδοτες = εἰδότες, *knew me*) = (?) כל־מחודעי (Gn 45¹).

v. 20. 𝔐 st. i is too long for the metre. Either בעורי or בבשרי belongs to st. ii (cf. 7⁵ 18¹²); we must therefore omit one of them here. For the language, cf. Ps 102⁶ (דָּבְקָה עַצְמִי לִבְשָׂרִי) לְ for בְּ, as in 29¹⁰). An emaciated person is said to be 'nothing but skin and bone'. The key to st. ii might perhaps be 13¹⁴ אשא בשרי בשני *I carry my flesh in my teeth*; said of running a great risk and escaping with difficulty (cf. the parallel stichus: *And I put my life in my hand* = 1 Sa 28²¹). We might then read ואתמל בבשרי בשני *And I have escaped with my flesh in my teeth*: i.e. like some animal impeded in its flight by carrying off its young in that way. St. i 𝔊: ἐν δέρματί μου ἐσάπησαν αἱ σάρκες μου = בְּעוֹרִי רָקְבָה בְשָׂרִי *In my skin rotted my flesh*, which Du says is 'clearly the correct text' (could one say בְּעוֹרִי בְשָׂרִי רָקְבָה, as Du writes?). For st. ii 𝔊 gives τὰ δὲ ὀστᾶ μου ἐν ὀδοῦσιν ἔχεται = ועצמ(ו)תי תֶּאֱחוֹנָה בשני; (For ἔχω = אחז, vid. 17⁹ 18²¹ 21⁶ 30¹⁶.) 𝔊 thus om. עור². Bickell, Du, accordingly read וַיִּתְמַלְּטוּ שִׁנַּי *And my teeth have slipped away* (or *out*: cf. 41¹¹); which is metrically too short, while שנים is strictly feminine. Possibly we should restore ותתמלטנה מבשרי שני *And my teeth have slipped forth from my flesh*; but obviously the term required is *gums*, not *flesh* (see OL s.v. מלט). (𝔊ᴬ for ὀδοῦσιν gives ὀδύναις = בעני (30¹⁶ 𝔊) for בשני; an interesting variant, exhibiting the common confusion of ע with שׁ.)

v. 21. *Pity me, you my friends,* (om. חנני² metr. gr.)
    For the Hand of Eloah hath stricken me! (1¹¹ Is 53⁴.)

𝔊 ἡ ἁψαμένη μού ἐστιν = לִנְגֹעָה (points only). κυρίου = יהוה pro אלוה, ut alibi ap. 𝔊.

v. 22.   Lit. *Why like El will ye pursue me,*
    And are not sated of my flesh?

(𝔊 again pl. ἀπὸ σαρκῶν μου. So also 31³¹.) The suggestion באל *like a hart* instead of כאל *like El* is plausible, but more obvious and commonplace. Besides, צוד would be more natural of hunting a hart (10¹⁶). According to 𝔐, Eyob accuses his friends of siding with his Divine Persecutor. 𝔊 διὰ τί με διώκετε ὥσπερ καὶ ὁ Κύριος. Cf. 13²⁸. 'For him (leg. אֹתוֹ) whom Thou hast smitten they pursue' (Ps 69²⁶; a psalm which contains other echoes of this ch.) St. ii *of my flesh*; i.e. with portions of it. Cf. 31³¹. *To eat pieces* of a man is an ancient and common Semitic metaphor for slander and calumny. The Assyrian word-lists prove that it was originally Sumerian. Thus we find EME-KU.KU (lit. *linguu-cat-cat* = 'One who devours with the tongue'), explained by the Assyrian *âkil qarṣi*, lit. 'eater of pieces', i.e. slanderer

(Br. 840); and the phrase *akâlu qarṣi*, 'to eat the pieces' of any one, 'to slander', is common in all periods of Assyrian. It is also found in Aramaic, both old (Inscrr.) and new (Dan 3⁸ 6²⁵); while in Arabic they say *'akala laḥmahu*, 'he eat his flesh', in the same sense. (Cf. also Ps 27²; where the phrase לאכל את בשרי *to eat my flesh* is used in much the same sense of false accusation.)

vv. 23-24. Since his persistent affirmation of a clear conscience and his arraignment of what he cannot but regard as unjust dealing on the part of God (if the traditional doctrine that all human suffering is penal be true), fall upon deaf ears and unsympathetic hearts, Eyob is fain to appeal to posterity:

> *O that my sayings might be written,—*
> *That my words might be inscribed in a roll,—*
> *That with stylus of iron and (with) lead*
> *They might be graven in rock for ever!*

In st. *a* I have substituted אֲמָרַי *my words* for אֵפוֹ וּ (אמר plur. 22²² 32¹⁴ 6¹⁰ ²⁵·²⁶ 8² 23¹² 33³ אֲמָרֵי 32¹² אמריו 34³⁷). 𝔐 is too long for the metre. The second מי יתן seems superfluous; I have therefore read וּמֵלִי בַסֵּפֶר יָחָקוּ in st *b*. If Duhm's בספרו *in his roll* be right, why not also בצורו *in his rock* in st. *d*? (For the construction מי יתן c Imperf. without Waw, see 6⁸ 14¹³.) In st. *c* leg. וּבְעֹפֶרֶת *and with lead* (i.e. with leaded lettering, for greater permanence), which gives a better-balanced rhythm. Duhm thinks it strange that Eyob should express so emphatic a wish that his words should be written in a book, and asks, Why should not Eyob write them down himself? Therefore, he concludes, that Eyob's wish is for a record in God's book of remembrance. The answer to Duhm's question, however, would seem to be that, although writing was freely practised in the patriarchal age to which the figure of Eyob belongs, it was confined, so far as we know, to an official class of scribes whose art and mystery it was, as is amply attested by the remains of Babylonian and Assyrian antiquity. Eyob was no more likely to write down his own compositions than a Bêdâwî poet of his own or any later age. And even if that were otherwise, Eyob's physical condition of extreme helplessness is conceived as precluding all possibility of such a thing.

𝔊 τίς γὰρ ἂν δῴη γραφῆναι τὰ ῥήματά μου (= 𝔐)
τεθῆναι δὲ αὐτὰ ἐν βιβλίῳ εἰς τὸν αἰῶνα (= וְיִתֵּן בַּסֵּפֶר לָעַד).

Cf. 29², τίς ἄν με θείη = מִי־יִתְּנֵנִי. The verb נתן is here taken by 𝔊 in the sense of *put* or *place*; a meaning which it bears in many other passages from Gn 1¹⁷ onwards. ויחקו is then omitted, perhaps as superfluous, if not also unintelligible; and the stichus is finished off with לָעַד = εἰς τὸν αἰῶνα, transferred hither from st. *d* (v. 24 *b*.) Thus it cannot be said with certainty that 𝔊 omits the second מי יתן (so Duhm and Kittel), but only that it understands and renders the verb נתן as it does in above eighty other passages of OT. Then, for v. 24, 𝔊ᴮ presents merely ἐν γραφίῳ σιδηρῷ καὶ μολίβῳ = st. *a*; but 𝔅ᵃᵇ ᴬ supply the other clause ἢ ἐν πέτραις ἐγλυφῆναι = בַּצּוּרִי יֵחָצְבוּן׃ . (𝔊 seems to give πέτραι plur. for צוּר, Is 2¹⁰, where, however, it perhaps read 'בצורי, cf. vv. 19, 21. So probably here.)

Theodotion's לְעֵד *for a witness*, instead of לָעַד *for ever*, is very attractive and may be right. At any rate, it correctly specifies the object of the desired record. Duhm calls it 'a not incorrect, but self-evident addition'. The same, surely, might be said of לָעַד. Eyob had said before, 16¹⁹, that his Witness was in heaven; but here he is longing for an eternal witness on earth.

vv. 25-27. It is generally recognized that this famous passage has suffered considerable corruption in the course of transmission. The ancient Versions diverge from the Hebrew text and from each other; and that text itself presents unmistakable evidence of those detrimental changes, many examples of which have already perplexed us in this and previous chapters of the book. Upon close scrutiny, however, one fact stands out clearly and conspicuously, which may prove to be a clue to the essential meaning of the passage, even if it should fail to enable us to restore the original text with anything more than a relative degree of satisfaction or certitude. Eyob affirms, with all the emphasis of solemn repetition, that he will eventually 'see God' (אחזה אלוה . . . ועיני ראו). The obvious implication is that this Vision of God will be the all-satisfying close of his prolonged and inexplicable sufferings. And Eyob does not hesitate to give his unfeeling friends, who have so long insulted his misery with groundless assumptions of his secret guilt, the stern and even savage warning, '*Fear ye the sword for yourselves!*' (v. 29); as though his own vindication was to involve Divine vengeance on their heartless and obstinate cruelty. *I shall see God! . . . My (own) eyes will behold Him! It is what I am waiting for with soul-consuming desire* (v. 27 *c*). The question at once suggests itself, did Eyob, *in fact* (i.e. in the development of his poetical history), ever 'see God'? In other words, is the *Deus ex machina* the culminating point and conclusion of the whole spirit-stirring drama? We know, of course, that it is. *Iahvah answered Eyob out of the storm-wind*—an immediate physical manifestation (38¹ 40⁶; cf. Ez 1⁴). We are left in no doubt about it by Eyob's own words (42⁵), which surely were not written without intentional reference to the present passage: *I had heard of Thee by hearsay; But now my own eye hath seen Thee!* (ועתה עיני ראתך; cf. ועיני ראו, v. 27 *b*). Eyob's prophecy, then, finds its fulfilment within the limits of the poem itself. He is not represented as looking forward to the establishment of his innocence after he had passed out of the body into the dim world of the dead ('after death, apart from the flesh': OL s. v. חזה); much less is he anticipating his own resurrection from the dead at the Last Day (so 𝔙). He simply declares his unalterable conviction that Iahvah, the God of righteous Retribution (אל נקמות Ps 94¹) will appear to right his lamentable wrongs in the present life (cf v. 29), before his disease has run its fatal course (16²²).

> Scio enim quod Redemptor meus vivit,
> Et in novissimo die de terra surrecturus sum;
> Et rursum circumdabor pelle mea,
> Et in carne mea videbo Deum meum.
> Quem visurus sum ego ipse,
> Et oculi mei conspecturi sunt, et non alius:
> Reposita est haec spes mea in sinu meo.

Thus does St. Jerome find in this passage a clear and precise statement of the faith of Christendom concerning the Resurrection of the Dead (cf. Joh 11²⁴). But what was his authority for the striking divergence of the second line from the Masoretic text? Did he possess a Hebrew codex written by some Pharisee (cf. Acts 23⁸) which actually gave it in the form וביום האחרון מעל עפר אקום ? Or did the Rabbi whom he consulted assure him that the line might be so emended? Or was the *First Pers.* of the verb here merely a guess of his own, based on the fact that the verbs of the following stichi are all in the *First Person* except the last? What is certain is that, with whatever written or oral assistance, the learned Father was working upon a Hebrew text not very different from 𝔐, and that he was by no means dependent upon 𝔊 or other antecedent versions. That he exercised a critical judgement upon the difficulties of his text is apparent from his rendering of the next distich (v. 26), which as it stands in 𝔐 cannot possibly be regarded as authentic: *Et rursum circumdabor pelle mea*,¹ 'And again shall I be encompassed with my skin' = עורי (ב)עורי נקפתי. Here instead of the baffling נקפו זאת he reads or corrects נִקַּפְתִּי, understanding the verb as Niphal Perfect (Prophetic) of נקף *to go round* (Is 29¹; Hiph. ch. 1⁵; 19⁶), although the Niphal of this verb has not been recognized elsewhere. It may be that St. Jerome's *rursum* is merely a loose rendering of אַחַר *afterwards*; but since עוד and עור are often indistinguishable in MSS, his rendering of the stichus may really preserve a conflate reading עוד עורי. In the remaining stichi his version agrees with 𝔐, except that in v. 26ᵇ he reads ובבשרי *et in carne mea*, instead of ומבשרי *et ex carne mea* (an important variation which supports our view of the general meaning of the passage), and in v. 27ᵇ he escapes the absurdity of locating the kidneys in the bosom by reading, as it would seem, בסלי *my hope* instead of כליתי *my kidneys*, and perhaps taking כלו *are consumed* as a defectively written כלוא *is confined, shut up*.

---

¹ Cf. Cic. *Univ.* 'Animum Deu) circum lelit corpor et vestivit extrinsecus'.

The Greek translator starts well, with an elegant paraphrase which reads almost like a reminiscence of the tragic tale of Prometheus:

οἶδα γὰρ ὅτι ἀέναός ἐστιν ὁ ἐκλύειν με μέλλων·
For I know that he that is to release me is eternal

(ἀέναοι, Aesch. *Suppl.* 554; τὸν ἐκλύσοντ' ἐμέ, Prom. Vinct. 800) = גאל . כי ידעתי (כי) גאלי חי is not so rendered elsewhere (ἀγχιστεύων, Le 25²⁵ f. Dt 19⁶ al.). 𝕲 פרקת here: cf. ופרקת = ἐκλύσῃς, Gn 27⁴⁰. חי is understood as *ever-living*, naturally enough. (Yet it is curious to observe that in Is 48¹² אחרן *the last* is rendered εἰς τὸν αἰῶνα = ἀέναος; for ואחרון is the next word in the Hebrew here, and 𝕲 apparently omits it.) The second stichus in 𝕲 runs 25 *b* and 26 *a* together thus: ἐπὶ γῆς ἀναστῆσαι τὸ δέρμα μου τὸ ἀναντλοῦν ταῦτα, *Upon earth may he raise up my skin which exhausteth or goeth through* (cf. Prom. Vinct. 375 ἀντλήσεις) *all this!* = על עפר יקים נקף עורי זאת (cf. Is 29¹). ('ז נקף) might be supposed to mean 'going the round of this' = completing this suffering. But possibly 𝕲 intended rather זאת נפק, an Aramaism = יוצא זאת *coming out of this*, reading נפק for נקפו.) This is no improvement on 𝔐, the text of which it really confirms, except in the apparent omission of אחרון (perhaps supposed to be covered by ὁ μέλλων) and ואחר. The next stichus is strangely represented by παρὰ γὰρ Κυρίου ταῦτά μοι συνετελέσθη, *For from the Lord all this was accomplished to me* = ומשרי כלו לי אלה instead of 𝔐's ומבשרי אחזה אלוה; which, again, is far from being an improvement. (Κύριος = שדי in eight other passages in Job.) כלו לי = μοι συνετελέσθη appears to come from the next verse. There can be little doubt that 𝔐 אחזה is right here. In the first two stichi of v. 27, 𝕲 had evidently a Hebrew text identical with 𝔐, although it has altogether missed its purport: ἃ ἐγὼ ἐμαυτῷ συνεπίσταμαι, ἃ ὁ ὀφθαλμός μου ἑόρακεν (𝕲ᴬ οἱ ὀφθ. μου ἑοράκασιν) καὶ οὐκ ἄλλος. For the third stichus 𝕲 gives: πάντα δέ μοι συντετέλεσται ἐν κόλπῳ = וכל כלו לי בחקי, instead of כלו כליתי בחקי; which does not help us at all, though it gets rid of the 'kidneys' in the bosom.

We may now submit a tentative reconstruction of the Hebrew:

כִּי אֲנִי יָדַעְתִּי גֹּאֲלִי
וְאַחַר עַל־עָפָר יָקוּם:
אַחַר בַּעֲדִי נְקָמוֹת אֵל
וּבִבְשָׂרִי אֶחֱזֶה אֱלוֹהַּ:
אֲשֻׁרֵנוּ וְלֹא אַחֵר (Is 42⁸)
וְעֵינַי יִרְאֻהוּ וְלֹא־זָר (Is 43¹²)
כָּלוּ כִלְיֹתַי בְּחֵבוֹתִי (3²¹)
[עַד־פִּי יָבֹא כִסְלִי:]

For I, I know my Avenger;
And at last He will rise up on earth;

I shall see, while I yet live, El's revenges, (Ps 58¹²)
And in my flesh I shall gaze on Eloah!
I shall behold Him and not Another,
And mine eyes will look on Him, and not a strange god!
My kidneys are wasted with my waiting
(*Until my hope shall come*).

v. 25. ואני ידעתי גאלי חי את *But I—I know my living Avenger* (Ho 2¹ al.) If the meaning were *I know* that *my go'el is alive*, we should expect כי after ידעתי, as in 9² ²⁸ 10¹³ 13¹⁸ al. Besides, the question of the *existence* of God is not raised in the book (as it might very well have been in connexion with the main problem). Both Eyob and his friends take it for granted throughout. חי, חיים, חיה are never predicated of God in Job (except in the common formula of the oath, 27²). Cf. 16¹⁹. The st. is also metr. too long (four stresses). The חי may be due to the חר of the following word. Otherwise, apart from the above considerations, we might read st. ii as follows: חי הוא ועל עפר יקום *He liveth and on earth will appear.* (For יקום cf. also 16⁸ Dt 19¹⁵, of a witness coming forward.) ואחר *and afterwards* or *by and by*, Ps 73²⁴. But את ואחרון (18²⁰; joined with גאל in Is 44⁶) may mean *And last of all, He will stand up* as a witness. *on earth*, על עפר; lit. *on* (*the*) *dust* = on the ground, as in 39¹⁴ (of the ostrich leaving her eggs on the bare ground), and 41²⁵ (*there is not on earth his like*, of the crocodile); Is 47¹ (*sit on the ground*). At present He is in high Heaven, 16¹⁹. The distich might also be read thus:

חי־הוא ועל־עפר יקום | ואני ידעתי גאלי
But I, I know mine Avenger; | He liveth and will rise up on earth!

v. 26. *And I shall see*; pointing וְאַחַר for את ואחר *And after*. The √ חור *to see* is attested by the Assyrian ḫâru, sehen, ansehen, anblicken, ersehen (HWB), a synonym of amâru, aṭû (2 R 35. 20, 21 ef; MA), as well as by the Aramaic (Syriac) ܚܙܐ *to see*. *in my lifetime*, lit. *in my continuance*; (בְ)עוּרִי for עורי, Ps 104³³. Perhaps simply עוֹרִי. *revenges*· 'The whirligig of Time brings his revenges' (Shakespeare). נקמות Ps 18⁴⁸ 94¹. Iahvah is אל נקמות *God of Requitals* or *Revenges*. For the sense, cf. also Ps 58¹²: חָזָה נָקָם *he hath seen vengeance*: Je 11²⁰ 51¹¹. וְאַחַר עוֹרִי נִקְּפוּ זֹאת את is usually rendered: *And after my skin, which they have struck off* (alluding to the ravages of his disease)—*this!* (so OL); that is, *this will happen!* But *after my skin* is an extraordinary expression to denote a point of time; and the pregnant use of זאת is both unparalleled and intrinsically improbable, although the Targum assumes it here: וּמִן בָּתַר דְאִתְפָח מַשְׁכִּי תְּהֵי דָא וּמִבִּסְרִי אֲחֲמֵי תוּב אֱלָהָא *And after my skin has been breathed into* (a reference to Ez 37⁹), *this will happen*; *And out of my flesh I will obtain* ... *God!* 𝔖 has the curious version ועל מטבכי הו

אתברך הלין ועל בסרי אן תחוא לאלהא עיני חזי נוהרא, בוליתי וג' *And against my skin these things have set themselves round about, and against my flesh. If mine eyes see God, they see light! For my reins are quite perished*, &c.; apparently reading ובעורי נקפו זאת ובבשרי וג', and taking נקף (like 𝔙) for נקף *to go round*. (A trace of the same thing may perhaps be recognized in 𝔊's παρὰ γὰρ Κυρίου ταῦτά μοι συνετελέσθη, since עורי might have been misread שדי, while συνετελέσθησαν = הקיפו in 𝔊 1⁵.) The proposed וְאַחַר עֵדִי נִקֵּף אָתִי *And Another as my Witness* (16¹⁹) *will raise himself with me* is dubious Heb. (וקף Ps 145¹⁴ 146⁸ only, of Iahvah lifting up the bowed or prostrate). A similar remark applies to וּמְשָׂהֲדִי: *And as my Testifier I shall see Eloah*.

v. 27. 𝔐 gives three stichi instead of four and, moreover, continues the context in ordinary prose style: אשר אני אחזה לי *Whom I shall gaze on for myself* ... Remembering Nu 24¹⁷, I long since conjectured אשרנו (20⁹) *I shall behold Him* for אשר אני *Whom I*; and אחזה לי, which looks like dittography from the preceding stichus, supplies material for ולא אחר *and not another* (cf. Is 42⁸), which provides a parallel to ולא זר (Is 43¹²), in the next stichus (where the Prophetic Perfect ראו may be right; cf. דרך in Nu l.c.). Thus the form of the distich, v. 27 *a b*, exactly reproduces that of Nu 24¹⁷ᵃ·ᵇ. The third stichus probably ended with בחבותי *through my waiting* (3²¹) corrupted in 𝔐 into בחקי, by loss of ת and confusion of בו with ק. Its fellow has disappeared altogether. Our כסלי (or כסלתי, 4⁶) may find some slight support in the *spes mea* of 𝔙 in the previous line.

v. 28 f. *If ye are saying, 'How shall we run him down,*
   And find the cause of the thing in him?'
   Be afraid for yourselves because of the sword!
   (Or, *Fear ye a Sword for yourselves!*)
   For Wrath will consume the unjust!

If ye are saying; among yourselves; laying your heads together to entrap me into an admission of guilt, in which you could recognize the 'root of the matter', the real cause of my calamities. Or else, *if ye are saying in your heart*, i.e. *thinking* (as Duhm takes it).

How? Heb. מה, which is so used Gn 44¹⁶. (Cf. 26² *How!*)

in him, Heb. בו. So about a hundred codd. and 𝔊 𝔗 𝔙, instead of the meaningless בי *in me* of the *Textus Receptus*.

How shall we run him down or *to earth*; lit. *pursue him?* 𝔊 has the instructive variant נדבר for נרדף: Τί ἐροῦμεν ἔναντι αὐτοῦ; = מה נדבר לו (13⁷: where לו = *for him*). Perhaps this is right, as it gives a good sense, and מה נרדף לו is rather strange: *If ye muse, What shall we say to him, That we may find in him the cause of the thing?*

v. 29. *Fear ye a Sword*; or *the Sword*. The Sword of Divine Justice is, of course, intended, which would avenge Eyob's wrongs upon his persecutors. Dt 32⁴¹ ⁴² Ju 7¹⁸ Is 34⁸ 66¹⁶. (𝔊 ἀπὸ ἐπικαλύμματος = מפני חפה, cf. Je 14³·⁴ ἐπεκάλυψαν = חפו. A curious error, due to illegibility of Heb. MS. Confusion of ב with פ, and *vice versa*, is very common; cf. v. 28.) *For wrath will consume the unjust* = כי חמה עולים תבער: see Is 42²⁵, where חמה *heat, hot anger*, and בער *to burn up* are similarly connected. 𝔐 כי חמה עונות חרב is ungrammatical and untranslatable, unless any one can find satisfaction in *For heat* (is) *sins of* (the) *sword*. 𝔊 θυμὸς γὰρ ἐπ' ἀνόμους ἐπελεύσεται, *For Wrath will come upon lawless ones* = תעבר כי חמה על עולי (ἐπέρχομαι = עבר 15¹⁹ Na 3¹⁹ al. More usually it represents בוא; e. g. 20²²). This תעבר may have been a misreading of תבער. For ἀνόμους, cf. ἄνομα = עולה 27⁴; τῶν παρανόμων = עול 27⁷. The verse ends with a third stichus, which is probably an interpolation: *In order that ye may know*—what? שדין K𝔊ᴬᴼˣ 𝔊 𝔚 *that* (there is) *a judgement*: Q שַׁדִּין, apparently the same. But שדין could hardly stand for שֵׁיֵשׁ דִּין (cf. Ps 58¹²); and if it could, ש = אשר is otherwise unknown to our book. שָׁרֵי is a probable correction (so Ew Di); and the original line may have been : למען ידעו שדי *That they* (𝔊) *may know Shaddai* (a marg. note). 𝔊ᴮ: καὶ τότε γνώσονται ποῦ ἔστιν αὐτῶν ἡ ὕλη = (ל) וְיֵדְעוּ אַיִן עֶצְם; but 𝔊ᴬ: καὶ τότε γν. ὅτι οὐδαμοῦ αὐτῶν ἡ ἰσχύς ἐστιν = (לָמוֹ) וְיֵדְעוּ אִין עֶצֶם (19⁷ 30²¹)—a difference of pointing. [In 29⁵ 𝔊 gives ὑλώδης, *woody, wooded*, where 𝔐 has שַׂדַּי *Shaddai*. But there 𝔐 בעוד שדי עמדי *While Shaddai was still with me* is obviously right, and 𝔊's ὅτε ἤμην ὑλώδης λίαν, *When I was exceedingly woody* (*substantial?*), a mere curiosity of interpretation. The passage, however, lends some support to the conjecture that ὕλη = שדי here. Perhaps αὐτῶν ἡ ὕλη = יערם, which might be a misreading of שדין; ש being broken up into י,ע, and ינ run together into ם.] It is natural to compare Ps 9²¹ יֵדְעוּ גוים אנוש המה : *Let the nations know they are* (but) *mortal men!*

Chapter 20.

v. 2. *Therefore*: לָכֵן: but 𝔊 לֹ(א)־כֵן *Not so*; but cf. st. ii *because of this*. For שעפים anxious *thoughts*, see note on 4¹³. *reply to me*: 13²² 33⁵·³² al. St. ii. *because of this*; scil. which thou hast just said. ואת (or אלה) must be restored to the text after the Prep. *they speak to me*: 19. ישיחו לי (cf. 12⁸ note) instead of the evidently corrupt חושי בי *my hasting in me*. Perhaps rather יש' בי *they muse* (or *complain*) *in me*. His indignant thoughts compel Zophar to speak again. 𝔊 'Not so did I suppose thou wouldst utter these contradictions; And you (!) have no better understanding than I.' (Illegible Heb. text.) But 𝔚 et mens in diversa rapitur = וּבְעֲבָר יָחוּשׁ לְבִי; and the occasional confusion of ם with ש (see 15²⁹) suggests יחום (יָחֹם) for יחוש, so that the st. might orig. have said *And with anger* (ובעברה) or *And within me* (ובקרבי) *my heart waxeth hot* (יחום לבי): Ps 39⁴. Others would read *And because of this my heart is stirred up* רחש לבי+ Ps 45·; but th... ...רחש... ...ou... not angry, emotion. On the whole, we may perhaps prefer the following version of the couplet:

Not so (𝔊) *do my thoughts respond to me;
But within me my heart waxeth hot.*

v. 3. A lit. translation of 𝔐 would be *The correction* or *chastisement of my reproach* or *ignominy* (i.e. *My shameful correction*; cf. Is 53^b) *I hear; And a spirit out of my understanding answereth me* (cf. v. 2). So 𝔊. St. i then refers to Eyob's scornful words and threats. But the Hebrew is strange. For כלמה (here only in Job) see Ps 44¹⁶ 69²⁰. Since st. ii continues the thought of v. 1, it seems probable that st. i. originally expressed something similar. We therefore suggest כליתי *my reins* instead of כלמתי (cf. Ps 16⁷ יסרוני כליותי *my reins corrected* or *instructed me*); a frequent parallel to לב *heart*, Ps 7¹⁰ al. Je 17¹⁰: *The monition of my reins* (my inmost thoughts and feelings) *I hear; And my intelligent spirit* (leg. רוּחַ מְבִינָה pro רוּחַ מִבִּינָתִי) *answereth me*. Cf. 𝔊 ἐκ τῆς συνέσεως = מִבִּינָה (a difference of points only). The ת of מבינתי really belongs to the next word, which should be תענני (not יענני as 𝔐), since רוח *spirit* is fem. (6⁴ 10¹² 17¹ 21⁴) in Job.—In the opening quatrain Zophar merely affirms that he speaks with all due deliberation, not offhand and without previous thought (cf. 11²).

v. 4. Reading הֲלֹא c 1 cod. (cf. 𝔊 μὴ ταῦτα ἔγνως κτλ.) instead of 𝔐 הזאת. St. ii. *from the placing of man on the earth*; viz. at his creation. To delete שים (Ki) would spoil both sense (see Gn 2⁸ וישם) and metre. 𝔊 gives the meaning correctly: ἀφ᾽ οὗ ἐτέθη ἄνθρωπος ἐπὶ τῆς γῆς.

v. 5. *joy*: רננת: lit. *shouting*; cf. Assyr. *rininu*, 'whining'. The √רנן *cry aloud*, usu. from joy, but also from grief (La 2¹⁹), may be akin to לנן or לון *to murmur* (cf. Sum. LIL, *the wind*, from its wailing), and to Assyr. *ramânu*, 'to thunder' (LIL = LIN = RIN, RIM). *soon over*: מִקָּרוֹב: an idiomatic phrase found in Ez 7⁸ Dt 32¹⁷ Je 23²³ ('at hand', 'anear' as opp. to 'afar', of place; then of time, 'not far', 'near' in either direction, past or future; e.g. 'lately', Dt 32¹⁷, 'soon' or 'shortly', Ez 7⁸, and adjectivally, 'not farreaching', 'short', as here). 𝔊 paraphr. πτῶμα ἐξαίσιον, 'The joy of the impious (plur.) is *a signal fall*': see 4¹² 9²² 18¹². (Did 𝔊 read פתאם for מקרוב and אֲבַד, Pr 11¹⁰, or איד = ἀπώλεια, for עדי־רגע, in a defaced text?)

v. 6. *his height*, or *growth*, *stature*. 𝔐 שיאו *his loftiness*; a ἅπ· with which we may perhaps comp. שַׁי, 'the Lofty' (?), as a name of Hermon. שְׂאֵתוֹ *his dignity* or *exaltation*, *majesty* (13¹¹) has been proposed. Perhaps שנאו *his growth*: cf. 8⁷·¹¹ 12²³ al. 𝔊 *his gifts* (שַׁי Ps 68³⁰ al.) supports 𝔐. 𝔙 superbia eius = נאותו. 𝔖 רומה *his height* (or *pride*). In st. ii, 𝔊 ἡ δὲ θυσία αὐτοῦ pro וראשו (? ואשו = ואשהו!).

v. 7. 𝔐 כגללו לנצח יאבד *Like his own dung he perisheth for ever*. 'The dung-heaps which are used as fuel and consequently disappear' (Dillon).

So RV: cf. Ez 4¹². But surely the disappearance of these would be gradual, and certainly not rapid enough for the figure. We may read בגדלו *In his greatness* (Ez 31¹·⁷) or, better, instead of כגללו לנצח, כגלל לפני־רוח *like a dustwhirl before the wind* (Ps 83¹⁴) or perhaps כגלגל ומץ *like a whirl of chaff and stubble* (cf. Is 17¹³). 𝔊 paraphrases with the unlikely guess ὅταν γὰρ δοκῇ ἤδη κατεστηρίχθαι, *For whenever he seemeth to be now firmly established, then* (&c. as 𝔐) = בגדלו *in his greatness* or *pride*. Instead of ראיו *they who saw him* 𝔊 εἰδότες = ידעיו *they who knew him*.

v. 8. Cf. Ps. 73²⁰. *Like a dream that flieth*: so 𝔊 ὥσπερ ἐνύπνιον ἐκπετασθὲν οὐ μὴ εὑρεθῇ (לא יִמָּצֵא): 𝔙 Velut somnium avolans non invenietur. Or *Like a dream he flieth away* (cf. Ps 90¹⁰), *and they* ('who saw him') *find him not* (so 𝔐). St. ii. *And he fleeth*: pointing וַיָּדֹד. 𝔐 יֻדַּד Hoph. *And he is made to fly, chased away* (cf. Hiph. 18¹³); which is hardly the way a dream departs. 𝔊 ἔπτη δέ = וַיָּדֹד; 𝔙 transiet.

v. 9. *that once glanced at him*; or *descried him* 28⁷: but in Ct 1⁶ שזף = שדף *to scorch*. (Perhaps distinct Roots. With שזף *look upon*, cf. צפה *watch, look out*, and perhaps Sum. SHAB, barû ša šîri, 'inspect, of flesh' or 'Seer of the omen'; with שדף *scorch*, cf. שבב *burn, flame*.)

beholdeth: leg. ישורנו pro 𝔐 תש' (due to preceding תוסיף). Though starred by the Hexapla, the verse is necessary to the completion of the quatrain. (This, however, might be effected by connecting v. 11 immediately with v. 8, as some prefer to do, and rejecting vv. 9, 10, as an insertion.)

v. 10 The resemblances noted between st. i and v. 19ᵃ (ירצו דלים = רצץ דלים) and between st. ii and v. 18ᵃ (משיב = תשבנה) have suggested that we have here a variant or a gloss upon those verses. The likeness, however, is not reflected in 𝔊.

In 𝔐, as it stands, the two stichi are not parallel. To remedy this, וילדיו *And his children* (cf. 𝔖) or וידיהם *And their hands* (i. e. his sons') has been proposed in place of ידיו *And his hands*. But the idea that the wicked man's sons are brought so low as *to court the favour of poor folk* by restitution of the gains of oppression, is more than dubious; and the meaning assigned to יְרַצּוּ (a scribal error for יְרַצּוּ ? cf. 𝔗 and v. 19) finds no support elsewhere (on √רצח see note 14⁹). We might get a parallel to ידיו *his hands* (st. ii) by reading כפיו *his palms* (16¹⁷ 31⁷; cf. Is 59³·⁶) instead of בניו *his sons* (st. i). St. i might then be restored to *His palms oppress* (יְרַצּוּ or ירצצו or, correcting the gend., תרצנה?) *the poor*; cf. 𝔊 *His sons may inferiors destroy* (𝔊ᴬ θλασιαν, ut v. 19); 𝔖 *His sons shall be broken by poverty* = 𝔙 Filii eius atterentur egestate (both pointing the vb. as Niph. יְרֹצּוּ). Hence some would render: *His sons are crushed* (as) *poor men*; a quite improb. construction. It will be noted that all the Verss. imply √רצץ > רצה. (RV marg. 'The poor shall oppress his children' = rg. of 𝔊, but sense improb., and incongruous with st. ii ap.

RV.) In st. ii, 𝔊 gives αἱ δὲ χεῖρες αὐτοῦ πυρσεύσαισαν ὀδύναις (-ας, B^{a.b} ℵ^{c.a} AC), *Let his hands signal to sorrows* (or *kindle sorrows*)! app. rg. תְּצִתְנָה or חִשְׁקָנָה for 𝔐 תְּשַׁבְּנָה. But 𝔊^A ψηλαφήσουσιν = תְּמַשֵּׁנָה *feel*, Gn 27¹², or תמשישנה, 5¹⁴ 12²³ (cf. Gn 31³⁴·³⁷), suggests the interesting sense *And his hands search through* ('finger'?) *their wealth* or *goods* (to claim them as his own, or otherwise annex them). 𝔊 ὀδύνας = אוֹנ׳ (= אונם in this case, not אוֹנוֹ as 𝔐). Perhaps, however, we should read some vb. meaning *to plunder*, e.g. תשסה or תשלנה or even תבצנעה. (Both 𝔊 and 𝔙 et manus illius reddent ei *dolorem suum* confuse אוֹן *wealth* with און *trouble, sorrow*.)

v. 11. 𝔐 lit. as RV *His bones are full of his youth.* So 𝔊, 𝔙; the latter explaining עֲלוּמוֹ by *vitiis* adolescentiae eius (cf. Ps 38⁸ 25⁷). If עַל be right, the verse simply means that the wicked man's youthful vigour (33²⁵) survives unimpaired to his dying day; a sense which is hardly suitable here. Besides, עֲלוּמָיו m. plur. does not agree with תִּשְׁכַּב. Read, therefore, עַוְלָתוֹ *his injustice*; which accords with v. 10.

v. 12. So 𝔊𝔙, with stop at the end of the verse. But it is better to extend the influence of the introductory particle אִם (𝔊 ἐάν, 𝔙 cum enim) to the three following stichi, as in our versions; thus connecting vv. 12, 13 with v. 14 as the apodosis. Injustice is sweet in the doing, but bitter in its results for the doer (cf. also v. 16).

v. 13. *Though he save* or *spare it.* He finds it so delicious, that he does not swallow it at once, but rolls it under his tongue, loth to let it go down. Cf. Pr 9¹⁷ᶠ· 20¹⁷. (𝔊 prefixes οὐ to st. i perperam. 𝔙 recte ut 𝔐.) (*holdeth it back*: יִמְנָעֶנָּה. 𝔊 συνάξει, cf. ἀδίκως συναγόμενος v. 15 = בלע. But possibly al. συνέξει is right.)

v. 14. *Into poison*: leg. לִמְרֹרַת: cf. 30²¹ 41²⁰ Ex 7¹⁷·²⁰. For the noun, *bitterness, gall, poison*, see 13²⁶ and v. 25 infr. 𝔊 here χολή, 𝔙 fel.

For st. i 𝔊 has καὶ οὐ μὴ δυνηθῇ βοηθῆσαι ἑαυτῷ, *And he will not be able to help himself* = ולא יכל לעזור לנפשו. Cf. with this the text of 𝔐 (c Apodot. ו) ולחמו במעיו נהפך. (𝔊 prob. intended by this app. incongruous substitution '*But he is obliged to swallow it*; he cannot help himself, keep it as long as he will in his mouth'.) In the closing st. 𝔊 χολή (not εἰς χολήν) ἀσπίδος shows that מרורת (not למרורת) stood in 𝔊's Heb. text. The Prep. must therefore have occurred in the previous st. Read therefore לְחֵמָה *into venom* (6⁴ Dt 32²³ Ps. 58⁵) instead of the jarring לַחְמוֹ *his bread* at the beginning of the verse, and so restore both symmetry and sense:

Into venom in his bowels it turneth,—
(Into) poison of asps within him.

v. 15. 𝔊 paraphrases *Wealth unjustly gathered shall be vomited forth.* St. ii: 𝔊 *Out of his house* (מביתו: 𝔐 recte מבטנו: see on 19¹⁷) *an angel will draw it* (יְמָשְׁכֵנִי ut Gn 37²⁸). Perhaps יַעֲלֶנּוּ *bringeth it up* or

יוֹצִיאוֹ *bringeth it forth.* 𝔐 יְרִשֶּׁנּוּ (see note on ירש 13²⁶. Not a Job word). ἄγγελος = אֵל (? אֱלוֹהַּ or אֱלֹהִים : cf. Gn 31²⁴ Ps 8⁶).

v. 16. *venom* : רֹאשׁ : which 𝔙 confuses with ראשׁ *caput*. 𝔊 θυμός, as in Dt 32³³. (Perhaps 𝔊 read חֵמָה 1. *wrath*, 2 *poison* : see v. 14.)

v. 17. 𝔊 *Let him not see a milking of nomads, Nor pastures of honey and butter !* (perhaps reading במלגות, and connecting the strange word with Gk. ἀμέλγω, *to milk*. Then νομάδων = רֵעִי, i. e. רֵעִים 1 C 27²⁹ and νομάς = נָוֶה or נְאוֹת Je 23³·¹⁰.) That 𝔐 cannot be original is certain ; the first st. being short, and the second redundant in more senses than one. פְּלָגוֹת (Ju 5¹⁵·¹⁶) is suspicious and should prob be פְּלַגֵּי, which is followed in the parallel passage 29⁶ by שֶׁמֶן *oil* (cf. Mi 6⁷ נַחֲלֵי שֶׁמֶן *torrents of oil*). Others have suggested יִצְהָר *fresh oil*, which, however, does not occur in א״מח, while, as we have seen, ‖ locc. favour שׁמן. (נהרי) looks like a var. of נחלי, or a gloss on פלגות. But cf. Ps 46⁵ נהר פלגיו ; the latter being the irrigating canals drawn from the main stream.)

v. 18. 𝔐 corrupt. Lit. *Returning* (or *about to return*) *gain* (יָגֵע ἅπ· one cod. יָגִיעַ *toil, produce* ; whence some read יְגִיעוֹ *his produce*), *and he swalloweth not ; According to the wealth of his exchange* (15³¹ 28¹⁷) *and he rejoiceth not* (39¹³ Niph). RV supposes st. i to mean : ' That which he laboured for shall he restore, and shall not swallow it down ' : cf. v. 10 and 15. But the oppressor's wealth is not the product of his own labour (יגיע). It is extorted from the poor (v. 19). 𝔊 εἰς κενὰ καὶ μάταια ἐκοπίασεν, πλοῦτον ἐξ οὗ οὐ γεύσεται = (?) לַשָּׁוְא יָגַע בְּחַיִל לֹא יִבְלַע (יטעם) : cf. 9²⁰ 39¹⁶ εἰς κενὸν ἐκοπίασεν = לריק יגעה : Is 49⁴ Je 51⁵⁸. בחיל . so fifty codd : for יגע ב see Jos 24¹³. γευσ· = יטעם : see 12¹¹ 34³ : πλοῦτος = חיל 21⁷ 31²⁵. For st. ii 𝔊 gives ὥσπερ στρίφνος ἀμάσητος ἀκατάποτος, *Like a tough morsel unchewed, not to be swallowed.* (See note on στρίφνος in 𝔊ᴮ* ap. Swete). This = ולא ילעם . . . כ. 𝔊 appears to have read ילעם (an Aramaism ; לְעַם, ܠܥܣ, *manducare, esse*, ' chew ', ' eat ') instead of יעלם *he rejoices* ; a better parallel to יבלע *he swallows* (7¹⁹). That 𝔊's version of the distich is more or less composite is evident : e. g. it bears traces of both בחיל and כחיל, while ἀμάσητος (fr. μασάομαι) = לא ילעם and ἀκατάποτος = לא יבלע. We may perhaps read, partly following 𝔊 :

לשוא יגע ולא יעיל
יחיל לתבואתו ולא ילעם:

He toils in vain without profit ;
He hopes for his crop and eats not.

Cf. also 𝔖 : *He will turn to labour and will not swallow ; Acc. to the power of his exchange he will not profit* (ܢܣܟܠ). 𝔙 Luet quae fecit omnia, nec tamen consumetur : iuxta multitudinem adinventionum suarum, sic et sustinebit -: ? יָשׁוּב יָגִיעוֹ וְלֹא יִבְלַע (בְּחֵיל מַקְמִיתוֹ ? וּתְמִידְתוֹ ?) וְלֹא יְסַבֵּל ?. Another attempted restoration is perhaps worthy of mention : לשוא י״ע

וְלֹא יֹאכַל בְּחֵכוֹ יִטְעַם וְלֹא יְבַלֵּעַ: *He labours in vain, and eats not; With his palate he tastes, and swallows not.* (𝔗 וְיָמַר pro יְבַלֵּעַ. Cf. 22²⁰ גָּמַר = אָכַל!)

v. 19. 𝔐 *For he hath crushed, he hath forsaken* (עָזַב), *the poor* is not in the poet's manner. 𝔊 πολλῶν γὰρ ἀδυνάτων (א^{c.a} AC rectè; B δυν. error script. see 5¹⁸ 31¹⁶) οἴκους ἔθλασεν: a better parallel to st. ii. Read perhaps מֹשָׁב the *dwelling*. For this word as syn. of בַּיִת *house* see Ex 12¹⁹,²⁰. (οἶκος is usu. בַּיִת, but sometimes אֹהֶל 12⁶ 15³⁴.) Otherwise, we might read עֹרֶף *neck*, 16¹², or זְרוֹעַ *arm*, 22⁹. 𝔖 *Because he thought to abandon* (= עָזַב = 𝔐) *the poor*. 𝔗 עִסְקָא = דָּבָר the matter *of the poor*. In st. ii read בָּנָהוּ c 𝔖𝔚 instead of יִבְנֵהוּ; cf. 𝔊 καὶ οὐκ ἔστησεν = וְלֹא הֱצִיבוּהוּ apparently. The well-known metaphor of 'building a house' = establishing or perpetuating a *family* (1 Sa 2³⁵ Ru 4¹¹) is not intended, the material house only being in question.

v. 20. 𝔐 cannot mean RV, for שָׁלֵו is not *quietness* (שַׁלְוָה Pr 17¹) but *quiet, easeful* (16¹² 21²³), and בַּחֲמוּדוֹ is not *aught of that wherein he delighteth* (מַחְמָד) but *in* or *with that*, &c. (cf. Ps. 39¹² Is 44⁹); and the vb. מלט Pi. requires an Accus. Obj. (6²³ 22³⁰ 29¹²). The √ חמד *desire, delight in*, does not recur in any of its forms in Job (though we might have expected the Niph. *desirable, valuable*, in ch. 28); which seems a suspicious circumstance, esp. when taken in connexion with the fact that the stichus in which it occurs is too short, while st. i is app. too long. 𝔊^B οὐκ ἔσται αὐτοῦ σωτηρία τοῖς ὑπάρχουσιν (𝔊^A οὐκ ἔστη αὐτῷ σωτηρία ἐν τοῖς ὑπάρχουσιν αὐτοῦ + *v.* 21 ᵇ). 𝔊 therefore appears to have read (יְשׁוּעָה) כִּי לֹא יֵשַׁע לוֹ *For he hath no safety* instead of כִּי לֹא יָדַע שָׁלֵו, and instead of בְּבִטְנוֹ *in his belly* either בְּבֵיתוֹ *in his house* (see on *v.* 15 and 19¹⁵ for the same confusion. τὰ ὑπάρχοντα = בַּיִת Gn 45¹⁸) or בְּאוֹנוֹ *in his wealth* (see *v.* 10; and τὰ ὑπάρχοντα αὐτοῦ = אוֹנוֹ 18⁷ 21¹³). The context favours the latter here (ב was repeated after אנו was misread טנו). Instead of the dubious בחמודו we propose (ו)בְרֹב חֵילוֹ *And by the greatness of his wealth* (τὰ ὑπάρχ. αὐτοῦ = חֵילוֹ 15²⁹), which at least restores the balance of the stichus. The vb. must be pointed Niph. יִפָּלֵט c 𝔊𝔖𝔗. Thus we get for the distich:

> *No safety for him in his wealth;*
> *Nor doth he escape by his great riches.*

For the general form of the verse cf. Ps 33¹⁶⁻¹⁸.

v. 21. 'There was nothing left that he devoured not' (RV) sounds plausible enough; but שָׂרִיד *survivor* (*v.* 26; 18¹⁹ Is 1⁹) is only used of persons. Hence, though 𝔊 supports 𝔐, we should read בְּאָהֳלוֹ *in his tent* (18¹⁹). 𝔖 מִן תּוֹלְדָתֵהּ *of his generations* or *race*: a paraphrase. 'Therefore his prosperity (lit. *good*) shall not endure' (RV = 𝔐) is not a good parallel to st. i. 𝔊 Τhrfor his good things will not flourish (ἀνθήσει = יִפְרַח: cf. 14). For טוּבוֹ *his good* read שְׁמוֹ *his name*. The vb. יָחִיל

shall be firm or *enduring* is doubtful both here and in Ps 10⁵, although the sense would suit. *His name* flourisheth (lit. *buddeth* or *sprouteth*) *not* is a beautiful metaphor for childlessness (cf. Nu 17²⁵ Ps 72¹⁷). Perhaps יחלף (Ps 90⁵·⁶) or יחליף (14⁹); or even ינון in the like sense (Ps 72¹⁷; cf. Sum. NUN *rabû*, NUM, LUM, *uššubu*, NUMUN, NÛ, *zêru*, 'seed', 'offspring').

v. 22. Lit. *when his sufficiency is full, he is in straits* (or *want*) שׂפק ἄπ· Aramaism? cf. vb. 1 K 20¹⁰ Ecclus 15¹⁸ סָפַק *suffice, abound.* But possibly שׂפק = צמק = לְפָמַץ *fist*, read backwards: cf. the phrase מלא קֻמְצוֹ *fulness of his fist*, Le 2² 5¹², and Gn 41⁴⁷ לקמצים *by handfuls*, i.e. *abundantly*.

In st. ii point עָמָל *suffering* instead of עָמֵל *sufferer* (3²⁰), c 𝔊 𝔙, both of which om יָד *hand, power.* Perhaps די *sufficiency, abundance* : *All plenitude of trouble attacketh him*; or read בְּכָל־דָּיוֹ עָמָל תְבֹאֶנּוּ *In all his plenty trouble attacketh him* (די prop. *overflow*, from דוה *to flow*; cf. שַׁי *gift* from שוה *to put* in the hand.)

v. 23. A tristich. St. i is obviously corrupt. It cannot mean *His belly shall be filled!* (Davidson, Driver); for בטן is fem. (15³⁵ Pr 18²⁰). The Hex. stars the line, but the mention of God is necessary to the context (cf v 15); and it is more prob. that either st. ii or st. iii is spurious. Read יהוה (אלוה ?) ימלא בטנו *Iahvah* or *Eloah filleth his belly*; | *He looseth against him* (or *sendeth into him* : Am 1⁴ Ps 104¹⁰) *the heat of his anger ;* *And He raineth upon him His* (?) *Terrors* (leg. בַּלְהוֹתָיו or simply בַּלָּהוֹת *terrors*, c 𝔊 ὀδύνας = בלה 18¹¹ 27²⁰: 𝔐 בִּלְחוּמוֹ, which Dr doubtfully explains *into his flesh*; cf. 𝔗 and Zp 1¹⁷: but the word evidently conceals the direct Obj. which should follow ימטר as in Ps 11⁶) פַּחִים) 𝔖 *And he will rain upon him* in his *valour* (בקרבתנותה), app. pointing בַּלְחוּמוֹ qs. *in his fighting*; cf. 𝔙 Et pluat super illum bellum suum, which suggests וימטר עליו מלחמתו (or וים' עליו בלי־מלח') *And He rains down upon him His battle* (or *the weapons of His battle*): cf. the next two verses.

v. 24. 𝔊 καὶ οὐ μὴ σωθῇ ἐκ χειρὸς σιδήρου. This may confirm the suspicion that וְאִם has fallen out at the beginning of the stichus *And if he flee from arms* (39²¹) *of iron*, | *The bow of bronze transfixeth him* : cf. also 𝔖 *He who fleeth from the corselet of iron*, &c.

v. 25. App. a tristich; grammatically incoherent, and metrically defective. Instead of 𝔐 שלף ויצא מגוה, which is really nonsense, 𝔊 has the excellent sense διεξέλθοι δὲ διὰ σώματος αὐτοῦ βέλος = וְיֵצֵא שֶׁלַח מִגֵּוִיתוֹ *And the missile* (Jo 2⁸ βέλος = שלח) *cometh out of his body* (𝔐 מגוה might be retained if pointed מִגֵּוֹה, i.e. מִגֵּוֹ *out of his back*). The suggestion that שָׁלַף should be read, on the ground of Syr. שלפא *a blade without handle or hilt*, is improb An *arrow* is intended, as the context shows. Cf. Ps 18¹⁵ 144⁶. שֶׁלַח recurs, 33¹⁸ 36¹². St. ii, *the flash*: i.e. the flashing steel of the barb. ברק 'lightning' is similarly used in the Psalms cited above; Hb 3¹¹. 𝔊 ἄστρα is a mere verbal error for ἀστραπή — בָּרָק, and ἐν διαίταις (-τῃ) αὐτοῦ = באהלו *in his tent* is due to the translator's eye having wandered to the end of the next verse, where that word occurs. St. iii. אימים (יפלו) עליו *Upon him fall terrors* (see Ps 55⁵) is prob. a gloss. (There seems no sufficient reason for regarding vv. 24–25 b ממררתו as an addition.)

v. 26. 𝔐 lit. *All darkness is laid up for his things laid up* (כל חשך טמון לצפוניו); cf. 𝔊^A ἐγκέκρυπται τοῖς ἐγκειμένοις αὐτοῦ· a not very appropr. sense, since it is for the wicked man himself > for his treasures that 'all darkness' = every kind of misfortune is reserved: cf. st. ii. צפן must be omitted (c 𝔊) as a marg. variant of טמון, which should be followed by לו or אליו (cf. 15²²). For the √ טמן *hide* see 3¹⁵ (3²¹ מטמונים *hid treasures*) 18¹⁰ 31³³ 40¹³. צפן *hide, treasure up,* also occurs some seven times in Job.

St. ii. For the anomalous pointing תְּאָכְלֵהוּ leg. the ordinary form תֹּאכַל implied by the Versions and given by seven codd. The curious phrase אֵשׁ לֹא נֻפַּח *a fire unblown* seems to mean not fanned by breath or bellows (מַפֻּחַ Je 6²⁹); i.e. not of human origin: prob. an allusion to 1¹⁶. We must read נְפֻחָה (cf. 41¹² נפוח Ecclus 43⁴ כור נפ׳) for נֻפָּח, as Pu. does not seem to be substantiated: cf. 𝔖 נורא דלא נפיחא and 𝔗 *the fire of hell which is not* נָפִיחַ *blown up*. 𝔊 ἄκαυστον but 𝔊^A ἄσβεστον *unquenchable, not to be blown out* = לֹא־תְכֻבֶּה (Pr 26²⁰; but not al. in Job).

St. iii is prob. an add. Cf. v. 21. The text is unsatisfactory, however we choose to vary the pointing of יֵרַע (𝔐). If אֵשׁ *fire* is the Subj. (RV), the word should at least be תרע (cf. תאכל ad init.). 𝔊 κακώσαι = יָרַע. 𝔖 misread ירע as יבש. The old conjecture יֵרֶע *shall be grazed upon* or *fed upon* = *consumed* is improb. and, indeed, unparalleled. If we read וּתְבַעֵר, we get good sense and a good parallel to st. ii: *And consumeth the survivor in his tent*. (The reading suggested by Ki יִדְעַךְ שָׂרִיב וגו׳ *The flame is quenched in his tent* is ingenious, but also incongruous with st. ii, though it might suit as a parallel to st. i, if we rejected st. ii as spurious.)

v. 27. The mode in which Heaven and Earth attest the guilt of the wicked man is made clear by v. 28. It is by the flood which sweeps his house away. (Instead of מִתְקוֹמָמָה לוֹ we might read תָּקוּם לְעֵד־בּוֹ *And earth stands up as a witness against him*. Cf. 𝔊 γῆ δὲ ἐπαναστείη αὐτῷ, 𝔙 et terra consurget adversus eum. 𝔐 seems metr. short.)

v. 28. 𝔐 *The produce* (יְבוּל always elsewhere of *yield of the soil*) *of his house shall depart* (יִגֶל; cf. Is 24¹¹ Pr 27²⁵); *Things flowing* or *running down* (נִגָּרוֹת; cf. La 3⁴⁹: corrupt) *in the day of his anger*. Supposing נאנרתו = נאנרות = נגרות *his ingatherings* or *stores* (cf. Pr 6⁸ 10⁵), we get a passable parallel. But the loss of crops hardly suffices as a climax or finishing stroke in the picture of ruin. Moreover, יגל ad init. may have been influenced by יגל v. 27 ad init.; and there is no immediate reference for אפו ביום, as God has not been mentioned since v. 23. Prob. we must read אידו *his* (the wicked man's) *ruin* (21³⁰) instead of אפו *his* (God's) *anger.* For יְגַל יְבוּל we suggest יִגַּר מַבּוּל (Hb 1¹⁵ Pr 21⁷) or perhaps נֵגֶר (Mi 1⁴ ⁶ 2 Sa 14¹⁴). There seems no reason why a late poet might not use מַבּוּל (Noah's *Flood*, Gn 6¹⁷+) of any great deluge or storm of destruction (cf. Ps 29¹⁰). (The word *מַבּוּל = מַנְבּוּל ?, cf. Assyr. *nabbaltu* = nanbaltu ?, the def. of Sum. IM-BAL, 'destructive wind', 'hurricane'. *Nabâlu* means to *throw down* or *destroy* cities. Since IM denotes both wind, *šâru*, and rain, *zunnu*, it seems not impossible that the old Heb. *mabbûl* may be a transformation of Sum. IMBAL) Others have proposed יִגֹּל יָבָל *The river rolleth away*; but neither גלל nor יָבָל *watercourse* or *canal, conduit* (Is 30²⁵ 44¹), for irrigation, seems to be so used. In st. ii for 𝔐 נגרות read גְּרָפוֹ *And sweepeth it away* (cf. Ju 5²¹ of a river). Ki אחו וַנֶגֶר; but what does this mean? 𝔊 ἑλκύσαι τὸν οἶκον αὐτοῦ ἀπωλεία εἰς τέλος ; ἡμέρα ὀργῆς ἐπέλθοι αὐτῷ. See Hb 1¹⁵ εἵλκυσεν αὐτόν = יִגְרֵהוּ; ἀπωλεία = אֲבוֹד Pr 11¹⁰, or אֵיד 21³⁰. As כָּלָה *destruction* may be ἀπωλεία (cf. vb. ap. 𝔊 7⁸ 9²²) and εἰς τέλος = לִכְלָה 2 C 12¹², כלה Ps 74¹¹, ἀπωλ· εἰς τέλος may be a dupl. equivalent of יְבוּל. For st. ii 𝔊 app. read עָלָיו יָבוֹא יוֹם אַף. 𝔊 *The foundations of his house shall be exposed* (= יִגָּל), *And he shall be drawn away* (נָגֹּשׁ = יִתְנַגֵּד pro נגרות) *in the day of wrath*; cf. 𝔙 Apertum erit germen (= בּוּלוֹ or יְבוּלוֹ?) domus illius | Detrahetur in die furoris Dei.

v. 29. Om. אָדָם *man*, which is implied in רָשָׁע (9²²⁻²⁴ 15²⁰ 24⁶ al), metri gratia. Cf. 27¹³ Is 17¹⁴ᵇ. *from Iahvah* = 𝔊 παρὰ Κυρίου, for which 𝔐 מֵאֱלֹהִים *from Elohim* may have been substituted.

St. ii. 𝔐 וְנַחֲלַת אֲמָרוֹ מֵאֵל *and the portion of his word* (= sentence ?) *from El*; but the second word is unknown in such a use, and the parallel locc. show that it is superfluous. See 27¹³ 31² Is 17¹⁴ 54¹⁷ Je 13²⁵. The objection to מוֹרָה = מֹרֶה *rebel* (Nu 20¹⁰) is that the √מרה is of doubtful occurrence in Job (see notes on 17² 23²) except in the Elihu-section (36²²). 𝔊 καὶ κτῆμα ὑπαρχόντων αὐτῷ (𝔊^AC αὐτοῦ) παρὰ τοῦ ἐπισκόπου = (Es 2¹¹) מֵיֶרֶץ (18⁷) אוֹנוֹ (27¹³) וְנַחֲלַת or מִדְרָשׁ (Dt 11¹²). Read backwards, either ידע or דרש indicates אֵל > שַׁדַּי: see 27¹³. But 𝔐 may be a perversion of וְנַחֲלָתוֹ מֵאֵת אֵל *And his portion from with* (i. e. assigned by) *El*: cf. Is 54¹⁷.

Chapter 21. *v.* 2. *Comfort.* 𝔐 תַּנְחֻמוֹת abstr. intens. plur., as 15¹¹. The m. form occurs thrice (see Je 16⁷ תַּנְחוּמִים); the sing. never Kittel's note 'l c 𝔊𝔖𝔗𝔙—מַתָּכֶם—' is therefore erroneous. 𝔊 mistakenly reads שִׁמְעוּ for שָׁמוֹעַ in st. i, and inserts a neg. in st. ii.

v. 3. *Ye may mock*: reading plur. תָּלִינוּ pro 𝔐 sing., c 𝔊𝔖𝔙, as the parallel vb. and the context require. (𝔊 again inserts a neg., rendering *Then ye will not laugh at me*. But Eyob hardly expected his friends to become mollified towards himself by what he was going to say. He only thought to silence them.)

v. 4. Lit. *I* f (לִ) *man is my complaining* (שִׂיחִי) *or men*. But a vb. fin. seems to be wanting; and 𝕲 *I will speak* (אֹמַר pro אָנֹכִי) may possibly be right. Leg. הַאָמֵר: *Do I make my plaint of a man? Or why should not my temper be short?* (For שִׂיחִי 𝕲 ἡ ἔλεγξίς μου: so 23²).

v. 5. *appalled* or *silenced* (16⁷ 17⁸ 18²⁰): cf. the parallel stichus and 40⁴. The mystery of the wicked prospering in a world governed by God overwhelms Eyob with trembling fears and uncertainties (v. 6, 7); and he thinks that, if his friends will but consider his presentation of the facts, they will have nothing left to say. Cf. Ps 17¹⁴ 37 73 Je 12¹. Whether he has sinned or not, it is a fact of common observation that the wicked often prosper; a fact which contradicts their theory of the relation between sin and suffering.

v. 6. *confounded*: or *dismayed*, נבהלתי; a vb. which 𝕲 curiously renders by σπουδάζω *to make haste*, 4⁵ 22¹⁰ (cf. 23¹⁶) as well as here (𝕲ᵀ recte θορυβοῦμαι, 22¹⁰ ταράσσει). Cf. Aram. (Tg.) בְּהִיל *to hasten*, trans. *bewilder, terrify*. The root is perhaps akin to בלל *mingle, confuse, confound* (Gn 11⁷), or to Sum. BUL, *to quake, tremble* (*naš̌u*) before a god; cf. also Aram. בַּל *heart* = Ar. بال. *seizes*: leg. אחזה fem. pro 𝔐 אחז masc.

v. 7. The moral problem which so greatly disturbs him. *mighty in power*: or *in riches* (חיל 5⁵ 15²⁹ al.) 𝕲𝕭𝕴. But 𝕾 makes the expression refer to physical strength: *And grow old as mighty men of valour* (= נבורי חיל), app. reading גִּבֹּרֵי pro גָּבְרוּ. Cf. Ps 73⁴. This may be right in sense, even if we keep נברו.

v. 8. St. i: cf. Ps 102²⁸ᵇ. The stichus is too long metr. It is prob. that עמם *with them* conceals the vb. of st. 2, viz. יעמדו or יעמרו Is 66²² Ps 102²⁷: *And their offspring* (5²⁵ 27¹⁴ 31⁸) *endures in their sight*. (𝕲 ὁ σπόρος αὐτῶν κατὰ ψυχήν (+ αὐτῶν 𝕲ᴬ) = כמו נפשם pro נכון לפניהם.)

v. 9. Lit. *Their houses are peace*; cf. 5²⁵. 𝕲 εὐθηνοῦσιν = שָׁלוּ *are quiet*, La 1⁵, or שלמו pro שלום; cf. 𝕭 securae sunt et pacatae.

v. 10. *Their bull*: שׁוֹרָם c 𝕲𝕭 pro 𝔐 שׁוֹרוֹ *his bull*. Similarly in st. ii פָּרָתָם *their cow* pro 𝔐 פָּרָתוֹ *his cow*, where 𝕲 αὐτῶν ἐν γαστρὶ ἔχουσα = פָּרָתָם *their fruitful one*, or הָרָתָם (cf. Ho 14¹). 𝕲ᴬ recte δάμαλις. As to the meaning, 𝕲𝕭 interpret both stt. of the female; but 𝕾𝕴 rightly understand the t. t. of st. i as referring to the function of the male. The √געל *to loathe, regard as foul*, may be compared with גאל II, and with בחל Syr. The primary GAL, ḤAL, is perhaps akin to Sum. GUL, *bad*. *calves*: תפלט Pi.; cf. Aram. use (Tg. Syr.) *spit forth, spue out*; here of easy delivery. (𝕲 διεσώθη, pointing as Niph.) Cf. מלט Pi. ova parere, Is 34¹⁵.

v. 11. *play about*: יְשַׂחֲקוּ ludunt, 40²⁰·²⁹ Zc 8⁵ (of children playing) pro 𝔐 יְשַׁלְּחוּ *send forth*, which does not seem very suitable (cf. Is 7²⁵ 32²⁰). Whither do they 'send forth their little ones' (ע׳ 19¹⁸)? Cf. Gn 25⁶. Moreover, st. ii is metr. short; and כְּמוֹ־עֵגֶל *lik- a calf*, Ps 29⁶, or כעגלים *like calves* may have fallen out before the verb.

𝕲 μένουσιν δὲ ὡς πρόβατα αἰώνια = עולם כצאן ישבו (Ps 9⁸).

v. 12. Lit *They lift up* (scil. the voice) *with* (accompaniment of) *labor and lyre* (cf. Ps 49⁵ᵇ). The 'pipe' (𝔗 אבובא) from Assyr. *imbûbu*, a *reed-pipe* or *flute*; cf. Ar. *'unbûb*, a *reed*) recurs 30³¹: see also Gn 4²¹.

v. 13. *They end*, or *complete*; reading יְכַלּוּ c Qerî, 𝕲 συνετέλεσαν, 𝕾𝔗 and 36¹¹ where the words are quoted. Cf. Is 65²² (where also the text is יְבַלּוּ *they wear out*). St. ii וּבְרֶגַע 𝔐 *And in an instant*: i.e. they know no lingering pains; their death comes swiftly, is a matter of a moment: see 7¹⁸ 20⁵ 34²⁰; 'a quick and easy death' (Driver). So 𝕾𝔚; but 𝕲 ἐν δὲ ἀναπαύσει ᾅδου ἐκοιμήθησαν connects רגע with √רגע II *be at rest* (Niph. Hiph. only), pointing וּבְרֹגַע or וּבְרָגְעוּ, and 𝔗 has וּבְמַרְגּוֹעָא (= מַרְגּוֹעַ? Je 6¹⁶), app. meaning the same thing. *And into the rest of the Grave* (var. *She'ol*) *they go down*: cf. 1 K 2⁶ ⁹ 2 K 22²⁰ Je 34⁵. But why not בְּשָׁלוֹם, as in these and similar passages, if that were the poet's meaning? No form or derivative of √רגע II occurs anywhere else in the book.

go down· יֵחָתּוּ = יֵחַתּוּ (cf. Pr 17¹⁰ Je 21¹³): metaplastic form from נָחֵת, an Aramaism used in poetry. 𝕲 ἐκοιμ = ישכבו (3¹³ 14¹² al.), or perhaps יָנוּחוּ *they repose*.

v. 14. 𝕲 has vbb. in sing., λέγει δὲ (𝕲ᴬ+ ὁ ἀσεβής), returning to the plur. in the next verse. Cf. note on v. 3ᵇ. κυρίῳ = לָאֵל.

v. 15. ἱκανός = שַׁדַּי; so 31² 39³². But 6⁴ κυρίου = שַׁדַּי (alii ἱκανοῦ, 𝕲ˣ σαδδαί: see Ez 1²⁴ 10⁵) This equivalent rests on a false etymology, viz. שדי = ש Pron. Rel. *He Who* + די (*is*) *Sufficient* (so Rabb.). In 5¹⁷ 8⁵ παντοκράτωρ, *Almighty* (so 15 times in the book). It is improb. that שדי as a title of God is akin to שֵׁד *demon* (Dt 32¹⁷), Aram. שֵׁידָא, Assyr. *šêdu*, which is used of evil spirits as well as good (*šêdu limnu*). Rather is this ancient word Shaddai, Σαδδαί, Σαδαί, to be compared with the Sumerian SATI (from SAD; cf. ITI from ID), *bâmâtu* (בָּמוֹת), *hills*, and SHAD, SAD, values of the mountain-symbol (𐎹), from which Assyr. *šaddû*, *šadû*, plur. *šadê*, *šadê*, *mountain*, is doubtless derived. The great gods Asshur and Bel were styled *šadû rabû* (Sum. KUR-GAL), 'Mighty Mountain'; cf. the Personal Name *Šaddâ-šû* (*his mountain*). There may be a trace here of primitive mountain-worship. In any case, it would seem that the old Heb. (originally Babylonian) Divine title Shaddai is nearer in meaning to עֶלְיוֹן ('the Most High') than to שֵׁד *demon*. (*šadû* also denoted an earthly *prince* or *potentate*: Anp. I. 22 al.)

v. 16. 𝔐 lit. *Lo, not in their* (*own*) *hand* (*is*) *their welfare: The counsel of the wicked is far from me* (מֶנִּי 22¹⁸ 30¹⁰ Ps 18²²). A parenthesis repudiating all sympathy with such impious sentiments. But this is improb. in the context which it interrupts. Nor can we suppose (with RV marg.) an interruption at this point by one of the friends. The verse looks like an interpolation by some scribe who felt bound to protest against such a flagrant impiety. 𝕲 ἐν χερσὶ γὰρ ἦν αὐτῶν τὰ ἀγαθὰ ἔργα δὲ ἀσεβῶν οὐκ ἐφορᾷ, omitting the Neg. Part. in st. i and app. reading טוֹב מַעֲשֵׂה instead of עֲצַת, טוּבָם, with רָחַק מִמֶּנּוּ ad fin. This is at least in better harmony with the context: *Lo, their prosperity is at their own command; The doings of the wicked are remote from Him* (far from the Divine notice). We get virtually the same sense if we read הֲלֹא Interrog. pro לֹא הֵן st. i ad init. *Is not their pr. in their own hand?* Possibly the orig. text was אֵין־לְאֵל יָדָם טוּבָם *Their weal is not subject to their own control*; &c. as in 𝔐. It appears, however, to be even more probable that the verse is a corrupt form of 22¹⁹: cf. 𝔊 הֵן לֹא בְיָדָם טוּבָם with הוּא מָלֵא בְתֵיהֶם טוֹב (st. ii is the same in both locc.). Further, it is possible that vv. 16–18 have been dislocated from one column to another and really belong to the speech of Eliphaz. They certainly fill up in a desirable manner the lacuna between 22¹⁸ and 22¹⁹.

v. 17. *How often*: כַּמָּה which in 13²⁵ means *How many?* and here is understood to mean *How seldom!* but may very well be *How often!* as in Ps 78⁴⁰. In that case we have an utterance in perfect harmony with the doctrine of the friends (cf. 18⁵,⁶ 22¹⁹). Moreover, it seemed strained and unnatural to make v. 18, which is much more forcible as a direct statement, depend on כמה (as well as st. iii, which is prob. spurious). 𝔊 οὐ μὴν δὲ ἀλλὰ κτλ. (אבן pro כמה; cf. 32⁸ 34³⁶) *Nay, but the lamp of the wicked will be quenched*, also treats the verses as a categorical assertion. St. iii, lit. *Portions* (or *Pains*) *He distributes in His anger*. The Asyndeton is strange and the sense doubtful. It is more likely that the stichus is an interpolation than that a parallel line has fallen out of the text. If a distich stood here once, it may have run somewhat as follows:

חבלים יאחזם באפו
חיל כיולדה:

Sorrows seize them *in His anger,—*
Pangs as of the woman in travail.

Or, as this couplet is in the *Qînah*-measure, יחילו כי׳ בחמתו *They writhe, like a woman in travail, at His wrath*, might be substituted for the second stichus.—𝔊 recte: ὠδῖνες δὲ ἕξουσιν αὐτούς (ἔχω = אחז, the proper term with חבלים): see Is 13⁸, of which the vs. may be a reminiscence; cf. also 18²⁰ 21⁶. For באפו 𝔊 ἀπὸ ὀργῆς = (ו)מאפו.

v. 18. *carries off:* נֻבְּתוּ *filches away* = 𝔊 ὑφείλατο, 27²⁰. (With נגב *steal*, str. *put aside*, cf. Sum. GUN, *idu*, 'side', as well as Ar. جَنب *side*, נגב = *side-at*.) For מֹץ 𝔊 κονιορτός cf. Dan 2³⁵ עוּר *chaff*; which 𝔊 perhaps read here (עוּר = מוֹץ misread backwards), if not עָפָר or אָבָק, 𝔙 *favilla*, *ashes* = אֵפֶר.

v. 19. St. i 𝔐 *Eloah stores up his trouble* (אָוֶן 15³⁵) or *wickedness* (22¹⁸) *for hi*. . . *ons*. This agrees neither with st. ii, nor with vv. 20, 21; in fact, while consistent with the doctrine of the friends (cf. 5⁴), it is quite contrary to Eyob's argument here, and the line is metr. redundant. We may regard אלוֹהַ as a marg. gloss and read הֲיִצְפֹּן: *Doth He store up his trouble for his sons?* Is that your contention? or else read אַל instead of אֱלוֹהַ (which is perhaps due to a scribe's mispointing the word אֵל *God*): *Let Him not lay up his trouble* (= the trouble due to him) *for his sons!* (𝔊ᴮ υἱούς is prob. a scribal error pro υἱοῖς 𝔊ᴬ. τὰ ὑπάρχοντα αὐτοῦ = 𝔐 אוֹנוֹ: see note on 20¹⁰.)

v. 20. *his ruin*: reading פִּידוֹ (12⁵ 30²⁴) or אֵידוֹ (v. 30, 18¹²+) pro 𝔐 בְּיָדוֹ, an otherwise unknown ἀπ᾽—𝔊 τὴν ἑαυτοῦ σφαγήν (cf. 10¹⁶), but 𝔊ˣ πτῶσιν.

In st. ii, 𝔊 om. חֵמַת (ἀπὸ Κυρίου = מִשַּׁדַּי) and seems to read אַל (or לֹא) יְפַלֵּט or יִמָּלֵט (v. 10, 22³⁰) pro 𝔐 יִשְׁתֶּה bibit. More probably, however, the translator merely intended a free rendering of a non-Hellenic metaphor like 'drinking the wrath of Shaddai' (Is 51¹⁷ Ps 75⁹ Je 25¹⁵).

v. 21. After his death the wicked man has no further interest (חֵפֶץ 1 *pleasure, delight*; 2. *business, affair*, Is 53¹⁰ 58¹³ Ec 3¹ al.—late usage) in the fortunes of his house. Cf. 14²¹. 𝔊 μετ᾽ αὐτοῦ = אִתּוֹ pro 𝔐 אַחֲרָיו *after him.* 𝔊 app. om. מה *what?*)

is cut short: חֻצָּצוּ plur., because מִסְפַּר חֳדָשָׁיו is equivalent to *all his months*; a *constructio ad sensum*. The vb. חצץ Pi. = Assyr. ḫuṣṣuṣu: e.g. *kîma qanê abi uḫaṣiṣu, like a reed of the sedge I cut off* (or *broke off*, Sum. ZUR), Anp. I. 27. The statement is not that 'the number of his months' is 'decreed' or predetermined by God (חרוץ 14⁵), but that it is exhausted (cf. Is 38¹²). It is not therefore an improvement to read חָרְצוּ here. 𝔊 διῃρέθησαν (διαιρ = חצה 2 K 2⁸ al.): so 𝔙 dimidietur.

v. 22. 𝔐 can only mean *Will he* (i.e. the wicked man) *teach knowledge to El* (emph.)? We might point יְלֻמַּד pro יְלַמֶּד. *Shall knowledge be taught to El?* Would you make your limited ideas of justice a canon for the Omniscient? (Cf. 𝔊 *Do ye teach?*) But 𝔊 הֲלֹא אֵל pro 𝔐 הַלְאֵל seems preferable (πότερον οὐχὶ ὁ κύριός ἐστιν ὁ διδάσκων σύνεσιν καὶ ἐπιστήμην;). Should we not rather observe what God actually does (vv. 23-33), in His dealings with man, than assert our own a priori notions of what He ought to do? *Shall not El teach knowledge* (Ps 94¹⁰)—teach us, e.g., that calamity is not an invariable consequence of sin?

the Heights: רָמִים: i.e. Heaven, Ps 78⁶⁹. (Perhaps the more usual מְרוֹמִים *id.* 16¹⁹ should be read in both places.) Cf. 25² and 4¹⁸; 22¹². So 𝔗 שְׁמֵי מְרוֹמָא *the highest heavens*; but 𝔙 excelsos, i.e. their inhabitants. 𝔊 φόνους = דמים simply confirms 𝔐 רמים. The proposed רְמִיָּה *treachery*, making the stichus a threat to the friends (cf. 19²⁹), is hardly prob. here.

v. 23. בְּעֶצֶם תֻּמּוֹ is difficult. 𝔊 ἐν κράτει ἁπλοσύνης αὐτοῦ, pointing בְּעֹצֶם תֹּ' (30²¹). The phrase might then mean *in the might of his completeness* or *perfection* = 'in his full strength': with all his faculties of mind and b.dy un.mpa'r.d.

entirely untroubled: reading שַׁאֲנָן c 1 MS. (12⁵, cf vb. 3¹⁸) pro 𝔐 שַׁלְאֲנָן (confusion with שלום?). 𝔊 εὐπαθῶν (= רענן Ps 92¹⁵). The √שאן *at rest, in peace*, cf. 3¹⁸ (of the grave), is prob. cogn. c ישן *asleep*; cf. Syr. שֵׁנָא *pax* and Assyr. *šittu* (shin-tu), *sleep*. For the prim. root cf. Ch. ch'in, ts'im, Jap. shin, An. têm, *to sleep, rest*, and perhaps Sum. SAN in U-SAN, *sleep* (U *šittu* + SAN). The prim. mg. is prob. *lie down*; cf. Assyr. *çalâlu*, id. (צל = צן), and שָׁלָה, שָׁלוּ *be quiet, at ease*, Assyr. *na'âlu, nâlu, lie down, sleep* (n = s).

v. 24. *his belly*: reading בִּטְנוֹ or מֵעָיו (= 𝔊 τὰ ἔγκατα αὐτοῦ, 𝔙 *viscera eius*) for the ἄπ. עֲטִינָיו. The word has been supposed to mean *milk-pails*; a bad parallel to st. ii. Cf. Pr 3⁸. The Versions agree in making some part of the human body to be intended (𝔗 ביזוהי *his breasts*; 𝔖 נבוחי *his sides*). The suggested Aramaism עטמיו *his thighs* or *flanks* (cf. 15²⁷) becomes plausible, if we point (c 𝔊 στέατος, 𝔙 *adipe*, 𝔖 חֶלְבָּא) *fat* pro חָלָב *milk*; but *milk* gives a better parallel to *moistened* (lit. *watered*, kept moist, not dried up) in st. ii. (Instead of עטיניו we might also read שארו *his flesh* as parallel to *his bones*; or שריריו *his muscles*, a Job-word, 40¹⁸. *His flesh* or *his muscle is fraught with fat*, &c.)

v. 25. It would improve the metre to read c 𝔊 𝔙 בְּמַר־נֶפֶשׁ *in bitterness of soul*, like 7¹¹ 10¹, pro 𝔐 בְּנֶפֶשׁ מָרָה *with bitter soul* (so 𝔖 𝔗). *tasted happiness*: lit. *eaten of good* (9²⁵ Ex 12⁴³ f.). The stichus seems too short. Perhaps מכל טובה *of any good*.

v. 26. *in the dust*: or *on the ground* (עַל־עָפָר), 19²⁵ 39¹⁴. 𝔊 ἐπὶ γῆς. *worms*: i.e. maggots: רִמָּה coll. 𝔊 σαπρία, *rottenness*. √רמם = Ar. رمّ *ramma*, *to decay*: cf. also Assyr. *ramû*, *become loose, go to pieces, decay*, of a foundation.

v. 27. *plots* or *devices*: מזמות: 42² Ps 10²·⁴ 21¹². *devise*: reading תַּחְפְּשׁוּ (written ? תַּחְפֹּשׂוּ), Ps 64⁷, instead of תַּחְמֹסוּ which takes an accus. obj. (15³³) > עַל. Perhaps, however, 𝔐 may mean: *And the devices against me wherewith ye deal violently* (contr. Accent.). 𝔊's text here was probably defective, but it gives ἐπίκεισθέ μοι for the verb (= תחברו לי 19³! q.v.). 𝔙 *et sententias contra me iniquas*. 𝔗 תַּחְשְׁלוּן *favours* תַּחֲרשׁוּ > תַּחְפְּשׁוּ (see Pr 6¹⁴·¹⁸ 𝔗). The Aram. חשל, like חרש, means *to forge, fabricate*, both lit. and met.

v. 28. *Ye say*: or *think* (say in your heart). The friends think that the ruin of Eyob's (the former 'Great Man's') house is ocular demonstration of the truth of their suspicions, and of the justice of their efforts to entrap him into an admission of guilt. Cf. 18¹⁵·²¹; also 8¹⁶·²² 15³⁴. (St. ii is overloaded metr. אהל may be due to dittogr. of איה, or to the influence of the parallel locc. Om. c 𝔙 et 1 cod.).

The godless: plur., indicating Eyob less directly, or rather perhaps including his dependents.

v. 29. An interesting reference to 'Travellers' tales', such as Orientals delight in, especially when full of the marvellous. With *passers along the way* or *wayfarers* (merchants, handicraftsmen, and the like), cf. the similar phrase Ju 5¹⁰ Stories of successful villainy are intended.

heed: or *regard* or *recognize* (הִכִּירוּ; Pi. here and 34¹⁹ only in Job; perhaps Hi. הַכִּיר which occurs six times). *their tokens*: or *signs, indications*, signal instances of the prosperous careers of men thoroughly wicked. (St. ii seems metr. short. Some word, e. g. זָרִים *strangers*, 15¹⁹, רוֹכְלִים *merchants*, Ez 17⁴, or אֱמֶת *of truth*, Jos 2¹², may once have followed אֹתֹת *tokens*, if that word itself be genuine.)

v. 30. 𝔐, if correct, should mean: *That the bad man* is held back (*reserved*: cf. 38²³) *for the day of ruin; To the day of outbursts* (of wrath, 40¹¹) *they are led* (cf. Is 53⁷); which is contrary to the context. We must at least read ביום for ליום in both stt. And since יום איד (without an individual reference) is an unlikely phrase, whereas יום עברה *day of wrath* occurs, Zp 1¹⁵, cf. ¹⁸ Pr 11⁴, and the verb חשׂך is common in the sense of *holding* a man *back* or *keeping* him *from* evil fortune (33¹⁸), while the first ביום, which overweights the stichus, may easily be dittogr. of the second, it seems natural to restore the verse as follows:

כִּי מֵאֵיד יֵחָשֵׂךְ רָע
וּבְיוֹם עֶבְרָה יִפָּלֵט׃

(𝔊 κουφίζεται = 𝔐: cf. Ezr 9¹³ ἐκούφισεν)

For יובלו (which recurs v. 32) יִפָּלֵט seems probable, and a better parallel to Ni. in st. 1. The plur. as parallel to the sing., st. i, is obviously corrupt. The יְ is either a relic of טְ־, or belongs to the next verse (וּמִי *And who* . . .). The plur. עברות may be Intens. (cf. 𝔙 diem furoris). The objection to עברתו *his* (God's) *Wrath*, is that God has not been mentioned since v. 22, which seems too far back for the reference of the suffix. (Might st. ii have been: בְּיוֹם עָבֹר מַבּוּל *In the day when the Flood overfloweth?*)

v. 31. None dares to rebuke the powerful wicked for his crimes; much less, to attempt his punishment.

Read perhaps וְזֶה (15¹⁷) pro 𝔐 וְהוּא: *And what he hath done, who can repay him?* cf. 𝔊𝔙𝔖: or 'ע הוא זה *And what* He (emph.) *hath done*, &c. But והוא begins the next verse.

v. 32. *And He* (emph.)—in contrast with other and better men—*is borne* (10¹⁹) or *conducted* (Is 55¹²) *to a stately tomb* or *mausoleum* (lit. *graves*: plur. excellentiae). (Was עברות יובל, v. 30, influenced by קברות יובל here? The scribe's eye may have strayed downward. This would account for the plur. עברות instead of עברה.)

St ii. 𝔐 lit. *And over a (the) mound he watcheth*: as though the dead man's spirit, or his sculptured image, stood on guard over his tumulus. But the stichus is metr. short; and on this ground, and because of the sense, we read עָלָיו י‎ ‎‎‎‎‎ ‎‎‎‎‎ instead of the simple prep. עַל: *And over him a mound keepeth guard* (to prevent disturbance of the body). גדיש *heap*, which was a heap of corn 5²⁶, is here a heap of earth or grave-mound (a barrow). 𝔊ᴮ ἐπὶ σωρῶν, but 𝔊ᴬ σωρῷ better. Σωρός = either a heap of corn or a mound of earth. (𝔊ᴬ ἐπὶ σορῷ = over a cinerary urn.) 𝔖 ܓܕܫܐ *gedšā, id.* The Aram. גְּדַשׁ *heap up* may be akin to Hb. גדל *grow up, become tall, great* (cf. מגדל *tower*), by interchange of *l* and *s*; the prim. root being perhaps גד = Sum. GID, *long (arâku).*

v. 33. clods of the glen or wâdy; scil. of which his tumulus is built. For רֶגֶב *clod, gleba,* cf. 38³⁸. √גֹב (= Sum. GAB, *breast*); a rounded protuberance or prominence; cf. Aram. גַּבְּתָא *hill,* Hb. גַּב *mound,* Ez 16²⁴: ר־נב = שׂ־נב (cf. שׂנב *be high,* 5¹¹): ארגב *cairn,* 𝔊 1 Sa 20¹⁹. 𝔊 χάλικες χειμάρρου, *pebbles* or *rubble of the winter torrent*: 𝔙 *dulcis fuit glareis Cocyti,* 'He was dear to the gravels of Cocytus' (taking נחל for the river of Hades). 𝔖 בלעין לה גפיפי נחלא *The winding hollows* (or *caves*) *of the wâdy swallow* (= *are greedy for*: see Payne-Smith, col. 538) *him*.

Sweet to him are the clods of the glen is a somewhat strange statement in this context. There is no reference to Hades (She'ol); for there is nothing 'sweet' in Eyob's conception of Hades (10ⁿ ᶠ·; cf. 3¹⁷⁻²¹ ᶠ·). Perhaps a better reading would be יִשְׁתֹּק בְּמוֹ־רִגְבֵי נחל *He is quiet* (*at rest* Ps 107³⁰) *among the clods of the glen* (שׁ ש = מ מ). Some reject vv. 28–33.

St. ii. *And after him all men march*: i.e. all go the same way, good and bad alike (cf. v. 26); all without distinction march to the same goal of the grave. The verb משך seems to be used intrans., as in Ju 4⁶, where 𝔊 ἀπελεύσῃ = ἀπελεύσεται here. (𝔐 adds a third stichus: *And before him* (they marched?) *without number.* This is clearly a marginal note.)

v. 34. Cf. 16². *with mere breath*: or *vainly, to no purpose* (הֶבֶל 9²⁹ 27¹² Is 30⁷). St. ii 𝔐 lit. *And your answers—treachery remains over*; an inadequate parallel, and an improb. form of sentence. Instead of נשאר, leg. שקר *falsehood* (13⁴), or שוא *emptiness, futility,* either of which would be a good parallel to הבל, and point מעל (a word not found elsewhere in Job) מֹעַל (= מוֹעִיל) *profiting, helpful* (15³ 21¹³ al.), supplying the neg. אין before it: cf. Je 16¹⁹. Further, since תשובות *answers* only recurs in 34³⁶ (Elihu-section) and not elsewhere in OT, we may get rid of the cumbrous ותשובתיכם and improve the syntax by restoring: ותשיבוני שקר אין־מעיל *And answer me* (13²² 20²) *with profitless falsehood!* 𝔊 τὸ δὲ ἐμὲ καταπαύσασθαι ἀφ' ὑμῶν οὐδέν = וְשָׁבְתִּי מִכֶּם אָיִן (!). 𝔖 *And the answer of his words is left before me.*

Chapter 22.—Eliphaz opens the third round with a third attempt to compel Eyob to an admission of guilt.

v. 2. benefit: or *profit*; 15³ 35³ 34⁹. Driver renders st. ii: '(No,) for he that is wise is profitable unto himself.' If, however, we read עלוי for

𝔐 עלימו in st. ii, הלאל can hardly be right in st. i. That the text is more or less corrupt is evident from the variations of the Versions. 𝔊 simply repeats 21²², word for word; 𝔖 *With God sayest thou, O man, That thou art equal with Him in wisdom?* cf. 𝔙. 𝔗 *Can a man teach* (יאלף) *God?* cf 𝔊 ὁ διδάσκων, 21²². *Can a man impart knowledge to El, That the sage should profit Him?* is at least good sense (for the constr. cf 3¹² 6¹¹ 7¹² 21¹⁵ et saep.). To make עליו refer to משביל > אל seems unnatural. Apart from the difficulty of the change of prep., לנפשו would have been more explicit than עליו in the sense of 'unto himself'. (If we might assume an Arabism עלים = علِم *wise*, doctus, עלים ומשביל would give for st. ii *That the wise and prudent should profit him?*)

v. 3. *Shaddai's concern* or *interest* (21²¹ חפץ). *perfectest* cf. Ps 18³³ 101². (𝔊ᴮ ἀπώσης is a mere scribal error for ἁπλώσης 𝔊ᴺ ᶜ·ᴬ·.)

v. 4. *godliness* or *piety*; lit. *fear*, scil. of God = religion or religiousness (4⁶ 15⁴, cf. 28²⁸). 𝔊 ἡ λόγον σου ποιούμενος = *or because He maketh account of thee*; taking מיראתך wrongly in the sense *from fear of thee*, which it might bear in a different context.

v. 5. The argument so far (vv. 2–4) seems to be this: Neither your wisdom or subtlety displayed in your special pleading, nor your boasted integrity, constitutes any claim upon God; and as you recognize with us that your affliction is from Him, and as He cannot, of course, be chastising you for godly living, it stands to reason that it can only be for unacknowledged sins. *Is not thy wickedness great?* We should say: *Must not thy wickedness be great?* What else necessarily follows from what I have said? Then vv. 6–9 suggest various sins of which a great man like Eyob might have been guilty (sins at all periods characteristic of the ruling classes in Israel according to the testimony of the Prophets), and of one or all of which the speaker assumes that he *must* have been guilty.

v. 6. *Doubtless*: כי lit. *For*. *distrainest upon*: or *exactest pledges from* (cf st. ii and 24³·⁹ Ex 22²⁶ Dt 24⁶·¹⁷). *thy kin*: lit. *thy brothers*; i.e. members of thy tribe or clan. (The verbs in vv. 6–8 are all impf., describing what Eyob habitually did. We must not therefore render *thou hast taken . . . stripped . . hast not given*, as RV, which would require the pf.)

v. 7. *bread*. לחם; but 𝔊 ψωμόν, *a morsel*; i.e. פת as 31¹⁷, where Eyob affirms the contrary of these charges; Pr 17¹. (A variant in the orig. text?)

v. 8. 𝔐 lit. *And the man of arm* (usu taken to mean *the powerful*, but the phrase occurs nowhere else in this sense)—*his is the land; And the face-uplifted* (i.e. the person of honour, the accepted or favoured one, 13⁸ Is 3³) *dwelleth in it*. This is explained as a covert reference to Eyob himself, 'insinuating that he was one of the class of powerful men who claimed all the land for themselves and ejected their poorer neighbours from it (Is 5⁸), by force or fraud': see Driver. So 𝔙: *In fortitudine brachii tui possidebas terram, Et potentissimus obtinebas eam.* But the Heb. can hardly mean this. (Did 𝔙 read יָרֵשָׁה ad fin.?) We propose תִּרְצֶה *thou favourest* pro 𝔐 הָאָרֶץ *the land*, and תֵּיטִיב *thou treatest well* in place of ישבה *dwelleth in it*, or perhaps הֵיטַבְתָּה *thou hast well-treated* (pf. as v. 9⁸). Cf. 24²¹ᵇ; Ma 1⁸. The form of such a statement certainly harmonizes better with the context on both sides of it:

The man that hath an arm (i. e. power) *thou favourest,*
And the person of rank thou treatest well.

Cf. 𝔊:

And thou didst admire the person of some,
And cause them to dwell upon the land.

𝔊: *There is a man who soweth* (וְזֹרֵעַ) pro 𝔐 (וּזְרוֹעַ) *for himself the land,*
And a lord of violence (מָרֵא קְטִירָא) *taketh it from him*.

v. 9. *empty-handed*: see Gn 31⁴² for the same phrase. Lk 1⁵³.

thou crushest: תְּדַכֵּא pro 𝔐 יְדֻכָּא. 𝔙 *comminuisti, rectè;* 𝔊 ὀρφανοὺς δὲ ἐκάκωσας, *And didst illtreat orphans*; a free rendering. 𝔖 ܟܟܒܬ *didst lay low*.

v. 10. *are about thee:* סְבִיבוֹתֶיךָ. 𝔊 ἐκύκλωσάν σε = fort. סְבָבוּךְ, cf. Ps 18⁶. For the paronomasia פַּחַד ... פַּחִים see Is 24¹⁷, and for פַּחַד פִּתְאֹם *a sudden alarm*, panic, or *scare*, Pr 3²⁵. פַּח, פָּחָא, ڤَخّ, 18⁹, is prop. *a bird-snare*, Ho 5¹ 9⁸: cf. perhaps Sum. PAG, *esirum ša iççuri, auceps*, or *cavea avium*(?). The Chinese say *T'ien chi kiang wang*, 'Heaven is letting down its net', scil. of calamities on the country (Shi III. iii. X. 6, 1). *alarmeth thee:* וִיבַהֶלְךָ. There is no need to point יְבָ֣, unless we read סבבוך ante. 𝔊 καὶ ἐσπούδασέν σε, as 4⁵ 21⁶, where see note. For *sudden scare* 𝔊 gives πόλεμος ἐξαίσιος, possibly reading חֶרֶב (5¹⁵) or קְרָב for פַּחַד. As to the translator's favourite adj. ἐξαίσιος, see 9²³ 18¹² 20⁵ 4¹² 37¹⁸.

v. 11. 𝔐 lit. *Or the darkness dost thou not see, And the multitude of waters which covereth thee?* This is taken to mean, Art thou altogether blind to the real significance of thy afflictions? But the Heb. is suspicious, there being nothing to justify the use of אוֹ, and the two members of the distich lacking symmetry and metrical precision. Read perhaps אוֹר חָשַׁךְ בְּאָהֳלֶךָ (after 18⁶): *The light is darkened in thy tent;* cf. 𝔊 τὸ φῶς σοι σκότος ἀπέβη. or אוֹרְךָ חָשַׁךְ וְלֹא תִרְאֶה *Thy light is darkened, and* (so that) *thou seest not*. But אוֹר does not usually take a suff. except with ref. to God (cf., however, 38¹⁵?).

multitude: שִׁפְעַת. So 38³⁴, where st. ii is repeated. The word seems to mean *overflow*, abundantia: see 2 K 9¹⁷. Cf. Syr. *pour forth, overflow, rise* (of a river in flood). √פע; cf. נבע, נבג, בוי, נבבו, שׁפך, Assyr. *tabâku*, &c. *pour*. (𝔊 κεκαλυμμένα δὲ ὕδωρ σε ἐκάλυψεν; but שִׁכְבַת מַיִם *a layer of waters*, cf. Ex 13¹⁴, is wholly improb. here, where the violent action of a flood is intended, not a gentle deposit of moisture like dew, Ex l.c.)

v. 12. Reading הַגְבִיהַּ pro 𝔐 גֹּבַהּ *height*. To make 𝔐 tolerable, בְּגֹבַהּ (so 𝔗 plur.) might be read: *Is not Eloah in the height of heaven?* (AV, RV) From such a height He necessarily sees everything on the earth (Ps 33¹³·¹⁴) But 𝔊 ἀρίμ = הַגְבִיהַּ is certainly preferable. It is possible that אֱלוֹהַּ, which 𝔊 omits, grew out of הֲלֹא (dittogr.) and that גבה was then added. The orig. v. may have been: הבט שמים וראה | ושור כוכבים כי־רמו *Look at the heavens and see, And behold the stars that they are lofty!* (cf. 35⁵ which may be an echo of this verse). 𝔐 רֹאשׁ, which is unique in its present connexion, may very well be a corruption of שׁוּר (written backwards). This relieves st. ii of its metrical overweight. In any case, the thought of vv. 12–14 is similar to Is 40²⁶·²⁷, and may have been suggested by that passage.

𝔊 μὴ οὐχὶ ὁ τὰ ὑψηλὰ ναίων ἐφορᾷ = הֲלֹא מַגְבִּיהַּ שִׁבְתּוֹ יִרְאֶה (cf. Ps 113⁵ ch. 5⁷; ἀπ' ναίων = κατοικῶν) or הֲלֹא שֹׁכֵן גֹּבַהּ יִרְאֶה (cf. Is 33⁵ שֹׁכֵן מָרוֹם; also Is 57¹⁵) Note 𝔊's omission of אֱלוֹהַּ. τοὺς δὲ ὕβρει φερομένους ἐταπείνωσεν; = יַשְׁפִּיל וּרְאֵה (עָרִיצִים?) אַבִּירִים (וּגְאוֹן?) וְרֹאשׁ (cf. 24²² Is 13¹¹), or something similar. (𝔊 hardly intended דָּאֹשׁ = דָּשׁ *treads down* or *threshes* by ἐταπείνωσεν. That verb is never used of God, and never so rendered by 𝔊.)

v. 14. *a cover'*. or *hiding-place, covert*, סֵתֶר Ps 18¹²; 𝔙 latibulum eius; 𝔊 ἀποκρυφῆς (𝔊ᴺᴬ ἀποκρυφή· recte), also pointing יֵרָאֶה (and *He is not seen*) St ii. In English we can say 'walk' or 'pace' the vault of heaven, but not, it would seem, in Heb הִתְהַלֵּךְ is usually followed by בְּ *in* (1⁷ 2² Gn 3⁸) or עַל *on, upon* (18⁸ 2 Sa 11²); one of which preps., probably the latter, may be assumed to have fallen out here. Cf. Is 40²² Pr 8²⁷. The חוּג, 𝔊 γῦρον (Ecclus 24⁵), *ring, circle*, also *round hole*, is the semicircular vault or firmament of the visible heavens. Cf. perhaps Sum. AGA, AGU, *crown, diadem* (from GAG; Ch 戹 ngo, ak. *a ring, a bangle*, from ngak). Cf. the verb 26¹⁰, and עוּג (*round*) *cake*.

v. 15. So 𝔐 and 𝔊 τρίβον αἰώνιον φυλάξεις = 𝔙 Numquid semitam saeculorum custodire cupis. But עַוָּלִים *the unjust* would supply the missing parallel to מְתֵי־אָוֶן *men of wickedness* (cf. 11¹¹); and אֲשֻׁר *step(s), track, path*, would do the same for אֹרַח *way* (cf. 23¹¹), at the same time getting rid of the prosaic אֲשֶׁר (points) which, besides, follows properly in the next stichus:

*Wilt thou keep to the way of the unjust,—
The track which men of wickedness have trodden?*

(𝔊 δίκαιοι ad fin. prob. scribal slip for ἄδικοι.) With this disappears the supposed reference to the Flood in אֹרַח עוֹלָם and the following verse.

v. 16. Reading בְּלֹא (ויִקָּפְצוּ?) c. 20 codd. and 𝔖: cf. 𝔊 οἱ συνελήμφθησαν ἄωροι and 𝔙 Qui sublati sunt ante tempus suum. 𝔗 adds explan. *from the earth*. *were snatched away*: קֻמְּטוּ lit. *were seized* or *grasped* (an Aramaism ἅπ. in OT, 16⁹ being corrupt). The root is clearly akin to קמץ and קבץ (Ar. قبض) *grasp, seize, gather*, &c. (Cf. Sum. GAM, *to bend, bow, curve*, as the fingers do in grasping. Hence קֹמֶץ, קוּמְצָא *fist, handful*, Ar. قبضة *handful*. √ √ם, √ב, are variants of the same orig. sound.) St. ii נהר יוצק יסודם. RV *Whose foundation was poured out as a stream*; but this would require כנהר, for נהר as a secondary predicate is not in the poet's manner. Besides, the sense required, as at once more natural and direct, is *Whose foundation the river dissolves* (or *washes away*). Cf. 14¹⁹ Na 2⁷. We might read יָצוּק *pours out* (Impf. of צוק 29⁶) or יִצֹּק *id*. (Impf. of יָצַק 1 K 18³⁴; script. plen.) or point יֹצֵק (cf. 𝔊) Ptcp. *effundens* or *effusurus est*, instead of יֻצַּק Ho. Impf. *is poured out* (cf. 11¹⁵ 37¹⁸ 38³⁸ where Ho. Ptcp. = *poured out* as metal, *cast, made firm*, and 41¹⁶·¹⁶ where יָצוּק Qal Ptcp. has the same mg.). Possible also is יַצִּיק Hi. Impf. *pours out* (Jos 7²³). In view of the general use of יצק in Job, it is perhaps not altogether improbable that the text orig. ran: וכהר יצוק יסודם *Though their foundation was firm set as a mountain* (Ps. 87¹ 125¹): יָצוּק Qal Ptcp. Pass. 𝔊 ποταμὸς ἐπιρρέων οἱ θεμέλιοι αὐτῶν (ἐπιρρέων = יֹצֵק intr. ?); which may be a false interpretation of the possibly correct reading (vid. supr.). The idea that the *foundations* of the wicked *are* (or *become*) *a stream flowing on and on*, is not probable.

v. 17. Cf. 21¹⁴·¹⁵. *Do for us*: reading לָנוּ c 𝔊 𝔖 pro לָמוֹ *to them*. *for us* > *to us*, on account of 21¹⁵. 𝔊 gives the verse differently, but with much the same mg. *Who say, Iahvah—what will He do to us? Or what will the Almighty* (= *Shaddai*) *bring on us?* (= יבוא עלינו cf. 34²⁸ 42¹¹ 𝔊; or perhaps יוביל לנו cf. 21³⁰). Verses 17–18 may belong to the marg. (a citation *memoriter* of 21¹⁴⁻¹⁶ ?).

v. 18. St. i has four stresses: leg. fort. וַיְמַלֵּא *though He filled*.

St. ii. *principles*: lit. *counsel* or *plan*: עֵצָה. See on 21¹⁶ᵇ.

from Him: ממנו = 𝔊 ἀπ' αὐτοῦ. 𝔐 מני *from me*; making the sentence a (needless) repudiation by the speaker of the axioms or standpoint of the wicked; cf. 𝔙: Quorum sententia procul sit a me! (This stichus also is metr. unsatisfactory.) Verse 16 described the catastrophe of the godless; vv. 19–20 describe the joy of the righteous thereat (cf. Ps 58¹¹). As the text stands, vv 17–18 disturb the connexion; but 21¹⁶⁻¹⁸, rightly translated and regarded as a continuation of 22¹⁶, would not have this effect:

> *How often* (כמה) *is the lamp of the wicked put out,*
> *And their ruin cometh upon them;*
> *They become like chaff before wind,*
> *And like stubble the storm carries off!*

Then would follow, quite naturally (22¹⁹)

> *The righteous see and rejoice,*
> *And the innocent mock at them,* &c.

v. 19. *rejoice*; ישׂמחו: so Ps 58¹¹ 107⁴². 𝔊 ἐγέλασαν = ישׂחקו. (The aorists of 𝔊 do not imply וַיְ ... רָאוּ, nor is that a preferable reading; cf. the following יִלְעָג.)

v 20. *our adversaries*: קָמֵינוּ (Ex 15⁷ al.) pro 𝔐 קִימָנוּ ἅπ· (vox nihili). This involves the plur. of the verb (𝔐 נכחד). 𝔊 ἡ ὑπόστασις αὐτῶν, *their substance*; 𝔙 erectio eorum; both perhaps implying קוּמָם *their rising up* or *standing* (or else יְקָמָם *their existing things*: Gn 7⁴ ²³ 𝔙 substantiam 𝔊 τὸ ἀνάστεμα; Dt 11⁶ 𝔙 substantia eorum but 𝔊 αὐτῶν τὴν ὑπόστασιν). It is in the destruction of the wicked themselves rather than their possessions that the righteous rejoice elsewhere (see the Psalms cited above); קָמֵינוּ is therefore to be preferred. With this is naturally involved the destruction of their belongings (? יְתָרָם *their abundance*, st. ii, cf. Ps 17¹⁴ Is 15⁷. But יתרם may mean *the rest of them*, i.e. the rank and file of their followers, who share the fate of the chiefs: cf. Dt 11⁶ Nu 10³²·³⁵). (𝔊 *If they are not humbled from their obstinacy, The rest of them also shall the fire devour!* does not certainly prove that 𝔊 read נכחדו pl. It may perhaps have read נכחד as 𝔐 with subj. קוּמָם *their upstanding, firmness,* or *opposition.* 𝔗 also may have had the same text.)

v. 21. *be reconciled with Him*: or *use thyself to Him*; *become familiar and friendly with Him*: 𝔗 אֲלַף עֲמֵיהּ *become used to Him*; 𝔙 acquiesce ei, *yield* or *assent to Him*; 𝔊 *make an agreement, come to terms with Him.* 𝔊 γενοῦ δὲ σκληρός, ἐὰν ὑπομείνῃς = הַקְשֵׁה־נָא אִם־תְּשָׁלָם; vid. 9⁴ ᵇ.) Driver: '*Accustom thyself to Him*, acquiesce in His dealings with thee.' For the Hi. of סכן (15³) see also Nu 22³⁰ Ps 139³ ᵇ. [If ס׳כן is a Saph. of כון Assyr. *kânu*, the idea of use and wont, habituation, familiarity, may be traced back to the primary mg. *fixed,* firm, right, regular, proper = Sum. GIN, GEN, *kénu, kéttu, kunnu,* &c. See note on 9⁴. מִסְכֵּן (Heb., Aram., Ar.), on the other hand, may, like its syn. Assyr. *muškînu*, have sprung from Sum. GEN, *little, weak.*]

be at peace: scil. with Him. Cf. Ps 7⁵ Ptcp. Or *be safe and sound, prosperous*: 9⁴. Perhaps we should read Hi הַשְׁלֵם *make peace* (with Him): Dt 20¹².

St. ii. 𝔐 is evidently more or less corrupt. 𝔊 εἶτ' ὁ καρπός σου ἔσται ἐν ἀγαθοῖς = אָמְנָם תְּבוּאָתְךָ בְּטוֹב. For εἶτα = אמנם see 12²; for ἐν ἀγαθοῖς = בטוב see 21¹³ 36¹¹; cf. v. 18 supr. תְּבוּאָתְךָ *thy crop* or *gain* (31¹²) is supported by 18 codd. as well as 𝔊𝔙𝔊𝔗. Others would read תְּבוֹאֲךָ *shall come to thee*, which is perhaps less prob. (cf. 20²² Ez 32¹¹ in both of which locc. as elsewhere בוא c suff. is used of evil haps). בְּטוֹב may be entirely consisting in good, wholly good, excellent (*B t' E ntiae*), cf. 𝔙 fructus optimos. Else we must keep 𝔐 טֹבָה *a thy well-being.*

בָּהֶם *Thereby*, lit. *By those* (things?), is doubtful. Why not f. בָּהּ or, as is much more usual, בּוֹ? Moreover, the precise reference of the pronoun (why plur.?) is not clear. בזאת would be more natural: cf. 𝕲 *dra*. Perhaps בְּכֵן *then* (Aramaism = אָז), Ec 8¹⁰.

v. 22. Eliphaz appears to pose as a prophet, or at least to lay claim to prophetic inspiration (cf. 4¹²ff); תּוֹרָה *teaching, instruction,* being either the oracular response of a priest, or the authoritative utterance of a prophet of Iahvah (both regarded as indicating or pointing out the Divine will to man, and so *teaching* him truth for conduct and belief: cf. 6²⁴ 27¹¹). Cf. Assyr. *têrtu, omen, oracle, command, law;* Sum. UR-UŠ = *têrtum ša ḫašê*, 'omen from the inwards (liver?)'; UZU UR-UŠ = (DP. šîr) *têrtum ša širi*, 'omen from inspection of the flesh'.

v. 23. 𝕲 *If thou wilt return and humble thyself before Iahvah*; reading either וְתִכָּנַע or וְתֵעָנֶה instead of 𝔐 תִּבָּנֶה *thou shalt be built up* (which is clearly wrong, as the Apod. is given in the next verse: the ו fell out after י, as often). The Ni. of neither of these verbs, however, occurs anywhere else in Job (ענה Pi. 30¹¹ 37²³; כנע Hi. 40¹²†). Read therefore וְתִפְנֶה *and turn* scil. to Him for help (5¹: cf. Is 45²²), or perhaps אם־תשוב ועל(אל)־ש׳ תפנה *If thou repent and turn unto Shaddai.* Prefix ו to תרחיק: *and banish* or *put far.*

v. 24. 𝔐 lit. *And set thou on the dust* (or *ground*) *precious ore* (?), *And in the rock of wâdys Ophir.* This cannot possibly be right. Eyob, who had lost all, had no gold left to sacrifice (see 1²¹). We propose תָּשִׁית בֶּעָפָר חָרוּץ וּבְצוּר נַחַל כֶּתֶם אוֹפִיר *Thou shalt make gold as dust, | And bullion of Ophir as the rock(s) of the ravine.* Cf. 27¹⁶ Zc 9⁵ 1 K 10²⁷. Instead of 𝔐 וְשִׁית 10 codd. or give ישית (cf. 𝔙 *dabit*), but 𝕲 θήσῃ = תשית (Gᴬ θήσεις). The על־עפר of 𝔐 may be due to a scribe's subconscious memory of the phrase which occurs 19²⁵ 20¹¹ 21²⁶. There appears to be no real authority for the supposed בֶּצֶר *precious ore, gold* (cf., however, 36¹⁹). The word may easily be a corruption of חָרוּץ *gold*; or it may be a disguise of צֶרֶף = Assyr. *ṣarpu, silver* (here only). 𝕲 ἐν πέτρᾳ = בְּצוּר (*pts*); cf. 𝔙 *silicem*. In st. ii some 65 codd. וּבְצוּר *recte pro* 𝔐; so 𝕲 καὶ ὡς πέτρα χειμάρρου Σωφείρ; cf. 𝔖𝔗. (It will be seen that 𝕲 *And thou shalt gather silver as dust, And as sand of the sea gold of Ophir* comes near to the prob. orig. text, and that AV is here preferable to RV. The verse is not an exhortation to the surrender of treasure which Eyob no longer possessed, but a promise of future wealth contingent on repentance: cf. 42¹¹.)

For כֶּתֶם אוֹפִיר, see 28¹⁶·¹⁹ 31²⁴ Is 13¹². Cf. further v. 21 (promise of *gain* תְּבוּאָה) and Pr 3¹⁴ (תבואה, חרוץ, כסף associated). For st. i we may also suggest וְכֶסֶף בֶּעָפָר תִּצְבֹּר *And silver as dust thou shalt heap up*: cf. 27¹⁶. (וכסף miswritten successively ובשף ?ושח.)

v. 25. Unquestionably corrupt as it stands in 𝔐. In fact, vv. 24—25 look like different attempts at restoring the same distorted text: cf. וּשִׂיחַ and וְשִׂדַי, בְּצֹר וּבַצּוּר and בְּצָרֶיךָ, אוֹפִיר (כֶּתֶם) and תּוֹעָפוֹת. 𝔊 st. i gives ἔσται οὖν σου (𝔊^A δέ σοι) ὁ παντοκράτωρ βοηθός ἀπὸ ἐχθρῶν = וְהָיָה שַׁדַּי צָרְךָ (בְּ)(טְ)צָרֶיךָ (cf. Ps 18³ צוּרִי = μου βοηθός); a sort of conflate reading. 𝔊 app. understood בְּצָרֶיךָ as mg. *against thy foes* (which it might mean in another context); so 𝔙 Eritque Omnipotens contra hostes tuos. But 𝔊 appears to have read before this word (בְּ)צ(וּ)רְךָ (as) *thy rock* (*Beth Ess.*); which may have been an alternative view of the obscure בְּצָרֶיךָ and, in any case, reminds us of the בְּצֹר וּבַצּוּר of v. 24. If we might read for בְּצָרֶיךָ (4 codd. and Qimḥi בְּצֹרֶךָ) the very similar צֹרְפָךְ or מְצָרְפָךְ *thy refiner*, we should at least get a line in perfect harmony with 𝔊 st. ii: καθαρὸν δὲ ἀποδώσει σε ὥσπερ ἀργύριον πεπυρωμένον (Ps 12⁷) = וּכְכֶסֶף צָרוּף יְטַהֲרֶךָ. The distich would then be:

> And Shaddai will become thy Refiner,
> And like silver refined will purify thee (37²¹).

It is, however, possible that 𝔖 has preserved the true reading: viz. בְּעֶזְרֶךָ (pro בְּצָרֶיךָ) *in* (= as, in the character of) *thine help*; for its version is: *And God will become in thine help* (حكـﻠـﻮﻧ). Indeed 𝔊 may have intended the same expression by βοηθός σου: see Ex 18⁴ Ps 70⁶ and other locc. ap. Concord. For st. ii (metr. short?), where a verb may be missing, 𝔖 gives: *And silver of countings* (i.e. in great quantity) *shall be thine*; but 𝔙 et argentum coacervabitur tibi = וְכֶסֶף יִצָּבֶר לָךְ (cf. Zc 9³ coacervavit), or perhaps תִּצְבָּר־לָךְ (*thou shalt heap to thyself*). הצב(ו)ר obviously resembles the difficult and prob. corrupt תּוֹעָפוֹת and also 𝔊's צָרוּף. 𝔗 st. i app. מִבְצְרֶ(י)ךָ *thy stronghold(s)* pro בְּצָרֶיךָ; in st. ii (וּמָמוֹן כְּסַף תְּקוֹף רוּמָא דִילָךְ) *And above silver shall lofty strength be thine* may imply: וּמִכְּכֶסֶף תּוֹעָפוֹת לָךְ. Cf. 𝔙 Nu 23²² 24⁸. It would make a good parallel to

> And Iahvah will be thy Refiner

if we might read: וְכַכֶּסֶף צָרוּף תּוֹפִיעַ

> And like silver refined thou shalt shine (3⁴ 10^{a.22}).

The phrase כֶּסֶף תּוֹעָפוֹת *silver of the summits* or *peaks* is improb. (cf. 28¹). Silver-mines are not usu. situated on hill-tops. But that תּוֹעָפוֹת means something like cacumina, *peaks, tree-tops*, is prob. from the three other locc. where the word occurs. In Nu 23²² 24⁸ the תּ of the wild ox are mentioned; and it is natural to compare the similar figure of Dt 33¹⁷ where the *horns* of the wild ox are spoken of. In Ps 95⁴ (the only other occur.) we have תּ' הָרִים *the tops of the mountains* (𝔙 altitudines montium); their 'horns', as they are called in the Alps. In the Psalm 𝔊 τὰ ὕψη τῶν ὀρέων recte. The √יעף may perhaps be compared with Assyr. *appu* (from *wa'pu*), 'top', e.g. *appu* u *išdi* top and bottom; *appu* ša iṣi, 'top of a tree' (cacumen). Cf. also the use of the Sum. SAG, *head, top* (*rêšu*), in the sense of *horn* (*qarnu*).

v. 26. St. i: see 27¹⁰ Is 58¹⁴. Perhaps a quotation. *lift up thy face* (11¹⁵): in renewed confidence and trust. 𝔊 om. כי *For*, 9³¹ 13²⁰: παρρησιασθήσῃ ἐναντίον κυρίου (a paraphrase as in 27¹⁰), ἀναβλέψας εἰς τὸν οὐρανὸν ἱλαρῶς.

v. 27. St. ii: 𝔊 δώσει δέ σοι ἀποδοῦναι τὰς εὐχάς = 'תש (נדר)(ו) וְיִתֶּן־לָךְ: cf. 6⁸. The stichus is metr. short. Perhaps rather לְאֵל *to El*, or לו *to Him*, the usual constr., has fallen out before תשלם *thou shalt pay*.

v. 28. *purpose*: or *decree*. (גזר here only in Job; an Aramaism in this sense. In Heb. it means *to cut in two*: 1 K 3²⁵.) For st. i 𝔊 repeats 8⁶ ἀποκαταστήσει δέ σοι δίαιταν δικαιοσύνης = וְשִׁלַּם נְוֵה צִדְקֶךָ: a better parallel. Was it orig. וְיָקֶם־לְךָ אֹהֶל צִדְקֶךָ *And He will raise thee up thy righteous tent* (Am 9¹¹)? Then יגזר might have originally stood as a mistaken gloss on יקם, and אמר have displaced אהל.

v. 29. St. i is corrupt. 𝔐 lit. *For they abased* (השפילו) *and thou saidst pride* (33¹⁷; an Aramaism גֵּוָה = גַּאֲוָה); which, however explained, is no parallel to st. ii *And the downcast of eyes he saveth*. See Dan 4³⁴ *And them that walk in pride* (בְּגֵוָה), *He is able to abase* (להשפלה), Is 2¹¹·¹² 5¹⁵ Pr 29²³, and ch. 40¹¹, which suggest a suitable parallel, e.g. כי השפיל גֵּאוּת אָדָם *For He abaseth the pride of man*. אֶת־אֲמַר גֵּוָה *the speech of pride*(?) is doubtful Heb. Cf. also Is 13¹¹ 25¹¹. Also אֶת־הָרָם וְגֵאֶה *the lofty and proud* is possible (cf. Is 2¹² but order reversed for the worse; and why אֶת?). Perhaps נבהות אדם *the haughtiness of man* (= ותאמר נוה): Is 2¹⁷. 𝔊 *Because thou didst humble thyself and didst say, I* (𝔊^A) *was haughty* app. = כי תשפיל ותאמר גאה (Aram. use of נאה?); but this cannot be right, and is prob. a guess. (In st. ii κύφοντα = שַׁח should be κυφέντα: scribal error? Cf. Is 2⁹ וישח = ἔκυψεν.) Cf. 𝔖: *Because he who humbleth himself hath said* (= thought) *that he will be exalted*, &c.

v. 30. St. i, besides being metr. short, contains the isolated expression אי־נקי *non-innocent*, which really contradicts st. ii, instead of presenting a parallel thereto. The idea that, if Eyob makes his humble submission to God, He will then 'deliver even the guilty for the sake of Job's righteousness' (so 𝔛; cf. 42⁸), is entirely foreign to the thought of Eliphaz. 𝔊 𝔙 om. the anomalous Neg. אִי, which 𝔖 turns into a Positive Ptc. by pointing אַי, אֵי *where* and rendering it *wherever he is* (איכא ראיתוהי): so 1 cod. and Ar.—The suggestion אֶת נָקִי is improb., the את being superfluous; and אִישׁ נָקִי *the innocent man* is contrary to the use of נקי, which is mostly substantival (exc. when joined with דם *blood*) like צדיק *the just man*. In fact, among all the forty-two occurrences of the word, neither of these expressions is ever found. אֵל *El* is therefore to be preferred. (For נקי alone, see 4⁷ 17³ 22¹ 27¹⁷; plur. 9²³.). The verbs ונמלט . . . ימלט do not seem very probable. It is not in the poet's manner to make one form of a verb parallel to another. Perhaps יִפְדֶּה *he ransometh* is indicated by 𝔊 ῥύσεται (5^{20} 6^{23} 33^{28}); and since verbs of saving and delivering are commonly followed by מִן, as in the locc. citt., אי may very well be regarded as a remnant of מִאָוֶן *from trouble*, or מֵאֵיד *from calamity, ruin*. In st. ii וְנִמְלַט (𝔊 καὶ διασώθητι 𝔊ᴬ melius διασωθήσῃ) is prob. right; cf. 6^{23} מוֹלֵט ′ = σώσαι με 29^{12}, אֲמַלֵּט = διέσωσα. See also $1^{15\,16\,17\,19}$ מלט Ni. = σωθῆναι and prob. 20^{20} (𝔐 Pi.).—The similar √פלט occurs in 21^{10} 23^{7} only (see notes ad locc.) —For 𝔐 כפיך ad fin. (𝔊 𝔗) leg. כפיו *his palms* (𝔅 𝔖 𝔄 𝔊ᶻ). The phrase בֹּר כַּפַּי ′ *purity of hands* (cf. Ps $18^{21\,25}$) is found nowhere else in Job; but בֹּר is connected with כַּפַּי, in a different sense, 9^{30} q.v The verse may be an addition in the vein of Elihu.

Chapter 23.—Eyob's seventh answer, chaps. 23–24.

v. 2. 𝔐 lit. :

Also (or *even*) *to-day rebellion is my musing* (or *complaint*);
My hand is heavy upon my sighing.

St, i cannot possibly be regarded as good Heb. for '*My complaint is still accounted of you rebellious*', viz. against God. The verse is certainly more or less corrupt. 𝔊 καὶ δὴ οἶδα ὅτι ἐκ χειρός μου ἡ ἔλεγξίς ἐστιν, καί (𝔊ᴬ om.) ἡ χείρ αὐτοῦ βαρεῖα γέγονεν ἐπ' ἐμῷ στεναγμῷ = כִּי־עַתָּה יָדַעְתִּי (כִּי)מְרִי שִׂחִי | (וְ)יָדוֹ כבדה על־אנחתי:. For καὶ δή = כי־עתה, cf. 6^3. ידעתי may have grown out of this; or it may be an accidental anticipation of v. 3^a. Possibly καὶ δή = 𝔐 גַּם־הַיּוֹם. It is self-evident from the following verses (3–15) that God must have been mentioned by name in this verse, as otherwise there is no visible reference for the 3rd Pers. Pron. throughout. Now מְרִי *rebellion* (chiefly Ez, e.g. 27^8) is not a Job-word; and if it were, it would not be in harmony with the context here. It probably conceals the Divine name שדי (מ or ש׳ = שׁ or ש׳, as in other instances; see 15^{29} 21^{33}; and ר=ר׳). Thus the original stichus may have been גַּם־הַיּוֹם לְשַׁדַּי שִׂיחִי *Still of Shaddai is my complaint*, scil. and not of man; see 21^4. Nothing thou hast said has altered my standpoint or modified my conviction, which is the same 'to-day' as it was yesterday. There is clearly a reference to Eyob's last (the sixth) reply, 21^{7b} (where 𝔊 μου ἡ ἔλεγξίς = שיחי as here). St. ii naturally enough adds: *And His Hand it is that is heavy on groaning me* (lit. *on my groaning*). Leg. וְיָדִי pro 𝔐 יָדִי c 𝔊 𝔖. (𝔊 𝔗 𝔅 read מַר *bitter* in st. i pro 𝔐 מְרִי *rebellion*. If we could dispense with all mention of God until v 16, the stichus *To-day also is my complaint bitter* would suit well enough.)

v. 3. St. ii. Leg. וְאָבוֹא *That I might come* Exc. ו post ו praeced The st. is metr. short, and תְּכוּנָה *preparation, things prepared* (Ne 2^{16}) is more than doubtful in the required sense of *fixed abode, seat*. We therefore restore שְׁבוּן (עָבְתוֹ) *His dwelling-place* (Ps 33^{14} 1 K $8^{13\,39}$+), which satisfies both ⟨sens⟩ and metr ⟨ ⟩ ⟨ ⟩ ils ilum ⟨ts⟩ מכי כסאי Ps 89^{15}, or שבת = sedes?). 𝔊 εἰς τέλος = עד־לכלה (!).—In st. i leg. דַּעְתִּי Inf. cst. c suff., ut 11⁵ Ex 16³, pro 𝔐 יָדַעְתִּי constr. anom. (Kittel dl. c 1 cod.— 𝔊 incert.).

v. 4. That I might... So 𝔊𝔙 (making verbs of 4–5 depend on *O that...*, v. 3). *my case*: מִשְׁפָּטִי (י exc. p. ו?—cf. 13¹⁸ ubi exc. p. י). So 𝔊 ἐμαυτοῦ κρίμα.

v. 5. Eyob cannot conceive, and would like to learn, how God could refute his contentions. *the words*: 𝔊ᴮ ἰάματα, prob. scribal error for ῥήματα (𝔊ᴺᶜ·ᵃᴬᶜ).

v. 6. Note the paronomasia in the Heb. (*habĕrob-kōaḥ yarîb 'immadî?*). Leg. prob. הברב־כֹּחַ *In the greatness of* His *strength* (Is 63¹ 30¹⁸ note). The ו fell out before י, as often elsewhere.

would He strive: 𝔊 ἐπελεύσεταί μοι = יבוא עלי pro ירוב עמדי; but the paronomasia as well as the legal force of ריב favours 𝔐.

St. ii is difficult, and the text uncertain if we may judge by the Versions. 𝔊 εἶτα (𝔊ᴬ καὶ εἰ) ἐν ἀπειλῇ μοι οὐ χρήσεται (𝔊ᴬ μοι in loc. ult.). Since ἀπειλή = אֵימָה *terror*, Pr 20² (a word found in 9³⁴ 13²¹, where Eyob expresses the same desire as here that God would meet him on equal terms, and not overawe him with His Majesty); and since χρῆσθαι c dat. pers. = עשה עם 13²⁰, or עשה ל Gn 16⁶, 𝔊 may perhaps indicate some such text as ואם לא באימה יעשה לי *Or not in terror deal with me?* Cf. 𝔊 *In greatness of strength He striveth with me: And if not* (ואן לא), *fear He putteth upon me.* 𝔙 Nolo multa fortitudine contendat mecum; *Nec magnitudinis suae mole me premat* (= ולא אכפו ישים בי *And not put His pressure on me;* אכפו pr 𝔐 הוא אך: cf. 33⁷). Since we desiderate a parallel question, we may assume that the sentence began with ואם־לא (ו exc. p. י; אם = אך) and render: *Or will* (would) *not He* (emph.) *listen to me?* (ישמע ut 15¹⁷ al. pr. 𝔐 ישם בי; a doubtful constr. Cf. 1⁸ 2⁸).

v. 7. 𝔐 lit. *There an upright one* (or *the upright*) *would be arguing with Him*. There is something strange about this oblique reference to himself, apart from the question of a suitable parallel to st. ii. We incline to read שָׁם יָשָׁר וְנוֹכַח עִמִּי *There* (i. e. at His 'fixed abode', v. 4) *would He contend and argue with me.* Cf. Ho 12⁵ (of which this verse may be a reminiscence: '*At Bethel he findeth him, And there he speaketh with him*'); Gn 32²⁹. Eyob implies that (like Jacob) he would come off victorious in the strife of words; i.e. that he would convince God of the justice of his case. 𝔊 ἀλήθεια γὰρ καὶ ἔλεγχος παρ' αὐτοῦ (? αὐτῷ =עמו); perhaps pointing יָשָׁר וְנֹכַח, or יֹשֶׁר וְהוֹכֵחַ, and in either case confirming ונוכח; cf. 𝔗 תמן תריצא ותקין עמי There *the upright and perfect* (will be?) *with me* (but Levy עמו *with Him*, as 𝔐). 𝔙 Proponat aequitatem contra me; misp[o]inting שָׁם pro שָׁם, taking נֹ(וֹ)כַח as the prep. (adv.) נֹכַח *in front*, [etc.] and not confirming ונ. 𝔖 *There uprightly I should plead* (or *strive*) *along with Him, and should be found guiltless* (implying text of 𝔐). See also Burney, *JTS.* Apr. 1910, pp. 436 f.

St. ii. *I should escape*: leg. וְאִפָּלְטָה pro 𝔐 וַאֲפַלְּטָה: cf. 22³⁰. The √פלט is prob. not genuine anywhere in Job. 𝔐 has it besides only in 21¹⁰, where it may be a t. t., but should probably be altered to תִּמָּלֵט. Moreover, פלט Pi. is always trans. Hence some would provide an Obj. by pointing מִשְׁפָּטִי *my cause* or *case* (c 𝔊𝔖𝔙) instead of מִשְׁפָּטִי מִ *from my judge*. But *I should secure, carry off*, or *deliver my cause*, is not a Heb. mode of saying *I should win my case*; and the most usual Subj. of פלט Pi. is Iahvah. Perhaps אֲבַטְּלָה might be read (an Aramaism; cf. Ec 12³) with מִשְׁפָּטִי: *And I should end my case for ever*; put a final end to my litigation. Cf. 𝔊 ἐξαγάγοι δὲ εἰς τέλος τὸ κρίμα μου. 𝔙 *Et perveniat ad victoriam iudicium meum* gives the general sense; but the particular meaning of the verse is that God will cease to persecute Eyob, when once the latter has succeeded in demonstrating his innocence.

v. 8. קדם ואחור may mean either *forward and backward, to the front and to the rear, before and behind* (cf. Ps 139⁵), or *eastward and westward* (cf. Gn 11² Is 9¹¹). Similarly, in the next verse, שמאל and ימין may be either *left hand* and *right* or *north* and *south* (Ez 16⁴⁶). As is well known, Orientals face the east, to determine the points of the compass.

He is not there: איננו: 𝔊 οὐκ ἔτι εἰμί = אינני *I am no more*: so Or^K but Or^Q as 𝔐 rectè. Cf. 𝔙 *Si ad Orientem iero, non apparet; si ad occidentem, non intelligam eum*.

v. 9. *I seek Him*: בִּקַּשְׁתִּיו (= 𝔖 ܟܒ̈) pro 𝔐 בעשׂתו *when He works*. Perhaps בשעתי *when I look*—a Job-verb, 7¹⁹ 10²⁰ 14⁶. *see Him*: אֶחֱזוּ pro 𝔐 אָחַז (Apoc. Impf. of חזה; cf. Mi 4¹¹), which 𝔙 *apprehendam eum* and 𝔊 κατέσχον (Gn 22¹³) confound with אחז *to seize*. *I turn*: (וְ)אֶעֱטֹף c 𝔖𝔙 (*si me vertam ad dexteram*) pro 𝔐 יַעְטֹף *He turneth*; an Aramaism (the word in 𝔖). Sole occurrence of a √עטף in Job. At the end read אֶרְאֵהוּ *I behold* or *perceive Him* pro 𝔐 אֶרְאֶה. (The fine quatrain, vv. 8–9, wanting in Hex., may be regarded as an apt marginal parallel to v. 3. Here it seems to interrupt the connexion of thought between v. 7 and v. 10.)

v. 10. 𝔐 דַּרְכִּי עִמָּדִי *the way with me*; an unlikely, if not meaningless expression in Heb.—𝔊 *For He knoweth already my way*; 𝔙 *Ipse vero scit viam meam*. 𝔗 also om. עמדי (without which the stichus is too short metr.). 𝔖 *He Himself knoweth my way* and my uprising (or *standing, steadfastness*, קִימִי) = וְעָמְדִי. This, which recalls the phrase 'Thou knowest my downsitting and my uprising', Ps 139², may be right, either in the sense of *my going and standing* (stopping), or in that of *my steadfast* or *persistent way*, or simply *the way wherein I stand* (? דֶּרֶךְ עָמְדִי *the way of my standing*; cf. Ps 1¹). If H̲e̲ t̲e̲s̲t̲ o̲r̲ t̲r̲y̲ m̲e̲: ב״י perhaps akin to ברר *c̲l̲e̲a̲n̲*. In Aram. (Sy̲) s̲u̲c̲h̲ w̲o̲r̲k̲ a̲s̲ t̲e̲s̲t̲i̲n̲g̲ p̲r̲o̲v̲e̲s̲ o̲r̲ a̲s̲s̲a̲y̲ f̲o̲r̲ a̲s̲s̲a̲y̲ fire.

The original idea seem to be that of looking into, or examining with the eye (cf. בחן *look-out, watch-tower*, Is 32¹⁴, and חור *to look at*): cf. Ps 11⁴. *I shall come forth*; scil. from the crucible; cf. Zc 13⁹. The ancients knew nothing of chemical assaying; fire was their only means of testing metals.

v. 11. *His steps* : 31⁷ (not elsewhere in Job); Pr 14¹⁵. Perhaps plur. always as in Ps 17⁵ al. (= vestigia eius, *His footprints* or *tracks* : so 𝔙). 𝔊 ἐξελεύσομαι δὲ (= אצא v. 10 !) ἐν ἐντάλμασιν αὐτοῦ (= ממצותו v. 12 ! —translator's eye wandered to next line, and overlooked אחזה רגלי).

v. 12. *from the commands* : מִצְוֹת = 𝔊 ἀπὸ ἐνταλμάτων, 𝔙 A mandatis (מ om. ante מ ; per contra 𝔐 ולא male add. 1 post ו).

in my breast or *bosom* : בחקי = 𝔊 ἐν κόλπῳ μου, 𝔙 in sinu meo pro 𝔐 מחקי which cannot mean מלחם חקי (Pr 30⁸); nor indeed can anything sensible be made of it. Cf. 22²². St. ii : four stresses. Leg. אֲמָרָיו *His words*?

v. 13. 𝔐 והוא באחד *But He is One* (Beth Essent.), i.e. ' one and the same, who will not change His purpose ', can hardly be right (= 𝔙 Ipse enim solus est ; et nemo avertere potest cogitationem eius). בָּחַר *He hath chosen* is not used in the sense required by the context. 𝔊 εἰ δὲ καὶ αὐτὸς ἔκρινεν = והוא מֵרִיב (cf. 10²). Perhaps מֵאֵל or הָאֵל *He pleaseth, willeth*, or *resolveth* (cf. 6⁹·²⁸) : *But He pleaseth, and who can turn Him back ?* (9¹² 11¹⁰). Cf. also Nu 23¹⁹·²⁰, which suggests והוא אמר . . . ישיבנה *But He hath spoken, and who can reverse it ?* Another possibility is חָפֵץ or יַחְפֹּץ (9³ al. Ps 115³ 135⁶), voluit, vult, or יחרץ decidit (14⁵).

v. 14. St. i is metr. short. ידעתי *I know*, fort. exc. p. ויעש : *I know that He will fulfil* (Is 44²⁶·²⁸) *my fate* (𝔐 חקי ; cf. 14⁵ ; fort. חקו *His decree concerning me* ; cf. 𝔊 𝔙).—St. ii. 𝔐 וכהנה רבות עמו *And like those things (there are) many with Him* ; very improb. (prosaic and a bad parallel to st. i). Fort. leg. וִיכַלֶּה רִבוֹת עִמִּי *And He will finish the strife with me* : רִיב 13⁸. God will not be diverted from His purpose, but will pursue His quarrel to the bitter end, regardless of Eyob's sufferings. (The verse may be an interpolation. It is apparently omitted by 𝔊, which gives instead of it a duplicate version of v. 15.)

v. 15. אבהל 𝔊 κατασπουδασθῶ (hic tant. ap. Job ; vid. 𝔊ᴬ Ps 2⁵ 6¹¹) = ἐσπούδακα v. 14ᵃ : cf. v. 16 4⁵ 21⁸ 22¹⁰. Eyob is ' dismayed ' or confounded at the thought of the Omnipotent Will as dealing out weal or woe to man without regard to moral desert. See what follows, ch. 24, and cf. 21⁶ff.

v. 16. *softened my heart* ; i.e. robbed me of all courage and confidence, and filled me with despair : cf. Is 7⁴. St. ii is metr. short. As parallel to לבי *my heart* insert נפשי *my soul* ; (בשׁ)נ הבהיל pro 𝔐 הבהילני ; cf. Ps 6⁴ ; or add מאד *greatly, sore* : Ps 6⁴·¹¹.

v. 17. The first stichus is overweighted, and the verse evidently corrupt. Who could be satisfied with such a rendering as '*For I am not undone because of the darkness* (i.e. his calamity), *Or because of my own face* (!), *which thick darkness hath covered*' (Driver)? Such a roundabout and prosaic statement is altogether unlike the usual style of the poet. Omitting the Neg. לֹא c cod. K⁴⁸ and reading נשׁמתי pro 𝔐 נצמתי (cf. 17⁸ 18²⁰ 21⁵·⁶), and in st. ii וְעַל־פָּנַי (21²⁶) pro 𝔐 וּמִפָּנַי (which may be due to the previous מפני), we get the more natural and more poetic statement:

> *For I am appalled before the darkness,*
> *And my face the gloom (30²⁰) hath covered.*

The 'darkness' is the mystery of the Divine dealings, which baffles and bewilders his mind. 𝔊 st. i· *For I knew not that darkness would come upon me* (= כִּי לֹא יָדַעְתִּי יָבֹא עָלַי חֹשֶׁךְ); πρὸ προσώπου δέ μου ἐκάλυψεν (𝔊ᴬ καλύψει) γνόφος (= וּלְפָנַי יְכַסֶּה אֹפֶל). 𝔊 gives the verse thus : *For I was not stilled from before the darkness, And from before the veil of the gloom.* It read נצמתי, as did also 𝔙 (Non enim perii propter imminentes tenebras, Nec faciem meam operuit caligo).

Chapter 24. Eyob continues his reply. He cannot understand God's toleration of the daily spectacle of oppression and crime.

v. 1. 𝔐 lit. *Why of Shaddai are not times laid up* (or *reserved*: 15²⁰ 21¹⁹)? or, more naturally, *Why from Shaddai are times not*(?) *hidden* (10¹³ 17⁴)? *And why have His knower(s) not seen His days?* The 'times' and 'days' are usually supposed to be those of Divine retribution and Judgement. Eyob, however, makes no reference to the prophetic doctrine of 'the Day' (never 'Days') 'of the Lord' (Am 5¹⁸ Is 2¹²). Moreover, acc. to the prophets, the Day of Iahvah *is* 'laid up' or in store for the wicked, and its coming is generally imminent. What Eyob demands is, why do so many wrongdoers prosper all their lives, if his friends are right in maintaining that God always dispenses prosperity and adversity according to human deservings? Instead, therefore, of the really irrelevant questions of this verse, we would restore

> מדוע לא־נצמתו ערי(צ)ים
> ור(ש)עים לא־חזו אידם (פידם 21³⁰):

Why are not oppressors annihilated,
And bad men see not their own ruin?

𝔊 διὰ τί δὲ Κύριον ἔλαθον ὧραι = מדוע משׁדי נצפנו עתים = 𝔐 since לֹא. 𝔊 continues the question with ἀσεβεῖς δὲ ὅριον ὑπερέβησαν κτλ. (v. 2) = ורשעים גבולות וגו׳, omitting v. 1ᵇ (st. ii). In Job ἀσεβής, which occurs some 23 times, always = רשׁע (as usu. elsewhere in OT). It does not, therefore, indicate רעים here, but רשעים. (רעים *bad men* occurs but once in Job, and that in the Elihu-section, 35¹²: the sing. רע is found in 21³⁰ only, where perhaps we should read רשע.)

v. 2. St. i is metr. short. It is natural to supply רֵעִים or רֵעָם *of neighbours* or *of their neighbour* (2¹¹ 16²¹ al.); cf. Dt 19¹⁴ Pr 22²⁸. The vb. יָשִׁיגוּ is a mode of writing יַשִּׂיגוּ: see the locc. citt. (שׁ = ס ut 5²⁶²). St. ii 𝕲 ποίμνιον σὺν ποιμένι ἁρπάσαντες, reading וְרֹעוֹ *and its shepherd* pro 𝔐 וַיִּרְעוּ et pascunt (scil. gregem), which is prob. right. They lift or snatch their weaker neighbour's flock; and then openly graze it as their own. But 𝕲 also gives a good sense: They appropriate flock and shepherd together (the shepherd being a slave).

v. 3. Cf. Dt 28²¹. *distrain*: or *take in pledge*: cf. v. 9 22⁶ Dt 24⁶·¹⁷.

v. 4. *from justice*: leg. מִדִּין as Is 10², where we have the same vb. Cf. also Am 5¹². 𝔐 מדרך *out of the way* (to which 𝕲 adds δικαίας). *the humble folk*: Qerî עֲנִיֵּי א׳ prob. rectè; vid. Is 10². So 𝕲ˢ𝕾𝔙𝔗. Ketîb עָנְוֵי א׳ = 𝕲 πραεῖς γῆς, 𝔙 mansuetos terrae; so Occ Orᴷ. The poor of the land hide, and dare not appear 'in the gate' to claim their rights at law.

v. 5. 𝔐 lit. *Lo, wild asses into the steppe they go forth in their work, seeking eagerly for the prey* (or *food* Pr 31¹⁵); *the 'Arabah* (*is*) *to him bread for the boys*. Textual corruption has obliterated metre, and turned the orig. distich into bald prose. A little adjustment makes the verse tell us that the despoiled poor seek a refuge in the waste land:

כְּמוֹ־פְרָאִים בַּמִּדְבָּר יָצְאוּ
כ(מוֹ). עֲיָרִים מְשַׁחֲרֵי לַטָּרֶף

Like (𝕲𝕾𝔗𝔙) *wild asses into the waste they go forth,*
Like (*wild*) *ass-colts in quest of forage.* (Cf. 7²¹ 8⁵ 11¹².)

𝕲 st. ii ὑπὲρ ἐμοῦ = עָלַי = עָלוּ ascendunt; prob. a marg. var. of יָצְאוּ (ἐξελθόντες); τάξιν prob. scribal error for πρᾶξιν (𝕲ᴺ; 𝕲ᴬ πράξει = לִפְעַל).

St. iii, as it stands in 𝔐, is really meaningless. Metrically, of course, it is superfluous; unless we suppose that it constituted the first member of a distich of which the second stichus has been lost. Possibly the line has grown out of marginal glosses or variants to the preceding distich: thus ערבה (ב) might be a var. of במדבר; (ללחם) לו לחם might be an explanatory gloss on לטרף; and לנערים may have originated in a correction or corruption of כעירים (כמרעירים), or whatever erroneous form had already displaced it. (𝕲 ἡδύνθη αὐτῷ = לוֹ עָרְבָה pts. 𝔙 praeparant panem = ערכו לחם cf. Pr 9².)

v. 6. 𝔐: *In the field they reap his fodder* (בְּלִילוֹ: 6⁵ Is 30²⁴); they cut the fodder for the cattle of the wicked man who is mentioned in st. ii. But this inversion is not natural. Hence RV: *They cut their provender in the field*: the term 'fodder' being here used 'to denote the coarse food of these unfortunates' (Driver). This, of course, would require בְּלִילָם.

𝕲 gives a double equivalent of בְּלִילוֹ, viz. πρὸ ὥρας = *before the time* (cf. 5²⁸ καθ' ὥραν)+οὐκ αὐτῶν ὄντα = בְּלִי־לוֹ (a field) *that is not theirs* (בְּלִי לָמוֹ ?). Prob. πρὸ ὥρας indicates another reading (not בַּלַּיְלָ *in the night*), viz. בְּלִי־עֵת (ב) *at the wrong time* (see 5²⁸ 38²³ for ὥρα = עֵת) for בְּלִילוֹ; and as a parallel term to רָשָׁע for which some would substitute עָשִׁיר *the rich*, 27¹⁹ tant. et dub.; vid. note ad loc.) seems desirable, we suggest בְּלִיַּעַל *the villain* or *the wicked, worthless*, or even *the man who ruined them* (cf. 34¹⁸ Na 2¹): *In the field* (בשדה) *of the wicked they reap* (Qerî יִקְצוֹרוּ; Ketîb Hi.; prob. a vox nihili; hic tant.)*; And the vineyard of the godless they glean* (יְלַקֵּטוּ c 2 codd. pro ἅπ. יְלַקֵּשׁוּ *despoil?*: vid. Le 19⁹ ¹⁰), as the poor had a customary right to do. The poor outcasts gather up what they can, to eke out a scanty subsistence—perhaps in the very lands of which the oppressor has robbed them. The reading בַּלַּיְלָ would imply that they do this surreptitiously 'in the night', as though it were not allowed by the churlish owner. 𝕍 Agrum *non suum* demetunt: et vineam eius, quem vi oppresserint, *vindemiant*. This refers the verse to the conduct of the local oppressors instead of the oppressed. (Some would transpose vv. 10–11 to follow v. 6.) 𝕲 paraphrases st. ii: ἀδύνατοι (== אביונים v. 4) ἀμπελῶνας ἀσεβῶν ἀμισθὶ καὶ ἀσιτὶ ἠργάσαντο, *The poor tilled impious men's vineyards without wages and without rations* (a guess at the meaning of the ἅπ. ילקשו, which is generally explained *they gather the* לֶקֶשׁ or *late-ripe fruit from the vineyard*).

v. 7. Cf. 31¹⁹ (also 26⁶); 22⁶; Is 20² ³·⁴. If אֵין־כְּסוּת might be read with but one accent, we might insert לְעוֹרָם *for their skin* (cf. Ex 22²⁶) or לָמוֹ *to them* after כסות, which generally has some defining term attached to it. St. i looks like a variant of v. 10ᵃ. One or the other may be an interpolation. 𝕲 γυμνοὺς πολλοὺς (רב add. gloss) ἐκοίμισαν (ילינו as Hi., 2 Sa 17⁸; but cf. 39⁹) ἄνευ ἱματίων, | ἀμφίασιν δὲ ψυχῆς αὐτῶν ἀφείλαντο (a different text? cf. 22⁶: ψυχῆς scribal error = ψύχους = קָרָה 37⁹)

v. 8. *storm*: of rain, זֶרֶם: cf. Is 25⁴ מַחְסֶה מִזֶּרֶם *a shelter* or *refuge from the rainstorm*. 𝕲 ἀπὸ ψεκάδων *from raindrops*.

v. 9. App. a variant of vv 2–3, and obviously out of place in a description of the sufferings of the homeless poor. *from the breast*: pointing מִשֹּׁד = 𝕲 ἀπὸ μαστοῦ pro 𝔐 מִשֹּׁד *from violence* (cf. 𝕍).

babe: עֻל *suckling* Is 49¹⁵ 65²⁰ only: pro 𝔐 עַל־ (which makes the line metr. short). 𝕲 ἐκπεπτωκότα δὲ ἐταπείνωσαν = וַיְעַנּוּ נֹפֵל a misreading of 𝔐. 𝕍 vulgum pauperem = עַם־עָנִי pro 𝔐 עַל־עֲנִי.

v. 10. The verse cannot reasonably be connected with the last. RV *So that* could only be supplied, if the rendering of v. 9 (*There are that pluck the fatherless from the breast*) were possible. But neither *There are* nor *So that* is either expressed or implied by the Heb.

go about. Pi. of הלך as 30⁻ Is 59 Ex 4 : of the lazy 'walk' in way of life. הלכו may have been substituted here for ילינו (v. 7), for the sake of varying the stichus, as 𝕲 γυμνοὺς δὲ ἐκοίμησαν (= ילינו Hi.) ἀδίκως suggests. (ἀδίκως = שקר *wrongfully* Ps 35¹⁹ 38²⁰; לבוש misread backwards?)

St. ii. In the midst of plenty the poor labourers are famished, unpitied by their cruel employer (cf. *vv.* 6, 11). 𝕲 *And from* (the) *hungry they took away the morsel* (τὸν ψωμόν = פַּת 31¹⁷ or לֶחֶם *bread* 22⁷ pro 𝔐 עֹמֶר *sheaf* Dt 24¹⁹); which would require וּמֵרָעֵבִים. Thus 𝕲 makes the whole verse refer to the conduct of the oppressor of the poor. Cf. 𝔙.

v. 11. *Between the twin rows*; prob. of olive-trees: Aram. שׁוּרְתָּא *a row, rank* (cf. Je 5¹⁰ of rows of vines?). Others: *Within their walls* (cf. RV); but the plur. of שׁוּר *wall* (Gn 49²²), not found in Heb., is שׁוּרִין in Aram. (= שׁוּרִים). The word is masc., like the cogn. Assyr. *dûru*, plur. *dûrâni*. The var. of two or three codd. שׁוּרוֹתִים suggests that שׁוּרֹתָם may be a contracted form of the dual > plur. c suff. (like עֵינַיִם = עֵינָם &c.) Etym. this שׁוּר may be akin to יָשָׁר *straight, upright.* 𝕲 ἐν στενοῖς ἀδίκως ἐνήδρευσαν = שֶׁקֶר (בצרות?) יָשׁוּרוּ (בְּמְצָרוֹת ; cf. 1 Sa 23¹⁴,¹⁹ ἐν τοῖς στενοῖς; Je 5²⁶ ἐνέδρ. (fort. ארבו > יָשׁוּרוּ; 38⁴⁰ La 3¹⁰ al.). 𝔙 Inter acervos eorum meridiati sunt (*they took a siesta*; deriving the ἄπ. יצהירו from צהרים *meridies* > וצהר *oil*).

winepresses: יְקָבִים prop. *vats*; used in sense of נתות torcularia (𝔙); Is 16¹⁰. (St. ii ap. 𝕲: ὁδὸν δὲ δικαίων οὐκ ᾔδεισαν: cf. vv. 4, 13. 𝔙 qui calcatis torcularibus sitiunt = 𝔐 recte.) It is needless to read the dubious וינמאו (cf. 39²⁴) pro ויצמאו. The poor vintagers dare not quench their burning thirst with the wine they are making for a merciless master.

The following verses (12–16) are all triplets instead of couplets. Indeed the tristich seems to be the dominant measure to the end of the section (v. 24), which may have been substituted for a rejected or lost portion of the original text. Some question the authenticity of vv. 5–24; others consider v. 25 the only relic of the original chapter. Without adopting an extreme view, which our scrutiny of the text so far hardly appears to justify, we cannot but recognize that the chapter shows many signs of corruption and interpolation.

v. 12. *the dying*; i.e. prob. murdered, or wrongfully slain by violence: pointing מֵתִים c 1 cod. and 𝕲 pro 𝔐 מְתִים *men*. 'City of men' is not a likely phrase. The city rings with the vain cries of victims of lawless violence or judicial murder. For ינאקו and חָלָל *fatally wounded*, see Je 51⁵² Ez 30²⁴ La 2¹². Perhaps בעיר *In the city* > מעיר *Out of the city*. 𝕲 οἱ (𝕲^A om.) ἐκ πόλεως καὶ οἴκων ἰδίων ἐξεβάλλοντο (𝕲^A ἐξέβαλον αὐτούς) =

pro 𝔐: מעיר ומבתים יקיאו (?)
                  מעיר מתים ינאקו

For the vb. cf. 20¹⁵ (= ἐξεμεσθήσεται lit.) Jon 2¹¹ ἐξέβαλεν. (קוֹא has been suggested; but Ni. of קיא is not used.) In st. ii 𝔊 νηπίων = עֹלָלִים (3¹⁶) *children* pro חללים *wounded* or *slain*. ἐστέναξεν μέγα (𝔊ᴬ μεγάλως) = fort. תשוע אל־אל *crieth for help* unto El (38⁴¹), which improves the sense: cf. st. iii, αὐτὸς δὲ διὰ τί τούτων ἐπισκοπὴν οὐ πεποίηται = והוא למה־זה לא־יישים לבו. 𝔐 תְּפִלָּה *tastelessness*, in the moral sense (1²²); but 'ת ישים cannot mean *imputeth it for folly*, or treat it (the despairing cry or the outrages) as a thing morally anomalous. We must point תְּפִלָּה *prayer* c 2 codd. and 𝔊, restoring ישמע *heareth* for ישים *setteth* (see note 23⁶ ad fin.; Ps 65²)

v. 13 𝔐 lit. *They* (emph.) *were* (or *have been = are*) *in* (? Beth Essent. Predic. or ? *among*, cf. RV) *rebellers of* (? *against*) *light*. But מרד requires ב *against* (Nu 14⁹), or עַל, עֲלֵי id. (late constr.). Moreover, the implied figure, if it relate to moral light, is foreign to Job. Perhaps המה מרדי באל *They are rebels* (cf. 𝔙 Ipsi fuerunt rebelles) *against El*. This seems to suit the ensuing distich (*in His ways ... in His paths*). 𝔊 ἐπὶ γῆς ὄντων αὐτῶν καὶ οὐκ ἐπέγνωσαν (𝔊ᴬ ἔτι ὄντων αὐτῶν ἐπὶ γῆς κτλ.) = המה היו (בארץ) בארץ (5⁶) (st. ii). 𝔊 further implies . (אמת?) ודרך משפט ולא־חלבו בנתיבתיו(־יה) *And the way of justice* (*truth*?) *they know not*, לא־ידעו *And walk not in its paths*. For st. ii, metr. short in 𝔐, read: לא־הלבו בדרך יהוה *They walk not in Iahvah's way* (cf. the ‖ st. iii). In st. iii three codd and 𝔊𝔙 point יָשֻׁבוּ *return* pro 𝔐 יֵשְׁבוּ *abide*. Perhaps אָשֻׁרוּ *go on* (Pr 4¹⁴ 9⁶).—After all, it is perhaps better to understand the phrase מרד (ב)אור lit., in the sense of hating daylight (cf. v. 17); as criminals whose misdeeds are perpetrated under cover of darkness naturally do (cf. Joh 3²⁰). 𝔐 may then be left pretty much as it stands:

> *These* (the following: Pr 30²⁴) *are rebels against daylight;*
> *They acknowledge not its ways,*
> *And abide not in its paths.*

v. 14. *Ere the dawn*: leg. בלא־אור or לא־אור. Cf. 15³². 𝔐 לאור *At the dawn* (Ps 30⁶); but vv. 13–17 describe the doings of nocturnal malefactors. לערב *At sunset* (Pr 7⁹) is less prob. לפני־אור would also be possible. 𝔊 γνοὺς δὲ αὐτῶν τὰ ἔργα παρέδωκεν αὐτοὺς εἰς σκότος has no apparent relation to the Heb. text. It resembles a Midrashic comment (cf. v. 12ᶜ). It may, however, be merely an unhappy misreading of an injured text (fort. = ? יכיר מעבדיהם ויסגירם לאפל: cf. 34²⁵ 16¹¹). Per contra, from st. iii to v. 18ᵇ 𝔊 reproduces 𝔐 practically verbatim. (Olim deerant ap 𝔊.)

He slayeth the poor and needy. The lawless oppressor murders whom he will with impunity, esp. the weak and helpless: cf. Ps 94⁶ (also Ps 9¹³ 10⁸⁻¹⁴). To read אֹיְבוֹ וְצָרוֹ *his enemy and adversary* is to miss the point, and is quite arbitrary. St. iii. Reading יהלך גנב *walks the thief* (Merx) pro 𝔐 יהי בננב. ...

v. 15. Fort. leg. סתר על־פניו *a covering upon his face* (cf. 21⁸ 29⁸ Je 13¹·²) or insert לוֹ or עָלָיו: (And) *a face-cover (he putteth) on himself* (cf. 22¹⁴).

v. 16. *they break* (lit. *dig*) *into*: plur. as required by context, though 𝔐 and Versions have sing. (influence of last verse). Cf. Ez 12⁵·⁷ Am 9². Burglary is, of course, intended, as in Ex 22² (noun), Mt 6¹⁹. 𝔖 פלש = Assyr. *palâšu*, 'bore or dig through' walls (also ears).

St. ii. 𝔐 יוֹמָם חִתְּמוּ לָמוֹ *by day they seal up* (Pi. hic tant.) *for* (?) *themselves* or *seal themselves up*; keep within closed doors. Perhaps ἄπ. Hithp. התחתמו *they seal them up close* (?). 𝔊ᴮ ἡμέρας ἐσφράγισαν ἑαυτούς, *By day they sealed themselves* (gen. temp. at 𝔊ᶜ ἑαυτοῖς, *for themselves*). It has been proposed to read יָמִים (*The days they seal up to themselves*; make no use of them); but this is hardly prob. (cf. 9⁷). יוֹמָם is a better parallel to בחשך. Perhaps, as the metr. halts, and חתם seems to require an accus. obj., we may read יומם חָתְמוּ (דְּ)לְ(תָ)(י)מוֹ *By day they seal their doors*; keep them fast closed. (Or דַּלְתָם? or פִּתְחָם *their gate?* The *waw* may belong to the next word.) They shut themselves in (and shut out the light? cf. st. iii). St. iii is defective metr. לִרְאוֹת may have fallen out before the similar אוֹר: *And they know not to see the light.* (If these triplets were originally distichs, the stichus might be a gloss on st. ii.)

v. 17. St. i is overweighted metr., and lacks a verb. Moreover, the occurrence of צלמות as the final word in both stichi is unparalleled in the book and improb. We might read יָחַת *scareth* (7¹⁴ 31³⁴) pro 𝔐 יחדו (which is said to strengthen למו and to mean, in conjunction therewith, *to them all at once*; a quite superfluous insistence upon the unity of feeling among the burglars); and, replacing למו by כלמו .or בלם, omit צלמות¹ as an accidental anticipation of צלמות², render *For the morning scareth them all.* (𝔊ᴬ διεσκέδασεν pro σκιὰ θανάτου = יחת; Is 9³.) St. ii would then follow quite naturally: *And they are familiar with the terrors of night* (ויבירו pro 𝔐 כי יכיר)—and therefore are not afraid of them. Note the return to the regular metrical form (the distich). 𝔙 Si subito apparuerit aurora, arbitrantur umbram mortis; et sic in tenebris quasi in luce ambulant may almost be called a fair paraphrase of this. The words in tenebris ... *ambulant* may lend some support to הליכות the *goings* (= *doings* Pr 31²⁷) pro בלהות the *terrors*; but בְּקָרוּ (? בִּקְּרוּ) *seek for* pro בֹּקֶר *morning* in st. i (𝔖 בעו) is wholly improb. Night comes without 'seeking'.

vv. 18-21 are supposed by Driver and others to 'express, in opposition to what Job has been saying, the view taken by his friends'. Hence RV marg. *Ye say, 'He is swift'*, &c. But there is no 'ye say' in the Heb., nor any hint of such a reference to the speaker's opponents. It is, in fact, only an expedient due to the vain endeavour to defend a desperately corrupted text.

v. 18. St. i, lit. *Swift is he upon the face of the waters*, is surely an extraordinary way of saying 'The sinner is rapidly borne away upon the stream'; and obviously there is no trace of parallelism between the three stichi of the verse. Leg. קללו לפני שמים *They are accursed before Heaven* (cf. 1 Sa 26¹⁹; or keep עַל־פְּנֵי = *in sight of*, cf. 1¹¹ 6²⁸ 21³¹); a good parallel to st. ii (rendering it needless to read הלקתו): *Accursed is their portion* (allotted ground, allotment) *in the earth*. St. iii, 𝔐 lit. *He turneth not the way of the vineyards.* Driver paraphrases stt. ii, iii: 'The passers-by, as they see his desolated homestead, utter a curse over it (5⁸); he no more revisits his well-planted vineyards', which would be good sense, if it did not read so much into the text which is not there (*the passers-by* . . . יפנה *revisits* . . . *his vineyards*). Instead of לאֹ־יִפְנֶה דֶרֶךְ כְּרָמִים some would read לא־יפ' דרך כרמם *the treader of their vineyard turns not* (cf. v. 11ᵇ 9ᵃ for דָּרַךְ). See Is 3¹⁴ 5⁵ Je 12¹⁰ (but could דרך in connexion with כרם have such a meaning?). Perhaps לאֹ־יִפְרֶה פִרְחָם בָּאֲדָמָה *Their sprout fruiteth not in the ground*; which is at least parallel to the preceding distich (and perhaps a gloss upon st. ii). If, however, we suppose the crimes of the wicked to be still the subject, we may read either לאֹ־יִפְנֶה דַרְכָּם מִדָּמִים *Their way turneth not away from bloodshed*, or לאֹ־יִפְנוּ מִדֶּרֶךְ דָּמִים *They turn not from the way of bloodshed*. Cf. Is 1¹⁵ Je 2³⁴ Ps 14¹, &c. But 𝔊 ἀναφανείη δὲ τὰ φυτὰ αὐτῶν ἐπὶ γῆς ξηρά seems to favour the former suggestion.

v. 19. 𝔐 lit. *Dryness* (?) *also heat snatch* (vv. 2ᵇ 9ᵃ) *waters of snow*; or (since the vb. is masc. plur.) *Snow waters snatch away drought* (and) *also heat; She'ol* (*those who?*) *have sinned*. St. i is metrically redundant; st. ii defective both metr. and gramm. 𝔊 (ἐπὶ γῆς ξηρά· added to v. 18) ἀγκαλίδα γὰρ ὀρφανῶν (-οῦ) ἥρπασαν = כִּי זְרוֹעַ יָתוֹם גָּזְלוּ׃ (a guess or substitution for an illegible text). Even in its present corrupt state, the verse has the look of a proverb. Assuming ציה to represent a verb, viz. a ἅπ. Aramaism צְוָה *to dry up* (= Syr. ܨܝ arefecit) and regarding גם as a double of חם, we get for st. i צוה חם מימי־שלג *Heat drieth up snow waters.* Cf. 6¹⁷. This leaves יגזל to supplement st ii, which might be restored thus: וּשְׁאוֹל יִגְזֹל חוֹטֵא *And She'ol snatcheth away the sinner.* Or we might treat חם as a marg. gloss on ציה *drought* (usu. *desert*), and suppose that the similar word יִשָּׂא has fallen out after וּשְׁאוֹל: *Drought snatcheth away* (leg. תגזל) *snow waters; and She'ol carrieth off the sinner.* Or, finally, we might read תַּחֲרִיב *drieth up* pro נַם־חֹם, and restore st. ii in the way first suggested.

v. 20. The opening distich is marred by being broken into three detached statements, the second of which, moreover, is not quite grammatical; and metre is, as usual, disregarded. Lit. *The womb* (whose?) *forgets him; the worm has sucked him* (𝔖 *them*); *he is no more remembered.* Reading רחם backwards we get מהר . . . (Pr 1ᵐ 2ʳ); implying that the sinner is soon forgotten. The rest w d necessary to complete

both sense and metre in st. i lurks under the disguise of the supposed Aramaism מתקו exsuxit eum (מתקתו would be necessary with Subj. רמה). viz. מקמו *his place;* i.e. his abiding-place or home (not his *city* in Job, but either his fixed abode or station, or his locality: cf. 2¹¹ 6¹⁹ 7¹⁰ 8¹¹ 14¹⁸ 18⁴·²¹ 20⁹ 27²¹·²² 28¹·⁶·ᵃˡ· 34²⁶ 37¹ 38¹²·¹⁹: hence רָחֹב pro רָחָם is less prob.; since the 'square' or *plaza* of a מקום is nowhere else mentioned in OT, nor is מקום thus subordinated to a limiting term anywhere in Job). After *His place forgetteth him to-morrow,* st. ii *His name is no more remembered* would naturally follow (שְׁמוֹ pro רמה): cf. 18¹⁷ and Je 11¹⁹ where the same words occur; and for the gen. sense of the distich 7¹⁰ 20⁹. That רִמָּה *worm* (7⁵ 17¹⁴ 21²⁶ 25⁶) has displaced (שְׁמוֹ) שְׁמוֹ *his name* in 𝔐 is perhaps due to the need of finding a suitable Subj. for the supposed verb מתקו exsuxit eum.—In st. iii 𝔊 𝔖 read עָוֶל the *unjust* pro עַוְלָה *injustice;* prob. rightly (cf. 16¹¹ 18²¹ 27⁷ al.). But the language is rather strange. Why *like a tree?* Trees are not specially brittle or liable to breakage (Ps 29⁵ Ex 9²⁵ are different). 𝔙 *sed conteratur quasi lignum infructuosum* = (?) וְשָׁבַר כָּעֵץ צָרִי. Read וְיִשָּׁלֵד (cf. Ez 19¹²) or rather וְשֻׁחָה (Je 11¹⁹ Dt 20¹⁹·²⁰ Ju 20²¹) *is felled* (שחה = Assyr. *šaḫâtu, to fall*).
𝔊 gives a quatrain for the tristich:

Then was remembered his sin (חטאו v. 19 pts.? עֹנוֹ יזכר pro ? עוֹד לֹא י׳.)
And as a mist of dew he vanished:
(? Aram. וּכְמוֹ־שֶׁלִי לֹא יָשְׁכַה cf. Pr 26¹ Ps 147¹⁶.)
And let there be repaid to him what he did, (וישלם לו כפעלו) cf. 34¹¹.)
And every unjust man be shivered, like a tree incurable!
(אִין־מַרְפֵּא a gloss, Ps 6¹⁰.)

The third line here is apparently a variant text of the fourth.

v. 21. RV marg. connects with last verse: *as a tree; even he that devoureth,* &c. As the dubious action of 'devouring' cannot be attributed to a tree, this must imply the reading עֹל in v. 20ᶜ. In such a sense, moreover, we should have expected אכל (Ps 14⁴ Pr 30¹⁴) > רעה *graze* or *feed on.* It is obvious, and prob. right, to read יָרֹעַ *he hurteth* or *ill-treateth;* a good parallel to לא ייטיב *doeth not good to,* st. ii. (The pointing יְרֹעֶה—app. by false analogy from יְהֵיטִיב—is prob. erroneous, and should be יָרֹעַ as elsewhere.) For the phrase *the barren that beareth not,* cf. Ju 13² Is 54¹.

v. 22. 𝔐 st. i lit. *And he draws* or *drags (off, away) mighty ones* (אבירים) *by his strength:* cf. Ps 10⁹ 28⁵. The word אביר is suspicious, since neither it nor its root occurs elsewhere in Job, except once in the Elihu-section (34²⁰). 𝔊 ἀδυνάτους = אֶבְיוֹנִים (see 5¹⁵ 29¹⁶ 31¹⁹), not אבירים, as has been supposed without reference to the usage of the translator. The [illegible] must ascribe yet another [illegible] ...his prey. (משך)

alone cannot mean *to prolong the life of*; the Obj. would have to be expressed: cf. Ps 36¹¹ Ne 9³⁰. Nor is it reasonable to supply *God* as the Subj. of the stichus, when the wicked is that of the immediately preceding lines.) As משך is followed by ב Instrum. (40²⁵ בחכה *with a fishhook*; Ps 10⁹ *with his net*), it is prob. that the forcible-feeble בחו conceals a similar phrase here (perhaps בחכה itself; cf. 𝔊 θυμῷ = בחמה—an easy misreading of that word—or even of בחרמו *with his net*: Ha 1¹⁵).

St. ii belongs to the next tristich: *He standeth* (8¹¹) *and trusts not*, has no confidence, *in his life* = While he subsists, he is always uncertain of life (quotation of Dt 28⁶⁶; on the ground of which we read בחיי instead of בחיין *in life*). The stichus cannot possibly mean *He riseth up, and no man is sure of life* (RV).

v. 23. 𝔐 lit. *He giveth him securely and he leaneth*; which is much too elliptical to be intelligible, to say the least. 𝔊 has an entirely different verse: *Having sickened, let him not expect to be healed; But he shall fall by disease*. St. i is perhaps a variant or duplicate of *v.* 22ᵇ; but the whole may possibly be merely a conjectural reading of 𝔐 somewhat as follows: נתלו־יתלה | אליבמח לחיות | וינע (14¹⁰) בסדרתו. 𝔙 Dedit ei (= 𝔐) Deus locum paenitentiae, et ille abutitur eo in superbiam (prob. = 𝔐 = ולבמח ישען); oculi autem eius sunt in viis illius (= 𝔐 c ר— pro הם—). We propose לארתן מבטח ישען־עליו ועיני אלוה על־דרכיו *Not enduring is his trust whereon he leaneth* (cf. 8¹⁴·¹⁵ where מבטח is immediately followed by ישען as here; 18¹⁴ 31²⁴ᵇ 2 K 18²¹); *And the eyes of Eloah are upon his ways*; i.e. marking them for retribution (cf. 11¹ 34²¹).

v. 24. Read רָמוּ כִמְעַט *High grown* (or *exalted*) *is he for a little while* (Is 26¹⁵), pro 𝔐 רוֹמוּ מְעַט *They are exalted a little while*. Perhaps יָרוּם (cf. prec. impff.). הֻמּוּ or רֻמּוּ is a doubtful form; and the plur. does not agree with the following ואיננו *and he is no more* (𝔊𝔙 *and they are*, &c.). 𝔊 πολλοὺς γὰρ ἐκάκωσεν τὸ ὕψωμα αὐτοῦ = כִּי רַבִּים הָרַע רוּמוֹ (not an improvement). *he is brought low*: leg. הֻמַּךְ sing. (Ho. ἅπ.). This implies ירום ad init. Perhaps וַיָּמֻךְ Qal (Ps 106⁴³). 𝔐 הֻמְּכוּ; but the final ו belongs to the next word, וּכְמַלּוֹחַ *and like the mallow* (sic leg. c 𝔊 pro 𝔐 כַּכֹּל *like all*). *he is plucked*: יִקָּפֵף (8¹² 30⁴ of the mallow), pro 𝔐 יִקָּבְצוּן *they are gathered together*. Cf. 𝔊 ἐμαράνθη δὲ ὥσπερ μολόχη ἐν καύματι = וּכְמַלָּח בְּקַיִץ? *cut off*: ימל sing. pro 𝔐 ימלו plur. (ו seq. *v.* 25). 𝔊 perhaps read יבל (αὐτόματος ἀποπεσών? cf. Is 34⁴). See note on 14¹; 18¹⁶. Ps 37² (both vbb.).

Driver assumed that vv. 22-25 express Eyob's own view, as opposed to that of the friends, viz. that 'God by His power preserves the powerful oppressor, ... ores him to hea... ... ... to describe 'how the sinner, though of course he must die like all other men, enjoys a long life' [But *a little while?*], 'and has at the end of it a quick and painless death (cf. 21¹³)'. In harmony with this, *cut off as the head of a corn ear* is explained to mean 'not prematurely, but only when fully ripe (cf. 5²⁶)'. But the text does not justify the statement that the sinner 'enjoys a long life', nor that his end is 'painless', but only that it is sudden and complete. The words מעט ואיננו are, in fact, fatal to this interpretation (cf. Ps 37¹⁰·³⁵·³⁶), although it must be admitted that it finds some support in the ancient Versions. There is, however, nothing in the text of 𝔐 to warrant the opinion that vv. 18-21 represent the view of the friends and vv. 22-25 the contrary view of Eyob himself (see the notes); and the fact that throughout the entire section, vv. 13-24, the tristich supplants the normal distich, may be taken as a clear indication that we have to do here with material foreign to the original poem. The views expressed are those of the friends, not Eyob's: cf. chap. 20. (Might these verses, in their original form, have belonged to Bildad's third speech, now unsatisfactorily represented by chap. 25?)

v. 25. Lit. *And if not, then* . . . 9²⁴ 17¹⁴ 19⁶·²³. (אֵפוֹ enclit., and as such metr. attached to prec. word. Leg. מי אפו. Cf. Gn 27³³?) *prove me liar*: Hi. cf. 6²⁸ Pi. 41¹ (41⁹ AV) Ni. *make my word naught*. For ישם cf. Mi 1⁶. אל nihil, ἅπ. Fort. לאין: cf. Is 40²³. 𝔙 ante Deum = לְאֵל pro לְאַל; at 𝔊 εἰς οὐδέν = לאין Is 40²³.

Chapter 25. Bildad's (?) Third Reply to Eyob.

It is difficult to believe that this lofty utterance was the original response of *Bildad* to the indictment of God's rule in chaps. 23 sq. Not only is it a response which is no answer to Eyob's allegations, but it is quite unlike Bildad's previous speeches. Indeed, as Driver has observed, vv. 4-6 repeat, partly in the same words, the argument of Eliphaz in 4¹⁷ (cf. 9²) and 15¹⁴⁻¹⁶; while vv. 1-2 remind us of Eyob's own words 9⁵⁻⁹·¹³ 26⁵⁻¹³. Has this virtual cento of previous thoughts, the brevity of which contrasts so strongly with the much longer and more characteristic replies of Bildad in chaps. 8 and 18, taken the place of an illegible or lost or rejected original? In itself, at all events, it is a fine and stately utterance and, as such, worthy of preservation, however much we may regret the missing portion of the original text.

v. 2. *Dominion and dread* or *awe, awfulness* = *A dread sovereignty*. Hi. Infin. Abs. המשל = *exercising rule* or *dominion*, here only. 𝔊 mispointed הַמְשֵׁל (cf. 27¹ 29¹ מָשָׁל = προοίμιον). *He maketh*, or *made*: עֹשֶׂה (so 𝔖) pro 𝔐 עֹשֵׂה = 𝔊 ὁ ποιῶν, 𝔙 qui facit. The allusion may be to the old myth of the War in Heaven between the Powers of Light and Darkness; esp. perhaps to the Babylonian legends of Creation (cf. 9¹³ 26¹²); or more generally, to the power of the Deity in raising and quelling storms. For מרומים = שמים (usu. מרום) cf. 16¹⁹ 21²². Instead of שלם

(שלם) *peace* 𝔊 app read תבל *the world* (τὴν σύμπασαν) Na 1⁵ or ארץ *the earth*, 2².

v. 3 Lit. *Is there a number to His troops* (invading or assailing *forces*)? They are innumerable. He is the Lord of the Hosts of Heaven, and therefore irresistible and omnipotent. For גדוּר/ see 19¹².

𝔊 curiously: *For would any one suppose that there is* παρέλκυσις πειραταῖς *delay to assailants?* For πειρ. cf. 19¹³. Pro παρελκ. 𝔊^Σ ἀριθμός. *his ambush*: אוֹרְבוֹ (cf. 31⁹) c 𝔊 ἔνεδρα παρ' αὐτοῦ. Either by open assault or by surprise-attack He vanquishes His foes. An app. better parallel; but if גדודיו = צבאתיו and denotes the stars, we may keep אורהו and render: *And upon whom ariseth not his light?* The meaning will then be that God is the Creator of both stars and sun. Cf. Ps 147⁴ Is 40²⁶.

v. 4. St i repeats 9²ᵇ verbatim. The meaning must be, How can a mere mortal be *justified*, i.e. held and treated as blameless (11² 40⁸) or perfectly innocent, in relation to God and judged by His standard, when things so far exalted above man in the scale of being as the moon and stars are not free from fault in His eyes (vv. 5, 6, with which cf. Ps 8⁴,₅)?

v. 5. *Lo, even the moon*: so 𝔙 Ecce luna etiam non splendet. But can הן עד־ירח mean this? 𝔐 עַד *as far as to* prob. conceals some other word. In Ps 89³³ עַד is app. an epithet or syn. of ירח *the moon* (cf. Sum. ID, ITU, ITI, *the moon*); and ירח here might conceivably be a gloss on the rare word עד. A verb, however, seems desirable: cf. 𝔊 ἡ σελήνη συντάσσει (= צוה pro עד: 38¹²: not יָעַד, which does not bear the required sense), καὶ οὐκ ἐπιφαύσκει. Perhaps: נער(ך) (נ exc. post נ) *Lo, the moon faileth, and shineth not* · cf. Is 40²⁶ ד(מ)ע *halteth* or *stoppeth*, is also possible: cf. Jos 10¹³ Hab 3¹¹. The ἅπ יאהיל pro יהל (see 31²⁶ 41¹⁰ also 29³) may be a scribe's error due to reminiscence of יאמין 4¹⁸ 15¹⁵. The moon 'stops' in its walk across the sky (31²⁶ הלך; ירח = 'the Traveller', cf. ארח).

St. ii is identical with 15¹⁵ᵇ, only substituting the stars for the heavens. For the ideas involved in the verse, cf. notes on 4¹⁸ 5¹ 5¹⁵, and the common formulas of the old Bab. exorcisms prescribed for the healing of the sick: *Like Heaven let him shine, Like Earth let him be bright!* (*Kíma šamé lelíl, kíma irçitim lîbbib*); *Let the man the son of his god shine, be bright, glisten!* (*amélu már ilíšu lilil lîbib limmir*).

v. 6. *a maggot* (רמה), associated with bodily decay and death (7⁵ 17¹⁴ 21²⁶) and the corruption of the grave (Is 14¹¹) Fort. of the same origin as רמ״ש *to crawl*   *a worm* (תולעה), as small and weak Ps 22⁷ Is 41¹⁴ (but also associated with the corruption of death, Is 66²⁴). The Sum. UĜ TURA *tultu*, UĜ DURRA (= TURA) *âkilu*, 'devourer' (אֹבֵל cf. 13²⁸ Dt 28³⁹). 𝔊 renders the two words σαπρία, *rottenness*, and σκώληξ, *worm*. The idea of 'uncleanness' or impurity was naturally associated with such creatures.

Chapter 26.—Eyob's answer to Bildad (vv. 2–4 only?).

v. 2. A bitter sarcasm. (𝔊𝔙 seem to have read מי pro מה in vv. 2, 3. 𝔊's *Whom art thou joining*—πρόσκεισαι = נלוית, cf. Is 56³,⁶—*or whom art thou going to help? Is it not him that hath much strength and a mighty arm?* app. involves confusion of לא with לו, as elsewhere, and is no improvement. Cf. also v. 3ª. ללא is treated as equivalent to הלא לו in both instances.)

v. 3. *How hast thou counselled him that hath no wisdom, And made him know sanity abundantly!* לָרַךְ *to the tender*, i.e. young and inexperienced, has been suggested in place of לָרֹב *in abundance*; but this hardly suits the case of Eyob, and the √רכך occurs only 23¹⁶ 40²⁷ with quite different implications. לְפֶתִי *to the simple* might serve; but there is no need to diverge from 𝔐, which is perhaps more pointedly ironical with its suggestion of abounding sagacity.

v. 4. *Whom* (אֶת־מִי): not *With whom*: cf. 31³⁷ 2 K 7⁹⁻¹¹. The meaning seems to be *Whom hast thou thought to instruct? And at whose inspiration hast thou spoken?* (Driver). Cf. Is 28⁹. Perhaps, however, the sense is rather *With whom have you been talking* (setting forth arguments)? I can scarcely credit your unaided powers with such extraordinary wisdom. אֶל־מִי would be possible (= the usual לְמִי): Ex 19⁹: cf. 𝔊 τίνι ἀνήγγειλας ῥήματα; The remainder of the chapter, vv. 5–14, is obviously out of connexion with what precedes, and has probably been dislocated from its original context. It may well have followed 25³, as the continuation of Bildad's monologue on the universal sovereignty of God, which then concludes naturally with 25⁴⁻⁶, after having run to about the average length. It is hardly necessary to point out the general harmony of the thoughts with 25² sq.

v. 5. From the realms of Heaven and the Upper Regions or 'Heights' (25²,³) the speaker passes to the Underworld of She'ol and the Deep: cf. Ps 139⁹⁻¹⁰. Verses 5–11, starred in 𝔊ᴴ, as wanting in the old text of 𝔊, cannot be brought into any reasonable connexion with vv. 2–4; not even on the highly artificial hypothesis that Eyob wishes to demonstrate that he 'knows God's greatness as fully as Bildad does' (Driver), as to which it may be observed that the poet's method is not exactly that of the rival singers in a Virgilian Eclogue.

St. i is metr. short and otherwise defective; e.g. יחוללו must mean either *are travailed with, brought forth*, as 15⁷ (cf. 39¹ Act.), or *are made to writhe, tormented* (cf. 15²⁰ Hithpol.), neither of which is suitable here. Perhaps מפניו has fallen out before מתחת, and we should read יחלו מפניו *shiver* (with fear) *before Him* (Je 5²²), or יח' מלפניו id. (Ps 114⁷); and since רפאים (ἅπ. in Job) in the sense of the Shades or denizens of She'ol is always anarthrous (seven times in OT, e.g. Is 14 26¹⁴,¹⁹ Pr 9¹⁸ al.),

26. 7

we may perhaps restore הלא רפ׳ וגו׳ *Do not the Shades tremble before Him?*
Cf. 𝔊 μὴ γίγαντες μαιωθήσονται κτλ. (taking ה as the Interrog. Part.).

St. ii. Reading מִשְׁכְּנֹתֵיהֶם (משכניהם is dub.) pro 𝔐 וְשֹׁכְנֵיהֶ֫ם. The world of the dead lay under the earth and the surrounding ocean. 𝔐 *Beneath the waters and their inhabitants*; but parallelism apart, a reference to the denizens of the water does not seem very relevant, though perhaps picturesque. As a parallel phrase to רפאים one might think of וְשֹׁכְנֵי מִתַּ֫חַת לַמַּיִם *And the dwellers below the Waters?* But the proposed הרפאים יחולו לו ויחתו מים ושכניהם *The Shades tremble at Him* (?), *And the Waters and their dwellers are dismayed*, although ingenious is not satisfactory; (1) because of הר׳ (vid. supr.), (2) because of the dub. constr. יחלו לו which, moreover, leaves the stichus metr. short, and (3) because st. ii is no real parallel to st. i, if it refer to the seas and their fishy inhabitants. The Shades do not live in the waters, but in a region far below them, viz. She'ol, which is immediately mentioned (v. 6)

v. 6. Abaddon: Destruction or Ruin (אבד *perish, be destroyed, ruined* of houses, Am 3[15] = Assyr. *abâtu, fall into ruin*); as Syn. of She'ol, virtually a Nom. Prop. (28[22] 31[12]). Only in Wisdom-Lit. (six times). see besides, Pr 15[11] 27[20] Ps 88[12]. Perhaps an old Canaanite word. Even the Land of Darkness (9[21]) lies open to the All-seeing (cf. Ps 139[12]).

v. 7. the North must be the northern sky: cf. Is 40[12] Ps 104[2] (נָטָה as here, of stretching or spreading out the heavens). *The Void* or *Waste* (תֹהוּ 6[18] 12[24] *desert*; Is 40[17] *nothingness, vacancy*) is the app empty air or vacant space between the northern vault of heaven and the earth. From this quarter of the heavens issued Theophanies (37[22] Ez 1[4]); and there (above the celestial Ocean) rose the divine 'Mountain of Assembly' in the farthest North, where the Most High was enthroned (Is 14[13,14]) The far North was vaguely known to be a land of mountains; and the same was assumed to be true of its heavenly counterpart.

St. ii may mean that the earth is suspended in space, with no solid support underneath (cf. 2 Sa 4[12] 'over the pool'). Hindu myth makes it rest upon a huge elephant, the elephant in turn standing upon a tortoise. As not being solid, the waters upon which the earth was supposed to rest (Ps 24[2]) might perhaps be regarded as 'nothing' (בלימה ἅπ. usually derived from בלי *not* + מה *anything, aught*; thus = *naught* ‖ תהו st. i): cf. 𝔗 *He set up the earth upon the waters, with nothing supporting it*). Since, however, תלה על is *to hang* a thing *on* (i.e. *from*) another, to let it *depend* from it, as a harp from a willow (Ps 137[2]) or a 'vessel' from a peg (Ez 15[3]), the earth, as standing under the hollow sky, might perhaps be said to be suspended on nothing. But, in that case, what of 'the pillars of heaven'? Cf. also 9[6] 38[6] 1 Sa 2[8]. Of course, we are dealing with poetry, founded more or less upon ancient mythical conceptions not upon scientific astronomy. (Is בלימה really בלי+מה, and so a Syn. of תהו in the sense of *vacancy, vacuity, the Void*, as the parallelism would suggest, possibly coined by the author? Then the meaning will be: *Who suspendeth Earth from Vacancy* or *the Air*. Or is it an old mythic name for the ocean Deep, *The Curbed* or *Bound One*, from בלם Aram. Heb., related to אלם *to bind*, Ps 32⁹? cf. Ps 24².)

v. 8. 'Another marvel of God's power: the waters upheld [צרר *bind* or *tie up*: Pr 30⁴: cf. Sum. SAR, *bind*] in the clouds, which yet do not burst under their weight. The Hebrews were unaware that clouds consist of the vapour of water, and do not contain actual water' (Driver). They were ignorant that matter might become solid, liquid, or aeriform under variable conditions. Cf. the questions in 38¹⁹·²⁰·³⁶·³⁷ and other wonders of nature, which were insoluble mysteries until the dawn of modern science.

v. 9. 𝔐 מְאַחֵז Pi. ἅπ. appears to mean *shutting in* (cf. Qal Ne 7³) or *enclosing*. The corresponding form in Assyr. (*uḫḫiz, uaḫḫiz*) means to *enclose* or *set* gems in gold, and also to *overlay* doors with gold or silver. Cf. also *iḫzu, setting*, and *fence* (of a field). 𝔖 אֲחַד *he shut, closed*, e. g. a door; Pa. *shut closely, fastened up*. The prim. idea of the √חד = חז is that of *grasping, holding, holding fast* (cf. Sum. GAD, *hand*); hence 𝔊 κρατῶν, 𝔚 qui tenet. Read perhaps מַחֲבִיא or מְחַבֵּא *hiding*. כְּסֵא = כִּסֵּא *throne* in 1 K 10¹⁹, and many codd. read the latter word here. So 𝔊 θρόνου. But we should expect כִּסְאוֹ *His throne* (so 𝔄𝔚), since the throne of God is never mentioned simply as 'The Throne'. Nor is there any other instance of כִּסֵּה = כִּסְאָה = כִּסְאוֹ. We must either read כסאו or point כֶּסֶה (Ps 81⁴) = כֵּסֶא *the full moon*, a glorious object in Eastern skies. The ? of the anomalous form פרשז, variously explained as Pil. of פרש (= פרשש) and as 'forma mixta ex פרז et פרש' (an improb. origin), may be an accident due to unconscious reminiscence of the preceding מאחז, and should prob. be וּפָרַשׂ *And spreadeth* (𝔚 et expandit super illud nebulam suam: cf. Ps 105³⁹): cf. 11¹³ 36³⁰.

v. 10. Pr 8²⁷ has בְּחֻקוֹ חוּג עַל־פְּנֵי תְהוֹם *when He drew a circle over the Deep*. Hence it is proposed to point חָג חֻק *He drew a circle* here; but חָג does not happen to occur elsewhere (cf. Ez 4¹), and חֹק is the *boundary* marked out for the sea, 38¹⁰, cf. Pr 8²⁹ Je 5²² Ps 148⁶ חק נתן. The verb חוג may very well mean *to mark out with a compass* (מחוגה Is 44¹³). The noun חוּג is the *arch, dome*, or *vault* of heaven in 22¹⁴. 𝔊 πρόσταγμα ἐγύρωσεν ἐπὶ πρόσωπον ὕδατος, 𝔚 Terminum circumdedit aquis.

St. ii may mean that the arch of heaven reaches on both sides to the point where light is merged in darkness, i.e. to the horizon-line of east and west. For תכלית *end*, see 11⁷ 28³.—According to the poet's Physics (which are mythico-phenomenal), Darkness is not merely the negation of Light, but both are substantive beings, having their separate though unknown abodes, 38¹⁹·—Perhaps עַד > עֲדֵי should be read, and the stichus rendered: *He hath determined the limit of Light along with Darkness*: cf. the possibly cogn. Assyr. *(w)adû*, *to fix* or *determine*, *appoint*. Pa *uaddi* (*Uaddîšumma šuknat mûši ana uddû ûmê*, 'He appointed him (i. e. *the Moon*), a creature of Night, to determine days' (Creation Tab. V). But, in view of 11⁷ 28³ 38¹⁹ᶠ, יָדַע *He knoweth* (*the limits of Light and Darkness*; knows them in their entirety) seems also possible. In either case we have a stichus of four stresses (cf. also st. i). The verse is perhaps an intrusion from the margin.

v. 11. *the pillars of Heaven* are only mentioned here. As Driver explains, they are prob. 'distant mountains, on which the vault of heaven was supposed to rest', like e. g. the classical Atlas. The mountains *rock* or sway to and fro (ירופפו ἄπ.) at Iahvah's *rebuke* (Ps 18¹⁶), Whose voice is the thunder. Cf. 9⁵ 36²⁰ 37² Ps 29³ᶠᶠ·⁶. 𝔊 ἐπετάσθη = יעופפו?; cf. 5⁷ Is 6² Ps 18¹²ᵃ. But רָפַף = *make tremble* (of a pillar), 𝕋J Gn 44¹⁶, 𝕋 מתרפפין = יתפלצון 9⁶ (of the pillars of the earth), Talm. רפרף is *to flap the wings* (of a bird) = Ar. رفّ, *to flutter, flap the wings*, and رفّ (= רפף) is *to glisten, flash, quiver*: see Lane.

St. ii is metr. short (cf. 9⁶). הרים *mountains* may have fallen out; or the verse may be a marginal intrusion. (תָּמַהּ Aram. הָמָא is cogn. c שָׁמֵם, דּוּם, דָּמָה, דָּמַם; cf. Sum DIM, *to bind fast*.)

v. 12. *stilleth*: or *stilled*, viz. at the Creation, when he fought and conquered Tiâmat (= Rahab), the great Dragon of the primeval Deep (תהום), as related in the Babylonian Epic of Creation, Tab. IV. See on 7¹² 9¹³. The rendering *he stirreth up* spoils the parallelism. 𝔊 κατέπαυσεν, *he quieted*. Cf. Ps 65⁷ 89⁹ 93⁴. There are many allusions elsewhere to Iahvah's quelling or quieting the sea, but few or none to His disturbing it (cf. Jon 1⁴): see note on רגע at 7⁵. Perhaps בקע, Ps 78¹³ [𝔊 transposes the letters, reading גער בים *who rebuketh the sea* (= Na 1⁴), 𝔅 *repente maria congregata sunt* (remembering Gn 1⁹) appears to have made אֲגַר of רגע (cf. Pr 6⁸ 10⁵ 𝔅)] Moreover, the language of vv. 12ᵇ 13ᵇ recalls that of Is 51⁹, and is obviously not independent of it (מחץ רהב, cf. 5¹⁴ Ju 5²⁶ for the verb; Is המחצבת רהב: חללה, Is מחוללת); but both that passage and Is 27¹ נחש ברח *the Fleeing Serpent*) tell not of *stirring up* or *exciting* but of quelling the Water-dragon. See also notes on 3⁸ 9¹³. 𝔊 ἔστρωται (𝔊ᴬ ἔστρωσε) τὸ κῆτος = חלל תנין: cf. Gn 1²¹ Is 51⁹ Ez 28⁷. (But κῆτος = לויתן 3⁸· κήτη τὰ ὑπ' οὐρανόν = עזרי רהב 9¹³.) For the general sense, cf. also Ps 74¹³.

v. 13. 𝔐 lit. *By His breath* or *breeze the Heavens are beauty* (ἄπ. שִׁפְרָה = שֶׁפֶר Gn 49²¹; Aram. שׁוּפְרָא). Perhaps rather הִשְׁפֵּר (Aramaism: cf. 𝕋J Gn 9²⁷): *By His breath the Heavens He made fair* (cf. Ps 33⁶); a better parallel to st. ii. Otherwise leg. שָׁפְרוּ (שָׁפְרוּ?) *become fair* Ps 16⁶. Cf. 𝔙 *Spiritus eius ornavit caelos*. (𝔐 takes חלל as in 15⁷ 19⁷; 𝔊 rectè ἐθανάτωσεν.) 𝔊 κλεῖθρα δὲ οὐρανοῦ δεδοίκασιν αὐτόν. προστάγματι δὲ ἐθ.

δράκοντα ἀποστάτην misreads ברוחו as בריחי *bars* and שפרה or שפרו as שערו *shudder* (? שׂעֵרָהוּ ; cf. Dt 32¹⁷); while the second line may be חלל בדברו נחש טרד (also due to misreading, as Is 51⁹ proves). This last, like חללה ידו נחש ברח ℨ, is a line of four stresses, and thus metr. abnormal. The simplest way out of this difficulty, which is a serious one, inasmuch as we have found the rule of the three-stress stichus rigorously observed hitherto, is to suppose that נחש ברח has been substituted for תנין *the Dragon* (= δράκων 7¹² Is 51⁹ and about 16 other locc.), having been orig. perhaps a marg. gloss by some one who remembered Is 27¹. (ידו *His hand* is supported by the 'arm of Iahvah', Is 51⁹; which makes ויחלל נחש ברח inadmissible.) The verse is gen. explained of the wind (God's 'breath', Is 40⁷) clearing the sky by blowing away the cloudrack after a storm, and of the slaying or driving away of the great Serpent which was believed to coil round the sun and obscure his light. (Winds were Merodach's chief instruments in subduing Tiâmat: Creation Tab. IV. Cf. Gn 1².) See notes on 3⁸. 𝕲 *By His Spirit He governeth the Heavens* (ברוחה שמיא מדבר) ; *And His hand killed the Serpent that fled.* The archetypal passage Is 51⁹, however, with its reiterated notes of time (*As in the Days of the Prime, the Ages of Eld*), seems to leave little room for doubt that the allusions are to the exploits of God in subduing the primeval monsters of the chaotic Deep at (and after?) the Creation of the World, as told in the sacred literature of the Babylonian priesthood.

v. 14. fringes of His Way: pointing דְּרָכוֹ c Ketîb 𝕲; cf. Pr 8²². God's 'way' is His course of action, or mode of creative procedure, of which only the *ends* or outer edges and outskirts (קְצוֹת Ps 19⁷), the mere extremities, are perceptible to man. Then בּוֹ will refer to דַּרְכּוֹ: *And what a whisper of a word* (= what a mere whisper) *is heard in it!* (cf. 4¹² 15⁸ Ps 92¹²) > *do we hear of Him!* [Since *m, n*, are interchangeable, e.g. שטן, שטם, the rare √שׁמץ may be cogn. c Assyr. *šanâçu, to revile, slander* (שני ; Abp.), and so c נאץ, irrisit, sprevit, as a Shaph. form of the same Prim. Root.] 𝕲 καὶ ἐπὶ ἰκμάδα λόγου, curiously taking שמץ as compounded of the Relative שׁ and ימצה (Le 5⁹) = *what is drained out, moisture* (cf. 𝔗 ומה די אתמצי מן קצת מלתיה). So 𝔅: *Et cum vix parvam stillam* (a little drop) *sermonis eius audierimus.* 𝕾 merely takes שמץ in the sense of שמצה (Ex 32²⁵): *And what evil word is heard against Him?* St. iii is prob. an addition: lit. *And the thunder of His prowess* (sing. so Ketîb 𝕲𝕾𝔗𝔅 ; plur. *feats of pr.* Qerî) *who discerneth* (or *considereth*, or *understandeth*)? 11¹¹ 23¹⁵ 30²⁰ 31³ 32¹² 37¹¹ 38¹⁸. 𝕲 σθένος δὲ βροντῆς αὐτοῦ (= וגבורת רעמו) τίς οἶδεν ὁπότε ποιήσει (a mistaken gloss). For רעם see 39²⁵; but read perhaps רא and גבורתו (Qerî): *And the sum* (Ps 119¹⁶⁰ 139¹⁷) *of His exploits who can perceive?*

Chapter 27. Hitherto the heading of Iyob's replies has been simply *And Iyob answered and said;* and a like formula has introduced the speeches of the friends Now, for no obvious reason, a new formula arrests our attention: *And Eyob again took up his* mashal, *and he said*: cf. Nu 23⁷˙¹⁸ 24³˙¹⁵˙²⁰. The same variation recurs, 29¹. There is, however, nothing in the form or diction of the contents of either chapter to distinguish them from previous discourses as specifically 'mashalic'. They are not characterized by terse maxims and proverbial similitudes like those which constitute the main contents of the book named after them (משלי 'Proverbs'); nor are they lyrical effusions like those of Nu ll. cc. (cf. also Is 14⁴ Mi 2⁴ Ha 2⁶), from which the new heading may indeed have been taken by an editorial hand.

No attentive reader can fail to perceive that Eyob's solemn reiteration of his innocence, vv. 2–6, forms a natural sequel to his ironical address to Bildad, 26²⁻⁴. It is also in perfect harmony with what he has often said before. But the transition from 26¹⁴ to 27²ᶠᶠ· is too abrupt to be original, and the gap is not adequately filled by the introductory formula.

That Eyob should have the last word in the argument with his friends, summing up his own case at great length, as he does in chaps. 29–31, is reasonable enough. What is not reasonable is that he should contradict himself, as he certainly does if 27⁷⁻²³ are correctly assigned to him. The wish *Let mine enemy be as the godless!* (v. 7) stands in strange contrast with the supposed speaker's idyllic picture of the lifelong felicity and peaceful end of the godless (21⁷ᶠᶠ ²³). The questions of vv. 8–10 are equally incongruous in the mouth of Eyob (cf. 21²⁰⁻³³). Does he include himself with the 'godless' whose cry God will not hear (v. 9)? But he has always steadfastly asserted his own righteousness, and has just declared it on oath ('As God liveth!'), although often complaining that God pays no heed to his appeals and protestations (cf 16¹⁷ᶠ· 19⁷ 23³˙⁸ᶠ 30²⁰). Not only so. The description of God's judgements on the 'godless' (vv. 13–23) is in perfect harmony with the doctrine of the friends and in perfect contradiction to his own view as expressed in chap. 21 (cf. 24¹). Evidently these sections are erroneously attributed to Eyob, owing prob. to accidental dislocations and lacunae in the Heb manuscripts and perhaps also to the unskilful patchwork or wilful alterations of editors. However that may be, the solution which recognizes in these verses a third speech of Zophar is, in all probability, correct. They agree in style and sentiment with his previous utterances (chaps. 11, 20), while symmetry of plan is restored to the book by assigning three speeches to each of the three friends (thus nine in all, corresponding to the nine discourses of Eyob) and concluding with Eyob's final restatement and summing up of his case.

v. 1. *his mashal.* A mashal is strictly a *likeness, equivalence,* and then a *comparison* or *similitude;* hence a *proverb* or brief popular saying, expressing supposed, between two different persons, objects, or sets of circumstances. (מָשַׁל Ni. to be or become *like*, Hi. to *liken*, Assyr. *mašâlu*, to be *like*, *equal*, *mišlu*, *half*, *equal part*, *tamšîlu*, *likeness*, *image*, may be referred to the Sum. MASH, *twin*, BAR, *half* = MASH, triliteralized by the addition of the Postposition LI, לְ *in* or *into*.)

𝕲 τῷ προοιμίῳ *in* (his) *proem* ore *xordium* (so also 29¹; cf. 25⁵). Did the translator confuse this word with παροιμία = מָשָׁל *proverb*?

v. 2. *As El liveth*: or *By the Life of El!*; formula of the sacred oath: lit. *El* (*is*) *living* (cf. Ps 18⁴⁷). When the oath is by the life of a human being 𝔐 is always careful to point חֵי instead of חַי (see 1 Sa 20² for both uses); a theological rather than a logical or grammatical distinction. *who hath set aside my right*: 𝕲 softens this into *who hath so judged me*.

v. 3. St. i is apparently a quotation or reminiscence of 2 Sa 1⁹, with נשמתי *my breath* pro נפשי *my soul* or *life*: cf. Is 42⁵. (The distich looks like an intruder. Perhaps some one thought it necessary to account for the prolonged eloquence of a sufferer so grievously afflicted. He still retains 'life and energy' enough for the lengthy discourse that follows. The verse interrupts the oath, the substance of which is suspended till v. 4. Eyob swears that all that he has said is true and sincere. In v. 4 𝕲 ἡ ψυχή μου = נפשי pro 𝔐 לשוני wrongly substituted, because the verb was understood in the sense of *musing* or *meditating* (Pr 24²) > that of *uttering* (תהגה Is 59³: so read here also pro 𝔐 'יה).

v. 5. *Be it far from me!* 𝔙 *Absit a me* ut iustos vos esse iudicem! 𝕲 μή μοι εἴη δικαίους ὑμᾶς ἀποφῆναι! It is gen. assumed that חלילה = *Ad profanum!* but חליל *profanus* does not otherwise exist, and the analogy of classical phrases like ἐς βάραθρον, *Pereat!* &c., would rather suggest a somewhat similar meaning. Conceivably, חלילה might be a noun fem. (מלעיל ante לִי, לְךָ) denoting 'the Pit', 'Perdition' (cf. Syr. חלילא, חליל *a hole, cavity*): cf. 1 Sa 24⁷ *Perdition to me from Iahvah if I do this thing*, &c.

Perhaps, however, חלילה has nothing to do with √חלל, but is a Neg. form of אחלי (2 K 5³ Ps 119⁵), qs* אַחֲלָיְלָה or אחליל א *O that not!* (an elliptical phrase = *May I not have my wish from Iahvah if*, &c.). St. ii is too long: om. ממני *from me* c 𝕲𝔙. *disown*: or *retract*, Is 31², or *cease affirming*.

v. 6. *let it go*: 𝔐 points אַרְפֶּהָ c Suff. as in 7¹⁹; some codd. 𝕲𝔖𝔙 carent Suff. ut Pr 4¹³ (same parallel).

In st. ii, keeping מימי *from my* (earliest) *days* (cf. 38¹² 1 K 1⁶), we might perhaps read חרפני pro 𝔐 יחרף : *My heart* (i.e. conscience) *hath never reproached me all my life*: cf. 𝔙 neque enim reprehendit me cor meum in omni vita mea. 𝕲 οὐ γὰρ σύνοιδα ἐμαυτῷ ἄτοπα πράξας may represent לא־יחרפני לבבי מאומה *My heart* (1 Sa 24⁵) *reproacheth me with nothing* (cf. Ju 8¹⁵ Ps 55¹³). Neither חָרַף Pi. nor יָחְפַּר (6²⁰ Ps 34⁶) is acc. to Heb. use. Perhaps מום לא־יחרפלי לבבי מום *My heart reproacheth me not with a fault* (11⁷ 31⁷). The י ad fin. may be dittogr. of foll. י. Cf. 𝔖.

v 7. St. ii seems too short. 𝔊 ὥσπερ ἡ ἀπώλεια τῶν παρανόμων (‖ ὥσπερ ἡ καταστροφὴ τῶν ἀσεβῶν) suggests that איד (= both καταστρ. and ἀπώλεια cf. 21¹⁷ ³⁰ 31³) may have fallen out (כאיד עול) *as the ruin of the wrongdoer*). Possibly also it would be an improvement to point אֹיְבַי and וּמִתְקוֹמְמַי plur. c 𝔊 (cf. Ps 59²), reading יהיו pro יהי.

v. 8. St. i is metr. over weight, as it would seem. We must in any case point יְבַצֵּעַ (6⁹ cf Is 38¹²). The phrase כי יבצע is usu. rejected as a gloss on the obscure כי ישל which follows. Of the emendations proposed we prefer כי ישא אל־ *When he lifteth up his soul* (in prayer) *to Eloah*. This, which is a known phrase (Ps 25¹ La 3⁴¹), appears to be supported by 𝔊 ὅτι ἐπέχει (= *animum advertit*) and 𝔖 *At the time when God is taking from him his soul* (שקל לה לנפשה = ישא לו נפשו), and agrees better with the context, vv. 9, 10. *When God draweth out* (יִשֶּׁל Apoc. Impf. of שָׁלָה = Syr. שלא *extraxit*; or יִשַּׁל or יָשַׁל from שָׁלַל id., Ru 2¹⁶) *his soul*, i.e. his life, apart from the strangeness of the phrase, does not suit the connexion. There is no question of *hope* in the actual hour of death for Eyob and his friends. The three verses (8–10) simply emphasize the idea that the prayer of the godless is vain. Nor is the more attractive ישאל *asketh* really at all probable; for שאל is never used of God's *demanding a man's life*, nor does the verb occur in Job in any other sense than that of asking questions (8⁸·²⁴ 12⁷ 21²⁹ 38³ 40⁷ 42⁴), except in 31³⁰ (of imprecating death on an enemy). Perhaps 𝔊 ὅτι ἐπέχει = כי יעצר (1 K 14¹⁰) = כי יבצע (al. ὅτι πλεονεκτεῖ). For st. ii 𝔊 gives πεποιθὼς ἐπὶ κύριον ἄρα σωθήσεται, = כי יציל אלוה נפשו? But cf also 11¹⁸ 12⁶. (𝔊ᴬ μὴ πεπ. ἐπὶ κ εἰ ἄρα σωθ. הֲכִי (ואם?) יציל וגו' *Is it that* (*Or will*) *Eloah deliver his life?* This may poss. be orig. Cf. 𝔙 *Quae est enim spes hypocritae si avare rapiat* (=𝔐), *Et non liberet Deus animam eius?*

v. 10. With st. i cf. Ps 37⁴ Is 57¹ (*alio sensu*). For 𝔊 ἐχ. παρρησ. cf. 22²⁶. *And call*: וקרא pro 𝔐 יקרא—an intolerable Asyndeton. Cf. 𝔊𝔙𝔖. After this verb we should expect לאלוה (12⁴ 19¹⁶), or אל־אל (so some codd); cf. 𝔖 Perhaps וקרא אליו *And call unto Him* (𝔊 om. אלוה). Yet cf. also Is 43²² קרא c Accus. Pers. 𝔊 st. ii might represent ואם קרא אם בקרא יעתר לו or וקרא ונעתר לו or even יעתר־לו. Cf. Gn 25²¹ for the second verb. But בכל־עת (Ps 34²), 𝔙 *omni tempore*, is supported also by 𝔖𝔗. (𝔊 ineptly turns the verse into a promise of mercy to the penitent. *But if he trust in the Almighty and call unto God continually, God will answer him and hear him.* Coloured by 𝔊?)

vv. 11, 12. If these two distichs really belonged to Eyob originally, we must suppose that they once introduced a very different account of 'the portion of the wicked' from that which follows them in the present text; an account like that which Eyob has already given in chap. 21, but perhaps going so far beyond it as to provoke editorial excision, although, of course, the loss of the original sequel may have been due to an *hiatus valde deflendus* in the Heb. manuscripts. Verse 11 would be fairly suitable in the mouth of either Eyob or Zophar (cf. Eliphaz, 15¹⁷); but v. 12 is certainly more pointed and forcible in the mouth of Eyob, as a challenge to the friends not to uphold arbitrary theories in the face of undeniable experience.

v. 11. *instruct you in*: Ps 25⁸ Pr 4¹¹ (בדרך) *in the way*; which would be not inappropriate here). *the Hand*: i.e. the Power, and its exercise, or His doings, mode of action. But 𝔊 τί ἐστιν ἐν χειρὶ K., *what is in Iahwah's Hand*; as if מה־ had fallen out after אתכם (𝔊 ὑμῖν). This perhaps agrees better with the parallel *what is with Shaddai*; i.e. in His mind or purpose (cf. 10¹³). אתך *thee* pro אתכם *you* is improb. since Eyob has always addressed the friends collectively, except in 12⁷,⁸ and 26²⁻⁴.)

v. 12. הֵן אַתֶּם should prob. be הֶן־אַתֶּם with a single stress, metri gratia. St. ii: *And why do ye vapour in vain?* or *And why will ye babble so idly?* by contradicting the evidence of your own eyes (or perhaps your own admission that God's ways are unfathomable and inscrutable to man, e.g. 11⁷⁻⁹). Cf. 𝔙 Ecce vos omnes nostis; et quid sine causa vana loquimini? 𝔊ᴮ *Behold, ye all know | That ye are adding vain things to vain*; a loose paraphrase, which 𝔊ᴬ corrects *Behold, ye all have seen*; | *But why do ye add*, &c.

v. 13. St. i is repeated from close of Zophar's second speech, 20²⁹; a fact which lends some degree of support to our attribution of the section. Like 20²⁹ᵃ the stichus is metrically redundant, and the superfluous אָדָם must be rejected here as there (cf. 9²²,²⁴ 15²⁰ 24⁶ al. for רשע). *from El*: reading מֵאֵל (cf. ׳מֵאֱלֹהַּ 20²⁹) pro 𝔐 עִם־אֵל *with El*, which echoes עִם־שַׁדַּי (v. 11), or may be mere dittogr. of the preceding ע. So 𝔊 παρὰ Κυρίου; but 𝔙 apud Deum = 𝔐. Perhaps rather מֵעִם־אֵל *from with El*; God has it in store and it comes from Him: cf. 𝔖 𝔗.

St. ii also appears overweighted (cf. 20²⁰ᵇ), and יקחו add. mars the parallelism. עָרִיץ *the violent man, the tyrant*, sing. as ‖ to רשע (15²⁰), seems preferable to the plur. (6²³: see note there), and agrees better with '*his* sons', &c., in what follows. (𝔊 δυναστῶν, 𝔙 violentorum = 𝔐. In accordance with this plur. 𝔊ᴮ continues with οἱ υἱοὶ αὐτῶν . . . χῆραι δὲ αὐτῶν, vv. 14, 15; but returns to the sing. in v. 16 ff. So also 𝔖.)

v. 14. *His sons grow up* or *are multiplied*: om. אם *If* (from v. 16?). 𝔐 must mean *If his sons multiply* (or *grow up*, 39⁴), (*it is*) *for the sword* = למו חרב יהיו; cf. 𝔊 εἰς σφαγὴν ἔσονται, 𝔙 in (? במו) gladio erunt. Cf. Je 15² אשר לחרב *They who are for the sword* . . . ואשר לרעב *and they who are for famine*, &c. לָמוֹ = לְ recurs 29²¹ 38⁴⁰. A more logical parallel to st. ii would be לְמוֹ־רָעָב it is *for hunger* (5²⁰). But see Je 15² (*plague, sword, famine = sword, famine, plague* here, vv. 14 f.). *his offspring*: צאצאים (׳צ 21⁸ = τέκνα; Is 48¹⁹ 61⁹ 65²³ = ἔκγονα) *issue*: a word peculiar to II Is and Job. 𝔊 suggests יצאו אם *And if they come* (or *grow*) up

(8¹⁶ 14²), with its ἐὰν δὲ καὶ ἀνδρωθῶσιν, προσαιτήσουσιν, *And if they have even grown up, they shall beg*. But this version perhaps merely indicates that the translator felt the difficulty discussed above. The slain could not hunger any more.

v. 15 *perish*: יאבדו pro 𝔐 יקברו *are buried*. *by the Plague*: בְּמָוֶת: lit. *by the Death*: cf. the old English designation of the Plague as the Black Death. 𝕲 τελευτήσουσιν = ימותו (1¹⁹ 3¹¹ 12² 14⁸ al.). To insert לא *not* before יקברו spoils the formal correspondence of the distich with v. 14 and yields a doubtful sense. (נקבר is joined with בְּ of the *place* of burial; and בְּמָוֶת can hardly mean *when they die* or *when dead*) St. ii occurs in Ps 78⁶⁴ in a similar context. There is little reason to read '*their* widows' instead of '*his* widows' (𝕲𝕾), as all the widows of the רשע's tribe or clan are regarded as belonging to the great man himself; and still less to point תְּבָכֶינָה Ni. (which is not used, though 𝕲𝕾𝖂 wrongly suggest it in Ps 78⁶⁴) as the widows would naturally weep over their loss on ordinary occasions, but not in times of general and overwhelming calamity (cf. Ez 24¹⁶ᶠᶠ).

v. 16 St. i = Zc 9³ᵇ where חרוץ *gold* in ‖, as 𝕲 here χρυσίον instead of מלבוש *clothing*, which, however, suits יבין better, and is required by the immediate context, v. 17ᵃ. For clothes as an important element of wealth, side by side with silver and gold, see Gn 24⁵³ 45²² Ex 3²² 2 K 5⁵ 2 C 9²⁴.

v. 17. Lit *He provides, and the righteous* (emph.) *puts on*. It is what always happens, according to the speaker. 𝕲 paraphrases: *All this just* (men) *will acquire* (περιποιήσονται, app. reading ירבש pro 𝔐 ילבש. Gn 36⁶). 𝕲 ἀληθινοί = נקי (hic tant.) perhaps indicates a variant יָשָׁר in 𝕲's Heb. text (cf. 2⁸ 4⁷ 8⁶ 17⁸).

v. 18. 𝕲 *And his house turns out* (ἀπέβη 22¹¹) *as moths and as a spider*, incorporating the two readings כעש *like the moth* (𝔐𝖂 *sicut tinea*, 𝕾 ברקבוביתא) and כעכביש *like the spider* (𝕾𝔄). The latter is prob. right; cf. 8¹⁴. 𝕲ᴬ completes the distich by add. ὁ πλοῦτος αὐτοῦ (עשרו, a relic of 𝔐 עשה נצר ? st. ii). St. ii was partially effaced in 𝕲's manuscript. The *booth* is the temporary screen against the sun, put up by the keeper of a vineyard (Is 1⁸), and soon blown down by the storms of winter.

v. 19. 𝔐 lit. *The rich man lies down* (in death?), *and is not gathered* (for burial, Je 8² 25³³, cf. also Ju 2¹⁰ 2 K 22²⁰). There is, however, something strange in this sudden transition from the רשע of the introduction (v. 13) to the עשיר. Prob. the latter is due to a misreading of the former word, written in the margin as a gloss. There is no more need to repeat the Subj. here than in vv. 16–18. But this leaves st. i metr. short; and as ולא יאסף is hardly a good ‖ to ואיננו, we restore ולא יוסיף לקום *and riseth not again*. After making this emendation, it was satisfactory to find that it was actually the reading of 𝕲 (ולא נוסף למסם); cf. also 𝕲 καὶ οὐ προσθήσει.

He openeth his eyes: i.e. app. in She'ol or Hades, the world of the dead (cf. 𝔙 which thinks of Ps 49¹⁸; Lk 16²³ 'in Hades he lifted up his eyes'; also Lk 12²⁰).

v. 20. *by day*: יוֹמָם (5¹⁴ 24¹⁶ tant.) pro 𝔐 כַּמַּיִם *like the waters*, i.e. a sudden inundation or flood, sweeping everything away. So the Versions; but the other agrees better with the parallel stichus. It may, however, very well be that vv. 20, 21 are explanatory of the general statement of v. 19: *He lieth down* (to sleep), *and riseth not again*; He wakes and finds himself whirled to destruction by flood and storm. Cf. 22¹¹·¹⁶.

We must point תְּשִׂיגֻהוּ plur. pro 𝔐 תְּשִׂיגֵהוּ with Subj. בַּלָּהוֹת (cf. 18¹¹), unless that noun be regarded as an Intensive Plur. = extreme terror: cf. Ez 26²¹ 27³⁶ 28¹⁹ where it is connected with אֵין as here (v. 19). See also 18¹⁴ 24¹⁷ 30¹⁵ Ps 73¹⁹ and esp. Is 17¹⁴ בַּלָּהָה Sing. ἄπ.). In some, if not all, of these locc., a late Sing. בַּלָּהוּת would suit. With st. ii cf. 21¹⁸ (37⁹ סוּפָה). 𝔊 γνόφος for סוּפָה as for שְׂעָרָה 9¹⁷.

v. 21. *Sirocco*: the burning wind from the E. and S.E. deserts (15²). 𝔊 καύσων, 𝔙 *ventus urens*. St. ii is metr. short. Fort. exc. בְּרֶגַע *in a moment* (cf. 20⁵ 7¹⁸ 21¹³ 34²⁰ Ps 73¹⁹). *whirleth him away*: cf. Ps 50³ 58¹⁰. 𝔊 λικμήσει, *winnow* (*him*) *away* (usu. = זָרָה: cf. Is 41¹⁶).

v. 22. Lit. *And he casteth at him* (cf. Nu 35²⁰) *and spareth not* (16¹³). Read וַיַּשְׁלֵךְ. *God* may be Subj. subaud., though we have to go back to v. 13 to discover this. Either אֵל has fallen out before עָלָיו, or the reference may perhaps be to the violent action of the wind hurling things upon its victim; but the former view is preferable. וַיַּשְׁלֵךְ sine Obj. is somewhat remarkable (cf. Nu l. c.). It seems to include all the calamities already specified, and to suggest others to the imagination, if any be omitted. The root occurs four times in Job (15³³ 18⁷ 27²² 29¹⁷) ac. to 𝔐; but two of these are dubious (see notes on 18⁷ 29¹⁷).

v. 23. 𝔐 (evidently more or less corrupt) lit. *He claps at them their palms, And hisses at him from his place*. The forms עָלִימוֹ, כַּפֵּימוֹ are foreign to the style of Job (cf. st. ii עָלָיו, the normal form). The ו of the second word may be dittogr. of the foll. ו; read therefore כַּפַּיִם, after La 2¹⁵ (although כַּפֵּי would also be possible, Nu 24¹⁰). But even so the Subj. of the verb יִשְׂפֹּק (= יִסְפֹּק; see locc. citt.) is not clear. It may be El (see note on v. 22). Iahvah jeers at His enemies, Pss 2⁴ 59⁹, and He 'hisses' to summon nations, &c., Is 5²⁶ 7¹⁸ Zc 10⁸. But שָׁרַק is more usual as an expression of human hatred and derision (La 2¹⁵·¹⁶ Je 19⁸ al.), and does not appear to be said of God in such a sense elsewhere. Moreover, the reference to God makes מִמְּקֹמוֹ *from his place* difficult, as in that case it would have to mean *from Heaven* (cf. Rabb. use of מָקוֹם), since 'יִשְׁרֹק עָלָיו מִמּ cannot mean *hiss him out of his place*, but only *hiss at him from his place*. Cf. Ez 3¹⁴ Mi 1⁰. מִמָּרוֹם *from the Height* has been proposed: but the usage of Job would require the plur. (16¹⁹ 25² 31²).

To read the verbs as plur. indef. (*they*, i.e. men, *clap, hiss*) is a doubtful expedient in the context; and the repetition of עליו, though not ungrammatical, is suspicious. The parallel passages cited above (add 1 K 9⁸ Zp 2¹⁵ Is 55¹² Je 50¹³) suggest

יספק עובר כפים
וישרק עלי כל מבות(י)ו:

The passer-by clappeth hands,
And hisseth at all his plagues.

Cf. 18²⁰ 21²⁰. (St. ii possibly וישרק עלי-יום פידו (אידו) *And hisseth at the day of his ruin.*)

Chapter 28. THE PRAISE OF WISDOM. *Other things accounted precious have sources whence man obtains them; but the source of Wisdom, the thing of supreme value, is beyond the search of man, and known to God alone.* Although this unique discourse begins with the word *For* (כִּי), it gives no justification for the statements which, in the present text, immediately precede it (27¹³⁻²³). It is equally out of all visible relation to the immediate sequel (chaps. 29–31), in which Eyob reviews at length his past life and affirms his blamelessness as stoutly as ever (cf. 27²⁻⁶) To secure a place for the chapter in Eyob's discourse, Bickell and others make it the continuation of 27¹¹,¹², while freely revising and rejecting more than half of its contents. Even this expedient, however, cannot hide from us the fact that the connexion so effected is only external. Instead of furthering, the chapter really interrupts the course and progress of the argument; and the conclusion of the whole (v. 28), however true in itself, is not the point of Eyob's previous or subsequent pleadings. (See the note ad loc., and cf. Pr 1⁷ 9¹⁰ Ec 12¹³). This conclusion, indeed, might have been more appropriately put into the mouth of one of Eyob's three antagonists, all of whom have maintained that Eyob's calamities are direct and irrefragable evidence that he has *not* 'feared God and departed from evil'; while he himself (in complete harmony with what may be called a postulate of the book, 1¹) has steadily and consistently affirmed the contrary. In the following chapters he reaffirms his consciousness of innocence and his confident readiness to confront his Divine Adversary if He will but vouchsafe him a hearing (31³⁵⁻³⁷); after which, no doubt, the original poem proceeded at once to the *dénoument* of Iahvah's answer out of the whirlwind (38¹).

As regards the substance of chap. 28, it must be admitted that the long description of the wonders of mining (vv. 1–11), and the elaborate enumeration of gems and precious metals which are worthless for the purchase of Wisdom (vv. 15–19), provide neither a natural sequel to Eyob's passionate protest, 27²⁻⁶, nor any clear fulfilment of the promise, 27¹¹. The latter passage (vv. 15–19), which might almost be an extract from the Book of Proverbs (cf. Pr 3⁴⁻ ᵛ⁴⁻¹ 16⁻ cf. also the lists of gems,

Ex 28¹⁷⁻²⁰ Ez 28¹³), is remote from the usual thought and diction of Job (cf. 21⁸ ff. 22²⁴ f. and the Prologue and Epilogue, where we find no mention of gems among the tokens of wealth). Lastly, if vv. 23-27 originally belonged here, we can only call them an inartistic anticipation of the Divine utterances, 38²⁶·³⁶ ff. (cf. also Pr 3¹⁹ f. 8²²⁻³⁰).

Throughout the chapter, with the exception of the last verse (see the note), 'Wisdom' appears to denote insight into the Creator's methods of working in the physical world (see the innumerable questions with which Iahvah confounds Eyob in chaps. 38 sqq.); a topic hardly discussed at all in Eyob's preceding speeches and in the long soliloquy with which he concludes his case against God and man. The poetical merits of the piece ought not to blind us to the perception of its irrelevance in its present context, nor to the probability that, if Eyob had raised the question, he would not have handled it in this fashion.

v. 1. The gap in style and sentiment, in thought and expression, between this and the last chapter, is too obvious to escape the notice even of a cursory reader. We should at least have expected the bridge of an introductory heading like that of 27¹. Assuming that the chapter was originally an independent piece drawn from another source, Duhm accounts for the opening Ptc. *For* by the ingenious supposition that the 'Refrain'

> *Wisdom, whence is it found?*
> *And where is the Place of Insight?*

(see vv. 12, 20) once preceded it. This expedient is at least preferable to rendering כִּי by *Surely*, which is against ordinary usage.

they refine: Rel. clause. For the verb, see Ps 12⁷. It occurs in another sense, 36²⁷ (Elihu).

v. 2. earth: or *the soil* or *ground* (עָפָר *dust*: 4¹⁰ 5⁶ al.). *it is taken* (Gn 3¹⁹·²³). There is no need to point יֻקָּח. St. ii lit. *And* (the) *stone, it poureth copper* (i.e. when smelted). The 'stone' is, of course, the 'Vein Rock' which is the matrix of the metal. Cf. Dt 8⁹ *A land whose stones are iron, and out of whose hills thou mayst hew copper.* The verb יָצוּק, which recurs 29⁶ (q.v.), should perhaps be pointed יָצִיק, *scr. plen.* = יָצִק, Impf. of יצק *effudit* > of the dub. צוק: see 11¹⁵ 22¹⁶ 37¹⁶ 38³⁸ 41¹³·¹⁶ Gn 28¹⁸. Moreover, the gender of אבן (1 Sa 17⁴⁹ et pass.) requires תִּצֹּק ('י due to influence of || 'יק). The Ho. תוּצָק (22¹⁶): *And the stone is poured out as copper* or *cast, smelted into copper* (cf. 1 K 7¹⁶·²³) seems also possible. 𝔊 *And copper is quarried like stone* (? תחצב: 19²⁴ Is 51¹).

v. 3. In 𝔐 a tristich. But תכלית is usually followed by a defining Genit. (11⁷ 26¹⁰), which in this case would naturally be some syn. of חשך, perhaps the אפל preserved in st. iii. The כל before 'תכל may well be dittogr., and instead of the Prep. ל usage suggests עד (although, as חקר takes a simple Accus. 5⁷ 13 29 32", a Prep. is hardly needed). Further, the phrase חשך וצלמות (3⁸ 10²¹, cf. 34²² Ps 107¹⁰ ¹⁴) justifies restoration of וצלמות, the last word of st. iii, to st. i. Thus we get the distich

קץ־שם לחשך וצלמות
ועד תכלית אפל הוא חוקר:

An end he puts to darkness and deathshade,
And the limits of gloom he explores.

The miner does this by opening to the light the mountain sides within which the metallic ores lie hidden. If the meaning be that the miner carries a lantern, why is not the lantern expressly mentioned?

v. 4. 𝔐 lit. *He breaks through* (or *into* or *open*) *the wâdy from with the sojourner* | *Which are forgotten* (masc. plur.) *by the foot* | *They hang* (?) (*far*?) *from men they waver* (*swing? wander?*). Another tristich, evidently very corrupt. It is generally taken for granted that the verse describes how the miner is let down deep into the earth by a rope. So Driver; who suggests אר *light* for גָּר *sojourner*. But even so, st. ii remains out of all grammatical connexion with st. i; and if we connect it with st iii (*They who are forgotten by the foot swing,* &c.), we violate the metrical structure and substitute prose for poetry. It is possible that the third line (דלו מאנוש נעו) has grown out of marginal variants or corrections of the second (הנשכחים מני רגל): see Duhm, who restores the verse as follows:

פרץ נחל מני רגל
דלו במושכה נעו

Man broke away a shaft under the foot;
So man hangs down swaying on the rope.

But here, as always, נחל means *wâdy, torrent-bed, ravine,* and *shaft* is only a guess from the context (*Thes.* 'Prob. *puteus metallicus*'). The phrase מני רגל can hardly stand for מתחת רגל; and if it could, the whole sentence would still be very strange Besides, ancient mines were worked by lateral adits rather than by deep vertical shafts (e.g. those of the old Egyptian sovereigns in the *Wâdy Maghâra,* or 'Valley of Caverns', in the Sinaitic peninsula).

Duhm regards עם גר, st. i, as an inferior variant of מני רגל, st. ii; and similarly, he takes הנשכחי as a variant of אנש נעו; both the latter being assumed to be perversions of the true reading בַּמְשֻׁבָה נָעוּ (38³¹; בַּמוּשָׁכַת?). This is certainly very ingenious, if nothing more. In any other context st. iii would naturally be rendered *They are brought low* (cf. Ps 79⁸ Is 19⁶); *away from man they wander* (cf. Gn 4¹² נע). Perhaps גלו should be read pro דלו (cf. 2 Sa 15¹⁹), so that the stichus would mean *They are exiled* (and) *wanderers from men*—a possible gloss on עם גר (*vid. infr.*).

A better sense emerges for st. i if we make the very slight change of pointing עָם *people*, pro עִם *with*, and connect the מ with the preceding נחל (thus gaining a Subj. for the vb. and an antecedent for the following הנשכחים, which otherwise, like the supposed miner, hangs in the air):

> *The foreign folk breaketh up the ravines,*
> *Forgotten of the foot* (i. e. long untrodden).

The mines and quarries of Sinai were worked by foreigners, Phoenicians and others. Cf. 𝔙 Dividit torrens a *populo peregrinante* eos quos oblitus est pes *egentis hominis, et invios* (dividing נעו ומאנוש דל). 𝔊 διακοπὴ χειμάρρου ἀπὸ κονίας = גר (עם)מֵ נַחַל פָּרֶץ (points; cf. Is 27⁹ 2 Sa 6⁸) only confirms 𝔐. οἱ δὲ ἐπιλανθανόμενοι ὁδὸν δικαίαν ἠσθένησαν ἐκ βροτῶν = הַשֹּׁכְחִים מַעֲגַל יֹשֶׁר דַּלּוּ מֵאֱנוֹשׁ (app. om. נעו).

An unfrequented glen might poetically be said to be 'forgotten of the foot' (of travellers); but to say of a man hanging by a rope in a shaft, or working underground, that he was 'forgotten of *the foot*' (instead e. g. of 'forgotten of *the passer-by*', עבר, or of the people above) would be an illogical obscurity of expression. The foot is not the organ of remembrance.

v. 5 'The earth provides man with food; *but,* not content with that, in his search for metals he overturns her ruinously underneath' (Driver): cf. RV which, however, would require נהפכה f. instead of נהפך m. 𝔐 St. ii is probably corrupt. 𝔗 thinks of the fire of Gehenna; but the reference may well be to precious stones (cf. v. 6). We might perhaps read אבני אש (נצפנו?) ותחתיה נחבו *And under her are hidden stones of fire* (Ez 28¹⁴ ¹⁶); or as the ספיר follows in v. 6, נֹפֶךְ וְיָשְׁפֵה *carbuncle and jasper* might be substituted for 𝔐 נהפך כמו אש: see Ez 28¹³ (Ex 28¹⁹) ישפה ספיר נפך. (It may be more than a mere coincidence that in the previous verse of Ez l. c. חכמה *Wisdom* is mentioned, as also before in vv. 3, 5, 7.) In st. i also (which has four stresses) we may suppose a ref. to gems > bread, reading מִנִּי־אֶרֶץ יֵצֵא לֶשֶׁם *Out of Earth cometh the jacinth* (Ex 28¹⁹); or perhaps יַהֲלֹם *the onyx* (?).

v. 6. *Her stones are the place of the sapphire* (𝔊 σαπφείρου; so 𝔖𝔗𝔙); others *lapis lazuli,* in view of st. ii, which is then supposed to mean *Which hath specks of gold.* But עֲפָרֹת plur. of עָפָר *dust, earth* (Pr 8²⁶ tant.) is improbable in this sense; and Ex 24¹⁰ Ez 1²⁶ 10¹ suggest a transparent > an opaque blue. 𝔐 *And dusts of gold it* (the place of the *sapph*r) *hath.* Either way we get an indifferent parallel. To correspond to *her stones* we should expect *her dust* (עפרתיה *her earths* or *clods?*); and we might perhaps read לָמוֹ ad fin. pro לוֹ: *And her clods have gold*: or keeping 𝔐 ועפרת זהב, we might render . *And they* (her stones) *have nugg..¹* (?) *of g ld.* (𝔖 seems to have read וערפת *And a dripping* (of gold), &c., instead of ועפרת, as it gives ܘܥܪܦܬ ܕܕܗܒܐ.) Ex 28¹⁸, where

נפך ספיר ויהלם are mentioned together, suggests the possibility of the line *And her dusts are gold and onyx* (?). 𝔊 καὶ χῶμα χρυσίον αὐτῷ, 𝔙 et glebae illius aurum. Perhaps וּבְרֶקֶת זָהָב לָמוֹ or וזהר ברקת למו *And they have the sheen of the emerald.*

v. 7. There is no visible connexion between this verse and the last.

RV's 'That path no bird of prey knoweth' (i. e., as Driver explains, the path found by the miner) is not a permissible translation. 𝔐 may be rendered *A (The) path, no eagle knows it, And the hawk's eye hath not descried it,* or *A (The) path which no eagle knows,* &c. Why should birds of prey and wild beasts be supposed unfamiliar with the mountainous scenes of mining operations? It is not the path to the mines, but the path to the 'place' of Wisdom that is hidden from the 'birds of the air' (v. 21). The mountains and deserts are the natural haunt of the birds and beasts of prey, and nothing, however remote, escapes their marvellous powers of sight. But Wisdom is beyond the range even of *their* almost miraculous vision. It is highly probable, therefore, that some reference to Wisdom preceded this verse; in fact, the refrain of vv. 12, 20:

> But Wisdom, whence cometh it?
> And where is the place of Insight?

We may then read נתיבו לא ידע עיט *The path thereto no eagle knows* (i. e. the path to the 'place' of Wisdom; cf. 38¹⁹ ²⁰).

v. 8 *Sons of Pride*: 41²⁶. (שחצא = *lion*, 𝔗 Ps 17¹²; but var. שחלא.) No doubt, majestic wild beasts are intended; cf. st. ii. 𝔗 בני אריון *sons of lions*; 𝔊 υἱοὶ ἀλαζόνων; 𝔙 filii institorum, *sons of pedlars*!

v. 9. *flint*: חלמיש. There can be little doubt that this word is etym. identical with the Assyr *elmešu, elmêšu, elmâšu, elmîšu,* a brilliant precious stone, the Sum. equivalent of which (SUD-AM) means *light (nûru)* or *glittering.* The Semitic word may be compared with the Sum. ĠAD, ĠUD, *bright,* GIR, *lightning,* GIRIM, *bright,* a kind of gem (*samtu*), GAR, AR, *light,* ĠUL, *joy* (brightness), MUL, UL (from GUL), *star, glitter* (cf. UL, *joy*), EL, *bright,* and MAŠ, *bright, shining.* The Greek ΑΔΑΜΑC, *diamond, steel,* may perhaps be of the same origin. 𝔊 ἐν ἀκροτόμῳ, *on* (the) *abrupt rock* or *precipice* (see also Dt 8¹⁵). 𝔙 ad silicem, *towards the flint*

St. ii seems hyperbolical, as a description of ancient mining. Cf. 9⁵. (It is possible that vv. 9–11 originally followed v. 4.)

v. 10. 𝔐 בצורות ἅπ. = בצורים (8 occ.): *In the rocks (cliffs) he cleaveth* (opens) *watercourses* (or *channels*); i e. either the damp, dripping tunnels or 'workings' themselves, or else gutters to carry off their moisture, which seems more likely. For יארים, str. *Nile-arms,* see Is 33²¹. Cf. also Ps 78¹⁵. An leg. בצורות לאור מבקע *Things inaccessible* (cf Je 33³) *he breaks open to the light* (?). 𝔊 δίνας δὲ ποταμῶν ἔρρηξεν, fort. מצולות (41²³), cf. note τὰ κοιλώματα τῶν ἰσταμένων ῥάγας, [illegible] f the *waters, the whirlpools* ($\mathfrak{G}^{B\,a\,mg.\,Inf}$); $\mathfrak{G}^{C}$ θίνας ποτ. = *dunes*. $\mathfrak{S}$ connects בצרות with √בצר.(vid. supr.). But $\mathfrak{V}$ In petris rivos excidit = $\mathfrak{M}$.

v. 11. This looks like a variant of v. 10.

St. i. $\mathfrak{M}$ lit. *From weeping the rivers* (or *canals*) *he bound up*; which is supposed to mean that the miner prevents water from percolating into the workings (Driver). Obviously this is no parallel to st. ii. Moreover, חבש Pi. does not recur in OT in the sense of *restraining*, nor is this Root found in Job except in 5¹⁸, where it has its ordinary meaning (34¹⁷ 40¹³ are corrupt: see notes). If with $\mathfrak{G}^{\Theta}$ (ἐξηρεύνησεν; $\mathfrak{V}$ scrutatus est) we read חפש *he searched*, and for the dub. מבכי substitute the very similar נבכי *springs* (38¹⁶ Pr 8²⁴ $\mathfrak{G}$), or מעמקי *depths*, we get a better || to st. ii.

$\mathfrak{G}$ βάθη δὲ ποταμῶν ἀνεκάλυψεν = נעמקי נהרות גלה; cf. 12²² Pr 9¹⁸. In st. ii leg. ותעלמות יצא לאור (or א לאור)(ותעלמות הוצי) *And hidden things he brings into the light*: cf 11⁶ 12²². ($\mathfrak{G}$ δύναμιν = 'תעלמ as in 11⁶.)

Do vv. 10, 11 refer to mining at all? Such words as יארים (plur. of יאר), the Nile), which commonly, if not always, means the arms and canals of the Nile in the Delta (Ex 8¹ Is 19⁶ 33²¹ Am 8⁸ Ez 29³ᶠᶠ ¹⁰ Zc 10¹¹), and נהרות *rivers*, plur of נהר (14¹¹ 20¹⁷ 22¹⁶ 40²³), appear altogether extravagant in their assumed application. The term נהר always implies a considerable volume of running water, denoting either an independent stream or a river-canal (Egypt, Babylonia), and is never app. used of an artificial channel or gutter for carrying off water, for which other terms were available, e.g. תעלה, Ez 31⁴. The word, in fact, is mostly used of the great rivers of the world, esp. the Euphrates, 'The River', 'The Great River', and the Nile (Gn 2¹³·¹⁴ 15¹⁸ 31²¹ Is 19⁶), and poet. of the ocean floods ('the running seas'), Jon 2⁴ Ps 24² 93³. We have not to think of the vast underground workings of modern mines and their methods of preventing and overcoming floods. The two verses almost appear to describe works of Divine rather than human activity (cf. v. 24; Ps 78¹⁵·²⁰ 105⁴¹ Hab 3⁹). Possibly, however (supposing the two verses still stand in their orig. context), the reference is to collecting gold and other precious things (e.g. pearls and other gems) from the beds of rivers. In that case, read 'מצולות יאר (cf. Is 44²⁷ Zc 10¹¹) as parallel to 'נבכי נהר, and translate

        The depths of Niles he cleaves .
        The sources of rivers he searches . . .

v. 12. *cometh it*: reading תבוא (v. 20) pro $\mathfrak{M}$ חמצא (dittogr. of v. 13ᵇ).

v. 13. *the way to her*: leg. דרכה c $\mathfrak{G}$ ὁδὸν αὐτῆς (cf. v. 23) pro $\mathfrak{M}$ ערכה *her price* (anticipation of v. 15).

v. 14. There seems no need to alter אמר: cf. Hab 3¹⁰.

v. 15. The ἅπ. סגור should prob. be pointed סָגֻר, which occurs 1 K 6·¹· 10²² in the phrase זָהָב סָגֻר *solid* or *massive gold* (as distinct from gilding or gold leaf?). סגור is lit. *closed*, i.e. app. *close* or *close-grained*.

Whatever the exact implication, the Heb. phrase certainly corresponds to Sargon's Assyr. *ḫurâṣu sakru* (=חרוץ סגור), *sekêru* (סכר) being the Assyr. equivalent of סגר *to shut, close up* (3^{10} 12^{14} 41^7). Perhaps זהב *gold* should be inserted here; the phrase being regarded metr. as a single word. 𝔊 συνκλεισμόν (so also Ho 13^8 where סְגוֹר is prob. corrupt). 𝔙 *aurum obrizum* (so 2 C 3^8 = זהב טוב *fine gold*); cf. *obrussa, assaying or testing gold by fire*; χρυσίον ὄβρυζον, *refined gold* (Ducange). Since the names of the metals are mostly colour-terms, e.g. זהב = צהב *bright, yellow*, חרוץ *ḫurâṣu*, id., it seems possible that סגור *sakru* may have sprung from Sum. SIG, *yellow* (cf. also SIG ⟨⊦⊰⟩ *bright, purified, refined* of silver, KUBABAR SIG DIM = kima çarpi çurrupi, 'like refined silver'; SHAG, *bright, purify*), triliteralized by addition of the Pp. R (RA, RU, IR); so that 𝔙 would be practically right.

v. 16. *poised* or *weighed*: תכלא = תכלה (La 4^2). So again v. 19^b, where we have the same stichus repeated with the var. טהור *pure* pro אופיר *of Ophir*. 𝔙 Non conferetur (cf. 𝔊) *tinctis Indiae coloribus*; perhaps connecting the late poet. בֶּתֶם *gold* with כתם Aram. *stain, defile*. The Rt. may be identical with that of דם *blood*, אדם *red*, Assyr. *adamu*, a syn. of *sâmu*, triliteralized by the Pref. כ *like*, or it may be compared with Sum. GUSH in GUSH-KIN, *gold*, ĠUSHA, an epithet of gold, *bright* or perhaps *red*, akin to ĠASH, ĠAD, ĠUD, *shining* + Afform. M; so that כתם would be 'red gold', as our own poets say.

onyx: so 𝔊 ἐν ὄνυχι τιμίῳ; cf. 𝔙 *lapidi sardonycho pretiosissimo*. 𝔐 שֹׁהַם (Gn 2^{12}) should perhaps be pointed שֹׁהֶם, related to Assyr. *sâmtu, sându*, as תהום to Assyr. *tâmtu, tâmdu*. The *sâmtu* was called in Sum. the 'sparkling' (GUG) or 'clear', 'pure' (GIRIM) stone; the latter perhaps indicating transparency. The Assyr. adj. *sâmu*, f. *sâmtu*, is somewhat vague in application, like other colour-terms. It covers various shades of brown (e.g. *imêru sâmu*, 'a dun ass'; *ḫurâṣu sâmu*, 'yellow gold'). The Heb. שהם was perhaps the beryl (so 𝔖𝔗) or chrysoberyl; but the data are insufficient for any certain identification of ancient with modern precious stones: see the Bible Dictionaries.

v. 17. Read זהב מזקק (1 C 28^{18}) pro 𝔐 זהב וזכוכית = 𝔊 χρυσίον καὶ ὕαλος, 𝔙 *aurum vel vitrum*. The sing. verb is against 𝔐 (cf. also v. 19^a); and however costly glass may have been in the author's time, it can hardly have ranked with gold as equally or more precious. If זכוכית be right, it must denote some kind of gem or precious stone (cf. v. 19). It is found nowhere else in OT; and ק is easily and often confused with כו or כי and ם with ת. (Is זכוכית due to recollection or imitation of Syr. and Talm. זגוגיתא *glass*?)

יערכנה = יערך לה (cf. Is 40^{18}) *is comparable* or *equal to it*.

St. ii. Leg. fort. פו יתמ׳ לאיכל *N*.. .. *ex hange* (cf. 42^2 Ho .. .. *h.m*. . כְּלִי (or כְּלֵי plur. 11 cold.

𝔊𝔖𝔗𝔙) פז is not found elsewhere, and the Neg. Ptc. (1 cod. Kenn.) and a verb seem desirable. Cf. 𝔙 Nec commutabuntur pro ea vasa auri = ולא יומרו בה כלי פז. The word פז is possibly from a √פזז = Assyr. *pazâzu*, 'to beat', 'crush'; cf. Ar. نفض (wrought) *silver*, from نفض *to break in pieces*. (On מופז see Burney ad 1 K 10¹⁸).

v. 18. The gems are again uncertain, as is shown by the Verss. 𝔊 μετέωρα καὶ γαβείς (= translit. of גביש); 𝔙 excelsa et eminentia; as if ראמות (Ez 27¹⁶) were רָמוֹת (Aram. רָאמָא *a height*), and גביש connected with Aram. גֻּבְשָׁא *a heap, hill* or with גְּדִישׁ (5²⁶ 21³²). 𝔗 סַנְדְלְכִין וּבְידוֹלִין *sardonyxes* (?) *and beryls* (the former is compared with the Greek σανδαράκ(χ)η, *orange colour*, σάνδυξ, &c. Carals is Qimḥi's interpr. of ראמות. Perhaps ת(ברק)ו אדם, associated with פטדה Ex 28¹⁷. As to גביש (𝔊ˣ ὑπερημένα cf. 𝔙), the mg. rock-crystal is only an inference from comparison of אל־גביש *hail*, Ar. جبس gibs, *gypsum*, the uses of the Gk. κρύσταλλος (*ice, crystal*), and the Eth. ebna barad, *hailstone, crystal*; which can hardly be regarded as certain. Possibly this ἄπ. λεγόμ. covers וּשְׁבוֹ (Ex 28¹⁹).

St. ii. 𝔐 מֶשֶׁךְ (𝔊 points מְשֹׁךְ ἕλκυσον, though Infin. would yield a better sense) is supposed to mean that the *drawing* (i.e. fishing, cf. 40²⁵) *up* of Wisdom is better than (the drawing up of) corals (see OL). This use of משׁך being dub. (cf. Gn 15²), we suggest מָכְשַׁת (= מָכָם) or מִכְסַת (= מכסת Le 27²³) *valuation, value, worth*. Otherwise, leg. מֶכֶר *price* (Pr 31¹⁰) or מחיר id. Rashi explains פנינים as *pearls*, but La 4⁷ implies something of a *red* colour, perhaps red coral, which is more valuable than the white kind (? ראמות): cf. Pr 3¹⁵ 8¹¹ 31¹⁰. 𝔊 τὰ ἐσώτατα = פנימים, 𝔙 de occultis.

v. 19. See on vv. 16ª, 17ª. The verse sounds more like an echo than a fresh note here; marring, as it seems to do, the climactic effect of the last. [It is difficult to believe that פטדת *topaz* (𝔊 τοπάζιον, 𝔙 topazius) is masc. 'יערכ is prob. due to v. 17. (𝔊 *the pearls of Cúsh and stones of the Ephod* app. gives two equivalents for כושׁ; פטדת כושׁ the latter identifying פטדת with פרתא = אפוד!)]

v. 20. For 𝔐 תבוא *cometh*, 𝔙 venit, which seems preferable also in v. 12, 𝔊 εὑρέθη = תמצא as there.

v. 21. *It is hid*: omitting 𝔐's initial ו c 𝔊𝔙𝔖.

all living: כל חי, including both man and beast, or either alone. See 12¹⁰ Gn 3²⁰ 6¹⁹ 8²¹. Here כל חיה *all* (the) *wild beasts* would perhaps give a better ‖ to st. ii: cf. vv. 7, 8, 5²²·²³ 40²⁰. But חיה without a defining genit. is not so used elsewhere in Job, except in the Elihu-section (37⁸).

v. 22. *Abaddon*: 26⁶ 31¹²: *Death* seems here to be a syn. of Abaddon or She'ol (Pr 5⁵, cf. chap. 38¹⁷), the place of the dead, Hades, > a personification of our last enemy in the modern fashion.

We have heard mere hearsay: lit. *with our ears*, as in 2 Sa 7²² Ps 44².

Cf. also 42¹¹. The dead know no more of Wisdom than they heard about her on earth.

v. 23. God: אלהים‎. This word, rare in Proverbs, occurs elsewhere in Job only in the Prologue and in the Elihu-section (32² 34⁹) and once in the phrase בני אלהים‎ 'The Sons of God' in the poem itself (38⁷). In 5⁸ 20²⁹ it is almost certainly corrupt (see the notes ad locc.). (With Suff. it is not found in Job, and only once or twice in Proverbs.) If original here, it adds force *pro tanto* to the argument against the authenticity of the chapter. 𝔊 ὁ θεός, but perhaps א‎ ᵃ·ᶜ·ᶜ·ᶜ AC 𝔖 = יהוה‎ is right (cf. v. 28).

discerneth: הבין‎: as in 38²⁰. In 13² 15⁹ al. *understand*; 6²⁴ *teach*; 9¹¹ 23⁸ *perceive*. (𝔊 εὖ συνέστησεν = הבין‎; so some codd.: but cf. the parallel ידע‎ and 38²⁰.)

v. 24. ends of the Earth: Is 40²⁸ 41⁵·⁹. Here only in Job. Cf. 26¹⁴ (קצות‎). *looketh to*: הביט ל‎ = *look at*, Ps 104³². The verb is abs. 6¹⁹ and prob. 39²⁹; takes an Accus. Obj. in Elihu-sect. 35⁵ 36²⁵. Not elsewhere in Job as here. *under the whole of Heaven*: Gn 7¹⁹ Dn 9¹². The phrase recurs in Job only 37³ (Elihu), 41³ ⁽ᴬⱽ ¹¹⁾. It seems to suit the context (and metre) better if we transpose תחת כל‎ and point כֹּל‎, as an accented word: *All things under the Heavens He seeth*, and therefore also the 'place'of Wisdom and the 'way' to it. Cf. 𝔊 εἰδὼς τὰ ἐν τῇ γῇ πάντα, 𝔙 et omnia quae sub caelo sunt respicit.

v. 25. 𝔐 לעשות‎ *to make*, connecting the verse with the last; as though stating the purpose of God's all-comprehensive survey (cf. Dr *in making*). But 𝔊 ἐποίησεν, עשה‎ *He made*; 𝔙 Qui fecit ventis pondus: i.e. at the Creation, which seems to be what is meant: cf. Is 40¹²·¹³ מים ... מדד‎ ... תכן ... רוח‎) 26⁸ Pr 30⁴. Read בעשותו‎ *When He made*, as v. 26, and connect with what follows. (𝔖 עבד‎ = הָעֹשֶׂה‎.) Cf. also Pr 8²⁷ ff.

v. 26. law: or *limit*: 26¹⁰ 38¹⁰. 𝔊 καὶ ἐποίησεν· οὕτως ἰδὼν ἠρίθμησεν = או ראה ויספר'‎ (= v. 27²) בעשותו‎. The translator's eye wandered to the line below. 𝔙 Quando ponebat pluviis legem.

St. ii is repeated in 38²⁵ᵇ. In both places we should prob. read plur. חֲזִיזֵי‎ after Zc 10¹ יהוה עשה חזיזים‎, where מטר‎ *rain* is connected with thunder. The meaning is not altogether certain. *Thunderbolts* or *levin-bolts* or *lightning-shafts* would suit. For the latter, cf. Je 10¹³ *lightnings for the rain He made*. The Jewish explanation *bright clouds*, i.e. clouds illuminated by lightning, seems to connect חזיז‎ with the root √חזה‎ *to see* (cf. 𝔖 here: *And a way* לחזוא דקלא‎ *for the shows of voices*): but this is a mere fancy. The Root חז‎ is a double (more primitive) form of חצץ‎, whence חֵץ‎ *arrow* (used of lightning, Ps 18¹⁵ Hab 3¹¹ חצציך‎ Ps 77¹⁸); and חָזִיז (?) חָוִיז‎ may thus be an old Syn. of חץ‎ or חצץ‎ *arrow, bolt*, used esp. of lightning. (Cf. Sum. ĠAZ. ĠAŠ. GAZ. *ḫarâḫu. ḫaṣâçu. ḫiṣṣû. &c.*)

v. 27. examined her: read ייסברה‎ { יעברה‎: h. שָׁבַר‎ *expect*,

Ne 2¹⁸·¹⁵) instead of 𝔐 ויספרה *and counted her exactly*, 'reckoned her up' (i.e. estimated her nature completely). Others would point 𝔐 as Qal (cf. 14¹⁶ 31⁴ 38²⁷) and render *took account of her*. Wisdom is regarded throughout as a substantive entity, not merely as a faculty or attribute of mind.

discerned (or *perceived*) *her*: reading הבינה as parallel to ראה > 𝔐 הבינה *prepared her* or *established her* (see note on v. 23). Cf. Pr 8²²⁻³⁰.

proved: lit. *searched her thoroughly* or *through and through*: cf. v. 3, 5²⁷ 13⁹ al. The verse does not assert that God *created* Wisdom. She is a primeval, nay eternal, Being, whose 'place' He knows; whom He 'saw' before the world was, and having realized her excellence, made use of her in Creation. See Pr 8 l.c.

v. 28. *And He said to the Man* (or *to Man*). This is obviously pure prose; an extra-metrical introduction of the following distich. Cf. Gn 3⁹·¹⁷. The whole verse may be regarded as a later addition, based upon such passages as Pr 3⁷ 9¹⁰ 15³³ 16⁶. The 'Wisdom' of the preceding poem (vv. 1-27) is not so much the practical wisdom which should govern conduct as knowledge of the methods and principles of the Divine working in the world of Nature (cf. vv. 26, 27).

Chapter 29.

v. 1. See the note on this introductory formula, 27¹. In the original text the ordinary heading ויען איוב ויאמר *And Eyob answered and said* may have introduced the unquestionably authentic discourse which follows (29-30).

v. 3. *let* ... *shine*: pointing בְּהִלּוֹ = בְּהָהִלּוֹ Hi. Inf. Cst. c Suff. pro 𝔐 בְּהִלּוֹ Qal Inf. (not found elsewhere). Cf. 31²⁶ 41¹⁰ (Hi. in both = *shine, yield light*) and Is 13¹⁰ (Hi. Trans. as here). The √ is common in Assyr. though not in Heb. (*elêlu*, 'to shine', 'be pure'; *kîma šamê lêhil*, 'like Heaven may he shine!'). *above* > *upon*: cf. 18⁶ 21¹⁷. 𝔊 ὑπὲρ κεφαλῆς μου. *By* (לְ *as regards, because of*) *His light*. Perhaps ולאורו *And by*, &c. (exc. ו post י), and ad fin. בחשך: Ps 23⁴ (exc. ב post כ). Cf. 𝔊 ἐπορευόμην ἐν σκότει = 𝔙 ambulabam in tenebris.

v. 4. St. i seems overweighted metr., and 𝔐 בימי חרפי *in the days of my autumn* (Am 3¹⁵) is somewhat strange. Possibly we should read חֶלְקִי *my health* (an Aramaism; cf. the vb. 39⁴ Is 38¹⁶) ἅπ. Cf. 𝔙 adolescentiae meae = עֲלָמַי (20¹¹ 33²⁵). But 𝔖 ܚܣܕܝ (חסדי) *my kindness* (Hebr.?), i.e. God's kindness or favour to me, would yield a closer parallel. A reference to Eyob's 'maturity' (RV 'in the ripeness of my days') does not seem relevant. 𝔊 ὅτε ἤμην ἐπιβρίθων ὁδούς (𝔊^AC ὁδοῖς) may be corrupt (? ΟΔΟΥC = ΟΛΟC, ΟΛΟΥC, ΟΛΟΙC? cf. 37¹¹ 𝔊ˣ ἐπιβρίσει = יטריח which suggests טרחי for חרפי and lends some support to the conjecture פרחי *my budding*, i.e. flourishing; cf. Ps 92¹⁵).

v. let ... : בְּסוֹד (𝔊ˣ περιέφρισσεν) instead of 𝔐 בסוד (15' 19¹⁹); cf. 1¹⁰

(שׂ = ס) 3²³: or rather (on account of the Prep. עֲלֵי) בְּסֹךְ (1 K 8⁷; cf. 40²²): cf. 𝔊 (שָׂכוּ). *When Eloah overscreened my tent.*

v. 5. St. ii is metr. short, and barely complete from the point of view of sense. נְעָרַי would most naturally mean *attendants* or *retainers* (Gn 14²⁴ 22³); and if we keep the pointing, we may suppose עֲדַת *company* (15³⁴ 16⁷) to have fallen out before it. Cf. הַנְּעָרִים (1¹⁵·¹⁷) 'the young men'; an expression used in the general sense of Eyob's sons, 1¹⁹: cf. v. 8. (24⁵ is corrupt.) We might point נְעֻרָי *my youth* (13²⁶ 31¹⁸) and insert בְּנֵי before it (Ps 127⁴); also prefixing ו to סבי' (so 𝔊𝔙), that letter having fallen out after י. This would give a reference to Eyob's sons: *And the sons of my youth were around me.* But a verb seems desirable, and perhaps עָמְדוּ *stood* has been accidentally omitted owing to its resemblance to עִמָּדִי *with me* in the previous clause. Then, keeping 𝔐 נְעָרַי, we might render: *And my young men stood around me.*

v. 6. *were bathed*: רחץ Intrans. as in Ct 5¹². Cf. Assyr. *raḫáçu,* 'to flood', 'to wash', 'bathe' (= Sum. RAG, RA, whence the Semitic Rt.).

my steps: הֲלִיכַי ἄπ. *curd* or curdled milk, the Arab *leben* of to-day (Ju 5²⁶), Heb. חֶמְאָה (20¹⁷), which must be read here with one cod. and 𝔊𝔙𝔗 (βουτύρῳ, butyro, בלווא) pro 𝔐 חֵמָה. Perhaps rather *liquid butter*, mod. Arabic *samn* (cf. Sum. LI = *šamnu*, 'oil', 'fat', LI-NUN, 'thick fat' = Assyr. *ḫimētu* = חמאה; and cf. Sum. LI with Aram. לווי).

St. ii has more than the normal three stresses, and is otherwise suspicious. Lit. 𝔐 says: *And the rock—it poured out with me canals of oil.* עִמָּדִי *with me* is prob. dittogr. (v. 5ᵃ); and צוּר *rock* may be a corruption of צְעָדַי *my paces* (31⁴) or footsteps (|| הֲלִיכַי). If this be right, we must restore יָצוּקוּ (יָצוּקִי? יָצוּקוֹ?) plur. for יָצוּק sing. Cf. 𝔊 τὰ δὲ ὄρη μου ἐχέοντο γάλακτι = וצעדי יצוקו חלב. Possibly the phrase פלגי שמן *streams of oil* is an intruder here from 20¹⁷ (see the note there); and the original text may have been וצעדי יצוקו חלב *And my footsteps ran with milk* (cf. in part 𝔊)—a better rhythm and sense than we find in 𝔐, which is perhaps coloured by reminiscence of Ex 17⁶ Nu 20⁸ ff.

v. 7. Instead of שַׁעַר the *gate* 𝔊 gives ὄρθριος = שַׁחַר (in the) *morning* or *early, at dawn* (cf. Ps 57⁹), while rendering עֲלֵי קֶרֶת ἐν πόλει. 𝔙 simply *ad portam civitatis* (cf. 𝔖 *When I went forth* to the gate *and called*; rg. קראתי instead of עֲלֵי קֶרֶת!). The Heb. might mean *went forth of* (i. e. through) *the gate* (cf. 31¹⁴ Gn 34²⁴ for the constr.); but as Eyob's place was outside the town, the meaning must be *to the gate*, and ע' קרת will be either *by* (i.e. beside) *the city* or *upon* (i.e. rising over) *the city*; the town-gate being a considerable structure, with a chamber over it. The open space within the gate was the רְחֹב or forum (st. ii) where justice was dispensed and public meetings were held. There Eyob was wont to sit as an honoured and righteous *qâḍi* or judge (vv. 11 17), whom all men feared and reverenced (vv. 8–10).

v. 8. The moment the younger men saw his approach, they fell back behind the elders (ונחבאו; Pf. of action simultaneous with the first-named). In st. ii 𝔊 perhaps read כלם *all of them* pro קמו *arose* : πάντες ἔστησαν.

v. 9. Lit. *Princes—they restrained* (or *stopped*) *words* (4², cf. 12¹⁹); they left off talking : 𝔙 Principes cessabant loqui ; 𝔊 ἁδροὶ (= גדולים *Great men*, Je 5ᵇ) δὲ ἐπαύσαντο λαλοῦντες. In st. ii leg. על־פיהם *upon their mouth* (21ᵇ Ju 18¹⁹) pro 𝔐 לפיהם. 𝔊 δάκτυλον ἐπιθέντες ἐπὶ στόματι (as we put the forefinger on the lips to recommend silence).

v. 10. 𝔐 : *The voice of leaders* (31²⁷; not elsewhere in Job) *they retired* (נחבאו). The verb is obviously dittogr. from v. 8. We should have expected *The voice of leaders was hushed* or *became dumb*. This might be either נאלם (which, however, does not occur elsewhere in Job) or ידם (v. 21, 30²⁷ 31³⁴) or יחריש (6²⁴ 13⁵,¹⁹); but Ez 3²⁶, with its parallel to st. ii, certainly favours נאלם. (ידום, however, might easily have fallen out after נגידים.) 𝔊 οἱ δὲ ἀκούσαντες ἐμακάρισάν με—a curious anticipation of v. 11ᵃ, due no doubt to eye-wandering.

The subject of vv. 7–10 is resumed somewhat awkwardly in vv. 21–25; a section which seems rather out of place as the sequel to vv. 18–20, but might very well follow as the continuation of v. 10, and should perhaps be restored to this place.

v. 11. Omit כי (from v. 12ᵃ). So 𝔙. Lit. *The ear, it heard and called*, &c. *And the eye, it saw*, &c. *bare me witness* : La 2¹³ Qeri (cf. Lk 4²²). The meaning appears to be, approved of his manifest integrity and benevolence. Neither this verb (העיד) nor the parallel (אשר) occurs again in Job. 𝔊 με ἐξέκλινεν (23¹¹ 24⁴ 31⁷ 36¹⁸) = וחטני pro והעידני (exc. ר and ע = ט). 𝔊 𝔙 𝔗 rectè ut 𝔐.

v. 12. The verse resembles Ps 72¹². Both there and here the pointing מֹשׁוֹעַ *from the noble* or *magnate* (𝔊 ἐκ χειρὸς δυνάστου) may be preferred (for שׁוֹעַ see 34¹⁹ Is 32⁵). 𝔊 ἐκ ἀλιτζανα = מִצַּר *out of distress* (or *from the adversary*, 6²³); but the other seems better. מֵרָשָׁע *from the wicked* (𝔊 9²²) or מִיַּד עָרִיץ (6²³ 15²⁰ 23¹⁷) is also plausible. 𝔐 מְשַׁוֵּעַ = 𝔙 vociferantem. But would the oppressed 'cry for help' in the court of justice ? In st. ii read לא pro ולא c 11 codd., 𝔊 𝔙 𝔖 (so 𝔊 𝔙 𝔖 Ps 72¹²).

v. 13. *on me.* The pronoun is emphatic by position.

For the verb in st. ii cf. Ps 65⁹. (Intr. Ps 32¹¹, 81².) 𝔊 στόμα δὲ χήρας με εὐλόγησεν app. preserves a different recension.

v. 14. Lit. *Right I put on, and it put me on* ; as though Justice invested itself with the person of Eyob, or, as we might say, became incarnate, took visible form, in him. Cf. Ju 6³⁴ *The Spirit of Iahvah put on Gideon*. As the body may be regarded as the flesh-garment of the spirit, so the Divine Spirit may enter into any man, clothing itself as it were with the vesture of mortality and for the time actuating both body and soul for its own purposes. St ii 𝔐 lit *Like robe and turban* (to me) (*was*) *my justice*; i.e. the justice he dealt out to suitors. 𝔊 (not understanding ולבשני) *And righteousness I had put on, And robed me with judgement like a double cloak* (διπλοῖς = מְעִיל 1 Sa 2¹⁹ al.); app. reading ובמעיל אצנוף משפטי *And like a robe I wrapped my justice* (about me). Perhaps, however, 𝔐 includes st. ii also under the government of לבשתי: *Like robe and turban* (I put on) *justice* (om. suff. י). Then 𝔊 will merely have supplied ἠμφιασάμην δὲ acc. to the sense (omitting צניף). 𝔖 *Truth I put on and it clothed me, Like the pall and the diadem of judgement.*

v. 16. Notice the alliteration and the assonance in st. i. 'אב אנכי לאב. *A father*: i.e. a protector and an adviser (Gn 45⁸). 𝔊 renders st. ii *And a cause which I knew not, I investigated*; implying that Eyob took all possible pains to ascertain the merits of any cause which came before him for decision, esp. in the case of the poor, instead of favouring the rich and powerful, as Oriental judges are only too apt to do. So 𝔙𝔖𝔗; but 𝔄 *And I did the best for him whom I knew not.* The Heb. might certainly mean *And the cause of one I knew not, I searched out.* This provides a closer parallel to st. i; but the other rendering seems to yield a preferable sense. Eyob would probably know who the suitors were who came before him; but not always who was in the right in any dispute that might arise

v. 17. *shattered* eagerly or with zest, as the form of the Heb. verb (Cohort. Impf. c Waw Conv.) implies. *grinders*: = 𝔊 μύλας, *dentes molares* (Galen). מתלעות = instruments of *gnawing* , √תלע, prob. cogn. c לוע, or לעע *to swallow* (cf. ב-לע), Syr. לתעא *the jaw*, לחך *lick up*, لَعِقَ *lick the fingers*, לתי־, לתא *the jaw*, לחם *to eat*, לקק *to lap* or *lick up*. Cf. תולעה *worm, grub, weevil, maggot*, as an *eater* or *gnawer* of vegetation and grain, or decaying bodies (Is 14¹¹); Dt 28³⁹. Assyr. *tultu, âkilu* (*eater*), *weevil, mealworm*, and the like. Prim. Root LAG (Sum), *eat* (?).

drew: rg. אשלוף, which usu. means *draw* a sword out of the sheath, instead of 𝔐 אשליך *cast.* Cf. Ju 3²², and Assyr. *šalâpu*, 'draw sword', but also *ašallapa lišânki*, 'I will tear out thy tongue !' 𝔊 ἐξήρπασα: a happy equivalent.

v. 18. 𝔐 lit. *And I said* (to myself), *Along with my nest I shall expire, And like the sand* (Gn 32¹³) *I shall multiply days.* This can hardly be right, since Eyob would not find any satisfaction, but rather the contrary, in the thought of his 'nest' (i e. his house or family; Nu 24²¹ Hab 2⁹) and himself coming to an end together. Nor is it any real help to take עם in the sense of *beside, close by* (Gn 25¹¹, 2 Sa 6⁷?); for if the meaning were *I shall die surrounded by my family* (Dr), we should have expected at least בקני *in my nest* or בתוך קני *in the midst of my nest.* Moreover, the parallelism of the two stichi has obviously been obscured. Prob. עם קני is a corruption of קֵץ and an ... (...). *And methought, I shall die an old man*—a good parallel to st. ii. Or we might read : עִם־זְקֵנַי *with the aged* (= עִם־זְקֵנִים); i.e. in their company, as one of them. Comparison, however, of 14⁸˙⁹ with vv. 18, 19, suggests that corruption has gone further, and that we should read וָאֹ׳ זָקֵן גֹּוֵעַ וְכַנַּחַל אַרְבֶּה יָמִים (cf. 𝔊) *And methought, My stock will grow old, And like the palm* (or read כאיל *like the terebinth*; a tree which attains to a great age) *I shall multiply days.* The context certainly favours the mention of a tree of some kind (cf. 'my root', 'my boughs', v. 19, and the same words, 14⁸˙⁹), and 𝔊 renders כחול (? כנחל; cf. Nu 24⁶) ὥσπερ στέλεχος φοίνικος = 𝔙 *sicut palma*: cf. Ecclus 50¹²ᶜ 𝔊 ὡς στελέχη φοινίκων = Heb. בערבי נחל (40²²). The Arab. نَخْل *naḥl* (נחל), *palm-trees*, first cited by Perles, confirms this emendation; although φοῖνιξ in 𝔊 gen. = תָּמָר (cf. στελέχη φοινίκων = תְּמָרִים Ex 15²⁷ Nu 33⁹).

For עִם קִנִּי אֶגְוָע (st. i) 𝔊 has the enigmatical-equivalent ἡ ἡλικία μου γηράσει (cf. יזקין = γηράσῃ 14⁸). What does ἡ ἡλικία μου (*age*, also *stature, height*) represent? Possibly קֹמָתִי *my stature* (קני misread 'קמ; cf. Ez 13¹⁸ πάσης ἡλικίας = כל קומה), or perhaps קָנִי *my stalk* (= my trunk or stature?); cf. 𝔖 which gives a double reading of קני עם (viz. עָם עָנִי *the poor folk* and עִם־קִנְיָנִי *with my property*—perhaps a scribal error for עִם־קָנֶה *like a reed*). 𝔊 (קני יזקין ? קומתי תזקין?) seems to omit עִם. For גֹּוִעִי *my trunk* or *stock*, cf. 14⁸ גּוַע (= 𝔊 τὸ στέλεχος αὐτοῦ) and Is 11¹. In both locc. גוע is associated with שׁרשׁ as here (v. 19). The Rabbinical exposition of v. 18 (Yalqût) which finds in it a reference to the fabled phoenix, 'the rare Arabian bird', which lives a thousand years, and is then consumed by a flame issuing from its nest, appears to depend on the ambiguity of the Greek word φοῖνιξ which may mean either a *palm* or a *phoenix* (Hdt. 2. 73 : cf. the proverbial φοίνικος ἔτη βιοῦν, 'to live as long as a phoenix'), and on the prob. corrupt phrase קני עם *together with my nest.* Beyond this fanciful interpretation of the passage, there is no evidence that חול ever meant a 'phoenix' (see Buxtorf, s.v. חול); nor does this view harmonize with the language of vv. 19, 20, which apparently describes the flourishing of a (palm) tree.

v. 19. 𝔐: *My root* (is) *open unto the water.* 𝔊 ἐπὶ = עֲלֵי, *upon, by, beside* (= 𝔙 *secus*) pro אֶל, *unto* or *towards* the water. Leg. fort. יפריח *will sprout* or *shoot* (14⁹). Cf. Je 17⁸.

my boughs : 14⁸ 18¹⁶ : קציר : confounded by 𝔊𝔙 with קציר *harvest.*

v. 20. 𝔐 lit. *My new glory* (is) *with me* (or *My glory* is *new with me* : but cf. ‖); *And my bow—in my hand it sprouts afresh* (תחליף : 14⁷ of a tree). An extremely improb. utterance in the context, though supported by the Versions. If קשתי *my bow* were right in st. ii, כדוני (i.e. כִּידוֹנִי) *my javelin* (39²³ 41²¹) might be read for כבודי *my glory* (𝔖 עמי *my people* = עמדי; om. כבו׳) in st. i. But Gn 49²⁴ is no real parallel; nor was Eyob's 'glory' new or fresh, but rather long-established. Instead of

חדש a verb-form is required (cf. 10¹⁷ Ps 103⁵ 104³⁰); and תחליף suggests a continuation of the tree-metaphor, which is otherwise prob. We would therefore read כפתי (15²²) *my branch* (cf. Is 9¹³) instead of כבודי, and תחדש *it renews* pro חָדָשׁ; and since a tree 'renews' its leaves, either עָפִים *leaves* (Ps 104¹²) or עָלֶה *its leaves*, or perhaps עֲנָפֶיהָ *its twigs*, pro עִמָּדִי. Then, in place of the strange וקשתי בידי, we adopt וינקתי עוד (14⁷, cf. also 8¹⁶ 15³⁰ Ps 80¹¹·¹²). We thus get a distich in perfect harmony with the context.

*My branch, it will renew its leafage,
And my shoot it will sprout again.*

v. 21. Continues the subject of v. 10 (vid. not. supr.)
Transpose ויחלו ודמו (Bateson-Wright), pointing וַיַּחֲלוּ וַיִּדְּמוּ. But 𝔊^AC adds πρεσβύτεροι = זְקֵנִים; and as st. ii is metr. short, we may perhaps prefer

וזקנים לי שמעו
יִחֲלוּ וידמו למר־עצתי :

*Elders to me did listen ;
They would wait and keep silence for my counsel.*

לְמוֹעֲצָתִי ('ca 35 manuscripts') cannot be right, for מוֹע is only used in the plur., and occurs nowhere else in Job, whereas עצה is fairly common in the book (eight or nine times). For ל = למו vid. 27¹⁴ 38⁴⁰ 40⁴.

v. 22. Lit. *after my speaking* (pointing דַּבְּרִי 21⁵ pro 𝔐 דְבָרִי *my word*). *would say* (Impf.) *no more*: cf. 40⁵ and note. *would drop* : 𝔐 תטף. As נטף (akin to שטף) is Trans. (Pr 5³ Ju 5⁴), we should perhaps read אַטֹּף *I would drop*, or אַטִּף Hi. (cf. Am 9¹³). The root does not recur in Job 𝔊 st. ii περιχαρεῖς δὲ ἐγίνοντο (= 3²²), ὁπόταν αὐτοῖς ἐλάλουν. app. a loose paraphrase. They found Eyob's discourse as refreshing as rain. (𝔊 perhaps read עלזו *they exulted* for עלימו *upon them*.)

v. 23. As the text stands, 𝔐 וְיַחֲלוּ *And they would wait* (in hope) is the natural sequel to יָטֹף. (There is no need to point וְיָחֵל Hi. as 32¹¹·¹⁶ Elihusection see 6¹¹ 13¹⁶ 14¹⁴ 30²⁶.) Omitting 1 c 𝔊𝔙𝔖, and regarding v. 22 as an interpolation, we may see in this verse a natural expansion of the יחלו of v. 21 : *They waited for me as for the rain*, | *And their mouth they opened wide* (16¹⁰ Is 5¹⁴) *as for the spring-rain* (leg. כַּמַּלְקוֹשׁ = 𝔊 דלרביעא איך, 𝔙 quasi ad imbrem serotinum). The verse may, however, have been suggested to an editor by חטף (v. 22), though it looks original. The conjecture כְּפִי הַסְּגַרְפוֹת *like the clods* (?) pro 𝔐 וּפִיהֶם פָּעֲרוּ *and their mouth they opened wide* cannot be called happy, since its only basis is a disputed passage in Joel (1¹⁷). 𝔊 paraphrases *As a thirsty land expecting the rain*, | *So they my speech* (𝔊^A + *were expecting*). Cf. אֶרֶץ צִיָּה Is 53². Have we here a trace of another recension of the Heb. text ?

v. 24. 𝔐 lit. *I laugh unto them, they believe not;* | *And the light of my countenance they cause not to fall.* Driver thought this might mean that 'Job's clear-sighted counsel encouraged them, if they were despondent [taking st. i as RV marg. *I smiled on them when they had no confidence*]; on the other hand (line 2), their despondency never clouded his cheerfulness' (*made his face fall*: cf. Gn 4⁵·⁶). This, however, reads too much into the text. It treats st. i as equivalent to אשחק ללא־יאמינו (cf. 26²); but even so, a reassuring smile is not the same thing as 'clear-sighted counsel', and the phrase 'the light of my countenance' (parallel to שחק) denotes the favouring look or smile of a superior (Ps 4⁷ Pr 16¹⁵) rather than his personal cheerfulness or buoyancy of spirit. Cf. the proposed emendation of st. ii וָאוֹר פְּנֵי אֲבֵלִים יָנְחֵם *And the light of my c. did comfort mourners* (from v. 25ᶜ); which, however, is metr. redundant, and associated with an ungrammatical alteration of st. i (אשחק אלהם ויאמינו; as if this could mean *I smiled at them, and they grew confident*). We can say in Heb. 'My c. fell (Gn 4⁵·⁶), but hardly 'the light of my c. fell'. יפילון must be corrupt; and we may perhaps read לְאוֹר פָּנַי לֹא־יְחִילוּן *The light of my c. they were not expecting*. The sense of the verse will then be that people stood in such awe of Eyob that, when he smiled graciously upon them, it came as a pleasant surprise, and they could scarcely credit their good fortune. For לא־יאמינו see 9¹⁶ 15²² 24²². 𝔊𝔚 support our view of st. i; but in st. ii they seem to have read יָפוֹל pro יפילון (𝔊 app. ילבן). 𝔗 וקלסתור אפי לא אסתכלון suggests a possible ואל־אור פני לא־יביטון *And at the light of my face they would* (durst) *not look*; i.e. they were so overawed by his presence. This agrees very well with st. i as we understand it. The stichus was wanting in the original text of 𝔊, as was also *v*. 25.

v. 25. A tristich, of which st. i has four stresses, while st. iii is incongruous with both the others. אבחר דרכם is prob. *I used to test* (Aramaic use of בחר: cf. Is 48¹⁰ Je 6²⁷) *their way*; i.e. their conduct or course of action (>*choose*, prescribe it for them). In harmony with this we propose וְאֶשְׁבְּרֵם *and examine them* (cf. Ne 2¹³·¹⁵), instead of וְאֵשֵׁב רֹאשׁ *and sit chief*. Eyob is still thought of as *qâḍî*, or judge and referee.

St. ii *And I used to dwell like a king in the host.* His authority was supreme among his people. 𝔊 ἐν μονοζώνοις = בנדוד (cf. 2 K 5² al.); 𝔊ˣ ἐν στρατοπέδῳ. It may be recalled that the Babylonian prototype of Eyob was, in fact, a king (see Introd.). St. iii, *As one who comforteth mourners*, has been regarded as a variant of v. 24ᵇ. If, however, instead of כאשר אבלים ינחם we read the very similar כשר אלפים במחנה *Like a captain of thousands in the camp* (or *army*) we get a good parallel to st. ii (מחנה = ינחם read backwards!). St. i may well be rejected as an intrusion.

Chapter 30. Eyob contrasts his present humiliations and sufferings with his happy past. (There is no real break between the chapters.)

v. 1. *They who are younger than I*: cf. 32⁶ for the phrase *young (little) in days*; and for the contrast 29⁸. This is not quite satisfactory. 𝕲 ἐλάχιστοι νῦν νουθετοῦσίν με ἐν μέρει = . . . צעירים יבינוני (cf. 32⁸ 𝕲 34¹⁶ 38¹⁸). The original text may have been something like צערוני בני עמים *The sons of the nations* (17⁶) *dishonour me* (an Aramaism: Qal? Pi.?); or, reading גרים or נכר(ים) for the third word, *The sons of aliens*, &c. Even young foreigners, whose fathers he had not thought good enough to serve as his shepherds, now jeer at Eyob.

v. 2. *it relaxed*: רָפָה־לוֹ *droopeth to itself* (Dat. Eth.) pro 𝔐 למה לי *What good was it to me?* The sequel implies that they had no strength. *With them*: lit. *upon them*: cf. Ps 42⁵˙⁷. We might perhaps read כֻּלָּמוֹ *They all* pro 𝔐 עלימו, or even עלמים *young men* (cf. 1 Sa 20²²): *Young men whose sap hath perished*. Instead of the dub. כלח we propose לֵחָם *their sap, freshness, vigour*, or כָּל־לֵחַ *all vigour* (see note on 5²⁶).

v. 3. *famine* or *hunger*: כָּפָן, an Aramaism: see on 5²². *they are spent*, or *come to an end*, גמרו (Ps 7¹⁰ 12²) pro 𝔐 גלמוד *barren*, Sing. (3⁷ 15³⁴), 𝕲 ἄγονος, 𝔙 *steriles*, which can hardly be right.

St. ii. 𝔐 *they who gnaw* (v. 17) *the desert*, which is metr. short. Some word has fallen out; perhaps עקרי *roots* (an Aramaism; cf. Dan 4¹²), which resembles the preceding הערקים (hardly ירק in the ציה). 𝕲 οἱ φεύγοντες ἄνυδρον, *who flee to the desert*; taking ערק in the Aramaic sense *to flee*: but 𝔙 qui rodebant *in solitudine*.

St. iii. One of the three stichi of this verse is metr. superfluous. It may be this one, but more prob. the first, which may be regarded as a marginal gloss. Then this distich הערקים וג׳ will correspond in form with the next הקטפים וג׳ (v. 4). 𝔐 אמש שואה ומשאה cannot possibly mean *in the gloom* (or *on the eve*) *of wasteness and desolation*. אֶמֶשׁ *last night*, Gn 19³⁴ 31²⁹, *yesterday* (cf Assyr *amšat, amtašt*, id., *ina amšat*, 'last night'), is certainly corrupt, although 𝕲 renders stt. ii, iii *Who were fleeing to* (the) *desert yesterday from straits and distress*. 𝔙 suggests אנוש (i. e. אֲנוּשִׁים): *squalentes calamitate et miseria*. Regardless of stichic division, 𝔗 renders the verse: *In want and hunger, childless, the wicked were fleeing into a land of drought, dark as evening; a place of destruction and unrest* (?) אֶרֶץ pro אָמֶשׁ). We might perhaps read טֶצֶא *the growth* or שָׂיא *the herbage* (cf. 38²⁷), though אֶרֶץ *land* would suffice. It seems possible, however, that the original distich ran

הערקים בארץ ציה
מקום שואה ומשואה

Who flee into the land of drought,—
The place of waste and wild.

v. 4. *who pluck*: 8¹² Dt 23²⁵. 𝕲 οἱ περικλῶντες is app. a scribal error for περικλῶντες (sic al..); (𝔥 ἅπαντ ξουτες. ..tv).: כלח. which appears to be related to מלח *salt* as 𝔊 ἅλιμα, *saltwort*, to ἅλς. Our own word 'mallow' appears to be identical with the Lat. malva, Gk. μαλάχη. 'Me pascunt olivae, Me cichorea levesque malvae' (Hor.); 'et gravi Malvae salubres corpori' (id.).

beside the bush: עֲלֵי־שִׂיחַ (v. 7, Gn 2⁸). Perhaps rather וַעֲלֵי שׂ׳ *and the leaves of the bush* (Ne 8¹⁵). 𝔊 ἐπὶ ἠχοῦντι = עֲלֵי־שׁוֹאָה (cf. Is 17¹²). Cf. 𝔙 Et mandebant herbas *et arborum cortices* (= what is *upon* the bush). (𝔊 om. vv. 3, 4.) 𝔊 adds ἄτιμοι δὲ καὶ πεφαυλισμένοι, ἐνδεεῖς παντὸς ἀγαθοῦ (𝔊^{ANB ab mg. inf.} + οἳ καὶ ῥίζας ξύλων ἐμασῶντο ὑπὸ λιμοῦ μεγάλου). This looks like an explanatory paraphrase of vv. 3, 4; perhaps preserving some variants, e.g. גָּדוֹל pro גַּלְמוּד, v. 3.

v. 5. St. i is metr. short, and מִן־גֵּו *from the middle* (Aramaic word), it correct, obviously requires a complement, e.g. הָאָדָם *of men*, or הָעִיר *of the city*. The latter word might have fallen out owing to its likeness to the following יְרִיעוּ. Perhaps מִן־גּוּר בָּעִיר יְגֹרָשׁוּ *From sojourning in the city they are driven out* (cf. Ju 9⁴¹ for the Constr.). Others read מִן גוֹי *from the nation* or *community*; leaving the stichus still too short. 𝔊 om. 𝔙 מִן־גֵּי (de convallibus).

St. ii. *shout against them*: cf. 2 C 13¹². If they see the outcasts coming, people raise a hue and cry against them as they would against a thief (24¹⁴). 𝔙 ad ea cum clamore currebant (? יָרוּצוּ pro יָרִיעוּ). (𝔊 understands the verse as describing the joy of the outcasts at finding their wretched fare.) 𝔊 ἐπανέστησάν μοι κλέπται = יָעוֹרוּ (יָעִירוּ) עָלַי גַּנָּבִים (cf. 14¹² 17⁸).

v. 6. מ בַּעֲרוּץ נְחָלִים *in the dreaded* (Sing.) *of the wâdys*, which is supposed to mean *in the most gloomy valleys*, but is prob. corrupt. Read מְעָרוֹת *caves*, 1 Sa 13⁶, or מְצָדוֹת *fastnesses*, Is 33¹⁶ (for שֹׁכֵן c accus. cf. Je 17⁶). *holes*: 𝔊 τρώγλαι, as also 1 Sa 14¹¹. They were Troglodytes; but these חֹרִים were holes in the 'dust', i.e. the ground. *rocks*: כֵּפִים Je 4²⁹ only. An Aramaism: cf. Syr. כֵּיפָא and Cephas. (Assyr. ka-a-pi ša šadê, 'the rocks of the mountains', and ka-bi alone 'the rocks'. Perhaps akin to Sum. GAB, 'breast', GABIRI, 'mountain'; cf. GABA-TINU, 'hill of life', i.e. the *mons Veneris*.) 𝔊 paraphrases the whole verse *Whose houses were caves of rocks*.

v. 7. bushes: שִׂיחִים; 𝔊 εὐήχων (cf. Ps 150⁵ = שֶׁמַע). Not a different reading; see note on v. 4ᵃ. *bray*: 6ᵇ. Cry out for want of food, like wild asses. *they huddle together*: lit. *are joined together*: יִסְפָּחוּ: which perhaps should rather be pointed Ni. (cf. Is 14¹), if the verb be genuine; but it seems very doubtful. 𝔊 διῃτῶντο, *they lived*, 𝔙 delicias computabant = יַחְפְּצוּ; but a parallel to יִנְהֲקוּ would be more satisfactory, e.g. יְרִיעוּ *they roar* (Is 42¹³) or *howl* or *yell*, or יִסְפְּדוּ *they wail* (Mi 1⁸). *scrub*: חָרוּל (Zp 2, plur. Pr 24³¹), a plant or shrub of unknown species, growing in neglected fields and wastes. 𝕲 φρύγανα ἄγρια, *wild brushwood*; 𝔙 sentes, *briers, brambles*. (The Syr. חוּרְלָא denotes a kind of *vetch* used as fodder.)

v. 8. Metrically dubious and otherwise suspect. St. i virtually repeats v. 1ª, and st. ii = v. 5ª, so that the whole seems superfluous. For נבל the *fool*, in wits and behaviour, see on 2¹⁰. The phrase בני בלי־שם cannot be exactly paralleled. בלי־שם should mean *without name* (fame, repute; cf. Gn 6⁴ אנשי השם the men famous in story); but if the sense be *sons of men of no name*, we miss אנשי. Cf. 8¹¹ 24¹⁰ 31³⁹ 38² for the use of בלי. Moreover, the tone of aristocratic contempt does not harmonize with the spirit of 31¹³ ff. (cf. esp. 31¹⁵); while, as regards form, the verse is rather prosaic than poetical. Perhaps בלי־שם has displaced בליעל (cf. 1 Sa 25²⁵). 𝕲 ἀφρόνων υἱοὶ καὶ ἀτίμων ὄνομα | καὶ κλέος ἐσβεσμένον ἀπὸ γῆς. This suggests for st. ii ושמעם נדעך מן־הארץ *All report of whom is extinct from the land*; making the two stichi parallel in sense, and restoring the metre. (κλέος = שמע 28²²; σβεσθήσεται = ידעך 18³·⁶ 21¹⁷.) It also gets rid of the isolated נכאו *they are scourged* or *smitten* (supposed Aramaism). It would give much the same sense if we read זכרם אבד מן־הארץ (cf. 18¹⁷ Ps 9⁷) *And their memory is perished from the land*; which is perhaps preferable in view of 18¹⁷.

v. 9. *But now*: ועתה, as in v. 1. It looks as if the curious section vv. 1–8, which is introduced by the same Particle of Contrast, might be an interpolation. Certainly v. 9 might immediately follow upon 29²⁵, at least as naturally as v. 1. Nothing necessary to the continuation of the sense would be missed, while what may seem to us an exaggerated and irrelevant insistence upon the wretched condition of Eyob's revilers would be avoided. It must, however, be recognized, in spite of manifold corruptions and obscurities of the text, that the section is picturesque, vivid, and poetical; and even if it did not originally belong here, we may be glad that it has been preserved.

And now I am become their song: La 3¹⁴ (cf. 3⁶³) Ps 69¹²: the subject of satirical allusions in popular minstrelsy and topical improvisations. (נגינה *music*, playing on stringed instruments, La 5¹⁴, and the verb נגן appear to be derived from the √NAG, *to strike*; cf. Sum. BA-LAG, *harp, lyre, music*, SIR BALAGA, *zamâr balaggi*, 'harp-music', 'harp-playing', BA-LAG ZURA-TA, *ina balaggi u ikribî*, 'with music and prayer'; and the Ch. 樂 lok, ngok, Annam. lak, fiiak, 'joy', 'music'.)

St. ii lit. *And I am become to them a word*; i.e. a *byword*, or perhaps *common talk*. (מִלָּה is not so used elsewhere.) 𝔙 proverbium; 𝕲 θρύλημα (= משל, 17⁶, which may be right here also).

v. 10. St. ii lit. *And from my face they have not withheld spittle*: cf. Is 50⁶. So 𝕲𝔙. See also the note on 17 .

v. 11. Very corrupt. For יתרו (Ketîb) or יתרי (Qerî; 𝔊𝔗; 𝔊 φαρέτραν αὐτοῦ = תליו; so 𝔅) leg. יתרם *their cord*, and point the two following verbs as plur., to agree with שלחו ad fin. (a syn. of פתחו 12¹⁵·¹⁸ 39⁸). For מפני (dittogr. from v. 10ᵇ) leg. פִּימוֹ (*of*) *their mouth* (Ps 17¹⁰ al.). The two stichi thus become parallel in meaning:

For their cord they have relaxed and abused me;
And the halter (Ps 32⁹) *of their mouth they have loosed.*

The meaning of יתר is determined by the parallel רסן (= 𝔊 χαλινόν; 𝔅 frenum). It cannot therefore be *bowstring*, as elsewhere, e. g. Ps 11², but a restraining cord or bond, as in Ju 16⁸⁻⁹. The verse means that Eyob's assailants have cast off all the restraint once inspired by respect or fear, and given free rein to their tongues (cf. Ps 39²). Duhm, adopting Q. יתרי and שלח Sing. (𝔊) or rather שלך, and regarding רגלי שלחו, v. 12, as a variant of רסן שלחו here, accepts Bickell's דגלי *my banner* pro רגלי *my feet*, and renders the verse thus violently emended:

For He hath loosed my bowstring and humbled me,
My standard He hath cast down before my face.

It is, however, a curious fact that throughout the entire OT we nowhere else find mention of the דֶּגֶל, *banner* or *standard*, of a single chief or king, but only of the standards of the tribes of Israel in the Book of Numbers. (For Ct 2⁴, vid. infr.) To us, no doubt, the supposed reference to Eyob's 'standard' is highly suggestive and poetical; but, as already indicated, neither in the heroic tales of the Conquest and the early Monarchy, nor in any of the old martial songs and patriotic psalms of Israel, do we find such reference to a standard. The fact makes it difficult to believe in the mention of one here. (Familiar as we are with the romantic associations called up by the words of Ct 2⁴, it is more than doubtful whether the text of that passage is sound. Read perhaps ויגר pro דגלו: *And he poured upon me Love.*)

v. 12. A tristich; text corrupt. The ἅπ. פִּרְחָח for which 25 codd. have פרחה and 𝔊 פרח (βλαστοῦ, cf. Nu 17⁸) is prob. a *vox nihili*. If the rare word עלמין *Youths* orig. stood where על־ימין *On the right* now stands, we might suppose that פִּרְחָם *soboles eorum*, a marg. gloss on that word, had crept into the text. But (י)על־ימין is in itself unobjectionable (cf. Ps 109⁶·³¹), although the word ימין is not common in Job (23⁹ 40¹⁴ all). Perhaps פרחח is a disguise of בְּחֶרֶב *with the sword*; so that st. i would be: *On my right they rise up with the sword* (cf. Am 7⁹). In st. ii שלחו prob. originated in dittography (v. 11ᵇ), and רגלי may have been added (cf. ברגליו . . . שלח, 18⁸). In that case we might read יסלו עלי ארחותיהם *They cast up against me their highway*, as the second member of the distich; cf. 19¹²ᵇ (𝔐 ארחות אידם. ויסלו עלי דרכם *the ways of their ruin* overloads the stichus metr., and cannot be right.) Another possible restoration of the distich might be :

עלמין יקומו לרגלי
יסלו עלי תרפותיהם

The youths start up in my track (cf. 18¹¹); *They lift high* (Ps 68⁵? or *heap up* Je 50²⁶?) *their taunts against me*.

v. 13. Another tristich, corrupt and entirely unmetrical. נתצו = נתסו (so five codd.) hîc tant. (perhaps an error of dictation). If we connect להיתי, which should be להותי (so Q, six codd., see notes on 6² ³⁰), with st. i we get a passable line : *They have broken up my path for my destruction* (? לַהֲוֹתִי *to make me fall*; an Arabism? cf. 37⁶ תֹּוָא). Then, reading יבלעו for the meaningless יעילו, and connecting the word with what follows, the second stichus will be *They engulf* (2³ 10⁸ 8¹⁸ 20¹⁵ 37²⁰) *them who have no helper*; or reading עצר pro עזר. *They engulf—there is none to restrain them* (12⁵ 29²:? בְּמוֹ). Cf. Is 3¹². (𝕲 st. ii ἐξέδυσαν γάρ μου τὴν στολήν = ויפשיטו מעילי; cf. 19⁹ Nu 20²⁶ ²⁸. 𝕲 st. iii βέλεσιν αὐτοῦ κατηκόντισέν με, *with His arrows He shot me down*: cf. 𝕲 ἀνοίξας γὰρ φαρέτραν αὐτοῦ, v. 11ª, and 7²⁰ 16¹²·¹³. This prob. represents a different text.)

v. 14. *outburst*. i.e. of waters: cf. 2 Sa 5²⁰ כפרץ מים *As (through) a wide breach*, scil. in my walls (Ne 6¹), is also possible; cf. 𝔅 Quasi rupto muro, et aperta ianua, irruerunt super me.

𝕲 app. from another text κέχρηταί (δέ) μοι ὡς βούλεται (ἐβούλετο), (*And*) *He uses me as He will(ed)*. Perhaps it read כְּחֶפְצוֹ *According to His will* pro כפרץ ad init.

St. ii can hardly mean 'In the midst of the ruin they roll themselves upon me' (RV). 𝔐 שאה תחת is *Under* (or *Instead of*) *the ruin* (v. 3; Is 47¹¹; or *the storm*; 𝕾 עלעלא; cf. Pr 1²⁷), but we seem to require another comparison. Leg. fort. כחת pro תחת; i.e. either כְּחַת (41²⁵; or בְּחַתַּת 6²¹), *Like a terrible storm*, or even כְּחָת (= כְּהָחַת; cf. 31³⁴), *Like the shattering* (Is 9²; or *terrifying*) *of the storm* (שָׁאָה akin to Assyr. šū, šūtu) *they rolled onward* (התנלגלו) or *whirled along*, storm-like : cf. גלגל *whirlwind*, Ps 77¹⁹. The translation *roll themselves upon me* is usu. justified by reference to the Hithpoel להתגלל עלינו Gn 43¹⁸; להתגדל; cf. 19⁶ and Is 10¹⁵); but Hithpalpel should have a different meaning. 𝕲 ἐν ὀδύναις (= v 15ª) πέφυρμαι, in griefs *I wallow* (cf. πεφυρμένος = מתגלל 2 Sa 20¹²)

v. 15. Another tristich. St. i may be an intrusion. The Hophal ההפך (here only in OT) should perhaps be Niph. נהפבו (v. 21; 19¹⁹ 20¹⁴), as 𝕲𝕾 (cf. 𝔅 Redactus sum in nihilum = לבלימה נהפכתי 26⁷ or simply נה' לבלי), or Qal הפך *He hath turned* (9⁵ al. 'הה dittogr.). The stichus is not parallel to either of the others; while they are mutually parallel, and make a good distich. In st. ii 𝔐 תרדף would naturally mean *Thou pursuest*; cf. 𝔙 abstulisti. 𝔊 ᾤχετο = תְּהֻלָּה (Mine honour *departeth*) gives a better parallel; but תְּחֵלִי (4¹⁵ 9¹¹ where it is joined with the syn. עָבַר as here; Is 21¹ of whirlwinds) seems better still. Others point Ni. תֻּרְדַּף and render: *Mine honour is chased as by the wind.* נדיבתי *my honour*; i.e. his princely dignity and reputation (Driver): cf. נדיב *noble*, 12²¹ 21²⁸. But 𝔊 ἡ ἐλπίς μου = תקותי (11 times) or תוחלתי; 𝔙 desiderium meum = 𝔊ˣ τὰ καταθύμιά μου (= חֲמֻדָּתִי, cf. Is 44⁹).

v. 16. St. i is metr. over weight with its four stresses. Om. 𝔐 וְעַתָּה *And now* (v. 9; dittogr.). Lit. *Upon me* (or *Over me*) *my soul is poured out*; my feelings overwhelm me. Cf. Ps 42⁵·⁶·⁷·¹². For the vb. (Hithpael), La 2¹² 4¹. Pro 𝔐 עֲנִי יְמֵי *Days of affliction* we might perhaps read, in view of the vb. יאחזוני *grip me* or *hold me fast*, חבלי עני *cords of affliction* (36⁸ cf. Is 13⁸) or יְדֵי עֳ *hands of affliction*; but hardly אמי עני *the terrors of a.* (אמי constr. plur. does not occur). But the following לילה *By night* certainly favours 𝔐: cf. 7³⁻⁵, ¹³ᶠ·

v. 17. St. i has become too long, owing to dittogr. of עלי from v. 16. Instead of 𝔐 (עָלָי) נִקַּר מֵ *He bored from off me*, read נָקְרוּן (מִ = וּן ut saep.); cf. ישכבון ad fin., which also confirms לילה: *By night my bones are pierced*; 𝔊 om. מעלי. For the vb. see Ju 16²¹ Is 51¹. 'Corroded' is not a possible rendering (RV marg.); nor is it likely that לילה is the Subj. ('The night gnaws away my bones'). It seems needless to suggest נָמֹקּוּ *decay*, or יִרְקְבוּ *rot* (cf. Pr 12⁴), since he means that his bones are racked and wrenched with pain. נִבְהֲלוּ *are troubled* (Ps 6³) would be better (cf. 𝔊 συγκέχυται = בלל Gn 11¹). *my gnawers*: cf. v. 3: i.e. my gnawing pains. Cf. Mk 9⁴⁴. 𝔙 Et qui me comedunt non dormiunt. (𝔊 τὰ δὲ νεῦρά μου διαλέλυται, *And my sinews* (10¹¹ 40¹²) *are relaxed* treats עֹרְקַי as an Aramaism; cf. Aram. ערקא *a leathern strap* or *thong*. So Nachmanid. App. also it omits לא and reads יְשָׁכָּרוּן pro יִשְׁכָּבוּן.) Add perhaps עוֹרִי *my skin* (or בְּשָׂרִי *my flesh*) in st. ii metr. grat. (pt. עֹרְקֵי): *And the gnawers of my skin rest not*.

v. 18. Very uncertain. A reference to God (RV marg. 'By *his* great force', &c.) seems improb., though the phrase בְּרָב־כֹּחַ is used in that relation 23⁶ (cf. Is 63¹); unless indeed the verse be an interpolation. If it were 'intended to describe how Job's garments are thrown out of shape, as they cling closely to his emaciated form' (Dr), it is surely obvious that 'clinging closely' would be the result of the limbs swelling rather than of emaciation, which would cause the clothes to hang loosely about the figure. The second member, *Like the neck* or *collar* (lit. *mouth*; Ex 28³²) *of my tunic he* (*it? they?* יַאַזְרֵנִי? so 𝔙) *engirds* (*engird?*) *me*, may suggest a parallel such as כבנפי לבשי יחבשני *Like the skirts of my raiment they enwrap me* (cf. Jon 2⁶): 'they', i.e. his gnawing pains, due to the eruptions or ulcers which covered him from head to foot (2⁷). 𝔊 supports 𝔐, except that it has ἐπιλάβετο = יִתְפֹּשׂ (1 K 11³⁰) pro יִתְחַפֵּשׂ: *With much* strength *He laid hold of my robe*, | *Like the orifice* (= 𝔐) *of my tunic He encircled me.* בְּפִי . . . יֶאַחְזֵנִי (*By the neck of my t. He* seizeth *me*) would improve this; but, as pointed out above, the reference to God is improb. in the context. 𝔐 יתחפש לבושי *my clothing* or ' coat ' (supposed by some to mean *my skin*) *is disguised* (= disfigured), is altogether improb. (cf. 1 Sa 28⁸ 1 K 22³⁰); and the emendation (י)בחשׁ (*my leanness* : 18⁶ see note) pro בה is little better (*Through my great leanness is my garment disfigured*). The supposed ref. to the ill fit of Eyob's clothes seems almost grotesque. The reading בשרי *my flesh* instead of לבושי *my garment* does not harmonize with st. ii. (𝔖 *I clothed me with my clothing and girt me with my tunic: They threw me into the mire*, &c., v. 19. Cf. 9³¹.)

v. 19. St. i is too short metr. and otherwise suspicious. *He hath cast me into the mire* would rather be יָרַנִי בַחמֶר (cf. Ex 15¹·⁴) than הֹרָנִי לח׳ (Hi. c ל = *shot at me*). We might read הוֹרִדַנִי *He hath brought me down* (cf. La 2¹⁰ Ps 55²⁴) *into the mire* (Is 10⁶), and insert אֵל *God* as the Subject, thus restoring both sense and metre. Since, however, the following verses appeal directly to God in the 2nd Pers., we should perhaps consider this verse as the beginning of the appeal (ה = vestige of אַתָּה *Thou*, emph., רני = דם), and read in closer parallelism with st. ii אַתָּה דִמַּתַנִי לַחֹמֶר *Thou, thou hast likened me to the clay*: cf. 𝔖 ἥγησαι δέ με ἴσα πηλῷ and 𝔙 Comparatus sum luto. He complains that God thinks of him as mere clay (cf. 10⁹), and treats him as of no more account than dust and ashes (42⁶ Gn 18²⁷).

v. 20. The rendering of st. ii in RV, *I stand up, and thou lookest at me*, is forcible (cf. Ps 22¹⁸ יביטו יראו בי), but unsatisfactory. The vb. התבונן (23¹⁵) does not mean *to look at* physically but mentally; i.e. to *pay attention to, give heed to, consider*. cf. 11¹¹ 23¹⁵ 26¹⁴ (see note). And metrical balance and parallelism are improved by repeating the Neg. Ptc. לֹא c 1 cod and 𝔙 (Sto et non respicis me). Further, עמדתי *I stood* seems dubious (𝔖 ἔστησαν δὲ καὶ κατενόησάν με, *They* stood, &c.; cf. Ps 22¹⁴). Does it mean *I stood* praying, or *I stopped* (32¹⁶ 2 K 13¹⁸)? 𝔖 עמדת *Thou stoodest* is not more prob. cf. 9¹¹ 23³·⁸·⁹. The parallelism requires the 1st Pers. Reading עָתַרְתִּי (33²⁶) or rather אֶעְתַּר *I supplicate* or *entreat* (22²⁷), we get the good || *I entreated, and Thou wouldst not regard me*.

v. 21. *Thou turnest* (or *art turned* or *wouldst turn*) *into a cruel* (41²) *one to me.* For the verb cf. 1 Sa 10⁶ and 41²⁰. So 𝔙 Mutatus es mihi in crudelem. 𝔖^A ἀπέβησαν δέ μοι ἀνελεήμονες, *They* (my foes) *turned out ruthless to me* (𝔖^B ἐπέβησαν prob. does not indicate a different reading, but a scribal error) Instead of תשטמני *assailest me* = 𝔙 adversaris mihi (see 16⁹ Gn 27⁴¹ 49²³ 50¹⁵ *bear malice against* one) 𝔖 ἐμαστίγωσάς με, didst *scourge* me; app. a (hypoth.) Denom. from שׁוֹט *scourge* (5²¹) תשׁטמני.

v. 22. עַל *upon* pro 𝔐 אֶל *unto*. So 𝔊𝔖𝔙. This must be right, whether we connect על־רוח with the preceding or the following vb. c 𝔖 (cf. Gn 31¹⁷

Ex 4²⁰ Dt 32¹³) as seems better in view of st. ii. 𝕲 ἔταξας δέ με ἐν ὀδύναις = ותשׂימני בכלחות (v. 14) or בְּשֹׁאָה (v. 15; cf. st. ii ad fin.).

St. ii is metr. short. The vb. תְּמֹגְגֵנִי can only mean *thou meltest* or *dissolvest, breakest up, shatterest* (cf. Ps 65¹¹ the hard earth with rain) *me with* . . ., if strict parallelism be observed. The remaining word תשׁוה (Ketib) Qerî תשׁיה (i.e. תֻּשִׁיָּה see note at 5¹²) is clearly corrupt. If 'my substance' were meant, the Pron. Suff. would be indispensable. בְּשֹׁאָה *in (with?) the storm* (RV), v. 14, or בִּתְשֻׁאָה *in the din or uproar*, 36²⁹ 39⁷, would make sense but not metre; to complete which we might perhaps read ותנגבני כמץ בשאה *And thou snatchest me away like chaff in the storm* (or leg. סוּפָה = שׁוּפָה?): cf. 21¹⁸ 27²⁰ᶠ· 𝕲 καὶ ἀπέρριψάς με ἀπὸ σωτηρίας = וַתְּשַׁלְּכֵנִי מִתְּשֻׁעָה?; 𝔙 elisisti me valide = 𝔐(?); 𝕾 *And Thou hast humbled me and brought me low.*

v. 23. *the Grave*: lit. *Death*, i.e. the place of the dead, used as a syn. of Abaddon, 28²², and She'ol, Ps 6⁶: cf. also 38¹⁷. The Prep. אֶל may have fallen out: cf. 10⁹. *House of Assembly* (בֵּית מוֹעֵד): cf. the *Mountain of Assembly*, scil. of the gods, Is 14¹³. (An leg. למות . . לבית . . כל?) 𝕲 οἶδα γὰρ ὅτι θάνατός με ἐκτρίψει = יְשׁוּפֵנִי, *will bruise or wear me down* (9¹⁷) pro 𝔐 תְּשִׁיבֵנִי. Seq. οἰκία γὰρ παντὶ θνητῷ γῆ = וּבֵית עָפָר לְכָל־חָי (עָפָר = γῆ ut 2¹² et saep.—pro מוֹעֵד).

v. 24. Neither RV nor RV marg. is satisfactory. The dub. עִי *a heap of ruins* (Mi 1⁶ cf. 3¹² Is 17¹) is improb. in the context, and, in any case, cannot mean *in his fall.* The phrase שָׁלַח יָד בְּ = 'stretch out hand against' one', Gn 37²² al., and אֶבְיוֹן, v. 25, suggest the ∥ term עָנִי here (cf. 24⁴·¹⁴ 31¹⁸). Read therefore בעני pro 𝔐 בעי. (The suggested טֹבֵעַ *sinking*, qs 'a drowning man', is improb. without some explanatory addition: cf. Ex 15⁴ Ps 69²). For אך ad init. אם should prob. be read (cf. 𝕲 εἰ); and for the ungrammatical words ad fin. (להן שוע), parallelism demands a verb. If now we read לה אשׁיע (*him I would help*; cf. 𝔙𝕾) there, and אשלח pro 'יש in st. i, we obtain:

> *If not against the poor I stretched hand,—*
> *If in his ruin him I did help:—*

a distich which essentially agrees with the immediate sequel (v. 25)

> *If I wept for him whose day was hard,—*
> *If my soul was grieved for the needy:—*

and obviates the necessity of alteration in v. 25, except omission of לא ad init. (dittogr. fr. v. 24?).

𝕲 εἰ γὰρ ὄφελον δυναίμην ἐμαυτὸν χειρώσασθαι = אשלח יד (l) בעצמי אחלי (or אם לא בנפשי cf. 9· Ps 81³ 119⁵) *Would that I might lay hands upon* (= kill) *myself!* (Perhaps אם לא עלי *O that against myself . . .* Cf. 𝕲

But not against me—ܠܝ—*will he extend his hand | And when I cry unto him he will save me.*) 𝔊 therefore prob. read אִם־לֹא ... אֶשְׁלַח יָד. When 𝔊 continues ἦ δεηθείς γε (A δεηθῆναι) ἑτέρου, καὶ ποιήσει μοι τοῦτο, it perhaps preserves traces of two guesses at the riddle of שוע להן, viz. לִי יַעֲשֶׂה and לו אשוע.

v. 25. For the phrase קשה־יום *one who has a hard day* or *time,* cf. 𝔊 1 Sa 1¹⁵ γυνὴ ᾗ σκληρὰ ἡμέρα (= קשת יום pro 𝔐 קשת רוח). Note the Aramaism עָנַם *to be grieved.* The word is of the same origin as אָגַם *troubled* (Is 19¹⁰), אֲגַם a *troubled* or *muddy* pool or marsh (Is 14²³), both found in Assyr. (*agamu,* 'trouble'; *agammu,* 'swamp').

vv. 24, 25 do not seem to belong here. They agree in form with 31⁵ᵃᵠᵠ· and may have belonged to that chapter, either as a marg. variant or a part of the original text (cf. 31¹⁶⁻²⁰). Vv. 27-31 might naturally follow v. 23

v 26. Perhaps a quotation from another source. The distich has four stresses in each member (Tetrameter) instead of the normal three (Trimeter). 𝔊 paraphrases (as in v. 25). *for good*: read לטוב pro 𝔐 טוב: cf. 3⁹ 6¹⁹ (also st. 11). For the sense cf. 3²⁵ᶠ· Je 8¹⁵. 𝔊𝔖𝔙 om. כי.

v. 27. *boiled*: רתחו (41²³ Hi. Causative), an Aramaism. Pointed Pu.; perhaps should be Qal (cf. Syr. use); but Ez 24⁵ has Pi. 𝔊 ἐξέζεσεν.

were not quiet: דמו Pf. 𝔊 σιωπήσεται = ירמו Impf. (*would not be quiet*): prob. correct. Fig. of 'the tumult of his emotions' (Dr). Cf. La 1²⁰. The parallelism is weak. For *met* or *confronted me,* cf. 3¹² Ps 18⁶ ¹⁹.

v. 28. *A mourner*: str. dressed as such: in dark and squalid attire (Dr). Cf. 5¹¹. The phrase קדר הלכתי occurs Ps 38⁷, where it is completed by the addition כל־היום *all the day,* which would suit here also instead of the strange בלא חמה *without the sun* (Ct 6¹⁰). For the form of the sentence cf. 24¹⁰. חמה *sun* (Is 30²⁶ Ct l.c.) does not recur in Job. Leg. מְנַחֵם *a comforter,* La 1², or נֶחָמָה *comfort,* 6¹⁰. בלא חֲמָה *without desire* (2 C 21²⁰ without regret?) is improb.; and 'I go darkened (in skin), but not by the sun' (cf. Ct 1⁶; but קדר is not a syn. of שחר) is simply a curiosity of interpretation. 𝔊 ἄνευ φιμοῦ (alii θυμοῦ = 𝔙 sine furore, 𝔖 דלא חמתא, pointing חָמָה; so three codd.), *without a muzzle* (scribal error in 𝔊?). *in the Assembly* is strange if the verse is genuine. Did he visit the Gate in the intervals of sitting on his heap? בְּקֹלִי *with my voice,* i.e. *aloud,* seems plausible; but בקהל suits קמתי *I rose.* The next verse, however, favours בקלי, since his mournful cries constitute his resemblance to jackals and ostriches: cf. Mi 1⁸.

v. 29. For תנים *jackals* (𝔙 draconum, confusing the word with תנין *a serpent*), 𝔖 ܝܪܘܕܝܢ = 𝔗, 𝔊 gives σειρήνων, *sirens* (so Is 34¹³ 43²⁰, = *ostriches* Is 13²¹!). For the two Sirens see Odyss. xii. 39 ff. (Since the Sirens were singers, and the word has no known etymon in Greek, we may compare the Sumerian SIR, *sing,* (also SUR *ziṅṅu*), and Heb. שיר *id.* The ... Greek myth ... refers to a primitive

Babylonia is greater than is commonly suspected; e. g. Σίβυλλα, *Sibyl*, *prophetess*, may ultimately be akin to ŠIB, *divination*.)

v. 30. 'My skin is black, *and falleth* from me' (RV). The supplement is inadmissible. 'Black' or even blackened skins do not necessarily 'fall' off. Read perhaps מֵחֳלִי *from disease* pro מֵעָלַי *from off me*. 𝔙 denigrata est *super me*; 𝔊 (ἐσκότωται) μεγάλως = עַד־מְאֹד (Ps 38⁷·⁸), but מחלי is a closer parallel. The verb שָׁחַר *be black*, ἅπ. (Hi. Ecclus 25¹⁷ = σκοτοῖ) is Aramaic. It is prob. a Factitive (שׁ) formation from √חר (cf. חרר st. ii), which means *be hot* (cf. fig. חרי־ה, חרי־א of *heat* of anger), *scorched*, *burned*, *charred*, and may ultimately be identical with *GAD* (*KAD*), *GAR* (*KAR*), *shine, burn*; cf. Sum. KAR-KAR, *shine*, ĠAD, ĠUD, *id.*, Mongol k'ara, *black*, Jap. kuroi, *id.* Things *burnt* become *black.* (שחר has no visible connexion with Sum. SHU-RIN, *tinûru*, clay 'firepot', תַּנּוּר; cf. SHU, *hand*, RIN, *bright, glowing*, qs the portable fire.) *my bones* or *limbs* (v. 17): pointing c 𝔊𝔙𝔖 as plur. עֲצָמַי > 𝔐 עַצְמִי sing. and reading plur. חָרוּ pro 𝔐 חָרָה (Is 24⁶). Yet cf. 2⁵ 19²⁰ (Sing. Coll. ?).

Chapter 31.

v. 1. *A covenant* or *binding agreement* (בְּרִית; cf. Assyr. birîtu, 'bond', 'fetter', fr. barû, 'to bind', fr. Sum. BAR, *id.*) *I made for* (= imposed on, cf. 40²⁸) *my eyes*. The gist of the covenant immediately follows: *I will never take notice of a virgin*. 𝔐 וּמָה (dittogr. of v. 2?) can scarcely be right. 𝔙 ut ne cogitarem quidem de virgine; 𝔊 καὶ οὐ συνήσω ἐπὶ παρθένον (the verse was wanting in 𝔊ᴴ); 𝔖 דלא, &c. *That* I would *not*, &c. Leg. אֲנִי אִם emph. Pron. + the strong Neg. in oaths (cf. 1¹¹ 6²⁸). The Ptc. might also be understood as Interrog. = *Num*? (6¹² Ju 5⁸): אִם(!) *And would I take notice, &c.?* The suggestion מֵהִתְבּוֹנֵן *From taking notice* (= *That I would not take*, &c.; מִן of a Neg. Consequence) is grammatically but not metr. suitable. (Mt 5²⁸ has been compared. There, however, the subject is *adultery*, i. e. illicit intercourse with a married woman, cf. 2 Sa 11², which is not the case here.)

v. 2. Lit. *And what is the portion of Eloah from above*, &c., as RV; but the meaning demanded by the context, according to some, must be as RV marg. For this sense we should have expected וּמַה־חֶלְקִי מֵאֱלוֹהַּ מִמַּעַל וְנַחֲלָתִי מִשַּׁדַּי מִמְּרוֹמִים: *And what* (would be) *my share from E. above, And my portion from Shaddai on high?* cf. 20²⁹ 27¹³. As, however, נַחֲלַת יהוה may possibly mean *portion* assigned by *Iahvah* (cf. Ps 127³), the synonymous חֵלֶק אֱלוֹהַּ and נַחֲלַת שַׁדַּי may perhaps bear the same unusual meaning here. But an entirely different sense for the whole verse may be obtained by rendering *And what is* (or *was*) *Eloah's award from above, And Shaddai's allotment from on high?* I jealously guarded my eyes, says Eyob (v. 1), and with what result? It is before you. God has rewarded me evil for good. [He has all along maintained this (to us) daring position, which, however, is quite in accordance with the presuppositions of the story (see the Prologue).]

Then v. 3 might ask in the same strain *Should not ruin* (befall) *the unrighteous, And misfortune doers of evil?* Why then has it befallen me, the righteous? Is it possible (v. 4) that God, like you, is blind to realities, and cannot see the blamelessness of my life?

(𝔊 καὶ ἔτι ἐμέρισεν κτλ. ἔτι is prob. a scribal error for τί, the reading of 𝔊ᴺᶜ·ᵃ; ἐμέρισεν = חָלַק 21¹⁷ or חָלָק 39¹⁷. 𝔙 Quam enim partem haberet in me Deus desuper, Et hereditatem Omnipotens de excelsis?)

v. 3. St. i is metr. short. נָכֹן *prepared* may have fallen out after אֵיד (18¹²); or perhaps rather יָבוֹא (3²⁵ 21¹⁷ +ʼאֵיד Pr 6¹⁵): *Should not ruin come to the unrighteous* (leg. plur. c 𝔖; cf. ‖ ad fin.), *And calamity* (נֵכֶר Ob 12?) or *hostility*(?) *to the evildoers* (34²², cf. 22¹⁵)? נֵכֶר is perhaps *estrangement, alienation*, as 𝔊𝔙 𝔖. (Pro הֲלֹא ad init. vs. 𝔊 οὐαί = הוי.)

v. 4. *Cannot HE* (or *Doth not HE*) *see my ways, And take account of all my steps* (14¹⁶ same phrase)? It is an impossible supposition; and therefore He must know my innocence.

Considerable difficulty has been felt about vv. 1–4, which appear to have been wanting in 𝔊ᴴ, upon which and other internal grounds some would omit them. The latter, however, are at least weakened by the interpretation suggested above. It is no doubt true that Eyob has declared that the wicked often prosper all their lives and enjoy a peaceful end (21⁷ᶠᶠ), and that vv. 2, 3 appear to contradict this. Driver, therefore, held that vv. 2–4 'state not what Job argues now, but the considerations which deterred him from sin in the past'; and, unless we suppose him exempt from temptation, it must be admitted that the instinctive fear of consequences (which we call conscience) was one element in Eyob's piety (cf. 1¹·⁵), until the catastrophe overwhelmed him with an agony of doubt, not of God's existence and power, but of His justice. Dr. E. J. Dillon, rejecting vv. 1–4 as having been 'substituted for the original verses', supposes that the lost pair of quatrains made Eyob declare 'that this great change of fortune is not the result of his conduct'. But, as we have seen, the Massoretic verses may imply this, although they do not directly state it.

v. 5. St. i is metr. short; and as we cannot speak of *walking with* שָׁוְא (7³), but only with *men of* 'ש, we insert (c 2 codd.) מְתֵי before it (11¹¹ Ps 26⁴; אַנְשֵׁי שָׁוְא does not occur). 𝔊 μετὰ γελοιαστῶν, *with jesters* (ἅπ.). St. ii. *hath hasted* or *hastened*: 𝔐 points וַתַּחַשׁ which looks more like Hi. than Qal (וְתָחָשׁ). No other instance of the Impf. Qal of חוש occurs. (Assyr. *ḫâšu* = Sum ĠAL = BU-LUĠ; ĠAL, *run, flow, gardru*; GIR-PAB-ĠAL, *take the road quickly*. ĠAL = ĠASH? GAR? *ḫâšu* is one of the synn. of *alâ'u*, 'to [...]': אֶל [...] מ עַל [...]. 𝔊 ἐς δόλον. חוש usually [...] Ps 22).

v. 6. App. parenthetic. *a true balance*: so אַבְנֵי צֶדֶק *true* (correct) *weights*, Le 19³⁸, opp. מֹאזְנֵי מִרְמָה *a false balance*, Pr 11³. *perfectness* or *integrity*: 2³·⁹ 27⁵. The verse reminds us of the old Egyptian doctrine of the Weighing of the Soul after death in the Hall of Judgement (*see* the *Book of the Dead*); where the heart of the deceased is placed in the one scale and the symbol of Truth in the other.

v. 7. St. i is overweighted. Leg. מִנִּי־דַרְכִּי pro מִנִּי הַדֶּרֶךְ. The Art. is superfluous. With the idea of st. ii, cf. v. 1.

St. iii is prob. an intruder in the text. 𝔙 Et si manibus meis adhaesit *macula* (𝔐 מְאוּם = מוּם: so some codd. 𝔗 Qerî): see note at 11¹⁵. Or ᴷ מְאוּמָה *aught*. 𝔊 sees an allusion to taking bribes.

v. 8. *another eat*: 𝔊 plur. It is needless to add any Obj. (e.g. בֹּל): cf. Is 65²² Mi 6¹⁵. Brevity may be the soul of force as well as of wit. St. ii has only two stresses. 𝔊 *And may I become rootless* on earth (ἐπὶ γῆς) suggests that מֵאֶרֶץ *from Earth* (cf. Ps 52⁷) may have fallen out after צֶאֱצָאַי *my offspring* (so also 5²⁵ + זַרְעֲךָ 21⁸ 27¹⁴; the only other occurrences of the word in Job). 𝔙 et progenies mea eradicetur = 𝔐. Perhaps we should read: וְצֶאֱצָאַי לֹא־יִשְׁרְשׁוּ בָאָרֶץ *And my offspring not take root* (Po. Is 40²⁴, cf. Je 12² ch 5³ Hi.) *in the land!* Cf. 18¹⁶·¹⁷. (Even in Is 34¹ 42⁵ צֶאֱצָאִים means *issue, progeny* > *produce*. The Earth is the Mother of All: cf. 1²¹.)

v. 9. *enticed*: or *deceived*: cf. v. 27, 5², Je 20⁷. The √פתה *to be open*, i.e. not shut, met. *unguarded, unsuspicious, easily deceived, simple*, is doubtless an offshoot of the Sum. BAD, *pitú*, 'to open'.

v. 10. *grind*: scil. with the handmill; usually the work of female slaves: Ex 11⁵ Is 47² (cf. Ju 16²¹). 𝔙 Scortum alterius sit uxor mea, assuming a sexual metaphor, in agreement with st. ii (𝔊 ἀρέσαι is prob. a scribe's error for ἀλέσαι = 𝔐); and so 𝔗. But there is no trace of this met. use elsewhere. If a free woman were degraded to a שִׁפְחָה, she would become liable to both services at the will of her master. (טחן Ar. طحن = Assyr. *ṭênu*, 'to grind', e.g. *ṭênu ša qêmi*, 'grind, of meal', קֶמַח: cf. Is 47².) Leg. אֲחֵרִים c 11 codd. ad fin. pro 𝔐 אַחֵרִין (Aramaism): 𝔊 om. 𝔊 τὰ δὲ νήπιά μου = וְעָלַי pro 𝔐 וְעָלֶיהָ. (Or עֹלְלַי La 1⁶ 4⁴.) In st. i leg. fort. לְאָדוֹן *for a master* > לְאַחֵר *for another*.

v. 11. St. i is metr. short. Lit. *For that is* (or *were, would be*) an evil *device* or *wickedness* (זִמָּה). We might insert עֲשׂוֹת *to do*, Pr 10²³, or add וּנְבָלָה *and folly*, Ju 20⁶ ch. 42⁸ (see 2¹⁰ note; 30⁸). For זִמָּה see Le 18¹⁷; here only in Job (17¹¹ is corrupt): cf. מְזִמָּה 21²⁷ 42². The vb. זָמַם (not in Job) springs from a Bilit. Root ZAM, make a *sound, noise* (Syr.), *speak* (Arab.), *speak to oneself or inwardly*, i.e. *think, plan, devise* (Heb., Aram.), cogn. c NAM in Heb. נְאֻם, NH. נים *to speak*, and Sum. NIM in I-NIM, E-NEM, *word* (NIM = ZIM, by a well-known phonetic change).

Grammat. Concord justifies the Qerî הִיא in st. i and הוּא in st. ii.

In the latter עָוֹן פְּלִילִים is an ungrammatical combination or mixture of עָוֹן פְּלִילִי (v. 28, and about 20 codd. here) and עָוֹן פלילים (so codd. mult.).

a criminal offence. an offence of which the law takes cognizance, or which renders one liable to its penalties. If the pointing עָוֹן be correct, we must read פְּלִילִי *iudicialis* (v. 28), an Adj. not found elsewhere; though the f. פְּלִילִיָה occurs as a Subst. in the sense of judging (Is 28⁷ = κρίσις 𝔊ˣ). It seems better to read עָוֹן פְּלִילִים in both verses. For פְּלִילִים *judges* (plur. tant.) we have only Ex 22²¹ (?) Dt 32³¹ beside the present loc. According to the law of Le 20¹⁰, the penalty of adultery was death; but the phrase *a crime of* (for) *judges* hardly seems to express so much, or indeed anything specially distinctive of adultery. 𝔙 renders *iniquitas maxima* (cf. 𝔊 v. 28 ἀνομία ἡ μεγίστη); and it is evident that the original phrase, whatever it may have been, was intended to emphasize the moral gravity of the offence rather than its legal consequences. Did the translator think of פֶּלֶא *wonderful, extraordinary*; or was his *maxima* merely determined by his just sense of the general import of the verse? 𝔖, with its עינא הי דנצעתא *est oculus fraudium* and חזא בלהין צנעתי *vidit omnes fraudes meas* confuses עון with עין, and appears to read נפתלים or פתלים for פלילים and פלילי: cf. 5¹³, where it renders נפתלים *the tortuous* by צנעתנא *versuti, fraudulenti*.

We perceive that 𝔖 and 𝔙 had a phrase more or less resembling עון פליל(ים) in their Hebrew copies; but what are we to say of 𝔊's θυμὸς γὰρ ὀργῆς ἀκατάσχετος, | τὸ μιᾶναι ἀνδρὸς γυναῖκα (*for a passion of anger not to be checked, | is the defiling a man's wife*)? Duhm, who translates the Hebrew text *For that is a deed of shame and rebellion, And that is an offence for the Criminal Court* (Denn das ist Schandthat und Abfall Und das eine Schuld fürs Halsgericht), speaks of 'the doubtful addition which LXX has instead of v. 11ᵇ'; and then, after remarking that 'Unfortunately not much can be made of the LXX' (Leider lässt sich mit der LXX nicht viel machen), he says 'I get a וְסָרָה out of their ἀκατάσχετος (סררה)'. But סָרָה is an adj. fem. of סַר *stubborn, sullen, refractory*, and is not used for the subst. (abfällig, nicht Abfall); and it is improbable that ἀκατάσχετος represents a single positive term like סוֹרְרָה *stubborn*. The verb κατέχειν, poet. κατασχεθεῖν, means *to hold back, check, restrain, bridle*, e.g. ἵππους (Aesch. Pers. 190) and metaph. ὀργήν, θυμόν, &c. (Soph. El. 1011); and the verbal adj. with privative prefix here used in connexion with θυμὸς ὀργῆς obviously means *uncontrolled, unbridled* rage or passion. In 3¹⁷ θυμός ὀργῆς renders the single word רֹגֶז; and it may stand either for חֵמָה (= θυμός, 6⁴ 19²⁹ 36¹⁷, et al. saep.), or for עַף (= ὀργή 15 times in 𝔊) here. It might also represent such a phrase as זעם ועברה, which might possibly be a distortion of זמה ונבלה (vid. supr.). Cf. also Is 30³⁰ 𝔊. But the Adj. ἀκατάσχετος also belongs to st. i and this may represent Het. לֹא־לְבִים (P j² l·h ⸱ (⸱ ⸱ ⸱ ⸱ לֹא־זָכִים

uncurbed, unbitted, by an Aramaism (cf. Aram. זְמָמָא *a muzzle* or *bit*, זָמַם to *bit* or *muzzle* an animal). We may therefore suppose that 𝕲's first stichus implies a Heb. line כי־הוא זעם לא־זמום *For that is* (a cause of) *indignation unbridled* (or כי־הוא זעם לא־לבלם); while its second stichus, τὸ μίανaι ἀνδρὸς γυναῖκa, instead of being a superfluous gloss on st. i, as Duhm supposed, may stand for אשת איש בעל (or לטמא אשת לחלל), which may have grown out of והוא עון פלילי׳ by more or less obvious and usual corruptions of letters (e.g. ע = שׁ, ב = פ, לי = ע). [In the other two passages also (Ex Dt) 𝕲 failed to understand פלילים (cf. also Is 16³ 28⁷, and the vb. פָּלַל Gn 48¹¹ 1 Sa 2²⁵ Ez 16⁵² Ps 106³⁰) in the sense of *judges* or *umpires*. If the √פלל really had the meaning of *intervening, mediating, interposing as arbitrator*, as well as *interceding, praying for*, in Heb., the primary idea will be that of *splitting, separating, coming between*; cf. Ar. فل *break* or *notch* the edge of a sword or anything else, e.g. *a tooth*; *break* (through?) or *defeat* an army; Sum. BAL, *break through, into*, BAL, *an axe*, BAL, *to dig, break up or open* the ground, and BAL, *to speak, break out* into speech or, perhaps, *open* the lips. Cf. the same Prim. Root in פלא, פלה, פלג, פלק, פלשׁ, פלח, &c.)]

Both here and in v. 28 the reference to 'judges' is surprising; cf. vv. 8, 10, 22, 40, where we have imprecations, but no prosaic allusion to legal penalties. The word פלילים may be corrupt in both places; and vv. 11, 12 are possibly an interpolation. (An leg. נפ(י)לים? Gn 6⁴.)

v. 12. St. i is overweighted metr., even after omitting כִּי (dittogr. of v. 11?). App. based on Dt 32²² (*unto Abaddon = unto She'ol*). Cf. 26⁶ Ps 7²⁷. 𝕲 ἐπὶ (𝕲ᴬ ἐκ) πάντων τῶν μερῶν = מכל עבריו 1 K 5⁴. The vs. has been influenced by v. 8 (ותוצאי ישרשו = ובכל תבואתי תשרש; יאבל—תאבל). *And would root out all mine increase* (תבואה *produce, crops*) looks like a variant or gloss on v. 8ᵇ, and seems improb. here as parallel to st. i. 𝕲 οὗ δ' ἂν ἐπέλθῃ, ἐκ ῥιζῶν ἀπώλεσεν = ובכל תבוא תשרש. We must read תִּשְׂרֹף *it burneth up* pro 𝔐 תשרש (Fire does not 'root up').

v. 13. 𝔐 violates the metre by wrong division of the stichi. Point ואמתי > עבדי, *in their quarrel*: or *when they contended (at law) with me*.

v. 14. rose up: יָקוּם. 𝕲 ἐτασίν μου ποιῆται (𝕲ᴺ ποιήσηται 𝕲ᴬᶜ ποιήσῃ) = יחקור. It is needless to point יָקֹם *avengeth*. But it is a plausible conjecture that this verse is out of place here and orig. preceded v. 18.

v. 15. Lit. *Did not—in the belly—my Maker make him* (not emph.)? i.e. Is he not human like me? of the same flesh and blood as I am?

One: emph. One and the Same Being, viz. God. *prepare us*: 𝔐 וַיְכֻנֶנּוּ: leg. Hi. וַיְכִינֵנוּ or Pol. וַיְכוֹנְנֶנּוּ. 𝕲 ἐν τῇ αὐτῇ κοιλίᾳ (האחד); perhaps meaning the womb of Earth, the Mother of All. (𝕲 γεγόναμεν = תַּכֹּן or וְנִכּוֹן; cf. Dt 17⁴.) 𝔐 (וַיְכֻנֶנּוּ?) may be intended as a contraction of וַיְכוֹנְנֶנּוּ *and constituted him*. *And formed him in the one womb* (בְּרֶ׳ אחד) is conceivably right.

v. 16. *from* (their) *desire*: cf. 21²¹ 22³: perhaps חֶפְצָם (Ps 107³⁰ 1 K 5²²f·). חֵפֶץ may mean *a thing desired* (cf. Pr 3¹⁵) as well as *delight, pleasure*. 𝔙 *Si negavi quod volebant pauperibus, Et oculos viduae expectare feci*: see note 11²⁰; 17⁶. For the Construction, st. i, cf. Nu 24¹¹ᵇ. 𝔊 paraphr. *And the poor* (ἀδύνατοι), *what want they ever had, failed not to get*.

v. 17. *my morsel*: פתי (Gn 18⁵). *ate*: 𝔐 אֹכַל. 𝔊 καὶ οὐχὶ ὀρφανῷ μετέδωκα implies the pointing אֹכֶל (אוכיל), a dubious Hi. form (cf. Ho 11⁴).𝔊𝔙 as 𝔐.

v. 18. 𝔐 lit. *For from my youth he grew up to me* (? גְּדֵלַנִי) *as* (*to?*) *a father*, | *And from my mother's belly I would guide her* (i. e. the widow). This cannot be right. גָּדַל Qal occurs nowhere else with any Suffix (cf. 2 Sa 12³); and the hyperbole of st. ii is extravagant and improb. If the verse be in its original place, the reference will naturally be to the adoption and rearing of orphans in childhood or infancy. (To get back to the widow, we must overleap v. 17.) *Nay, but from his youth* (ני— pro י—) *I brought him up, as a father* (גִּדַּלְתּוֹ pro גְּדֵלַנִי; or simply גִּדַּלְתִּי), *And from his mother's womb I would guide him* (אִמּוֹ pro אִמִּי and אַנְחֶפוּ pro אַנְחֶנָּה)! The changes proposed are slight and easy; and the passage thus becomes similar to 29¹⁶ (*A father was I to the needy*; cf. also 29¹²). The view of my late acquaintance Dr. Merx, however, is very attractive. Pointing גִּדְּלַנִי *He* (i. e. God) *brought me up* (cf. 𝔊 *pains reared me*) pro 𝔐 גְּדֵלַנִי, and reading נָחַנִי *He guided me* [38³² ? יַנְחֵפִי] pro 𝔐 אַנְחֶנָה, Merx made this verse the immediate sequel of v. 14 (transposed to this place):

> *What should I do, if El arose?*
> *And if He visited, what should I answer Him?*
> *For from my youth He fostered me as a Father,*
> *And from my mother's womb He guided me.*

𝔊 lends some support to the former view (ἐξέτρεφον ὡς πατήρ . . . ὡδήγησα). 𝔙 *Quia ab infantia mea crevit mecum* (= 𝔐) *miseratio* (כְּאָב pro כָּאָב): cf. 𝔊.

v. 19. St. ii, lit. *And there was no covering to the needy*; which does not seem quite coherent with st. i. 𝔊 καὶ οὐκ ἠμφίασα αὐτόν, *And I clothed him not*. Should we read וְאִם לֹא כִסִּיתִי לָאֶבְיוֹן *And if I covered not the needy* (Is 11⁹ ?כסה ל)? אם may have been misread אין, and then לֹא omitted.

v. 20. *his loins*: 38³ 40⁷. 𝔊 ἀδύνατοι· perhaps חַלָּשִׁים pro 𝔐 חֲלָצָיו (cf. Jo 4¹⁰); or אֶבְיוֹן from v. 19 fin. (The metaphor may have seemed improbable to the translator.) In st. ii לֹא may have fallen out before the verb 𝔊 supplies οἱ ὦμοι αὐτῶν, *their shoulders* (vv. 22, 36) as the Subj. of the verb: making the stichus too long.

v. 21 sh⸱ ⸱ ⸱ ht⸱ ⸱ u u i ⸱ a ⸱ ⸱ ⸱ ⸱ ft⸱ ⸱ ₃ ⸱ ha⸱⸱ ⸱ ⸱ ⸱ ⸱ ⸱ ₂. a nst.

The phrase denotes a menacing gesture (cf. Is 11¹⁵ 19¹⁸), or perhaps a contemptuous one (cf. Ecclus 12¹⁸). The √נוף is cogn. c נוע and זוע, and also prob. c עוף and־עפעפים. (For the permutations of initial sound, vid. Proc. Brit. Acad. VII, *Shumer and Shem*, pp. 9 ff. 31.)

at the orphan: cf. 5⁴. עֲלֵי־תֹם *against an unoffending or honest man* (1¹·⁸ al.) has been suggested pro 𝔐 עַל־יָתוֹם. Cf. 8²⁰ Ps 64⁵ for תֹּם alone. But the change is not imperative. St. ii. *When* (or *Because*) *I saw my help* (= Concr. *helpers*, supporters or partisans) *in the Gateway*: cf 127⁵. 𝔊 *confident that I have a great surplus of help* (בַּשַּׁעַר pro תֻּשָּׁאֵר).

v. 22. Cf. the imprecation of Hammurabi: 'May Nergal ... smash his limbs *like an image of clay!*' (*biniátišu kíma ςalam tittim lihpuš!* Cod. Ham. XLIV. 37–39). שְׁכֶם *shoulder*, (upper) *back*, is prob. a Factitive formation (כם+ש) from the Prim. and widespread Root *GAM, KAM*, to *bend, bow* (cf. Gn 49¹⁰) = Sum. GAM; cf. the Chinese, kung, kwañg, 'the upper arm', kín, kien, kieng, 'top of shoulder'. 𝔊 ἀπὸ τῆς κλειδός, *from the collar-bone*; 𝔙 a junctura sua = משכמה (so point! instead of 𝔐 ה Raphat. et post מקנה). 𝔊 ἀπὸ τοῦ ἀγκῶνος, *from the elbow*, which may be right (קָנֶה *reed, stalk*; hîc tant. hoc sensu).

v. 23. 𝔐 lit. *For a dread unto me* (was) *ruin of El*; but, since אֵיד אֵל cannot mean 'calamity *from* God' (RV), but only *calamity* endured by *God* (30¹², the supposed parallel instance, is corrupt: vid. not. ad loc.), it is evident that the stichus is in need of revision, as indeed the collocation of similar letters אלי איד אל suggests at first sight. Read כִּי פַחַד אֵל יְאַתֵנִי (3²⁵, cf. 16²²), or perhaps יְאָחֲה־לִי (cf. 37²²). 𝔊 φόβος γὰρ συνέσχεν με = כִּי פַחַד יֹאחֲזֵנִי; and the verb may be right: cf. 18²⁰ 21⁶ ἴσχεν 1 K 6¹⁰ συνέσχεν. 𝔙 curiously: Semper enim *quasi tumentes super me fluctus* (אִיד נֵל!) timui Deum; 𝔖 *Because the fear of God shook me* (אֹיַעְתַּנִי), *And His breaking* (ruin, חברה) *came upon me* (אתא עלי). St. i might perhaps have been כִּי פַחַד אֵל יָבוֹא (א)לִי *For dread of El used to come to me*. St. ii 𝔐 lit. *And from* (= *because of*) *His loftiness* (מִשְּׂאֵתוֹ) *I was unable* (i. e. could do nothing). For שְׂאֵת *exaltation, majesty*, see 13¹¹ 41¹⁷ and cf. Le 13²·¹⁰·²⁸ a 'rising' = a swelling or eruption of the skin. 𝔊 καὶ ἀπὸ τοῦ λήμματος αὐτοῦ (λῆμμα = שְׂאֵת Hab 1⁷. Usu. = מַשָּׂא prophetic 'burden') οὐχ ὑποίσω (4² = יוּכַל; but Am 7¹⁰ = לְהָכִיל *bear, endure*): cf. 𝔙 Et *pondus eius* ferre non potui. Possibly וּשְׂאֵתוֹ וגו' *And His storming* (?) *I could not endure*: cf. 30⁸·¹⁴·²² Pr 1²⁸ 3²⁵.

In any case, the distich is an unsuitable sequel to the imprecation of v. 22. Hence some have transposed it to precede v. 15. More probably it is an interpolation.

v. 24. (*yellow*) *gold*: זָהָב, the ordinary term for gold, prob. cogn. c צהב *shn* ... bronze, *y-le-v*, of hair (η Arab. *ṣ-du-h*, η hair of men, camels, the lion. Cf. perhaps Sum. ZA-BAR (ZAB-BAR? ... *laming, copper*,

31. 30   NOTES ON THE TEXT   363

ZEB, *bright, beautiful.   my confidence*: *my stay*: 8¹⁴.   (*red*) *gold*. כֶּתֶם
28¹⁶ note. (𝔊 εἰς χοῦν μου, *my heap* of earth, my *rampart*? cf. 39¹¹ χοῦς
= עָפָר. For λίθῳ πολυτελεῖ = כֶּתֶם cf. Is 13¹² 28¹⁶ Pr 25¹².)

v. 25. *much*: כַּבִּיר so Is 16¹⁴. For this poet. syn. of רַב see 8² 15¹⁰ al.

v. 26. For the worship of the heavenly bodies, universal in the ancient
East (and in the West among the Maya and Nahua-Aztec peoples of
America), cf. Dt 4¹⁹ Je 44¹⁷ ff. Ez 8¹⁶.

the sun. אוֹר (str. *light*) so here only. Cf. Is 18⁴ עֲלֵי אוֹר 'in the sun').
as it shone: = 𝔊 τὸν ἐπιφαύσκοντα: so 25⁵ 41¹⁰. 𝔊 strangely adds
ἐκλείποντα, *in eclipse*: 'Or see we not Helios that shineth *while being
eclipsed* | And Selene *declining*? (φθίνουσαν· ἅπ.) *For it is not in their
power*'. 𝔊 perhaps read ירק *pale* pro יָקָר *splendid*; or else קֹדֵר *dark*
(Jo 2¹⁰), which it may have transposed and rendered ἐκλείποντα, taking
הָלַךְ as *departing*. Possibly τὸ ἐπιφαύσκοντα ἐκλείποντα combines two
readings, viz. כְּרִיהֵל *when he shone* and יָכְהֶה *was dim* (Is 42⁴). But there
can be little doubt that 𝔙 has understood the verse rightly: Si vidi solem
cum fulgeret | Et lunam incedentem clare.

v. 27. *was seduced*, Niph. (וַיִּפְתְּ) as v. 9 Je 20⁷, pro 𝔐 Qal. The
meaning seems to be (*cor meum*) *sibi persuaderi passum est*. 𝔊 ἠπατήθη.

my hand hath kissed; as in throwing a kiss to a person at a distance.
Kissing the images of gods is a well-known Oriental mode of worship.
Cf. Ho 13² 1 K 19¹⁸.

v. 28. If genuine, the verse is parenthetic, rather than apodotic. There
is no apodosis to vv. 16–20, 24–25, 29–34; the fact being that all these
formally hypothetical propositions are virtually emphatic denials of the
sins enumerated. See notes on v. 11. Certainly trust in riches (vv. 24,
25) was not 'an iniquity to be punished by the judges' (RV). The verse
looks like an interpolation.

I had been false (or *lied*) *to* . . . , cf. 1 K 13¹⁸. Perhaps we should read
בָאֵל pro לָאֵל: *I should have denied* (or *disowned*) *El above* (cf. 8¹⁸ Is 59¹³).

v. 29. *If I rejoiced*. The Impf., as in the other instances (vv. 7, 13,
16, 19, 25 f.), expresses habitual conduct: *If I was wont to* . . or *If I
would* . *ruin*: פיד: 12⁵ 21²⁰ al. *was elated*: or *exulted*; וְהִתְעוֹרַרְתִּי
roused myself, was excited: see 17⁸. 𝔙 exultavi. Cf. Pr 24¹⁷ where this
Schadenfreude (we have no word for it in English) is the subject of a
warning. 𝔊 gives an apparent variant: καὶ εἶπεν ἡ καρδία μου Εὖγε
= לִבִּי הֶאָח וְאָמַר *And my heart would cry*, '*Aha!*' 39²⁵ Ps 35²¹·²⁵ Ez 36².

v. 30. Lit. *And* (*But*) *I have not given my palate to sinning*, | *To
asking his life with a curse*. The Pf. here and elsewhere expresses habit,
with a picturesque difference from the Impf.; as though one said 'I have
never once done it!' 𝔊 has a different verse: *Let, then, my ear hear my
curse* | *And* ·   ·, · (Λ on.)   ·   ·   ·   · · · · Λ ; *ple
abused!* =

תִּשְׁמַע אָזְנִי אֶת־אָלָתִי (Cf. 𝔐 st. ii.)
וּלְמִלָּה לְעַמִּי אֶהְיֶה: (Cf. 30ᵃ θρύλλημα = מִלָּה.)

which has at least the merit of not involving another parenthesis, and of being a possible conclusion. As to *asking the life of enemies*, i.e. praying for their deaths, see 1 K 3¹¹ (with a curse, Nu 22⁶·¹¹ 23¹ff·).

v. 31. RV is not a possible equivalent of 𝔐; and RV marg., which divides the stichus between a wish and a categorical assertion, sins against poetical construction. As in other passages of our book, however, e.g. v. 35 infr., מִי יִתֵּן must introduce a wish. Accordingly, st. ii, as it stands in 𝔐, can only mean *Oh that with his flesh we were not surfeited!* which might conceivably be the expression of a regret that repletion prevented them from eating more of such good fare. This would agree with v. 32; but the two verses need not be closely connected, and *flesh* (בשר), a frequent word in Job, does not occur in this sense elsewhere in the book (2⁵ 4¹⁵ 6¹² 7⁵ 13¹⁴ 14²² 19²⁰ 21⁶). Even if בשרו could mean *his meat* (שְׁאֵר Ps 78²⁰·²⁷), מְתֵי אָהֳלִי *the men of my tent* can hardly be *my guests*, but rather my household or dependents (cf. 19¹⁹ Gn 34³⁰). 𝔊 αἱ θεράπαιναί μου = אַמְהֹתַי (19¹⁵, v. 13 sing.). But the occurrence of the phrase וּמִבְּשָׂרִי לֹא תִשְׂבָּעוּ *And (why) are ye not sated with my flesh?* i.e. *Why do ye not weary of slandering me?* would seem to be almost decisive; and then the stichus must mean *O that we could speak enough ill of him!* in this case, perhaps, as a churlish, mean, and niggardly master, and inhospitable to strangers (cf. 1 Sa 25). The second Neg. must be omitted c 𝔊𝔅 (due to dittogr. or 19²²). Others omit יִתֵּן and take נִשְׂבַּע as Niph. [ἄπ.] Pf. 3 Sing.: *Who with his flesh hath not been satisfied?* i.e. Who has not enjoyed his lavish hospitality?

(𝔊 *And if often my handmaids said,* | *O that we might be filled with his flesh!* plur. τῶν σαρκῶν αὐτοῦ so 2⁵ 4¹⁵ 19²⁰ al. ten times. 𝔊 adds the epexegetical gloss λίαν μου χρηστοῦ ὄντος, *when I was all too kind*.)

v. 32. Cf. Ju 19²⁰. We must, of course, point אֹרֵחַ *traveller, wayfarer* (Ju 19¹⁷) pro 𝔐 אֹרַח *the way*, c Versions.

v. 33. *If I covered my transgressions*; i.e. concealed them: Pr 28¹³ (the same phrase). כְּאָדָם *like men*; as men usually do. Cf. 𝔙 quasi homo. But מֵאָדָם *from men* would be better, in view of v. 34; cf. Gn 18¹⁷ הַמְכַסֶּה...מֵאַבְרָהָם. (בְּאָדָם 'unter den Menschen' will not do; בְּ = *cover with*, Gn 38¹⁴ Ps 147⁸. כְּמַדִּי Ps 109¹⁹, or כְּאַדֶּרֶת as with *a mantle*, cf. Ps 104⁶, might also be suggested, but מֵאָדָם is perhaps preferable.)

in my bosom: an Aramaism; חֹב = חוּבָּא. So 𝔙𝔗; 𝔊 בְּטוּשְׁיָא *in secret*. 𝔊 paraphrases εἰ δὲ καὶ ἁμαρτὼν ἀκουσίως | ἔκρυψα τὴν ἁμαρτίαν μου, app. supposing that st. i was another way of saying אִם־חָטָאתִי בִּשְׁגָגָה, and omitting בְּחֻבִּי as a gloss on עֲוֹנִי (owing to confusion with Aram. חוֹבָא

debt, sin). Perhaps we should read בְּחֵ(י)קִי *in my bosom* (cf. 23¹²) and וָאֶטְמֹן (18¹⁰ 40¹³) c 𝔙 *Et celavi* in sinu meo, &c. (Cf. 𝔊.)

v. 34 A tristich. *I dreaded*: אֶעֱרוֹץ. Not so elsewhere c Accus. Obj. In 13²⁵ Trans. (*to scare*). Cf. Jos 1⁹. 𝔊 *For I turned not away from a mob of multitude* | *In order not to confess* (Le 5⁵ Ps 32⁵ הוֹדָה) *before them* (a loose paraphr. which app omits st. ii) ; | *And if also I suffered a poor man to go forth of my door with empty bosom* = ואבין לא אצא פתח, which might be due to misreading of 𝔐 וארום לא אצא פתח (*So that I kept quiet, nor went forth of the doorway*; prob. a marg. gloss).

v. 35 𝔐 מי יתן לי שמע לי *Who will give to me one listening to me?* is barely metrical; and if we suppress the first לי (after six codd. 𝔊ᵃ 𝔙 𝔖) it becomes less so. The restoration of a single letter will yield a satisfactory line, viz. מי־יתן אל ישמע־לי *O that El would listen to me!* St. ii, though metr., is even more dub. 𝔐 הן תוי שדי יענני *Lo my mark! let Shaddai answer me!* (תָו *mark*, Ez 9¹·⁴†). 'Job speaks, as he has often done elsewhere, in legal phraseology. Here, he says, is my solemn signature to these protestations of innocence; let the Almighty refute them, and "answer me", if He can!' (Driver). In Ez l.c., the only other place where it occurs, תָו is a mark made with ink on the forehead, prob. a cross (cf. +, ×, the oldest shapes of the letter Tau). No instance can be adduced of its use in the sense of a man's 'mark' appended to a written document by way of signature, as in the case of the illiterate to-day (cf. the thumbnail impressions on Babylonian Contract Tablets). But even if it were so used, it does not appear that Eyob had actually signed a written statement of his case; in fact, the next stichus makes him utter a wish for a document recounting the charges against him, which he would joyfully receive, as affording him something definite to answer and disprove. How could he exclaim 'Here is my signature!' before he had actually set it on any document? Are we to suppose that he held up a sort of stamp or seal engraved with a Tau? Moreover, as 𝔐 gives it, the verse is a tristich; and the parenthetic st. ii robs st. iii of all possible grammatical connexion (e.g. with st. i, as RV). There is no trace of תָוִי *my mark* in the Versions. 𝔊 χεῖρα δὲ κυρίου (= שַׁדַּי 6⁴·¹⁴ al.) εἰ (= הֵן) μὴ ἐδεδοίκειν (!); 𝔗 *Lo, my desire* (= תַּאֲוָתִי pro תָוִי) *is that Shaddai answer me!* So 𝔙 Ut *desiderium meum* audiat Omnipotens. 𝔖 *If it be* (תְּהִי) הֵן תְּהִי pro הֵן תָוִי), *let God answer me,* | *And write,* &c. (st. iii). St. ii might be restored thus: וְיֵאֹת שׁדי ויענני *And that Shaddai would come and answer me!* But, since God *does* as He desires (אָוָה 23¹³), וְיֹאֶה or וְיִתְאַוֶּה may have been the missing verb (cf. 𝔊𝔗𝔙), which would account better for the תוי of 𝔐: *And that Shaddai would will it and answer me!* A line may have fallen out either before or after st. iii, which still hangs in the air. To fill up the gap Duhm suggested מי יתן־לי מְגִלָּה (? *that I will it will* כֻּלָּה)

Ps 40⁸ Ez 3².³ Je 36¹⁴ᶠᶠ·); making a good connexion with st. iii (iv): *And the writing which mine opponent hath written!* But the repetition of מִי יִתֵּן within the bounds of the same quatrain seems strange; and מְגִלָּה *roll* does not occur elsewhere in Job. Perhaps Eyob does not so much assume the existence of a Divine catalogue of his offences as express the wish that God would prepare one and submit it to his scrutiny. He would have the Almighty state His case in writing (in a סֵפֶר); as he wished his own case might be stated, 19²³. Hence 𝔊𝔙 may be right with יִכְתֹּב instead of כָּתַב: *An indictment let mine Adversary write* . . . Then might follow וְיֹדִיעֵנִי עַל־מָה יְרִיבֵנִי: *And show me why He contends with me!* (cf. 10²) as the missing st. iv; or something similar (e.g. וְעָרֹךְ לְפָנַי מִשְׁפָּטוֹ *And set out His case before me!* cf. 13¹⁸ 23⁴; or simply וְיָשֵׂת נֶגְדִּי אֶת־עֲוֹנִי *And set before me my sin!*).

Is 30⁸ might also suggest וְעַל־לוּחַ חֻקַּהּ עֹנִי *And on a tablet inscribe* (19²³) *my sin!*, and Is 50⁸ וּמַכְתָּב בַּעַל מִשְׁפָּטִי *And a written account my prosecutor!* 𝔊 συγγραφὴν δὲ ἥν εἶχον κατά τινος = אִישׁ רִיבִי? וְסֵפֶר כְּתָב = 𝔐.

v. 36. I would wear it as a badge of honour; I would glory in it as evidence of my innocence. *I would bind it*: Pr 6²¹ only. (The √עָנַד may be cogn. c אֶגֶד *bind*, Talm., cf. אֲגֻדָּה, עָקַד *bind*, Arab. *tie fast*, Syr *bend*, and קד in קָדַר *bend, bow*, *GAD = *NGAD = *NAD? Cf. Sum. GAR, GUR, *to bend, bow*; KUR, KEŠ, *to bind.*) Cf. also Pr 7³ Dt 6⁸ᶠ· *a crown*: Sing. c 2 codd. and 𝔊𝔖𝔙 pro 𝔐 plur. Cf. 19⁹. *upon my brows*: lit. *upon me* (עָלַי pro 𝔐 לִי: as Pr 6²¹). 𝔊 (in continuation of v. 35, st. iii) ἐπ' ὤμοις ἄν περιθέμενος στέφανον ἀνεγίνωσκον, (And the writing which I had against any one) *on shoulders putting round* (as) *a crown I used to read.* This app. omits אשאנו *I would bear it*, adding ואקראנו *and I would read it* at the end (a gloss? cf. Dt 17¹⁸·¹⁹; or misreading of אקרבנו, v. 37 ad fin.?).

v. 37. Driver explained the verse: 'I would also declare to my Judge every action of my life, and present (marg. RV) the indictment fearlessly before Him.' All his actions, however, are supposed to be already recorded in the 'indictment'; and it is difficult to believe that the repeated Suffix נּוּ ־ can refer first to the Judge and then to the document. Its use in both stichi of v. 36 to indicate the document makes the same reference here most natural in both stichi. *The tale* (i.e. sum; or *account*, Ju 7¹⁵; cf. the verb chap. 15¹⁷) *of my doings* (steps = proceedings) *I would declare* (or *avow, proclaim*) *it,—Like a prince* (29¹⁰) or *As to a prince* (cf. 𝔙) *would I present it!* Since st. ii halts metr., we may perhaps see in כמו the vestige of כמלי (26⁴) *Like the words of a prince or noble* (and therefore a true statement and above suspicion) *I would bring it on forward!* cf. Is 41·). We may even suggest אקראנו *I would read it aloud* (Je 36⁸·¹⁵·²¹) pro אקרבנו ;מ or, retaining the latter, *As the gift of a prince* (כמו מתן נדיב 12²¹ 21²⁸ Pr 19⁶) *would I receive* (?אקבלנו) *it!*

He is sure that a Divine account of his actions could contain nothing against him. If only God would give him a written statement of what He well knows, Eyob would exhibit it to all the world as irrefragable proof of his innocence. Cf 𝔙 *Per singulos gradus meos pronuntiabo illum, Et quasi principi* (=כנגיד) *offeram eum*. 𝔊 καὶ εἰ μὴ ῥήξας αὐτὴν ἀπέδωκα, Οὐθὲν λαβὼν παρὰ χρεωφιλέτου = ואם־לא פרצתי ואשיבנו ומיד נשה לא־אקבלנו: *And I would have rent and given it back, Accepting naught from a debtor!*

Verses 38–40 are evidently out of place. They belong somewhere in the previous series of hypothetical paragraphs (vv. 5–34). They may have originally followed v. 8 or v. 34. 'Most of the paragraphs in this chapter begin with *If*; so that a scribe might easily have omitted one accidentally, and afterwards, discovering his mistake, have added it at the end of the chapter' (Driver), to which vv. 35–37 form a natural conclusion.

v. 38. *cry out*: as wrongfully appropriated by fraud or violence: cf. 24² Dt 19¹⁴ 1 K 21 Is 5⁸.

v. 39. *its produce without payment*: lit. *its strength* (בֹּחַ Gn 4¹²) or *virtue, goodness, without silver* (Is 55¹); i.e. without payment for the rent of the land, or as wages to the labourers: cf. Je 22¹³ Ma 3⁵.

𝔊 + μόνος = לְבַדִּי (v. 17); a gloss which violates the metre.

snuffed at: i.e. despised, made of no account: cf. Ma 1¹³: cared nothing whether he lived or starved. cf. Pr 12¹⁰. Others · (the life of its owner) *I caused (him) to breathe out*, which would require הפחתיו (c Suff.). Cf. Je 15⁹. 𝔊 ἐκλαβὼν ἐλύπησα (cf. 3⁵ ἐκλάβοι); but 𝔊ᴬ ἐκβαλών = הרחתי (Je 29¹⁸) seems the better reading.

its owner > *its owners* (Ex 21²⁹ 22¹⁰ Is 1³); Plur. of Dignity. Cf. 𝔊 κυρίου τῆς γῆς.

v. 40. *the brier*: 2 K 14⁹ 𝔊 κνίδη, *a nettle*; 𝔊ᶿ ἄκανθα, *thorn, thorn-bush*; 𝔊ˣ ἄκανος, kind of *thistle* 𝔙 *tribulus*: cf. Vergil's *Lappaeque tribulique*.

noisome weeds: בָּאְשָׁה *stinking thing*, Coll. Cf. באשים *labruscae*, *wild grapes*, Is 5²·⁴. 𝔊 βάτος, *bramble-bush* or *wild raspberry*; 𝔙 *spina*.

The words of Eyob are ended. Prob not part of the original text, but a colophon added by a scribe or editor, as is commonly the case in manuscripts. 𝔊 καὶ ἐπαύσατο Ἰὼβ ῥήμασιν, as an integral part of the text, 32¹ (cf. 𝔖 31⁴⁰). Cf. Ps 72²⁰. Possibly 𝔊 is right in connecting the words with the introduction to the Elihu-section: תמו ... וישבתו.

Chapters 32–37. *The Episode of Elihu.* It is now generally recognized that the figure of Elihu was unknown to the original poet. See the Introduction. When however the text has been cleared of some of the manifold and glaring corruptions which ... it ... ian reader at all events will hardly fail to admit that these chapters have great and substantial merits of their own and were well worthy of preservation, at least as an appendix to the matchless original.

Chapter 32.

v. 1. *these three men*: i. e. Eliphaz, Bildad, and Zophar, neither of whom, according to the existing recension of the text, has said a word since chap. 25. In the interval editors would appear to have forgotten their existence. See the remarks on 26⁵ᶠᶠ· 27¹¹ᶠᶠ· 28. 𝕲 οἱ τρεῖς φίλοι αὐτοῦ = שֶׁל רֵעָיו (cf. 2¹¹). Not a various reading, but explanatory. *because he was righteous in his own eyes*; and they had failed to convince him. 𝕲 ἦν γὰρ Ἰὼβ δίκαιος ἐναντίον αὐτῶν (so 𝕾; בְּעֵינֵיהֶם pro 𝔐 בְּעֵינָיו); implying that Eyob's arguments had convinced them of his innocence, which can hardly be the author's meaning: cf. 42⁷ᶠ· and v. 3.

v. 2. Cf. these fuller details of Elihu's parentage and tribal connexions with the little told of Eyob's three friends, 2¹¹. 𝕲 adds τῆς Αὐσείτιδος χώρας, *of the land of Uç*: 1¹. An obvious gloss. Buz was the brother-tribe of Uç, to which Eyob belonged (Gn 22²¹). (Copt. ⲥⲱⲃⲏⲧⲕⲉ is a mere curiosity pro 𝕲 Βουζείτης.)

v. 3. *but let Elohim appear unrighteous*: adopting the traditional correction of the Scribes (*Tiqqûn Sôpherím*) הָאֱלֹהִים pro 𝔐 אִיּוֹב. 𝔐 must mean: *Because they found no answer* (to Eyob's arguments), *and (because) they treated Eyob as guilty*—or *and (so) condemned Eyob*: cf. 9²⁰ 10² 15⁶. But by their failure to refute Eyob's arguments, they seemed to leave the Divine justice unvindicated. 𝕲 *because they were not able to answer in opposition* (ἀντίθετα, things opposed) *to Eyob, and they made him to be ungodly* (καὶ ἔθεντο αὐτὸν εἶναι ἀσεβῆ· so 𝕲ᴮᴺ*ᴬ²ᶜ but 𝕲ᴺᶜ·ᶜᴬ*𝕲ᴴ ᵐᵃʳᵍ· εὐσεβῆ, *godly*; implying וַיַּרְשִׁיעוּ pro וִיַצְדִיקוּ).

v. 4. 𝔐 חִכָּה אֶת־אִיּוֹב בִּדְבָרִים *waited for Eyob with words* can hardly be right. חכה is usu. *to wait*, abs., or *to wait for* c לְ (3²¹ Is 8¹⁷), and is nowhere else found c Accus. Pers. We therefore read בִּדְבָרָם אֶת־אִיּוֹב (Gn 17³ 50¹⁷). This is confirmed by st. ii. Elihu waited, because he did not venture to speak before his seniors had finished what they had to say. 𝕲 Ἐλιοῦς δὲ ὑπέμεινεν δοῦναι ἀπόκρισιν (τῷ) Ἰώβ smooths over the difficulty by a loose paraphrase (cf. v. 5 15² 33⁵ 35⁴ for δοῦναι ἀπόκρ.), which does not help.

v. 6. After the usual form of heading the words of Elihu follow in the same metre as the original poem.

in years: lit. *in days* (𝕲 τῷ χρόνῳ so again v. 7 Gn 26¹·¹⁵ al.; but v. 4 ἡμέραις; cf. 1 Sa 1³). *all of you*: בְּלְּכֶם inserted metr. grat.; cf. 27¹². *aged*: 12¹² 15¹⁰ 29⁸ יְשִׁישִׁים pec. to Job; but cf. יָשֵׁשׁ or ? לָשֵׁשׁ 2 C 36¹⁷. The √ישש is perhaps akin to √קשש *dry, withered*: cf. Aram. קשיש *elder*). *therefor·*: עַל־כֵּן and דֵּעַ *knowledge* or *opinion* (vv. 10, 17; 37¹⁶) = דֵּעָה (10⁷ 13·15²) occur only in the Elihu-section of Job (דֵּעִים, רֵעִי, עַיִן,

nowhere else). *was I fearful*: וחלתי (ἅπ.) = Aram. דְּחַל *to fear* (of which חל might be the older sound: cf. the Zenǧirli inscrr.). In Aram. (Tg. see Levy HWB) וְחַל is *to run* or *flow*, of liquids, and *to crawl, glide*, of reptiles (cf. ⊥ וְחִיל *worm* 13¹⁸). Hence others would render וחלתי here *I held back*, comparing Arab. جل ; *to withdraw, retire to a distance, to hang back, lag behind* (see Lane). The Primary Root of חל in these various senses may be Sum. GAL, *to run, flow* (= חל), *quick motion* (like that of a lizard or a snake when startled) being the primitive idea. 𝔊 ἡσύχασα = חרלתי (14⁴); but 𝔖 רחלת *I feared*. With st. 11 cf. 13¹⁷ 15¹⁷ (𝔐 אֶתְכָם not אִתְּכֶם is prob. right) 36².

v. 7. Lit. *I said, Days*, &c. Cf. 𝔙 Sperabam enim quod aetas prolixior loqueretur. 𝔊 awkwardly inserts a Neg. in both members, and points יָדְעוּ *they know* pro יְדִי(עוּ) *they teach* in st. ii. Metre demands וְרֹב־שָׁנִים instead of וְרֹב שָׁנִים.

v. 8. *But*: or *Still*: אָכֵן (Ps 31²³ Is 49⁴) not elsewhere in Job. Lit. *But indeed the* (or *a*) *spirit is* (not *there is a spirit*) *in man*.

Moreover, a ‖ to *Shaddai* is wanted, prob. אֵל: cf. 33⁴. *informeth*: or *maketh intelligent*. We should have expected תְּבִינֵהוּ (Is 40¹⁴) > 𝔐 תָּבִין (here only), as אנוש even in Coll. sense takes Sing. Predicates and Pronouns of reference (7¹⁷ 9² al. 33²⁶ 36²⁵). 𝔊 app. תביג׳ (cf. 𝔊ᴬ* + σε, 𝔊ᴬ + με = ־ני).

v. 9. *seniors*: רַבִּים: cf. Gn 25²³ רַב *the elder* opp. to צָעִיר *the younger*, v. 6). The לא is emphatic, and therefore stressed separately. 𝔊 οἱ πολυχρόνιοι, 𝔙 longaevi (= רַבִּים). Perhaps רַבֵּי יָמִים (hic tant.); cf. 𝔖, which implies רַב יָמִים, and phrases like רַב בֹּחַ.

v. 10. 𝔐 שְׁמָעָה *hearken thou!* Sing. cannot be right, as he is addressing the Three. Read therefore שִׁמְעוּ c 𝔊𝔙𝔖: *Therefore I say, 'Hearken ye to me!' And I too*, &c. ואחוה. (Exc. 1 post י)

v. 11. A tristich, and certainly corrupt on other accounts. St. ii עד־תבונתיכם looks like dittogr of (עדיכם אתבונן) v. 12ª; and מלין (st. iii) is the natural parallel to דברי (st. i), while אזין (st. ii) may conceal the vb. required by metre and sense in st. iii, possibly אָאזין (or Pf.) *I weighed* or *pondered*, which is followed by חִפֵּר Ec 12⁹ as here by תָּחִ׳. We might also read אאזין *I gave ear* (so 5 codd. 𝔊𝔙𝔖) *unto* (ער) Nu 23¹⁸; cf. התבונן עד v. 12 38¹⁶ ? leg. על = אל in all, as Ps 39¹³) *your reasonings*, and make the stichus the first of v. 12 (also a tristich), thus turning it into a quatrain. But the plur. of תבונה is not found again in Job, and is strange in this sense, while v. 12ª is metr. short. Both may be rejected as accretions to the genuine text, which may have run thus:

  Lo, I waited for your words,—
  I pondered (*or* gave ear) while ye sought what to say:
  And behold, Eyob had none to confute him,
  To rebut his speeches, among you!

v. 13. Lit. *Lest* (cf. 36¹⁸ Is 36¹⁸) *ye say, 'We have found Wisdom!'* (Pr 3¹³), i.e. We have discovered that it is folly to argue with him; he is too clever or subtle a reasoner for us. Or perhaps, '*We have come upon* (unexpected) *Wisdom!*' in Eyob; a wisdom which only God can overcome (st. iii; Driver). *rout him*: or *drive him off*: 13²⁵ Ps 1⁴ (נדף). One cod. has יהדפנו *thrust him out* or *away* (18¹⁸). For st. ii 𝔊 has only Κυρίῳ προσθέμενοι = באל דבקנו (cf. Dt 13⁵) or נרבק; but 𝔙 Deus proiecit eum, non homo = 𝔐.

v. 14. 'Job has not yet tried conclusions with me' (Dr); and I have something fresh to say. 𝔖 *I will not speak against* (him) (mere) *words*; app. reading אֶעֱרֹךְ אֵלָיו, which is perhaps to be preferred, as a better ∥ to st. ii. But cf. 33⁵. (𝔊 *But to a man permit to speak such words* looks like a guess at the reading of a defaced text.) א exc. p. א, unde אֵלָיו (sic 2 codd.) mut. in אֵלִי.

v. 15. Prob. a gloss. St. i לא ענו עוד *they have not answered again* = v. 16ᵇ; and העתיקו ונו׳ *They have removed words from themselves* (cf. 9⁵) seems rather strange. (Cf. also עתק Qal Intr. 14¹⁸ 18⁴.) 𝔊 ἐπαλαίωσαν = 𝔐 (cf. 21⁷ עתק *grow old*). Of course we might take Hi. here as Intrans. (Gn 12⁸): *Words have departed from them*; but cf. 𝔙 Abstulerunt que a se eloquia. In any case, the 3rd Pers. of the verbs suspends the direct address to the Friends and implies the beginning of a soliloquy or *sotto voce* address to himself.

v. 16. St. ii leg. ולא pro 𝔐 לא. (ו exc. p. ו.) So many codd.

v. 17. 𝔐 אַעֲנֶה app. the (non-existent?) Hi. Point אֶעֱנֶה Qal, ut v. 20. Cf. 15² for ענה c *Accus. rei.* Instead of 𝔐's isolated חלקי *my share* (𝔙 partem meam) leg. לקחי (with) *my learning*, which seems a better parallel to דעי. Yet cf. חלק Pr 7²¹. Does 𝔐 mean: *I also will let my persuasiveness answer*? St. ii = v. 10ᵇ. Instead of this verse 𝔊 ὑπολαβὼν κτλ. = ויען אליהוא ויאמר *And Elihu answered and said* (!).

To cancel v. 10 and transpose vv. 15–17 to follow v. 9, as has been proposed, does not eliminate the difficulty of the 3rd Pers., v. 15, unless, contrary to the context, we suppose v. 9 to have a particular > a general reference.

v. 18. In st. i Qerî et Codd. circa 20 מָלֵאתִי rectè. But the stichus is metr. short (כִּי is metr. a Proclitic). Perhaps אֲדַבֵּר *I will speak* has fallen out before כִּי; cf. 𝔊 Πάλιν λαλήσω· πλήρης γάρ εἰμι ῥημάτων. Others would read אָנֹכִי *I* (emphatic) pro 𝔐 כִּי *For*.

in my bosom: lit. *of my belly.* For the belly (בֶּטֶן) as the seat of the mind or intellectual faculties, cf. Pr 22¹⁸ ch. 15³⁵ Ps 40⁹ (מעי). Grotesque as this may seem to us, we must remember that antiquity knew absolutely nothing about the physiology of man. If even an Aristotle could regard the brain as a cold mass intended to act as a counterpoise to the excessive heat of the heart, we can hardly be astonished at the crudeness of Hebrew notions on the same subject. It is interesting to find that similar ideas have always prevailed among the Chinese, with whom 肚 tu, *the belly*, is also the temper or mind; cf. the phrases tu-li ming-pai, 'to understand', 'be intelligent' (*belly-in clear-bright*), ta tu-tzŭ-li yiu hioh-wên, 'He is a man of learning' (lit. *he in the belly has learning*).

constraineth: or *urgeth*: Ju 14^{17} 16^{16} (הֵצִיק). 𝕲^{x} συγκαίει = הצית or הדליק. (𝕲 ὀλέκει, ? חויק *injureth*: Aram.)

v. 19. Cf. Mk 2^{22} ff. Leg. הֵן pro 𝔐 הִנֵּה metr. gratia (cf. 8$^{19f.}$ al.), et תבקע pro 𝔐 יִבָּ (cf. 15^{23} al.). The word יין yain, yein, *wine*, is interesting as a culture-term, and as being apparently of the same origin as Φοῖνος, *vinum, vinea*, and other 'Aryan' terms. It was natural that, as in other instances, with the plant its primitive name should spread over the whole world. The initial w (= m) appears in Ethiop. ወይን: wain, *vine, vineyard, wine*, Ar. وَيْن wain, *black grapes*, Assyr. inu (2 R 25. 38: Sum. MU-TIN = GESH-TIN). The same word may be recognized in the Sum. MUN, an intoxicating liquor or fruit-syrup (*tâblu*, *šikaru ša KASH*), and in the Chinese 酉 醖 wên, yün, ún, *fermented liquor, wine, spirit made from fruit*. 𝕲 *But my belly is as* a skin boiling over with new wine (γλεύκους ζέων), *fastened* (= not opened); a paraphrase of 𝔐. In st. ii 𝕲 read חרשים *smiths* pro חדשים *new*, and understood אבות *skins* as skin (leather) *bellows* (ἢ ὥσπερ φυσητὴρ χαλκέως ἐρρηγώς).

v. 20. Lit. *I will speak, that there may be relief* or respite *to me*: 1 Sa 16^{23} tant. Cf. the noun Ex 8^{11}. The primary root of רָוַח is *RAG̓*, which we see also in רחב *broad, wide, open* (cf. Ps 4^{2}), from which it has sprung by Internal Triliteralization: cf. Eth. ረሐወ raḥ-awa, *open*, as well as the Ar. رجو, *be wide*, with weakened Gutt. *RAG̓* becomes *RAB* in רבב (cf. Assyr. *rap-âšu*, *widen, broaden, multiply*). It is perhaps ultimately identical with Sum. RA(G), LAG̓, *walk, go*, the idea being freedom of movement, room to go.

v. 21. 𝔐 Lit. *Let me not lift up a man's face!* See 13$^{8. 10}$. *And to no man* (+כל) *will I be indulgent* or *And no man will I address endearingly*, אֲכַנֶּה (v. 22). The word is only found besides in Is 44^{5} 45^{4}, where it is usually explained *to betitle* or *give a title of honour*. But the clue to the meaning of this rare Heb. verb seems to be given by the Assyr. *kunnû* (Pael), 'to treat tenderly', 'to be indulgent to', 'to spare', 'cherish', or the like (Sum. GEME-DUGA 𒊩 𒅗 𒁹 written *woman* + *mouth*; also 𒊩 ZUR *kunnû*, id., written *young one*). Thus Is 44^{5d} might mean *And shall use 'Israel' as a pet-name* or title of affection (but point יְכֻנֶּה Pass. *shall be endearingly called 'Israel'*), and Is 45^{4} *I did lovingly address thee* (אֲכַנְּךָ = Assyr. *ukannika*), or *cherish thee*. 𝔙 Et Deum homini non aequabi<ı>, reading וְאַל לְאָדָם לֹא־אֲדַמֶּה (cf. Is 40^{18} 46^{5}), which is possibly right. But 𝕲 ἀλλ᾽ μὴν οἶκ αἰμσ̇τν οἱ μὴ ἐντραπῶ. *I will not pay regard* or *respect to a mortal* (= אבנה ?).—𝔐's אל should prob. be כל; or if we retain אל we must add כל.

v. 22. *For I know not showing favour*: reading (ל)שאת פנים) after 𝔊 (θαυμάσαι πρόσωπα: cf. 13¹⁰ 22⁸) instead of 𝔐 אבנה, which is hardly grammatical (repeated from v. 21ᵇ). 𝔊𝔗 seem to imply לכנות Infin.

carry me off: ישאני: perhaps a play on the different meanings of נשא with reference to the preceding לשאת (cf. Gn 40¹³·¹⁹). But 𝔊 εἰ δὲ μή, καὶ ἐμὲ σῆτες ἔδονται suggests something very different, viz. ואם־לא יאכלני עש *And if not, may the moth devour me!* (? עש for עש' = עשני): cf. Is 50⁹ 51⁸.

Chapter 33.

v. 1. St. i has four stresses in 𝔐. The introd. ואולם seems superfluous. See 11⁵ 12⁷ 17¹⁰.

v. 2. *palate*: or mouth: cf. 12¹¹ 20¹³. (חך, Syr. ܚܢܟܐ, Ar. ‎ﺣﻨﻚ, may be from √חך *bend, curve*, cf. חנה, ܓܢܐ, c Afform. כ, and thus mean 'curve-like', the *arched* roof of the mouth. √חך is weakened from GAN, GAM, Sum., *bend, bow*.)

v. 3. 𝔐 lit. *The uprightness of my heart* (are?) *my words; And the knowledge of my lips pure*(ly?) *they have spoken*. The verse is metr. faulty and grammat. improb. Instead of 𝔐 ישר we might perhaps point יִשַׁר Juss. of שָׁרָה (37⁵): *Let my heart release words of knowledge* (leg. אִמְרֵי־דַעַת Pr 19²⁷ pro 𝔐 אִמְרֵי וְדַעַת); or else read יָשִׂחַ *museth*. Others may prefer the ἅπ. רָחַשׁ *is astir with* words of knowledge (Ps 45²). All these conjectures, however, leave the stichus with four stresses. Read perhaps יֶשׁ־בְּלִבִּי אִמְרֵי דַעַת *There are in my heart words of knowledge*; or יִשְׂלְבִי אָמַר דַעַת *Indeed my heart speaketh knowledge*.

St. ii. *My lips shall speak* (Pf. Fut. Cert.) *what is purified* of error or falsehood. Cf. Zp 3⁹ and perhaps Ps 2¹² (בר).

v. 4. This verse, which some would reject as a variant of v. 6 or 32⁸, might better follow v. 6; while v. 5 seems a natural sequel to v. 3.

did give (or *giveth*) *me life*. 𝔊 ἡ διδάσκουσά με = תְּחַוְּנִי (cf. 32⁶) pro 𝔐 תְּחַיֵּנִי.

v. 5. St. i is metr. short. Add מִלִּין: see 35⁴. (𝔊 + πρὸς ταῦτα = לָאֵל from v. 6ᵃ? cf. Ju 5²⁹.) So 𝔖.

Marshal them: ערכה, which implies מלין as the Obj. (32¹⁴; cf. 13¹⁸ 23⁴). 𝔊 ὑπόμεινον = עמדה. 𝔊𝔙𝔖 connect לפני with'התיצ; but cf. 23⁴.

v. 6. 'I am *in the proportion of thee* (כפיך) as regards God, i.e. I stand towards God even as thou dost' (OL), does not seem very probable. It is certainly an odd way of saying 'I am a man like thyself'. It is not easy to parallel such a use of כְּפִי. Read perhaps כָּמוֹךָ *like thee* (cf. 𝔖), *et post* לֹא־אֵל pro 𝔐 לָאֵל: *Lo, I, like thee, am but human* (lit. *am not El*, am *no god* or *a non-god*, Dt 32²¹ al.). 𝔙 *Ecce, et me sicut et te fecit Deus* (perhaps כמוך פעל אל; cf. Is 45⁹). 𝔊 paraphr. *From clay hast thou been prepared* (διήρτισαι hîc tant.), *thou as also I; From the same (clay* ⵏᴬ) *we have been prepared* (διηρτίσμεθα).

St. ii. *From clay was I nipt off, I also,* is now generally recognized as a clear allusion to the Babylonian myth which relates how the goddess Aruru (who according to one of the Creation-legends was Merodach's partner in the creation of man) 'washed her hands, *clay nipt off,* threw on the waste, (and made) Engidu, created a warrior' (NE I. ii. 34 sq.). The tîtɩ ɩqtariç (טיט יקטרץ) of that passage throws welcome light on מחמר קרצתי here.

v. 7. A reference to Eyob's own words, 9^{34} 13^{21} 23^2. *my palm*: כפי = ⵏ ἡ χείρ μου (confirmed by 13^{21}, cf. 23^2) pro 𝔐 אכפי ἄπ. [The Syr אכפא is *care, necessity,* and the verb *to be careful, anxious, urgent*; meanings unsuitable here, as affording no parallel to אימתי and not agreeing so well as כפי (= ידי) with the verb תכבד (sic leg. pro יך): 23^2. Ps 32^4.] 𝔗 טוני *my burden*; ⵏ *my anxiety for thee*; both imply 𝔐. 𝔙 *eloquentia mea* = אך פי *surely my mouth* (cf. Ex 4^{11}) = 𝔐 divided!

v. 8. *a sound of words*: 𝔐ⵏ𝔗. But ⵏᴬ + σου· so ⵏ𝔙 *the sound of thy words.* The latter agrees better with st. 1 *thou hast said.* Leg. מליך pro מלך. (In st. i זאת *this* may have fallen out after אך; cf. v. 12. Its restoration would improve the rhythm.)

v. 9. Leg. וּבְלִי pro 𝔐 בְּלִי (1 exc. post י). So 𝔙 *et absque delicto clean*: leg. בַּר parallel to זך as in 11^4 = ⵏ ἄμεμπτος in both locc. In $1^{1.8}$ 9^{20} ἄμεμπτος = תָם *blameless,* of which 𝔐 חַף might be a misreading; but 11^4 seems decisive for בַּר. As to חף, the Mass. note זעירא ח׳ prescribes writing it with a small ח, as though some doubt attached to the letter, or as if it had been supplied by conjecture. The Syr. חָפָּא is *soap, soaping, shampooing*; but there is really no evidence for the ἄπ. חַף *clean* in Heb. usage, and the word is almost certainly corrupt. *I have no guilt*: so 𝔐, but 𝔙 *et non est iniquitas in me* (בי pro 𝔐 לי) is probably right.

v. 10. *pretexts*; lit. *occasions,* i.e. *grounds of quarrel,* reading תֹּאֲנוֹת (Ju 14^4; cf. the vb. Hithp. 2 K 5^7) pro 𝔐 תְּנוּאוֹת *frustrations* (cf. Nu 14^{34}). ⵏ תשׁאות (μέμψιν 39^7, cf. 36^{29}) *shoutings.*—Cf. 10^{13-17} and for st. ii see 13^{24b}. In אויב *foe* we may recognize an allusive play on the name איוב.

v. 11. A virtual quotation of $13^{27a.b}$. Point יָשֵׂם (יָשִׂים); 𝔐 יָשֵׂם after 13^{27}. Perhaps עַל should be inserted before כֹּל; cf. 14^{16}. [The suggested וְהוּא *But He* pro הן *Lo* ad init. (enclitic) spoils the metre.]

v. 12. 𝔐 הן־זאת לא־צדקת אענך *Lo, (in) this thou art not right* (or *hast not spoken the truth*: Arab. use?): *I will answer thee: For* (or *That*) *Eloah is greater* (?) *than man.* Cf. RV and RV marg. The first stichus is disjointed and unnatural, whichever way we take it, and the use of ירבה in st. ii is unique. ⵏ Πῶς γὰρ λέγεις Δίκαιός εἰμι καὶ οὐκ ἐπακήκοέν μου, Αἰώνιος γάρ ἐστιν ὁ ἐπάνω βροτῶν = (9· 14) תֹּאמַר צִדֶקְתִּי אַךְ (היך)

צָעַקְתִּי וְלֹא אֶעֱנֶה, which suggests צעקתי pro צדקתי here. But this anticipates the next verse. Cf. also 30²⁰. Nothing can be made of 𝔊's st. ii. Did 𝔊 think of עֵתִּיק יוֹמִין (Dan 7⁹) and suppose יְרָבֶּה = רַב יָמִים? The conjecture מַעֲלִים *hideth* (42³) pro 𝔐 ירבה, on the ground of 𝔊 (αἰώνιος = מעולם), is very improbable. Perhaps the anomalous ירבה is a distortion of חֲיָרִיב, and we may read הֲיָרִיב אֱלוֹהַּ עִם־אֱנוֹשׁ *Will Eloah contend with a mortal?* Eyob had often desired that God would meet him fairly, and argue out his case with him; neither overawing him with His Majesty, nor confounding him with His Terrors. Cf. 9³,¹⁴⁻²¹ 10² 13³,¹⁹ 23³⁻⁷; 40²⁻⁹. But another possibility is אֵיךְ תֹּאמַר צָדַקְתִּי אָנֹכִי הֲיָרִיב אֱנוֹשׁ עִם־אֱלוֹהַּ *How couldst thou say, 'I* (emph.) *am righteous'? Should a mortal contend with Eloah?* (אֲעָנֶךָּ pro אנכי.)

v. 13. Lit. *Why toward* (= against) *Him hast thou contended* (or *made complaint*), *For that all thy* (leg. c 𝔙 דְּבָרֶיךָ pro 𝔐 דְּבָרָיו—) *words He would not answer?* (= That He would not answer any of thy protests or appeals?). For רִיב אֶל cf. Je 2²⁹,³³ 12¹. (We might also read אִתּוֹ *with Him,* Is 45¹.) 𝔙 Adversus eum contendis, | Quod non ad omnia verba responderit *tibi*. (𝔐 דְּבָרָיו his *words* refers to אֱנוֹשׁ, *v.* 12ᵇ.) The root רִיב *strive, quarrel, contend* (esp. at law), is prob. cogn. with רהב, and the orig. idea may be that of *clamour,* noisy contention (cf. the Syr. use). Both may be Internal Triliteralizations of the same primitive root (cf. perhaps Sum. RI, *blow, rage,* of the wind = RIG, RIB?; or R-B = L-B in Assyr. *labâbu,* 'rage'). 𝔊 λέγεις δέ (= וַתֹּאמֶר explanatory add.) Διὰ τί τῆς δίκης μου οὐκ ἐπακήκοέν μου (sic 𝔊ᴮ, om. AC recte) πᾶν ῥῆμα = בכל דבר לא יענה (13ᵉ) מְדוּעַ רִיבוֹתִי (misreading of 𝔐).

v. 14. God, on the contrary, does speak to man (1) in dreams, vv. 15-18, and (2) in the visitations of sickness, vv. 19-28.

לֹא יְשׁוּרֶנָּה cannot mean '*though man regardeth it not*' (RV). The Subj. of the vb. must be אֵל as in st. i: so the Verss. But the vb. itself is corrupt. Read perhaps יְשַׁנֶּה *he changes it* (i.e. what He says):

    For at one time (or *once*) *El speaketh,*
    And at a second He changeth it not. (Cf. Ps 89³⁵,³⁶.)

בְּאַחַת scil. פַּעַם; בִּשְׁתַּיִם scil. פְּעָמִים. The purpose and purport of the Divine word is always the same. Or we may read לֹא יִשְׁנֶה *he repeats not,* i.e. does it not again, or speaks not a second time: cf. 29²² 40⁵:

    For, once for all, El speaketh,
    And doth it not again.

Cf. 𝔙: Semel loquitur Deus, et secundo id ipsum non repetit. 𝔊 לֹא מוֹסִיף *he addeth not* (cf. 𝔙 29²² 39³⁵ᵇ = 𝔐 40⁵). Considering, however, that בַּחֲלוֹם *In a dream* immediately follows, defining the mode or method of God's speaking (cf. also v. 19 במבאוב), it will prob. be best to translate the verse thus:

> For in (or *with*) *one thing speaketh El,*
> *And in two* (or *a second*) *He changeth not.*

Cf. Ma 3⁶. The other possible emendation לא ישיבנה (Nu 23²⁰ Am 1³) *He doth not reverse it* (viz. His intention) certainly accounts more easily for 𝔐's לא ישורנה *He seeth it not*

v. 15. Cf. 4¹³. 'Elihu' accepts Eliphaz's source of Divine intimations. Leg. בחזיון (+ב) c 6 codd. 𝔊𝔙𝔖. 𝔐 wrongly turns the distich into a tristich by interpolating 4¹³ᵇ (*When sound sleep falleth on men*). *slumbers*: Pr 6⁴·¹⁰ Ps 132⁴ †. (Instead of בחזיון 𝔊 ἐν μελέτῃ = בהגיון *in meditation,* Ps 19¹⁵ La 3⁶²; a respectable variant.)

v. 16. *bareth* or *uncovereth men's ear*: 𝔊 men's *intelligence* or inward perception (νοῦν). Cf. Assyr. *uznu, uzunu,* ear, attention, intelligence. For the Heb. phrase see 36¹⁰ 1 Sa 9¹⁵ 20².

St. ii. 𝔐 ובמסרם יחתם, which is metr. defective, is supposed to mean *And on their discipline setteth seal.* But חָתַם בְּ is to seal *with* (e.g. a ring). The other would be חָתַם בְּעַד (9⁷ and the corrupt 37⁷ q. v.). 𝔊 ἐν εἴδεσιν φόβου τοιούτοις αὐτοὺς ἐξεφόβησεν = ובמראה מו(ו)ראים (אימים) יחתם *And with an appearance of terrors affrighteth them.* 𝔖 *And in their rebellion humbleth them.* (𝔊 ובמראי מראים fort. dittogr.) This, however, is not quite satisfactory. ובמסר אלהים יכ(ו)חם *And with Elohim's monition He warneth them* is perhaps preferable: cf. 5¹⁷ 13¹⁰ 36¹⁰ Pr 3¹¹·¹². Or read: ובמראה אלהים יחתם *And with divine apparition alarmeth them.*

v. 17. 𝔐 להסיר אדם מעשה is quite impossible, unless we point מַעֲשֹה *from doing.* The most natural emendation is מִמַּעֲשֵׂהוּ *from his doing(s).* מ might easily have fallen out between the two מ's, and ו before the following ו. So 𝔊 מעבדוהי *from his works*; cf. 𝔙 Ut avertat hominem *ab his quae facit.* But 𝔊 has the more definite ἀπὸ ἀδικίας = מֵעַוְלָה 11¹⁴ 15¹⁶ (cf. 34²² ἀδικίαν = עול, 36³³ ἀδικίας = 𝔐 עלה) or possibly מֵאָוֶן *from wickedness* (ἐξ ἀδικίας 36¹⁰). מֵעשֶׁק *from oppression* is less likely. This noun does not occur elsewhere in Job, although we have the verb עָשַׁק = ἀδικεῖν once (10³; 40²³ is corrupt).

St. ii must continue the statement of God's purpose. But to '*hide* pride from [a] man' (RV) is altogether improb. 𝔙 'to *free* (or *deliver*) him from pride' (et liberet eum de superbia) is much more natural (though not as a translation of 𝔐). Even if גֵוָה *pride* (22²⁹ Je 13¹⁷ Dan 4³⁴), an apparent Aramaism, be right—and parallelism requires some kind of sin—it is still difficult to guess what vb. has been supplanted by יכסה. 𝔊 τὸ δὲ σῶμα αὐτοῦ ἀπὸ πτώματος ἐρρύσατο = וגויתו מסיר יפדה *And his body* (perhaps גֵוָה cf. Ne 9²⁶) *from disaster* (31²⁹) *to ransom* (פדה 5²⁰ 6²³ ῥύομαι) or ‹ ? › (יצה Ps 144· Aram.). 𝔖 *A[nd ? h]' a₁ f [i]' man*

He covereth. As פֶּן *turn out or away* is the parallel to הָסִיר in Zp 3¹⁶, it may perhaps be so here also. (Cf. Gn 24³¹ Le 14³⁶ *clear out or up, empty* a house, Is 57¹⁴ *clear* the way of obstacles.)

v. 18. *He holdeth back*: the verb seems to be co-ordinate with יגלה *v.* 16 > with יכסה *v.* 17. Perhaps we should read לחשך *To hold back*; cf. להסיר *v.* 17. But 𝔊 ἐφείσατο δὲ = (וְ)יחשך.

into She'ol: 𝔐 בשלח (but 36¹² בְּשֶׁלַח) *by a missile* is extremely improb. The usual parallel to שחת *the Pit* is שאול *Hades* (cf. 17¹³,¹⁴ Ps 16¹⁰ 49¹⁶); and the idea that עבר בש׳ might mean *rush upon missiles* [and perish] (OL 1019 col. 2) is wholly incredible. Elihu may be thought laboured and longwinded and deficient in originality; but his defects are mostly to be ascribed to corruptions of his text rather than to ignorance of Hebrew and the rules of Hebrew verse. For עבר *to pass away, vanish* cf. 30¹⁵ 34²⁰. 𝔊 om. vb. *And his life from* אבדנא = Abaddon, syn. of She'ol, 26⁶ al.

v. 19. A second mode of Divine warning. Cf. 5¹⁷,¹⁸. 𝔐 וְהוּכַח (Hoph. here only) can hardly be right. 𝔊 πάλιν δὲ ἤλεγξεν αὐτὸν ἐπὶ (𝔊ᴬᴺ ἐν rectè) μαλακίᾳ ἐπὶ κοίτης = (v. 15) וַיּוֹכִיחֵנוּ בְּמַכְאוֹב עַל־מִשְׁכָּב (cf. 13³⁰ 22⁴) or perhaps, prefixing או *or*, או הוֹכִיחוֹ (cf. 2 Sa·7¹⁴) or או הוֹכֵחַ וגו׳ (abs.) *Or He chideth* (or *correcteth*). 𝔙 Increpat quoque per dolorem in lectulo.

St. ii. *strife*: רִיב. Some codd. 𝔊𝔖𝔙 רֹב *multitude*: see 4¹⁴ (= *all his bones*). דּוּב (ἅπ.) *pining* through disease (cf. Le 26¹⁶) may be suggested. *The strife* (or *pining?*) *of his bones is perpetual* would be a good description of rheumatic pains. But אֵיתָן (= איתן 12¹⁹) seems doubtful. A verb was to be expected: cf. 𝔙 Et omnia ossa eius *marcescere facit*; 𝔊 *And the multitude of his bones are benumbed* (ἐνάρκησεν). Did 𝔊 think of Syr. ܚܢܢ (חנן) *to be or become numb, rigid?* *And all his bones He stiffeneth* (?? יָתֵן) would not be incongruous with st. i.

v. 20. *his soul*: lit. *his life* (חיתו *v.* 18) = his appetite (38³⁹), for which we have the syn. *his soul* (נפשו) in st. ii.

loatheth: 𝔐 וְחָמְתוּ וגו׳ app. *So that his life makes nauseous to him bread* (וְהֶם c dupl. accus.). We must read either וְהֵמַת (an archaism like אָזְלַת Dt 32³⁶) or וְהָמְסָה *maketh stinking or foul*; an Aramaism (cf. 𝔗 38¹⁴ וְחָיִם *soiled*, of a garment; Syr. ܦܣܝ *to be greasy, dirty, rank or stinking*; ܦܣܐ *stinking*, &c. Arab. زَهِمَ *stink*, of flesh, زَهِم *fat*, زُهَم *stench*, &c.).¹ 𝔊 *And all food of corn he cannot receive*; where βρωτὸν is perhaps an error for βρῶμον (βρόμον), *stink*: cf. 6⁷ᵇ. σῖτον = לָחֶם as in 6⁷ 30⁴. Possibly, however, 𝔊 represents וְהָמַם כָּל־מִחְיַת לָחֶם. Cf. Ps 107¹⁸. *dainty fare*: מַאֲכַל תַּאֲוָה *food of desire.* 𝔊 βρῶσιν ἐπιθυμήσει, pointing מַאֲכַל תַּאֲוֶה.

v. 21. 𝔐 corrupt in both stichi. Neither *His flesh is consumed away*,

---

¹ With this root cf. Sumerian SIM, Chinese -ing, *scent, smell.*

that it cannot be seen (ראי = *seeing*), nor *His flesh is*, &c., without (healthy? l) appearance ('ר = appearance 1 Sa 16¹²), as OL takes it, is at all prob. מראי (or the word it conceals) should rather express the cause of the wasting (e.g. מרעב *from famine* or want of food, cf. the last verse and Gn 41³⁰, or מדוי *from sickness* Ps 41⁴ see note on 6⁷ and cf. Le 26¹⁶, or as others suggest מרוי or מרזון *from leanness or emaciation*, Is 10¹⁶ 17⁴ Ps 106¹⁵?). But the stichus may be a reminiscence of Pr 5¹¹ᵇ, and we may read ושארו instead of מראי *His fleshly tissue wasteth* (ו exc. p. 1; W = ײַ). Cf. also Ps 73²⁶ כָּלָה שְׁאֵרִי וּלְבָבִי.

The לא ראו of st. ii looks like a variant or marg. gloss on מראי, as if it meant (so that) *they were not seen*. But the Pu. of ראה is unique (why not the usual Ni. נראו?). The Ketîb שפי *bareness* (?), *a bare height*, is dub. in Nu 23³ and occurs nowhere else (plur. שפיים Is 41¹⁸ + seven times). The Qerî שֻׁפּוּ should mean *are broken* or *crushed* (ע שִׁפְיָן: cf. Ps 51¹⁰,¹⁹); but this does not suit here. The bones may also be spoken of as *dried up* (Ez 37¹¹ יבשו cf. Pr 17²²) or *watered* (cf. 21²⁴ Pr 3⁸). We therefore suggest ושפו pro ויבשו and either בלא־רוי (=בלא־רוי, cf. Ps 23² נאות = נוֹה) *without moisture* or רוו? ויריון? (?ולאירוון) *and are not watered* pro לא ראו. See also note on ברי 37¹¹. כלה and יבש are ‖ Is 15⁶. 𝔙 Tabescet caro eius (om. מראי) et ossa, quae tecta fuerant, nudabuntur (= Qerî: *and bared are his bones which were not seen*). 𝔊 *Until his flesh have rotted* (מרקב pro מראי?) ‖ *And he show his bones empty* (!).

v. 22. Verses 20, 22 look like an expansion of Ps 107¹⁸. St. ii is metr. short and, moreover, הַמְמִתִים *the slayers* (supposed to mean Angels of Death) is a strange parallel to השחת *the Pit* of Hades (v. 18), for which 𝔊 gives εἰς θάνατον while rendering למתים ἐν ᾅδῃ = (ב)שאול *in She'ol* (the usual ‖ to שחת Ps 16¹⁰ al.). Read either לבית (ה)מתים *to the House of the Dead* (cf. 17¹³ 30²³) or למקום מתים *to the Place of the Dead* (cf. note on 34²⁶, Ec 3²⁰). 𝔊 לָמוּת *to Death* (cf. 28²²·38¹¹). (The references Ex 12²³ 2 Sa 24¹⁶ Ps 78⁴⁹ all relate to the *coming or sending* of Destroyers to men; here, on the contrary, the man's life 'draws nigh' and comes to the verge of the grave.)

v. 23. *beside him*: or *over him*, or perhaps *on his behalf*: lit. *upon him* (עליו). *an Angel*: or *Messenger* (the proper meaning of the word: the √לאך is internally triliteralized from לך which we see in ה־ל־ך *to go*, perhaps weakened in ש־ל־ח *send*, i.e. *cause to go*: cf. Sum. LAG *go*, Caus. *lead, bring, drive*, RA-G? *alíku*). A prophetic or priestly messenger might be intended (cf. Is 42¹⁹ Ma 2⁷). The מֵלִיץ *Interpreter* (Gn 42²³) or Envoy, Ambassador (2 C 32³¹; cf. 2 K 20¹² סְפָרִים *letters*, סֹפְרִים? *scribes*), is a person qualified to explain the terms of one language in those of another, and so to serve as a medium of communication between people of alien speech. Here as in Is 43⁻ may signify the priest (Ma 2⁷ ...

the Divine meaning of events ... not necessarily an 'Angel'. [The primary sense was perhaps simply *speaker*. The Canaanite לִיץ√ may be akin to לְעוֹ Ps 114¹, and even to לָשׁוֹן the *tongue*, as the organ of speech: cf. Sum. LI, *cry aloud, sing*, I-LU, id., *wail* (so the Assyr. *turgumannu*, 'dragoman', *interpreter*, from *ragâmu, cry out, lament*, &c.); LI-LIZ (= LIZ-LIZ), also read LI-LESH, *guitar-playing* (= Ch. *li*).] *one out of* (= among) *a thousand*. The phrase implies the rarity of the interpreter's gifts. Hardly one man in a thousand could play the part. Cf. Ec 7²⁸ אָדָם אֶחָד מֵאֶלֶף מָצָאתִי *One man in a thousand have I found*; Ct 5¹⁰ דָּגוּל מֵרְבָבָה *gazed at among a myriad*. (Not *one of the thousand*; implying that there were many capable of such a service. Spiritual gifts are rare. Ec l.c. suggests the rendering *One Interpreter among a thousand*, in spite of the Accents. אֶחָד would be superfluous, if it were not emphatic.) 𝔙 thinks of an Angel of Intercession, and joins מֵלִיץ with מַלְאָךְ, to the detriment of the metre: Si fuerit pro eo angelus *loquens*, unus de millibus. 𝔊 *If there be a thousand death-bringing Angels, not one of them shall wound him. If he have purposed in his heart to return to the Lord* (22²⁸ Ma 3⁷), *And announce to a man his own blame, And show his folly* (ἄνοιαν = אִוֶּלֶת Pr 22¹⁵; but 𝔊ˢᵐᵃ ἀνομίαν = אָוֶן, עָוֹן, פֶּשַׁע, רִשְׁעָה(?)): a notable expansion of the verse, app. reading stt. i, ii, somewhat thus: אִם־יֵשׁ (עָלָיו) מַלְאָכִים מְמִתִים | לֹא־יִן(פְּ)צַ(ע) אֶחָד מִנִּי־אָלֶף. The θανατηφόροι = מְמִתִים obviously belongs to v. 22 ad fin. (ubi 𝔙 *mortiferis*). 𝔊's next line is app. a gloss (אִם־יֹאמַר בְּלִבּוֹ אָשׁוּב אֶל־אֵל or the like), while the next corresponds to 𝔐's st. iii לְהַגִּיד לְאָדָם יָשְׁרוֹ. For לחג' 𝔊 (ἀναγγείλῃ δὲ) יַגִּיד *And he declare* (or *explain*) to the man; and instead of the dubious ישרו *his uprightness* (יֹשֶׁר semper sine Suff. Pr 14² leg. יָשָׁר) 𝔊 τὴν ἑαυτοῦ μέμψιν (v. 10 39⁷ tant.) suggests פִּשְׁעוֹ *his transgression* (v. 9 34⁶·³⁷ 7²¹ al. Mi 3⁸). The stichus seems, indeed, to be a reminiscence of Mi 3⁸ (לְהַגִּיד לְיַעֲקֹב פִּשְׁעוֹ *To declare to Jacob his transgression*); an impression confirmed by the addition in 𝔊 τὴν δὲ ἄνοιαν (ἀνομίαν?) αὐτοῦ δείξῃ, which recalls the closing stichus of Mi l.c. וּלְיִשְׂרָאֵל חַטָּאתוֹ *And to Israel his sin*), and suitably converts 𝔐's tristich into a quatrain. A line like וְרִשְׁעָתוֹ יְחַוֵּנּוּ *And to make known to him his sin* may have fallen out between ישרו and ויחננו, owing to the resemblance of letters.

v. 24. Unmetrical and corrupt. By inserting the Subj. אֱלוֹהַּ between the two verbs in st. i, and restoring נַפְשׁוֹ (Ex 30¹² Pr 13⁸) or לְנַפְשׁוֹ (Nu 35¹¹ Pr 21¹⁸) after כֹּפֶר, as necessary to sense as well as to metre (exc. ante רטפש), we get a passable tristich:

      And Eloah be gracious to him and say,
      '*Redeem him from descending to the Pit;*
      I have found a ransom for his life!'

read to him: פְּדָהוּ pro 𝔐 פְּדָעֵהוּ (some codd. פְּרָעֵהוּ which is no improvement). Cf. v. 28 and Ho 13¹⁴ *Out of the hand of She'ol will I redeem them; From Death will I ransom them.* Cf. also Is 35¹⁰ 43³ Je 31¹¹; Ps 49⁸ ¹⁶ and chaps. 5²⁰ 6²³. Since it is always God who delivers from Death (to whom can כְּדֵהוּ *Redeem* thou *him* refer?), we should prob. restore אֶפְדֵּהוּ *I will redeem him.* (It is possible that 𝔊 τὴν δὲ ἄνοιαν αὐτοῦ δείξῃ is not an addition but represents another reading of ויחננו ויאמר, e.g. חָטָא יֹאמַר or וְיַחֲנֵנוּ אִוַּלְתּוֹ.)

𝔊 ἀνθέξεται τοῦ μὴ πεσεῖν εἰς θάνατον = (v. 22) יִפְדֵּהוּ מֵרֶדֶת שַׁחַת. Instead of כפר מצאתי 𝔊 gives a complete distich: ἀνανεώσει δὲ αὐτοῦ τὸ σῶμα ὥσπερ ἀλοιφὴν ἐπὶ τοίχου | τὰ δὲ ὀστᾶ αὐτοῦ ἐμπλήσει μυελοῦ =

ויחדש בשׂרו כשׂיח בקיר
ועצמתיו יסלא (ישבע מ)מח

Cf. Ez 13¹²⁻¹⁵ and for the second line 9¹⁸ 19²² 21²⁴. Possibly ויחדש שׂארו in the first line is a perversion of ויחננו ויאמר, and עצמתיו—בקר מצאתי of כפר; but the whole distich looks like an alternative or doublet of v. 25. It seems probable that 𝔐's third stichus ([נפשו] מצאתי כפר) is a marg. gloss: cf. v. 28.

v. 25 The ἅπ. Quadrilit. רֻטֲפַשׁ, an anomalous form which can hardly be right, may have grown out of an exaggerated י mistaken for ר (as in some other instances), the original word being יטפש, or may be due to dittogr. of the preceding ר, in which case the word might have been the Pf. טפש. 𝔊 *And he will soften* (or *make plump*: ἀπαλυνεῖ: cf. 2 K 22¹⁶ רַךְ = ἡπαλύνθη) *his flesh like an infant's* (reading בַּנַּעַר pro מִנֹּעַר) | *And will restore him when become a man among men* (reading יָשִׁיב pro יָשׁוּב); which is mainly a paraphrase of 𝔐. The Syr. word טַרְפַּשְׁתָא *lean flesh* suggests no suitable sense for רֻטֲפַשׁ (*His flesh is* become thinner *than that of childhood*: but children are normally plump and fat). The Aram. טפשׁ *to be fat* (cf. 𝔗 Is 6¹⁰ 'ט = השמן) favours טָפַשׁ or יִטְפַּשׁ: cf. Ps 119⁷⁰ טָפַשׁ בַּחֵלֶב לִבָּם (Cf. also Assyr. *akala tapšāku,* 'with food I am waxed fat', *tupuš ašnan,* 'fatness of wheat', as an offering, cf. Dt 32¹⁴.)

Does the verse continue the Divine utterance (cf. 𝔙 Consumpta est caro eius a suppliciis; Revertatur ad dies adolescentiae suae! 𝔗 אִתְחַלָּשׁ *His flesh is* weakened ... *Let him return,* &c.); or does it express its immediate consequence? In the one case, we must render: *Let his flesh wax fatter,* &c. (or *His flesh shall wax,* &c.; cf. 𝔖 *Let his flesh* be changed *like as it was in his childhood*); in the other, *His flesh waxeth* (or *will wax*) *fatter,* &c., *He returneth* (or *will return*: 𝔐 יָשׁוּב. *Let him return* would require יָשֹׁב, not יָשׁוּב as Kittel suggests), &c.

v. 26. An וְיֶעְתַּר pro 𝔐 יֶעְתָּר? cf. vbb. seqq. *with joy*: תרועה *joyful shouting* 8²¹. So 𝔊ᴬᶿ ἐν ἀλαλαγμῷ An accompaniment of psalmody in public worship (Pss 27 33 al.) ... *H. Fa.: ...ev.\i is the Sanctuary* for worship: cf. Gn 33¹⁰ (joined with רָצָה as here) Ps 42³ Is 1¹² (pointing לִרְאוֹת). 𝕲 app. misread ויבא pro וירא and בתורה or בתודה pro בתרועה (cf. 8²¹ 22²²).

St. iii may be an addition. It perhaps means: *And he restoreth to the man his wellbeing* (cf. Pr 8¹⁸) > *his righteousness*: cf. 42¹⁰ᶠᶠ. Instead of וישב we might perhaps read וישלם (𝕲 ἀποδώσει, cf. 22²⁷ 34¹¹; yet cf. also 39¹²): *He recompenseth to the man his righteousness* (i.e. his penitence regarded as such): but hardly ויספר or ובשר (!).

v. 27. 'The restored sinner is here represented as giving public expression to his gratitude in a short psalm of confession and thanksgiving' (Driver). *He singeth unto* (Pr 25²⁰) *men*: pointing יָשֵׁר (?) יָשֵׁר or יָשִׁיר pro 𝔐 יָשֹׁר *he looketh* (= יָשׁוּר) 𝔙 *Respiciet* homines. 𝕾𝕿 think of יָשָׁר *straight*. (שִׁיר *to sing* may be compared with Sum. SIR, SUR, *zamâru*.) 𝕲's paraphrase εἶτα τότε ἀπομέμψεται ἄνθρωπος αὐτὸς ἑαυτῷ λέγων may indicate the same root יָשַׁר (reading perhaps יָשֵׁר עליו אנשים) or, pointing יְיָשֵׁר, יָסַר = יָשַׁר *to correct, admonish*: cf. 𝕲 v. 23ᶜ τὴν ἑαυτοῦ μέμψιν, 𝔐 יָשְׁרוֹ. *I sinned*: חטאתי. 𝕲 οἷα συνετέλουν; = מה־עשיתי. 𝕲 continues: καὶ οὐκ ἄξια ἤτασέν με ὧν ἥμαρτον = וַאֲשֶׁר הֶעֱוֵיתִי לֹא־שָׁוָה לִי. Cf. 11⁶. 𝔐's וְיָשֹׁר (𝕲 ואשר) looks like dittogr. of ישר ad init. vers., and ויש׳ העויתי is a dub. phrase, for which we might substitute וְדַרְכֵי הֶעֱוֵיתִי *and my way I made crooked*, after Je 3²¹ La 3⁹. St. ii לֹא־שָׁוָה לִי *He was not like* (or *equal*: Is 40²⁵ Pr 26⁴) *to me* cannot be right. It offends both metre and sense. Read perhaps וְלֹא־שִׁלַּם פָּעֳלִי לִי *And He requited not my work to me* (cf. 34¹¹ 36⁹), or וּכְעֲוֹנֹתַי לֹא־עָשָׂה לִי (Ps 103¹⁰) *And acc. to my sins He did not unto me*. If שָׁוָה לְ could mean *to do equal things to, deal equally or in like manner with* a person, the reading וְאֵלֶּה לֹא־שָׁוָה לִי might be adopted as involving the least change in the traditional text. (שׁוה *lie flat, be level, equal*, may be cogn. c נוח *lie down*, since primitive N may become Š both in Sumerian and Semitic.)

v. 28. Cf. v. 18. 𝔐 *He redeemed my soul from* passing into the *Pit* overweights st. i. Read מִנִּי־שָׁחַת (v. 18) and om. מֵעֲבֹר. 𝕲 σῶσον = פָּדָה ut 𝔐 v. 24. So 𝕾𝕿. *my soul ... my life*: so rightly Ketîb 𝕲𝕾; *his soul*, &c., Qerî 𝕿𝕍.

v. 29. *Twice, yea thrice*: i.e. two or three times, more than once. Lit. *two beats, three* (beats: subaud. פְּעָמִים). 𝕲 ὁδοὺς τρεῖς, *three ways*: cf. v. 14. 𝕲 pointed פְּעָמִים שׁ׳ (*three footsteps*) instead of שׁ׳ פַּעֲמָיִם (the Dual).

v. 30. God's purpose in warning the sinner by dreams or sickness. Cf. 𝕍 Ut revocet animas eorum a corruptione, et illuminet luce viventium. (𝕲 ἀλλ᾽ v. καὶ ἐρύσατο κτλ., 𝕲 מהסך Ptcp. But 𝕿 ut 𝔐𝕍 rectè). St. ii is dub. The Niph. Infin. לֵאוֹר (ἀπ. = להאור) would seem to require a following לוֹ to give it a personal reference (cf. 2 Sa 2⁰¹: Ps 76⁶ is corrupt). Read either לְרַאֹתוֹ (= לְהַרְאֹתוֹ) Hi. Inf.) *to let him look* (on the light of life), cf. v. 28ᵇ; or לְהָאִיר ('הח אור בו =) לָאִיר *to let shine on him the light*, &c. (cf. Ps 119¹³³ for the Construction). 𝔊 = :לְהוֹר' בְּאוֹר חַיָּי (ἵνα ἡ ζωή μου ἐν φωτὶ αἰνῇ αὐτόν); wrongly making vv. 29, 30, the close of the penitent's psalm. Cf. Is 38¹⁹ חי חי הוא יודך. It has been suggested that we should read בארץ החיים *in the land of the living* > באור הח' *on the light of life*. For the former phrase see 28¹³ Is 38¹¹ (53⁸) Ps 27¹³ 116⁹ al. The other does not seem to be found elsewhere except in Ps 56¹⁴ and Joh 8¹². Light and Life, however, are connected together in 3¹⁶ ²⁰ Ps 36¹⁰, and אור החיים suits the present context better (unless we choose to substitute ארח הח' *To show him* the way *of life*: cf. Ps 16¹¹). 𝔊 may be right with its לראות באור הח'= למחוא נוהרא דחיא *To behold the light of life*. We need not resent an original phrase in Elihu, even if it should clash with a theory.

Verses 31–33, which have somewhat the effect of an anticlimax here, might well be transposed to precede 34¹⁸, where the change to the 2nd Pers. Sing. seems to require some such introduction.

v. 31. 𝔊's καὶ ἐγώ εἰμι λαλήσω, which 𝔊ᴬ corrects with ἵνα λαλ., is a slip due to mechanical word-for-word translation.

v. 32. Lit. *If there be words*. The *be* (יֵשׁ) is emphatic, as always: If you really have anything to say in reply.

v. 33. *teach*: Pi. of אלף *learn* Pr 22²⁵: 15⁵ 35¹¹ (all). Aram. = Heb. למד. The Bilit. Root is *LAP, LAB*, which we see in Assyr. *labû*, 'surround', e.g. with walls, Perm. *lâbi, lâpi*, Pi. *lubbû*, 'enclose', 'bind', *ulâpu*, 'bond', 'league', *lapâtu, lupputu*, 'handle', 'touch', with the hand (cf. also note on 6¹⁸), cognate with *LAM* in *lamû*, 'surround', לָוָה אלם 'bind', לְאֹם 'tribe', 'people', Assyr. *limu = kimtu*, 'family', cf. Ar. غَيَّ la'ama, 'bind up' a wound or rupture, Sum. LIM, 'a thousand', as a number of things *bound together*, cf. Heb. אֶלֶף 'thousand', 'a family', Sum. LAB, 'mighty', Aram. אַלִּים 'be strong', well-knit or bound together, and (since L and D interchange) with Sum. DAB, *lamû*, 'surround', 'seize', 'grasp', 'hold', *sandqu, tamâḫu*, DIB, 'take', 'grasp', 'catch', 'bind', *çabâtu, aḫâzu, tamâḫu, kamû*, &c., DUB, 'surround', *lamû, saḫâru*, DIM, 'to bind', 'fasten', *sandqu (lâ sanqu*, 'unbound', i.e. rebellious, unsubmissive), 'a rope', *riksu*. The character ⌐▯⌐ LU, DIB, the Determinative of oxen and sheep, orig. a picture of a fold or enclosure with a rod or crook inside it, suggests the idea of *enclosed* (i.e. stalled or folded) animals, as opposed to wild ones roaming at large. The primary meaning of *alpu*, אֶלֶף 'ox', may have been the *bound* (i.e. tamed and submissive to the yoke); cf. אַלּוּף *tame and gentle*: that of אלף *to learn*. Pi. *to teach*, may have been *to .... , grasp ... in* ideas, and ? ...... & , respectively (cf. Assyr. *ḫ.zu, aḫâzu*, 'to learn', Shaph. *šuḫuzu*, 'to teach', and קַח learning, teaching, from לָקַח to take).

Chapter 34. The heading *And Elihu answered and said*, repeated chap. 35¹, seems perfectly irrelevant in both instances, as none of his hearers has made any reply to what he has said hitherto. The formula of 36¹ *And Elihu* added *and said* (i.e. said further) would be more suitable; but both may be due to some later editor who thought it desirable to break up Elihu's lengthy address into sections, with formal headings like those of the original poem.

v. 2. Elihu appeals to the wise in general, not to the three Friends of Eyob, who (in his opinion) had so signally fallen short of Wisdom (cf. *vv.* 10, 34: see also 35⁴).

v. 3. Quotation of 12¹¹ (from marg.?). *tasteth food*: so 𝔊𝔙𝔖. 𝔐 *tasteth to eat* (לֶאֱכֹל) has prob. grown out of אכל לו יט' *tasteth* for itself *food*: see 12¹¹. 𝔊𝔙𝔖 naturally omit the *Dat. Commodi*. (This is more probable than that they read לֶאֱכֹל, since טעם does not occur c לְ of Direct Obj.)

v. 5. A reference to Eyob's words 9²⁰·²¹ 27².

v. 6. St. i has only two metr. stresses, and מִשְׁפָּטִי looks like dittogr. of v. 5 ad fin. The line cannot mean *Notwithstanding my right I am accounted a liar* (RV; pointing אֲכַזֵּב?); אַכְזָב is *I lie*, 6²⁸ Pr 14⁶. 𝔐 is tolerant of no meaning but *Against my right I lie* (or Interrog. *shall I lie?* cf. AV). We might read עָלַי שֹׁפְטִי יְכַזֵּב *Against me my Judge lieth*; i.e. by treating him as guilty when he was innocent (cf. 9²⁸⁻³¹). For יב' cf. 𝔊 ἐψεύσατο; for עָלַי see 𝔖; for שֹׁפְטִי 23⁷. Possible also seems אַכְזָר *cruel*: see 30²¹ 41²: but the former suggestion yields a better parallel to st. ii *Deadly is my wound, without fault* (of mine). Perhaps עָלַי מַכָּאֲבִי יכוב *Against me* my pain *lieth*: cf. 33¹⁹ Je 30¹⁶ (אָנוּשׁ מַכְאֹבֶךָ). His sufferings falsely suggested that he must have been a great sinner.

St. ii. אָנוּשׁ *sore, incurable*, is a natural epithet of wounds and pain (Je 15¹⁸ al.); but 𝔐 חִצִּי *my arrow* can hardly be a fig. equivalent of *my wound*, and if we read חִצוֹ *His arrow* (cf. 6⁴) the epithet becomes suspicious. Read therefore מַחֲצִי (Is 30²⁶) or פִּצְעִי (9¹⁷ Gn 4²³); cf. the verb מחץ 5¹⁸ 26¹².

v. 7. St. i is metr. short and begins with unusual abruptness. Restore וְאוּלָם *But* (cf. 33¹); of which וארח (v. 8) may perhaps be a distortion. *Howbeit, what man is like Eyob?* Or read מִי־הוּא כ' *Who then is a man*, &c. (4⁷ 13¹⁹ al.). In st. ii אשר Relat. may have fallen out before ישתה *drinketh in*; but 15¹⁶ᵇ (of which the stichus is obviously an echo) suggests אִישׁ שֹׁתֶה *One that drinketh* (i.e. revelleth in) לַעֲג (*stammering, jabbering*, of a foreign tongue; then *mockery*; and in the sphere of religion *blasphemy*: akin to לעו and לִיץ Pr 1¹).

v. 8. St. i is metr. too long. Omit the strange אָרַח which is found nowhere else as a Verb. Fin. (Ptcp. only, in sense of *traveller*) and may perhaps have originated in dittogr. of the following word (see also note on v. 7ᵃ), and read וּלְחֶבְרָה *And is for joining with*, &c. (for the Constr. see OL s v. לְ 7. h.), or else understand the two Infinn. in the ordinary sense of purpose · *To ally himself with* . . . *And to walk with* . . . Cf. 22¹⁵ Ps 1¹ for the thought. (𝔊 ὁδοῦ pointing אֹרַח, and prefixing οὐχ ἁμαρτὼν οὐδὲ ἀσεβήσας, a mistaken gloss.)

v. 9. *gaineth nothing*: לֹא יִסְכָּן 15³ 22² 35³. Or *profiteth not, is of no use*. 𝔊 *For say not that* 'There will be no visitation (10¹² Nu 16²⁹) *of a man!*', *When* (there will be) a visitation to him *from* (the) *Lord*. Due perhaps in part to deliberate alteration. But 𝔊 may have pointed יָסֻבֻּן or even read יָפְקַד in a similar sense: cf. the T. A. use of the vb. *sakânu*, 'see about', 'attend to', 'look after' (= פָּקַד), e.g. *liskin šarru ana mâtišu*, 'let the king look after his country!', and of (*amêlu*) *sukinu*, 'overseer' (= פּוֹקֵד), 'superintendent' (syn. *râbiçu*). The ultimate Root may be Sum KIN = Bab. *štê'u*, 'look for', 'seek', 'attend to', 'care for', from *še'u* = שָׁעָה.

St. ii is metr. short. Moreover the sense of 𝔐 is unsatisfactory. Read בִּרְצוֹת עִמּוֹ א׳ *When Elohim is well-pleased with him*, pro 𝔐 עִם־א׳; thus restoring both metre and sense. For the Constr. cf. Ps 50¹⁸.

v. 10. A tristich. By inserting חֲכָמִים הַאֲזִינוּ *ye wise give ear!* after לָכֵן (cf. v. 2) we turn st. i into a suitable distich, making a quatrain of the verse. *men of mind* (lit. *heart*): recurs v. 34 only. *to deal wickedly*: leg. מֵהַרְשֵׁעַ (Ps 106⁶ Ne 9³³ Dan 12¹⁰) > מֵרֶשַׁע (Qal Infin. is not found). St. ii is clearly mutilated. Read וּגְלֻשָׁרַי מְעַוֵּת צֶדֶק; cf. 𝔊 ταράξαι τὸ δίκαιον: 8¹ᵇ ταράξει τὸ δίκ. = יְעַוֵּת צֶדֶק and v. 12 ταράξει κρίσιν = יְעַוֵּת מִשְׁפָּט.

v. 11. *For* according to *a man's work*: leg. כִּי כְפֹעַל א׳ (כ׳ exc. post כִּי). *causeth to befall him*; cf. Nu 32²³. (𝔊 read וּבְאֹרַח pro יָבֹא׳ and pointed יַמְצִאֶנּוּ: *And in a man's path He findeth him*. A good sense, but not so close a parallel.)

v. 12. For the strong asseverative אַף־אָמְנָם see 19⁴ (𝔊 ναὶ δή) Gn 18¹³. *dealeth not wickedly*. לֹא־יַרְשִׁיעַ: see note on v. 10. We need not substitute יִרְשַׁע for this well-attested late use of Hiph. 𝔊 *And thinkest thou the Lord will do absurd things* (ἄτοπα = אָוֶן 4⁸ 11¹¹ 36²¹ שָׁוְא 35¹²) = אַף־אָמַרְתָּ אֶל יַרְשִׁיעַ prob אָמְנָם misread אָמְרַתְ om. (לֹא).

v. 13. *Who made the Earth His charge?* or made Him responsible for the care of the Earth, made Him its פָּקִיד or Overseer? For פָּקַד עַל in this sense cf. 36²³ Nu 4²⁷ and Aram. usage. (Leg. הָאָרֶץ or simply אֶרֶץ pro 𝔐 אַרְצָה > אַרְצָה = אַרְצוֹ *his earth*; cf., however, 37¹³ Pr 8³¹.) 𝔊 ὃς ἐποίησεν τὴν γῆν as add. to v. 12. To bring st. ii (𝔐 lit. *And who set the world all of it?*) into parallelism with st. i read שִׁפִּי עַל pro 𝔐 שָׂם *And who set Him over the whole world?* Cf. Gn 47⁶ Ex 1¹¹ Ps 105²¹ (שָׂמוֹ). 𝔊 suggests (וּמְלֹאָהּ?) וּמִי־עָשָׂה תֵבֵל וְכָל־בָּהּ *And who made the world and all therein (and the fullness thereof?* Ps 50¹²)? ἡ ὑπ' οὐρανόν = אֶרֶץ 2² 38¹⁸,²⁴,³³ 42¹⁴ חֵבֶל Pr 8²⁶.

God is no Delegate or Viceroy. As Creator, He is supreme over all and accountable to none.

Verses 14, 15 are an expansion of Ps 104²⁹ᵇᶜ: תֹּסֵף רוּחָם יִגְוָעוּן וְאֶל־עֲפָרָם יְשׁוּבוּן: *If Thou gather in their spirit, they expire, | And unto their dust they return.*

v. 14. The best that can be made of 𝔐 is: *If He were to set His heart upon* (= give sole attention or confine His regard to) *Himself,—His spirit and His breath to Himself gather in* … Apart from the strange idea (unique in the OT) of God's fixing His attention upon Himself, which is no ‖ to the second stichus, st. ii itself at once arouses suspicion by its metrical redundancy (four stresses). Read יָשִׁיב (c 5 codd. Or^K and 𝔊 מִפְּנָא) pro 𝔐 יָשִׂים, and om. לְבּוֹ (added after יָשִׁיב had become יָשִׂים). This yields the satisfactory distich:

אִם־יָשִׁיב אֵלָיו רוּחוֹ
וְנִשְׁמָתוֹ אֵלָיו יֶאֱסֹף:

If He cause His spirit to return to Him, | And gather in His breath to Himself. Cf. Ps 104²⁹,³⁰. The verse constitutes the Protasis to the Apodosis which follows in v. 15. Cf. also 12¹⁰.

v. 15. In st. ii עַל should rather be אֶל (Gn 3¹⁹): cf. 𝔊 εἰς γῆν. 𝔊 adds the gloss ὅθεν καὶ ἐπλάσθη: cf. 10⁸,⁹ Gn 2⁷,⁸,¹⁹.

It is futile for a mortal to question the justice of his Maker. However it may be with inferior potentates, the supreme Judge, the absolute Lord of all living, must be supposed superior to every form of injustice. Cf. Rom. 9¹⁴⁻²¹.

v. 16. 𝔐 וְאִם־בִּינָה RV marg. *Only understand!* (cf. Gn 23¹³) is dub. Hebrew. Read בִּינֹתָה (plene): *And if thou hast understanding* (for the form cf. Dan 9²): cf. בִּנְתָּה Ps 139²: or perhaps add לְךָ after בִּינָה (which would justify the accentuation). 𝔊 εἰ δὲ μὴ (!) νουθετῇ (cf. 38¹⁸); 𝔙 Si habes ergo intellectum.

v. 17. 𝔐 הַאַף שׂוֹנֵא מִשְׁפָּט יַחֲבוֹשׁ would be extraordinary Heb. for *Shall even one that hateth right govern?* (RV). For √חבש see the note on 28¹¹. It occurs but once in Job, and that in the ordinary sense (5¹⁸). Read הֲאֵל לְשׂוֹנֵא־מִשְׁפָּט תַּחְשׁוֹב *Accountest thou El the foe of right?* cf. 13²⁴ 33¹⁰ and 𝔊^A οὐκ οἴει. In st. ii the Asyndeton צַדִּיק כָּבִיר is improb. Read צֶדֶק *justice* (‖ to מִשְׁפָּט, st. i; 29¹⁴ 35² 36³) and cf. 8³. This gives us: *Or condemnest thou the Justice of the Mighty One?* (כַּבִּיר Abs. of God; so ʾhere only: cf. 36⁵). (𝔊 ἄνομα = לֹא־מִשְׁפָּט: καὶ τὸν ὀλλύντα τοὺς πονηρούς = מַשְׁבִּית רְשָׁעִים: aliouter = כָּבִיר α_A d 15¹ cf. Dan 7⁹.) 𝔙 sanari potest = יְחַבָּשׁ; st. ii Et quomodo tu eum qui iustus est, *in tantum condemnas?* = 𝔐; taking כביר as Adv. = *greatly*.)

v. 18. Point הָאֹמֵר (c cod. 1 𝔊𝔙𝔖), referring to אֵל v. 17. God proves His Justice by administering His rebukes to high and low alike, without fear or favour (vv. 18, 19). For *worthless* see note on 34⁶ בליעל pro בלילו). St. ii in 𝔐 has only two stresses. Read perhaps רשע(ים) לנדיבי (עמ)ים: cf. Nu 21¹⁸ Ps 47¹⁰ (or keep אל־ and read אל־מלך in st. i). Possibly רָשָׁע is a gloss on בליעל which has displaced (על) הַשּׁוֹפֵךְ בּוּז (*Who poureth contempt upon nobles*: cf. 12²¹) Or, assuming that אֲשֶׁר ad init. v. 19 may be a disguise of some other word belonging to the end of this verse, we might read ר' לנדיבים יקרא (17¹⁴) or רשעים לנדיבי ארץ: 𝔙 qui vocat duces impios. Cf. Is 32⁵.

v. 19. St. i seems overloaded: om. אשר *Who* (see last note). *showeth no partiality*: 13⁸·¹⁰ 32²¹. *preferreth to*: lit. *regardeth before*... נִכַּר לִפְנֵי. Pi. so here only (cf. 21²⁹). Perhaps הכיר Hi. (six times in Job, e.g. v. 25); cf. Dt 1¹⁷ לא תכירו פנים במשפט *Ye shall not recognize faces* (show partiality) *in judgement*. (The Semitic √נ־כר I. *attend to, regard, know*, may perhaps be compared with Sum. ⟨⊢⊰⟩ KUR *paqâdu*, and √נ־כר II. with Sum. ⊢ KUR *aḫû, šanû, nakru, nakâru, nukkuru*, &c., 'other', 'another', 'different', 'strange', 'foreign', 'enemy', 'to be or become other', 'to change', 'alter', &c. The primitive Root is triliteralized by the Pronom. Preform. נ = Sum. NA, NI, is, ille, iste.) Instead of שׁוֹעַ *noble* or *generous* (Is 32⁵) it seems natural to read עָשִׁיר *rich*, on account of the parallel דָּל *poor* (Ex 30¹⁵ Pr 10¹⁵). St. iii, which 𝔊 app. omits, is probably a gloss, though apt enough in sense; unless, perhaps a line has fallen out before it. (𝔊's version of the two preceding stichi appears to be more or less conflate: *Who was not abashed at an honoured one's face* = אֲשֶׁר לֹא חָפֵר מִפְּנֵי נִכְבָּד cf. Dt 28⁵⁰ Is 1²⁹, | *Nor knows to give honour to great ones, so that their faces be admired* = וְלֹא־יָדַע לְהַכִּיר פְּנֵי גְדֹלִים cf. Dt 1¹⁷ Je 5⁵ 2 K 10⁶ [ἄδροί = גדלים but 29⁹ ἄδροί = שָׂרִים]: לָשֵׂאת פְּנֵיהֶם, cf. 13¹⁰ 22⁸. Possibly st. ii was originally something like וְלֹא־יָדַע or וְלֹא־יַכִּיר פְּנֵי נְדִלִים: or even וְלֹא־יִקַּר נְשׂוּאֵי פָנִים 22⁸ Is 3³ 9¹⁴ 13¹¹.)

v. 20. Another tristich. St. i 𝔐 lit. (*In*) *a moment* (Ps 6¹¹ Is 47⁹) *they die and* (at) *midnight* (Ps 119⁶² Ex 11⁴ חצות הל׳). The second Adv. phrase is dub. Read perhaps וְיִחָצְצוּ pro 𝔐 ל' וחצות (21²¹). St. ii יְנֹאֲשׁוּ Pu. here only. *A people are convulsed* (OL) or *The people* (i.e. of these potentates) *are shaken* is not prob. in the context, which relates to God's overthrow of the Mighty. (געש is prop. and nearly always used of physical convulsions. Cf. Ps 18⁸ Je 25¹⁶ dub. cf. 46⁷·⁸ sim.). And why not ינעש עם ויעברו? Read יָנֻעוּ עַם־עָשׁ (9²⁴) or יִ' כָּעָשׁ *They expire like the moth* [...]

Job; the plur. אבירים occurs in 24²²ᵃ (a similar statement). Read either ויסיר אבירים *And He removeth the mighty ones*, &c.; or ויסורו אבירים *And the mighty ones depart*, &c., c 1 cod.: cf. 𝕲. The former seems preferable on account of v. 21 ; cf. 12²⁰·²⁴: but the stichus is prob. an addition based on La 4ᶜᵈ Dan 2³⁴ 8²⁵ (*without hand*; i.e. without human, or by supernatural agency). 𝕲's version of this verse does not so much indicate a difference of reading as a guess at the meaning of a more or less injured text identical with that of 𝔐. κενὰ δὲ αὐτοῖς ἀποβήσεται τὸ κεκραγέναι καὶ δεῖσθαι ἀνδρός (𝕲ᶜ αὐτοῖς) = ריק יתמו צוחם למו ושועם (רנע = ריק; ין[י][ע]שו עם = ושועם; חצות לל' = צוחם למו; יתמו = יתמו). The second stichus is ἐχρήσαντο γὰρ παρανόμως, ἐκκλινομένων ἀδυνάτων = ויעברו ויסורו אביונים. Here עבר is understood in the sense of *transgressing*; and אביר is misread אביון as in 24²². Cf. also 24⁴ (*They turn the needy out of the way*) which seems to have influenced 𝕲's interpretation here. Further, 𝕲 may have taken לא ביד in the sense of 'without strength', as an epithet of אבינים, and so omitted it as already implied in ἀδυνάτους.

v. 21. Cf. 31⁴.

v. 22. Cf. Ps 139¹¹ᶠ· Am 9³. It is impossible to escape the notice of the Allseeing (or, as we say, the Omniscient), and so to evade His Justice. 𝕲 gives a free paraphrase of both verses.

v. 23. 𝔐 lit. *For not upon a man setteth He* (scil. *His heart* or mind) *still* (or *again*), | *To go* (= That he should go) *unto El in the judgement.* God has no need to investigate like an earthly judge: He knows (cf. 11¹¹). But the Heb. is doubtful, and the two stichi have a look of incoherence. Read either עֵת *a time* (cf. Ec 8⁵·⁶ + ומשפט) or מוֹעֵד *a set time* (Ex 9⁵; see Bateson-Wright) instead of 𝔐 עוֹד *still.* (? יָשֵׂם־עֵת.) Cf. 9¹⁹ᵇ. Point perhaps לַהֲלֹךְ *to bring him*.

St. ii. Cf. 22⁴ᵇ. Perhaps אֶת־אֵל pro 𝔐 אֶל־אֵל; cf. Ps 143². There may be an allusion to Eyob's desire to argue his case with God (13¹⁸ᶠᶠ· 23⁸ᶠᶠ· 31³⁵ᶠᶠ·) as in a court of justice. Cf. 9³². God knows without inquiry whether a man is guilty or not, and smites at once when He pleases (v. 24). 𝕲 ὁ γὰρ Κύριος πάντας (𝕲ᴬ τὰ πάντα) ἐφορᾷ (28²⁴) = כי הכל אל מבט (due to omission and transposition of letters).

v. 24. *He breaketh:* יָרֹעַ (Je 15¹² Ps 2⁹). Aramaism = יְרוֹעַ (יָרֹעַ?): see note on 20¹⁰. 𝕲 ὁ καταλαμβάνων = יֵדַע (cf. 𝕲ᴺᴼᴸ Je 15¹²). *without trial*: lit. *without* (leg. בְּלֹא pro 𝔐 לֹא) *search* or investigation. For לֹא־חֵקֶר *beyond search* see 36²⁶ and cf. 5⁹ 9¹⁰ 8⁸ 11⁷ Pr 25²·²⁷. For the sense of st. i cf. perhaps 11¹¹. With st. ii cf. 8¹⁹ 18²⁰(?) 21⁸·³³?. Instead of this verse 𝕲 repeats 5⁹, except that it has ὁ καταλαμβάνων here in place of τὸν ποιοῦντα μεγάλα there. Did it understand כביר as equivalent to גדלות and אחר to נפלאות? 𝔙 *Conteret multos et innumerabiles*: cf. 31²⁵ Is 16¹⁴ and chap. 36²⁵.

v. 25. 𝔐 לָכֵן *Therefore* seems inconsequent here. 𝕲 om. 𝔙 *Novit enim*

We might read הַפֵּר, making יַכִּיר more emphatic (*He well noteth,* &c.); or אָכֵן *But indeed* (32⁸); or כִּי־הוּא *For HE* (emph.) *noteth,* &c. לָכֵן (or עַל־כֵּן? vid. v. 27) may belong to v. 26. *their doings*: מַעְבָּדֵיהֶם: an Aramaism (Dan 4³⁴†); here only in OT. Heb. Elsewhere Elihu uses the ordinary words מַעֲשֶׂה (v. 19, 33¹⁷? 37⁷) and פֹּעַל (v. 11 36⁹·²⁴ 37¹²); and it is possible that this verse as far as לָיְלָה merely preserves variants to verses 20, 21, as some think, and that the closing vb. וירבאו should begin verse 26 (so 𝔖 but not 𝔊). It is perhaps an improvement of 𝔐 to read וַהֲפָכָם *And He overthrows them* (9⁵†) pro וְהָפַךְ. *are crushed* 5⁴†. Cf. 4¹⁹ 6⁹ 19² 22⁸ for other forms of the verb.

v. 26. 𝔐 lit. *Under the wicked He slappeth them in*(to) *the place of seers*; which is neither sense nor metre. Read

לָכֵן יָחַת רְשָׁעִים
סְפָקָם בִּמְקוֹם רְפָאִים׃

Therefore He shattereth (Is 9³) *the wicked ;* | *He hath smitten* (?) *them into the place of the Dead* (i.e. She'ol). *Therefore*; viz. for the reason assigned in the next verses. (For לָכֵן or עַל־כֵּן see verses 25, 27.) The verse might perhaps be better restored as follows:

יַנְחֵת רְשָׁעִים שְׁאוֹל
וְסְחָפָם בִּמְקוֹם רְפָאִים׃

He makes the wicked go down to She'ol (cf. 21¹³) | *And casts them down* (Pr 28³ סוחף) *into the Place of the Dead.* 𝔊 ἔσβεσεν δὲ ἀσεβεῖς looks as if וירבאו was read וינכאו (cf. 𝔊 30⁸) or וירעבו (18⁵·⁶) and תחת omitted. St. ii ὁρατοὶ δὲ (ἐγένοντο 𝔊^A) ἐναντίον αὐτοῦ (v. τῶν ἐχθρῶν) suggests that 𝔊 pointed רָאִים or read רָאוּ (33²¹), while representing ספקם במקום either by קָדְמוֹ *before him* (Aram.) or by לפני קמ(ים) *before enemies.* 𝔖 renders the verse: *And they shall be humbled under the wrong of their deeds in the fearful place* (reading מוֹרָא pro ראים).

v. 27. Because: אשר(־)על־כן; usu. compared with כִּי־עַל־כֵּן (Gn 18³ al.). But אשר alone might mean *because* (𝔊 ὅτι), and על־כן, as we have seen, may not belong here. (𝔙 ingeniously: Qui quasi de industria = 𝔐.) Some would delete this verse as a gloss; which is probable (see next note).

v. 28. If verse 27 is genuine, this one states either the consequence or (ironically) the purpose (cf. 𝔙) of the oppressive behaviour of the wicked, as though they were bent on their own ruin. But it seems more natural that the Subj. of both stichi should be the same, viz. God ; in which case the verse expresses the Divine purpose in the destruction of the oppressors (v. 26): *To bring in to Himself* (אֵלָיו c 2 codd. 𝔙 ad eum) *the outcry,* &c., *And to hear* ⸱⸱ ⸱⸱ *f r h* לִ⸱ שַׁוְעַת P- 1⸱⸱ ⸱⸱⸱ 𝔐 צְעָ֫קַת ; ⸱ ⸱ ⸱ 35⁴ ⸱ *f the oppressed.* Cf. Gn 4 19⸱⸱.

v. 29. 𝔐 יַשְׁקִט (יִשְׁקֹט ? cf. יַסְתֵּר) may mean *show quietness* = keep quiet (37¹⁷); or we may point יִשְׁלָט *be quiet, inactive* (Is 18⁴), which comes to the same thing. Instead of 𝔐 יַרְשִׁעַ *condemn* (verses 12, 17), which is incongruous with the previous verb, we propose (יַרְעִשֵׁנוּ) *make Him spring up* (39²⁰) or יְעֹרְרֶנּוּ *rouse Him* (41² ⁼ ¹⁰ cf. 8⁶). For the general sense of the verse cf. Is 51⁹ Ps 44²⁴ᶠᶠ. *Awaked! why sleepest Thou, O Lord? ... Why hidest Thou Thy Face?* (Also 13²⁴ Ps 30⁸ 78⁶⁵ Is 54⁸ al.); 19²⁷ *I shall see Him*; 35¹⁴. Men 'see' God in His active intervention to help and save.

It is only by forced interpretation that anything can be made of st. iii as an integral portion of this verse (cf. RV). Perhaps it really belongs to verse 30, which is metr. and otherwise defective. We might read:

אִם־עַל־גּוֹי אַפּוֹ יֵחַר
וְיַמְלִךְ חָנֵף עֹשְׁקֵי־עָם:

If against a nation His Wrath be kindled,
And He make king a profane one (8¹³), *an oppressor of the people:*

such a one e.g. as Antiochus Epiphanes. For חרה אף על see 19¹¹ Zc 10³; usually c ב, 32²·³ 42⁷. Or read יַחַד pro יֵחַר and וְהִמְלִךְ pro מִמְּלֹךְ, concluding with מְעַשְּׁקֵי־עָם (Pi. ἅπ. cf. Is 23¹² Pu.): *And should He be wroth against nation or man,* &c. (The repeated אָדָם is certainly dubious; and חנף occurs nowhere else as epithet of אדם: cf. 36¹³. 𝔐 may mean: *That a profane man, one of the snares of the people, reign not*; but the phrase is unique and improb. 𝔙 *propter peccata populi* = app. מְעַקְּשֵׁי עָם or מְעַקְּשׁוֹת עָם. 𝔊 ἀπὸ δυσκολίας λαοῦ = מִקְשֵׁי־עָם cf. Dt 9²⁷ or מַהֲקָשׁוֹת־עָם.) It is possible that st. iii of v. 29 is spurious. In that case v. 30 might perhaps be restored as follows:

מִמְּלֹךְ אָדָם חָנֵף
מַקְשֶׁה עֻלּוֹ עַל־עָם:

Who maketh a profane fellow king, | *Who maketh hard his yoke on the people* (1 K 12⁴). Cf. 𝔙 *Qui regnare facit hominem hypocritam propter peccata populi* = 𝔊 βασιλεύων ἄνθρωπον ὑποκριτὴν κτλ.

v. 31. 𝔐 *If* (or *When* or *For*) *unto El hath he said?* is evidently due to wrong division of the letters. Read (יֹאמַר ?) כִּי אֶל־אֱלוֹהַּ אָמַר *If* (*When*) *unto Eloah he* (i.e. the tyrant; or *it*, i.e. the oppressed nation) *saith*: cf. 7¹³ 19²⁸. In st. ii pro 𝔐 נָשָׂאתִי *I have borne* read נְשָׂא־לִי *Forgive me!* (cf. Ps 10¹² Ho 1⁶ Is 2⁹). We can hardly understand *my punishment* (עֲוֹנִי Gn 4¹³), since his punishment has not been mentioned. And to supply the missing third stress add עוֹד *again* after אֶחְבֹּל (see note, v. 32): *I will deal wrongfully no more!* (This seems better than pointing נִשֵּׂאתִי Ni. *I have lifted myself up*, in the unusual sense *I have been haughty* or overbearing; cf. Pr 30⁹). We might perhaps point נִשֵּׁאתִי *I was beguiled* (Is 19¹³). With אחבל cf. Assyr. *ḫabâlu*, 'injure', 'ruin', 'destroy'; e.g.

Sargon Cyl. 50: *Kîma zikir šumîa, ša ana naçâr kitti û mîšari, šutešur lâ lî'i, lâ ḫabâl enši, imbûinni ilâni rabûti*, &c. 'In accordance with the import of my name (qs *šarru kênu*, 'righteous king'), which the mighty gods called me, that I might keep righteousness and justice, deal justly by the powerless, *and not wrong the weak*,' &c. (He goes on to say that he paid the full value for a site which he required.) 𝔊^Θ ὅτι πρὸς τὸν ἰσχυρὸν ὁ λέγων (הָאֹמֵר) Εἴληφα, οὐκ ἐνεχυράσω (l. חבל Dt 24⁶·¹⁷) = 𝔐, but misconstrued. 𝔙 *Quia ergo ego locutus sum ad Deum, te quoque non prohibebo* = (אני) אל־אל אמרתי גם־אחך לא־אחבל (taking חבל in sense of *binding?*). For חבל see further note 17¹ Ne 17.

v. 32. 𝔐 *Apart from* (that which) *I see, do Thou* (emph.) *teach me !* But the use of בלעדי *apart from, besides*, is unique (not elsewhere c verb: hence 𝔊 ἄνευ ἐμαυτοῦ = בלעדי); and the word may well be dittogr. of עד (בל) עוד (v. 31 *ad fin*). Restore אם־אחטא *If I err*, or אם־חטאתי *If I have erred*; cf. 𝔙 *Si erravi, tu doce me.* Or we might substitute הארח *the way* (Pss 25⁴ 27¹¹) pro אחוה *The Way do Thou teach me!* Then (st ii) *And if* (ואם: exc. ¹ p. ¹) *I have done wrong*, &c. 𝔙 si iniquitatem *locutus sum*; perhaps reading מָלָתִי pro פעלתי 𝔐.

v. 33. A strangely incoherent tristich, with metr. short third line. The cumbrous st. i perhaps preserves the remains of a complete distich, which may have run somewhat thus ·

הֲמֵעִמְּךָ יְשַׁלֶּם אֱלֹהַּ ·
כִּי מוּסַר שַׁדַּי מָאָסְתָּ:

Is it by thy thinking (lit. *from thee*) *that Eloah should requite, That thou despisest the chastening of Shaddai?* Cf 5¹⁷. Instead of הֲמֵעִמְּךָ (מעם 2 Sa 3²⁸) read perhaps הֲכְטַעֲמָךְ *Is it according to thy taste* (judgement, 12²⁰) *that*, &c., or המטעמך.

The meaning may perhaps be: Would you deny a *locus paenitentiae* to the wicked ruler? Does your notion of Divine Justice involve his instant destruction, even if he repent and promise amendment? (Cf. 33²²⁻²⁸.)

The reference may be to the repentant nation rather than to the oppressive monarch; in which case we must render v. 31ᵃ *When unto El it* (i.e. the nation) *hath said*.

v. 34. 𝔐 lit. *Men of heart will say to me, And the wise man who listens to me*. It makes a better couplet to read יאינו pro יאמרו and ישמע pro שמע. This improves the parallelism, and yields a distich which is more in the manner of Elihu.

v. 36. St. i is overweighted in 𝔐 (four stresses). אבי יבחן may have grown out of אבחן by dittogr. of the first two letters. *I will test Eyob unto the end.* 𝔊 Οὐ μὴν δὲ ἀλλὰ μάθε, Ἰώβ, | μὴ δῷς ἔτι ἀνταπόκρισιν ὥσπερ οἱ ἄφρονες = אבל תבין איוב! עד נצח אל תשב כאנשי און. 𝔙 gives the literal meaning of 𝔐's st. 1: *Pater mi, probetur Iob usque ad finem*: but for st. ii it gives *ne desinas ab homine iniquitatis* = אַל תָּשֵׁבת מֵאֱנוֹשׁ אוֶן (pts!).

v. 37. A tristich, and otherwise corrupt. St. i *For he adds to his sin* (i.e. the sin which had caused his calamities) *rebellion* (in exclaiming against the Divine Judge) may pass muster all right; but st. ii 𝔐 ביננו יספוק *Between us he claps* (scil. his hands? cf. 27²² La 2¹⁵) can hardly be regarded as satisfactory. Inserting כפים *hands* as necessary to sense and metre, we get the tolerable stichus *Among us he claps his hands* (in scorn); viz. against God, as appears from st. iii *And multiplies his words against El* (leg. וירבה pro 𝔐 וירב and על־אל pro 𝔐 לאל). Perhaps the superfluous ביננו is a disguise of (ע)לשדי *Against Shaddai* (parallel to *El*). St. i may be rejected, except the introductory כי. Others reject st. ii. 𝔊 *That we add not upon our sin ;* | *But transgression upon us will be reckoned* (עלינו pro ביננו and יסָּפֵר pro יספוק), *speaking many words before the Lord*. 𝔙 *Quia addit super peccata sua blasphemiam* (= 𝔐 st. i) *inter nos interim constringatur* (= Aram. ביננו יָחַץ); *et tunc ad iudicium provocet sermonibus suis Deum* (= וְיֶרֶב באמריו עם־אל).

Chapter 35. For the heading see note on 34¹. Pro 𝔐 אליהו read, of course, אליהוא as elsewhere.

v. 2. *Right:* or *just* (מִשְׁפָּט): 34⁴. The parallel in st. ii is צֶדֶק > צִדְקִי 𝔐.

    This dost thou reckon as right,—
    Think (or *Call*) *it just with* (or *before:* cf. 4¹⁷ 9² 25⁴) *El,—*

Leg. צדק עם־אל pro 𝔐 צדקי מאל. *This:* viz. *That thou sayest,* &c. (v. 3). Is *that* demand consonant with ideal right and truth?

𝔊 paraphrases: *Why didst thou think this in* (ב pro ל?) *judgement? Who art thou that thou saidst, 'I am just before the Lord'?* צדקתי עם־אל 25⁴ ἔναντι Κυρίου ut hic; cf. 9² παρὰ Κυρίῳ). 𝔊ᴮ om. v. 3; 𝔊ᴺᶜᵃᴬᶜ add hic ἢ ἐρεῖς τί ποιήσω ἁμαρτών; = אם־תאמר מה־אפעל מחטאתי (a mutilated form of v. 3; both v. 2ᵇ and v. 3 are starred in Hexapl.): cf. 𝔙 *vel quid tibi proderit, si ego peccavero* = ומה־יעיל אם־חטאתי.

v. 3. Continues the rhetorical question of v. 2. For the verbs see 15³ 22² 34⁹. In st. i leg. לי pro 𝔐 לך, and perhaps ומה pro מה as in 21¹⁵ (a virtual parallel), st. ii. The usual rendering of 𝔐 is *What shall I gain more than from my sin* (i.e. more than if I had sinned); but the natural meaning of the Heb. surely is: *What advantage shall I gain from my sin?* Read therefore מחטאים *more than sinners* pro 𝔐 מחטאתי (and insert אני metr. grat.?). Eyob had more than once argued that God makes no difference in His treatment of just and unjust (9²² al.).

v. 4. Lit. *I, I will return thee words* (i.e. arguments). In st. ii add שלשת *three* p. את c 𝔊 metr. grat. et sens. (The v.l. ורעיך, though gramm. correct, is too short metri.). Cf. 2¹¹ 32¹.

v. 5. Cf. 11⁷⁻⁸ 22¹² Is 40²⁶ 55⁹. The idea here seems to be that God is too high above man and, therefore, too remote from him, to be affected by his conduct. (Or can it be meant that the majestic march of Heaven goes on day by day, unaffected by anything that happens here below? Cf. verses 6, 7.)

St. ii. *the Skies*: שְׁחָקִים. So 36²⁸ 37¹⁸ ²². *Clouds?* 38³⁷. Often a mere syn. of שָׁמַיִם: Dt 33²⁶ Ps 68³⁵. The Sing. שַׁחַק *fine dust* (on a balance: Is 40¹⁵†) recalls Na 1³ וְעָנָן אֲבַק רַגְלָיו, and suggests an original connexion with the Sumerian 𒊕 SAĜAR, *epru*, 'soil', 'dust'. The verb occurs 14¹⁹ (= *terunt*: cf. Aram. *to beat small, pound* or *pulverize*).

far above thee: lit. *which are higher than thou*. There seem to be four stresses here. Perhaps כִּי has fallen out after מ, and מִמֶּךָ been added: cf 𝔅 *et contemplare aethera quod altior te sit*: 𝔊 ὡς ὑψηλὰ ἀπὸ σοῦ: *And see the Skies, how high from thee!*

v. 6. 𝔊 ܠܗ = לוֹ *to Him* in both stichi (so 2 codd.), which may be right, as ב עשׂה does not seem to be used in the general sense of affecting another by one's behaviour, and st. i = st. ii (𝔊 om. in both stichi.) Cf. v. 8 With verses 6, 7 cf. 22³ ⁴ (Eliphaz). Verses 8, 9 were starred in Hexapl.

v. 8. Man can do good or harm only to his fellows, not to the Most High. (It does not seem to be meant that right or wrong conduct benefits or injures the doer himself.)

v. 9. *oppressors*: pointing עֲשׁוּקִים c 1 cod. and 𝔗 (מְלוֹמִין) 𝔅 (calumniatorum). 𝔐 עֲשֻׁקִים *oppression*; an abstr. like עֲלוּמִים: Am 3⁹ Ec 4¹. Some codd. have עֲשָׁקִים defect. (? עֲשָׁקִים cf. 10³ 34³⁰ Ec 4¹) Pro 𝔐 יַזְעִיקוּ leg. fort. יִזְעָקוּ or יְצַעֲקוּ (cf. v. 12): La 3⁸ וַאֲשַׁוֵּעַ וְאֶזְעָק ut hic.

the mighty: perhaps רַבִּים (cf. 34²⁴); but 𝔐 רַבִּים seems defensible in the same sense: cf. Is 53¹². 𝔅 tyrannorum. 𝔊 πολλῶν = 𝔐. 𝔗 *princes* (דוּרְבְּנַיָּא); cf. Sing. 34²⁰ = אַבִּיר; perhaps errors for רַבְרְבָנַיָּא or רוּרְבָנַיָּא et Sing.). Keeping עֲשׁוּקִים, we might read רָמָה pro רַבִּים: see 38¹⁵.

v. 10. If the verse is in its proper place, אָמְרוּ and עֹשָׂיו must be read c 𝔊. The anomalous form עֹשָׂי (Paus. pro עֹשַׂי = עֹשָׂיו) need not detain us. It requires no grammatical subtleties to account for it, if the final נוּ— was dropped inadvertently before the following נ(וֹ)תֵן Cf. עֹשֵׂנִי 32²². (For אַיֵּה cf. 15²³.)

vv. 9–13 seem to assert that the cries of the oppressed are merely instinctive, like those of a wounded animal. Not being inspired by faith, they make no appeal to God. This, however, does not agree with 34²⁸

v. 10. Cf. 36¹³. *Where* (21²⁸) *is Eloah my (our) Maker?* A mode of invoking Divine aid which was probably as ancient as it seems to us peculiar: see 2 K 2¹⁴ and cf. Dt 32³⁷ Je 2⁶ ⁸ Ps 42⁴ ¹¹. Leg. fort. אֱלֹהַי ישׁענוּ (cf. Is 17¹⁰ al.) > אֱלוֹהַּ עֹשֵׂינוּ (at cf. Is 51¹³) St. ii is usually taken to mean, 'Who enables those whom He has delivered to utter songs of thanksgiving in the night; cf. Ps 42 ' (Driver). If this is right, it confirms ישענו in st. i. The 'night' might be metaph. for the night of sorrow; times of affliction and calamity. But the phrase is unique and far from perspicuous. נֹתֵן (sine לנו or לי; cf. v. 7, 36⁸) would naturally mean, Who *putteth* (Ps 40⁴), *setteth*, or *appointeth*, acc. to context; while the constr. נתן בְּ is used of *giving* or *exchanging* one thing *for* (= תחת) another, which may even suggest בִּילָלָה pro בלילה (*Who giveth songs* for wailing: cf. Is 15⁸ 61³). 𝕲 ὁ κατατάσσων φυλακὰς νυκτερινάς = נֹתֵן (ב)לילה (א)שמרות (cf. 7¹² 20⁸ Ps 90⁴ 77⁵), *Who ordereth* (the) *night-watches* or *setteth watches in the night*. The 'night' (lit. or fig.) is not indefinitely long, but limited by periods marked off by the Divine Will. See also Ex 12⁴² Dt 16¹ Is 21⁸·¹¹. As astrological ref. seems not impossible (cf. v. 5; and v. 11 *Who teacheth us*, viz. by observation of the nightly heavens?). In that case, perhaps זמרות should be טזרות (38³²). Or is the reference to 'the music of the spheres'? Cf. 38⁷.

v. 11. An apparent allusion to Eyob's words 12⁷·⁸; cf. also 28⁷·⁸·²¹. The beasts and birds know what they see; knowledge of the Unseen is restricted to man (cf. 28²⁸). מאלפנו = טלפנו (Aram. 15⁵ 33²³ Pr 22²⁹†). The form corresponds to Syr. ܡܰܐܠܶܦ = (ܡܰܐܠܦܰܢ) fr. ܐܠܦ. 𝕲 ὁ διορίζων με = מבדיל(נ)י (*Who separateth me* from the four-footed things, &c.; om. verb in st. ii).

v. 12. *There* (in the case imagined; picturing an instance: cf. Pss 14⁵ 36¹³). Leg. fort. הֵם *They* (emph.); i.e. the wronged. *They cry, and He answereth not*. Cf. Mi 3⁴ אז יזעקו אל־יהוה ולא יענה אותם; where the reason is added ad fin. vs. כאשר הרעו מעלליהם. And since a parenthesis in st. i is improb., מפני גאון רעים (st. ii) should perhaps be emended into מפני גאון רעתם (נֹדֶל?) *Because of their overweening* (or *great*) *wickedness*. The word רעים *bad men* (Je 15²¹ Pr 4¹⁴ 15⁸) occurs here only in Job (cf. Sing. 21³⁰). For רעה *wickedness* see 20¹² 22⁵; and for מפני רע' Je 44³ Ho 10¹⁵. גאון *pride* seems hardly a suitable term for the violence which provokes cries for help (cf. Ps 123⁴); and elsewhere in Job (37⁴ 38¹¹ 40¹⁰†) the word has the good sense of *majesty* or loftiness. We should rather have expected a word like חָמָס *violence*, or לחץ *oppression* (36¹⁶ Ps 42¹⁰ cf. Is 19²⁰ᵇ), if st. ii expressed the reason for the outcry of the wronged. There may, however, very probably be a reference to Eyob's complaint, 19⁷: *Lo, I cry ... and am not answered* (Ni. cf. also 11² Pr 21¹³) and 30²⁰. In that case, we may read יַעֲנוּ pro 𝔐 יַעֲנֶה: *There they cry, unanswered*, | *Because of the insolence of wicked ones*. (This may lessen the objection raised above, without anticipating the reason of their cries not being heard which is given in the next verse.)

v. 13. Cf. Hab 1¹⁵. Since שוא is masc., read ישורנו pro 𝔐 ישורנה ad fin. vs.; unless we prefer to substitute שועתם *their cry for help* pro שׁוְא *emptiness* (i.e. a cry *void* of religious content or significance; a *vain* or ineffectual plaint). 𝕲 renders שמע by ἰδεῖν as in Is 30¹⁰; and instead of st. ii (which seems metr. short) it gives: *For the Almighty Himself is a beholder of those who perform the lawless things* (τῶν συντελούντων τὰ ἄνομα· cf. 34⁸·²² Je 6¹³ Pr 1¹⁹), app. a paraphr of : ושׂרי הא ישׁורנו (ἀνόμων = שׁוא 11¹¹). Read perhaps וש׳ הוא לא־ישׁור *And Shaddai, HE will not notice it.* 𝔊 adds καὶ (Α ὃς) σώσει με = וישׁיעני *And will save me* (22²⁹), which may be a var. of ישׁורנו (which perhaps should really be read ישׁיענו : see next note) But a line like (? שׁקר אָוֶן 11¹¹) ושׂרי לא־יקשׁיב מרמה *And Shaddai hearkens not to deceit* (31⁵) would be a better and more metrical parallel. Cf. Ps 66¹⁸.

v. 14. 𝔐 lit. *Yea, when thou sayest thou seest Him not,* | *The cause is before Him and thou shouldst wait for Him;* or perhaps rather: *Much less* (will He give heed) *when thou sayest thou canst not see Him;* | *The cause is before Him and thou art waiting for Him* (i e. to give judgement. cf. 13¹⁸⁻²²). Neither sense is satisfactory, and the Heb. is open to question; e. g. לא תשׁורנו after (ו)לא ישׁורנ, v. 13, apart from the repetition, ought either to be כי לא תשׁ׳ or else the direct לא אשׁורנו *I see Him not.* The Subj. of לא תשׁ׳ can hardly be the same as that of תאמר. (Cf. 𝔙 Etiam cum dixeris · Non *considerat* (=לא יש׳).) Eyob, however, had said the contrary (19²⁵ אשׁורנו). Read, perhaps, לא ישׁורני *He will* (doth) *not regard me,* or לא ישׁיעני *He will not save me* (cf. 𝔊). (𝔖 seems to have read לא ישׁבחנה in v. 13 and לא תשׁבחנו *thou wilt not praise Him* here) The line might then be rendered: *Yea, though thou sayest (thinkest?), He will not save me;* or *Dost thou really say,* &c. (cf. Gn 3¹).

St. ii דום לפניו ותחלל לו is app. an echo of Ps 37⁷ דום לי׳ והתחולל לו *Be still for Iahvah and wait patiently for Him.* (דם Defect. might easily have been misread דין). Cf. also Hab 2²⁰ Zp 1⁷. (חולל Polal. 39¹ peperit, Polal 15⁷ Pass., cf. 26⁵ Hithpol *writhe in pain* 15²⁰.) Perhaps it should be : תדם לפניו ותתחולל־לו (*Even if thou think, He regardeth me not, Thou shouldst be dumb before Him, and wait for Him*).

𝔊 κρίθητι δὲ ἐναντίον αὐτοῦ, εἰ δύνασαι αἰνέσαι αὐτὸν ὡς ἔστιν = לפניו ודין (ותהלל לו(?)) (cf 𝔖) אם־תוכל לשׁבחו It looks as if st. i were omitted (owing to homoeoteleuton?); or possibly the two stichi of the verse were transposed 𝔖 *And even if thou hast said thou will not praise Him, judge* (plead) *before Him and* supplicate *Him* (= והתפלל לו).

v. 15. The pointing is anomalous, and the verse otherwise corrupt. Moreover the phrase פקד אפו is contrary to usage. It should at least be פקד באפו *He visited* or *punished with His anger* (cf. 31¹⁴ Ps 89³³). We may perhaps restore וְעַתָּה כִּי־אֵין־פָּקַד בְּאַפּוֹ *And now, because He is not visiting with His anger;* cf. 𝔊 καὶ νῦν ὅτι οὐκ ἔστιν ἐπισκεπτόμενος ὀργὴν αὐτοῦ (i.e. fort punishing Eyob's anger??—an leg. ὀργῇ?). The stichus, however, seems overweighted; and it is possible that אפו is a gloss: *And now, because he is not visiting* (or *attending, giving heed:* cf. 7¹⁸ 31¹⁴), | *Nor marketh* (or *noticeth* or *careth for*) *rebellion much* (leg. בפשׁע or בפשׁע a rebel), E cf. 37¹⁸ᶠ· Je 38²⁴. But 𝔊 seems to have read פשע (sine ב): καὶ οὐκ ἔγνω παράπτωμά τι σφόδρα (an παραπτώματι Cas. Dat.?). παράπτωμα = פשע 36⁸. (Verses 15, 16 are starred in Hexapl.). For st. ii we may perhaps suggest וְלֹא־יָרַע בְּפֶּשַׁע מְאֹד *Nor hurteth He the rebel greatly*: cf. Zp. 1¹² (constr. Je 25²⁹ 1 C 16²²).

v. 16. *multiplieth*: יַכְבִּר an Aramaism : cf. Syr. and Old Aram. (S. A. Cook, *Glossary*, Z^{P⁴}) 36³¹ (cf. also כַּבִּיר *much* 31²⁵). 𝔊 βαρύνει = יכביר.

For v. 15 another conjecture may be offered, viz. וְעַתָּה כִּי־אֱלוֹהַּ פָּקַד (cf. 7¹⁸ 31¹⁴) *And now, because Eloah hath visited*, וְלוֹ־יָרְעָה נַפְשׁוֹ מְאֹד *And within him his soul is sore shaken* (cf. Is 15⁴); *Eyob idly*, &c. (v. 16). Eyob's flood of futile talk is the mere delirium of his intense affliction. (St. ii might also be וְלוֹ־הֵרַע בְּפֶשַׁע מְאֹד *And hath hurt HIM sore for transgression*: Je 31²⁰ ב *because of*.)

Chapter 36. *v.* 2. *wait for*: כַּתַּר an Aramaism ἅπ. (In Heb. *surround* Ps 22¹³.) *a little*: i.e. a little waiting, or a little while. So here only. Cf. Is 28¹⁰·¹³† (a little amount or quantity). St. ii, as 𝔐 has it, can only mean: *For Eloah still hath words* (i.e. arguments). לאלוה is perhaps a scribal error for לאליהוא: *For Elihu still hath somewhat to say*: cf. 𝔊 ἔτι γὰρ ἐν ἐμοί ἐστιν λέξις: 𝔙 adhuc enim habeo quod pro Deo loquar.

v. 3. *from afar*: לְמֵרָחוֹק 39²⁹ 2 Sa 7¹⁹, cf. also 2 K 19²⁵. Does Elihu perhaps mean *I will lift my cognisance* (or *thought*) *to Him that is far away*; or *I will bring forward my knowledge for the Distant One* (i.e. God; cf. st. ii)? Cf. Ps 139² בנתה לְרֵעִי מֵרָחוֹק (where some codd. לְדֵעִי). A closer parallel; cf. however, 𝔙 Repetam scientiam meam a principio.

My Maker: פֹעֲלִי so here only (= עשי cf. 35¹⁰). 𝔊 ἔργοις μου = לְפֹעֲלַי (pts.).

v. 4. 𝔊 connects אמנם, ἐπ' ἀληθείας with v. 3, omitting introd. כי and continuing with καὶ οὐκ ἄδικα ῥήματα = ולא־שׁקר מלים; thus making st. i part of v. 3ᵇ, in total disregard of the metrical structure.

indeed: אָמְנָם 34¹² (19⁴·⁸). Here perhaps אֲמָנִים: *For faithful, not false, are my words*. 𝔊 gives only ἀδίκως συνίεις = לא־שׁקר תרע (cf. Ex 36¹) for st. ii (dittogr.). 𝔐 תמים דעות עמך; upon which Driver remarks, 'Elihu means himself.' But cf. 37¹⁶, where the phrase (? דעות) תמים דעים denotes God, the *Perfect* in all kinds of knowledge. Should we read here עמדי pro עמך (*The Perfect in Knowledge is with me*)? Elihu seems to claim inspiration, 32⁸·¹⁸. Cf. also 1 Sa 2³† אֵל דֵּעוֹת יְהוָה. If *One that is perfect in knowledge* be the meaning (RV), we should expect אִישׁ תּ׳ דֵעוֹת; otherwise the natural meaning of the phrase will be 'The Perfect in Knowledge', which even Elihu would hardly claim to be. The two stichi, in any case, do not hang well together; and perhaps we should read אָמַרְתִּי (or וָאֹמַר) pro תמים: (*And*) *I* (*will*) *declare knowledge with thee*: cf. Ez 13⁷ Ps 40¹¹ for אמר.

v 5. ²כַּבִּיר is prob. dittogr. of ¹כַּבִּיר. 𝔐 lit. *Lo, El (is) mighty and despiseth not* (sine Obj.); *Mighty (in) strength of heart.* This leaves something to be desired in the way of perspicuity and relevance to context. St. ii is metr. defective. We would read יָמָס (Is 13⁷), or point יִמָאַס (7⁵? Ps 58⁸), pro 𝔐 יִמְאָס; and in st. ii (which seems to be an echo of 9⁴) אַמִּיץ כֹּחַ וַחֲכַם לֵבָב *Strong in power and wise of heart.* Cf. also Is 40²⁶·²⁸. 𝔊 γίγνωσκε δὲ (𝔊^A γινώσκω δὲ ἐγὼ) ὅτι ὁ Κύριος οὐ μὴ ἀποποιήσηται τὸν ἄκακον = 8²⁰ (הֶן־אֵל לֹא־יִמְאַס תָּם) ὁ γὰρ Κύριος οὐ μὴ ἀποποιήσηται τὸν ἄκακον. This suggests הֶן־אֵל תָּמִים לֹא־יִמְאָס for st. i here; but this obviously does not cohere with what follows in 𝔐. (St. ii and vv. 6-11 were wanting in the original text of 𝔊.) 𝔖 *Lo, the mighty God despiseth not* him who is pure as milk (בְּרוֹר כֶּחָלָב pro כַּבִּיר כֹּחַ לֵב).

v. 6. St. i insert נֶפֶשׁ (Gn 19¹⁹, cf. Ez 13¹⁹) or אָדָם (27¹⁵) metr. grat. *the right:* 27² 34⁵. Leg. fort. לָעָנִי (*And giveth* justice *to the opp*) on account of יִתֵּן (cf. Zp 3⁵). The usual phrase is עָשָׂה מִשְׁפָּט: see Dt 10¹⁸ 1 K 8⁵⁹ Is 10² al. We incline to read יָדִין pro יִתֵּן (cf. Je 21¹²): *And the cause of the oppressed He judgeth.*

v. 7. A tristich. The rendering of RV implies יֹשִׁיבֵם pro 𝔐 וַיֹּשִׁ׳, and is merely a desperate expedient. Cf. 𝔙 Non auferet a iusto oculos suos *et reges in solio collocat* in perpetuum, et illi eriguntur. Possibly st. i should be read *He withdraweth* (v. 27, cf. 15⁴·⁸) *not justice from the humble* (מַצְדִּיק עֵינָיו pro 𝔐 צֶדֶק מֵעָנָו), and the line be regarded as a var. or gloss to v. 6ᵇ (unless its fellow stichus be lost) Then ואת may conceal a verb, viz. וִיאַת or וִיתָא Hi. (ἅπ. cf. Is 21¹⁴ הֵתָיוּ Imp.) or וָיָבֵא: *He bringeth kings to the throne, | And seateth them in splendour, and they wax proud* or *behave haughtily:* Zp 3¹¹ Is 3¹⁶. (For the supposed Hi. form of אתה, cf. וַיֵּאת Qal Is 41²⁵.)

לָנֶצַח, usually *for ever,* may here have the meaning *in splendour* or *glory* (1 C 29¹¹, cf. 1 Sa 15²⁹ La 3¹⁸?); acc. to the Aram. use of the Root (cf. Syr. ܢܨܚ *bright,* ܢܨܚ *shine out, flame upwards, be brilliant,* and צַח *dazzling, glowing,* צָחָה canduit, La 4⁷; Sum. ZAG, a value of the Fire-character, ZA, *bright, shining,* ZAL, id.).

v. 8. The consequence of their sinful pride. Leg. אֲסוּרִים pro 𝔐 אֲסָרוּן; or, as the metre halts, and אֲסוּרִים looks genuine (it is not likely to have been substituted for a finite verb), and as some verb fin. seems needed to complete the sense as well as the metre, insert יֵלְכוּ after it (Is 45¹⁴ ubi leg. fort. אַחֲרַיִךְ יֵלְכוּ בַזִּקִּים et om. יַעֲבֹרוּ dittogr., cf. also Is 49⁹ 61¹ Ps 146⁷): *And if bound they walk in fetters;* like prisoners of war, e. g. Manasseh, 2 C 33¹¹ (ubi leg. בַּחֲבָלִים pro בַּחֹחִים); to the story of whose captivity, repentance, and restoration vv. 8-11 allude, though not exclusively (cf. 2 C 36⁶·¹⁰ Jehoiakim and Jehoiachin; 2 K 24²·¹²·¹⁵; Zedekiah 2 K 25⁶·⁷). ילכברון exc. aliter ילכו.

caught (or *taken*) *in the cords* (or *snares*: 18¹⁰ Ps 18⁶) *of distress* (or *oppression*: עֳנִי): cf. 2 C 33¹¹ (?) וילכדו את־מנשה בחבלים. Ps. 107¹⁰⁻¹⁴ אסירי (עני וברזל).

v. 9. With the whole passage, vv. 7-15, cf. 33¹⁴⁻³⁰ 34²⁴⁻³².

they dealt arrogantly: or *were overbearing, played the tyrant*: יתנברו (15²³ of impious defiance of God. Is 42¹³ of God as displaying puissance— 'playing the hero' (G. H. Box)—against His foes).

v. 10. *and He open their ear*: so v. 15ᵇ 33¹⁶. 𝕲 ἀλλὰ τοῦ δικαίου εἰσακούσεται = וְיִגַּל אָזְנוֹ לַמִּישָׁר (or לְמִשְׁפָּט, or לַמִּישָׁרִים) (?); misunderstanding the phrase גלה אזן (1 Sa 9¹⁵ al.). *And bid them return*: ויאמר כי יש'. 𝕲 καὶ εἶπεν ὅτι ἐπιστραφήσονται, *And said that they will return*; the usual meaning of כי אמר does not denote purpose (= *ut* c Subjunct.), cf. 𝔙 *et loquetur ut revertantur*, but simply introduces the Object-clause (like ὅτι followed by the Indic.): *And say that they should return*; cf. אשר Ne 13¹⁹.

v. 11. St. i is metr. short. Leg. fort. אם־ישמעו עליו ויעבדנו *If they hearken unto him* (2 K 20¹² על = אל) *and serve Him*.

they complete their days: they are not untimely cut off (Ps 55²³), but bring their lives to a full end, dying in a good old age. The stichus is an echo of 21¹³ᵃ; see the note there. (70 codd. יבלו ut Is 65²² ubi leg. יכלו ut hic). Stt. ii, iii make a distich which might have been modelled on Ps 78³³: ויכל בהבל ימיהם | ושנותם בבהלה; but st. iii, which is metr. short, is superfluous here: cf. 21¹³ᵃ. (שניהם ἅπ.; בנעימים Ps 16⁶ = *in the pleasant places*. Cf. נעמות *pleasures* Ps 16¹¹.)

v. 12. Om. ישמעו dittogr. (v. 11). *into She'ol*: בשאול pro 𝔐 בשלח 33¹⁸ᵇ (ubi 𝕲 ἐν πολέμῳ): cf. 𝕊 ܟܐܟܒܢܐ = באברון. For עבר, see 30¹⁸ 34²⁰. (*rush upon* weapons [and perish] OL is improb. Jo 2⁸ is no parallel. השלח there may perhaps mean the outer *wall* of the city; cf. Assyr. *šalḫu, salḫu*: 'And behind the *wall* they alight (or drop), *and are not stopped* thereby': leg. fort. ולא־יעצרו.)

𝕲 quite differently: *But impious ones He saveth not, because of their not willing to know the Lord*, | *And because, though warned, they were disobedient* (ἀνήκοοι ἦσαν = לא ישמעו Pr 13¹ᵇ) = ורשעים לא־יושיע בְּשָׁלָא (cf. Je 7²⁵) ולא־ישמעו בְּשָׁלְחוֹ | ויאבו (יחפצו f. 21³ᵃ) לרעת אל. 𝕲's st. ii looks like a var. rendering of st. i.

v. 13. 𝔐 חנפי לב *the godless in heart* is a dubious phrase (elsewhere only in the corrupt line Ps 35¹⁶ᵃ). The sing. חָנֵף (7 times in Job) is never qualified by a following genitive. For חנפים plur. abs., see Is 33¹⁴†. Read perhaps 'וחנפים בלב וגו *And the impious, in heart they lay up anger* (cf. Ps 13³ Pr 26²⁴); resenting their misfortunes as unjust. An indirect thrust at Eyob. Or: וחנ' רב יָשִׂימוּ *But the godless are greatly confounded* (21⁸); 'וְאֶל לֹא־יִשׁ *And to El they cry not*, &c, *when He hath bound them* (cf. v. 8): but perhaps we should read יִסְּרָם *chastised them*, or

יְיַסְּרֵם *chastiseth them*, pro 𝔐 אֲסֻרִם. Cf. 33¹⁶ 36¹⁰ Dt 8⁵. (The verse was starred in Hex.)

v. 14. *their soul dieth*: תָּמֹת pro 𝔐 תָּמֹת Juss., which seems due to reminiscence of the phrase תָּמֹת נַפְשִׁי *let my soul* (i.e. me myself) *die!* Nu 23¹⁰ Ju 16³⁰ (only). If בַּנֹּעַר *in childhood* or boyhood is right, בָּעֲלָמִים *in youth* will naturally follow in the parallel stichus, as in 33²⁵, instead of 𝔐's בַּקְּדֵשִׁים in cinaedis (1 K 14²⁴ 15¹² 22⁴⁷ 2 K 23⁷), which 𝔊 pointed בַּקְּדֹשִׁים (ὑπὸ ἀγγέλων); cf. 5¹. Such a statement was not likely to be made of bad kings generally. Moreover, st. ii being metr. short, we may insert תַּחֲלֹף *passeth away* (9²⁶) as Predicate of חִיתָם. *And their life, it passeth away in youth*: cf. 𝔊 ἡ δὲ ζωὴ αὐτῶν τιτρωσκομένη ὑπὸ ἀγγ. (20²⁴ תְּחַלְּפֵהוּ = τρῶσαι αὐτόν): or perhaps חָלְתָה *sickeneth* (cf. 2 K 20¹). 𝔙 Morietur *in tempestate* (cf. I נָעַר *growl, roar*; = 𝔐? at fort. בַּסַּעַר), et vita eorum *inter effeminatos* (= 𝔐). 𝔗 הַיָּה מָרֵי וְגוּ = בַּקְּדֵשִׁים pro 𝔐 בַּקְּ (a natural guess, based on the idea that the Hieroduli were shortlived). 𝔖 בכפנא *by famine*.

v. 15. The verb יְחַלֵּץ seems almost to demand מֵעֳנִי > 𝔐 בַּעֲ; cf. 𝔙 Eripiet *de* angustia sua pauperem; Pss 116⁸ 140². 𝔐 may perhaps mean *by* or *through* (בְּ instrument.) his affliction. Trouble is not punitive but remedial. The verse begins a new paragraph. St. ii. Cf. v. 10. Leg. אָזְנוֹ *his* ear c 𝔙 aurem *eius* pro 𝔐 אָזְנָם *their* ear. 𝔖 *their way* = אָרְחָם. 𝔊 ἀνθ' ὧν ἔθλιψαν ἀσθενῆ καὶ ἀδύνατον = כי לחצו עני ואביון *Because they oppressed the poor and needy*, a good reason for the statement of the last verse. But 𝔊 continues: κρίμα δὲ πραέων ἐκθήσει = וינל משפט ענים or ומשפט ענים יתן (v. 6ᵇ repet.; cf. Es 9¹⁴ 𝔊), which agrees better with 𝔐's st. i (as emended) than with its own. It seems possible that the verse originally ran: יחלץ עני מעניו | ויצל מלחץ אביון *He draweth the poor out of his misery,* | *And snatcheth away* (?? וְיִנָּצֵל cf Ho 13¹⁴ Ps 72¹⁴) *the needy from the oppressor* (or *from oppression*).

v. 16. A very corrupt tristich 𝔐 lit. *And also he enticed thee* (v. 18) *out of the mouth of straits* | *Breadth not narrowness* (37¹⁰ Is 8²³) *under her* | *And the quiet* (17¹⁶?) *of thy table (which was?) full of fatness*. Sticklers for the purity of the Massoretic text may defend this nonsense. We prefer to do our best to relieve 'Elihu' from the discredit of it. The verse appears to continue the subject of v. 15, viz. the restoration of the repentant oppressor. We may therefore suggest for st. i: וְאֹתוֹ הִסִּיע מִנִּי־צָר (29¹² יְמַלֵּט) *And him* (the penitent; as distinguished from the reprobate, v. 13 f.) *he bringeth out* (Ex 15²² Ps 80⁹) or *delivereth* (6²³ 29¹²) *from straits*. Cf. 𝔙 Igitur *salvabit* te de ore, &c. (יְשִׁיעֲךָ?). מִפִּי־צָר could only mean *out of the mouth of the* adversary (*not* straits· cf. Ps 22²¹); and מִנִּי = מִן is common in Job, and might easily be misread מִפִּי. 𝔐 הֱסִיתְךָ *incitavit te* seems to have been copied inadvertently from v. 18 infr. Then the parallel st. ii might be read: וְהִרְחַב־לוֹ מֵיצַר (מָצִיר). תַּחְתִּי. *And the narrowness* (37^{10}) *under him* (v. 20, 40^{12} Ps 119^{143} Ex 10^{23}) *becometh broad*, or better: וְיִרְחַב־לוֹ צַעֲדוֹ תַּחְתָּיו *And he maketh broad his footsteps under him*: cf. Ps 4^2 18^{37} ch 18^7 Pr 4^{12} 18^{10}. St. iii may have grown out of dittogr. (נחת of תחת st. ii; מלא רש׳ of מלא רש׳ v. 17). [𝔊^{BA*} καὶ προσεπώπατησεν prob. scribal error for καὶ προσέτι ἠπάτησεν (𝔊^{Nc.a}) = ואף הסית; ἄβυσσος = רחב = 𝔐; καὶ κατέβη = וְנָחַת pts.; κατάχυσις = מוּצָק qs de יצק *effudit* (= 𝔐). 𝔊 om. לֹא.] *His table is filled with fatness*: perhaps due to reminiscence of 2 K $25^{29f.}$ (Evil-Merodach's kindness to Jehoiachin).

v. 17. 𝔐 lit. *And with the judgement of the wicked thou art filled; Judgement and justice, they lay hold*. Dividing the letters differently, and following 𝔊 οὐχ ὑστερήσει = לֹא־יֶחְדַּל (cf. Ps 39^3 Nu 9^{13}), we submit וְדִין רְשָׁעִי(ם) לֹא־יֶחְדָּל *But the doom of the godless faileth not* for st. i; and for st. ii צדק ומשפט יתמכום *Justice and judgement lay hold of them*. (Cf. 𝔊 οὐχ ὑστερήσει δὲ ἀπὸ δικαίων κρίμα = the entire verse!) The Pron. Suff. ם־ is possibly concealed under כי v. 18, where that Conj. is not wanted. V. 17 thus becomes a natural sequel to v. 16.

v. 18. Corrupt. Some would render: *Because* there is *passion*, (beware) *lest it incite thee to mockery*. Driver: *For beware lest wrath* (i.e. resentment at God's dealings with thee) *allure thee into mockery*. But the note of Eyob's language is hardly 'mockery'. As to כי *For* see on v. 17^b. *Beware* (cf. v. 21) may be recognized in חמה *See!* (חֲמֵה); an Aramaism mispointed חֵמָה *wrath* in 𝔐. (For פֶּן, see also 32^{13} Is 36^{18}). The Subj. of the verb יסיתך is prob. concealed under the dubious בשפק, for which we may substitute שחד (parallel to כפר Pr 6^{35}; cf. st. ii). St. ii gives a clue to the right reading of st. i (cf. also v. 19^b and 𝔊). We thus get the distich:

> *See that a bribe seduce thee not,*
> *Nor abounding graft incline thee!*

In this and the following verses Elihu hints, under cover of precepts couched in proverbial form, that Eyob may have been guilty of certain sins common at the time among the rich and powerful.

v. 19. On st. i Driver truly remarks: 'Throughout this line RV. and RVm. are both extremely questionable. The Hebrew text must be corrupt; but no convincing emendation has hitherto been proposed.' Now in 6^{22} בֹּץ means *wealth*; and in $28^{17.19}$ ערך is used of *comparing* one valuable thing with another (cf. Is 40^{18} Ps 40^6 89^7). And since בצר, pointed בֶּצֶר (22^{24}) may be a syn. of חרוץ *gold* (see note on $22^{24f.}$), and שֻׁע may denote *safety, welfare*, we may recognize in these words the two terms necessary to a comparison, and suppose that the question originally ran: *Shall thy welfare be valued in gold?* היערך or היערך שׁעך אל־בצר (אל־ישׁעך בצר). St. ii certainly lends itself to and almost demands this view of the sense; whether we understand the ἀπ. מאמצי *vires* as denoting the *resources* or *rich supplies* of wealth, or prefer to substitute some other word for it, e.g. אֹצָרוֹת *treasures* or מַצְפּוּנֵי *hoards* (Ob 6). Leaving st. ii as it stands in 𝔐, we might also read st. 1: הַיַעֲרֹךְ לְיֶשְׁעֲךָ אוֹצָר (but perhaps 'Elihu' wrote שׁוּעֲךָ לְאוֹצָר).

It is evident that vv. 18-19 are closely connected in sense. 𝔊 *But wrath* (וחמה) *upon impious ones will be | On account of impiety of gifts* (= שַׁחַד Pr 6³⁵) *which they used to receive upon injustices. Let not the mind wilfully turn thee* (μή σε ἐκκλινάτω = אַל־יֻטְּךָ v. 18 ad fin.) *from a prayer* (שׁוע) *of powerless ones in straits* (ἐν ἀνάγκῃ ὄντων = 𝔐 בְּצָר) *| And all* (accus.) *who strengthen* (pointing מְאַמְּצֵי) *might* = 𝔐. A paraphrase of a misunderstood and partially corrupted text.

v. 20. St. i is metr. short. 𝔐 lit *Pant not for* (5⁸ 7²) *the night | That peoples may go up under them* (where they stand?). This is obviously corrupt Driver: 'Challenge not the Divine judgement ("night" being named as a time of disaster, xxxiv. 20, 25), which may prove to be of a kind in which whole peoples perish. Job had often desired to meet God in judgement (e.g. xiii. 22, xxiii. 3-7).' But Eyob had never expressed a wish for a catastrophic 'judgement' or 'Day of the Lord'. What he craved was a personal interview with his Judge, that he might vindicate his cause face to face with his Divine Adversary. Elihu may be supposed to be indirectly accusing Eyob of another fault, viz. tippling; which is associated with taking bribes in Is 5²²·²³ as, possibly, here. Cf. 1⁴·⁵·¹³. 𝔊 μὴ ἐξελκύσῃς τὴν νύκτα = אַל־תִּמְשֹׁךְ הַלַּיְלָ׳ (Gn 37²⁸ Ps 36¹⁰) *Draw not out* or *Prolong not* (Is 13²²) *the night* seems to give the clue, and perhaps we may venture to insert בַּיַּיִן *with wine*, for the sake of metre and sense: as we might say, 'Drink not far into the night.' But Pr 23³⁰ suggests the possibility of אַל־תְּאַחֵר עַל־הַיַּיִן *Linger not over the wine* בַּלַּיְלָ׳ *in the night* (cf. Is 5¹¹). Cf. also Ec 2³. An fort leg. אַל־תִּמְסֹךְ (תמסך) שֵׁכָר הלַּ׳ *Mingle not strong drink in the night* (??). At 𝔙 Ne *protrahas* noctem. In accordance with this, we propose עַד־לַעֲלוֹת יוֹם תַּחְתָּיו *Until Day* (= שַׁחַר Gn 19¹⁵ 32²⁵) *go up in its place*, instead of 𝔐's unintelligible לַעֲלוֹת עַמִּים תַּחְתָּם. For עַד־לַעֲלוֹת see 1 K 18²⁹.

v. 21. *Beware! turn not* . . . Cf. Ex 10²⁸ (וְאַל׳] Ju 13⁴). 𝔊 μὴ πράξῃς = אַל־תִּפְעַל pro 𝔐 אַל־חֵפֶן אֶל־. fort. recte. St. ii leg. 'בְּחַרְתְּךָ בְעֹ *thou wast tried with affliction* (Aram. use; בְּחַר = בֹּחַן); see Is 48¹⁰ בְּחַרְתִּיךָ בְּכוּר עֹנִי: *I have tested thee in the furnace of affliction*. עַל־זֹה *on account of this*, viz. אוֹן: cf. 34³⁶. (An leg. נבחנת et hic: cf. Gn 42¹⁵?). So 𝔊 *For because of this thou wast tried with poverty*. (𝔙 Hanc enim coepisti sequi post miseriam; mistaken paraphr. of 𝔐.)

v. 22. Begins a new paragraph. *doeth loftily*. יַשְׂגִּיב = 𝔊 κραταιώσει, cf. Ps 139⁶. Better perhaps נִשְׂגָּב Ptcp., cf. 𝔙 excelsus; Is 2¹¹ 33⁵. *And who*: וּמִי pro 𝔐 כִּי x. p t) *t*) *i. 2 n /* : שֹׂדֵ׳ . . I- 30 . 𝔊 διοικηστής

= Aram. שְׂרָא (haud recte). Cf. v. 10 33¹⁴ᵈ· 35¹¹. God teaches by affliction. (𝔙 paraphr. Et nullus ei similis in legislatoribus; understanding מוֹרֶה as a teacher of the Torah.) מרא, however, gives a closer parallel to st. i.

v. 23. Cf. 34¹³ᵃ. God chooses His own course and methods of procedure, in absolute independence of all His creatures.

who shall say; i.e. having given Him a charge, and found Him unfaithful to it. Leg. מי יאמר pro 𝔐 מי אמר (cf. 𝔙 and RV who *can* say). 𝔊 τίς δέ ἐστιν ὁ ἐτάζων αὐτοῦ τὰ ἔργα; 𝔙 Quis poterit *scrutari* vias eius? יחקר (3 2¹², cf. La 3³⁹) pro יפקר(?); ἔργα = ארחות *paths* 13²⁷, דרכי *ways* 34²¹. But פקד was perhaps understood by 𝔊𝔙 in the sense of *visiting to test or try* (cf. 7¹⁸ 31¹⁴); and no difference of reading seems to be implied. In ordinary use, מי פקד עליו דרכו would mean *Who hath (ever) punished Him for His way?* (cf. Am 3² Ho 4⁹); which would agree very well with 𝔐 st. ii (but cf. 34¹³); *And who*, i.e. what human judge, *hath ever said* in giving judgement, '*Thou hast done wrong*'? The Almighty is superior to all jurisdictions; none can question His justice, or call Him to account for His doings. (𝔊 st. ii = וּמִי אָמַר פָּעַל *And who saith, 'He hath done,'* &c.)

v. 24. magnify: or *praise*: Hi. שׂנא (8¹¹ 12²³†). Aramaism peculiar to Job.

So only here. 𝔙 Memento quod *ignores* (? תִשָּׁא = תָשֶׁה *forgettest*? or לֹא־תֵדַע v. 26) opus eius. 𝔊 μνήσθητι ὅτι μεγάλα ἐστὶν αὐτοῦ τὰ ἔργα (שַׂגִּיא פֹּעַל cf. v. 26 37²³) may be right. St. ii 𝔐 אנשים אשר שררו, 𝔙 de quo *cecinerunt* viri But שׁוֹרֵר Pol. of שׁיר is so used nowhere else (Zp 2¹⁴ Impf. sine Obj. Ptcp. *singer*, 1 C 6¹⁸ al.); and 𝔊 ἦρξαν = שָׂרוּ (Ju 9²² Is 32¹), i.e. שׂרו in the unpointed text. And as שָׂרוּ *have ruled* gives no satisfactory sense, while שׁוּר *to see* is a favourite word in Job, we may perhaps point שָׁרוּ *have seen*. The idea that God's creative power is visible in His works is emphasized in the next couplet (cf. Ro 1²⁰). If we go a step further and read מֵאֲשֶׁר pro 𝔐 אֲשֶׁר, we seem to recover a stronger distich than that of 𝔐:

> Remember that great is His work
> Beyond what mortals have seen.

For the construction, cf. Jos 10¹¹ Ju 16³⁰ Ec 3²². For אנשים 37²⁴. (It is perhaps worthy of note that, as שׁור, חזה, הביט, occur together in vv. 24, 25, here, so do שׁור, חזה, ראה, in 19²⁶·²⁷.) As regards 𝔐, it may be remarked that, while appeals to men and other creatures to sing to the Lord are common in OT poetry, the statement that men in general do sing of God's work would be unique in the sacred literature of the Hebrews. (Otherwise, one might be inclined to read אַנְשֵׁי קֶדֶם *the men of old* pro 𝔐 אנשים, and to think of the famous Babylonian Epic of

Creation with which the Jews must have become acquainted during the Exile, if not long before.)

v 25. Vv. 25–8 def. in 𝕲. *All mankind*: insert בְּנֵי? cf. Ps 33¹⁴. St. ii read וא׳ יביטנו *And a mortal may behold it* (i. e. God's work) *far away* (and therefore imperfectly: 26¹⁴): 39²⁹ Gn 22⁴. Cf. 𝔙 Omnes homines *vident eum* (i. e. God); unusquisque intuetur procul. The verse, however, does not affirm universal intuition or recognition of the existence of God (a question not raised in the book). 𝕲 curiously: πᾶς ἄνθρωπος εἶδεν ἐν ἑαυτῷ (= חזה בו); of inward consciousness of God; or perhaps rather, of seeing in his own being a 'work' of God: ὅσοι τιτρωσκόμενοί εἰσιν βροτοί, app. pointing אנוש first as אֱנוֹשׁ and then as אָנוּשׁ (conflate rend); but more prob. 𝕲 represents : כל־אנוש (יבים) מֻדְקָר (cf. Pr 12¹⁸).

v. 26. Is this verse a variant of *v* 22? It might, no doubt, begin a new paragraph or strophe; but st. ii ('the number of His years', cf. Ps 102²⁵·²⁸) seems hardly relevant to what follows. We might perhaps read מעשיו *his works* pro שניו *his years*.

beyond knowledge: וְלֹא־נֵדָע, lit. *and we know not*. Point perhaps נֻדָּע (= נוֹדַע). *unknowable*, i. e. not fully known, cf. 26¹⁴ Ps 77²⁰. ²ולא om. ו (ditt.). So 𝔙. Or read בְּלֹא *without*.

vv. 27–33. Rain and clouds as instances of the work (or works) of God (v. 24). Nothing was then known of the real genesis of these physical phenomena (cf. 28²⁵ᶠ 38²⁸·³⁴ ff. Ec 11³ 1 K 18⁴⁴ᶠ. Is 5⁶ Je 10¹³ Ps 135⁷ Gn 1⁶ᶠ· 7¹¹). In dealing with these corrupt and difficult verses we must not, therefore, read into the text any of the more exact ideas of modern science, such as are represented by such t. t as Evaporation, Rarefaction, Condensation. To the Hebrew mind, every shower that fell was a fresh miracle; every thunderstorm, nay, every single raindrop, was the immediate handiwork of God.

v. 27. St. i. The verb גרע (a younger by-form of גדע *cut off*? cf Aram. use of גְּזַע *shave*) means to *cut off from* so as to *lessen* or *diminish* (Ex 5⁸ Ec 3¹⁴, see notes on v. 7 15⁴·⁸) > either to 'draw up' or to 'draw down': *For He maketh small the drops of water* (AV). St. ii further explains: *And bindeth up the rain in His mist*; or *And squeezeth*, compresseth, *the rain into His mist* (Gn 2⁸ אֵד) Cf 26⁸ *Who bindeth up* (צֹרֵר; so Pr 30⁴) *water in His clouds*; which suggests the reading וַיָּצַר (or יָצֹר?). So 𝕾. But the word וקים *fetters* and the Aram. קְפָן *to bind* (only in Ptcp. Pass. קְפִיק *bound*; cf. also the NH use) suggest the possibility of ויקן. 𝔗 יָלְפוּן = יָקְפוּ: see 29⁶ for this equivalence. 𝔗 renders the whole verse: *Because He withholdeth* (יִמְנַע) *the drops* (or streams: טִיפֵי v. טוֹפֵי) *of water*; *They trickle the rain to* (?) *His clouds*. 𝕲 *If He count* (נָמְנָא = 𝔗 ימנע?) *the pillars of Heaven* (= עמודי שמים!), *And bind up* (יֹצֻר = צֹר vid. supr.) *the drops of rain by itself* (= לבדו; misreading of אֵד לאדו). 𝔙 Qui *aufert* (= אֵד) stillas plu · · · · · · · יציר · · · · · · *instar* gurgitum (= מִי ?). 𝕲 ἀριθμηταὶ δὲ αὐτῷ σταγόνες ὑετοῦ = וְיָמֹנוּ־לוֹ נִטְפֵי מָיִם (cf. 1 Sa 24¹ ἀρίθμησον = מְנֵה): so 𝕾 (cf. 𝔗 יִמְנַע); καὶ ἐπιχυθήσονται ὑετῷ εἰς νεφέλην = וְיֹצְקוּ מָטָר לְאֵדוֹ (Le 21¹⁰). The proposed reading נֹטְפִים מִיָּם (He withdraweth *drops from the sea*) suggests the formation of clouds by the process of evaporation; but this hardly agrees with st. ii, and cf. 14¹¹. In Gn 2⁶ the אֵד ʻused to go up from (out of?) the earth' (not the sea), ʻand water all the face of the ground'. (Can this baffling word be a transcription of the Sumerian ID, *river*? 𝕲 πηγή there, but νεφέλη 'here.) And in 1 K 18⁴⁴ it is ʻa little cloud' that the servant sees ʻgoing up from the sea' (עָב קְטַנָּה . . . עֹלָה מִיָּם), not ʻdrops of water', which soon overspreads the sky, and is followed by a downpour of rain (cf. v. 28). Instead of יָזֹקּוּ (Pi. here only) we might perhaps read יֶאֱסֹר, *colligit* (Pr 6⁸); and for לְאֵדוֹ either בְּאֵדוֹ or בְּנֹאדוֹ (Ps 56⁹) or בְּאֹבוֹ *in His water-skin* (32¹⁹ plur.), cf. 𝔗 Pss 33⁷ 78¹³.

v. 28. *Wherewith the skies flow down,— (Wherewith) they drop,* &c. See Dt 32² for both verbs. Cf. also Pr 3²⁰ Is 45⁸. *on the ground*· עֲלֵי־אֲדָמָה pro 𝔐 עֲלֵי־אָדָם *on man*: surely, an obvious correction, cf. Dt 32². 𝕲 *Which the heavens send down* in the season (= בְּעִתּוֹ Dt 11¹⁴) | *And the clouds drop upon men, and they rejoice greatly*. Instead of the dubious רָב ad fin. vers. we might read עָבִים *clouds* (including the superfluous אַף = ים—ad init. v. 29?), or perhaps רְבִיבִים *in showers* (=רָב + אַף + אִם?); cf. Ju 5⁴ Dt 32² Ps 72⁶. The original distich may have been either

Wherewith the skies drizzle in its season,
And the clouds drop on the ground
(or, *They drop on the ground in showers*).

It is hard to account for 𝔙. Qui (imbres) de nubibus fluunt, st. i, raises no difficulty; but whence came st. ii, Quae (nubes) *praetexunt cuncta desuper*? *praetexunt* looks like an error for *praetegunt* (or *praetexerunt*) = יַעֲרֹפוּ qs *overcloud, becloud* (cf. עָרִיף, עֲרָפֶל); and *cuncta desuper* may perhaps paraphrase עֲלֵי רָב־אָדָם (cf. Pr 20⁶) or עֲלֵי כָל־אֲדָמָה; cf. 𝕲 ἐσκίασεν δὲ νέφη (= וַיַּעַרְפוּ?, cf. Assyr. erpu, erpitu, urpatu, *cloud*) ἐπὶ ἀμυθήτῳ βροτῷ, *and clouds shadowed over untold* (8⁷) *man* = וַיַּעַרְפוּ עָבִים עֲלֵי רָב־אָדָם 𝕲's st. i ῥυήσονται παλαιώματα, *Ancient things will flow* (cf. Wordsworth's ʻthe most ancient heavens') depends on misreading שְׁחָקִים as עַתִּיקִים antiqua (so again 37¹⁸ ²¹).

𝕲 has here an interesting addition, consisting of two distichs, which in Hebrew might have run somewhat as follows:

עֵת שָׂם לְמִקְנֶה
וְיָדְעוּ מָקוֹם רִבְצָם׃
עַל־כָּל־זֹאת לֹא־יִשֹּׁם לְבָּךְ
וְלֹא־יֵהָפֵךְ לְךָ בְּנֶוֶךָ׃

For מקום cf. 38¹² and for רבצם Je 50⁶. For ישם cf. Is 52¹⁴ Je 2¹² (fort. יָמַס לבך Jos 2¹¹). For יֵהָפֵך לבך Ex 14⁵ (an יִשְׁנֶה מַעֲמָךְ(?). בנוך Aram. *within thee*. (Pro ² לבך leg. fort. בלך Aram. *thy heart, mind*. Cf. Sum BAL, *speak = think?*). The two couplets are probably a marginal citation; or they may belong to a different text of Elihu.

v. 29 begins a new paragraph. (Verse 31 should perhaps precede it. The rains make the ground productive, Le 26⁴ Dt 11¹⁷ Is 5⁸ 55¹⁰ al.)

Who: מִי (or וּמִי *But who?* so 𝔊) pro 𝔐 (יבין) אַף אִם *Also if* (*he understand*). 'Yea, can any understand' (RV) is not a translation of 𝔐 (See note, v. 28.) *spreadings*: מפרשי = 𝔊 ἀπεκτάσεις (hic tant.); cf. v. 30 ἐκτενεῖ = פרש and ἐκτείνων = נטה, syn 26⁷ Ps 104³; Ez 27⁷ מפרשך *thy spread* of sail. One cod. מפלשי (37¹⁶ ubi leg. מפרשי ut hic) The wonder was the rapid spread of a small cloud over the whole sky (cf. 1 K 18⁴⁴ᶠ·). St. ii תשאות סכתו is metr. short. 𝔊 ἰσότητα σκηνῆς αὐτοῦ (? תְּשֻׁאֹת. cf. 30²² Ketib). 𝔊 gives the verse thus: *And who understandeth? And He spread the clouds from the multitude of His pavilion(s);* 𝔗 st. ii רִכְפַת עֲנָנַיָא טְלָלֵיה *the mass* (or *pack*) of His clouds, *His shelters,* (*screens?*). רִכְפַת = הָמוֹן *noise, noisy crowd, mob, mass, bulk,' quantity* (cf. Je 51¹⁶ Ps 65⁸ Job 31³⁴ 2 C 11²³ 31¹⁰). In 26¹⁴ it represents רַעַם *thunder* (see note ad loc.), which might suit here · סֻכָּתוֹ [רַעַם] הְּשֻׁאוֹת *The thunder-crashes of His covert* (תשׁ 39⁷ Is 22²). But the thunder comes in, with a special introduction, later on (37¹ᶠᶠ·). Here therefore it seems better (cf. the ‖ stichus) to insert רַעַם > עָנָן, and either to point הַשָּׂאוֹת (?) *upliftings, risings* (cf. the word נשיאים *rising mists* Ps 135⁷ Je 10¹³ 51¹⁶) or to read מַשְׂאוֹת (cf. Ju 20³⁸·⁴⁰, sing. of smoke). *The rising of the cloud-masses His covert*. cf. Ps 18¹² 105³⁹ פָּרַשׂ עָנָן לְמָסָךְ. 𝔙 om. תשאות: Si voluerit extendere nubes | quasi tentorium suum = עבים לפרוש אם־יאבה סכתו;

v. 30. 𝔐 lit *Lo, He hath spread over Him* (or *it*, i.e. the cloud) *His light, | And the roots of the sea He hath covered*; instead of which we propose: עָלָיו־אוֹר (עָב) הִן־פָּרַשׂ כָּסָה | עָנָן וְשֶׁמֶשׁ בָּעָנָן *Lo, He spreadeth the cloudmasses over the light, | And the sun with clouds He covereth*: cf. Ez 32⁷ שמש בענן אכסנו; Ps 147⁸. 𝔙 is merely an incorrect paraphrase of 𝔐 (continuing the construction from v. 29). Instead of אורו *His light* 𝔊ᴮ ἡ ᾠδή (ungrammat. error; leg ἠδώ c 𝔊ᴺᶜ·ᵃ = אֵדוֹ *His mist* v. 27? 𝔊ᴬ τὸ τόξον = יורה 1 C 10³): 𝔗 מיטרא *the rain*. 𝔖 *Lo, He spreadeth above them* (i.e. the clouds) *His light* (= 𝔐).

v. 31. See note ad. v. 29. *nourisheth* or *feedeth*: יָזוּן Aram. (cf. Je 5⁸ Ho. Ptcp.) pro 𝔐 יָדִין *judgeth* (‖ grat.). Driver explained ידין as follows: 'The storm is the agent both of judgement, and, by fertilizing the earth, of beneficence.' But, so far, we have had to do with the rise and spread of clouds; we have not yet come to the storm. Besides, if ידין were

D d 2

right, st. ii ought to run: *He giveth* and withholdeth *food*. The parallelism demands a different expression.

in abundance: לְמַכְבִּיר. So the word is gen. understood (=לָרֹב OL), but the expression is very strange in such a sense. Elihu has already used יַכְבִּיר *he makes many* or *multiplies* (35¹⁶); and according to this, and the ordinary use of ל נתן, 𝔐 יתן אכל למכביר should mean *He giveth food to the multiplier* (or *to him who sheweth greatness*). Read rather: יתן אכל לכל־בשר *He giveth food* to all flesh (Ps 136²⁵), which also suits the parallel stichus better. (𝔊 למכביד cf. Is 6¹⁰ 𝔊. 𝔙 *et dat escas multis mortalibus* = לְכַבְּדִים? So 𝔊 ﺣﺴﻨﺎًl *to many*.)

v. 32. 𝔐 lit. *Over the two palms Light hath covered* (כסה על) is *to cover over*, 21²⁰ al.) | *And He hath laid charge on her* (!) *against an intervener* (or *assailant*). This, of course, is unintelligible. אור is masc. always (Je 13¹⁶ is corrupt); some codd. עליו recte. But כסה אור prob. means *He covereth the Light* (𝔙 abscondit lucem). The poet is still describing cloud-effects. Then על־כפים must be a distortion of some word denoting the means or instrument; e.g. בערפ(י)ים (Is 5³⁰) *with clouds*, or בערפל *with cloudmurk*, or בעבים *with clouds* (Ps 147⁸ המכסה שמים בעבים; Ez 32⁷). In st. ii we might read ויצר עליו *and besiegeth it, shutteth it in* במפגיע (so some codd pro 'במ) *like an assailant*; or possibly כמפרש *as with a sheet*. v. 29 (cf. Ez 27⁷ Is 29³). This is not entirely satisfactory, though we do speak of clouds 'sailing' over the sky, but it involves less change, and seems to agree better with the context, than וַיְקַלְעֵהוּ בְמַפְגִּע | עַל־כַּף יְפַלֵּס הָאוֹר *On palm He poiseth the lightning* | *And slingeth it forth at the mark* (7²⁰ 1 Sa 25²⁹). The idea of weighing light or lightning on the palm (or in the 'bought' of a sling, 1 Sa 25²⁹) is at once unique and improbable. The lightning is fig. God's 'arrow' (Ps 18¹⁵ Dt 32⁴¹f. Hab 3¹¹), 'sword' or 'spear' (Dt 32⁴¹ Na 3³ Hab 3¹¹), but never His 'sling' or 'stone' (אבני־קלע 41²⁰). He 'slings *out*' people, but not '*at*' them (1 Sa l c., Je 10¹⁸); not even at Ejob whom He attacks in so many various ways, and whom He makes the target of His 'arrows' (cf. 6⁴ 9¹⁷ 7²⁰ 16¹²f. 20²⁴f.). For the light and lightning, see also 37⁵ ¹¹ ¹⁵ 38¹⁹ ²⁴ ³⁵. Perhaps st. ii orig ran: ויצו עליו מהופיע *And chargeth it not to shine forth* (37¹⁵) cf. Is 5⁶ על־העבים אצוה מהמטיר. 𝔊 = ויצא עליהם ויפגיעַ־בו. 𝔛 *Because of hand*-rapine *He withholdeth the rain* (איד i.e. אד pro אור ut v 30); *And chargeth it* to descend *because of one praying* (= 𝔐; cf. Is 53¹² 59¹⁶: 𝔙 et praecipit ei ut rursus adveniat). Driver's comment on this verse forcibly illustrates the impossibility of extracting any probable sense from the traditional Hebrew text. Assuming the translation *He covereth His hands with the light; And giveth it a charge against the mark* (?), he explains as follows: 'Jehovah is represented poetically as plunging his hands into the flood of light about him, for the purpose of taking lightning-flashes out of it.' Compare this grotesque notion with the language describing Iahvah's mode of action with lightning in other passages cited above.

> v. 33.   *The noise thereof telleth concerning him,*
> *The cattle also concerning him that cometh up* (!).

This is perhaps the best that can be made of 𝔐; and so Driver takes it, with the comment, 'The thunder (line 1), by its sound, and the cattle (line 2), by their presentiments of a coming storm, alike announce that Jehovah is approaching in the thunder-cloud. But in line 2 many moderns (changing only some of the vowel-points) prefer to render, *As one that is jealous with anger against unrighteousness.*' The thunder, however, is not mentioned in the verse (unless we read רַעְמוֹ pro רֵעוֹ 𝔐); and even if רֵעַ could mean *noise* (which is dub.), to attribute noise to light is certainly strange. It reminds one of 'making a noise like a turnip'. In ordinary Heb. יַגִּיד עָלָיו רֵעוֹ means *His friend* (𝔊𝔖𝔗𝔙) *tells upon him* (1 Sa 27¹¹ Es 6²), as we still say in colloquial English; and so 𝔗ⁱ understands it: *He who telleth* a slander (lit. *a third tongue,* cf. Gn 1¹⁸ 𝔗) *against his friend, Jealousy and wrath upon him will go up* = עָלָיו (?) יַגִּיד (מַגִּיר); רֵעוֹ קִנְאָה וְאַף עָלָיו עוֹלֶה ; a bit of gnomic wisdom, quite irrelevant to the context, which appears to have suggested the pointing מִקְנֶה(וּ) אַף עַל־עוֹלָה mentioned by Driver. But how strange is אַף in the connexion, whether as Conj. or as Subst. *(anger)*! Cf. 𝔊 *He declares to his friends his possession,* | *And also to the unjust* = יַגִּיד עַל־רֵעוֹ מִקְנֵהוּ וְאַף עַל־עַוָּלִים. This, though conflicting with the context, shows at least a truer apprehension of Hebrew idiom than RV. Possibly we may recognize an Aramaism in יַגִּיד (נְגַד) *draw, draw out, spread,* e.g. a tent, Je 6³ 43¹²), and read יְרִיעָה *curtain* pro רֵעוֹ. *He draweth over it* (the light) *a curtain.* St. ii is very difficult; leg. fort. מְקוֹם אֹהֶל עַלְעוֹלָה *The place of the tent of the storm* (see 𝔗 4¹⁶; Aram., NH): cf. Is 54² (+יְרִיעוֹת), Ps 18¹². (Or חֶבְיוֹן אַפֵּי עלעולה *The veil of the face of the storm:* cf. Hab 3⁴: or even מְקוֹם אֹרֶב עלעולה *The lurking-place of the storm.*)

So far the poet would seem to have been describing the darkening of the skies, overcast with clouds that shut in the light, before the coming of a storm. He passes on, with hardly a pause, 37¹⁻⁵, to speak in awe-struck tones of the most terrifying of all displays of the Might and Majesty of God—the thunder which is His actual Voice, and the lightning which He wields at will.

Chapter 37.   *v. 1. At this too:* 𝔐 אַף־לְזֹאת (אַף־עַל־זֹ'?)   But why אַף? Nothing alarming has been spoken of hitherto. Perhaps אַךְ (cf. Le 11²¹ אַךְ אֶת־זֶה *But this*). Since, however, there is no real break between this verse and 36³³, we might perhaps read (בְּ)פַלָּצוּת *With terror* (21⁶ 9⁶ Is 21⁴): *With terror my heart trembleth* (1 Sa 28⁵); viz. at the thunder and lightning: cf Ex 19 . S. ii . metr. short:

add בְּקִרְבִּי *within me* (Ps 55⁸ al.). The word fell out owing to homoeoteleuton c לבי ad fin. st. i   For נתר *leap or spring up*, see Le 11²¹ Dr.
(𝔊 ἀπερρύη = וַיִּבֹּל? cf. Ps 1⁵.)

v. 2. St. i is metrically too long. Leg. שְׁמַע c 𝔊 (𝔊^{Nc aA} + Ἰώβ) 𝔖
pro 𝔐 plur et om. שמוע (dittogr.).   *to the rumble of His voice* 𝔊 ἐν
ὀργῇ θυμοῦ Κυρίου = בְּרָגְזוֹ אֵל pro 𝔐 קֹלוֹ; cf. 3ⁿ θυμὸν ὀργῆς = רֹם.
𝔐 is, of course, correct; the thunder is the Voice of Iahvah: Ex 19¹⁶
Ps 29.   *mutter*: הָגָה (Ez 2¹⁰) any *low, deep sound*; cf. the verb הָגָה used
of the *growling* of a lion and the *moaning* of a dove or a mourner, and
(Hi.) the *muttering* of wizards: prob. cogn. c הָמָה. (Is יהוה, as distinct
from יהו, יה, to be derived from a √הוה=המה, and so 'The Thunderer'?
cf. the Bab. *Gamar-Iãma* = Gemariah.)   𝔙 *bene*: Et sonum de ore
illius procedentem. (ובהנה?)

v. 3. Cf. Ps 19⁵. *He letteth it go*, lit. *looseth it*; יִשְׁרֵהוּ Aramaism: 𝔗
30¹¹ Ex 3⁵ CIS 145 A⁷ *to liberate* (S. A. Cook, *Gloss.*, p. 117), שרה, ישרה
Impf. But read perhaps יְשַׁלְּחֵהוּ (12¹⁵ or 1 Sa 20²⁰). (𝔊 ἀρχὴ αὐτοῦ confirms 𝔐: cf. Ezr 5² שָׁרִיו *inceperunt*. 𝔙 considerat = יָשׁוּר. 𝔖 ישבחונה
they praise him.)   *corners*: lit. *wings* = skirts, ends: 38¹³ Is 11¹².
Unto: אֵל = עַל; an leg. עַד? 𝔙 super (= עַל) terminos terrae. Here
God's 'light' is the lightning.

v. 4. *After it*: i.e. the 'light', which the thunder always follows
(because, though the flash and the explosion are simultaneous, light
travels far more swiftly than sound).

His Voice: reading קֹלוֹ c 2 codd. pro 𝔐 קוֹל; cf. the ‖ stichus The
third stichus appears to be a mutilated distich.   Read perhaps

וְלֹא־יְעַקֵּב שִׁפְעַת מָיִם
כִּי־יִשָּׁמַע קוֹל רַעְמוֹ:

And He keeps not back the multitude of waters (22¹¹ 38³⁴),
When His Voice of Thunder is heard (Ps 77¹⁸ ¹⁹);

or perhaps רַעַם קֹלוֹ (cf. 26¹⁴). עָקַב *to hold back*; an Aramaism (𝔗: cf.
Gn 22¹² NH). It is possible, however, that עקב *to heel*, i.e. *seize by the
heel*, was used in the sense of *holding back* (cf. Ho 12⁴). In Syr. Pael
is *to trace out, investigate*: so 𝔙 here *et non investigabitur* (pointing
וְלֹא יְעַקֵּב).

v. 5. St. i is metr. redundant, besides being a feeble repetition of v. 4ᵇ
(ירעם בקול) and grammatically dubious. בקולו, no doubt, is mere dittogr.;
and ירעם has displaced some similar word, e.g. ידענו (= יוֹדִיעֵנוּ) *showeth
us* (cf. Ps 88¹³), or יפעל *doeth* (33²⁹), or יראנו *maketh us see* (Mi 7¹⁵ Ps 78¹¹).
בעל נפלאות (= עשה נפ׳ everywhere else, 5⁹ Ps 136⁴); because עשה follows
in st. ii, with which cf. 5⁹ 42⁷. The verse evidently begins a new paragraph or strophe, dealing with other wonders of the natural world as the

immediate work of God. (𝕲ᶜ adds here the two verses which follow v. 28 in 𝕲ᴮᴬ. Vid. supr.)

we know not how: lit. *and we know not* (8⁹ 36²⁶ᵃ 42³). 𝕾 *and is not known* (pointing נֹדָע pro נֵדַע): cf. Pss 76² 77¹⁰

v 6. The כי *For* is explicative (cf. 36²⁷ ³¹). הֱוֵא אָרֶץ *Fall to earth!* (supposed Arabism; cf. هوى *to fall*) seems very unlikely. Perhaps הַרְוֵה־אָרֶץ *Water the earth!* (cf. Is 55¹⁰). St. ii presents a clear example of dittography in וגשם מטר(וֹת); and עזו ad fin., as an epithet of מטר, is difficult. A verb seems wanting; a need which might be satisfied by reading וּלְגֶשֶׁם וּמְטָר תָּעֹז *And to the downpour and the shower, Be strong!* or וּלְגֶשֶׁם מָטָר תָּעֹז *And to the torrent-rain, Prevail thou!* (cf. מְטַר גֶשֶׁם Zc 10¹ and for משם 1 K 18⁴⁴ᶠ·). (Ez 38²² suggests וגשם ימטיר עָלֶה *And downpour he raineth upon her*, i. e. upon the earth.) An objection to st. i as it stands in 𝔐 (as also to the emendation suggested above) is that it has four stresses, and so is metr. redundant. הואארץ may be a disguise of a single word (א ditt.), e.g. הָאָצֵר *Be stored up!* (cf. 38²² אצר Is 23¹⁸ אצרות שלנ N1.). And עזו ad fin. may represent וּ(שׁ+טֹף) (belonging to v. 7):

For to the snow He saith, Be amassed!
And to the torrent-rain, Overflow!

(גֶשֶׁם is rain in *body, bulk*, or *mass*, qs 'solid rain'; i. e. the heavy continuous torrential rains of the rainy season in tropical and subtropical countries. Cf. Aram. גושמא *the body* (Syr. נְשִׁים *embodied, material, solid*), Ar. جِسْم *the body, a body, a solid*, and by rhotacism גֶרֶם, גֶרֶם *body, self, bone* as solid; וֶרֶם *rainstorm*. But גרם *cut off* = נִדָם, גֶם, &c.)

v. 7. Heavy snows and rains 'seal up' (cf 24¹⁶) mankind, i. e. keep them under cover, and stop all out-of-door work. Wild beasts find shelter and hibernate in their dens (v. 8). Pro 𝔐 בְּיַד leg. בְּעַד (9⁷; 33¹⁶ is corrupt: see note there). In st. ii om. כל (dittogr. fr. st. 1) and read אֲנָשִׁים (v. 24, 36²⁴) pro 𝔐 אַנְשֵׁי (ס exc. ante ט): cf 𝔙 ut noverint singuli opera sua. The meaning seems to be, as Driver put it: that they may 'recognize His hand in their enforced inactivity'. (𝕾 *That every* man .might know τὴν ἑαυτοῦ ἀσθένειαν, *his own weakness*; the little he can do; a paraphrase? 𝕾 *And He maketh known to the world His works*.) If חָתַם בְּ, which usually means *to seal with* (instrum.), could also bear the sense *to set a seal upon* (like the Aram. equivalent רְשַׁם בְּ), we might transpose יד and מעשה, with this resulting distich:

במעשה אדם יחתום
לדעת כל־אנוש ידו:

On man's work He setteth a seal | That every mortal may know His Hand. Cf. Ps 109·⁷.

v. 8. *into a lair*: בְּמוֹ־אָרֶב pro מ' אֶרֶב בְּמַאֲרָב? see 38⁴⁰ Pss 10⁸·⁹ 104²² (where man's labour is mentioned in the next verse). 𝔊 ὑπὸ σκέπην (= אֹהֶל 21²⁸). ἐπὶ κοίτης = מעון'; sic 38⁴⁰ Je 10²¹.

v. 9. The insertion of תֵּימָן *the South* after (הַ)חֶדֶר, on the ground of 9⁹ (where see note), violates the metre with a fourth stress. The '(store-) chamber of the stormwind' is the magazine (cf. Ps 135⁷) in which God holds it in reserve, as He holds the snow and hail in other 'treasuries' (38²²ᶠ·). 𝔊 ἐκ ταμείων = חדרים (Pr 7²⁷ 24⁴ Ps 105³⁰). Leg. fort. מִנִּי־חָדָר *Out of the Storehouse.* (ταμεῖον, late form of ταμιεῖον.) Cf. the classical myth of the Cave of Aeolus and the Winds. It was not then known that the winds are caused by variations of atmospheric temperature. סוּפָה prob. *turbo, cyclone*; cf. 𝔙 tempestas. 𝔊 ὀδύναι; prob. a scribal error for αἱ δῖναι (*ut alii*), *the whirlwinds*. Cf. 𝔗 וְעַלְעוּלָא *the stormwind*; 𝔖 ܟܘܒܝܬܐ *a sudden storm* of wind, snow, or sand.

The metr. defect of st. ii may be supplied by inserting תֵּאתֶה *cometh* (cf. v. 22) as ‖ to תבא st. i. But what is מְזָרִים? The expression can only mean *from the scatterers*; improb. supposed to be an epithet of the winds, as scattering the clouds and bringing cold. Read מִמְזָוִים *out of the garners* (Ps 144¹³) or storehouses; a suitable ‖ to חדר(ים) (so Driver). 𝔊 *And from downpour* (זריפתא); a guess. 𝔗 וּמִבָּוַות מָזָרִים *And from the window of the mezārím* (Heb. word repeated, because not understood). 𝔊 ἀπὸ δὲ ἀκρωτηρίων, *from the ends or extremities* (i.e. of earth or sky?); or *from the peaks or summits* (ἄκρων τῶν ὀρέων) = מְנֵי־הָרִים? 𝔙 Et ab Arcturo frigus; which perhaps implies ἀρκτῴων cr ἀρκτούρου in 𝔊 pro ἀκρωτηρίων

v. 10. Cf. 38²⁹ᶠ· Is 40⁷. Point יֻתַּן *is yielded, produced*, pro 𝔐 יִתֵּן Impers. The *breath of El* is the icy blast of the north (Ecclus 43²⁰). Four stresses: ? יַקְפִּר *it freezes* (cf. NH). St. ii *And the breadth of the water is in constraint* (OL; cf. RV); 'I.e. *narrowed, contracted*,—the edges of the stream being frozen' (Dr): qs √צוק (32¹⁸; 36¹⁶ᵇ? vid. annot.). But surely the wonder is not the gradual narrowing of the stream or pool, which at first would hardly be noticed; but the whole breadth of it becoming solid, as molten metal does when it cools (cf. מוּצָק v. 18 √יצק 38³⁸ vid. ad 11¹⁵ 22¹⁶ 41¹⁰·¹⁶). An leg. c cod. 1 בְּמוּצָק *like a casting* (1 K 7³⁷)? If the meaning were *And the breadth of waters is narrowed*, would not יוצק (or 'ויצר לר' מ) be the natural way of expressing it? Cf 𝔙 Et rursum latissimae *funduntur* aquae (√יצק), 𝔗 בְּאִתְּכָבוּתָא *in pouring out* or *casting*: cf. 28² 41¹⁶. 𝔊 very strangely: οἰακίζει (adnot. διασχίζει ǀ χωρίζει· ἅπ ἀλλήλων Bᵃ ᵐᵍ· ⁱⁿᶠ) δὲ τὸ ὕδωρ ὡς ἐὰν βούληται. This seems to imply (? כחשק) מַיִם כִּרְצֹנוֹ (בְּחֶפְצוֹ) (v. 12ᵇǀ) וְחֵבֶל ; thus at least favouring 'כ > ב with the last word.

v. 11. St. i is supposed to mean *Also He ladeth the thick cloud with moisture* (RV); but the ἅπ. λγ· רוי from רוה 'v. i' n.' *fill*) is dubious, and the m. ture of the clouds is no longer the poet's topic (see v. 6 36²⁷ᶠᶠ·).

𝕲 (ἐκλεκτόν = בַּר *pure* Ct 6¹⁰) and 𝔙 *frumentum* (= בַּר *corn* Am 5¹¹), in fact, treat ב in בָּרִי as Rad. Hence we may conjecture בָּרָד *hail*, which is associated with lightning ('Fire' of God, Ex 9²³ᶠ), snow and stormwind, Ps 148⁸, and is a frequent accompaniment of thunderstorms (perhaps 𝕲 misread ברד as ברר = ἐκλεκτόν Is 49²), and would naturally not be omitted here (cf. Ps 18¹³); or else בָּרָק *lightning*—a closer ∥ to st. 11. The vb יפריח, also ἅπ., can hardly be regarded as certain. 𝔙 *Et nubes spargunt* (Ps 147¹⁶) *lumen suum* app. read יפזר pro יפריח; in harmony with יפיץ, st. ii. We might do worse than adopt this: *The heavy cloud scattereth Hail* (or *the Flash*), | *The thundercloud streweth His* (*its?*) *Light*. (𝕲 καταπλάσσει, *plasters over or besmears* = ימרח (Is 38²¹) pro 𝔐 יפריח; but the var. 𝕲^{Nc.aA} καταπλήσσει, *terrifies* = יבעת 7¹³ 14²¹ suits ἐκλεκτόν, the *Chosen* or *Pure* One, better.) Elsewhere in OT the √טרח only occurs in the Subst. טֹרַח a *burden* Is 1¹⁴ Dt 1¹² · cf. the NH (Tg Talm) use of the verb. The proposed Arabism יִמְרֶה proiecit (abiecit) is improb. (אף ברק ימרח עב *Also the clouds hurl lightning*). The clouds pour down rain; but the Heb. poets do not conceive them as hurling the lightning (cf. Ps 18¹⁵ 29⁷ 77¹⁸ 144⁶). Possibly we should read יַבְרִיחַ or יָטֹרד (the latter Aram., Assyr., TA, Ar.) *Also the flash pulleth the clouds to flight* | *His light scattereth the cloudmass.* In any case, we must point עָנָן in st. ii pro 𝔐 עָנָן c 15 codd. 𝕲𝔅𝔗. From moment to moment the whole sky is lighted up, and the clouds appear to have vanished

v. 12. The verse contains two distichs. RV treats it as a tristich; metr. overweighting st. 1 (and also st. ii?). But והוא (which prob. refers to the lightning > to the cloud; cf. המתהפכת Gn 3²⁴) demands a verb or Ptcp. as its Predicate, e.g. מְסֻבָב (so 𝕲 or יסובב), of which the ἅπ. מְסִבּוֹת (supposed to be used Adv. in the sense of *all around, in all directions*) might be an easy corruption. Adding שמים as Obj. of the verb (cf. Pss 26⁶ 59⁷), we get the stichus *And it* (emph.) *goeth about the heavens* (Otherwise, מסובב might be regarded as a gloss on מתהפך *turning -round and round*, of the appearance of zigzag lightning; and so st. i would be: *And it turneth about at His steerage*, Pr 1⁵ plur. Qerî hic rectè.) Then the purpose of these quickdarting motions of the lightning is expressed in the words (st. iii or ii?): *That it* (not *they*: the מ belongs to בל: cf. Lc 5²⁴ 11³⁴) *may do whatever He commandeth* (leg. לִפְעֹל מְכָּל־אֲשֶׁר יְצַוֶּה). St. iv (iii ?), defining the place, is perhaps not indispensable to the sense *Upon the face of the world of His earth*. The phrase תֵּבֵל אָרְצָה (so point c 𝕲) is from Pr 8³¹ (משׂחקת בתבל ארצו); a passage of which we have had earlier echoes in Job. It is found nowhere else in OT, תבל being gen. used as a poet. syn. of ארץ and always anarthrous (Ps 24¹). The word is prob. a Canaanite loan from Assyrio-Bab. *tabalu*, the *land, dry land*, syn. *nabalu*, id., as opp to the ··· and ···

Heb.) The primitive meaning is perhaps that which *bears*, is firm, *terra firma* (as we say 'The ice will bear'): cf. Sum. MAL (= BAL?) = GAL, *kânu*, 'be fixed' or 'firm', *naśû*, 'to carry': cf. also סבל *bear a burden*; יבל *bear, bring*. (Possibly the meaning is land as *rising above* the water, *surmounting* it: cf. Sum. BAL, to *scale* walls and mountains, TA-BAL, *surmount, overstep*, &c.). 𝔙 paraphrases the verse: Quae (i. e. nubes) lustrant per circuitum, quocunque eas voluntas gubernantis duxerit, ad omne quod praeceperit illis super faciem orbis terrarum. 𝔊 καὶ αὐτὸς κυκλώματα διαστρέψει | ἐν θεεβουλαθωθ(κυβέρνησις Pr 1⁸ 11¹⁴ al.) εἰς ἔργα αὐτῶν· | πάντα ὅσα ἂν ἐπιτείληται αὐτοῖς, | [ταῦτα συντέτακται παρ' αὐτοῦ, vers. dupl.] ἐπὶ τῆς γῆς (= 𝔐). 𝔖 is much nearer the mark: *And it* (His light) *circleth and turneth about* (מתחפך ומתכרך); *to do the purposes all that He commandeth them, on the face of the world of His earth.*

v. 13. Both stichi are metr. short. In the first we might read אף or אפו for אם² (cf. Is 10⁶ שבט אפי) and לערץ for לארצו (Is 2¹⁰): *Whether for a Rod of Wrath, to awe*. The ו belongs to אם *seq*. For שבט see also 9³⁴ 21⁹. (Instead of לערץ leg. fort. יְרִיצֵהוּ: *Whether for a Rod of Wrath He cause it to run*: cf. Ps 147¹⁵.) In st. ii there can be little doubt that we must read יוצאהו pro 𝔐 ימצאהו. The line may then be completed either thus: ואם־לעשות חסד יוצאהו *Or to do mercy He send it forth*: or ואם־לחסד וֶאֱמֶת יוֹצְ' *Or for mercy and faithfulness He send it forth*. Possibly, however, the whole verse should be read:

אם־לשבט אף על־עריץ
ואם־לחסד לארצו יוצאהו:

Whether for a Rod of Wrath upon the Tyrant, | *Or for mercy to His land, He send it forth*. God's lightnings deal out both judgement and mercy; cf. Jos 10¹⁰,¹¹ Ps 18¹⁴ 144⁶ Is 30³⁰ f. But the verse may very well be a marginal intrusion; inasmuch as the whole passage, 36²²–37¹², dwells rather on the wonder and mystery of the works of God than on His use of them for moral ends. 𝔙 took שֵׁבֶט in the sense of *tribe*: 𝔊 ἐὰν εἰς παιδείαν qs שבט = castigatio; 𝔖 שַׁבֶּט = *sceptre* = sceptriferi; 𝔗 app. שֶׁטֶף *rain-flood*, 38²⁵, pro שֵׁבֶט, with the following extraordinary version or rather perversion: *Whether the rain of vengeance in the seas and wildernesses, or the heavy rain for the trees of the mountains and valleys (?), or the gentle rain of mercy for the fields of fruit and vineyards, He supply him* (= ימצאהו; cf. Nu 11²² al.).

v. 14. Begins a new strophe or apostrophe. Cf. 33¹,³¹ 35², &c. Whether we connect it with the first or the second stichus (𝔐), עמד gives one stress too many for the metre. It is probably an insertion by some one who remembered locc. like 1 Sa 9²⁷ 12⁷. The sense is complete without it.

v. 15. The verse is suspicious on several grounds; st. i being metr. overloaded, and הופיע being app. *Trans.* in st. ii, although it is *Intrans.* everywhere else (cf. 3⁴ 10² Pss 50² 80² al.). *Knowest thou* (i.e. Understandest thou? cf. 37²⁹), *when Eloah attends to* (שׂוּם sc. לֵב 1⁸ Is 41²⁰) *them?* cannot be regarded as a satisfactory sense. 𝔍 *Knowest thou when God imposeth* a decree *upon them?* (cf. RV), *And made shine the clouds of His rain?* But there is no clear reference for עליהם in the preceding context; and we may well be uncertain as to the relation of this verse to the following, which also begins with התדע and mentions the clouds. Is either, in whole or in part, a dupl. or var. of the other? OL, citing Je 38²⁴ for the Constr., renders· *Dost thou know about God's enjoining upon them?* and so *v.* 16. *Dost thou know concerning the balancings of clouds?* But we cannot avoid asking 'Enjoining what?' and 'Upon whom?' cf 34²³ᵃ. (And what is the connexion of thought with v. 17?) 𝔊 hardly helps us with *We know* (𝔊ᴬ *Thou knowest*) *that God set* (= made) *His works | By making Light out of Darkness* (a ref. to Gn 1²·³) = נֵרַע כִּי־שָׂם אֵל פְּעָלָיו מוֹפִיעַ אוֹר מֵעָנָן. 𝔙 Numquid scis quando praeceperit Deus *pluviis* (cf. 𝔍 supr.), *ut ostenderent* lucem nubium eius? (= והופיעו plur. *Trans*). 𝔊 הֲא תֵדַע *Behold, thou knowest* pro התדע alioq. = 𝔐.

It seems possible that vv. 15, 16, should be transposed:

Knowest thou the spreadings (מפרשׂי pr 𝔐 מפלשׂי ut 36²⁹) *of cloud* (om. עָל),— *The doings* (leg. מִפְעָלוֹת Ps 46⁹ pro 𝔐 מפלאות voc. nil. 6 codd. נפלאות) *of the perfectly Wise* (leg. דעות 36⁴ 1 Sa 2⁴)*,— *When He setteth* (om. התדע¹ ut dittogr.) *His tent* (אהלו pro 𝔐 אלוה) *upon them, And the light of His thundercloud shineth forth?* Cf. 36²⁹ ³⁰ Ps 18¹²·¹³. [The variation of the phrase מברשׂי עב 36²⁹ which meets us here, מפלשׂי עב, supposed to be a mode of writing מפלסי ע', is not prob., whether we take it to mean *weighings out* or *levellings* of the clouds. The point is their *spreading* over the heavens: cf. 1 K 18⁴⁴ᶠ. 𝔊's διάκρισιν νεφῶν may = מפרשׂי עב (cf. Le 24¹²).] We may also suggest a bolder reconstruction of the two verses, viz.:

הֲתוֹדַע מְפָרֵשׂ עָבִים
וּתְאַלֵּף תְּמִים דֵעוֹת
בְּשׂוּם עָב לְבֻשׁוֹ (מְעִילוֹ)
וְהוֹפִיעַ אוֹר עֲנָנוֹ:

Dost thou teach (32⁷) *Him that spreadeth the clouds,*
And instruct the Perfectly Wise,
When He maketh the cloudmass His cloak (cf. 38⁹),
And the light of His cloud shineth out?

(Or read for the third line: בִּלְבֹשׁ אֱלוֹהַּ עֲרָפֶל *When God clotheth Himself with cloudgloom*: ⁶²¹· Ps 97⁴ Is 59⁷.)

* עַם רֵעִים i found nowhere else, and רֵעִים 'ת· 11 d ·', , ¡gì'

𝕲 v. 16ᵇ ἐξαίσια δὲ πτώματα πονηρῶν = רָעִים (מִפְלַח?) וּפִתְאוֹם אֵיד; cf. 9²³ 22¹⁰ 18¹² 31²⁹ Pr 29¹⁶ (but also Job 16¹⁴ 20⁵). This appears altogether improbable.

v. 17. Apparently a sarcasm. *Thou whose garments are* (unbearably) *hot, When the earth is still* (Is 57²⁰ ch. 34²⁹) *from the South*; i.e. 'in the sultry stillness preceding a sirocco' (Dr). How can you pretend to be His equal or mentor, Who at will wraps the fiery stormcloud about Him? (Cf. Ps 104².) Perhaps we should read מֵחֹרֶב *from the heat* (Is 4⁶ 25⁶ al.) pro מִדָּרוֹם *from the South* (i.e. *on* the south; cf. Gn 2⁸). 𝔙 seems more natural than 𝔐: *Nonne* vestimenta tua calida sunt, Cum *perflata fuerit* terra Austro? = (fort.) בְּהַשֵּׁב בָּאָרֶץ דָּרוֹם | הֲלֹא בג׳ חמים *Are not thy garments warm | When He maketh the Southwind blow over the land?* Ps 147⁸ Is 40⁷. 𝕾 *Thy clothes grow warm; And wilt thou* remove (rg. ? וְתַעְתִּיק cf. 9⁵ 32¹³ pro 𝔐 בהשקט) *the land from the south? And wilt thou extend with Him*, &c. (v. 18). דָּרוֹם (mostly in Ezekiel) is probably of Babylonian origin. In Babylonia the south was the region of clouds and storms. For the Rt. we may perhaps compare Sum. DA-RI, 'to blow hard' (*zâqu*), from RI, id.; qs DARIAM, the 'stormy' or 'blustering' region.

v. 18. Leg. הֲתַרְקִיעַ. The verb רקע is *to beat out* metal (Pi. Nu 17⁴), and so *to spread out*, e.g. the earth (Is 42⁵ 44²⁴ Qal Ptcp.); whence רָקִיעַ the *firmament* or solid arch of the visible heavens (Gn 1⁶ al.), upholding the waters of the celestial ocean. The prim. Rt. is seen in רַק (רקק) *thin*, qs *beaten out*; cf. Sum. RAG, *strike, thresh* (and perhaps RA, RA-G, *walk*, str. *tread, tramp, stamp?*), cogn. c DAG, DA, *outspread, broad,* רַּךְ *thin*, רקק *pound, beat small*, and דכא, דבך, דך, &c.

Like Him (lit. *with Him*: 9²⁵ 40¹⁶) *didst* (or *canst, couldst*) *thou beat out the Sky* (v. 21, 35⁵ 36²⁸ 38²⁷), *Hard* (Ez 3⁹) *as a cast-bronze mirror?* The idea seems to be: How canst thou match thy wisdom with God, unless indeed thou wast His partner in Creation? cf. 9⁸ 15⁸ 38 *passim*. An leg. וּתְחַזְּקֵם pro חֲזָקִים? sive וְתַחֲזִיקֵם? cf. 𝕾 *Wilt thou spread out* (or *make firm*: ܦܡܐ Qal) *with Him the Firmament* (ܠܪܩܝܥ = ܒ.ܪܩܝܥ), *To support* (it) *together?* 𝔙, freely but with elegance: Tu forsitan cum eo fabricatus es coelos, Qui solidissimi quasi aere fusi sunt. *mirror*: רְאִי (ἅπ.) = מַרְאָה Ez 38⁸ (also ἅπ.). For מוצק *poured out, molten, cast*, see v. 10. Ancient mirrors were of burnished metal, usually bronze (copper). I possess Etruscan and old Chinese specimens.

v. 19. *Teach* us: so 𝔐. Some codd. and 𝕲 𝕾 𝔄 *Teach* me. *What we shall* (or *should*) *say to Him* (or *of Him* Ps 3³; but cf. 23⁵). The words are apparently ironical. St. ii: cf. 13¹⁸ 23⁴ 32¹⁴ 33⁵ for עָרַךְ *to arrange* a case, or words. But מִפְּנֵי חֹשֶׁךְ (23¹⁷) *because of* (the) *darkness*, i.e. of ignorance (Driver) is hardly what we should expect from Elihu. 𝕲 καὶ παυσώμεθα (𝕲ᴬᶜ παυσόμεθα) πολλὰ λέγοντες. Perhaps

וַעֲרֹךְ (וְלַעֲרֹךְ) מִלִּים נַחְשֹׁךְ *And from marshalling words let us refrain.* At 𝔙 nos quippe involvimur tenebris. 𝔊 *And we will not hide* (נִסְתָּתַר; perhaps rg. נַעֲרֹק *flee*, Aram., or scribal error pro נסתדר; cf. 𝔗) *from the darkness.*

v. 20. 𝔐 היספר is very dubious (RV *Shall it be told him that I would speak?*). Read rather היכעם (or הֲיֻחַר לוֹ אַף) *Will He be annoyed or angry?* or היסער *will He storm, be enraged?* (cf. 38¹), and metr. grat. either אֵלַי *at me* (2 C 16¹⁰) or אֶל *El.* In st. ii we might transpose the verbs and read אם־יבלע איש כי־אמר *Will He swallow up a man for mere speech?* (כִּי² may be dittogr. But אִם־כִּי־אָמַר אִישׁ יְבֻלָּע *Or because a man hath said, will he be swallowed up?* would also satisfy both metre and sense. Cf. 𝔙 etiamsi locutus fuerit homo, devorabitur; 𝔊 *And if the man speak, he will be swallowed up.*) 𝔊 app. = הֲסֻפַּר וְסֻפַּר לִי בִּי־אִישׁ עֹמֵד אבלע (or כִּי אֶעֱמֹד וְאִישׁ אֲבַלֵּע). Note the conflate equivalent of היספר, and לִי pro לוֹ. Om. כִּי־אדבר.

vv 21–22 appear to herald the Theophany (ch. 38), which is the dramatic climax of the poem. At all events, we are reminded of the thrilling anapaestics with which Aeschylus closes the great lyrical drama of *Prometheus Bound*:

καὶ μὴν ἔργῳ κοὐκ ἔτι μύθῳ
χθὼν σεσάλευται κτλ.

is not seen: leg. fort. יֵרָא pro 𝔐 רָאוּ (= רָאוּי? cf. 𝔊 οὐχ ὁρατὸν τὸ φῶς, and 41²⁵ הֶעָשׂוּי). *dim*: בָּהִיר ἅπ. is compared with Syr. ܟܳܗܝܳܐ *dusky, dim, pale,* of colour; ܟܳܗܝܽܘܬܐ *dimness, faint light;* ܨܰܦܪܐ *dawn, twilight;* ܟܳܗܝܳܐ ܢܽܘܗܪܐ lux subobscura; ܥܢܳܢܐ ܟܗܝܬܐ *a faint cloud;* ܟܳܗܶܐ *dim, uncertain* See also Levy, s. v. בְּהִירָא *cloudy*. 𝔊 τηλαυγές, *far-shining,* 𝔖 ܢܰܗܺܝܪ *bright*; cf. שבהר, שבהורא, in Tgg. Jer. and the Syr. equivalent forms. St. iii, which is extra-metr. as such, may begin the next distich: *But the wind hath passed over and cleared them* (𝔊 ὥσπερ τὸ παρ' αὐτοῦ ἐπὶ νεφῶν: perhaps another interpr. of st ii: ἐπὶ νεφῶν = בשחקים: cf. 35⁵ 38³⁷; but cf. 38¹ 40¹ νεφ. = סערה; an leg. וְרוּחַ סְעָרָה תְּטַהֲרֵם *But the stormy wind cleareth them*, cf. Ez 1⁴), *And out of the North a Brightness cometh* (v. 22; leg זֹהַר Ez 8² Dan 12³ pro 𝔐 זָהָב et וּמִצָּ ad init. 𝔊 ἀπὸ βορρᾶ νέφη χρυσαυγοῦντα = ? עָב זָהָב or זָהֹב = צָהֹב: 𝔊 om. vb.). The clue to the gen. sense seems to be given by the description of the Theophany, Ez 1⁴: *And I saw and, behold, a wind of storm came from the North,* (and 𝔊) *a great cloud* (*therein* 𝔊) *with brightness around it and selfcatching* (? leg. מִתְלַחֶכֶת *selflicking*) *fire* (cf. לָשׁוֹן אֵשׁ Is 5²⁴ and 1 K 18³⁸) For *the North* and the Mountain of the Gods, see 26⁷ Is 14¹³ and cf. Ps 48³ Ez 8⁵ ¹⁴.

Then follows in 𝔐: עַל־אֱלוֹהַּ נוֹרָא הוֹד *Upon* (or *Beside*) *Eloah awful is* (*the*) *Glory;* ιv. 23) *Shaddai, u h ι n ' f und Him.* (𝔊 22 , 23 =

עֲלֵיהֶם נוֹרָא הוֹד וְהָדָר מִשַּׁדַּי : וְלֹא מְצָאֻנוּ שׁוֶֹה לְכֹחוֹ שֹׁפֵט צֶדֶק לֹא־יְעַנֶּה). We may perhaps substitute the more coherent distich : עֲלָעֳלָה נוֹרָא מְאֹד *His tempest* (36³⁸) *is exceeding awful ;* וְשַׁדַּי לֹא־נִמְצָא בוֹ : *But Shaddai is not to be found therein* (cf. 1 K 19¹¹ᶠ). Yet עַל־לֹא' נָאוֹר הוֹד seems possible, cf. Ps 76⁵·⁸ ; etc. ut 𝔐. The word הוֹד *splendour, majesty,* which appears rather isolated in Semitic (not akin to Ar. هاد *repent, speak or go or behave gently :* see Lane), is perhaps akin to Sum. 𐐙 UD ; a primitive Asiatic word for *the Sun, light, bright* (Tibetan *od* ; cf. also Sum. ĠUD, *bright, shine*). Slight changes in the remainder of v. 23 give the distich יַשְׂגִּיא בֹּחַ וּמִשְׁפָּט | וְרֹב צַדִּיק לֹא־יְעַנֶּה : *He showeth great Might and Justice, And the cause of the righteous He humbleth* (? *perverteth* or *wresteth* : יְעַנֶּה 33²⁷ or יְעַנֶּה La 3⁹) *not.* For שׂנא cf. 36⁽²²⁾²⁴. If שַׂגִּיא (36²⁶) were right, we should expect הוּא שׂנִיא : *He is great in power* (בְּכֹחַ 36²²?) *and justice.* V. 24 adds the concluding remark that it is because God combines irresistible power with inflexible justice that man pays Him worship and service, instead of disregarding Him altogether, as despair might induce him to do. Cf. Ps 130⁴ 𝔊 points יְרָאוּהוּ (cf. יִרְאוּךָ 1 K 8⁴⁰) : *Wherefore men will fear Him* (which seems less apt in the context), and continues with *And the wise in heart also will fear Him* (יִרְאֶה pro 𝔐 יִרְאֶה) ; which is quite improb. 𝔙 suggests וְלֹא־יִרְאוּ (et non audebunt contemplari) : cf. Ps 11⁷ Mt 5⁸. But it is doubtful whether חַכְמֵי לֵב *the wise of heart* (Ex 28³†) can mean *wise in their own conceit* (= חֲכָמִים בְּעֵינֵיהֶם Is 5²¹, cf. Pr 3⁷ Sing.). God Himself is חֲכַם לֵבָב (9⁴) ; cf. חֲכַם לֵב Pr 10⁸. In spite of 𝔙 (omnes qui sibi videntur sapientes), the sense must be either *God regards not human wisdom*—He baffles and confounds it (cf. 5¹² ¹³ 12¹³·¹⁷ ²⁰·²⁴ 1 Cor 1²⁵ 3¹⁹), *or the wise fail to apprehend God by their Wisdom* (וְלֹא־יִרְאֻהוּ) . they do not *see Him* (23⁹, cf. 42⁵).

Chapter 38 *v. 1. And Iahvah answered Eyob out of the storm* (or *whirlwind*) cf. 2 K 2¹·¹¹ · app. the storm whose rise is described 37²¹ᶠ. 𝔊 *But* after Elihu had ceased from speaking (τῆς λέξεως· 36² λέξις = מִלִּים : cf. also 29⁹), *the Lord said to Eyob through a whirlwind* and clouds (cf. add. ἐκ τοῦ νέφους 40¹ and Ex 24¹⁶ Mk 9⁷). λαῖλαψ = סְעָרָה (= סַעַר Je 25³² ; סוּפָה 21¹⁸) ; 𝔙 turbo, de turbine.

v. 2. If עֵצָה *advice, counsel, purpose, plan, wisdom,* meant 'God's *plan,* or method, of governing the world, which Job had "darkened" or obscured, by rashly declaring it to be arbitrary and unjust' (Dr), we should have expected עֲצָתִי *My plan.* The meaning seems rather to be. Ignorance, however eloquent, is not illuminating—contributes nothing towards a wise conclusion. The problem is only made more obscure by talk which is not founded on full knowledge of all the pertinent facts. 𝔊 ὁ κρύπτων με βουλήν (מַעְלִים) pro מַחְשִׁיךְ ut 42³) : haud recte. 𝔙 Quis est iste *involvens sententias sermonibus imperitis?* is nearer to the true sense. 𝔊 st. ii συνέχων δὲ ῥήματα ἐν καρδίᾳ, ἐμὲ δὲ οἴεται κρύπτειν ; (= בְּלֵב pro

88. 8 NOTES ON THE TEXT 415

מחשיך מלין בלב וטמני יעלים (at cf. מַחְשִׁיךְ = fort. (?) = מַחֲשִׁיךְ pro (!) מַחְשִׁיךְ and בְּלִי
34¹⁴ εἰ γὰρ βούλοιτε συνέχειν = אם־יישים אליו לבו).

v. 3 *like a mighty man*· pointing כְּגִבֹּר c cod. Ken¹¹⁷ 𝔖𝔗 pro 𝔐𝔊𝔙 כְּגֶבֶר. Many codd. and 𝔊𝔙 אשאלך sine ו. But the stichus is metr. short already; and the ו (= י) may be a relic of אני or אנכי *I* (emphatic)· *I myself will question thee,* &c. But perhaps אשאלך וְאַתָּה הוֹדִיעֵנִי *I will ask thee, and do thou* (emph) *inform Me !* (cf. 𝔊 σὺ δέ μοι ἀποκρίθητι) —an ironical demand—would be better.

v. 4. *Where wast* would express the sense more clearly. The verb is emphatic, not the pronoun *If thou knowest insight* means *If the ultimate truth of things is open to thy vision*, if thou canst penetrate the mysteries of being. The phrase ידע בינה occurs Pr 4¹ Is 29²⁴ (Dr). [The Assyr. use of *îdû* = ידע suggests that the primary meaning of this verb was *to see*. Cf. the Sumerian IDÊ, 'eye' (= IGI); which may be akin to DAG, DI or DE, *bright, shine*: cf. also DI, *judgement*.]

v. 5. *her measurements*. מְמַדֶּיהָ (?) מֵמַד ἅπ. looks like an error pro מדיה (dittogr. מ post מ). *since thou must* (or *shouldest*) *know*; ironically spoken. Or *if thou know* (Impf.): Pr 30⁴.

v. 6. *bases*: or *plinths, pedestals*, on which rest the *pillars* supporting the earth (9⁶ Ps 75⁴ 104⁵). 𝔊ᴮ κρίκοι (= κίρκοι); but 𝔊ᴬ στύλοι, 𝔙 bases. The word אֶדֶן (Ct 5¹⁵) is perhaps akin to the Assyr. *adannu* (also *adinnu*), a syn. of *dannu*, 'strong', 'firm'; ארון *lord* may be simply 'mighty one'. *planted*. lit. *sunken*. Pr 8²⁵. 𝔊 πεπήγασιν.

v. 7 The language of this verse recalls the time when (as in Babylonia) the stars, 'the Host of Heaven', were regarded as divine beings, 'Sons of Elohim' or 'Angels' (cf. 25⁵ Dt 4¹⁹ 32⁸ 𝔊ᴸ Am 5²³ Is 40²⁶?). 𝔊 gives the doctrinal paraphrase *When the stars came into being, all my angels praised Me with loud voice* (om. בקר). 𝔖 read ברא *He created* pro ברן *when shrilled* or *cheered*. The *stars* of Morning occur nowhere else. For the Morning Star see Rev 2²⁸ (cf. Is 14¹²). The phrase כוכבי בקר may perhaps be compared with כוכבי נשפו *its* (morning-)*twilight stars,* 3⁹ (cf. 7⁴).

v. 8. *And who shut the Sea in*. If 𝔐 וַיָּסֶךְ is right, it must be regarded as immediately consecutive to ירה v. 6, while v. 7 will be parenthetic. But why not read c 𝔙 מִי סָךְ (Quis conclusit *ostus mare*)? For the verb cf. 1¹⁰ 3²³. 𝔊 ἔφραξα δὲ θάλασσαν πύλαις = ואסך (or ואשך cf. Ho 2⁸ and 𝔊). 𝔖 *And shut* (ܐܚܕ) *the doors of the sea* As דלתים recurs v. 10, we should perhaps read: בחול *with the sand* (cf. Je 5²²) or בחיל *with a rampart* pro 𝔐 ברלתים (the ים — might be dittogr. of ים seq.); or even בנבול (?) בנבלות *with a boundary* Je 5²² Ps 104⁹. Cf. the Syr. phrase ימסא סנירין בחלא *the seas confined by the sand*.

St. ii. *burst forth*: ניח 40²³ (Trans. Mi 4¹⁰); cogn. c נ־גח *thrust* (cf. the labialized נ־בע, בע, expressing various kinds of *tufa* s.). After בני־

another ו has fallen out : leg. וּמֵרֶחֶם. Lit. *When he burst forth, and from the womb began to issue*. 𝔊 ὅτε ἐμαίμασσεν (Ep. = ἐμαίμα), *when it was eager*, &c. (The add. μητρὸς αὐτῆς = אִמּוֹ spoils the metr.)

v. 9. עָנָן and עֲרָפֶל occur together some six times. חֹשֶׁךְ Dt 4¹¹ might perhaps be added here st. ii metr. grat. (חשך ערפל חת' *And mirk of clouds his swathingband*). But possibly אחתל (Qal? Hi.? Pi.? cf. Ez 16⁴) or אחבש (cf. Ez 30²¹) has fallen out before the ἄπ. חתלתו (*And cloud I bound on as his sw.*). 𝔊 ἐσπαργάνωσα, pointing חֲתַלְתִּי or חֲתֻלָּתִי; cf. 𝔙 et caligine *illud quasi pannis infantiae obvolverem*. (𝔖 *He made the clouds his clothing*, &c., ut 𝔐.)

v. 10. 𝔐. וָאֶשְׁבֹּר *And I broke* finds no support in the Versions, and is intrinsically improb. 𝔊 ἐθέμην δὲ (αὐτῇ ὅρια) suggests ואשית (cf. 14¹³ תשית לי חק), which we adopt. 𝔙 *Circumdedi* illud terminis meis; 𝔖 *And he made* for him a statute; 𝔗 *And I cut* (ופסקית) i.e. determined *for him my decree*. Leg. חק c 𝔊𝔖 pro 𝔐 חקי (י dittogr. seq. ו). Cf. also Je 5²² Ex 23³¹. Otherwise we might read חקו *his* boundary (Pr 8²⁹). The idea that 𝔐 may mean *And I made its boundary a line of broken rocks and cliffs* (see Dr) is more ingenious than probable.

With st. ii cf. what is told of Merodach in the Bab. Epic of Creation, Tab. IV : *He drew a bolt, a watch he set; Not to let her waters forth them he charged* (*išdud parku maççaru ušaçbit | mêša lâ šuçâ šûnûti umtâ'ir*). This refers to the waters above the firmament, the celestial ocean.

v. 11. Each member of this distich has four stresses in 𝔐. We may perhaps regard וַיֹּאמֶר as extra-metrical, like the introductory heading v. 1; or we might omit it, inasmuch as the following words may be taken as defining the nature of the *limit* or expressing the *decree* (חק). This seems better than to omit either תבוא or ולא־תסיף, weakening the force of the line. For the latter, 𝔊 ולא־תעבר (cf. 9¹¹ 14⁵ Je 5²²). St. ii is corrupt. The best that can be made of 𝔐 is *And here shall one set* it (the חק) *in* (or *against*) *the swell of thy waves*; which is forced and unlikely. 𝔊 ἀλλ' ἐν σεαυτῇ συντριβήσεταί σου τὰ κύματα וּבְכָה יִשָּׁבְרוּ גַלֶּיךָ (which may imply the mispointing of a v. l. ובכה = וּבְכֹה *and here*: cf. Gn 31³⁷). Cf. 𝔙 et hic *confringes* tumentes fluctus tuos. 𝔖 *And here* thou shalt stay (ܬܟܠܐ), &c. It will be noticed that 𝔊 omits גאון, which possibly originated in dittogr. of גליך; or נאונך and גליך may have been var. readings of the ancient text. Either וּפֹה יִשָּׁבֵר גְּאוֹנֶךָ (*And here shall thy swell be broken!*), or וּפֹה יִשָּׁבְרוּ גַלֶּיךָ (*And here shall thy waves break!*), would yield an adequate sense and rhythm. Cf. the phrase משברי ים Ps 42⁸ 93⁴. (Possibly we might read תְּשַׁבַּח pro ב ישית : *thou shalt still thy waves*. Cf. Ps 65⁸ 89¹⁰. The suggested וּבְכֹה יִשָּׁבֵת גְּאוֹן גַּלֶּיךָ is metr. redundant.)

v. 12. 𝔐 lit. From thy days *hast thou commanded the Dawn?* Even if this could mean *Ever in thy life began hast thou*, &c., the question would be irrelevant; for what of the time before Eyob's birth? 𝔊 ἢ ἐπὶ σοῦ συντέταχα φέγγος πρωινόν; *Was it in thy time that I ordered* (or *arranged*), &c. = הֲבְיָמֶיךָ צִוִּיתִי וגו׳; cf. v. 4, 14⁷. 𝔙 Numquid *post ortum tuum* praecepisti diluculo = 𝔐. We propose המוצאו צוית לבקר *Didst thou appoint his going forth* (rise or starting-point) *to the Dawn?* Cf. Ps 19⁷ 65⁹. In st. ii leg. c 𝔙 וְיָדַעְתָּה (cf. Ketîb for the verb). Qerî divides the letters wrongly (יִדַּעְתָּ הַשַּׁחַר). שחר should be anarthrous, like the parallel בקר. The Pi. of ידע here only (unless it should be read in Ps 104¹⁹ also). Perhaps we should read (וְיָעַדְתָּ(ה) *And didst thou appoint* (? לַשַּׁחַר) *the Dawn his place?* So also Ps 104¹⁹: *The sun He appointed his* (place of) *going down* (? יער c dupl. Accus.): cf. 2 Sa 20⁵ Je 47⁷.

v. 13. 𝔐 lit. *That it* (the Dawn) *might seize on the wings* (corners or ends or skirts) *of the Earth | And the godless be shaken out of her*. Some see a reference to 24¹³⁻¹⁷, and suppose the meaning to be that light exposes and disperses evil-doers. But a reference to 'the godless' is quite out of place in this poetical description of natural phenomena. Nothing of the kind occurs in the previous (vv. 4–11) or following context (vv. 14–41; chap. 39: for v. 15 see note); and the ע *suspensum* (רשעים) indicates conjectural restoration of a lost letter, which might perhaps be פ (רשׁפּים) *flames, flashes* of light; cf. 5⁷). *Shaken out* does not seem very suitable as a description of the fires of dawn flashing up from the far ends of earth. Perhaps וְנֵעֹרוּ (14¹² Je 25³²): *And that flames might awake out of her* (or וְיָעִיר or יתערר: *And that it might stir up flames*, &c.: cf. Ps 57⁹); or possibly וּלְבָעֵר (וְיִבְעַר) *And that it might kindle*, &c. The fires of dawn seem to spring up out of the ground at the horizon. 𝔊 ἐκτινάξαι = לְנַעֵר. (וַיְנַעֵר חֹשֶׁךְ ממנה *And shake Darkness out of her* may also be suggested.)

v. 14. *She* (the Earth) *changeth* (or *is transfigured*) *like the clay of the seal* (חותם; ? חתום *sealed*): cf. Driver's comment: 'As the clay takes shape under the seal, so the earth, formless in the darkness, receives shape and form in the light.' In a sense, the light may be said to create anew the world which disappears in darkness. Cf. Gn 1²,³. We are reminded of the miracle by which Merodach, the Bab. God of the Morning Light, convinced his peers of his claim to supremacy:

> *They placed between them a single garment,—*
> *Unto Merodach, their first-born, spake they:*
>
> '*Thy destiny, Lord, be before the gods!*
> *Speak destruction and creation; let them be done!*
>
> *Open thy mouth, be the garment destroyed!*
> *Speak it again, l. th, ar, n: wh l l'*

He spake with his mouth, the garment was destroyed;
He spake it again, and the garment was created anew.

When the gods, his fathers, had seen the issue of his mouth,
They rejoiced, cried in homage, 'Merodach is King!'
                                    (Creation Tab. IV, 19–28.)

The test was, of course, the power of creating and destroying by a mere word. Gn 1³ Ps 33⁶.

St. ii is metr. short, since כְּמוֹ is proclitic (cf. 6¹⁵ 14⁹ al.). Moreover, the sense is obscure. OL *And they* (terrestrial things) *stand forth* (in the light) *like a garment*. But the def. Subj. is lacking (RV supplies *all things*!); and how can *in the light* (באור) be omitted? and what can standing forth *as a garment* mean? Driver explains (continuing the sentence quoted above) 'and the things upon it stand out *each in its proper colour and relief*, like a garment *in folds*'; but there is nothing in the Heb. to suggest the phrases we have ventured to italicize. Others think that the earth is compared to a carpet embroidered with many-coloured designs (reading וְתִצָּבַע or וְתִצְטַבַּע *and she is dyed*; cf. Ju 5⁵⁰ Je 12⁹ and Aram. use of the verb); but לְבוּשׁ is not a carpet. 𝔙 *et stabit sicut vestimentum* = וְתִתְיַצֵּב כְּמוֹ לבוש. Adopting this form of the verb, and restoring בָּאוֹר after it, we get the tolerable sense and rhythm: *And standeth in the light as* (*in*) *a garment*: cf. Ps 104²: or, pointing לָבֻשׁ, *like one apparelled*. (Ps 65¹⁴ might suggest וְתַעֲטֹף אוֹר כְּמוֹ־לְבוּשׁ *And she donneth light as a garment*.) Further, in view of the Aram. (Syr.) use of √צבת, we might possibly read : וְתִצְטַבֵּת אוֹר כְּמוֹ־לְבוּשׁ *And adorneth herself with light as a garment*.

𝔊 very differently : ἢ σὺ λαβὼν γῆν (𝔊ᶜ γῆς) πηλὸν ἔπλασας ζῷον | καὶ λαλητὸν αὐτό(ν) ἔθου ἐπὶ γῆς; cf. 10⁹ πηλόν με ἔπλασας. λαβὼν γῆν (γῆς) may be due to הארץ . . . אחז v. 13; but cf. Gn 2⁷. πηλόν = חֹמֶר as usually (or טִיט Is 41²⁵ both); ζῷον = חַיָּה (חַיּוֹת) = 𝔐 חוֹתָם. The language is evidently influenced by Gn 2⁷·⁸·¹⁹ 𝔊. Perhaps 𝔊 read or guessed at a text something like this:

הֲיָצַרְתָּ מֵחֹמֶר חַיָּה
וַתְּשִׂם מְמַלֵּל בָּאָרֶץ:

Lastly, we may observe that it would yield a closer parallel to st. i, if we might read רפש (Is 57²⁰) pro לבן(ו)ש, making the line וְתֻצַּר כְּמוֹ־טִיט וָרֶפֶשׁ *And taketh shape like clay and mire*.

v. 15. The distich is perfect, but seems out of place, and may be an intrusion. It is certainly improb. that *their light* can mean darkness, even ironically (Dr). 24¹⁶·¹⁷ does not justify this interpretation. Cf. 18⁵. For st. ii, see Ps 37¹⁷. (𝔊 makes the verse interrog., reading . . . וְתִמְנַע וּזְרוֹעַ רָמִים תִּשָּׁבֵר *Didst thou take from the wicked the light* | *And the arm of 'h haughty n.. didst thou break?*)

v. 16. *springs*: so 𝔊 πηγήν: cf. 𝔙 *profunda* maris; so 𝔖. The rare נִבְכֵי (see 28¹¹ 𝔊 βάθη, Pr 8²⁴ τὰς πηγάς, 𝔐 נבכי) may be cogn. c Assyr. *labâku* (Sum. 𝐃𝐔𝐑 *labâku* and *raṭbu*); cf. *labâku*, 'pour out' and Syr ܠܒܟ *rise, spring up*, and נָבַע *well up, flow*, &c. The 'fountains of the great Deep' (Gn 7¹¹ Pr 8²⁸) which supply the terrestrial seas from the abyss of 'the waters under the earth' (Ex 20⁴ Ps 24² al) appear to be intended.

the bottom: חֵקֶר *search*, and that which demands it; something *hidden* or mysterious and beyond human investigation. 𝔊 (*ἐν*) ἴχνεσιν (so ἴχνος 11⁷); but 𝔙 et in *novissimis* abyssi deambulasti? (= in the *extremest* parts). (For the possible etymology see note on 11⁷.)

v. 17. Gates of Death: cf. Ps 9¹⁴ 107¹⁸. As elsewhere, מוֹת is here a syn. of שְׁאוֹל, and denotes the place of the Dead, which was believed to lie below the subterranean waters of Ocean (26⁵). There is something wrong with st. ii. 𝔐 lit. *And the gates* (שַׁעֲרֵי rep.) *of Gloom* (צַלְמָוֶת 10²¹ *Land of Gloom*) *seest thou?* We might read, after 10²¹, וְאֶרֶץ צַלְמָוֶת רָאִיתָ *And the Land of Darkness hast thou seen?* or we might suppose that the repeated שַׁעֲרֵי has supplanted דַּלְתֵי *doors* (v. 10). The phrase *Doors of Darkness* sounds well enough in English; but we should have expected שְׁאוֹל > צַלְמָוֶת, which is hardly used in this concrete way as a name or syn. of She'ol elsewhere (cf. 𝔊 ᾅδου = שְׁאוֹל). 𝔊 seems to incorporate duplicate pointings in both stichi. ἀνοίγονται δέ σοι φόβῳ πύλαι θανάτου | πυλωροὶ δὲ ᾅδου ἰδόντες σε ἔπτηξαν; = הֲנִגְלוּ לְךָ (בְ)שַׁעַר שַׁעֲרֵי מָוֶת | וְשֹׁעֲרֵי שְׁאוֹל רָאוּךְ וַיִּרְאוּן: Interesting as this may be from the point of view of mythology, it is hardly probable, as such a ref. to the 'Porters of Hades' would be quite isolated in the entire OT. (שַׁעַר שַׁעֲרֵי may be mere dittography.)

In the Bab. legend of the Descent of Ishtar, when the goddess arrives at the 'Gate of the Land of No-return', she demands admittance of the Porter, who passes her through seven successive gates, at each of which she has to surrender some part of her ornaments and clothing, until at last she is quite naked (cf. 1²¹).

v. 18 Hast thou considered (𝔐 'הִתָב; an leg 'הֲהִתְ?)· or *discerned*, or *ascertained*, 26¹⁴. עַד should prob. be עַל (31¹ Ps 37¹⁰) or אֶל Is 14¹⁶ (cf. Nu 23¹⁸ עָדַי). In v. 16 also עַד may have displaced the more usual אֶל (cf. v. 22) *breadth*: 𝔐 רַחֲבֵי ἅπ. (The Sing. רַחַב 36¹⁶ is prob. corrupt: see note there.) The breadth of the earth both ways (from N. to S. and E. to W.) may be intended; but why not read רֹחַב הָאָרֶץ *the breadth of the earth* (Gn 13¹⁷) instead of 𝔐 רַחֲבֵי אֶרֶץ? Cf. 𝔙 Numquid considerasti *latitudinem terrae?* 𝔊 νενουθέτησαι τὸ εὖρος τῆς ὑπ' οὐρανόν;

how great it is: reading כַּמָּה = 𝔊 πόση τίς ἐστιν pro 𝔐 כֻּלָּהּ *all of it* (i. e. the earth). Cf. Zc 2⁶ לִרְאוֹת כַּמָּה רָחְבָּהּ *to see how great is its breadth*.

v. 21. This ironical remark seems to have been displaced in 𝔐. Following v. 18, it completes the quatrain. Cf. v. 4, 15⁷.

v. 19. 𝔐 can hardly mean *Where is the way to the dwelling of light?* as RV (= אֵי־זֶה דֶרֶךְ יִשְׁכָּן־אוֹר). The ה of הדרך might be dittogr. of the preceding ה. But *the way* (to where) *light dwelleth* (cf. 1 K 13¹² 2 K 3⁸) is not exactly parallel to *the place of darkness*. איזה הדרך is prob. due to v. 24, which begins so. We may either read ארץ pro הדרך after 𝔊 (ποίᾳ δὲ γῇ αὐλίζεται τὸ φῶς;), *Where is* the land *where Light dwelleth?* or more simply איזה ישכן אור *Where dwelleth Light?* Light and its negation are regarded as separate entities, each having its own proper abode, from which it issues in its turn to cover the earth.

v. 20. Might be understood ironically: *For thou takest* (i.e. *conductest*) *it unto its bourn* (or *territory*: fines), | *And discernest the paths to its house*. For לקח אל of *taking to* a place, see Nu 23²⁷. Cf. 𝔙. There is no reason to alter either verb. The rendering of RV: *That thou shouldst take it*, &c., is also possible: cf. 𝔙 Ut ducas unumquodque ad terminos suos, | et intelligas semitas domus eius. (𝔊 εἰ ἀγάγοις με = כִּי תִקָּחֵנִי pro כִּי תִקָּחֶנּוּ 𝔐 is not prob.)

v. 22. Snow and Hail, again, like Light and Darkness, are regarded as independent substances (not as forms of water), amassed in unknown 'storehouses', whence God brings them forth for His purposes.

sawest thou: or *didst* or *canst thou see?* תִרְאֶה as in v. 17. But 𝔊 ἑόρακας, 𝔙 aspexisti suggest רָאִיתָ. (In st. ii 𝔊 ἐπί = עַל pro 𝔐 אֶל.)

v. 23. *I reserved for the time of stress:* cf. 21³⁰. So 𝔙 Quae praeparavi in tempus hostis (= ווו. צָר). An leg. צָרָה ut Ps 37³⁹ al. 𝔊 ἐχθρῶν צָרִים. By God's ordinance the elements play a part in the drama of human struggle and conflict: cf. Jos 10¹¹ Ju 5²⁰ᶠ. Is 28²¹ 30³⁰ Ps 18¹³ᶠᶠ. 77¹⁷ᶠᶠ. Ex 14²¹. (Was the original rhythm שֶׁחָשַׂכְתִּי לְעֵת צָרָה?) 𝔊 ἀπόκειται (𝔊ᴬ pl.) δέ σοι εἰς..., *And hast thou them laid up for...?* A mistaken paraphrase.

v. 24. Cf. v. 19. 𝔐 = either *Where is the way*, (to where) *the light* (= lightning, 37³·¹¹) *divideth itself?* or *Where is the way* (along which) *the light*, &c. (= 𝔙 Per quam viam spargitur lux etc.). 𝔙 seems to transpose the verbs of the two stichi, as it continues with *dividitur* aestus super terram? But 𝔊 πόθεν δὲ ἐκπορεύεται πάχνη (𝔊ᴬ φῶς) = אֵי מֶה יֵחָלֵק כְּפוֹר *Whence cometh the hoar frost?* cf. 2² 41¹¹ v. 29 for the equated words. This looks like a variant of v. 29; but st. ii ἡ διασκεδάννυται νότος (= קָדִים Ex 10¹³ 14²¹) εἰς τὴν ὑπ' οὐρανόν; = 𝔐. (If πάχνη = קִימוֹר here, as in Ps 119⁸³, it would be strange that 𝔊 should use it again (v. 29) to represent the totally different כְּפֹר.) The idea of *the east wind* (15²) being *scattered* over the earth cannot be regarded as appropriate or natural. The winds may scatter things, but are not themselves scattered. The verb פוץ Hi. is used 37¹¹ 40¹¹. app. in relation to lightnings or thunderbolts (cf. also Ps 18¹⁵). We might therefore read בְּרָקִים pro ℳ קָרִים and וְיָפֵץ (or אֲשֶׁר־יָפִיץ) pro יָפִץ: *And (Which) scattereth lightnings upon the earth*. It seems possible, however, that both in v. 19 and here הדרך has displaced ידרך, in the rare poet. sense of *marching on* or *forth* (cf. Nu 24¹⁷ Ju 5²¹). In that case, we might read

אי־מזה ידרך אור
מפיץ ברקים עלי־ארץ:

Whence marcheth forth the lightning | *Scattering flashes over the earth?* (ישכן and יחלק v. 19 being regarded as conjectural supplements after the corruption of the previous word).

v. 25. The words seem to imply a material conduit (תְּעָלָה Is 7³), conveying the water of the torrential rains (the 'downpour') from the celestial ocean above the Firmament. שֶׁטֶף *overflow, flood*, Na 1⁸, is correctly paraphrased vehementissimo imbri by 𝔙 and ὑετῷ λάβρῳ, *violent rain* by 𝔊 — *bolts* reading לַחֲזִיז plur. (cf. Zc 10¹) pro ℳ לַחֲזִיז. 𝔊 (ὁδὸν δὲ) κυδοιμῶν (*And a way*) *of uproars* (Epic word; ἅπ. in 𝔊). But cf. 28²⁶ᵇ (same Heb. st.).

v. 27. the desert waste: see 30⁵. St. ii ℳ lit. *And to make sprout the outgrowth* (or *growing-place*) *of herbage*. Instead of מֹצָא *outgoing* it is better to read מְצִיָּה *out of the dryness*, i.e. the parched land or arid desert: see 30⁵. Perhaps rather צָמָא (? צְמֵאָה) *the thirsty*: Is 44³. In that case, render: *And to make the thirsty ground sprout grass* (dupl. Accus. ut Ps 147⁸).

v. 28. The 'rain' here may perhaps mean the gentle showers falling in drops (cf. st. ii), as distinct from the torrential downpour of v. 25. The ideas of paternity and generation, so strange to us in such a connexion, would not appear so to the ancient world. (In Sumerian 𒀀 A, 'water', is also 'seed', 'to beget', 'father', &c.) According to the transparent myth, Heaven is the husband of Earth.

𝔊 𝔙 *Who is the father of rain?* in closer agreement with the parallel stichus. *the drops of dew*: so 𝔗 טַלָּא רְסִיסֵי (cf. Ct 5²); 𝔙 stillas roris; 𝔊 βώλους δρόσου, *lumps of dew* (cf. Ecclus 22¹⁶); 𝔖 simply ܓܐܒ̈ܐ *the drops* (of rain?). אֶגְלֵי ἅπ. may be etym. akin to עָגֹל *round*, עָגִיל *ring*, &c. (√נגל+א, ע, Preform. Cf. גלל *roll*.)

v. 29. For קֶרַח *ice* see 6¹⁶ 37¹⁰. Prim. √קר; cf. קָרַר, קֹר *cold*. But the original meaning may be *smoothness, cleanness, brightness, whiteness*, rather than *coldness*; cf. קָרַח *make bald* = גָּלַח *shave* = נָלַב; חור (Intern. Tril.) *be white*; Sum. 𒆗 𒆗 KAR-KAR, *glitter*.

who bare it: or *who begat it*. If a *mother* were intended (cf. st. i), ילדתו would be more natural than ילדו. But הוֹלִיד was *begat* in the last verse (where 𝔙 Qui- _nuit_, as here: cf. also 𝔊).

v. 30. *stiffen*: reading יִתְקַפְּאוּ, of which 𝔐 יִתְחַבָּאוּ *are hidden* might perhaps be a mishearing in dictation; cf. Ex 15⁸ תחמות קפאו *The Deeps congealed* or *became solid*; chap. 10¹⁰ Hi. *didst curdle me* like cheese; קפאון *ice*, Zc 14⁶. 𝔐 admits of the rendering *As with stone* the waters are hidden; but *are covered* or *shut in* would be more natural, and יתחבאו is not a good parallel to יתלכדו, st. ii, which recurs, 41⁹⁽ᴬᵛ¹⁷⁾, of the *sticking together* or closeness of the crocodile's scales, and may be regarded as an Arabism: cf. لَكِدَ *become matted together*, of hair; *stick or cleave to*, of dirt; Conj. 5 تَلَكَّدَ (= התלכד) *it clave together, one part to another*; *he became thick and compact* in flesh (Lane). It is evident from 41⁸ that לכד may be used as a syn. of דבק *cleave* or *stick to* (cf. also 41¹⁰⁽²³⁾). Others would transpose the two verbs of the verse; but 'The surface of the Deep *is hidden*' does not seem a likely statement. Cf. 𝔙 In similitudinem lapidis aquae *durantur*, Et superficies abyssi *constringitur*. 𝔊 Like stones the waters *become hard* (מתקשין; perhaps reading יתחבאו pro יתחזקו).

If we do transpose the verbs, we might perhaps read יתרבדו for יתלכדו; getting the sense

> *As with stone the waters are bespread* (or *confined*),
> *And the face of the Deep is hidden.*

Cf. רבד *bespread*, P 7¹⁶, or Arab. رَبَدَ *shut in, confine*.

𝔊's version is altogether off the lines both of the Heb. and of probability. It seems to have read

> כִּיבְלֵ(י) מַיִם יֵחַת
> וּפְנֵי תהו מִי־כִלָּה׃

Cf. Is 44⁴ ῥέον ὕδωρ; Is 29²¹ ἀδίκοις; chap. 11²⁰.

In st. ii perhaps rather (יַתִּיךְ) וּפְנֵי תֹעָה מִי־הֵתִיךְ (ἔτηξεν: cf. Na 1⁶).

Thus 𝔊 ἡ καταβαίνει ὥσπερ ὕδωρ ῥέον; | πρόσωπον δὲ ἀσεβοῦς τίς ἔτηξεν; (so 𝔊ᴺᴬ but 𝔊ᴮ ἐπτηξεν) seems to imply 𝔐 as read in a partially defaced text.

v. 31. For the constellations named in this verse, see notes on 9⁹. It is natural to read מַעֲנְדוֹת *bonds* (cf. the verb 31³⁶ Pr 6²¹) instead of 𝔐 מַעֲדַנּוֹת *delights* (ἅπ.); cf. 𝔊 συνῆκας (החשביל?) δὲ δεσμὸν Πλειάδος. 𝔗 הֲתִקְסוֹר שֵׁירֵי כִימְתָא *Dost thou bind on the chains of Kîmah?* (What are these 'chains'? Are they the links that bound the Seven Sisters together in a single group or cluster, or perhaps fastened them to their place in the Firmament?) But 𝔙 Numquid conjungere valebis *micantes stellas* Pleiadas? suggests a different pointing of 𝔐 (מְעֹרְפוֹת?), as if the word were derived from מָעַד *quiver, tremble*, and so *twinkle*, or *sparkle*. 𝔊 *Dost thou shut* (the door) *in the face of Kîmah?*

St. ii. *the fetter* : 𝔐 מֹשְׁכוֹת ἅπ. supposed to mean the cables with which the rebel giant is *dragged* across the sky. But the phrase מוסר פתח

38. 32   NOTES ON THE TEXT   423

(12¹⁸) and the question עָרוֹד מִי פִתֵּחַ וּמֹסְרוֹת (39⁵) suggest the reading מֹסְרוֹת = מֵיסְרוֹת *bonds* or *shackles*. 𝕲 καὶ φραγμὸν (= מְשׂוּכַת; Is 5⁵) Ὠρίωνος ἤνοιξας; differs from 𝔐 in vocalization only. 𝔙 *gyrum* Arcturi, the *ring* (or *course*) of Arcturus; cf. 𝕲 *Or the path* (שְׁבִיל) *of the Giant hast thou seen?* 𝔗 *And the cords which draw Orion* (נִיפְלָא) cf. נְפִלִים Gn 6⁴) *wilt thou loose?*

v. 32. כִּימָרוֹת, 𝕲 Μαζουρώθ (מַזָּרוֹת), usually identified with מַזָּלוֹת 2 K 23⁵ (𝕲 τοῖς μαζουρώθ; 𝔙 duodecim signis), is probably a corrupted form of the name of some single star or constellation, rather than that of the Zodiac, or the Babylonian Stations (*manzazu, manzaltu, mazaltu*) of the Great Gods (3 R 59, 35a; Creation Tab. V al.). The parallelism requires this; and it is supported by the Sing. Suff. of בְּעִתּוֹ *in his season*. So 𝔙 Numquid producis *Luciferum* in tempore suo, 𝕲 ܥܶܢܠܬܳܐ (ענלתא) *the Wain*; but 𝔗 שָׁטְרֵי מַזָּלַיָּא (cf. 9⁹ v. 38) = מַזָּלוֹת. What the original term was can no longer be determined with certainty. It may well have been partially assimilated to Mazzaloth by some scribe or editor who took their identity for granted. S. Jerome seems to have connected the word מַזָּרוֹת or מְזוֹרוֹת(?) with זָהַר *shine*, Ar. زَهَرَ id., of the heavenly bodies, perhaps مَزْهُور *mazhûr, shining*; cf. أَزْهَرَ the planet Venus. In Is 14¹² he has *Lucifer* for הֵילֵל *The Shining One*. Conjecture in such a case appears almost hopeless; but if we are to think of a single star, we may perhaps suppose a מֵזוֹרָק = Arab. مِزْرَاق *mizrâq, a lance*. The Babylonians knew of a Lance-star, *kakkab mešrê*, Sum. MUL KAK-SIDI; an expression which is also equated with *šukûdu* and *tartaḫu, spear* or *javelin*. Cf. a passage in the Hunting-inscription of Assurnâçirpal, 1 R 28, col. 1, 13-15, which reads: Ina ûmât kuççi ḫalpê šûrîpi, ina ûmât nipiḫ MUL KAK-SIDI ša kîma êrê içûdu, 'In the days of cold, frost, snow, in the days of the (heliacal) rising of the Lance-star, which glowed like (burnished) copper'. The appearance of this star in the morning twilight was thus associated with the winter season. It has been identified with Antares, the principal star in Scorpio. However that may be (the Chinese call β Bootes 天矛 T'ien-mau, Heaven's Lance), it is perhaps possible that מַזָּרוֹת has grown out of מַשְׂרוֹ(ן) (Masrô), which in Hebrew might represent the Assyr. *Mašrû* (cf. *šâpiru* = סוֹפֵר, *šakan* = כֵּן, *šigaru* = סוּגַר, and T. A. *zûkin*, an attempt to reproduce in cuneiform the Canaanite pronun. of סוֹכֵן = *sâkin*)   St. ii ap. OL *And the Bear with her children, wilt thou lead them?* The Arabs call the four great stars of this constellation نَعْش Na'sh, the Bier, and the three stars of the tail بَنَات نَعْش the Daughters of the Bier, i.e. the mourners following it. Hence Gesenius proposed to read עָשׁ both here and in 9⁹, as an apocopated form of נָעָשׁ = نعش; which is certainly an attractive conjecture, though it would seem to require בָּנֶיהָ בִּנְתֵיה (a⁻ ⁸ نعس) *f* see Lane . 𝔗 i . . ('.. .,.-hen (i.e. the Pleiades; וְנַחְתָּ], which others suppose to mean Ursa Minor) *with her brood wilt thou lead?* (It is at least a coincidence, if nothing more, that *ki*, 'the fowl', is the animal associated with Mao, the Pleiades, in Chinese astronomy.) 𝔊 *Or dost thou stand before* (or *preside over?*) *'Iyúthā* (= עיש pointed עָיִשׁ or עָיִשׁ; cf. אִיוֹב Arab. *'Ayyúb*). 𝔊 evidently read פְּנֵי׳ *face* pro בְּנֵי׳ זּג. Amid all the uncertainties of the text, we may perhaps hazard the conjecture

התציא תַּמּוּז בְּעִתּוֹ
וְעֶשְׁתַּר(תּ) עַל־בְּנָהּ תְּנַחֵם:

Canst thou bring forth Tammuz *in his season,*
And comfort Ishtar for her son? (cf. Je 31¹⁵).

The reference would be to the return of spring, and the revival of vegetation from the death of winter. In Babylonian myth Ishtar was (among other things) Venus, the Evening Star (cf. 𝔙 *Vesperum*); and it seems possible that Tammuz (DUMU-ZI, *Du'dzu, Dûzu*, also *Tamûzu*), her spouse and son, may have had some legendary connexion with the Morning Star (𝔙 *Luciferum*), although none such has yet been established. (Tammuz and his fellow-god NIN-GISH-ZI or GISH-ZIDA stand 'in the gate of Anu', the god of Heaven, in the legend of Adapa.) However that may be, Ursa Major is out of the question, since, as Burney has pointed out, the four stars or constellations appear to be introduced as betokening changes of weather by their rising and setting (the whole context, vv. 22–38, relates to such changes); whereas Ursa Major never sets, but is always visible in the northern sky, and could not therefore be supposed to have any meteorological significance. (If, as Burney thinks, *EB* s. v. STARS, עיש is the Pleiades and כימה Canis Major, the Great Dog which lies at the feet of Orion the Hunter southward, perhaps בינה = כימה, with interchange of n, m, such as we find elsewhere, and כינה may be compared with the Aryan base *KWAN*, Gk. κυν-, Lat. can-, Chinese 犬 k'üen, F. k'ëing, hound, Irish and Gaelic *cu*, dog, Welsh *ci*, Chinese 狗 kou, J. ku, dog. The last is the sixteenth of the 28 Chinese Zodiacal signs = α, β, γ Aries. Cf. also Sum. UR-KU, *kalbu*, dog.)

v. 33. For *the laws of Heaven* see Je 33²⁵ (cf. 31³⁵). Perhaps הֲיָדַעְתָּ (cf. v. 12): *Didst thou appoint the Heavens laws?* (or *impose decrees on the Heavens?*). So Ps 104¹⁹ might be read שמש יעד מבואו *The sun He appointed its setting-place.* We get much the same sense if we point the verb as Pi. הֲיִדַּעְתָּ: *Didst thou make the Heavens to know laws?* (so also Ps l.c.). But 𝔊 *Knowest thou* τροπὰς οὐρανοῦ *the turnings* (i.e. the solstices) or *changes* (of weather) *of heaven?* a doubtful interpretation. 𝔙 Numquid nosti *ordinem caeli?* 𝔖 *Knowest thou* the law (νόμος) *of the heavens?* 𝔙 continues: Et pones *rationem eius* in terra? (= משפטו pro

38. 36   NOTES ON THE TEXT   425

𝔐 (משטרו); but 𝔊 quite differently ἢ τὰ ὑπ' οὐρανὸν ὁμοθυμαδὸν γενόμενα; = בארץ (שנעשו) אם יחד מעשים; omitting תשים (ἴδου may have fallen out of 𝔊). The adv. יחד = ὁμοθυμαδόν ten times in Job (יחדו = ὁμοθ. three times also). Possibly 𝔊 read or guessed מעשיו *his works* pro משטרו, which is an obscure ἄπ. 𝔗 *Canst thou set* שטריה דגלעליה (acc. to ChWB *sein kreisendes Himmelsgewölbe*) *upon the earth?* but בארץ makes any such reference improbable; otherwise we might compare the Assyr. phrase *šitir šamê* (also *šitirtu šamāmi*), meaning the starry firmament ('The writing of Heaven'?) in astrological sense. משטר, which OL renders *rule, authority* ('of the heavens over the earth', but? the Suff.), in form corresponding exactly to the Assyr. *maštaru*, 'a writing', 'inscription', can hardly be correct, unless it be supposed to mean (written) *decree* (leg. משטרך?). We propose משפטך *thy statute, ordinance*, parallel to חקות. Or *dost* (didst, canst) *thou lay thine ordinance on Earth?* (cf. 𝔊).

v. 34. *whelm* (lit. *cover*) *thee*: so 𝔊𝔙𝔗; but 𝔊 ὑπακούσεταί σου = תַעֲנֶךָ. 𝔊 appears to have read וְיִשָּׁטֵף מים יענך | התקרא לעב ב(קול)ך; cf. *v.* 25 (שטף = ὑετῷ λάβρῳ). For שטף מים see Ps 32⁶. This may indicate a real variant. St. ii 𝔐 repeats 22¹¹ verbatim.

v. 35. St. ii 𝔙 Et *reverentia* dicent tibi, Adsumus. The added word seems to make the sense clearer. Has וישובו fallen out before ויאמרו? This would agree better with the verbs of st. i. The lightnings would naturally say, 'Here we are!' i.e. ready to do thy bidding, either when they came at call (which would imply התקרא . . . ויבואו in st. i), or after they had fulfilled one task and returned ready for another. But perhaps the metre is against this (cf. 23⁵ 37¹⁹); and logical precision need not be pressed in poetry.

v 36. RV *Who hath put wisdom in the inward parts? Or who hath given understanding to the mind?* But, as Driver remarks, a reference to the intelligence of man [in general] is not favoured by the context. If we could be sure that טֻחוֹת meant *kidneys* (so 𝔗 כָּלְיָין and Jewish interpr.), we might read מי שחן[לך] וגו' *Who hath set* thee *wisdom*, &c., or simply add the Suff. to the word and read בְּטֻחוֹתֶיךָ *in thy reins*, as Gesenius virtually did when he rendered the stichus thus: *quis renibus* tuis *indidit* hanc *sapientiam?* sc. qua omnia illa cognita et perspecta habes. 𝔗 gives the same rendering in the equally difficult Ps 51⁸ (the only place where the word recurs). The kidneys (כליות) are associated with the mind Je 12² Pr 7¹⁰ 16⁷ al.; and in Chinese *sin fuh shên ch'ang*, 'heart and belly, kidneys and bowels' = the whole mind. Antiquity knew nothing of the real functions of the heart and reins; and the brain is not mentioned in OT at all. In st. ii we might perhaps read לְשָׂכָל (= לְסָכָל), *to a fool* instead of 𝔐 לשכוי (cf. 𝔊ˣ μεμωραμένῳ); cf. Ec 1¹⁷ שכלות. The verse would thus be a sarcasm: cf. v. 21. As, however, the context is concerned with the clouds and connected phenomena, it has been supposed that מחות may mean *dark or heaven-covering clouds* and שכוי *cloud-appearances or shapes* (Aram. סְכָא *see, look out*); and that the idea of the verse is that the clouds, by their motions and varying shapes, evince intelligence! Those who can may accept this view. It is not much more probable than the identification of שכוי with NH שֶׂכְוִי *gallus* (𝔗² st. ii : *Or who gave to the cock-of-the-wild understanding to praise his Lord?* 𝔗¹ is more sensible with ללבא *to the heart*). In all probability, both בטחות and לשכוי are corrupt. The curious translation in 𝔊 (τίς δὲ ἔδωκεν γυναιξὶν ὑφάσματος σοφίαν ἢ ποικιλτικὴν ἐπιστήμην; *Who gave to women spinning-craft or broidering skill?*) app. reads טוות *women who spin* (see Ex 35²⁵ᶠ·) for 𝔐 טחות, and perhaps שֵׂכֶל *skill* (cf. 𝔊Σ μεμωραμένῳ = the same letters pointed differently: vid. supr.) for שכוי. 𝔖 *Who put wisdom in concealment* (בְּכַסְיָא; בְּכַסְיָא ?; cf. Ps 51⁸)? *Or who gave form* (חֶוְוָא) *to the understanding* (= בטחות ut 𝔐; שכוי לבינה?).

v. 37. *Who counteth* (mustereth?) *the clouds by wisdom?* Cf. Ps 147⁴; מונה ... לכוכבים; Is 40²⁶. The idea seems to be that of mustering them skilfully like a flock. Perhaps, however, we should read יפרש = יפרס *spreadeth out* (cf. 36²⁹ 37¹⁰). 𝔙 *Quis enarrabit caelorum rationem* (= 𝔐, om. בחכמה). 𝔊 = 𝔐; perhaps pointing יְסַפֵּר. *waterskins* (נִבְלֵי): or *jars, pitchers*. *tilleth* (יַשְׁכִּיב): or *poureth out*; a possible Arabism (سكب *pour out*, both Trans. and Intr.). So here only in OT. The √שכב is etym. *cause to bend, bow, or incline, make bending*, &c.; being derived from the Causative or Factitive ש and כב = קב, נב, *bend, bow*, &c. Possibly, וְיִבְלֵי שָׁמַיִם מִי יִשְׁפּוֹךְ *And the streams of heaven* (Is 44⁴) *who poureth out?* (cf. Ps 22¹⁵). 𝔊 οὐρανὸν δὲ εἰς γῆν ἔκλινεν; = (?) ולתבל שט׳ מי ישכיב. 𝔙 Et *concentum* caeli quis dormire faciet? = 𝔐 (but taking נבלי in the sense of *harps* or *lutes*, and thinking of 'the Harmony of the Spheres'). 𝔖 *Who numbered the clouds in his wisdom? And the pillars of heaven who set up?* (Perhaps תמרי pro 𝔐 נבלי and יציב pro ישכיב.) 𝔗¹ *Who shall count the Seven Heavens by wisdom; And the measures* (פִּילָוֶות); but Ms בִּילָוֶות *curtains*) *of the heavens who shall lay out* (or *set up*; יַשְׁרֵי) = 𝔐. 𝔗² *Who shall count the stars of the heavens by wisdom; And the clouds which are likened to the waterskins of the heavens, who shall lay out?* (מַן יַשְׁכִּיב; ut 𝔐). Neither 𝔗 suggests any difference of reading. נבלי cannot mean *meteor* (cf. Assyr. *nablu*, 'fire'), if only because of v. 38. It seems possible that v. 36 is a variant of v. 37, or *vice versa* (repetition of חכמה, vv. 36ᵃ 37ᵃ, with ‖ בינה in 36ᵇ but not in 37ᵇ). Verse 36 may once have read:

מי ישפר עבות בחכמה
או מי נבלי שמי׳ יטנה :

*Who telleth the clouds by wisdom,
Or counteth up the waterskins of heaven?*

v. 38. Lit. *in the pouring* (בְּצֶקֶת) Infin. of יצק *pour, cast*, as in Ex 38⁲⁷; used Intrans. as in 1 K 22³³) *of the soil into the casting*; i.e. into solid lumps. (בצק *to swell* is improb. here.) דבק and יצק occur together again, 41¹⁵, in a similar sense. This determines the meaning here.

In st. ii, which is metr. short, יָחַד *together* may have fallen out at the end, or perhaps דָּבָק Adv. Infin. before ירבקו (41⁹). For רגבים *clods* see 21³³. 𝔙 Quando fundebatur pulvis *in terra* looks as if 𝔙 read בארץ instead of למוצק, cf. 𝔊 κέχυται δὲ (𝔊ᴬ γὰρ) ὥσπερ γῇ (= בארץ) κονία. So also 𝔊 *Who poured the dust* upon the earth (על ארעא)? But 𝔗 *When the dust* was founded for a foundation (איחתאם לשיתאסא; cf. v. 4) = 𝔐. In st. ii 𝔙 (Et glebae compingebantur) agrees with 𝔐. So also 𝔗 *And the clods* (גרגישתא 21³³) *clave together*. 𝔊 *And the cliffs* (שְׁקִיפָא) *who fashioned?* The text of 𝔊 is uncertain and prob corrupt. κεκόλληκα (𝔊ᴬ -κεν) δὲ (𝔊ᴬ γὰρ) αὐτὸν ὥσπερ λίθῳ κύβον (𝔊ᴬ κύβον λίθοις). Did 𝔊 read וּכְאָרְגַּב אֲבָנִים *And like a cairn of stones* (cf. 1 Sa 20¹⁹) and point ירבקו?

v. 39. *satisfy* lit. *fill the life* (= *soul* 33¹⁸·²⁰ Ps 143³, and so *appetite, desire*; cf. נפשי 23¹³). 𝔊 ψυχάς. 𝔙 animam. Cf. Pr 6³⁰ (מלא נפש). The more usual phrase is מלא בטן *fill the belly* (20²³). 𝔗 פרנסותא *food* = מִחְיָה. 𝔊 δρακόντων = פתנים (20¹⁶) or תנינים (7¹²) pro כפירים by confusion of letters.

v. 40. *in their lairs* or *haunts*. במעונתם (𝔐 + Suff.). 37⁸ᵇ Ps 104²². The addition of the Suff. improves both metre and sense. So 𝔊 ἐν κοίταις αὐτῶν. 𝔊 gives for the whole verse: *Who multiplied the animals in the wild?* (reading מי ישניא במדבר חַיִּת pro כי ישחו במעונ', with חית repeated by inadvertence from v. 39ᵇ).

The Heb. מָעוֹן, מְעוֹנָה *dwelling-place* has nothing to do with Arab. عَانَ *help*. Cf. perhaps Sum. EN, E, EŠ, *house*, or UN (from GUN), *dwelling* (*šubtu*). 𝔙 in antris = בַּמְּעָרוֹת *in the caves* (dens of wild beasts, Is 32¹⁴). St. ii 𝔙 Et *in specubus* insidiantur (parallel to *in antris*); a paraphrase. 𝔊 om.; 𝔗 ut 𝔐. 𝔊 ἐν ὕλαις, *in brushwood* = 𝔐 בסכה prob., which should perhaps be בְּסֻכָּם *in their covert* or *thicket*: cf. Je 4⁷ id. 25³⁸ Ps 10⁹ 76³. The verse resembles 37⁸. The conjecture בְּסֻכָּךְ seems needless. 𝔐 לְמוֹ־אָרֶב looks strange; cf. בְּמוֹ־אָרֶב 37⁸, and see the note there. Leg. either לֶאֱרֹב *to lie in wait*, or בְּמַאֲרָב *in ambush* (= 𝔊 ἐνεδρεύοντες).

v. 41. A tristich; but st. iii may be marginal. Would the young 'wander' (𝔊 *faint*) from the nest if left unfed? We should perhaps read: יִפְעוּ סָבְלִי אָכְלָה *They scream for lack of food*. But the objection to a tristich remains, unless we suppose that a line has been lost; e.g. ומי יביא אליו טרף *And who bringeth him the prey?* as st. ii.

cry to El: cf. Ps 147⁹ᵇ. 𝔊 πρὸς Κύριον = אל יהוה. 𝔊 πλανώμενοι τὰ σῖτα ζητοῦντες = יתעו לבקש אכל: Ps 104²¹ chap. 39²⁹ (τὰ σῖτα = אכל). *They wander to seek food* may be right.

Chapter 39.—The division is quite arbitrary, and far from happy. The same general subject is continued—the marvels of the animal world as ordered by God not man.

v. 1. St. i appears to be metr. overweighted, unless we point עֵת־לָדַת, so as to secure but three stresses for the line. Even then, יעלי־סלע (here only: cf. Ps 104¹⁸) is questionable as representing a single stress; cf. e.g. 13⁴. Further, the recurrence of ידעת עת לדת in v. 2ᵇ is suspicious. We might perhaps read היערת ליעלי סלע *Didst thou fix the time for the chamois?* (cf. 1 Sa 20⁵). The phrase עת לדת (cf. Ec 3²) would then be a marginal gloss. תֹּאֲנָה *rutting-time* (Je 2²⁴) is not a prob. substitute for it. St. ii add וְ *And* (𝔊 δέ) or אִם *Or* (𝔙 vel).

v. 2. Instead of st. ii (𝔙 Et scisti tempus partus earum?) 𝔊 gives: ὠδῖνας δὲ αὐτῶν (v. 3ᵇ) ἔλυσας (v. 5ᵇ); = וְחֶבְלֵיהֶן תְּפַתֵּחַ *And their pangs dost thou loosen?*

v. 3. *They bow*; sc. in travail: 1 Sa 4¹⁹. *They liberate*: תפלטנה (21¹⁰; cf. סלט Is 34¹⁵) pro 𝔐 תפלחנה *they cleave* or *split* (16¹³). So 𝔙 pariunt (cf. 21¹⁰ vacca *peperit*). St. ii lit. *Their pains* (Ho 13¹³) *they send forth*; i.e. their young, the cause of their pains—a quite possible metonymy, though apparently not found elsewhere. Others would transpose ילדיהן—חבליהן (𝔐 —; הם ; 11 codd. Kenn הן—); but this involves an unlikely change of Subj. in st. i (*They bow; their pains pierce them through*). 𝔊 ὠδῖνας αὐτῶν ἐξαποστελεῖς = חבליהם תשלח' = 𝔐. 𝔙 et rugitus emittunt (app. taking חבל' in sense of *cries* of pain). Instead of st. i, 𝔊 gives us ἐξέθρεψας δὲ αὐτῶν τὰ παιδία ἔξω (A ἄνευ) φόβου; = וְתַרְבֶּה ילדיהן מִפָּחַד or something similar. Illegible text? But in 𝔖 the whole verse appears thus: *And when they bow and bring forth*. Possibly פרי *fruit* or בני *sons* has fallen out before חבליהם, as st. ii is metr. short: *The fruit* (or *sons*) *of their sorrows* (cf. Gn 35¹⁸) *they let forth*. But a more satisfactory suggestion will be found in the next note.

v. 4. St. i has four stresses. It seems prob. that יחלמו (leg. וְהֶחֱלִימוּ) belongs to v. 3ᵇ, which would then run: *Their pains they cast forth, and are well*; i.e. after delivery they recover health (Is 38¹⁶) at once; an appropriate reference to the ease with which such animals bring forth their young. The verb חלם (cf. Syr. ܚܠܝܡ *strong, well*), like the n. בַּר (Aram. בְּרָא) *the open country*, is an Aramaism. Pro יחלמו 𝔊 ἀπορρήξουσιν, 'break away'; cf. 𝔙 separantur = יִפָּרְדוּ? but 𝔖 יִגָּמְלוּ *are weaned* (*Their sons grow up and are weaned*; for the verse). לָמוֹ: 𝔙 ad eas is prob. right (cf. 𝔊 αὐτοῖς) > Dat. Ethic. The adult offspring forsake their mothers for good. *Pro בבר 𝔊 ἐν γεν(ν)ήματι = בפרי; 𝔙 (pergunt) *ad pascuum* = (?) יעברו) במדבר (בְלִבְר).

v. 6. *the salty waste*: reading אֶרֶץ מְלֵחָה *the land of saltness* (Je 17⁶, cf. Ps 107³⁴) *metri gratia*. 𝔐 om. ארץ. 𝔊 ἁλμυρίδα, *saltness* (Diod.) and *salt soil* (Theophr.). 𝔙 in terra salsuginis.

v. 8. *he rangeth*: pointing יָתוּר pro 𝔐 *ἀπ.* יְתוּר. The verb (Nu 13²·¹⁶ ᵃˡ) means to *search* or *explore*; and is perhaps cogn. c שׁוּר *to see, look at.* 𝔊 κατασκέψεται; 𝔙 circumspicit; 𝔗 אַיִּיל *explores* (so Nu 13²). 𝔖 *In the multitude* (of mts. is his pasture); mispointing יֶתֶר *abundance.* 𝔙 montes pascuae suae = הָרֵי מִרְעֵהוּ.

v. 9. *The wild ox* (*Bos Urus*), רֵים, or רְאֵם (Nu 23²² al.), is the *rîmu* or *rêmu* of the Assyrian inscrr The name is perhaps triliteralized from the Sumerian RU(M), *to thrust or knock down* (*nakâpu*), written ⟨𝈙𝈘⟩ (⟨ *throw down* + 𝈘𝈙 *bull*), specially used of butting animals. Assurbanipal says: *Bêlit unâkip nakirêa ina qarnâteša gašrâte*, 'Belus knocked down my foes with her mighty horns' (Abp 9⁷⁸). Cf. also ⊢𝈙⟨𝈙 RI (RIM?), *to cast down* (*ramû*), and 𝈖 RIM, *enemy* (*âbu*). 𝔊 μονόκερως; 𝔙 rhinoceros; but 𝔖𝔗 רֵימָא, רֵימָנָא (= 𝔐). The Arabs give the name to the *Antilope Leucoryx*; but the context shows that no antelope can be intended here (cf. also Is 1³ Pr 14⁴). In st. ii read עָלַי pro עַל־ metr. gr.

v. 10. St. i has four stresses, and is otherwise questionable. It cannot mean RV; and if it could, *Canst thou bind the wild-ox with his band in the furrow?* (so 𝔗) is poor sense. The 'binding' or harnessing would be done *before* the 'furrowing' or ploughing began. The repetition of רֵים is obviously superfluous (𝔊 om.). 𝔊 δήσεις δὲ ἐν ἱμᾶσι ζυγὸν αὐτοῦ = הַתִקְשָׁר בַּעֲבֹתִי עָלוֹ *Wilt thou bind on with cords his yoke?* (ζυγός = עֹל 24 times. But cf. Is 5¹⁸; Ps 2³ עֲבוֹתֵימוֹ = τὸν ζυγὸν αὐτῶν; also Ecclus 33³¹.) 𝔙 Numquid alligabis rhinocerota ad arandum loro tuo? (ad *arandum* = paraphr. of בְּתֶלֶם *in the furrow?*). 𝔖 *Dost thou bind the yoke upon the neck* (קְדָלָא *nape*) *of the wild-ox?* This lends some colour to the suggestion הַתִקְשָׁר בְּעָנְקוֹ עֲבֹת *Wilt thou bind* on his neck *the cord?* (assuming an Aramaism עֲנָק = אוּנְקָא, and transposing תֶלֶם and עִמְקִי st. ii). For st. ii 𝔊 gives ἤ ἑλκύσει σου αὔλακας ἐν πεδίῳ; = אִם־יְשַׂדֵּד תְּלָמֶיךָ בַּשָׂדֶה *Or will he drag thy furrows* (31³⁸ Ps 65¹¹) *in the field?* 𝔖 *Or dost thou plow* (דְּבַר פְדָנָא *drive the yoke* or *plow*) *in the rugged place?* But 𝔙 aut confringet glebas vallium post te? = 𝔐. 𝔗 implies 𝔐 in both stichi. (For גְלִימְתָא or וַּלְמְתָא = עֲמָקִים cf. v. 21 בַּעֲמָק = בִּגְלִימָא.)

Evidently the text is uncertain. We may perhaps offer the conjectural emendation:

הֲתִקְשְׁרֶנּוּ בַּעֲבֹתַי עֻלָּךְ
וְאִם־יְשַׂדֵּד חֲלָמֵי אַדְמָתָךְ:

Canst thou bind him with the cords of thy yoke?
Or will he harrow the furrows of thy land?

Cf. 40²⁹ᵇ l. 2ⁿᵈ (וישׂדד אדמתו). 'Will he harrow the valleys (cf. Ps 65¹⁴) *behind thee?'* is unlikely; unless the meaning be 'behind thy back', i.e. when left to himself (cf. v. 11).

v. 11. 𝔙 Numquid fiduciam habebis in magna fortitudine eius = הֲתִבְטַח בְּרָב כֹּחוֹ *Wilt thou trust in the greatness of his strength?* yields a better rhythm; but 𝔊 𝔖 𝔗 support 𝔐 (בו and בי both enclitic). *Thy labour*: i.e. thy fieldwork, or possibly thy produce (cf. v. 12).

v. 12. Q יָשִׁיב seems preferable to K יָשֻׁב *he will return* or *come home*, when his work is done. Cf. 𝔊 𝔙 𝔗. (𝔖 *Dost thou trust him to purge thy floor,* | *And gather in thy seed?* app. reading וְזָרָה גרנך ורעך יאסף.) St. ii 𝔐 is too brief for sense and metre. It may be supposed that, owing to similarity of letters, דָּגָן *corn* has fallen out before גרנך. This would give us *And gather in the corn of thy threshing-floor.* Or we might read: וְגָרְנָה דְּגָנְךָ יאסף *And into the thr. gather thy corn* (cf. Mi 4¹²). 𝔙 et aream tuam congreget? = 𝔐. So 𝔊.

v. 13. The context (vv. 14–18) shows that the ostrich, with its apparent lack of parental instinct, its proverbial stupidity, and its marvellous running powers, is intended; but no ingenuity can extract any reasonable sense from this verse as it stands in 𝔐. RV is simply childish. The אִם which introduces st. ii indicates a double question, such as we have in vv. 9, 10; 11, 12. We propose

(ה)בבת יענה תתעלס
(ו)אם תאהב חסרת עצה :

Joyest thou in the ostrich, | *Or lovest her that lacketh counsel?* בת יענה is the usual name of the ostrich (30²⁹ plur. בת היענה Dt 14¹³); but יענים (La 4³ Q only) is not prob. here, if only because of the fem. Sing. in vv. 14 ff. We might perhaps read נעלסתה *hast thou rejoiced?* pro 𝔐 נעלסה, but Ni. occurs nowhere else, while Hithp. is found Pr 7¹⁸ in a sense that suits the parallel line. With חסרת עצה cf. חסר לב Pr 7⁷ al. (fem. of חסר here only).

𝔊 πτέρυξ τερπομένων (𝔊^{Nc.cA} + νεελασα, i.e. נעלסה translit.), ἐὰν συλλάβῃ ἀσίδα καὶ νεσσά = הרה ! אם הרתה חסידה ונצה (συλλαμβ. = הרה as oft; the other words translit.). τερπομένων = רננים (pts.): Zc 2¹⁴. Did 𝔊 read אפרי (Syr. *bring forth*) for אברה? 𝔙 Penna struthionis similis est pennis herodii (the heron) et accipitris (v. 26) = כְּנַף יְעֵנִים ? נִמְלָשָׁה עִם־אֶבְרָת חֲסִידָה וָנֵץ: (see La 4³, 𝔙 sicut struthio = בענים Q). Cf. 𝔗 *The wing of the cock of the wild which lauds and praises* (cf. 𝔗 38³⁶), *is it the pinion of the stork* (or *heron*) *and the hawk* (Levy: *and its plumes*)? = 𝔐? 𝔊 כְּנַף רננים = כַּנְפֵי שַׂבָּחִין; understanding רננים of shouting or singing praise to God (cf. Ps 5¹² al.): cf. 𝔗. It renders: *The* kenfai-šabbāḥîn *magnifies* (or *rouses*) *herself and soars* (!), *and comes and nests* (!). About ostriches the poet was evidently better informed than his translator.

v. 14. *leaveth her egg to the earth*: cf. v. 11ᵇ Ps 16¹¹ לשאול. 𝔙 *in* terra; but 𝔊 εἰς γῆν = 𝔐. *layeth them* · תַּגִּיחֵם pro 𝔐 תְּחַמֵּם = 𝔊 θάλψει, 𝔖. מחממא, 𝔙 calefacies. But 𝔗 תרנור *collect* or *heap up*; sc. her eggs: Is 34¹⁵. Did 𝔗 read תחמר *heapeth* (NH Aram.)? Cf. Heb. חֹמֶר *a heap*. *And heapeth them on the dust* makes good sense; but the point is that the ostrich takes no care at all for her progeny, but leaves them to chance. (𝔙 *When she forsaketh her eggs on the ground*, tu forsitan in pulvere calefacies ea, *wilt thou perchance warm them in the dust?* is ingenious, but hardly correct.)

v. 15. *press it*: or *squeeze* and so *crush* it: זוּר Ju 6³⁸ Is 1⁶. *It*; i.e. one or other of the eggs. Or the fem. Sing. may be Coll. 𝔊 σκορπιεῖ = תְּזָרֶה (pts); but 𝔙 (rectè) *conculcet ea*.

v. 16. The verb masc. cannot be right, with verbs and Suffixes fem. preceding and following. We must either point הַקְשִׁיחַ Infin. Abs., or c 2 codd. Kenn read הִקְשִׁיחָה *she deals hardly with* . . . *her young*: בנים is used of eggs and young birds Dt 22⁶ᶠ· לְלֹא לָהּ (making them) *into none of hers* (OL) or *according to not hers*. But it is simpler to read בְּלֹא (Ob 16): cf. 𝔙 Duratur ad filios suos *quasi non sint sui* 𝔊 ὥστε μὴ ἑαυτῆν (? ἑαυτῇ) = 𝔐 לְלֹא לָהּ. 𝔗 *She warms* (*broods*, שׁיחנא) *over the sons that are not hers* (דִּי לָא דִילַהּ); 𝔖 *She has multiplied the sons* that are not hers (ut 𝔗); app. reading השׂגיאה pro הקשיח (error of dictation?). 𝔊 𝔗 𝔖 favour הַקְשִׁיחַ > הַקְשִׁיחָה. In view of Is 63¹⁷ תַּקְשִׁיחַ לִבֵּנוּ (the sole recurrence of the verb), הִקְשִׁיחָה לִבָּהּ לְעֻלָּלֶיהָ *She has hardened her heart to her* (*unhatched*: cf. 3¹⁶) *young* seems possible.

St. ii lit. *Fruitless* (*For emptiness* or *naught*) *is her labour without fear* (i. e. apprehension of possible mischances and provision against them). But a verb יָגְעָה would be more natural (cf. Is 65²³ Le 26²⁰, also Is 49⁴): 𝔙 Frustra laboravit; 𝔊 εἰς κενὸν ἐκοπίασεν ἄνευ φόβου. 𝔐 can hardly mean: 'Though her labour, in laying and sitting on the eggs, be in vain, she is unconcerned about it' (Driver) = לָרִיק יְגִיעָהּ בְּלֹא־פָחַד. The point is that she is careless about the safety of her eggs (v. 14); she lacks *foresight* to provide against danger (v. 17). We may suggest לָרִיק יָגְעָה לְהַפְרִיחַ: *In vain hath she laboured to have young*. הפריח Denom. from אֶפְרֹחַ *young bird* (but cf. 14⁹); cf. Ar. فرخ 2. *to hatch*: or בְּהַפְרִחַ *at laying?* or even לְפָרֵחַ (Arabism).

v. 17. It is hardly necessary to remark that popular ideas about the ostrich are based upon imperfect observation. The habits of this bird are peculiar, but neglect of its young is far from being one of them. Three or four hens deposit their eggs in the same nest or hole in the soil; and the male shares with them in the duty of brooding. A number of eggs are dropped about outside the nest, which are afterwards broken to feed the young when hatched. This may explain v. 14. (See *En‑yc. Brit.*, s. v. Ostrich.   ...ade h r for₆ :: שָׁה. The expression is rather strange. We should rather have expected *has withheld from her.* 𝔙 *Privavit* enim *eam* Deus sapientia; 𝔊 ὅτι κατεσιώπησεν αὐτῇ ὁ θεὸς σοφίαν (= החשה? Ne 8¹¹); 𝔊 again השניא *has multiplied*; but 𝔗 as 𝔐.

v. 18. *What time in the race she flieth*; or *When she flieth along in the race*: reading בעת במרון תאביר pro 𝔐 בעת במרום תמריא. The comparison of the ἅπ. תמריא with Ar. مَرَى is altogether improb. (see Lane Suppl. p. 3019: 'The wind *tamrī-ssaḥāba* draws forth the clouds'). On the other hand, the Denom. אבר Hi. *to wing*, i.e. *work or ply the wings* occurs, v. 26, of the flight of the hawk, and might be used here of the swift 'flying', i.e. running, of the ostrich (cf. 𝔗 טָיְפָא = שׂט 9³⁶). Cf. also 𝔗 5⁷ 20⁸ (טוס = עוף). That the poet did not think of the ostrich as 'soaring on high' (as 𝔗 seems to do) is evident from st. ii.

במרום *in the height*, whether of the air or of high ground, suits neither the bird nor its hunters. It is on the plains of the desert, not among the mountains, that the running powers of the ostrich are seen at their best. Read therefore בְּמֵרוֹץ and cf. Ec 9¹¹. 𝔊 ἐν ὕψει ὑψώσει = במרום תרום; cf. 𝔊 במרומא תתרים איך דקלא *In the height she raises herself* like a palm-tree (כתמר; a double rendering). 𝔙 in altum *alas* erigit; perhaps to suggest the flapping of the bird's wings as it flies along the ground.

vv. 13–18 are starred in Hexapl. and are said to have been wanting in the original text of 𝔊; but there seems no sufficient reason for rejecting a section which is quite in character with the others, and as lively and striking as any in the chapter.

v. 19. *strength* or *prowess* (נבורה). *Terror*: אֵימָה (v. 20) pro 𝔐 רַעְמָה ἅπ., usually identified with רַעַם *thunder* (26¹⁴ 39²⁰). 𝔊 φόβον = אימה (9³⁴ 41⁶ al.). 𝔊 ὅπλα *armour* (a guess?); but 𝔗 תוקפא *might* (= עָצְמָה? a good parallel to נבורה). Leg. fort. רום *haughtiness* (Is 2¹¹) vel רוֹמָה (Mi 2⁸). The tossing of a horse's neck might inspire fear; but רעם or רעמה *thunder*, however appealing to the imagination and however poetical it may sound, is really inappropriate here, for the simple reason that a horse's neck or mane emits no sound, whereas the √רעם and its derivv. always denote some kind of sound (cf. 𝔙 aut circumdabis collo eius *hinnitum*? i.e. 'neighing' or 'whinnying'). The same objection lies against rendering רעמה (רעם) *vibration*, which is supposed to be equivalent to *quivering mane* (OL). In this sense רעש would suit better than רעם; but the mane is a feature of lions as well as horses, and does not seem to be either distinctive or poetical enough without further qualification.

v. 20. St. i is metr. short. Perhaps ארץ or אדמה has fallen out before (or after) כארבה: *Dost thou make him shake* the earth *like the locust?* Cf. Jo 2⁴·¹⁰, where the locusts are compared to horses, and earth and air tremble and quake at their onset. Or, since 'running' is repeatedly ascribed to the locusts (Jo 2⁴·⁷·⁹), Iahvah's 'army', we might read הַתְרִיצֶנּוּ בָאָרֶץ כָאַרְבֶּה *Dost thou make him run on the earth like the locusts?* 𝔙 Numquid *suscitabis eum* quasi locustas? (תְּעִירֶנּוּ?). 𝔊 περιέθηκας δὲ αὐτῷ (cf. v. 19ᵃ) πανοπλίαν; (= הֲתַעְטֵנוּ חֲלִיצָה? cf. 2 Sa 2²⁰ Is 61¹⁰) bears little resemblance to 𝔐. St. ii is almost certainly corrupt. Lit. *The glory* (or *majesty*) *of his snorting is a terror.* So 𝔙 gloria *narium eius* terror (pointing נְחִירָיו = נְחִרוֹ nares eius 41¹² pro 𝔐 נַחְרוֹ ἄπ.); cf. 𝔗 *The splendour* of the chain *of his nostrils is a terror.* The analogy of the context, however, requires a second question: cf. 𝔊 *Or dost thou terrify him with terror?* (𝔊 is dubious). We suggest הֲתוֹרֶנּוּ נַחֲרַת רַעֲמָה *Dost thou teach him his snort of thunder?* (רַעֲמָה v. 19ᵇ trs. Je 8¹⁶ chap. 12⁷,⁸ Is 28⁹). (𝔊 δόξαν δὲ στηθέων αὐτοῦ = ? וַהֲוֹד חֲדָיו: Aram. חֲדִי = στῆθος. Is τόλμη 𝔊ᴬ τόλμῃ an error for τολμᾷ: *And the glory of his breast dost thou dare?*)

v. 21. St. i 𝔐 is metr. too long with four stresses. Leg. בְּכֹחוֹ, and transpose בָעֵמֶק to st. ii (cf. 𝔊). *He paweth*: leg. יַחְפּוֹר *fodit* c 𝔊𝔙𝔖 pro 𝔐 plur. The distich thus becomes:

יַחְפּוֹר וְיָשִׂישׂ בְּכֹחוֹ
בָעֵמֶק יֵצֵא לִקְרַאת־נָשֶׁק׃

He paweth and exulteth in his strength; | He goeth forth into the valley to face arms. Cf. Ju 5¹⁶ Ho 1⁵ Is 61¹⁰ al. שִׂישׂ בְּ. For נֶשֶׁק 20²⁴ Ps 140⁸. 𝔊 *Digging in the plain he prances, | And goes forth into the plain in strength.* 𝔊 appears to repeat בָעֵמֶק; but εἰς πεδίον may represent another expression, e.g. בְּנַחַל, which we actually find in 𝔖 (*He paweth in the vale and exulteth* in the wâdy | *And goeth forth to the encounter in arms*) 𝔊 connects לִקְרַאת נָשֶׁק with the next verse.

v. 22. *He laugheth at fear* (פַּחַד), *and is not terrified* (scared, dismayed), besides being something of an anticlimax, does not suit the parallel stichus. If we read רֹמַח pro פחד we get a good parallel: *He laugheth at the spear*, &c. After נֶשֶׁק *arms* or *battle*, v. 21, the mention of particular weapons is natural; and this is continued in v. 23. 𝔊 has συναντῶν βασιλεῖ (but 𝔊ᴺᶜ·ᵃᴬ βέλει) prob. = לִקְרַאת נֶשֶׁק יִשְׂחַק. Possibly 𝔊 substituted נָשִׂיא *ruler* or *lord* (Is 3¹² 60¹⁷ Zc 10⁴) for נֶשֶׁק. Three codd. have פַּחַת *pitfall* instead of פחד; which might perhaps be understood of pits dug in the battlefield to hamper cavalry. So 𝔊 נִמְצָא *pit*. If this be right, יֵחַת might be from נחת > חָתַת (21¹³): *He laugheth at the pitfall and descendeth not* (into it) Some think that 𝔊 βασιλεῖ = לְפַחַת (the word being mistaken for פֶּחָה constr. פַּחַת *pasha*); which does not seem very probable. 𝔊 om. וְלֹא־יֵחַת (a good paronomasia with לְפַחַת).

v. 23. *rattleth*: 𝔐 תִּרְנֶה ἄπ. The more usual form תָּלֹן (√רנן) has been proposed; but √רנה may be defended on the analogy of הִנֵּה, הִנַּג, קִצֵּץ, קָצַה, and the Aram. רְנָא יְ־רָן *think*. Moreover the suggested division of the letters תרן האשפה (pro אשפה 𝔐) is improbable, because אשפה *the quiver* (Is 22⁶ only; elsewhere c Suff.) is not found c Artic., and all the other instruments of war mentioned in the context are anarthrous. 𝔊 ἐπ' αὐτῷ γαυριᾷ τόξον καὶ μάχαιρα = עָלָיו תִּרְנֶה קֶשֶׁת וְחָרֶב׃. 𝔊's Heb. text may have been corrupt here; but 𝔊 prob. failed to understand להב and כידון (the latter also in 41²¹). The verb γαυριᾶν (= שיש v. 21) occurred 3¹⁴ (οἳ ἠγαυρῶντο ἐπὶ ξίφεσιν = הבנים חרבות למו), where 𝔊 evidently misread רגים pro בנים. This favours the reading תִּרְנֶה here. 𝔗 has חַרְבָּא שְׁנָנָא *the sharp sword* for לַהַב *flame* = flashing blade or head (cf. Ju 3²² 1 Sa 17⁷). For אשפה 𝔗 has זינא *the weapon*; but 𝔊𝔙 קטירקא *pharetra* rightly. 𝔙 (st. ii) *vibrabit hasta et clypeus* is interesting, as suggesting a verb pro לַהַב, which indeed one would have expected.

v. 24. *In his eagerness*: or *rage*: בְּרָגְזוֹ: cf. 𝔊 καὶ ὀργῇ. 𝔐 ברעש ורגז; but one or the other of the two nouns must be a gloss, as this gives a line with four stresses. 𝔙 *Fervens et fremens* sorbet terram = 𝔐 (so 𝔊𝔗). *he diggeth into the ground*: i.e. makes holes by pawing it in his impatience to charge. The verb יגמא, AV RV *he swalloweth* (cf. Gn 24¹⁷ Hi. *let drink*), is usually compared with Aram. גְּמַע, גְּמָא *to sip or suck in* (𝔗 v. 30 = ילעלעו); cf. 𝔙 sorbet: and this is understood of galloping swiftly (cf. 𝔊 רהט על ארעא *he runneth over the ground*). But the charge does not begin before the trumpet gives the signal; and 𝔗 עביד גומתא בארעא *he makes a pit in the ground* appears to refer the verb to Aram. גּוּמְתָא, NH גּוּמָא *pit* or *hole*. We might even read יגמיץ *he digs* (Aram. גְּמַץ) pro גמא. St. ii 𝔐 can hardly be right. A verb is desiderated after כי יאמין (cf. v. 12, 9¹⁶). And if we read בְּקוֹל pro כי קול 𝔐, the sentence will naturally mean *And he trusts not in the sound of the trumpet* (cf. 4¹⁸ 15¹⁵·²²·³¹ 24²² 29²⁴). The sense might perhaps be: *He does not 'believe in' the sound of the trumpet*; i.e. he is so impatient to be off, that he thinks the signal will never be given. 𝔗 = 𝔐. 𝔊 *And he is not afraid of the sound of the horn.* 𝔊 *And he will not believe until the trumpet have signalled.* But *He does not stand still at the sound of the trumpet* would suit the context better; and perhaps the Hi. (or Ni. ?) of אמן may bear this sense here, though it is not so used elsewhere. Cf. Ex 17¹². In any case, ולא ימין ולא ישמאיל בקול שופר *And he turns not to the right nor to the left*, &c., is non-metrical and pure prose.

v. 25. The repetition of שופר is suspicious, and the phrase בדי ש' (supposed to mean *As often as the trumpet soundeth* = מִדֵּי הַשָּׁמִיעַ?) is anomalous. 𝔗 בְּמִיפַת שׁוֹפָרָא *With enough of the trumpet* = 𝔐; but 𝔊 בקלא (אמר) At the sound (*he saith*), omitting שופר. This may suggest the reading בְּקוֹלוֹ *At the sound of it*; cf. 𝔊 σάλπιγγος δὲ σημαινούσης (λέγει εὖγε). *But when trumpet signalleth*, &c. We might read בְּמִשְׁמַע *At the sound* (P-150), or תרועע, perhaps מִדֵּי שְׁמַע or מִדֵּי יִשָּׁמַע *As often as he heareth it*; but the required sense seems rather to be *The moment he hears it*

The verse, as it has reached us, is a tristich; and, as the zeugma *he scents the battle, the thunder ... and the shouting* seems rather too bold, sense as well as metre may justify the assumption that a line has fallen out after st. ii (unless st. i be somehow a variant of v. 24ᵇ, which seems possible); e.g. לֹא־יֵחַת מִקּוֹל נְבָרִים *He is not daunted by the cry* (cf. Is 31⁴) *of the warriors*, or לֹא־יְחִתֶּנּוּ קוֹל גִּבֹּ׳ *The cry of warriors daunts him not.* In st. iii 𝔐 = 𝔐; but 𝔊 gives *And makes the princes tremble* (מוֹעַ) *with his neighing* = וירעש שרים בתרועה, while 𝔊 has the strange equivalent σὺν ἅλματι καὶ κραυγῇ (*From afar he gets scent of war*) with a bound and a cry = רַעַם שָׂרִים וּתְרוּעָה pro 𝔐 עִם־רַעַשׁ וּתְרוּעָה.

v. 26 *ply his wings*: יאבר *make wing, wing it, wing his way*, or simply *fly* (cf. v. 18ᵇ note) > *soar* (יַנְבִּיהַ עוּף, cf. v. 27, 5⁷, but also Is 40³¹). 𝔊 ἕστηκεν ἱέραξ, *Doth the hawk exist?* = 𝔖 ܪܒ ܗܘܐ (*hath the hawk come into being?*); both prob. reading יברא (or נברא) *is the hawk created?* pro 𝔐 יאבר (why not יאביר?). *And spread*: וַיִּפְרֹשׂ or וּפָרַשׂ pro 𝔐 יִפְרֹשׂ. The bird flies south at the coming of winter. (After ἀναπετάσας τὰς πτέρυγας 𝔊 adds the gloss ἀκίνητος, *motionless*; which may imply for ἕστηκεν the more usual meaning *stands still* or *stops* (יעמר pro יאבר); i.e. the bird hangs motionless in the air, looking southward.)

v. 27. St. ii וכי appears to be corrupt; and this is borne out by 𝔊, which makes a single tristich of this and the following verse:

אִם־עַל־פִּיךָ יִנְבַּ(י)ה נֶשֶׁר
וְאַיָּה עַל־קִנָּהּ תָּשְׁכֹּן וְתִתְלוֹנָן
עַל־שֵׁן סֶלַע וּמְצוּדָה׃

At thy command doth the eagle (or griffon-vulture 9²⁸) *mount up* (sc. עוּף 5⁷) *And the vulture* (γύψ = איה 28⁷) *on her nest alight and lodge | On the point* (ἐξοχῇ = שֵׁן *tooth* here only; cf. 1 Sa 14⁴) *of the crag and fastness* (𝔊 ἀποκρυφῷ *hiding-place?* but 𝔊ᴬ ὀχυρώματος)? Thus 𝔊 om ירים and סלע¹, besides reading ואיה pro 𝔐 וכי. 𝔖 *Upon the word of thy mouth is the eagle lifted up* (? נתתרים = יַנְבַּה = 𝔊 ὑψοῦται) | *When he raiseth his nest* (וכי pro כי) *to the crag | And alighteth and lodgeth on the tooth of the crag?* (Thus another tristich; but 𝔐 not so.) The objection to 𝔊's γύψ v. 27ᵇ is that the following verses refer to a single bird which, like the נשר ἀετός of st. i, is of the masc. gender. Perhaps, therefore, we should emend v. 27ᵇ by reading וּלְךָ instead of וכי: *And for thee set high his nest?* (cf. Je 49¹⁶ᵇ); or else וּכִדְבָרְךָ *And at thy word*, &c. It may be noted that 𝔐 st. ii is metr. defective, having only two stresses, besides being grammatically dubious. Then we supply עַל־ before וּסֶלַע v. 28; and סֶלַע need not be regarded as dittogr., since it emphasizes the idea of inaccessible rocks (cf. 𝔙). The proposal to make a distich of the two verses by reading

אם־על־פיך ירים קנו
ויתלנן על־שן־סלע ומצורה:

At thy command doth he set high his nest,
And lodge him on tooth of crag and fastness?

makes the whole section (verses 26–30) refer to the hawk (נץ) only. But v. 30ᵇ is characteristic of eagles and vultures (נשר) rather than the hawks (cf. 9²⁶ Pr 30¹⁷˙¹⁹ Mt 24²⁸). Moreover, st. ii in the suggested form is metrically overweighted.

v. 29. *searcheth*: חפר, lit. *diggeth* (v. 21, 3²¹ Gn 21³⁰ Jos 2⁸). *see far away*: or *to a distance*; *to what is far off*: cf. v. 25, 28²⁴ 36³: > *behold it* (i. e. the food) *afar off*. So 𝔖; but 𝔊𝔙 *from afar* (πόρρωθεν, de longe) *his eyes look out* (σκοπεύουσιν, prospiciunt).

v. 30. 𝔙 *Pulli eius* lambent *sanguinem* (om. ו ad init. recte: dittogr.); 𝔖 ܠܚܒܒ *lap* or *lick up*; 𝔗 נמען *sip* or *suck in* (cf. v. 24); 𝔊^A ἐστομισμένοι. Hence it is proposed to read יְלַעְלְעוּ (√ לוע or לעע) pro 𝔐 יְעַלְעוּ ἅπ. But lapping, licking, and sucking are not bird-actions. We might read יִבְלְעוּ *swallow* or *gorge* (20¹⁵ al.); or יָלַע (cf. 𝔖: Ob 16 is dub.) or יְלַעְלְעוּ, in the sense of drinking. (√ לע = LAG = Sumerian ⊢≡𒅅 NAG *drink*, *give drink*, Assyr. *šatû*, *šaqû*.) 𝔊 φύρονται ἐν αἵματι, *are mixed* (or *wetted*, *defiled*) *with blood* (= יְלַבְּשׁוּ acc. to 𝔊 7⁵).

St. ii 𝔐 ובאשר חללים שם הוא *And where the slain are, there is he* is terse and vivid, but not a close parallel to st. i. The letters sufficiently resemble ובשר חללים ישבעו *And are glutted with the flesh of the slain* (cf. Ez 39 ¹⁷⁻²⁰). Possibly ישאפו *are fain for*: cf. 5⁵ 7².

Chapter 40. v. 1. *Iahvah*: 𝔊 + ὁ θεός = אלהים (Gn 2⁴ al.); app. combining a suggested substitute with the original reading. The verse is starred in Hex. Cod. 1 (Kenn. 431) om. The Versions make verses 1–5 the conclusion of chap. 39; which is certainly more suitable (cf. 40⁶˙⁷ c 38¹˙³).

v. 2. The pointing of 𝔐 seems questionable. If the meaning of st. i be *Will the caviller* (or *faultfinder* OL) *still contend with Shaddai?* (Dr), why the Infin. Abs. (הֲרֹב), so used nowhere else in the book, instead of the usual Impf. (הָרִיב)? And why is עוֹד *still* (or some equivalent word) omitted? Moreover, the ἅπ. יִסּוֹר *reprover* is very dubious. 𝔊 Μὴ κρίσιν μετὰ Ἱκανοῦ ἐκκλινεῖ; = הֲרַב עִם־שַׁדַּי יָסוּר. This might mean *Shall strife with Shaddai end?* (סוּר Am 6⁷). Cf. also 𝔙 Numquid *qui contendit cum Deo* (= רָב Is 45⁹) *tam facile conquiescit?* (= יָסוּר *turns aside*, *gives up*). 𝔗 app⸺s t⸺ have read הֲרַב עִם־שַׁדַּי יַסֵּר *Will h⸺ wh⸺ contendeth with Shaddai b⸺ adm⸺nt ⸺d?* This is rather attractive; esp. if we read for st. ii וּמוֹכִיחַ אֱלוֹהַּ יַעֲנֶה *And is he who chideth Eloah answered?* 𝕲 *Many are the counsels of God* (= רַב עִם־שַׁדַּי סוֹד) | *And he who reproveth God giveth answer* (=וּמוֹכִיחַ אֱלוֹהַּ יַעֲנֶה). St. ii 𝔐 is lit. *The reprover of Eloah should answer it* (viz. the argument of chaps. 38–39). 𝔗𝔙 *should answer Him*. But it yields a better parallel to treat st. ii also as Interrogative (cf 𝕲 ἔλεγχων δὲ θεὸν ἀποκριθήσεται αὐτήν;). The original form of the verse may have been

הֲרָב עִם־שַׁדַּי יוֹסֵר
וּמוֹכִיחַ אֱלוֹהַּ יַעֲנֶה:

Is the disputer with Shaddai corrected | *And the critic of Eloah answered?* (For רִיב עִם see 9³ 13¹⁹ 23⁶; and for יַעֲנֶה Ni. 11² 19⁷.) The meaning will be: Are you now satisfied, or do you require further proof of the folly of arguing against the Supreme?

v. 4. I am little: or *light, slight, insignificant, of small weight or account*. The √קל may be recognized in שְׁקַל, ܩܠ, ቀለለ: *lift up, weigh (make hang)*, Assyr. *šaqâlu*. The primary Root is probably the Sum. 𒄑𒃲 GAL *to lift* (*našû*). 'Light' = easy to lift.

𝕲 τί ἔτι ἐγὼ κρίνομαι, νουθετούμενος καὶ ἐλέγχων Κύριον ἀκούων τοιαῦτα οὐθὲν ὤν, (= לָמָּה עוֹדָנִי רָב | יוֹסֵר וּמוֹכִיחַ יהוה | שֹׁמֵעַ כָּהֵן כַּלֹּתִי); app. prefixing a variant rendering of v. 2 to הֵן קַלֹּתִי. For the equations cf 13¹⁹ Pr 9⁷.

v. 5. Once... And twice: Ps 62¹² cf. ch. 33¹⁴. *repeat it*: אֶשְׁנֶה pro 𝔐 אֶעֱנֶה *answer*. The vb. שָׁנָה תְּנָא Assyr. *šanû, do (or say) twice, repeat*, is of the same origin as שְׁנַיִם *two*, and is also cogn. c תְּאֹם *twin* (Intern Trilit from *TAM = TAN = SHAN*); cf. the Sum. TAM, TAN, DAM, *brother, companion, spouse*, and TAB (= TAM), *companion, twin, to double, repeat*; and the Chinese shwan, shan, san, *to bear twins*, shwang, *two, a pair*, and the old Egyptian sen, *two*, sen, *brother, companion*.

Some would transpose verses 4–5 to precede 42²; and cancelling v. 6 (= 38¹) and v. 7 (= 38²), they would transfer verses 8–14 to follow immediately on v. 2. Considering the manifold uncertainties of the text, we prefer the traditional arrangement.

v. 6. out of the stormwind: leg. מִן־הַסְּעָרָה ut 38¹. 𝕲 ἐκ τοῦ νέφους = מִן־הֶעָב (38³⁴ al. Ps 104³) or מִן־הֶעָנָן (38⁹ al.). Cf. 38¹. 𝔄 *out of the clouds*. For *cloud* and *whirlwind* combined in Theophany see Ez 1⁴ and cf. Na 1³.

v. 7. like a man: so 𝔐 כְגֶבֶר, 𝕲 ὥσπερ ἀνήρ, 𝔙 sicut vir; but 𝔗 נִבְרָא הֵיךְ = כִּגְבַר *like a mighty man* or *champion*, and so 𝔖. St. ii should perhaps be אֶשְׁאָלְךָ וְאַתָּה הוֹדִיעֵנִי. So also 42⁴. (Or אִשׁ והוד' דֵּעָת *I will ask, and teach thou me wisdom*. Cf. Is 28⁹ 40¹⁴.) Cf. 𝕲 σὺ δέ μοι ἀπόκριναι

v. 8. הַאַף Gn 18¹³ ch. 34¹⁷. 𝕲 Μή = אַל; but cf. 15⁴ אַף־אַתָּה תָּפֵר יִרְאָה where also הַאַף Interrog. should prob. be read · st. (ii). For תָּפֵר *annul*, *make void, frustrate*, cf. also 5^{12} Is 14^{17}. Eyob had all along affirmed his own innocence, and maintained that God was dealing with him unjustly (cf. esp. 27^{2-6}). On current theories he could not logically do otherwise. (𝕲 softens תַרְשִׁיעֵנִי *dost thou make me wicked*, i.e. *condemn me as guilty of injustice*, 9^{20} 10^2 15^6 al., into *thinkest thou that I have dealt at random or perversely*—ἄλλως—*with thee?*)

v. 9. *Hast thou*; reading אִם *Num?* pro וְאִם *Or hast thou* ..., as the second member of a Disjunctive Question (*Utrum—An*); cf. 34^{17}. 𝔙 *Et si habes*... implies אִם; so also 𝔗 וְאִין. But 𝕲 איח לך *Hast thou? arm*: וְרוֹעַ as five times in Job. אָזְרוֹעַ once (31^{22}); cf. Aram. אֶדְרָע.

v. 10. *grandeur*: גֹּבַהּ *loftiness*. 𝕲 δύναμιν = גְּבוּרָה (12^{13}+): so 𝕾. 𝔙 *in sublime erigere* = גְּבַהּ Imperat. (pts.).

v. 11. '*Scatter* the outbursts (or overflows) of thine anger' is strange. If lightnings be intended (OL), ברקי אפך or בְּרָקִים בְּאַפֶּךָ would be more natural. For הָפֵץ see 37^{11} 38^{24} Ps 18^{15}. 𝕲 *Pour out* (אשור) *the fury of thy wrath* suggests שְׁפוֹךְ (Ho 5^{10} Is 42^{25} La 4^{11}, ch. 12^{21} al.) = הפץ misread backwards (?). But 𝔙 *Disperge superbos in furore tuo | Et respiciens omnem arrogantem humilia* gives a better parallel. 𝕲 is peculiar: ἀπόστειλον δὲ ἀγγέλους ὀργῇ = באפך שלח מלאכים (Ju 9^{31} et saepius): cf. Ps 78^{49}. משלחת מלאכי רעים | ישלח בם חרון אפו עברה וגו'. St. ii πᾶν ($\mathfrak{G}^A$ πάντα rectius) δὲ ὑβριστὴν ταπείνωσον = 𝔐 since ראה et 1^2 et Suff. Verbi = וכל נאה השפיל which some have adopted. But השפילהו improves the rhythm and gives a more lively sense: *And every proud one—bring him low!* Did 𝕲 read אבירים (= ἀγγέλων, Ps 78^{25}) or צירים (Pr 25^{13}) pro עברות in st. i? For the former, cf. 24^{22} 34^{20}. *Scatter the mighty* (or *haughty*; רְהָבִים? Ps 40^5) *in thine anger* would be a fair parallel (cf. 𝔙).

v. 12. 𝔐 repeats ראה כל נאה (v. 11^b), and 12^a looks like a mere variant of 11^b. The poet may have intended to lay emphasis on the overthrow of the proud. Both stichi are good metre as they stand. But 𝕾 omits 12^a, and 𝕲 ὑπερήφανον δὲ σβέσον = ?רְ(ע)ד ורם; cf. 38^{15b} and Is 2^{12} כָּל־גֵּאֶה וָרָם = ὑβριστήν (= נאה v. 11^b) καὶ ὑπερήφανον. Instead of הבניעהו *humble him* 𝔗 gives וְתַבְרְגִיהּ *and shatter him!* but 𝔙 *et confunde eos*. St. ii 𝔐 וַהֲדֹךְ ἄπ. Since a √ הדך is unknown in Semitic, we must either point וַהֲדֹךְ (Aram. דְּכַךְ; but no Aph.), or read וְדֻכָּה or וְדַכֵּה *and crush* (*down*) (for דָּכָא see 4^{19} 6^9 19^2 al.). The Ar. هدم = هدل *pull down* buildings seems apocryphal (see Lane Suppl.). *where they stand*: or *in their place*: see 34^{24} 36^{20} Ex 16^{29} al. Cf. 𝔙 *et contere impios in loco uo*; 𝕾 *And throw down the sinners in their place* (ברוכתהח); 𝔗 *And pulverize the guilty in their places* (בְּאַתְרֵיהוֹן). 𝕲 (haud recte) σῆψον δὲ ἀσεβεῖς παραχρῆμα = וְהָמֵק רְשָׁעִים פִּתְאֹם (cf. Zc 14^{12}).

v. 13. Cf. Is 2^{10} *hide thyself in the dust!* Also Gn 35^4 Ex 2^{12} (*hide* = *bury*). It is difficult to believe that בֶּעָפָר can be correct ad fin. (cf. טמנם

ad init.). The context suggests that 'She'ol, the dark and hidden abode of the dead' (Dr), is meant. Cf. 𝕭 *Et facies eorum demerge in foveam*; 𝕲 *And* their faces *imprison in the dust!* (ܣܚܦ ܐ ܒܬܫܘܝ). 𝕿 *Their faces* כבוש בטומעא = 𝔐? 𝕲 τὰ δὲ πρόσωπα αὐτῶν ἀτιμίας ἔμπλησον = (La 3¹⁵) וּפְנֵיהֶם הַשְׁבַּע בְּקָלוֹן or (Ps 83¹⁷) וּפְנֵיהֶם מַלֵּא קָלוֹן. Cf also 10¹⁵. We might read וּפְנֵיהֶם תַּחְבֵּא (חָבֵא?) בְּצַלְמָוֶת *And their faces hide thou in darkness* (or בִּשְׁאוֹל *in She'ol* or בַּאֲבַדּוֹן *in Abaddon* 26⁶ al.); or, keeping חָבוֹשׁ, *And their faces bind about* (= enwrap, shroud) *with darkness* (בַּעֲלָטָה? בְּעֻפָּתָה). See Ez 16¹⁰ for the constr. NE 127 *kullat tênišêti ttûra ana ṭîṭi*, 'All mankind had returned to clay' may perhaps suggest חֲבָא בְטִיט *conceal in clay*.

v. 14. St. i וְגַם־אֲנִי אוֹדֶךָ is metr. defective (two stresses only). Leg. כִּי־אַף נַם־אֲנִי *For then* (emphat.) *I also*, &c. Cf. 11¹⁵ 13²⁰ 22²⁸.

St ii. Cf. Ps 44⁴ᵇ Is 59¹⁶ᶜ. The irony of this and the preceding verses appears somewhat irrelevant. Eyob has never made any such claims. That God does, in fact, always destroy the wicked (cf. vv. 11–13) had been the steady contention of the Friends. Eyob had argued from his own case that, when He pleases, He destroys good and bad alike, without difference or discrimination. The description of the hippopotamus and the crocodile (40¹⁵–41³⁴) might very naturally follow immediately upon that of the other creatures, ch. 39; in which case 40¹⁻¹⁴ would be an editorial interpolation.

v. 15. *the riverhorse* = Gk. *hippopotamus*; the most prob. meaning of the Heb בְּהֵמוֹת qs 'the monster-beast' or 'the super-cow' (*Plur. Intens.* of בְּהֵמָה *beast* or *cattle*). Ps 73²²† (with which cf. ch. 7¹² תַּנִּין). The word has been referred to a supposed Egyptian *pehemaut*, compounded of p *the* + ih *ox* + mw *water*; but no such compound has yet been found in the Eg. monuments. 𝕭𝕲𝕬 Behemoth, ut NPr. 𝕲 θηρία Plur. et ἐσθίουσιν in st. ii (𝔐 recte יֹאכֵל Sing.); so 𝕿 בְּעִירָיָא, at seq. יֵיכוּל. St. i is non-metrical and prosaic: 'Lo, now, Behēmôth *which I made* along with thee' (𝕭 Ecce Behemoth quem feci tecum), i.e. thy fellow creature. 𝕲 ἀλλὰ δὴ ἰδοὺ δὴ θηρία παρὰ σοί (*beside thee*) om. אֲשֶׁר עָשִׂיתִי recte. But corruption has gone further than the addition of this gloss. The monster would hardly be 'beside' the poet at the time of writing (παρὰ σοί = *beside thee*, or *apud te*, or *coram te*). The word עִמָּךְ (prob. due to reminiscence of Ps 73²² בְּהֵמוֹת הָיִיתִי עִמָּךְ) may be a disguise of some other word descriptive of בְּהֵמוֹת; e. g. קָנֶה (cf. Ps 68³¹ חַיַּת קָנֶה *the beast of the reeds* = the crocodile). We might then restore בְּהֵמַת קָנֶה *the brute of the reeds*; no bad name for the hippopotamus. Or we might suppose אֲשֶׁר עָשִׂיתִי עִמָּךְ to be a gloss on an original מַעֲשִׂי *my work*. Possibly, however, the altered word was עֹלָה *coming up* (scil. from the water; cf. Gn 41² Je 49¹⁹); הִנֵּה־נָא בְהֵמוֹת עֹלָה *Lo, now, the riverhorse cometh up!* presenting a picture of the huge animal climbing up from the river the banks: cf. st. ii *Grass, like the oxen, he eateth* (Is 11⁷ᵇ). The hippopotamus, we are told, still abounds in many of the river-courses of Africa; and its food is chiefly rank grasses and aquatic plants. It can walk quite rapidly under water along the bottom of rivers; and climb up steep banks and precipitous ravines with ease (EB. s. v. *Hippopotamus*).

v. 16. *in the thews* בִּשְׁרִירֵי (ἅπ.); but 𝔊 ἐπ' ὀμφαλοῦ = 𝔙 in umbilico; so 𝔗 בפרת דבריסיה. (𝔖𝔄 give only *and his strength in his side(s)* for the whole verse.) Cf. Ez 16⁴ שָׁרֵּךְ *thy navel-string*; Ct 7⁵ שררך 𝔊 ὁ ὀμφαλός σου. The context suggests the meaning *sinews, muscles,* or *thews* for this ἅπ. The √שׂרד seems to denote *hardness, firmness, strength*; but the original idea may have been that of *binding*, being *bound*, as in the case of other words denoting strength; cf. שַׁרְשְׁרָה Assyr. *šaršarratu*, 'chain' (Sum. SHER, *to bind*).

v. 17. 𝔊 ἔστησεν οὐρὰν ὡς κυπάρισσον, *He set up a tail as a cypress*; 𝔙 Stringit (*he draws tight*) caudam suam quasi cedrum; but 𝔗 כָּפֵף *he bends*; 𝔖 זָקֵף *he sets up* or *erects*, &c. The meaning of the ἅπ. יַחְפֹּץ is far from clear. OL *he bendeth down* (*extendeth down stiffly*) *his tail like a cedar* (comparing Ar. خَفَضَ *he lowered* a thing: e.g. a bird its wings). But why *like a cedar*? The cedar is a tall (Am 2⁹) straight tree, with widespreading branches; a frequent symbol of majesty and strength. It seems a ridiculous exaggeration to compare the short thick tail of the hippopotamus, with its few tufts of hair at the end, to such a stately tree. Such a comparison suggests a mythically gigantic creature rather than an animal actually existing in ancient or modern times; but there is nothing mythical in the rest of the section, nor any touch incongruous with a poetical description of the hippopotamus. Lane, however, registers another meaning of خَفَضَ, viz. *he remained, stayed,* or *abode in* a place. Regarding יחפץ as an Arabism in this sense, we may render: *His tail is as rigid* (firm or inflexible) *as a cedar*. An Intrans. > a Trans. verb is required by parallelism; and the simile ceases to appear inapt, in view of the short, round, stiff-looking tail of the animal (see the engravings in Smith's BD).

St. ii. *The muscles* or *sinews* (גִּיד) 10¹¹ Gn 32³³; cf. Sum. GID, *long, extend*) *of his thighs are interlaced* or *woven together, close-knit* (leg. פַּחֲדֵי יְשׂרָגוּ pro 𝔐 פַּחֲדֵי יְשׂרָגוּ; Qr פחדיו). 𝔙 nervi *testiculorum* eius perplexi sunt; cf. 𝔗 *The veins of his testicles* are intertwined (וְתִכְנֵיָא דְּפַחְדְּרוֹהִי וגו' see 𝔗ᴼ Le 21²⁰ פחדין = אישך); but such a fact would hardly be open to observation of the living animal. We must therefore accept the equation of the ἅπ. פחד with the Ar. فَخِذ *thigh*. 𝔖 renders: *And erected are the sinews of his loins* (ܚܒܠ ܘܦܨܝܥܘܗܝ): according to PS سمفܩ means *testiculus*: femora: venae iugulares /). For שׂרג = Aram. סָרֵג, see La 1¹⁴ Hithp. שׂרך Pi. Je 2²⁵ is of the same origin. The prim. Rt. is seen in אָרַג *weave*. 𝔊 τὰ δὲ νεῦρα αὐτοῦ (𝔊^A +ὥσπερ σχοινία) συμπέπλεκται = (וְגִידָיו שֹׂרְגוּ (כַּחֲבָלִים *And his sinews are intertwined like ropes*.

v. 18. *tubes*: or *pipes*: 'אֲפִיק: see 6¹⁵ 12²¹ 41⁷.

lengths of wrought iron. As the hollow bones containing the marrow are poet. called 'bronze (or 'brazen') pipes', so the solid ones (ribs, &c.) are *beaten lengths of iron* (? ממטול ברזל); cf. Ar. مَطْوَل *iron beaten into a long shape*; i.e. forged into bars: see Lane): another Arabism. 𝔐 כמטיל ברזל *like a beaten length of iron*; but why the Particle of Comparison (𝔊 om.; cf. st. i), and why not Plur. כְּמָטִלֵי (ut אֲפִיקֵי st. 1)? If we might read some word denoting *rods*, e.g. מַטּוֹת or even שְׁקֵלוֹת instead of מָטִיל, we should be rid of this isolated Arabism. גרמו *his bones* (Pr 17²²; Aram. גרם = Heb. עצם) may perhaps mean here *his limbs*, i.e. his legs. 𝔊 *His ribs* or *sides* (πλευραί = צַלְעֹתָיו Gn 2²¹) *are brazen ribs* | *And his backbone cast-iron* (σίδηρος χυτός = מוצק ברזל) cf 38³⁸ 1 K 7¹⁶) מוצק or מוּצָק seems at least preferable to מָטִיל (hardness and rigidity being the idea > flexibility). 𝔙 Cartilago illius quasi laminae ferreae, *His gristle is, as it were, iron plates*. But 𝔗 *His limbs* (אברוי) *are strong as tanks!* (פְּצִידֵי) *of brass* | *His bones are as a load* (הֵיךְ מַטְלָנָא) or *bars* (מָטְלַיָּא) *of iron* cf. 1 Sa 17⁶ 𝔗 = 𝔐 כידון *lance* מַטְלָנָא (Regia מַטְלוּתָא) connects 𝔐 מטיל with מָטָל (cf. גֵטֵל *burden* Pr 27³) improbably. 𝔖 *His bones are strong as brass and as iron* simply evades the difficulties of the verse.

v. 19. *prime fruit*: the first product of El's creative activity (Dr). For ראשית דרכ' see Pr 8²² and cf Gn 49³. Instead of דַּרְכֵי אֵל leg. fort. דְּרָכַי *my Way* metr. grat. (st. i has four stresses); cf. 41¹⁴ (1st Pers.) and 26¹⁴ note. 𝔊 τοῦτ' ἐστιν ἀρχὴ πλάσματος (al. ὁδῶν) Κυρίου; 𝔙 Ipse est principium viarum Dei (= 𝔐); 𝔖 *He is the head of all the creatures of God*; 𝔗 = 𝔐. 𝔊𝔖 paraphrase דרכי (or perhaps read ברא Gn 5¹).

St ii is more difficult, and certainly corrupt. הָעֹשׂוֹ יַגֵּשׁ חַרְבּוֹ *Let Him who made him* (but הָעֹשׂוֹ = עֹשׂוֹ is a solecism) *bring near His sword!* is obvious nonsense.¹ 41²⁰⁽³³⁾ הָעָשׂוּ לִבְלִי־חָת has suggested the correction הֶעָשׂוּי לִנְגֹשׂ חֲבֵרָיו *He who was made master of his fellow*(*creature*)*s*. The hippopotamus might perhaps be regarded as lord (נֹגֵשׂ *driver* 3¹⁸) of the amphibia, hardly of the land-animals; but what then of the 'leviathan', which is also an amphibious creature, and so far one of his חברים? 𝔙 Qui fecit eum applicabit (?יַגִּישׁ) gladium eius = 𝔐; but 𝔗 דְּעַבְדֵיה יְקָרֵב סַיְפֵיהּ *He who made him, let His sword come nigh!* (יַגֵּשׁ?); 𝔖 (God) *Who made him, that he might make war* (לָגֵשׁ חַרְבּוֹ = וַיִדְכֵּי מַבְכֵּל). 𝔊 is more helpful. πεποιημένον ἐνκαταπαίζεσθαι ὑπὸ τῶν ἀγγέλων αὐτοῦ (41²⁵ᵇ) =

---

¹ The rendering 'He who made him *that he might apply his sword*' (i.e. his sharp teeth or tusks which shear off the grass as neatly as a scythe) is little better. As a version of the Hebrew it is ca[...]b[...]if[...] n[...]   [...], L t   [...] [...] [...] gr[...] e incongruity with [...].

הֶעָשׂוּ (עָשׂוּי ?) לִשְׂחוֹק לְרַבָּו ? *Made for a jest to His Great Ones* (i. e. the Angels? or perhaps לַחֲבֵרָו *to His Companions*, in the same unusual sense). Ps 104²⁶ לויתן זה יצרת לשחק־בו *The leviathan whom Thou didst fashion to sport with* may very well have been in the poet's mind. ('The comp. vb. ἐγκαταπαίζεσθαι only here and 41²⁵; the simple form παίζειν = שָׂחַק v. 29 and eleven times al.; cf. ἐμπαίζειν = צָחַק Gn 39¹⁴·¹⁷.) Possibly he wrote הֶעָשְׂתִי לִשְׂחוֹק בּוֹ *whom I made to sport withal*; or if 𝔐 is right in st. i, בּוֹ עָשָׂהוּ לִשְׂחֶק *He made him to sport withal*. The metre would be improved by reading הוא ראשית דרכו | אלה עשהו לשחק־בו: *He was the firstfruits of His Way*; | *Eloah made him to play with*. Cf. v. 9; Pr 8³⁰.

v. 20. 𝔐 lit. *For* būl (supposed = יבול *produce* 20²⁸ Ju 6⁴) *the mountains bear for him* (cf. Ps 72³) | *And all the living creatures of the field sport* or *play* (v. 29, Zc 8⁵) *there*: 'without fear', explains Driver, 'because the monster lives only upon grass'. But this last fact has already been stated, v. 15ᵇ; and 'the mountains' are not the usual feeding-grounds of the hippopotamus, nor the playground of 'the beasts of *the field*'.

The two stichi hang loosely together, without any real parallelism of ideas. It seems possible that the ἅπ. בול = Assyr. *būlu*, beasts, four-footed animals, wild and tame; e.g. *būl çēri umam çēri . . . ušēlī*, 'The cattle of the field (and) the wild beasts of the field . . . I put aboard' (NE xi. 86). Then בול הרים will be a good parallel to חית השדה in st. ii; and if we point יִשָּׂאוּ (or read יִשְׁתָּאוּ cf. Gn 24²¹ + לָהּ), we get the excellent sense *The cattle of the hills gaze at him* (in wonder), which is naturally followed by *And all the beasts of the field are astounded* (תשם 17³; 𝔐 ישחקו perhaps from v. 19ᵇ; or תישׁוֹמם Is 63³ 59¹⁶). The land-animals are amazed at the sight of the monster coming up out of the water and grazing on the banks of the river.

𝔊 ἐπελθὼν δὲ ἐπ᾽ ὄρος ἀκρότομον = כבוא אל־הר (ה)חלמיש; cf. 20²⁷ 28⁹ Dt 8¹⁵ ἐκ πέτρας ἀκροτόμου = מצור החל׳ | ἐποίησεν χαρμονὴν τετράποσιν ἐν τῷ ταρτάρῳ = כל־חית בשאול ישמח. The word τάρταρος occurs nowhere else in either OT or NT (cf. ταρταρώσας 2 Pe 2⁴). Is the text of 𝔊 sound, or is there a trace of mythology here? (For χαρμονή = שִׂמְחָה see 20⁵ τετραπ. = חיה Nu 35³). 𝔗 = 𝔐; בול = עלל; יבול = 𝔙 Huic montes *herbas* (יבול pro כי יבול ?) ferunt | omnes bestiae agri ludent ibi (= 𝔐 om. ו ad init.). 𝔖 *And the multitude* (ורוב pro כי־בול) *of mountains bear* (sc. fruit? ܡܩܒܠܝܢ) *for him* | *And every beast of the field under his shadow lies down* (ישכבו + צל תחת from v. 21).

v. 21. צאלים *thorny lotus-trees* (Zizyphus lotus) occurs again in the next verse. 𝔊 ὑπὸ παντοδαπὰ δένδρα κοιμᾶται. Cf. v. 22, μεγάλα δένδρα (another guess at the meaning of צאלים). Leg. fort. מצולה *the deep* (water) pro צאלים; cf. 41²³ Zc 10¹¹ (of Nile) Ps 69³·¹⁶ (of a swamp), and בצה (8¹¹) *marsh* or *swamp* ad fin. vs. Possible also seems אֲגָה (9²⁶) or גֹּמֶא the *papyrus* (8¹¹); cf. 𝔊 παρὰ πάπυρον, st. ii, and the Egyptian hunting-scene

40. 23 NOTES ON THE TEXT 443

(Wilkinson, iii. 71). But the former is preferable. 𝔙 Sub *umbra* dormit
(= צֵל vel fort. מִצְלָּה?); 𝔗 תְּחוֹת טְלָלַיָּא יְגְנֵי *Under the shadows he lieth*.
(An objection to joining שָׁם v. 20 with v. 21 is that it would overload the
stichus metrically.)

St. ii 𝔊 παρὰ πάπυρον καὶ κάλαμον καὶ βούτομον. In 8¹¹ βούτομος =
אָחוּ *reeds* or *rushes* (Gn 41²). It perhaps denotes the flowering rush
(*Butomus*). In Gn 49² 𝔊 gives ὄχθη, *bank* of a river; and it might well
be that the Heb. word is akin to אח which is common in Assyr. in the
sense of *side* or *bank* or *shore* (*aḫ Puratti*, *aḫi tâmtim*), as well as in that
of *brother* (qs *side-one*). Παρά suggests that 𝔊 read בסתר as Aram. בסכר
Beside. Κάλαμος = קנה (Assyr. *qanû*, Sum. GIN, GI) as elsewhere (sixteen times), cf. Is 19⁶ καλάμου καὶ παπύρου = קָנֶה וָסוּף (*ibid.*⁷ καὶ τὸ ἄχι τὸ
χλωρόν = *and the green* אָחוּ, 𝔐 corrupt). 𝔙 in secreto calami et in
locis humentibus = 𝔐. 𝔗 אַרְקָא (= אֶרֶץ, אֲרִי) interpr. בִצָּה.

v. 22. 𝔐 is again dubious. Lit. *The lotus-trees screen him, his shade*;
but בצל(ל)ם instr. *with their shade* would have been more normal (cf.
La 3⁵⁴ Ps 91⁴). Perhaps we should read צֻלּוֹ for צִלּוֹ, in the sense of
when lying down or *resting* (cf. Assyr. *ṣalâlu*) or being *submerged* or
immersed in the water (cf. Ex 15¹⁰): *The lote-trees screen him lying down*,
which agrees with st. ii. 𝔙, *Protegunt umbrae* (= צֶלָּיִם יָסֻכּוּ) umbram
eius; but 𝔊 σκιάζονται δὲ ἐν (𝔊ᴬ om. ἐν) αὐτῷ δένδρα μεγάλα = וַיִּסְכְּרוּ לוֹ
צֶאֱלִים בְּצֵלָם? (see note on v. 21). We should have expected σκιάζουσιν δὲ
ἐπ᾽ αὐτῷ κτλ. (An leg. σκιάζοντα δὲ ἐστιν αὐτῷ κτλ.?) But the sequel
σὺν ῥαδάμνοις καὶ κλῶνες ἀγροῦ—better ἄγνου 𝔊ᴺᶜ·ᵃᴬ—shows that 𝔊 really
meant *And great trees with branches, and boughs of the willow*—the *vitex
agnus castus*—*are overshadowed by him*; supposing the monster to be of
a fabulous height and size. Cf. Le 23⁴⁰ ἄγνου κλάδους (= κλώνας) ἐκ
χειμάρρου = עַרְבֵי נָחַל *willows* or *poplars of the wâdy*. For ῥάδαμνος
(= ὀρόδαμνος) vid. 8¹⁶ 14⁷ 15³². 𝔊 may therefore imply something like

וְסֻבְּכֵי צֶאֱלִים (אֵלִים) צְלָלוּ־בוֹ
וְעַרְבֵי נָחַל:

And the thickets of lote-trees (or *terebinths*) *are shadowed* (Ne 13¹⁹) *by him* |
And the poplars of the wâdy. 𝔊 *Shadows* (cf. 𝔙) *encircle him* | *And
willows of the wâdy encircle him* (كَمْ مَيْمَ bis).

v. 23. הֵן *If*; 12¹⁴ 23⁸. Instead of 𝔐 יַעֲשֹׁק *oppress* (10³) we might
perhaps read יָשֹׁק *overflow* (Jo 2²⁴ 4¹³); cf 𝔊 ἐὰν γένηται πλήμμυρα, *If a
flood arise*. Neither יָשֹׁל *run*, scil. *upon him* (surely בוֹ must be expressed
Is 33⁴ Jo 2⁹), nor יִשְׁקַע *sink* (Am 9⁵ of the fall of the Nile) is prob.
(Would the fall of the Nile alarm the animal?) Cf. 𝔊 ܐܘ مَلْأ *If
the river leap up* or *rise*. 𝔗 הָא יִמְלוֹם נַהֲרָא = 𝔐; 𝔙 Ecce absorbebit
fluvium, *Lo, he will swallow down a river* (יִלְעַע? וִילַע). 'The River'
(נָהָר) is prob. the Nile, as in Is 19. St. ii is metr. t. . . long (four stresses).

יַרְדֵּן, 𝔊 ὁ Ἰορδάνης (sic 𝔙 𝔖), may easily be a marginal gloss on נָהָר. The correct gloss would have been יְאֹר (Is 19⁷) or הַיְאֹר *the Nile.* The hippopotamus was unknown in the Jordan valley. For יָגִיחַ *break* or *burst forth,* see 38⁸. 𝔊 here προσκρούσει, *will strike against* (יָגַע or יִגַּח?); 𝔙 influat (cf. 𝔗 נָגִיד *floweth*).

v. 24. St. i is metr. short (only two stresses), and is obviously incomplete as regards the sense. 𝔐 בעיניו יקחנו lit. *With his eyes he will take him.* RV (= AV marg.) is, as Driver says, contrary to Heb. idiom. It is likely that מי־הוא (an emphatic *Who?*) has fallen out after the similar letters פיהו (v. 23 end), and that בעיניו is a corruption of בְּצִנִּים (cf. note on 5⁵ Pr 22⁵) or בצנות (Am 4²) *fish-hooks* or *barbs* (√ צנן is prob. cogn. c שנן *sharpen,* שֵׁן *tooth*); or בְּצַמִּים *with a gin* (but see note on 18⁹; בְּמָצוֹר *with a hunting-net?* 19⁶): cf. (ו)במוקשים st. ii. 𝔊 *In his eye will he receive him (it)?* = 𝔐. 𝔙 In oculis eius *quasi hamo capiet eum* (= 𝔐 + explanatory addition). 𝔖 𝔄 read בַּעֲנָנָיו pro 𝔐 בעיניו: 𝔖 *In his clouds will he take him* | *And in his net* (كَمَرْتِبَاه) *will he be held* or *caught* (يَاخُشْ)? 𝔄 *In a cloud wilt thou take him* | *And in a net wilt thou hold him?* 𝔗 בתוקליא ינקוב נחיריה *With snares will he pierce through his nose?* = 𝔐 c אפו recte pro אף ad fin. 𝔙 Et in sudibus (*stakes*) perforabit nares eius. St. ii is suspicious, if only because of באפו and תקוב in v. 26. 𝔖 𝔄 suggest (2¹⁰) קְדְמוּנִי מוֹקְשֵׁי Ps 18⁶ (30²⁷ יְקַדְּמֶנּוּ (תְּ)יְקַדְּמָנּוּ or וּבְמוֹקְשִׁים יְקַבְּלֶנּוּ מוֹת); and the verse may perhaps be restored thus:

מי־הוא בצנים יקחנו
ובמוקשים מי יקדמנו:

Who with fish-hooks can take him, | *And with snares* (or *baits*) *who confront him?* (or *receive him?*). It is, however, possible that the verse is a marg. variant or even comment on v. 26, and refers to the capture of the crocodile: *In his eyes he pierceth him* (יקבנו?); or if we keep 𝔐 יקח *he taketh him*; cf. Pr 6²⁵); *With baits he pierceth his nose.* Cf. Hdt. ii. 70 ἐπεὰν νῶτον ὑὸς δελεάσῃ περὶ ἄγκιστρον κτλ. After swallowing the bait, the reptile is dragged ashore by the rope attached to it. Attracted by the cries of a sucking-pig on the shore, the crocodile meets the floating bait (within which a hook is concealed) as he swims towards the bank. When he is dragged to land, the hunter smears his eyes with mud, and he is then easily dispatched. The marginal note might conceivably refer to this procedure, rather than to spearing in the eye (cf. 𝔙): *Through his eyes he takes him,* &c. (= 𝔐 c אפו pro אף ad fin.). At the present day the Nubians harpoon the hippopotamus, securing the rope round a tree; or catch the poor creature in covered pitfalls, or by means of a sort of booby-trap.

בְּעֵינָיו cannot mean *in his own sight* (cf. Pr 1¹⁷) = though he be on the watch (EB). It must be instrumental, like the parallel במוקשים. Nor is

בִּשְׁנָיו a suitable substitute (מִי הוּא בְּשִׁנָיו יִקָּחֶנּוּ *Who will take him by the teeth?*); for the Heb supposed would rather mean *Who will capture him with* (instr) *his* (i.e. the captor's) *teeth?* (cf. Pr 6²⁵), and the idea of seizing the animal, whether hippopotamus or crocodile, by his teeth (יֹאחֲזֻנוּ 18¹), in order to cope with or capture him, is not likely to have occurred to the poet or to any sane writer.

v. 25. Chap. 41 begins here in AV. For לִוְיָתָן 'Leviathan', here certainly the crocodile of the Nile (described side by side with the hippopotamus, as in Hdt. ii. 68–71), see 3⁸. The word is possibly an old dual of לִוְיָה *wreath, circlet*—לִוְיָתִי = לִוְיָתָן—meaning *Double-coils, Coil upon Coil*, and would thus suggest an animal of the serpent kind, and might easily gather mythical associations; cf. Ps 74¹⁴ (104²⁶ the 'Sea-serpent', probably a huge decapod or cuttlefish) Is 27¹.

Canst thou draw up: leg. הֲתִמְשֹׁךְ (𝔐 + הֲ Part. Interrog.) c Cod. Kenn 157. Certainly not אִם from v 24 ad fin. For the verb cf. Gn 37²⁸. 𝔙 *An extrahere poteris Leviathan hamo | et fune ligabis linguam eius?* 𝔊 ἄξεις δὲ δράκοντα ἐν ἀγκίστρῳ κτλ. 𝔖 *Wilt thou take the Dragon* (ܬܢܝܢܐ חַנִּין Gn 1²¹ Is 27¹) *with a net?* A δράκων is a big snake, either real or fabulous (one with three heads springing from a single neck is described *Il.* xi. 39 f.). St. ii *And with a cord canst thou sink* (*pull* or *press down* OL RV) *his tongue?* So 𝔐 lit. The cord, of course, is attached to the hook. This is not satisfactory. The ancients supposed that the crocodile had no tongue; that organ in these reptiles being attached all round to the bottom of the mouth (EB., s.v. *Crocodile*). The teeth and sawlike tail are their most formidable weapons. We might perhaps read וְתִקְשֹׁר תְּקַשֵּׁר עַל־שִׁנָּיו *And canst thou bind cords on his teeth?* (v. 29 Gn 28³⁸). Others would justify תַּשְׁקִיעַ by reference to the Samaritan use of the Rt. (שקע *bind*); but this does not seem prob., as the verb is not isolated in Heb. (cf. e.g. Ez 32¹⁴) הַעֲקֹד would be possible in the same sense (Gn 22⁹). 𝔊 περιθήσεις (𝔊^A δεσμήσεις) δὲ φορβεὰν περὶ ῥῖνα αὐτοῦ (= אַפּוֹ from v. 24 fin.). Cf. Pr 7³ קָשְׁרֵם = περίθου αὐτούς (𝔊^A σύνδησον). 𝔖 *With a cord wilt thou take him* (ܒܚܒܠܐ as in st. 1) *by his tongue?* (perhaps reading חַבְלָא); 𝔗 *And with a cord canst thou bore through* (תִקְרַח) *his tongue?* 𝔙 *Et fune ligabis linguam eius?*

v. 26. *a rushen rope* or *line*; lit. *a rush*, as Is 58⁵ (where 𝔊 κρίκος, *a ring* or *nose-ring*, as here). 𝔙 *Numquid pones circulum in naribus eius?* 𝔖 *Dost thou put* a bridle in his mouth? (ܒܦܓܘܕܬܐ ܒܦܘܡܗ); perhaps due to reminiscence of Is 37²⁹. 𝔗 *Canst thou put* a hook (אוּנְקְלָא = ὄγκινος, uncinus) in his nose? 𝔊's *ring in his nostril* would seem to be for the purpose of leading him about, or perhaps rather for ornament; cf. 𝔊 st. ii *And with an armlet wilt thou pierce his lip?* (ψελίῳ δὲ τρυπήσεις τὸ χεῖλος αὐτοῦ; = 𝔙 *Aut armilla perforabis maxillam eius?* but 𝔊ᵃ χαλινῷ, *with a bridle* : cf. Is 37·ı. Possibly 𝔊 may have been thinking of the Egyptian custom of adorning the tame crocodiles kept in the temples of Thebes and lake Moeris with eardrops (ἀρτήματα) and anklets (ἀμφιδέαι): see Hdt. ii. 69. But the Greek of vv. 25 f. has been influenced by reminiscence of 2 K 19²⁸ (Is 37²⁹): καὶ θήσω τὰ ἄγκιστρά μου ἐν τοῖς μυκτῆρσίν σου καὶ χαλινὸν ἐν τοῖς χείλεσίν σου: and the passage refers to the difficulty or impossibility of capturing the crocodile by the ordinary methods of the fisherman, owing to its gigantic strength, formidable weapons and armour, and fiercely untamable nature. The question of various readings of the Heb. text, therefore, hardly arises in this instance. (𝕲 δήσεις is a corruption of θήσεις; חוֹחַ *bramble* 2 K 14⁹ should prob. be חָח *hook* or *ring*, Is 37²⁹; so eight codd. Kenn. 𝔗 as 𝔐: בְּסִילְוָא *with a thorn*; 𝕾 ܒܡܣܩܗ *in his leap* or *springing*: cf. ܣܦܩ *spirited*?) The sense seems to be: Can you catch a crocodile with hook and line, as you would catch a fish? (V. 24 might very well follow here, if we might restore it somewhat thus:

הַבְּצָמִים תִּקָחֶנּוּ חַי
וּבְמוֹקְשִׁים תַּחֲזִיק בְּאַפּוֹ:

Canst thou take him alive in a trap, | *And with bird-snares* (Am 3⁵) *catch him by the snout?*)

v. 27. Lit. as 𝔙: Numquid multiplicabit ad te preces, aut loquetur tibi mollia: cf. Pr 15¹. When caught, will he beg for mercy or release, in mild conciliatory speech?

v. 28. *Will he make* (lit. *cut*) *a covenant* or *contract with thee?* 𝔙 Numquid feriet tecum pactum? Will he agree to conditions of perpetual service? *Wilt thou take him*: 𝕲 𝔙 prefix *And*; making the connexion with st. i clearer. 𝔗 *Wilt thou* sell him *for a working slave for ever?* But the sense of the verse seems rather to be: Will he agree to perpetual service, on condition that you spare his life?

v. 29. *a pet sparrow.* צִפּוֹר, like Assyr. *iççuru*, is simply *a bird* of any sort. Roman ladies appear to have made pets of sparrows (cf. the well-known elegy of Catullus on the death of Lesbia's sparrow, *Passer deliciae meae puellae, Quīcum ludere*, &c., Carm. II, and the use of *Passer, passerculus*, as terms of endearment in Plautus); and several varieties of the bird are common in Palestine. The English name is referred by Skeat to the Teutonic base SPARWA, *to flutter*; so that, in spite of the resemblance of sound, it can hardly be related to the Heb *çippór*, Assyr. *iççûru* (= *içpûru* with Regressive Assimilation; cf. Arab. عَصْفُور), which appears to mean *whistler* (cf. Assyr. *çapâru*, 'whistle', 'pipe', 'twitter', 'mutter', &c.; Ar. صَفَرَ *to whistle*, of a bird).

St. ii is metr. short (two stresses). 𝕲 ἢ δήσεις αὐτὸν ὥσπερ στρουθίον παιδίῳ: supplies the desiderated parallel comparison: ὥσπερ στρουθίον = כְּבַת־יַעֲנָה *lik an* *str* *h* (cf. 30⁰ στρουθῶν, Is 34¹ στρουθίων). In Pr 26²

כַּצְפוּר is followed by כִּדְרוֹר *like the swallow* (𝔊 ὥσπερ . . . στρουθοί), and דְּרוֹר is parallel to צִפּוֹר in Ps 84⁴ also (where 𝔊 has τρυγών, *turtledove*); perhaps, therefore, it may be read here. The context implies some captive wild bird; כְּיוֹנָה *like a dove*, therefore, seems less suitable, as these birds are too tame to need any 'binding' to prevent their escape. (𝔊's word here παιδίον = לְנַעַר' is due to misunderstanding a scribal abbreviation.) στρουθίον = צִפּוֹר elsewhere in 𝔊 (seven times; e.g. Ps 84⁴ = 83⁵ 𝔊) 𝔊 *And wilt thou keep him for the days of thy youth?* misreading ותשטרנו לימי נעְרוֹתֶיךָ (pts.). כְּעָגוּר *like a crane* (Is 38¹⁴ Je 8⁷) seems also possible.

v. 30. *partners*· i.e. in fishing (cf. Lk 5⁷·¹⁰ μέτοχοι, κοινωνοί). חַבָּרִים *socii*; so pointed here only. 𝔙 *amici* = חֲבֵרִים. 𝔖 ܐܒ̈ܠܐ *partakers, associates, partners* 𝔊 ἔθνη (by inadvertence from st. ii; or did 𝔊 read נכרים *foreigners*?). 𝔗 seems to have read חכמים *wise men* pro חברים. *bargain about*: יכרו עליו (6²⁷); or *make trade of him*. C Accus. *buy* (Dt 2⁶). With √-כר cf. מדכר *sell*, and Sum. GAR, *do, put, give, put down* (cf. mgs. of נתן); MUN-GAR, NIG-GAR, *goods, property, treasure* (*makkûru*) 𝔙 concident eum: *cut him up* (= יכרתו); 𝔊 ἐνσιτοῦνται, *make a meal of*; ἅπ. כרה III. *give a feast*; cf. 2 K 6²³ and Assyr. *iškunu kêrêta*, 'they made a feast'). So also 𝔗. 𝔖 *assemble over him* (יָקְוּ or יָקַהֲלוּ) pro יכרו. Error due to dictation?).

St. ii. *share or divide him*; the Subj. being the partners. Cf. Ex 21³⁵. But 𝔊 μεριτεύονται (ἅπ. = μερίζονται) δὲ αὐτὸν Φοινίκων ἔθνη (AC γένη); and 𝔙 divident illum negotiatores? perhaps implying עַם *folk* pro 𝔐 בֵּין *between*. בְּנֵי pro בין would yield a similar sense: *Shall sons of Canaanites* (= Canaanites) *divide him?* i.e. share him out (cf. Ex 23³⁵). A closer parallel to st. i. 𝔊 *And will they divide him among many?* (app. rg. כְּנִשִּׁין Aram. *multitudes* pro 𝔐 כְּנַעֲנִים *Canaanites* or *traders*, Pr 31²⁴). The question of the verse seems to be: When caught, is the monster cut up and distributed for sale like a big fish? (presumably for human food: crocodiles, though extremely unpalatable to Europeans, are eaten by the people of the Upper Nile; and the flesh of the native species is sold in the markets of Siam)

v. 31. *spikes*: or *barbs*: שְׂכּוֹת ἅπ. cf. (שֵׂךְ), שִׂכִּים *thorns* ‖ צְנִינִם Nu 33⁵⁵; Assyr. *sikkatu*, 'plug', 'peg', or *šikkatu*, 'point', 'peak', of a mountain; *thorn-hedge* (cf. Is 5⁵); Ar. شَكَّ *pierce through*. The Versions misunderstood the word: 𝔙 Numquid implebis *sagenas* pelle eius? (rg שְׂבָכוֹת *nets*, 18⁸, pro בְּשֻׂכּוֹת); 𝔊 *Wilt thou fill his skin* with flesh? (בשר); 𝔗 *Canst thou fill his skin with* bowers? (במטללתא = סֻכּוֹת *booths* = 𝔐 שֻׂכּוֹת). 𝔊 πᾶν δὲ πλωτὸν συνελθὸν οὐ μὴ ἐνέγκωσιν βύρσαν μίαν οὐρᾶς αὐτοῦ (𝔊ᴬ more grammat. ἐνέγκῃ); a marvellous version, app. rg. שָׂבִיּוֹת (Is 2¹⁶ πλοίων) pro שֻׂכּוֹת. Possibly וְנָבוֹ he has war a nap. var. of עורו

his skin (suggested by *his head* in st. ii), so that βύρσαν μίαν οὐρᾶς αὐτοῦ is conflate. 𝔊 may thus represent (וגבו) התמלא בל־שכיות עורו; πᾶν δὲ πλωτὸν συνελθόν being merely a periphrasis of the plur., and the whole paraphrastic. (Since ἤνεγκε = הביא as a rule, 𝔊 may indicate הֲתָבִאן, כל־שכיות עורו *Could all ships bring his skin?*)

St. ii. 𝔙 *Et gurgustium piscium* capite illius? where *piscatorum* (the hut *of fishermen*) would seem more natural. The notion of *hut* is due to connecting צִלְצָל *spear* (fr. צלל I. *quiver, whizz*) with צֵל III. *shadow* (cf. Gn 19³ צֵל). So 𝔗 *And his head with the screen* (גְּנוּנָא) *of fishes*, cf. 𝔗 v. 22. 𝔊 *with the shadow of fire* (ܢܘܪܐ scrib. error pro ܢܘܢܐ). 𝔊 καὶ ἐν πλοίοις ἁλιέων κεφαλὴν αὐτοῦ = ראשו (pro רַגִּים דָּגִים *fishes*) ובצלצל דיגים; taking צִלְצָל to mean a *fishing-smack* (cf. Is 18¹ Οὐαὶ γῆς πλοίων πτέρυγες = הוי ארץ צלצל כנפים).

v. 32. 𝔐 lit. *Set thy hand upon him;* | *Remember the battle; add not!* The meaning seems to be Try it once, and you will never do it again. (Leg. אם־תשים?) 𝔙 nec ultra addas *loqui*, 'and *say* no more!'; wrongly supposing לדבר to be the suppressed Infin. But st. ii seems somewhat disjointed, and זְכֹר may be the Infin. (= לזכר cf. Gn 8¹¹ al.): *Thou wilt think of a battle no more* (לא pro אל). 𝔊 ἐπιθήσει should be ἐπιθήσεις (𝔊^ΑΛαC). Perhaps וּזְכֹר (cf. 𝔖𝔄). After πόλεμον (= מלחמה) 𝔊 adds the explanatory gloss τὸν γινόμενον ἐν σώματι αὐτοῦ (i. e. the 'battle' which the assailant experienced in his own person); while 𝔊^Νc·aAC add to this καὶ μηκέτι γινέσθω = ואל תוסף.

Chapter 41. Continues the same subject.

v. 1. Corrupt. St. i is metr. short, הן being always a proclitic (8¹⁹·²⁰ 13¹ al.). 𝔐 lit. *Lo, his hope hath proven false* (Pr 30⁶); cf. 24²⁵ Hi. The word לֹחֲמוֹ *of his assailant* (cf. Ps 35¹), or נִלְחָם בּוֹ *of him that fights against him*, may have fallen out after the preceding מלחמה (40³²): *The hope of his assailant proveth vain!* (תוחלתו pro תחלת לחמו).

𝔊 οὐδὲ ἐπὶ τοῖς λεγομένοις τεθαύμακας; = st. ii (rg. הֲנַם אֶל־אֲמָרִים תֵּפָּל). (𝔊^ACvid.Nc·a prefix οὐκ (οὐχ) ἑόρακας αὐτόν; which does not help much as a substitute for st. i (= הן תחלתו pro הלא חזיתו). 𝔙 Ecce spes eius *frustrabitur eum*, *Lo, his hope* will disappoint him (= יכזבנו Pi. or Hi.?). St. ii 𝔐 ייטל הנם אל־מראיו *Even at his appearance will he be thrown?* (RV inserts a 'not'; but see Heb.). The ה is dittogr. from the previous word, and must be omitted. מַרְאָיו *his visible form* or *appearance* (Gn 41²¹) = מַרְאֵהוּ. The crocodile is such a terrible-looking creature that his would-be assailant is 'knocked down', as we say, at the very sight of him. 𝔙 Et *videntibus cunctis* praecipitabitur (= וּבְכָל רֹאָיו יָטַל; cf. Is 8¹⁶): כל pro אל 𝔐 ut saep. 𝔊 οὐδὲ δέδοικας ὅτι ἡτοίμασταί μοι (𝔊^A σοι); = v. 2ᵃ. 𝔊 renders the verse: *Lo, loosed is thy foot* | *And also God will bear his bitterness* (= הֵן תּוּחַל רַגְלְךָ | וְגַם אֵל מָרוֹ יִטֹּל = corruption of 𝔐).

v. 2. St. i. RV *None is so fierce that he dare stir him up* makes good sense, but is hardly warranted by the Heb., is a bad parallel to st. ii, and ignores the fact that the stichus is metr. short (two stresses), and that אכזר (30²¹) prob. refers to the beast rather than to the man. The line may be restored thus הוא אכזר מי יעירנו *He is fell; who shalt arouse him?* (הוא pro לא and מי pro כי, as is almost demanded by the following ומי; יעירנו Ketib pro Qerî יעוּרנוּ). Then naturally follows st. ii : וּמִי הוּא לְפָנָיו *And who* (emph.) *before him can stand?* (לפניו pro לפני, c 27 codd. et 𝔗MSS.). The proposed לֹא יִזְכֹּר *He remembers not* (40³²ᵇ) leaves st. i metr. short, and is otherwise not much better than the fanciful זָר מַלְאָךְ *A hostile Angel* (pro לא אכזר). 𝔊 οὐδὲ δέδοικάς ὅτι ἡτοίμασταί μοι; = לֹא יָגֹרְתָּ (תירא? תפחד?) (cf. 3²⁵ 9²⁸; התעתד 15²³); corrupt reading of 𝔐. In st. ii τίς γάρ ἐστιν ὁ ἐμοὶ ἀντιστάς; = 𝔐. 𝔙 Non quasi crudelis suscitabo eum = לא בּאכזר אעירנו pro 𝔐 לא אכזר כי יעירנו; Quis enim resistere potest vultui meo? = 𝔐. 𝔗 *He is not cruel because he* rouses him | *And who* (emph.) *before him shall take his stand?* 𝔊 He will not go far when he is roused | *And who is there that shall stand before me?*

v. 3. St. i is again too short. 𝔐 cannot mean *Who hath first given unto* me (??), *that I should repay him?* (RV). By reading מִי־הוּא קִדְּמוֹ וַיִשְׁלָם *Who hath ever faced him and remained whole?* (or מי־הוא יְקַדְּמֶנּוּ וְיִשְׁלָם *Who can face him and remain whole?*), we restore the balance of the metre, and get rid of the dubious Hi. (cf. Am 9¹⁰), as well as of the awkward reference to God (cf. v. 2ᵇ). See 9⁴ 30²⁷. 𝔊 ἢ τίς ἀντιστήσεταί μοι καὶ ὑπομενεῖ (= וּמִי יְקַדְּמֵנִי וְיִשְׁלָם; cf. 9⁴ 22²¹ 𝔊). St. ii 𝔐 lit. *Under all the heavens to me he (belongs)* does not cohere with what precedes. '𝔊 as 𝔐; but 𝔗 attempts better sense with *Is not all under the heavens mine?* and 𝔙 with Omnia quae sub caelo sunt, mea sunt (both trs. תחת כל). 𝔊 εἰ πᾶσα ἡ ὑπ' οὐρανὸν ἐμή ἐστιν, *If all the earth is mine* (connecting this as Protasis with v. 4!) For ἡ ὑπ' οὐρ. = אָרֶץ see 2² 34¹³ 38¹⁸,²⁴ 42¹⁵; = תבל 34¹³: תַּחַת שָׁמַיִם Dt 25¹⁹ 29²⁰. Instead of לי־הוא, however, לֹא־אֶחָד *not one* (14⁴ᵇ) or perhaps לֹא־הוּא (but cf. Je 5¹¹), or לֹא־הָיָה, *he exists not*, there is none such.

v. 4. In 𝔐 st. i has only two stresses, while st. ii has four. The metrical balance may be restored by transferring דבר to st. i. Then, instead of the dubious בריו *his parts*, i. e. members (see note on 18¹³), read מדיו *his dress, garb*, esp. military *array*: see 1 Sa 4¹² 17³⁸ (where שריון also occurs as here, v. 5) בריך מתים due to reminiscence of 11³ יתרישו. לֹא־אַחֲרִישׁ דְּבַר מַדָּיו *I will not be silent about his array* agrees with what follows in v. 5 (לבושו *his* warrior's *apparel* or *cloak*; cf. 2 Sa 20⁸ Is 63¹). St. ii should be (וּ)גְבוּרָתוֹ וְחֵיל עֶרְכּוֹ *(And) his might and the strength of his utjil [or a] utr m nt*). Both בְּבוּרָד (30) in ! חיל (p. 33⁷) are used of physical strength; and the *vox nihili* חָיִן may be exchanged for the latter with some assurance. For עֲרְפּוֹ we might substitute עֶרְיוֹ *his attire*, if it were not sufficiently justified by עֶרֶךְ בְּגָדִים *an outfit* or *suit of clothes*, Ju 17¹⁰. Cf. עדה ‖ לבש 40¹⁰. 𝔊 οὐ σιωπήσομαι (= 𝔐 לֹא־אַחֲרִישׁ) διʼ αὐτόν (= בְּיָדוֹ ? pro 𝔐 בריו); καὶ λόγον δυνάμεως ἐλεήσει τὸν ἴσον αὐτοῦ = וּדְבַר גְּבוּרוֹת יָחֹן עֶרְכּוֹ *And with a word of power he will favour his equal* (dupl. accus. ut Ju 21²²: ἴσον: cf. 28¹⁷·¹⁹ יֵעָרְכֶנָּה = ἰσωθήσεται αὐτῇ) = text of 𝔐 slightly altered. 𝔙 Non parcam ei (? לֹא־אַחֲרִישׁ עָלָיו ? בְּעַדוֹ) et verbis potentibus (וּדְבַר גְּבוּרוֹת) et ad deprecandum compositis (וְלִחֹן! עָרוּךְ). 𝔖 *And I will not keep silence on* (ܚܠܝܗ) *his strength* *And on the sinews of his might.* 𝔗 takes בַּדָּיו as *idle talk* (11³) or *lying* (כַּדְבֻבַיָּה), and renders וְחִין עֶרְכּוֹ by וּבְעוּתָא דַעֲלַוֵיהּ *and the entreaty that is upon him*; app. an allusion to the fabled 'crocodile tears' (חִין connected with חנן as in 𝔊𝔙).

v. 5. Lit. *Who hath stripped off* or *removed* (גִּלָּה Is 22⁸ 47² of removing a covering or veil) *the face of his coat* (i.e. his skin, 30¹⁸) *?* exposed the skin by stripping off the armour of scales which covers it. Read prob. יְגַלֶּה (י om. post י); so 𝔊 τίς ἀποκαλύψει κτλ. 𝔙 Quis revelabit faciem indumenti eius? But the idea required by the context (st. ii) is rather that of penetrating or piercing through the hard surface; and Is 36⁶ (וּבָא בְכַפּוֹ וּנְקָבָהּ *it will go into his hand and pierce it*) suggests the reading יִקֹּב pro גִּלָּה: cf. v. 26. (יָגֹל fr. √נגל seen in מַגָּל, Ar. مِنْجَل *a toothed sickle* is also conceivable: *Who can gash the surface of his coat?*) In st. ii we must read סִרְיָנוֹ *his body-armour* or *coat of mail* c 𝔊 θώρακος αὐτοῦ (so Je 46¹; = שִׁרְיוֹן 1 Sa 17⁵·³⁸ שִׁרְיָן Is 59¹⁷. See also v. 18 infr.) pro 𝔐 רִסְנוֹ *his halter* or *bridle*. It is absurd to suppose that 'his double bridle' (RV) can mean his two rows of teeth. סריונו is a suitable parallel to לבושו (1 Sa 17²⁸ Is 63¹·²). The obvious answer to the question of RV *Who shall come within* (?) *his double bridle?* is, Anyone who chooses—at his own risk. *go into* means *penetrate*, as in Is 36⁶. The expression *his double mail* might perhaps denote his scales and hide together (Dr); but more probably the meaning is that his armour is twice as strong as any coat of mail, and quite impenetrable (as we might speak of a sevenfold shield). 𝔙 Et *in medium oris eius quis intrabit?* (perhaps reading בְּקֶרֶב פִּיו or בְּקִרְבוֹ pro בכפל, and supposing that רסן might mean the *place* of the bridle, i.e. the mouth: cf. 𝔗). 𝔊 recte εἰς δὲ πτύξιν θώρακος αὐτοῦ τίς ἂν εἰσέλθοι; 𝔖 *And when the net falleth*, &c. (בְּנְפֹל pro בכפל; רשת, מצוד, or some other syn. pro רסנו). 𝔗 as 𝔐 (*Into the doubling of his halter*, i.e. the place where it doubles, *who durst enter?*—Levy CHWB s. v. פְרוּמְבְּיָא = φορβεία compares χαλινοί, *bits*, and also *the corners of a horse's mouth where the bit rests*).

v. 6. *his mouth*: reading פִּיו 15³⁰ 23¹² al. or פִּיהוּ 3¹ 35¹⁸ 40²³ pro 𝔐 פָּנָיו *his face*. So 𝔖. Cf. the parallel *his teeth*. *can open*: Impf. יפתח pro

𝔐 פתח. So 𝔊 τίς ἀνοίξει, 𝔙 Quis aperiet; but 𝔗 as 𝔐. (𝔖 wrongly divides these vss.: *Who openeth the circle of his teeth, the terror that is in the valley* = בנאוה : אימה.) pro 𝔐 אימת ניא or אימה בניא.

v. 7. 'Crocodiles', we are told, exhibit 'a partial dermal skeleton, developed in the leathery integument, consisting of numerous square bony plates, keeled in the centre, and forming a complete dorsal shield' (EBr s.v.). This confirms the conjecture גַּוָּה *his back* (1 K 14⁹) or גֵּוֹה *id*. (Pr 10¹³ Is 50⁶) pro 𝔐 גַּאֲוָה *pride*. (גו) *dorsum* does not occur elsewhere in Job: see note on 30⁵.) *His back is furrowed with shields*; a picturesque description of its appearance. Lit. *His back is gullies* (or *watercourses, channels*) *of* (i.e. formed by) *shields* (i.e. shield-shaped plates). For אפיק see notes on 6¹⁵ 12²¹ 40¹⁸ and cf. Is 8⁷ Ez 6³. The grooves between the rows of bony plates running along the animal's back are compared to the gullies between mountains.

The use of the word אפיקי, however, seems questionable; and a verb would conduce to perspicuity, e. g. יקיפו (1⁵ 19⁶ and 1 K 7²⁴): *His back shields encompass* (or *enclose*); possibly, perhaps, in view of Ex 14²² 15⁸, גוה יקפא למגנים *His back is hardened* (10¹⁰) *into shields*. In any case, it is the 'shields', not the hollows between their rows, that are important to the armature of the crocodile. St. ii is also difficult. סָגוּר Sing. must refer to גוה, not to מגנים א' Plur. (OL, RV). סָגוּר חוֹתָם צָר וז (*Shut is a narrow seal !*) is really meaningless. It certainly cannot mean *closely joined* (?) *as with tight seal* or (pointing חוֹתָם צר) *with seal of flint*. We may perhaps read סָגְרוּ בְּחוֹמַת צֹר *They* (the shields) *shut it in as* (*with*) *wall of flint*. 'Seal' (9⁷ 14¹⁷) is not likely, for a seal could be broken. Verses 8, 9 describe how closely the 'shields' are set.

𝔊 τὰ ἔγκατα αὐτοῦ ἀσπίδες χάλκεαι | σύνδεσμος αὐτοῦ ὥσπερ σμιρίτης λίθος. גו treated as an Aramaism (גו, גַוָּא *middle, the inside*, viscera or 'inwards'); cf Ps 51¹² ἐν τοῖς ἐγκάτοις μου = בקרבי. But 21²⁴ τὰ ἔγκατα αὐτοῦ = עֲטִינָיו (!). ἀσπίδες χάλκεαι, cf. 40¹⁸ πλευραὶ χάλκεαι = אפיקי נחשה (!). 𝔖 (for the verse) *His mouth is fastened and bound and sealed*. 𝔙 Corpus illius quasi scuta fusilia, | compactum squamis se prementibus גֵּוָתוֹ pro 𝔐 גַּאֲוָה; כ)מוּצָק מגן) might account for *quasi scuta fusilia*, cf. 1 K 7³² (³³) ad fin., and for ἀσπίδες χάλκεαι also, if we might suppose χάλκεαι to be a scribal error for χωνευταί: thus מוצק pro 𝔐 אפיקי). In st. ii 𝔙 perhaps read סָגוּר בְּחוֹתָם צָר *enclosed with tight* (צָר) *seal* (qs Coll. = the plates or 'shields'); or במחבת צר ס' *shut in with an enclosing plate* (cf. Ez 4³ Ct 8⁹), regarding צָר as Ptcp of צור (Ps 139⁵). 𝔗 st. 1ᵃ גְּוִיָּתְנוּת פַּצִּידַיָּא · תְּרִיסִין לֵיהּ. Var. הֵיךְ גְּיוֹתָנוּת פַּצִּידַיָּא קְלִיפוֹהִי *Like the swell of ponds* (or *rivers*) *are its scales* = אַחִיר בְּחוֹתָם צָיִר סְגַנָּיו (גְּנָוַת אַפִּיקִים סְגָנָיו (cf. 𝔐); st. 2 (v. צָיִיר) (צָאִיר) *shut in with a close seal*. 𝔊 σύνδεσμος (𝔊ᴬ καὶ σύνδεσμοι, 𝔊ˣᶜ σύνδ. δὲ) αὐτοῦ = סָגְרוֹ(וּ) pointed וסגרוֹ? ὥσπερ σμιρίτης λίθος = כְּמוֹ־שָׁמִיר *like adamant* (?) pro 𝔐 כחיתם צר. Σμίρις l·······, or σμῖρις Hesych. is said to be Corundum or emery powder. The phrase is only found here. (Schol. σφραγὶς στενή = 𝔐.)

v. 8. Lit. *One to one they approach* (Constr. Is 65⁵); i.e. the 'shields' are set close, side by side.   *space*: or *interval*: pointing רֶוַח (Gn 32¹⁷) pro 𝔐 רוּחַ *wind* or *air*. (This and the last verses were wanting in 𝔊 originally.)

v. 9. This verse is an evident var. of *v.* 8. Cod. Kenn. 34 omits it, and it is starred in 𝔊ᴴ.   *clinging*: lit. as 38³⁸ *they are joined. They hold together*: see note on 38³⁰ᵇ.

v. 10. *his snorting*: lit. *sneezing*. Point עֲטִישָׁתוֹ Sing. c 𝔊𝔙𝔗 > Plur. 𝔐. The word happens to be ἅπ. in OT, but the Root עטש *to sneeze* occurs in Ar., Aram., Eth., as well as NH. It is doubtless an onomatopoeia. The allusion of the stichus may be to the flash of the spray shot up in the sunlight from the reptile's nostrils (cf. vv. 11 sqq.). It is curious to note that the Ar. عَطَسَ *to sneeze* means also *to dawn*, and العُطَاس is *the daybreak*. For יהל see 31²⁶ Is 13¹⁰. 𝔊 *And his orbs* (*eyes* ܡܙܠܐ) *are filled with light* | *And his eyes* (ܟܣܡܬܗ) *are as the rays of dawn* (ܐܟܡܦ ܥܕܢ); cf. Sum. ZALAG shine, firelight, and ܟܣ id.). A better parallel; but how did 𝔊 read עטישתיו? אישון ' עיניו *the pupil of his eyes*? The crocodile's red eyes 'are said to appear gleaming through the water before the head comes to the surface' (Driver).

v. 11. *flames*: לַפִּידִים lit. *torches*. Perhaps *flashes*; cf. Ex 20¹⁸ Na 2⁵. (The √לפד may be cogn. c נבט Assyr. *nabâṭu*, to shine.) 𝔊 λαμπάδες καιόμενοι, *burning torches*. 𝔊 perhaps chose λαμπάς (12 times) to represent לפיד because of the likeness of sound.   *sparks*: כִּידוֹדֵי (ἅπ.) from √כיד = Ar. كَدَّ *emit fire* (of firestick); akin to √קד in קָדַח *be kindled*, קָדַח *bore, kindle*, قَدَّ *strike fire*, and יָקַד, יָסַד, קָדַד *be kindled, burn*.

escape or *slip out*: יִתְמַלְּטוּ (19²⁰ only). Whether we retain 𝔐 (and a verb of motion suits the ‖ יהלכו), or read יתלהטו (ἅπ. Hithp.; cf. *v.* 13) after 𝔊 (cf. 𝔙 Sicut taedae ignis *accensae*), which is less prob. (as is also the treatment of the כ in כידודי as Caph Compar. ap. 𝔊𝔙), 𝔊 καὶ διαρριπτοῦνται (Is 62¹⁰†) ἐσχάραι πυρός lends some support to 𝔐 (διαρρ. = יוטלו or יְתוֹרָטוּ ἅπ.??; cf. 16¹¹). ἐσχάρα, *hearth, brazier, firewood, altar*, which represents some eight other Hebrew words in 𝔊, may well equal כידודי here. 𝔖 has a double rendering: And there go forth out of his mouth torches | *Like coals of fire, and like sparks of fire which are flaming*.

v. 12. *like a boiling pot*: כְּדוּד נָפוּחַ: lit. *like a pot blown* (under); i.e. with breath or bellows (מַפֵּחַ Je 6²⁹); cf. סִיר נָפוּחַ id. Je 1¹³ and כּוּר נָפוּחַ *a blown furnace* or *crucible* Ecclus 43⁴. There is a difficulty about the last word in the verse. 𝔐 וְאַגְמֹן *and rush(es)* 40² gives no good sense, at first sight. Possibly, however, the rushes are the fuel which, when blown into a flame, cause the pot to boil and steam. Perhaps באגמון (cf. Zc 12⁶). St. ᵘ ap 𝔊 ‏كَأَنَّهُ مِنْ فَوْهِ قِدْرٍ مُسَجَّرَةٍ‎ *like the flame round a pot which is heated*; 𝔙 sicut ollae succensae atque *ferventis*; ־ כִּיפָא דְּעָבַד נְפִיחַ דּוּדָא הֵיךְ 𝔗 *like a boiling pot which makes a jet* (*Wasserstrahl*, Levy). Perhaps an Arabism אָנוּג (‏أَجَّ‎ *the fire burned fiercely, flamed or blazed*) might be suggested pro אַגְמוֹן: *Like* (or *As of*) *a pot blown and blazed under*, or *blown under and heated*. 𝔊 (καπνὸς) καμίνου καιομένης πυρὶ ἀνθράκων = בוּר בָּעֵר בְּאֵשׁ נֶחָלִים: reading בוּר pro כְּדוּד (which is suspiciously like כִּידוֹדֵי codd. כְּדוּדֵי v. 11), and perhaps anticipating the נֶחָלִים of v. 13.

v. 13. *his breath*: נַפְשׁוֹ; not *his fury* (OL); cf. vv. 10–12. 𝔙 rectè · *Halitus eius prunas ardere facit.* There can be little doubt that נֶפֶשׁ, Assyr. *napištu*, orig. meant *breath*. (Cf. the analogy of רוּחַ *breath, wind, spirit*, and רֵיחַ *scent* or *smell*, str. *what is inbreathed* or *inhaled* = נֶפֶשׁ Is 3²⁰ = Assyr. *nipšu*, *smell, odour*: *çiru iteçin nipiš šammu*, 'A serpent smelt the scent of the herb', NE xi. 304. The vb. *napāšu* is *to breathe, blow*, and also *to expand, broaden*; breathing *expands* the chest · cf. *šittu kîma imbari inappuš elišu*, 'Sleep like a (sudden) blast bloweth over him' (NE xi. 210). The prim. Root may be Sum. 𝄃𝄃𝄃 PESH, *napāšu, rapāšu*. Cf. also נשׁף *to blow*.) 𝔊 ἡ ψυχὴ αὐτοῦ ἄνθρακες (תלהט exc. ante וְלַהַב). St. ᵘ = v. 11 st. 1. The verse may be a variant of that. 'No smoke without fire', says the proverb. The comparison of the monster's hot breath, steaming from nose or mouth in the sunlight, to smoke and sparks, is intelligible; and travellers' tales may have made him a fire-breathing animal. The poet probably depended on report for his description of the crocodile.

v. 14. 'The vertebrae of the neck bear upon each other by means of rib-like processes, the neck being thus deprived to a great extent of its mobility; hence the difficulty experienced by crocodiles in turning' (EBr s. v.) St. i: so 𝔊𝔙𝔖𝔗. For יָלִין *abides* see 17² 19⁴ Is 1²¹.

St. ii: *boundeth Panic* · יָדוּץ דְּאָבָה. Both words ἅπ. The former might be an Aramaism (‏דּוּץ‎ 𝔗 Pr 23²⁴ *exult*; Syr ‏ܕܨ‎ *leap or dance for joy*). So 𝔈 ‏ܣܠܩ‎ ‏ܕܨ‎ *exsultat timor*, and 𝔗 דְּאָבוֹנָא תְּדִיץ = 𝔐. But 𝔊 τρέχει = יָרוּץ *runneth* may be right for the verb. Instead of the noun דְּאָבָה (= דְּאָבוֹן Dt 28⁶⁵) *faintness, faintheartedness*, 𝔊 gives ἀπώλεια = אֲבַדּוֹן 26⁶ 28²²; which, though adopted by some, does not suit here, since it means *the Place of Perdition* (syn. She'ol). Besides, ἀπώλεια = אֵיד 21³⁰ 30¹² 31³ Pr 1²⁶ al., and many other Heb. words: see, e.g., 11²⁰ 20⁵ ²⁸. 𝔊ᴬ has ἐκλιμία, *extreme hunger*; 𝔙 *egestas*, *want*: both prob. representing דְּאָבָה. Perhaps רְעָדָה *tr* n ‥ (4⁴) may be suggested; but no change is really necessary. Cf. Hab 3. The reference to the neck seems rather strange; and a line like בצעדו ילך עז *In his steps* (= Behind him; cf. Dan 11⁴³) *marcheth Fierceness* (or עַז ἄπ. *Quaking, Panic?*) would improve the parallelism.

v. 15. 𝔐 מפלי בשרו *the fallings* or *hanging parts of his flesh* is very doubtful (מפל Am 8⁶†). The crocodile has no visible loose flesh. We may perhaps read 'כפלי בש *the folds* (or, according to the Eth. use of the Root, *the parts*; but cf. v. 5) *of his flesh*. The verb דבקו should be pointed as Pu. דֻּבָּ֑קוּ (cf. v. 9 38³⁸), since the Qal is not used abs. in Job (see 19²⁰ 29¹⁰ 31⁷). Cf. 𝔙 *Membra carnium eius cohaerentia sibi*; 𝔊 σάρκες δὲ σώματος αὐτοῦ κεκόλληνται (= Pu.); 𝔗 שַׁלְדֵּי בִּסְרֵיהּ מִתְאַדְּקִין *The lumps* (?) *of his flesh stick together* (cf. Syr. ܐܰܕܳܐ *carcase, trunk*); but 𝔖 *Goodly* (ܡܚܣܢ) *is his flesh and fat* (= וברי?); a guess at a defaced text. St. ii. *It* (i.e. his flesh) *is firm* (lit. *cast* 28²) *upon him, it cannot be shaken*; as it might, if it hung loose. 𝔊 καταχέει merely mistakes יָצוּק as Impf. instead of Ptcp. But 𝔙 *Mittet* contra eum *fulmina* appears to read יָבְרֹק or יִבְרוֹק (Ps 144⁶) pro יָצוּק, and וּבַל יִפֹּטוּ (*et ad locum alium non ferentur*; a paraphr.) pro בַּל־יִמּוֹט. The word יצוק (repeated twice in v. 16) certainly seems dubious; and 𝔊ᴴ, *stars the whole stichus*. 𝔗 = 𝔐: יִתְחַסַּד עֲלוֹי דְּלָא תְזוּעַ. 𝔖: ܘܡܣܬܡܟ and *he is supported* (connecting בל ימוט with v. 14: ܘܠܐ ܠܒܗ ܙܐܥ *And his heart quakes not*).

v. 16. Instead of the repeated יָצוּק (3ᶜᶜ; unique in the book), we seem to require here other words expressive of hardness and solidity, e. g. חזק or קשה. Thus we might restore

לבו קשה כמו־אבן
וחזק (יחזק?) מפלח תחתית:

His heart is solid as a stone | And harder than the nether millstone: cf. Ez 2⁴ 3⁷·⁹ Je 5³. Perhaps יצוק should be kept in st. i; or שָׁרוּר *firm, solid*, be read as an Aramaism (cf. Syr. ܫܪܝܪܐ ܟܐܦܐ *solid rock*). 𝔊 πέπηγεν, *is solid* (= נִצָּב Ex 15⁸; or קָפָא ibid.); in st. ii ἕστηκεν, *it stands firm* (= יַצִּיב? cf. Gn 43⁹ 2 Sa 15²¹ 𝔐 (וַיַּצִּיקוּ): both prob. represent 𝔐 (יָצוּק). 𝔊 did not understand פלח *millstone* (Ju 9⁵³), which it renders ἄκμων, *an anvil*. The phrase ἄκμων ἀνήλατος, *a stubborn* (unmalleable) *anvil* occurs only here. 𝔙 *Cor eius indurabitur* (יֻקְפַּץ? cf. 11¹⁵ *stabilis*; 22¹⁸ 37¹⁸) *tanquam lapis | Et stringetur quasi malleatoris incus* (יֻצַּק from צוּק I. cf. 37¹⁰ and Aul. Gell. *mare gelu stringi et consistere*; and מַחַת or מְחַתָּה pro תַּחְתִּית). 𝔗 = 𝔐. 𝔖 st. ii: ܘܢܦܫܗ ܐܝܟ ܥܣܩܐ܂ *And firm as flint* (= כמו־חלמיש† pro כפלח תחתית).

v. 17. Read (with many codd.) משאתו pro 𝔐 משתו, and point either מִשֵּׂאתוֹ *At his uprising* (= 𝔙 *cum sublatus fuerit*), or rather perhaps *At his* [majesty] (cf. 13¹¹ 31²³); or מִשֵּׁאתוֹ *At his storming* (30¹⁴ Pr 3²⁵) or ons [?] 𝔖 *from fear of him* (cf. 𝔗 31:). In view however, of La 3⁴⁷

הַשֵּׂאת וְהַשֶּׁבֶר (codd. 𝕲𝖁 שׁ) and st. ii 'מִשֶּׁבֶר, we may prefer to point מִשֵּׂאתוֹ *At his noise* or *uproar*. The noise will be that of his rush or breaking through the reeds, since the crocodile utters no cry (though the poet may have imagined or heard that he does): cf. בְּנֵי שֵׁת Nu 24¹⁷ = בְּנֵי שָׁאוֹן Je 48⁴⁵. We may then restore in the parallel stichus, which in 𝔐 is metr. short (two beats only), מְשַׁבְּרוּ אַבִּרִים pro 𝔐 מִשְׁבָּרִים. We thus get a fairly satisfactory verse:

> *At his noise heroes are afraid,*
> *At his crashing the brave take to flight.*

This involves little or no change in st. i; and, as regards st. ii, אַבִּרִים exc. p. עֲבָרוּ owing to similarity of letters. For אֵלִים (so 𝖁 *angeli*; cf. Pss 29¹ 89⁷ Is 9⁷ Ez 31¹¹ 32²¹ al.) some codd. have אֵילִים (Ex 15¹⁵ Ez 17¹³). 𝕲𝕿 אִתְבַּהּ, תקיפיא *the mighty*. In st. ii 𝕲 seems to have read מִשְׂרָרִים *the strong* (Aram.) pro מִשְׁבָּרִים and יחתו pro יִתְחַטָּאוּ. *Miss* or *lose themselves* = are bewildered, lose their heads, is questionable, in view of the mg. of חטא Hithp. in the only other occurrences (Nu 8²¹ 19¹² al), viz. *to purify oneself* (see 𝖁). The Eth. use ተጠፍአ *aufugit* (Gn 16⁶.⁸) may give the true sense here (Burney), though that meaning is isolated in OT. 𝕿 מִן־תַבְרַיָּא יְדוּן עֲלֵיהוֹן; app. reading יְחַטְּאֵם *he finds them guilty*. 𝕲 renders the verse very strangely: στραφέντος δὲ αὐτοῦ φόβος θηρίοις τετράποσιν (40¹⁵) ἐπὶ γῆς ἁλλομένοις = ¹⁷: בְּשֻׁבוֹ מָגוֹר לְחַיָּה | בַעַר מִשְׂחָקַת (due to misreading of similar letters). But possibly ἁλλομένοις is an error for ἁλωμένοις = 𝔐 יִתְחַטָּאוּ (so also in Eth.).

v. 18. Leg. אִם־תַשִּׂיגֵהוּ pro 𝔐 מַשִּׂיגֵהוּ (ungrammat.) c 𝕲𝖁; or simply תשׂיגהו c 𝕿, in the same sense (so cod. Kenn. 180). The rare בְּלִי *not* should prob. be בַל as in v. 15 *Should the sword reach him, it standeth not*; gets no hold; fails to penetrate his hide and glances off.

In st. ii מַסָּע *a dart* is very doubtful; and the same may be said of שִׁרְיָה *javelin* (?). Both are ἅπ. λεγόμ. A verb is wanted > the three nouns. Note also the Asyndeton. Cf 𝕲 (text incert.) and 𝕊 *The spears of captains he beareth*; יִשָּׂא pro מַסָּע and שָׂרִים pro שִׁרְיָה! (cf. 𝕲ᴺᵃ·ᵃC δόρυ ἐπηρμένον = חֲנִית נְשֻׂאת : Οὐ μὴ ποιήσωσιν = מַעֲשׂוֹת; so that 𝕲's text here is conflate.) 𝖁 has only *Neque hasta neque thorax* (𝕲 θώρακα, 𝕲ᴬ θώραξ) 𝕿 also seems to have thought of נשׂא, for it has מוּרְנִיתָא וְקִלְעָא דְמַטְלָא אַבְנִין *the spear and the sling that lifteth stones*, and the cuirass (וְשִׁרְיָנָא). We might perhaps read חֲנִית תָסַע מִשִּׁרְיָנֹה *The spear starteth off from his mail* (cf. Nu 11³¹ נסע); or חֲנִית מֵעֵץ שְׁבָרָה *The spear-head breaks off from the shaft*, or מַטֵּה חֲנִית שָׁבַר *The staff of the spear is broken*.

v. 19. Perhaps רֹקַב > רִקָּבוֹן (נ dittogr.); 𝕲 ξύλον σαθρόν, 𝖁 *lignum putridum*. (Neither word occurs elsewhere.)

v. 20. The rhythm is inconsistent. There would appear to be only two beats in st. i, but four in st. ii. חֵץ *arrow* may have fallen out before בן in st. i; and in st. ii we should perhaps read בְּנֵי for אבני (cf. Zc 9¹⁵). 𝔙 *vir sagittarius* probably = 𝔐; but 𝔊 οὐ μὴ τρώσῃ αὐτὸν τόξον χάλκειον = לֹא־תַחְלְפֶנּוּ קֶשֶׁת נְחוּשָׁה: see 20²¹ᵇ 𝔊. 𝔖 *He fleeth not from the bow.* 𝔗 בְּיַרְוָא דְקַשְׁתָּא = 𝔐. St. ii 𝔊 ἥγηται μὲν πετροβόλον χόρτον (cf. v. 19ᵃ) = לקש יחשב אב' קלע. 𝔊 thought a *ballista* was intended. Cf. Wisd. 5²² ἐκ πετροβόλων. 𝔖𝔗 both read נֶחְשְׁבוּ *are accounted* (cf. 𝔊) pro 𝔐 נֶהְפְּכוּ *are turned*; but cf. v. 21ᵃ. 𝔙 rightly as 𝔐: In stipulam *versi sunt* ei lapides fundae.

v. 21. 𝔊 ὡς καλάμη = 𝔐 בְּקַשׁ. (καλάμη = קַשׁ Ex 15⁷ and in five other places; never = קָנֶה, which is κάλαμος 40¹⁶ and twelve times al.) 𝔐 נחשבו should be נחשב־לו in agreement with the Sing. Subj. (cf. 𝔊ᴬ ἐλογίσθη αὐτῷ). תּוֹתָח ∥ כִּידוֹן must be some kind of missile, e.g. *dart* or *javelin* > a *club* (RV). It may be a Hebraized form of the *tartaḫu* of Assyrian historical texts, which probably means a sort of light spear or javelin (certainly a missile weapon: see Lehmann *Šamaššumukin*, p. 67, l. 22). Possibly, however, תותח is a corruption of רמח *spear*, incorrectly written רומח plené. 𝔊 σφῦρα (אᶜ·ᵃ σφυραν אᶜ·ᶜ σφυραι), i.e. σφῦρα, *hammer, mallet* (Ju 4²¹ מקבת Is 41⁷ פטיש); cf. 𝔙 Quasi stipulam aestimabit *malleum*; 𝔗 נרניא *clubs* (but the Syr. ܢܰܓܳܪܳܐ is *axe*). 𝔊 transposes the two stichi, and seems to read תהום *the deep* pro תותח: *He laughs at the spear* (ܣܰܦܳܐ) | *And the Deep is counted to him as the dry land.*

רַעַשׁ *shaking* (𝔊 σεισμοῦ ut Am 1⁴); cf. 39²⁴. 𝔙 Et deridebit *vibrantem* hastam. 𝔊 πυρφόρου (sc. ὀϊστοῦ or βέλεος) a *fire-bearing* shaft or bolt (= 𝔐 כידון); cf. Ar. كاذ *emisit ignem*, and כידודי v. 11. 𝔗 רְגוֹשׁ רוּמְחָא *noise of the spear.*

v. 22. Lit. *Under him* (are) *the sharpest of potsherds*; app. meaning the scales of his belly, which leave an impression on the mud where he lies. (חַדּוּד = חַד *sharp* here only.) This agrees with st. ii: *He spreads* (17¹³) *a threshing-sledge* (Am 1³) *upon the mire*. The implement intended is still used in Syria; 'a board, about 7 ft. long by 3 ft. broad, set underneath crosswise with sharp pieces of hard stone or basalt, which, being drawn round the threshing-floor by a yoke of oxen, shells out the grain, and cuts up the straw into chaff' (Driver). 𝔊 ἡ στρωμνὴ αὐτοῦ, *his bed* (17¹³) is a paraphr. of תַּחְתָּיו *that which is under him*, and implies no different reading; and the same may be said of ὀβελίσκοι ὀξεῖς, *sharp spits* (or *obelisks*; cf. 𝔙) = חַדּוּדֵי חָרֶשׂ: 𝔙 Sub ipso erunt *radii solis*. Both identify חרש with חֶרֶס *the sun* (9⁷). 𝔊ᴬ ὀξυντῆρες *sharpeners*, 𝔊ᶿ σιδήρια *iron tools* pro ὀβελίσκοι are other unhappy guesses at the meaning of 'חד. 𝔗 תחותוי פרידין וחרדין היך חספא *Under him are stones which are sharp as a potsherd* = 𝔐. (𝔖 om.) In st. ii 𝔙 gives Et secernet sibi aurum quasi lutum, *And he will set apart for himself gold as it were mire*; app. reading יְפָרֵד pro יְפָרֵשׂ and taking חָרוּץ as 𝔊 χρυσός (Pr 8¹⁰·¹⁹), though the word does not occur elsewhere in Job. 𝔊 is even more marvellous: πᾶς δὲ χρυσὸς θαλάσσης ὑπ' αὐτὸν ὥσπερ πηλὸς ἀμύθητος, *And all the gold of the sea is under him like untold clay!* (cf. 27¹⁶ ותחתיו כל חרוץ ים כמו טיט רב 36²⁸ ἀμύθ.). יָם *of the sea* is evidently from the next line. 𝔗 דהבא ימוך (סְוָה) סנינא עלוי סאן *He spreads* (?) *the pure gold upon the mire*. (The emendation הֵחַת חֲרוּדִי חָרָשׁ *He hath broken the sharp weapons of the smith* seems superfluous after vv. 26–29. The simile of the verse is surely apt and pictorial enough to satisfy us.)

v. 23. *maketh boil*: Hi. Cf. 30²⁷ Pu. צוּל, the Root of צוּלָה, מְצוּלָה, *deep water, the deep*, is perhaps to be compared with צלל Assyr. *çalâlu*, *sink, be submerged* (מצולה = *place of sinking?*). The Nile may be meant both by this word מצולה and by ים *the sea* (Is 19⁵ Na 3⁸). In st. ii 𝔐 יָשִׂים *he makes* is prob. right; cf Gn 13¹⁶ for the Constr. The suggested יָשִׂם *he wastes* is certainly no improvement, as it spoils the parallelism Both stichi refer to the trail of froth and foam which marks the monster's movement through the water. כמרקחה *like an ointment-pan*; viz. when it bubbles and throws up white scum in boiling down the oil and spices to be compounded. 𝔊 ἥγηται (יַחְשֹׁב) δὲ τὴν θάλασσαν ὥσπερ ἐξάλ(ε)ιπτρον (*as an unguent-box*); 𝔙 paraphr. Et *ponet* (= יָשִׂים) quasi *cum unguenta bulliunt* (𝔙 adds ים *mare* to st. i agst. metr. and sense) 𝔗 יַמָא יְשַׁוֵי הֵיךְ מְתִיבְלָא *The sea he makes like a pan* = 𝔐. 𝔖 om. Possibly we should read בַּקַלַחַת *like a cauldron* (|| to בַּסִיר: cf. Mi 3³).

v 24. Further, description of the appearance of the water as the long reptile swims through it There seems no reason for changing a word in st. i, except that we might add the 3rd Pers. Suff. to נתיב *a path* and read נתיבו *his path* or *track*; the ו having perhaps fallen out before the following י. *Behind him shineth his track* (or, *Behind him he maketh his path shine*; יאיר may be either Trans. or Intrans.): i.e he leaves a track of glistening spray behind him. Cf. 𝔙 Post eum lucebit semita = 𝔐; 𝔗 בַּתְרוֹי יְנַהַר שְׁבִילָא. To read יְאוֹר *the Nile* pro יָאִיר is to substitute prose for poetry.

St. ii· *The Deep might be reckoned white-haired*; a beautiful simile for the 'hoary foam' of the troubled water. Point יֵחָשֵׁב pro 𝔐 יַחְשֹׁב (v. 21; Is 29¹⁷). 𝔖 ܘܠܐܒܫܐ ܡܚܫܒ ܠܗ ܠܣܡܩܐ And as dry land the Deep is *reckoned to him*; reading ליבשה pro 𝔐 לשיבה: i.e. he is equally at home in the water or on the land. a good sense, but not a good parallel to st. i. 𝔙 aestimabit abyssum quasi senescentem = 𝔐. So 𝔗 יחשוב תהומא לשיבותא. 𝔊 (om. st. i) app. gives a double version of st. ii: *And (he regards) the Tartarus* (lowest depth?) *of the abyss as a captive* (ὥσπερ αἰχμάλωτοι = בַּשִּׁבְיָה pro 𝔐 בשיבה· cf. Is 52·1: He r ⋅ l r l i r s as a *walk* (εἰς περίπατον, cf. Ez 42⁴·¹¹). In view of this we might perhaps hazard the conjectural verse : .

אפיק יאור נתיבו
יחשב תהום לשבילו :

The bed of the Nile is his pathway ; | *He regardeth the Deep as a road*: cf. Ps 77²⁰. But 𝔐 suits the context better, and is far more poetical.

[The √שיב, ساب, Assyr. *šâbu*, was originally a colour-term, denoting *bright, white, whitish, grey*, esp. of the hair; cf. 3 R 65, 7ᵇ : *If his head be full of grey hairs*, &c. (SAG . DU-*su šibâti mali*), said of a newborn child (Omen-text) The analysis may perhaps be the Factitive שׂ, שׁ, +אב *bright, white*, &c., which we see in אבב Assyr. *abâbu, ebbu* : cf. also perhaps שבב, *šabâbu*, 'blaze', שָׁבִיב *flame* 18⁵.]

v. 25. *earth* : עָפָר as 19²⁵. *his like* or *likeness* : מֹשֶׁל *ȧπ*. 𝔊 ὅμοιον αὐτῷ; 𝔙 *potestas quae comparetur* ei. 𝔊 hardly suggests מְשָׁלוֹ (KB). Perhaps we should point מֹשְׁלוֹ (Is 52⁵ Je 30²¹) : *There is not on earth one that ruleth him* = his master. 𝔊 *And his power on the dust walketh* (reading אוֹן wrongly for 𝔐 אֵין and app. טְהַלֵּךְ for משׁלו). 𝔗 שׁוּלְטָנֵיהּ *his ruler* (cf. Mi 5¹); cf. st. i.

St. ii is very dubious. 𝔐 seems to mean *He who was made for* or *into* (Ju 8²⁷) *a lack-fear* or *fearlessness* (חַת *fear* Gn 9²); but both metre and parallelism are defective. 𝔙 ut 𝔐. qui factus est ut nullum timeret. 𝔗 (*whom He made that he might not be broken*, scil. with fear : cf 1 Sa 17¹¹) = paraphr. of 𝔐. 𝔊 πεποιημένον ἐνκαταπαίζεσθαι ὑπὸ τῶν ἀγγέλων μου = 𝔊 40¹⁹ᵇ ; see the notes there. The angels are introduced because it seemed irreverent to speak of the Creator as 'sporting' with His creature. The anomalous הֶעָשׂוּ (it should at least be הֶעָשׂוּי Ex 3¹⁵ 38²⁴) cannot be accepted ; and לְבַעַל חַיִת pro 𝔐 לִבְלִי חָת, (why not לִבְלָהוֹת ? cf. note 26²⁰), is hardly convincing. *He who was made a lord of beasts* is a phrase without parallel in the OT, and coheres but awkwardly with st. i. 𝔊 seems to have read הֶעָשָׂה (וְעָשָׂה) לְשַׁחַתִּבְלִי *Who hath made for the Pit of Destruction every high one that he seeth* ; connecting the words with v. 26ᵃ (cf. Is 38¹⁷), and perhaps omitting חָת. Upon the whole we incline to prefer : אֵלֶהּ עָשָׂהוּ לְשַׂחֶק־בּוֹ (*There is nothing like him on earth ;) Eloah made him to play with*. The poet is utterly at a loss to account for the existence of such a strange outlandish creature, and can only suppose it to be a kind of freak or sport of the Creative Power.

v. 26. 𝔐 lit. *Every high one he seeth* = 𝔙 Omne sublime videt · = 𝔗 יָת כָּל גּוּבְהָא יָחֱמֵי (cf. 𝔊 supr. cit.) = 𝔊 πᾶν ὑψηλὸν ὁρᾷ. But this is manifestly an unsuitable sense, not to mention the suspicious אֶת־ and the metrical shortness of the stichus. We might accept the corrections אֹתוֹ and יִירָא (cf. Ec 12⁵) : *Him every high* (or *haughty*) *one feareth*. But perhaps we should read עַל־כָּל־גָּבֹהַּ וָרָם יָנְאָה *Above all that is high and lofty*

42. 3   NOTES ON THE TEXT   459

he is exalted; or בָּאָרֶץ on the earth may have fallen out after נִכְבַּד, or even the emphatic Adv. Infin. נָאֹה (He is supremely exalted; cf. Ex 15¹).

The phrase בְּנֵי שָׁחַץ recurs from 28⁵†; see the note there. Levy CHWB cites from Sifri a saying about Rome: 'מלכות זו משתחצת ומתנאה וגו This kingdom was proud and haughty, &c. The Prim. Root may perhaps be recognized in Sum. 𒄤𒍝 𒄤𒍝 ĠA-ZA, ĠAZ, bear, lift, e.g. SAG-ĠUL ĠAZA, mukîl rêš limutti, 'lifting a head of enmity', i.e. hostile; said of the Seven Evil Spirits. The Ar. شخص to rise (of a star) may be a loan-word. Or, since Heb. שַׁחַץ, in the only other place where it occurs, denotes beasts of prey, such as the lion, we might compare ĠAZ, ĠAŠ, to smash, break in pieces, kill (=GAZ; cf. SA-GAZ, robber, bandit). The שׁ is, as usual, Factitive.

It should be noticed that st. ii has four stresses, while st i has only two. Possibly the verse is an interpolation. The statement that an amphibious and ungainly reptile like the crocodile is monarch of all the wild beasts seems very improbable (cf. Pr 30³⁰ Dan 4⁷ff ¹⁷ Pr 19¹² 20² Ju 14¹⁸ 2 Sa 1²³). If, however, we make the slight change of אל for אֵת in st. i (as elsewhere), and read וִימְלֹךְ pro הוּא מֶלֶךְ, st ii, we arrive at a verse which is metrically correct and forms a passable conclusion to the whole: El seeth every high one (cf. 28²⁴); | And is sovereign over all the sons of pride (including the crocodile). 𝔙 super universos filios superbiae. 𝔊 And he (the crocodile) hath become king over every creeping thing (كلّ خدم أسفل) suggests שֶׁרֶץ pro שַׁחַץ; cf. Gn 1²⁰⁻²¹ Le 10⁴¹. Cf. also 𝔗 And he is king over all sons of fishes (בְּנֵי כַוָּורֵי; cf. Gn 1²⁶); and 𝔊 αὐτὸς δὲ βασιλεὺς πάντων τῶν ἐν τοῖς ὕδασιν. But 𝔊ˣ βρομώδους, stinking thing = שֶׁקֶץ (Le 11¹⁰ ⁴¹).

Chapter 42. Realizing his own ignorance and impotence, in view of the inexhaustible wonders of the natural world, Eyob now makes humble submission to the absolute Lord of All.

v. 2. Clearly we must read יָדַעְתִּי c 𝔊 οἶδα, 𝔙 Scio, 𝔗 יְדַעִית, 𝔖 ܝܶܕܥܶܬ, Qerî and numerous codd. pro Ketib ידעת. Eyob confesses God's omnipotence: Scio quia omnia potes; so 𝔊. In st. ii leg. מְאוּמָה c 𝔊 ἀδυνατεῖ δέ σοι οὐθέν > 𝔐𝔙𝔖𝔗 מְזִמָּה device or purpose (21²⁷). The former suits the parallelism better. In any case, 𝔐 יבצר (Gn 11⁶) should be תִּבָּצֵר. Nothing is cut off or shut off from Thee; i.e. unattainable by Thee. (בצר looks like a labialized form of קצר.) If the meaning were No thought (or purpose) is hidden (cf. Je 33³) or withheld from Thee we should expect כָּל־מְזִמָּה: cf. 𝔙 (et nulla te latet cogitatio) and 𝔗.

v. 3. The non-metrical interpolation מִי זֶה מַעְלִים עֵצָה בְּלִי־דָעַת (reminiscence of 38² with מעלים pro מחשיך and om. במלים ante בלי; cf. 𝔊𝔖) must, of course, be rejected, as making the verse an incoherent tristich and interrupting the connexion of thought: That being so (Thou being what Thou hast now shown Thyself to be in Knowledge and Power), in my ignorance I have spoken too boldly on things beyond my grasp. Cf. Pr 30¹⁸ Ps 131¹. ⅏ *Therefore hast Thou shown me what I have not understood | And I have not known what things were too great for me.* 𝔊 τίς δὲ ἀναγγελεῖ μοι ἃ οὐκ ᾔδειν | μεγάλα καὶ θαυμαστὰ ἃ οὐκ ἠπιστάμην; Possibly the verse should be restored as follows :

לכן הגדת־לי לא־אבין
נפלאות ממני לא־ארע:

*Therefore thou hast shown me what I discerned not,
Wonders beyond me that I knew not.*

v. 4. Another interpolation. St. ii (metr. short) occurred 38³ᵇ 40⁷. For st. 1 see 33³¹. It is perfectly irrelevant, and greatly weakens the effect of the emphatic statement which follows (v. 5), if 'Job repeats, in line 1, the substance, and in line 2 the actual words, of God's challenge to him in xxxviii. 3, prior to confessing (v. 5) his inability to meet it, and retracting (v. 6) his former presumptuous utterances' (Driver). If the verse were genuine, it would naturally be taken to mean a demand for further discussion; but such a demand would absolutely contradict the spirit of the context (vv. 2, 5, 6).

v. 5. *By mere hearsay* : לְשֵׁמַע אֹזֶן *according to ear-hearing*: cf. Is 11³ לְמִשְׁמַע אָזְנָיו. The verse obviously contrasts mere hearing about God with personal vision, viz. the Theophany of 38¹ in which Eyob recognizes the fulfilment of his confident hope that he would one day 'see God', Who would 'stand up on the earth' and openly vindicate His servant's innocence (19²⁵⁻²⁷).

mine own eye hath seen Thee : עֵינִי רָאָתְךָ : cf. 19²⁷ ועיני ראו.

v. 6. The effect upon Eyob of the vision of God. 𝔐 cannot mean either AV or RV. The text is evidently corrupt, and st. ii is metrically short. אֶמְאַס cannot mean *I abhor myself*, nor yet *I reject* (*it*), viz. what I have spoken (Driver; cf. RV marg. *loathe* my words). An Object is certainly required if מאס here is *to reject* (5¹⁷ 8²⁰ 9²¹ 19¹⁸ 30¹ 31¹³ al.); and נחם על usually means *to repent of* some action (Am 7³ ⁶ Je 8⁶), and can hardly express *repent* (sitting) *on* dust, &c. Cf. Jon 3⁶ וישב על־אפר; Lk 10¹³. We have, however, already had an instance of another מאס (Aram.), meaning *to run, flow, melt away* (7⁵ Ps 58⁸ Ni.; cf. Tg. Ps 38⁶ מָאִיס). We might therefore point אֶמָּאֵס *I dissolve*; cf. 𝔊 διὸ ἐφαύλισα (= אֶמְאַס 31¹⁹) ἐμαυτὸν καὶ ἐτάκην, *Wherefore I slighted myself and melted* —a conflate rendering. Then, with the further change תחת *in my stead* or *place* (cf. 36²⁰ 40¹² notes ; Hab 3¹⁶), or possibly תחתיך *under Thee* (Mi 1⁴) pro ונחמתי, we have a good line : *Therefore I begin to melt on the spot.* According to ancient belief, the sight of God must cause instant dissolution (Gn 16¹³ Ex 3⁶ 1 K 19¹³ Is 6⁵ also Gn 32³⁰ Ju 13²² al.). Even the mountains 'melted at the Presence of God' (Mi 1· Ps 97⁵, cf. Is 64¹):

much more might flesh and blood, the unstable substance of poor humanity, be expected to do so.

𝕲's form of st. ii is ἥγημαι δὲ ἐγὼ ἐμαυτὸν γῆν καὶ σποδόν. This might represent ונחשבתי לעפר ונו׳ *And take myself for dust*, &c. (ἡγέομαι = חשב five times in Job, 13²⁴ 19¹¹ 33¹⁰ 41¹⁹ 35²?); or perhaps וְדָמְתִי or וְאֶדָּמֶה *And I become like* Is 14¹⁴ (which would account for 𝕲 ואשתוק = וְאֶדֹּם or וְדָמְתִי *and am still*) But if our restoration of st. i is right, we may suppose that st. ii was originally a reminiscence of 30¹⁹, ואתמשל (or תכמשלתי אל Is 14¹⁰) בעפר ואפר *And I (am) become like dust and ashes*; a natural result of dissolution. (𝕾 *Therefore I will* be still | *And shall be raised to life*—ܘܐܬܢܝܚ?—*on the dust*, &c. 𝕿 *Therefore I despised*—מָאֵסִית—my riches | *And was comforted for* my sons who are *dust and ashes !*) The idea that Eyob needed repentance for his presumptuous language, and that he expressly admits it in this final utterance, finds explicit statement in 𝔙: Idcirco *ipse me reprehendo* | et *ago poenitentiam in favilla et cinere*. That idea is, however, wanting in 𝕲 𝕾 𝕿; while, as we have seen, the text of 𝔐 is questionable on grounds both of grammar and metre. That the hero of the poem, for whose moral excellence Iahvah Himself vouches in the Prologue (1⁸ 2³), and whose language about God, which so greatly shocked the three Friends, actually receives the stamp of Iahvah's approbation in the very next verse (v. 7), should here fall into an agony of penitence, is extremely improbable. It would, in fact, stultify the main argument of the book, which hinges on the assumption of Eyob's perfect integrity and piety.

The Prose Epilogue.

Iahvah declares Eyob to have been right in his contentions as against the Friends, and bids them seek his intercession on their own behalf, lest punishment befall them (vv. 7-9). Eyob is restored to twice his former prosperity, and dies in a good old age (vv. 10-17).

v. 7. Iahvah: 𝕲 ὁ Κύριος. 𝔙 om. bis. The prose-narrative relating the happy conclusion of the trial of Eyob naturally reverts to the Divine Name used in the Prologue.

these words 𝕲 prefixes *all* (πάντα = כל), which may well be right. Instead of *Mine anger is hot against thee and against thy two friends* 𝕲 gives ἥμαρτες σὺ καὶ οἱ φίλοι σου = חטאת אתה ושני רעיך. Cf. 1²¹ 2¹⁰. (A remarkable substitution; perhaps preserving a real v. l.) *of Me* · אֵלַי מ׳ = עָלַי; cf. Je 27¹³. For אל used in different senses in the same verse, cf. 1 Sa 3¹². But 𝕲 ἐνώπιόν μου, 𝔙 coram me (so 𝕾 𝔄) = לְפָנַי: cf. 1 K 3²²ᵇ, Ju 11¹¹. The variant makes little or no difference to the general sense. Eyob had spoken quite honestly of God's dealings with man; the three Friends, in their anxiety to maintain the doctrine that all calamities are penal visitations, had ignored notorious facts of human experience. (The omission of all reference to Elihu would seem to indicate that he played no part in the original drama: see *Introd.*) נְכוֹנָה *what is fixed, certain, right* or *correct*; a syn. of אֱמֶת: Ps 5¹⁰†. 𝕲 ἀληθές; 𝔅 rectum; 𝔖 ܟܐܢܘܬܐ *justice*. Cf. כֵּן *right, true*, Gn 42¹¹ Nu 27¹ al. (The Sem. כון *kânu* كَانَ ، كُنْ *be fixed, established*, and so *to be*, is probably identical in origin with Sum. 𒁺 GIN or GEN, *kânu*, *kunnu*, 'stand firm', 'establish', *kêttu*, 'right', 'truth', 'justice'; also *alâku* 'to walk', as involving the *upright* position. The primitive form of the character is a human *foot*, which naturally symbolizes either standing fast or motion.)

v. 8. *seven bullocks and seven rams*: Nu 23¹·²⁹ Ez 45²³. Eyob was to act as priest: cf. Gn 12⁷·⁸ 22²⁻¹³. If Iahvah was originally a designation of Sîn, the moon-god, and identical with El-sheba', *the god Seven*, under which title he may be supposed to have been worshipped at Be'er-sheba' (see Burney *Judges*, pp. 43 f. 249–53 ff.), we may see a reason for the number of the sacrificial victims required by traditional use for His burnt-offering. Such ideas were, however, remote from our author's mind and age. To him sun, moon, and stars are alike subordinate to Iahvah (see 9⁷⁻⁹ 25⁵ 31²⁶); sacred numbers were probably a matter of ritual tradition about the original significance of which he felt no curiosity; and he appears to use the various Divine Names transmitted from the past as mere poetical variants of each other. But as in the Prologue he traces the misfortunes of his hero to the initiative of Iahvah, so he ascribes to Him (the God of prophetic revelation) the personal intervention which satisfies Eyob (38¹; cf. Gn 22¹·¹¹·¹⁴), and his subsequent restoration to health and wealth.

for his intercession I will accept: lit. *for his face I will lift up* (Gn 19²¹ 1 Sa 25³⁵). Pro 𝔐 כִּי אִם־פָּנָיו leg. כִּי אֶת־פָּנָיו (at 𝕲 ὅτι εἰ μὴ κτλ. = 𝔐). *that I may not wreak destruction upon you*: reading בְּכָלָה (Le 26¹⁸) or בַּלָּהָה (Is 17¹⁴; plur. five times in Job, 18¹¹ al.) pro 𝔐 נְבָלָה *folly* (2¹⁰), which seems too strong a term for the inconsiderateness of anger. 𝕲 paraphr. *For, save on his account, I would have destroyed you*; but 𝔅 ut non vobis imputetur stultitia = לבלתי יחשב לכם נבלה. 𝔗 *that I may not do to you* קְלָנָא *a shameful act* (Dt 22²¹). 𝔖 *that I put you not to shame* (ܕܠܐ ܐܚܣܕܟܘܢ ܒܡܟܠܠ). Regarded as a mere *façon de parler* or popular phrase, 𝔐 may be right· *that I may do you no fool-mischief*, play no fool's trick with you, do you no foul wrong, by dealing with you like a נָבָל. (Or cf. Ps 18²⁷ᵇ.)

The closing sentence of the verse is repeated, perhaps accidentally, from v. 7. 𝕲 varies it thus: *for ye spoke not against my servant Eyob a true thing*; 𝔅 has ad me = אֵלַי instead of *coram me* this time.

v. 9. *and Zophar*: וְצֹפַר c codd. mult. and 𝕲𝔅𝔖 (exc. ١ post י). 𝔗 צוֹפָר.

v. 10. The Trans. use of שוב in the phrase שוב שבות *to turn the captivity* of a nation or individual (Ps 126¹·⁴) and fig. *to restore their fortunes or prosperity* (cf. also Is 52⁸ Ez 16⁵³ Ho 6¹¹ Am 9¹⁴ Na 2³) seems an inexplicable divergence from the ordinary intrans. use of the verb. We should have expected Hi. (cf. the Aram. Aph.). It may be an isolated survival of the vaguer or more comprehensive use of the Root in the primitive stage of the language. (The bilit. √שב is possibly identical with Sum. TAB *double, repeat, add,* &c. Cf. the use of שוב to denote the repetition of an action, and the Syr. ܬܘܒ *again*. To do a thing again may be to reverse it. But perhaps we should rather compare Sum. DUB *go round, surround*; ŠUB *bend, a bow*; ŠUB *turn, turn round (lapátu)* =ŠEB *id.*¹) Q שבות, K שבית *captivity*, Coll. *a body of captives*, or prisoners-of-war, from שָׁבָה (Aram. שְׁבָא, Ar. سبى) *to take captive* men or cattle as booty of war, may be compared with Sum. DAB, DIB, *kamû*, 'to take prisoner', *çabâtu* 'to seize', 'take', &c (√שב = tab, dab). *his friends*: 𝔐 רֵעָהוּ ut 1 Sa 30²⁶. An רֵעֵיהוּ? The uncontracted form here only in Job; 32³ has רֵעָיו. In 12⁴ 16²¹ רֵעֵהוּ is Sing. as in Gn 11³ et saep. al.

increased all that was Eyob's to double. Read prob. אֶל־ pro אֵת־ (cf. Ez 23¹⁴) = עַל (Dt 1¹¹). His possessions were doubled, but not the number of his children (cf. 1²·³).

v. 11. *His brothers*, or *kinsmen*, members of his tribe, and his *acquaintance* are mentioned 6¹⁵ 19¹³, but his *sisters* nowhere else; cf. 1⁴ 17¹⁴. *feasted*: lit. *eat bread*: Lk 14¹⁵. *condoled ... and comforted*: 2¹¹. *an ingot*, scil of silver? The קְשִׂיטָה Gn 33¹⁹ Jos 24³²† (cf. Gn 23¹⁶) was prob. a definite weight of unstamped metal, used as money. 𝔊 ἀμνάδα μίαν, one *ewe-lamb* = 𝔙 *ovem unam*, 𝔗 חוּרְפָא חֲדָא *one lamb*, 𝔖 ܐܡܪܐ ܚܕ. The Midrash Gen. Rab. 79 gives a triple explanation of קשיטה; viz. *ounces*, *lambs* (טלאים) and *shekels* (סלעים). In Gn 31⁴¹ 𝔊 δέκα ἀμνάσιν = עשרת מנים. Was the translator thinking of מנים *manehs* or minas, or was he merely misled by the assonance of the two words? In the case before us, a shekel seems too little, and a maneh (50 or 60 shekels) would hardly be too much for a congratulatory present. Perhaps קשיטה was an old Canaanite equivalent of the Bab. and Aram מנה; and, like מנה, the word might etymologically denote a definite or specific *portion* of metal (cf. Ar. قسط *divide up or distribute* property, apportion a tax, &c.). Or should we rather compare Aram. קַשִּׁיטָא (קַשִּׁיט) קְשִׁיט *just, right, true*, and Ar. قسط, قسط *just* and *a balance* for weighing?

𝔊 expands the verse thus : *Now all his brothers and his sisters heard*

---

¹ שוב has lost the initial sound in Ar. آب *return*. If the primary notion was *bent, rounded*, we might comp אוב *skin-bottle* as a round thing, and אפף *surround*, and אופן *wheel* (Al AB ; p. o כב נוב, &c).

all that had befallen him, and they came to him, and all who had known him from the first: and having eaten and drunk at his house (παρ' αὐτῷ) they comforted him, and marvelled at all that the Lord had brought upon him: and each gave him one ewe-lamb and a tetradrachm of gold and silver (καὶ τετράδραχμον χρυσοῦ καὶ ἀσήμου: but 𝔊^{NAC*} χρυσοῦν ἄσημον, i.e. a tetr. of gold uncoined). The substitution for ואיש נום זהב אחר *and each an ear-ring* (Gn 35⁴) *of gold* is curious. Is it a trace of a second interpretation of קשיטה? נום, which is also *nose-ring*, an ornament worn by women (Gn 24²²·³⁰·⁴⁷ Is 3²¹) as well as pigs (Pr 11²²), may perhaps mean simply *ornament* (cf. Assyr. *nazâmu*¹ in *ušazzimšû*, 'I adorned it', Muss-Arn. p. 660, col. 2); but is more prob. to be connected with the primitive Root נום *shine* in Assyr. *zîmu*, Aram. זיו *splendour, sheen,* e.g. *zîm kakkabi*, and as plant-names *zîm hurâci*, *zîm kaspi*, qs 'Goldbright', 'Silverbright'. The Syr. ܙܡ *tie* a tree, ܡܚܒܠ the *tie* of a vine, suggests, however a different origin for נום, viz. the Sum. DIM (= ZIM) *bind, tie*, which is done by putting one thing round another; hence perhaps נום is simply a ring, whether for the ears or the nose. 𝔙 recte: et *inaurem auream unam*.

v. 12. The numbers specified are in each case exactly twice as many as those named (2³) for the palmy days before calamity fell upon him (cf. Is 61⁷ Zc 9¹²); a fact which indicates that we are not dealing with plain history but edifying parable. 𝔊 adds νομάδες = לעות *grazing* or *at feed* (cf. 1 C 27²⁹) to אתונות *she-asses*.

v. 13. וַיְהִי־לוֹ *And there came to him* = *and he got*; i.e. in the course of time. The number of his new family was the same as that of the old which had perished. See notes on 1². (His wife and his servants are not mentioned.) It is improb. that the form שִׁבְעָנָה is a blend of שִׁבְעָן (dual of שֶׁבַע = 2 × 7 or 14) and שִׁבְעָה; for שִׁבְעָן is a *vox nihili*, some codd. and all Versions have שִׁבְעָה, and the inserted נ is an inadvertent anticipation of the נ of the next word (בנים). If the number of the sons was doubled, why not also that of the daughters?

v. 14. The name of the eldest daughter יְמִימָה (perhaps יְמוֹמָה) may be compared with Aram. יְמָמָא 𝔗 Gn 1⁵ (𝔖 ܐܝܡܡܐ) *Day* as opp. to Night (= Assyr. *immu* in *immu u mûša*, 'day and night'). It thus indicates the father's sense of having emerged from the darkness of adversity into the light of restored prosperity. [The Ar. يَمَامَة *wood-pigeon* (Kâm. ap. Frei.; not in Lane) is in any case less appropriate.] So 𝔊 'Ἡμέραν, 𝔙 Diem (and 𝔖𝔄); 𝔗 יְמִימָא = 𝔐.

The second name, קְצִיעָה, 𝔊 Κασίαν, 𝔙 *Cassiam*, is the Cassia-tree, or wild Cinnamon (Laurus Cassia, L.), the bark of which is aromatic, and also its powdered bark which is used as a spice or aromatic (Ps 45⁸†). Cf. our own 'Myrtle', 'Rose', 'Violet', &c., as female names. The third name, קרן הפוך *Qéren-happûḵ*, 'The Horn of Antimony' = 𝔙 Cornu stibii, refers to the practice of darkening the eyebrows and eyelashes with powdered antimony, as Oriental women still do, to make the eyes appear more brilliant by contrast. Cf. 2 K 9³⁰ Je 4³⁰. 𝔊's Ἀμαλθείας κέρας, 'Amaltheia's Horn', is more curious than illuminating. The Greek phrase was used proverbially in the sense of 'horn of plenty' (Anacr. 8 al.); and 𝔊, not recognizing the word פוּךְ, and misreading הָפוּךְ for הַפּוּךְ, may have supposed that the name was *Horn overturned*; scil. in order to pour out the contents, as in the case of the fabled goat or nymph that suckled Zeus, according to the well-known Greek legend. It is doubtful scholarship and mere indulgence of unbridled fancy to interpret the three names as 'Lengthener of Days', 'Shortener of the Thread of Life', and 'Horn of Plenty' ('an astral-mythological allusion; Amaltheia is a constellation'); and to suppose that they 'contain a play upon the Oriental prototype of the three Greek Fates' (Jeremias, *OTLAE*, II. 253 ET.).—These names were evidently intended to suggest that Eyob's daughters were beauties of the first rank (cf. v. 15).

v. 15 Leg. נִמְצְאוּ c 2 codd. and 𝔊𝔖𝔚 pro 𝔐 נִמְצָא.

in all the land: or *earth*, as 𝔊 ἐν τῇ ὑπ' οὐρανόν, 𝔚 in universa terra. 𝔐 לָהֶם אֲבִיהֶם, אֲחִיהֶם, neglecting the gender of the Pron. Suff. Several codd. correct, reading לָהֶן, &c.

an estate among their brothers: cf. Nu 27⁴·⁷.

v. 16. *after this*: i.e. after giving his daughters their portions; or more prob. after all the events of his restoration. Cf. 𝔚 post haec. But 𝔊 μετὰ τὴν πληγήν, *after the stroke* (πληγή. ἄπ in Job = מַכָּה or נֶגַע).

a hundred and forty years: i.e. twice the period of the usual term of life (Ps 90¹⁰); so that in this respect also he was doubly compensated for all his sufferings, and might be considered to have attained to a truly patriarchal age. (Cf. Gn 11²⁶·³². If Eyob was about 65 at the time when his troubles began, he reached the same age as Terah, viz. 205.) 𝔊 *Now Eyob lived after* the Stroke *an hundred* (and) *seventy years*, and all the years he lived (were) two hundred (and) forty (and eight: 𝔊^(Nc aAC)). According to this, he was 70 or 78 at the time of the catastrophe.

and saw: K וַיַּרְא rectè; Q וַיִּרְאֶה. *four generations*: but as only three generations are mentioned, including himself, we must either take בְּנֵי בָנָיו in the wider sense of his sons' descendants or posterity, or suppose that וְאֶת־בְּנֵיהֶם *and their sons* has fallen out of the text. This last statement was not in the original LXX.

v. 17. *sated with life*: lit. *satisfied with days* (Gn 35²⁹ P)

𝔊 adds: *But it is written that he will rise again with those whom the Lord raiseth.* Is this a reference to 19²⁵ff., or to some Midrash? 𝔊 adds further: *He is explained ut of the Syria..........Auulic* land on the borders of Idumaea and Arabia. Formerly he had the name of Jobab (see Gn 36³¹†). And taking an Arabian wife, he begets a son named Ennōn; but he himself was of a father Zerah, a son of the Sons of Esau, and a mother Bozrah (Gn 36³³), so that he was fifth from Abraham. And these are the kings that reigned in Edom, which country he also ruled: first Balak the son of Beor, and the name of his city was Dennaba, and after Balak Jobab who is called Job; and after him, Husham who was a Duke from the Temanite country; and after him, Hadad the son of Barad (Heb. Bedad) who smote Midian in the plain of Moab, the name of whose city was Geththaim (Heb. עוית).

Now the Friends who came to him (were) Eliphaz of the Sons of Esau (Gn 36¹⁰), Baldad the Tyrant (or Prince Pr 8¹⁶ Hab 1¹⁰) of the Sauchaeans, Sophar the king of the Minaeans (𝔊ᴬ + Teman son of Eliphaz Duke of Idumaea. He is explained out of the Syriac book as dwelling in the Ausitic land on the borders of the Euphrates. Formerly he had the name of Jobab. And his father was Zareth from the sunrising) Ζάρε or Ζάρεθ = זרח, which means sunrise These attempts to fix the place of Eyob in history obviously depend upon the fanciful identification of the patriarch with Jobab (Gn 36 l c.); but it is hardly necessary to state that the resemblance of the two names is merely one of sound, and that no etymological relation is traceable between them. See *Introd.*

APPENDIX.—ALTERNATIVE VERSION OF CHAP. 3.

CHAPTER 3.—1 *Afterwards Eyob opened his mouth and cursed his day.*
2 *And Eyob answered and said:*

3 Perish the day I was born,
And the Night that said, 'A man is conceived!'
4 [*That Day become Darkness!*]
Eloah above heed it not,
And no Radiance shine upon it!

5 Darkness and Deathshade befoul it!
Clouds settle upon it!
[*Benightings(?) of Day affright it!*
6 *That Night—utter gloom seize it!*]
Be it not one among the Days of the Year—
Into the tale of the Months let it come not!

7 That Night become stone-barren!
No joyous birth-shout enter it!
8 Ban it they who curse the Day (?)—
Adept in rousing the Dragon!

9 Darkened be its twilight Stars!
[*Let it wait for the Light and there be none!*]
Let it not look on the Eyelids of Dawn!
10 Because it shut not my womb-doors,
And hid not sorrow from mine eyes.

11 Why began I not to die from the womb—
From the belly came not forth to expire?
12 Wherefore did knees receive me,
And breasts when I began to suck?

13 For now I had lain down, and were still—
I had slept; then rest were mine!
14 With Kings and Councillors of State,
Who rebuilded ruins for their pleasure.

15 Or with Princes who had much gold,—
Who filled their houses with silver;
16 Or like a buried abortion I should be,—
Like babes which never saw Light.

17 [*There the wicked cease from troubling;
And there the weary rest.*]
18 Together the prisoners repose;
They hear not the taskmaster's voice·
19 High and low are there;
And the slave is free from his lord.

20 Why is Light given to the suffering,
And Life to the bitter in soul—
23 To the man whose way is hidden,
And Eloah hath 'hedged him about'—

21 Who wait for Death in vain,
And dig for it as buried treasure;
22 Who rejoice to see She'ol,—
Are glad when they find the Grave?

24 [*For before my bread my sighing cometh,
And I pour out my groans like water.*]
25 If I dread a thing, it cometh upon me,
And what I fear befalleth me:
26 I have neither ease nor quiet,—
No rest, and Wrath cometh.

NOTE.—*Perhaps the last three quatrains should rather be read as follows:*

20 Why is Light given to the sufferer,
And Life to them that are sorrowful,
21 Who wait for Death, and there is none,
And who dig for it like buried treasure—

23 To the man whose way is hidden,
And Eloah hath 'hedged him about',
22 Who rejoiceth when he seeth She'ol,—
Is glad when he findeth the Grave?

25 For a dread I had, and it reached me,
And what I feared came upon me:
26 I was neither secure nor quiet,
I rested not, and yet came Trouble

GENERAL INDEX

INTRODUCTION to the Book, pp. 1-34.
  Author's argument and its limitations, 1-4.
  Analysis of the interpolated Elihu-section, 4-7
  The Praise of Wisdom, chap. 28, another interpolation, 7-8.
  Originality of the book, 8.
  The name Job, or rather Eyob, identified in Babylonian, 9.
  The so-called 'Babylonian Job', 9-11.
  Text and Translation of 'The Babylonian Job', 12-30.
  Story of Nebuchadnezzar's Fall and Restoration, Dan 4, compared with the older legend, 30-31.
  Date of the Book of Job uncertain. Apparent implications of the internal evidence, 31-34.

Note on the prosody of the poem, 34.

A revised translation of the book, 35-94.

Commentary on the traditional Hebrew text and the ancient versions, 95-466.

Appendix.—Alternate Version of Chap. 3, 467-8.

Index Rerum, 470.

Index to Notes on Hebrew Words (mainly philological), 471-5.

Sumerian with Semitic Glosses, 476-9.

INDEX RERUM

'Amalthea's Horn', p. 465.
Angels, 140 f.; 'The Host of Heaven', 145; Invocation of, 145; 'Sons of God', 101 f., 140; Messengers of Gods, 33 note, cf. 181; evil, 123, cf. Ps 78^{40}; demons (Babylonian), ubiquity of, 103, 105 f.
Antiochus Epiphanes, possible reference to, 388.
Apocalyptic or Eschatological element wanting in Job, 233, 399.
Babylonian cosmogony, allusions to:
    Man made from clay by the goddess Aruru, 142, 373; created before the beasts, rivers, mountains, vegetation, &c., 239.
    Division of Primeval Waters, 166, a boundary fixed for the Sea, 416, and paths for the Heavenly Bodies, 181.
    Primeval War between the Powers of Light and Darkness, 318; 'Helpers of Rahab' (*Tiâmat*), 184; Rahab or Tiâmat subdued, 323 f.
    Light, as daily creating the world anew, 417 f.
    The North and the Mountain of the Gods, 321, 413.
Belly as the seat of intelligence, 370 f., and the kidneys associated with mind, 425.
Benê Kèdem, 98.
Chaldeans, 108.
Confusion of ס and שׂ in old script, 305
Creation of Man, 142, 194.
'Day of Iahvah', no reference in Job, 309, 399
Earth as the Great Mother, 110.
Father as family priest, 99.
'Fire of God', 108.
Horus, an Egyptian sun-god, 181.
Laws of Hammurabi quoted, 362.
Mythical conceptions of physical phenomena (Snow, Light, Darkness, &c.), 420; Father of Rain and Dew, 421; Constellations, 422 f.
Necromancy, 137.
Numbers seven and three, 97.
Oath, formula of the sacred, 326.
'Pillars of Heaven', 323.
Play on the name Eyob, 373.
Prayer in healing sick (Bab.), 319.
Rebuilding ruins brings a curse, 245.
Sabeans, 107.
Satan, The, 102-104; cf. 123 f. (Evil Spirits).
Shaving the head a sign of mourning, 109.
She'ol, conceptions of, 198; its locality, 321; the dead ignorant of events on earth, 236; pains of decay (?), 237; porter of She'ol, 419.

INDEX TO NOTES ON HEBREW WORDS
(MAINLY PHILOLOGICAL)

אָבָה	188 f.		בהיר	413
אָבָה	170		בהל	290
אברק	321		בהמות	439 f.
אביר	316		בול	442
אבר	232		בז	168
אגל	421		בוס	168
אגר	33, 173		בור	266
אוה	170		בזה	168
אויל	145		בחן	307
אָחוּ	443		בחר	307
איוב	9, 95		בלג	189
איתנים	216		בלימה	321 f.
אַל	145		בלם	322
אֶל	158, 212		במות	182
אלוה	212		בצר	302, 398
אלהים	97, 101, 138, 339		בקר	202
אלח	241		בר	190
אליל	220		ברית	190
אללי	195		ברח	229
אָלַף	381		בת יענה	430
אֶלֶף	381			
אַלּוּף	381		גב	296
אמל	145		גבר-	232
אפיק	441, 451		גע	197
ארגב	296		גיד	440
ארי }	135		גיח	415, 444
אריה }			גלד	252
אֵשׁ	232		נגב	256, 292
אתמול	176		נרם	407
			נשם	407
בגד	245			
בדיו	263, 449		דאבה	403

דְּי	287	חמר	286
דֶּגֶל	350	חטט	247
דניאל	9	חטץ	247
דקק	412	הנף	177, 244
דרום	412	חנק	167
		חף	373
האביר	435	חצה	149
הוא	407	חצץ	149, 293
הוד	414	חקר	202
הוות	165	חרב	232
הלך	248	חרה	232
הלל	340	חרנפר	181
הרס	213	חרס	181, 232, 456
התחטא	455	חרף	200
הָתֵל	221	חרר	232
זהב	337, 362	טָחוֹת	425 f.
זהם	376	טחן	358
זור	272	טפל	220
זך	190	טרח	409
זכה	190		
זכוכית	337	יאל	145
זלעפה	246	יאל	158
זמם	358	ידע	415
		יהוה	211, 406, 462
חבל	388 f.	יין	371
חרה	231	יבח	220
חדוד	456	ילעלעו	436
חוג	299	יפע	192
חול	344	יקוט	177
חוץ	149	ירח	319
חור	279	ירט	252
חרש	357	ירק	169
חזיז	339	ישן	294
חץ	450	ישש	368
חַךְ	372		
חַפָּה	207	כאב	237
חלילה	326	כבר	232
חלף	234	כחד	245
חדד	194, 197 f., 206	כחש	250, 353

INDEX TO NOTES ON HEBREW WORDS 473

בידור	452	מענדרות	422
בידון	456	מקום	316
כימה	182 f.	מרץ	163
כלה	208	משטר	425
כלם	200	משל	325 f.
כִּנָּה	371	מתים	199
כֵּסֶא	322	מתלעות	343
כסיל	182 f.		
כפיר	283	נאף	170
כפר	190	נבל	229
כרר	202	נְבֵלָה	229
כֶּתֶם	337	נְבֵלָה	116, 462
		נבכי	419
לאה	250	נגן	349
לאם	381	נוה	185
לבב	203	נוח	185
לביא	283	נוץ	362
לויתן	124, 445	נום	464
לילית	266	נחושה	160
לין	378	נחשת	160
ליש	283	נחשתן	124
לפיד	452	נין ונכד	267
לפת	162	נבונה	462
		נבח	220
מאם	168, 460	נכר	385
מַבּוּל	289	נמלה	145
מום	205	נפל	229
מורש	259 f.	נפש	453
מזיח	218	נשב	170
מזרות	423	נשם	170
מלאך	377	נשף	170
מלאכי	32 f.	נתך	194
מליץ	377 f.		
מלל	229	סבל	410
מסה	168, 172	סנור	336 f.
מַפָּה	187	סר	227
מסס	168	סור	239
מסכן	301	סור	232
מָצַע	455	סחיפה	236
מעוז	427	סכן	23, l. 14

סלף	217	קמל	145
ספח	236	קנה	443
סרס	213	קרח	421
		קש	226
עויל	273	קשה	226
עון	225	קשת	226
עיש	182 f.	קשיטה	463
עטישה	452		
עלים	297	ראם	429
עלמין	350	ראש	229
ענר	366	רבב	371
ענק	167	רנב	296
עצב	193	רגל	172
ערל	157	רן	172
ערץ	226	רנע	172
		רחב	374
פז	338	רוּחַ	138, 255
פח	298	רָוַח	371
פיר	209	רֶוַח	452
פימה	244	רחב	371
פלא	196	רחץ	341
פלט	307	ריב	374
פלל	360	ריר	157
		רמה	319
צאלים	442	רמח	433
צבא	170	רנן	282
צול	457	רסס	213
צחנה	273	רעמה	429 f.
צלצל	448	רענן	247
צמים	147, 264	רפאים	189, 320
צמת	161	רצה	231
צנים	444	רצח	213
צפור	446	רצץ	213
צרר	235	רקע	412
		רק	169
קדש	145	רקק	169
קדקד	229		
קטל	224	שאון	294
ריר	202	שאף	170
לילתי	4:7	שבה	463

שביב	263, 458	שלת, שלו	210, 294
שגג	214	שלח	248
שנה	214	שלך	248, 264
שגע	214	שלל	210
שדד	210, 242	שמר	173
שדי	212, 291	שמץ	324
שהם	337	שנה	437
שוא	171	שנים	437
שואה	351	שפח	236
שוב	463	שפע	298
שוה	185, 201	שקה	214
שור	173	שקל	155
שורות	312	שרר	440
שזף	283		
שחד	248, 398	תאם	437
שחח	185	תבל	409
שחל	283	תהום	184
שחץ	459	תולעה	319
שחק	235, 391	תועפות	303
שחת	185	תּוּר	173
שטח	219	תורה	302
שׂטם	250	תושיה	214, 354
שׂטן	250	תותח	456
שיב	458	תלע	343
שׂיח	238	תם	96
שכב	426	חמה	323
שֹׂכוי	425	תמול	176
שְׂכוֹת	447	תעב	190
שכם	216, 362	תפת	257

SUMERIAN WITH SEMITIC GLOSSES

A *mû, mê, banû*, water, beget, 131, 421.
AG (AGA, AGU) *agû*, crown, 299.
ANSHU *imêru*, ass, 216.

EDIN *çêru, edinu*, plain, wilderness, desert, 142.
EL *ellu*, bright, pure (cf. UL *nabâṭu*, glitter), 212.
ELALU *zammêru*, singer, *lallarâte*, outcries, wailing (cf. ILU); ELLU *id.*, 195.
ER *dimtu, bikîtu, bakû*, tears, weeping, to weep, 131.
EME *lišânu*, tongue, speech; EME-KUKU *âkil qarçi*, slanderer (Sum. *tongue + eat*), 274.
EME-SIG *qarçu*, calumny, slander (Sum. *tongue + base*), 220.
EN *enu*, priest, *bêlu*, lord, *šarru*, king.
EN, ENE, *ittu*, time, 176.
ENEM *amâtu*, word (see INIM), 358.
EN-ZUNA (? ZU-ENNA) *Sîn*, the Moon-god, 123.
ESIR *sulû, sûqu, šulû*, road, street, 232.

ID, I, *nâru*, river, canal, 402.
ID, ITU, ITI, *arḫu*, moon, month, 319.
IDE, *înu, ênu*, eye (also IGI), 415.
ILU *nubû*, wailing, 195, 378.
IM, EN, *šâru*, wind, storm, 289.
IM, IN, *ulluḫu, šanû*, dye, stain, taint, 241.
IM-BAL *nabbaltu*, tornado, 289.
IM-GAL *šûtu, mêḫû*, south, south-wind, 123.
IM-GI L *imḫu u* hurricane, 123.

IM-SUB *kê mašši*, melting-pot (from IM *ṭîṭu*, clay), 160.
INIM *amâtu*, word, 358.

UD, U, *ûmu, urru*, day, (*ilu*) *Šamaš*, the Sun, 414.
U, UA, *šammu*, vegetation, plants, greens, *rîtu*, pasture, *mâkalu*, food, 131.
UG (GUG? MUG?) *mîtu*, dead, *mûtu*, death, 197.
UG̱ = G̱UG̱ = RUG, 169.
UG̱ *ru'tu, rûtu*, spittle, UG̱-RIA *rusû, ruḫû*, bewitching (*spittle + let flow*), 157.
UG̱, UG̱U, general name for various kinds of insects, grubs, and other vermin (*kalmatu, mûnu, sâsu, paršu'u*, &c.); UG̱-TUR (DUR), *tultu*, worm, maggot, *âkilu*, moth-grub, 319.
UL *ullu, ulçu*, joy, 158.
UR *kalbu, labbu, nêšu*, dog, lion, 135.
UR-KU *kalbu*, dog, 424.
URIG *urqitu*, greens, 247.
UZU *šîru*, flesh, 302.
UZU UR-UŠ, (*šîru*) *têrtum ša šîri*, omen from inspection of the flesh, 302.
USAN, USA, *šittum*, sleep, 294.
USHUM-GAL *ušumgallu* ('Great Worm'), *bašmu*, a serpent (mythical?), 123.

BAD *pitû*, open, 146, 152.
BAD *nisû*, far, depart, 209.
BAL *nabalkutu, pilaqqu*, break through, axe, 183, 196, 360.
BAL *ebêru*, get over, 410.
BAL *tabâku*, pour out, 156.
BAL *dabâbu, tamû*, speak, say, 229.

BA-LAG *balaggu*, harp, 349.
BIL *qalû*, *šarâpu*, BI-BI *šahânu*, burn, 114.
BUL *nâšu*, quake, 290.
BAR *ahâtu*, side, 183.
BAR, BA, *parâsu*, *zâzu*, *pitû*, *mišlu*, split, divide, open, half, 183.
BAR *namâru*, *nûru*, *šamšu*, shine, light, sun, cf. PAR *namru*, bright, 190.
BUR *bûru*, *hurru*, *šuplu*, pit, hole, bottom, 184.

PA .... Ê *šûpû*, shine forth, 292
PAG *esirum ša iççuri*, auceps, cavea avium? 298
PAR *namru*, bright, shining, 190.
PESH, PI, *napâšu*, *rapâšu*, breathe, blow, expand, *erû*, become pregnant, 245, 453.

GAB *irtu*, breast, 296.
GABA-TINU 'hill of life'?, 348.
GABI-RI *šadû*, mountain, 348.
GAB-RI *mahâru*, to 'breast', confront, 232
GAB *bi'šu bîšu*, stinking, foul, bad, 171, 190, 241.
GIB, GIG, *marçu*, *murçu*, *ikkibu*, sick, sickness, pain, 237.
GU *šasû*, *apâlu*, *qibû*, speak, 241.
GU BUR, *huburu*, abyss?, 184.
GUG *samtu*, sparkling? (cf. GUB *ellu*), 337.
GUN *kišâdu*, neck, 167.
GAD *kitû*, clothing stuff of some kind, 245.
GAD *qâtu*?, hand, 248.
GAD *ellu*, *ebbu*, *namru*, bright, pure, 231.
GID *arâku*, be long, 296.
GAL *našû*, *šaqâlu*, lift, 155.
ĜAL *garâru*, flow, run, 357, 369.
ĜAL *zâzu*, split, halve, 183
GUL *abâtu*, *ubbutu*, perish, destroy, 208.
ĜUL *limnu*, bad, hostile, 290; *zâru*, hate, 273.
ĜUL *šulputu* destroy 20⁰
ĜUL *ḫidûtu* rejoice, 107.

GAM, GAN, *kamâsu*, *kanâšu*, *qadâdu*, bend, bow, 177.
GEMF, GEM, *sinništu*, *amtu*, *ardatu*, woman, maid; GEME-DUG *kunnû*, greet (or treat) tenderly, 371. (Cf GEN, GÊ, *amtu*.)
GEN, GÊ, *šerru*, *la'û*, *çihru*, little, weak, 301.
GUM, ĜUM, *ḫamâšu*, *ḫašâlu*, grind, pound, 247.
GIN *çalmu*, dark, 146.
GIN, GI, *qanû*, reed, 146.
GIN *šadû*, mountain?, 182.
GAR *šakânu*, *šarâqu*, make, put, give (cf. MUN-GAR *makkûru*, goods), 447
GAR *uḫḫuzu*, *esêru*, *abbuttu*, *lânu* (= INGAR), enclose, bind, fetter, wall, 202.
ĜAR, GISH-GAR, *eçêru*, *uçurtu*, enclose, bounds, 202.
GÍR *birqu*, lightning, 232.
GI-RIM *ellu*, *samtu*, clear, pure, a gem (cf. RIN *ellu*), 337.
GISH *išâtu*, fire, 232.
GISH, GESH, *içu*, tree; GESH-TIN *înu*, *karanu*, vine, wine ('Tree of Life'), 371.
GUSH-KIN *ḫurâçu*, gold, 337.

KA *pûm*, *pû*, *appu*, mouth, face, 220.
KA-GÁL (*pît pî*), 'Open-mouth', 123
KASH *lasmu*, fiery, impatient?, 146
KESH *riksu*, bond, 226.
KA-ZAL *tašîltu*, pleasure (' ace-bright '), 231.
KA-SHU-MAR, KA-SHU-GAL, *appa labânu*, to cast down the face (in prayer), 229.
KIN *še'û*, seek, look for, attend to, 383.
KU(N), KUKKU, KU-KU, *ṭâbu*, *dašpu*, good, sweet; KU *matqu*, mead or metheglin: cf. GIN *ṭâbu*, 273
KU, KUÉ, *akâlu*, to eat, 131.
KU-BABBAR, *ṣ[ar]pu*, *kas[p]u*, silver, 337.

KAR, *kîru*, wall, 202.
KAR-KAR *nabâṭu ša tîme*, shine of day, 421.
KUR *šadû*, mountain, 239; KUR-GAL *šadû rabû* (title of a god), 291.
KUR, KURUM (i. e. KURU), *paqâdu*, look after, entrust. &c., 385.
KUR *nakru*, enemy, 385.

DA(G), DA; cf. DA-GAL *rapšu*, broad, 412.
DAB, *lamû*, *saḫâru*, surround = DUB, 381.
DIB *aḫâzu*, *kamû*, *çabâtu*, *lamâḫu*, seize, catch, take, 463.
DAG *ebbu*, *ellu*, *namru*, bright, shining; cf. DI, DE, *nabâṭu*, *nummuru*, glitter, brighten, &c., 415.
DAG *naparkû*, give way, cease, 161.
DAL *naprušu*, fly away, 222.
DIM *sanâqu*, bind, fasten; *riksu*, bond, rope, 323.
DIM *kîma*, like, 337.
DUMU, DAMU, *mâru*, child, son (also daughter, *mârtu*), 424.
DI *dênu*, judgement, 415.
DIM-MER, DI-MER, DIN-GIR, DI-GIR, *ilu*, *iltu*, god, goddess, 144.
DUN *palânu*, eat, swallow, 147.
DA-RI *zâqu*, blow hard, 412.
DAR-LUGAL. *tarlugallu*, Aram. *tarnegôlâ*, cock, 123.
DUR *labâku*, *raṭbu*, to flow?, watered, moist, fresh, 419.

TA *ina*, *kîma*, in, with, like = DA *idu*, *ittu*, side, 160, 410.
TAM *talîmu*, brother; TAN *ḫawiru*, spouse; TAB *tappû*, companion (cf. DAM *mûtu*, *aššatu*, spouse), 437.

LAL, LA, *enšu*, weak, *maṭû*, to minish, 250.
LAB *šâtuqu*, vast, huge, immense, 381.
LAG = NAG (*aqû*, *atû*, irrigate, drink), swallow, eat?, 343.

LAG *nûru*, *namru*, light, shine (cf. LAG in ZA-LAG), 181, 189. Cf. RA (RAG ?) *illu*, *ebbu*, *namru*, bright, pure.
LI in LI-DU, *zamâru*, sing, 378.
LI-LIZ *lilisu*, guitar-playing (Chinese *li*), 378.
LI *šamnu*, oil, fat (Ch. *ni*, *li*, fat), 341.
LI-NUN *ḫimêtu*, butter, 341.
LÙ *amêlu*, man; LÙ KINGA *mâr šipri*, messenger, 123. (Cf. NU *amêlu*, *zikaru*; Ch. *nu*, *lu*, slave.)
LUG *palâḫu*, be afraid, 181.

RAG, RA, *raḫâçu*, to flood, wash, 341 (cf. LAG, LUG *misû*, to wash, str. make bright or pure).
RAG, RA, *rapâsu*, to strike, thresh, 412. (Cf. LAG *mašâdu*, to smite.)
RI, (RIG), *zâqu*, to blow hard; *ziqqu*, blast, 138, 374.
RIG in U-RIG, green (Ch. *luk*, Jap. *ryoku*, green), 169.
RU *banû*, build, make, 142 (= DU).
RUZ (RAZ) in SHU-RUZ, *kabâbu*, *šabâbu*, *šamû*, burn, sparkle, shine, 231.

MAL = BAL = GAL, *nabâlu*, *labânu*, throw down, 229.
MUL *kakkabu*, star; *nabâṭu*, *namâru*, shine, 212, 423.
MULU - BABBAR Μολοβοβαρ, 184.
MIM, NIG (ning), NIN, *mamma*, *mimma*, *mumma*, any one, any thing, 205.
MUN *šikaru ša* KASH, *ṭâbtu*, must, 371.
MU-TIN (= GESH-TIN) *inu*, vine, wine, 371.
MUN-GAR *makkûru*, goods, 447.
MU(N)-SUB *šimetan*, *lilâtum*, evening, 125.
MASH *mašû*, *tu'âmu*, twin, 181 (= MAN *mašû*).
MASH *ellu*, *ebbu*, bright, pure; *âšipu* purifying priest, exorcist (also *mašmašu*).

MUSH *çiru*, serpent (cf. Jap. *mushi*, worms, *ma-mushi*, viper), 125.
MEZ, *edlu*, ME, MU, (MISH, MESH, MUSH) *zikaru*, male, man, 199.

NA, NU, *rabáçu*, lie down, *ulúlu*, *çalálu*, &c., 146.
NAG = SHAG 195. NAG *šatú*, to drink, 131.
NAM-LÙGAL, *amélútu*, mankind, 142. (With LÙGAL cf. Arab. *rag'ol*, man.)
NIG, LIG, *kalbatu*, bitch; *néšlu*, lioness, 135.
NU, LA, *lá*, not, 131.
NUM, LUM, *unnubu*, *uššubu*, to grow luxuriantly, to plant, 287.
NUMUN, NU, *zéru*, seed, 142, 287.
NUN *rabú*, great; *rubú*, prince, 287.

ZAG flame? cf. ZA in ZA-LAG *núrum ša išáti* (= אשׁלי), 190.
ZA-BAR *ebbu*, *ellu*, *namru*, bright, gleaming; *siparru*, copper, 362
ZEB *tábu*, good, beautiful, 362 (cf. DUG and ZAG *tábu*).
ZIB, (ZIG), *šimtan*, twilight, evening (cf. SUB in MU-SUB), 125.
ZAG *tamélu*, address to a god, 238.
ZUR *kunnú*, treat tenderly, 371.
ZUR *ikribé*, prayers, 349.

SHAB *baqámu*, *haráçu*, *šarámu*, split, &c., 136; *barú ša širi*, inspect flesh of victims, 283.
SHIB (in I-SHIB *išibbu*, diviner, sorcerer) divination, 356.
SHAG, SHA, *damáqu*, *dummuqu*, to be bright, pure; to purify metals, 190, 194, 337.
SHUB *lapátu*, to bend, bow, turn round (also SEB), 463.
(SHAD,) SAD, SATI, *bámátu*, mountains (cf. *satum* = *šadú*; Assyr. loanword), 212.
SHID *atmú*, speech, 239.
SHA-KAN *iméru*, ass, 216.
SHEN *ebbu*, *ellu*, bright, pure, 194.
SHER *rakásu*, *riksu*, *qaçáru*, bind, bond.
SHER *šarúru*, splendour; SIR, SI, *núru*, *namáru*, light, to shine, 173.
SHUG, SHUKU, *kurummatu*, sustenance, bread, 131.
SHU-RIN *tínúru*, clay oven, firepot, 356.
SUB (GEN-TA-) *limmašiš*, *limlessí*, let him be purified! 160.
SAG *mámítu*, charm (cf. ZAG *tamélu*), 238
SAG-DU *qaqqádu*, head, 458.
SA-GAR *epru*, dust, earth, 235.
SIG *damáqu*, *dummuqu*, *çurrupu*, to be bright, pure, to purify, smelt or refine metals, 194, 337 (cf. SHAG).
SIG *arqu*, green, yellow, 337.
SIG *šipátu*, *šupátu*, fleece, woollen stuff, 177.
SIL, SUL, *súqu*, *sulú*, road or street, 232. (Cf. SIR in E SIR.)
SIR, SUR, *zamáru*, sing; *çaráhu*, shriek, scream, 355.
SIR BALAGGA *zamár balaggi*, harp-music, 349.
SIR *šerú*, depart (cf. SUD and E-SIR), 232.
SIM in IR-SIM, *armannu*, *eréšu*, smell, fragrance, 376.

PRINTED IN ENGLAND
AT THE OXFORD UNIVERSITY PRESS

CPSIA information can be obtained
at www.ICGtesting.com
Printed in the USA
BVHW041751090122
625832BV00017B/304